Ouran High School Host Club

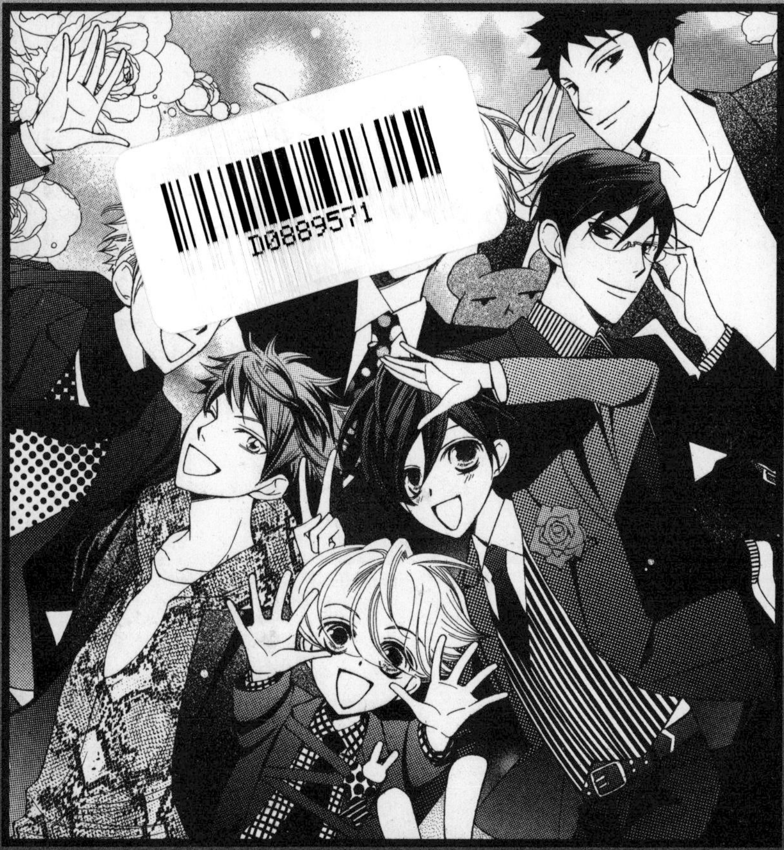

Vol. 18

Bisco Hatori

Ouran High School

Host Club

Vol. 18

CONTENTS

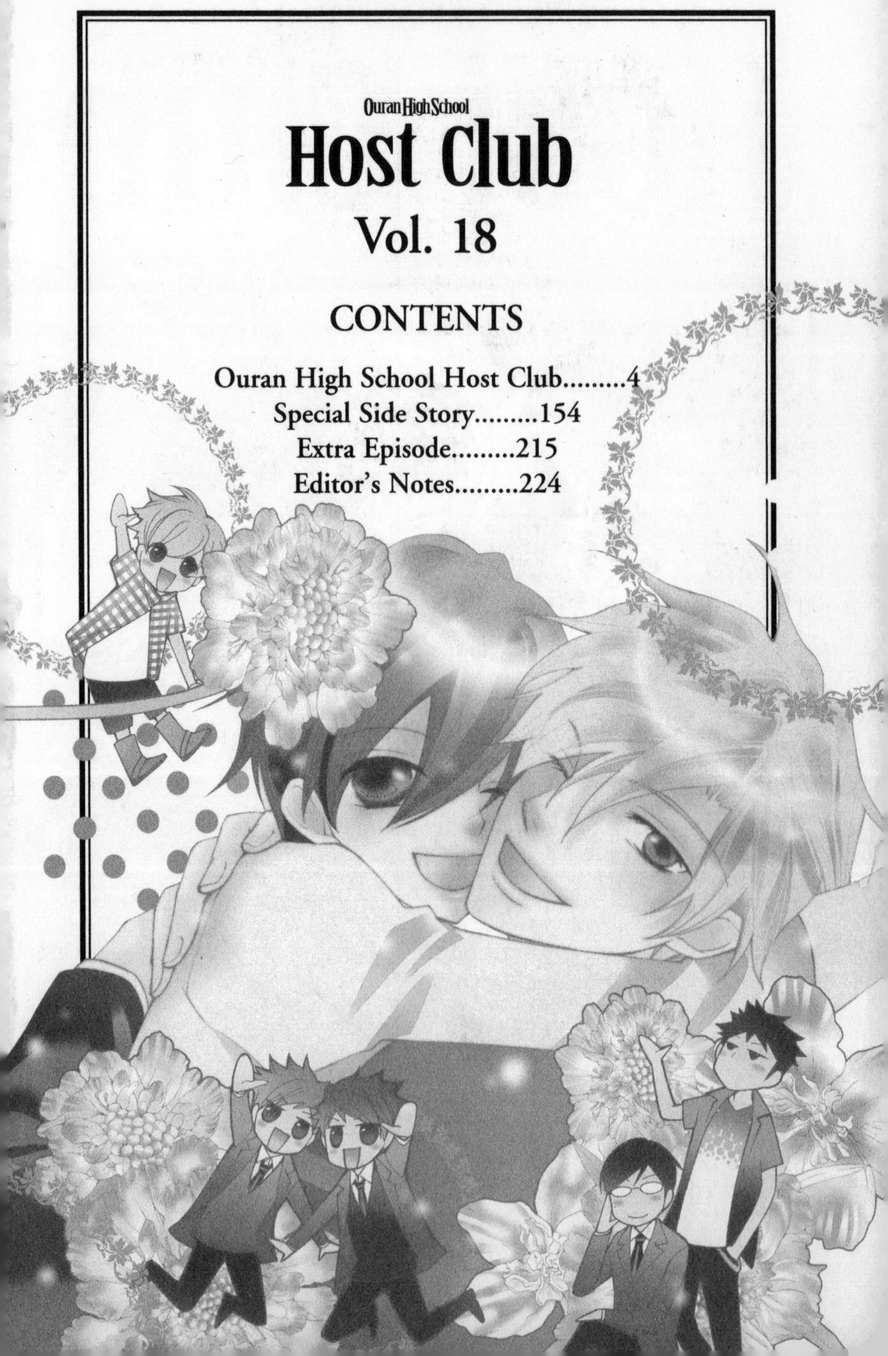

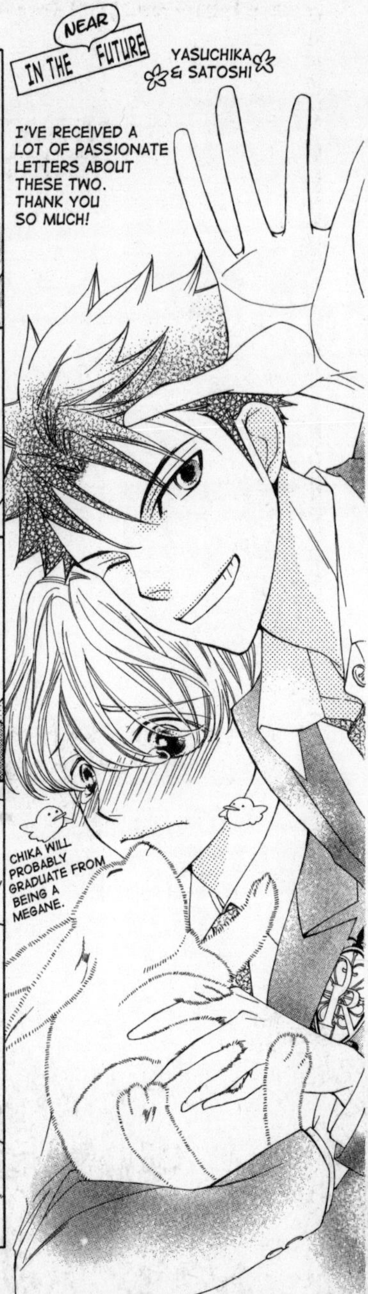
IN THE NEAR FUTURE
YASUCHIKA & SATOSHI
I'VE RECEIVED A LOT OF PASSIONATE LETTERS ABOUT THESE TWO. THANK YOU SO MUCH!
CHIKA WILL PROBABLY GRADUATE FROM BEING A MEGANE.

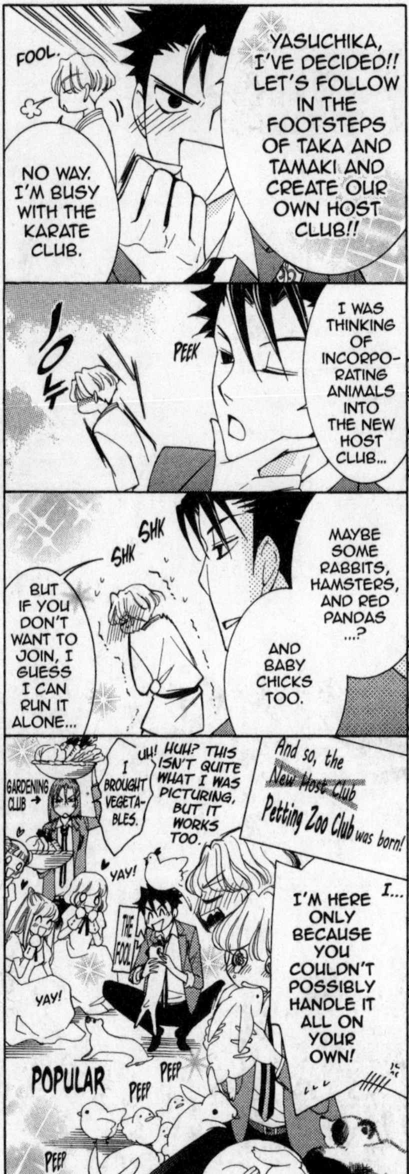
YASUCHIKA, I'VE DECIDED!! LET'S FOLLOW IN THE FOOTSTEPS OF TAKA AND TAMAKI AND CREATE OUR OWN HOST CLUB!!
FOOL.
NO WAY. I'M BUSY WITH THE KARATE CLUB.
I WAS THINKING OF INCORPORATING ANIMALS INTO THE NEW HOST CLUB...
PEEK
JOLT
SHK
SHK
MAYBE SOME RABBITS, HAMSTERS, AND RED PANDAS ...?
AND BABY CHICKS TOO.
BUT IF YOU DON'T WANT TO JOIN, I GUESS I CAN RUN IT ALONE...
And so, the ~~New Host Club~~ Petting Zoo Club was born!
HUH? THIS ISN'T QUITE WHAT I WAS PICTURING, BUT IT WORKS TOO.
UH! I BROUGHT VEGETABLES.
GARDENING CLUB
I... I'M HERE ONLY BECAUSE YOU COULDN'T POSSIBLY HANDLE IT ALL ON YOUR OWN!
YAY!
THE FOOL
YAY!
POPULAR
PEEP
PEEP
PEEP

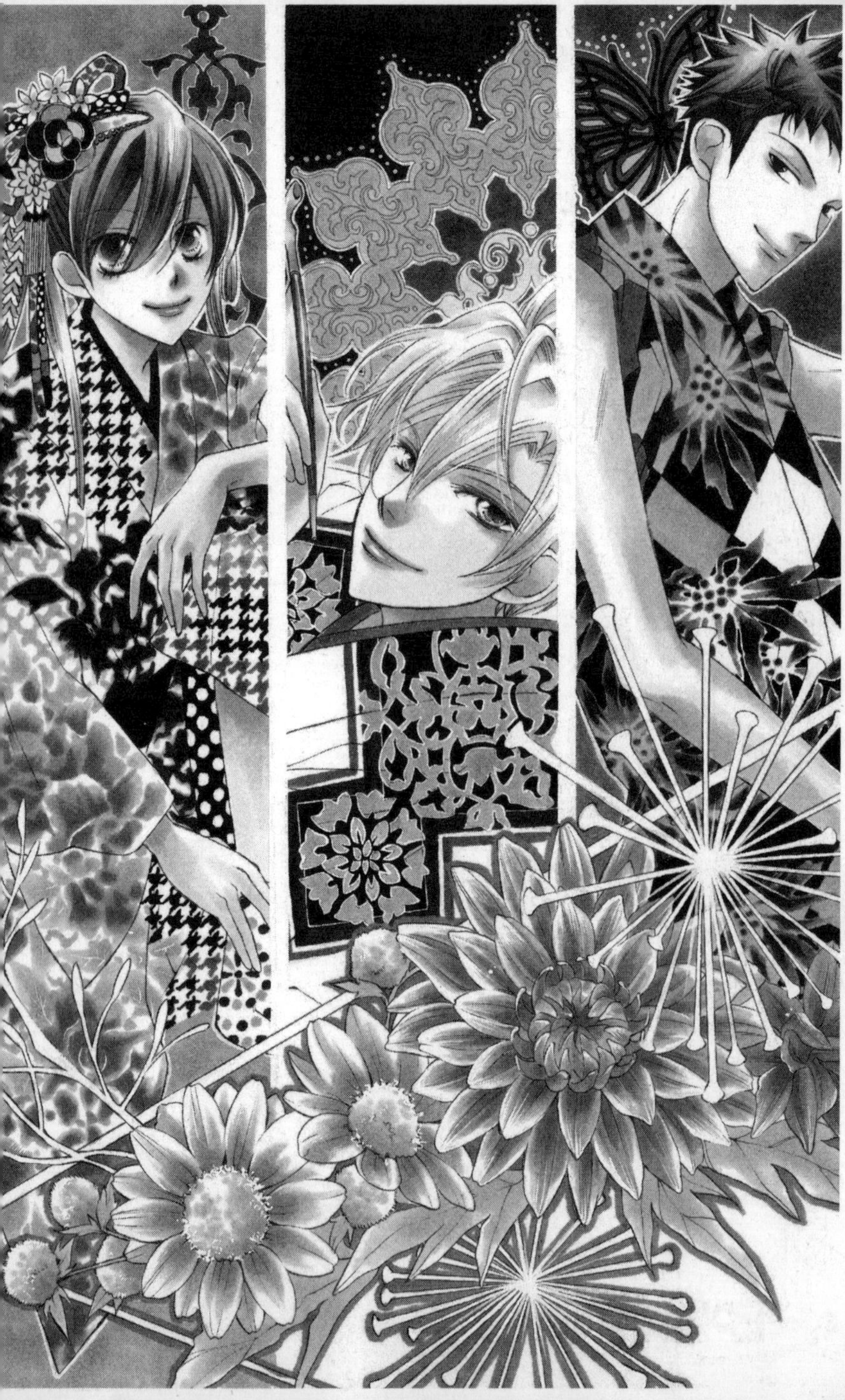

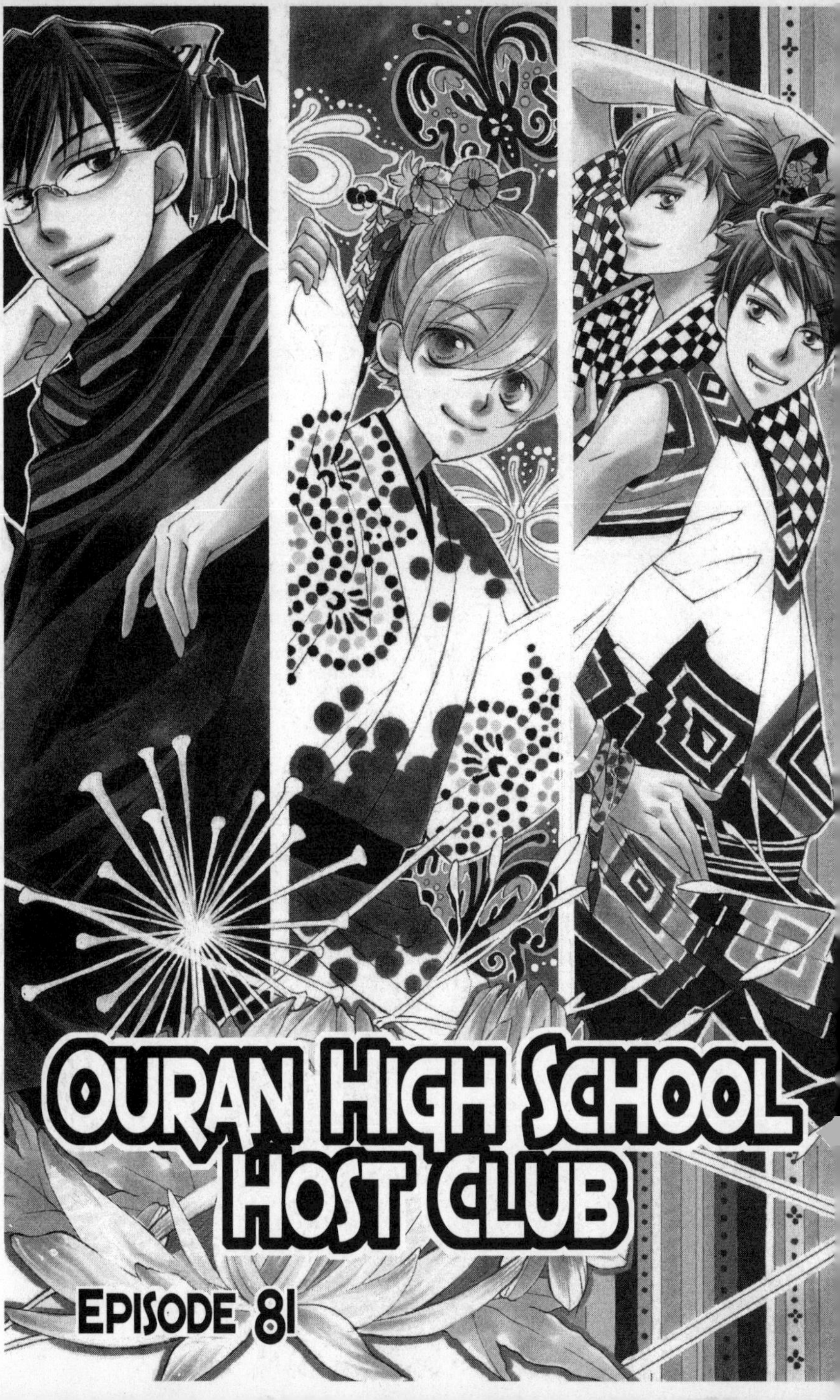
OURAN HIGH SCHOOL
HOST CLUB
EPISODE 81

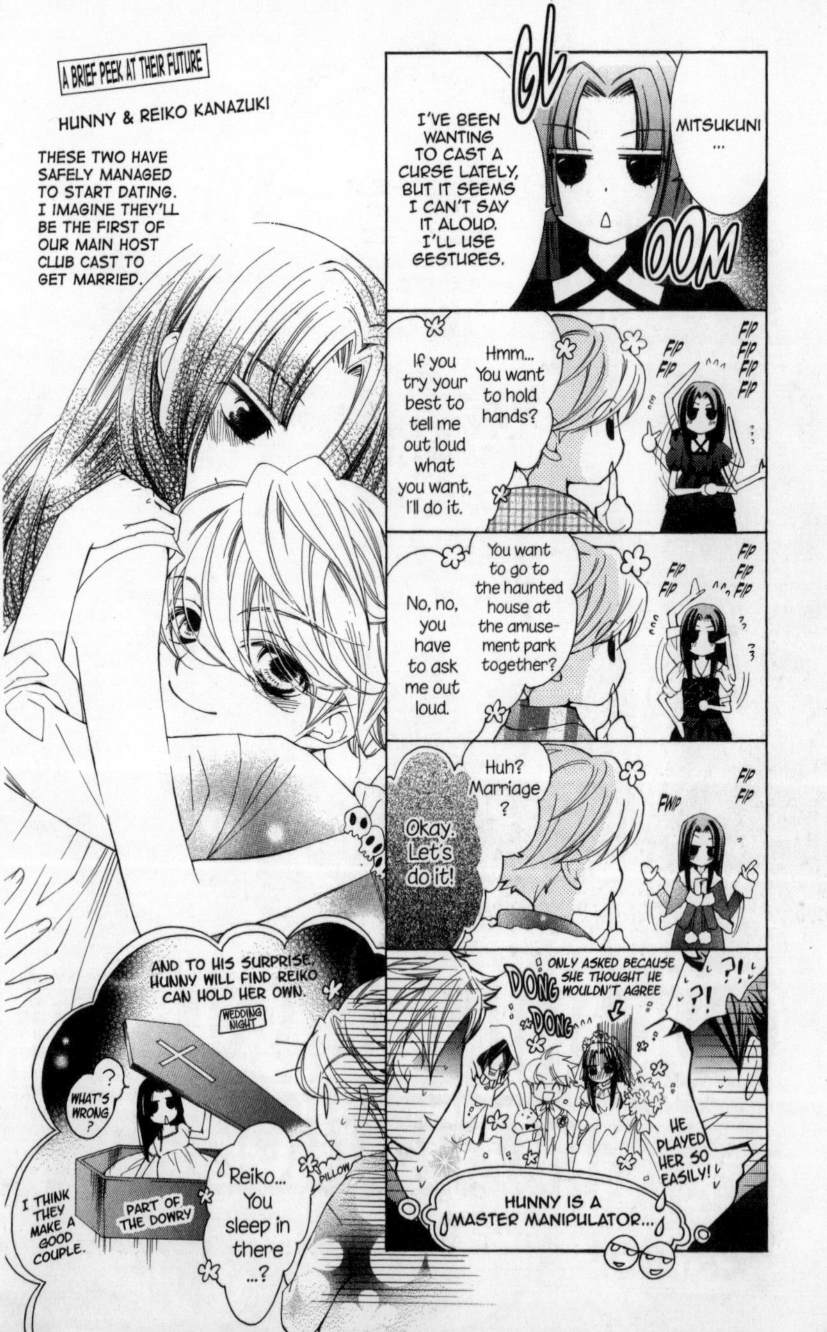
GLOOM
MITSUKUNI ...
I'VE BEEN WANTING TO CAST A CURSE LATELY, BUT IT SEEMS I CAN'T SAY IT ALOUD. I'LL USE GESTURES.
FIP FIP FIP FIP
FIP FIP
Hmm... You want to hold hands?
If you try your best to tell me out loud what you want, I'll do it.
FIP FIP FIP
FIP FIP
You want to go to the haunted house at the amusement park together?
No, no, you have to ask me out loud.
FIP FIP
FWIP
Huh? Marriage ?
Okay. Let's do it!
?!
?!
ONLY ASKED BECAUSE SHE THOUGHT HE WOULDN'T AGREE
DONG
DONG
HE PLAYED HER SO EASILY!
HUNNY IS A MASTER MANIPULATOR...
A BRIEF PEEK AT THEIR FUTURE
HUNNY & REIKO KANAZUKI
THESE TWO HAVE SAFELY MANAGED TO START DATING. I IMAGINE THEY'LL BE THE FIRST OF OUR MAIN HOST CLUB CAST TO GET MARRIED.
AND TO HIS SURPRISE, HUNNY WILL FIND REIKO CAN HOLD HER OWN.
WEDDING NIGHT
PILLOW
Reiko... You sleep in there ...?
?
WHAT'S WRONG ?
PART OF THE DOWRY
I THINK THEY MAKE A GOOD COUPLE.

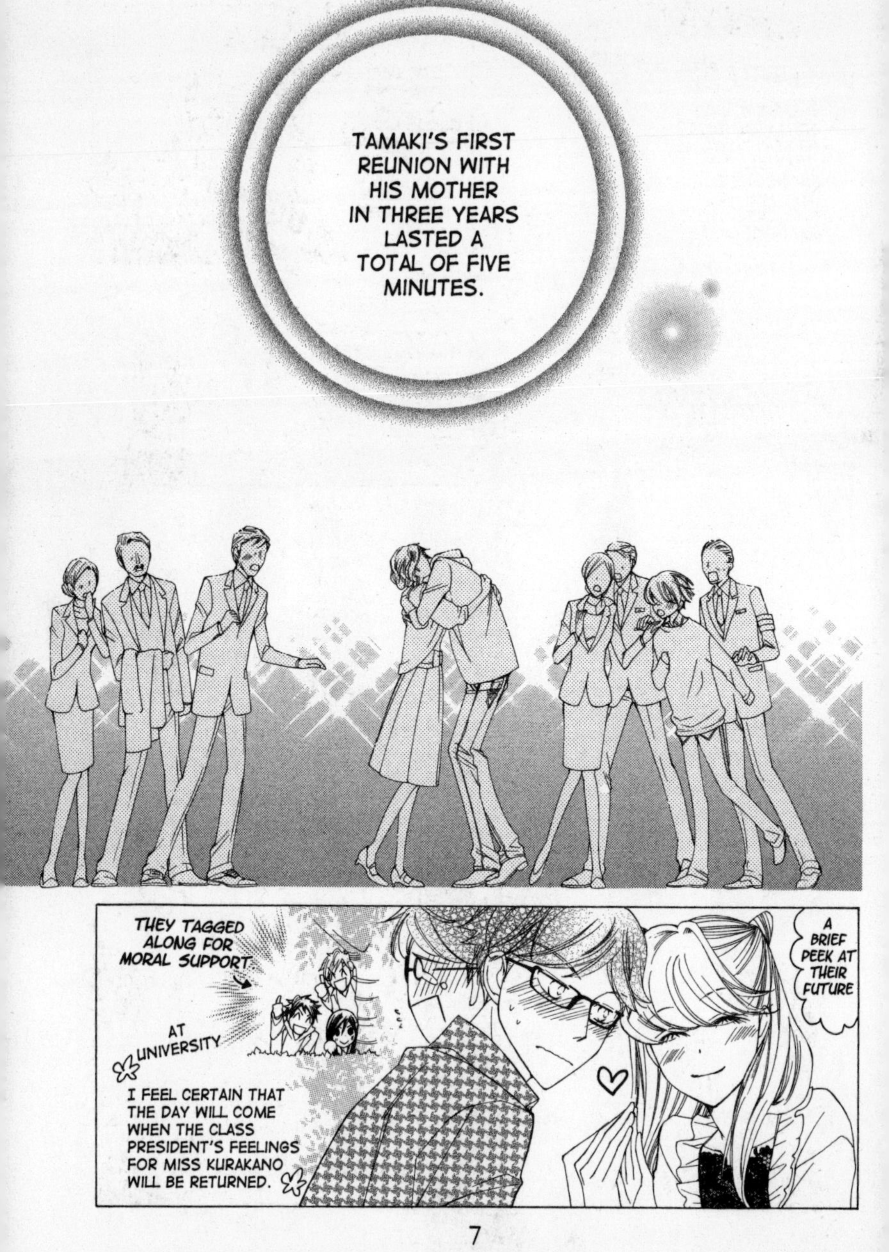
TAMAKI'S FIRST REUNION WITH HIS MOTHER IN THREE YEARS LASTED A TOTAL OF FIVE MINUTES.
A BRIEF PEEK AT THEIR FUTURE
THEY TAGGED ALONG FOR MORAL SUPPORT
AT UNIVERSITY
I FEEL CERTAIN THAT THE DAY WILL COME WHEN THE CLASS PRESIDENT'S FEELINGS FOR MISS KURAKANO WILL BE RETURNED.

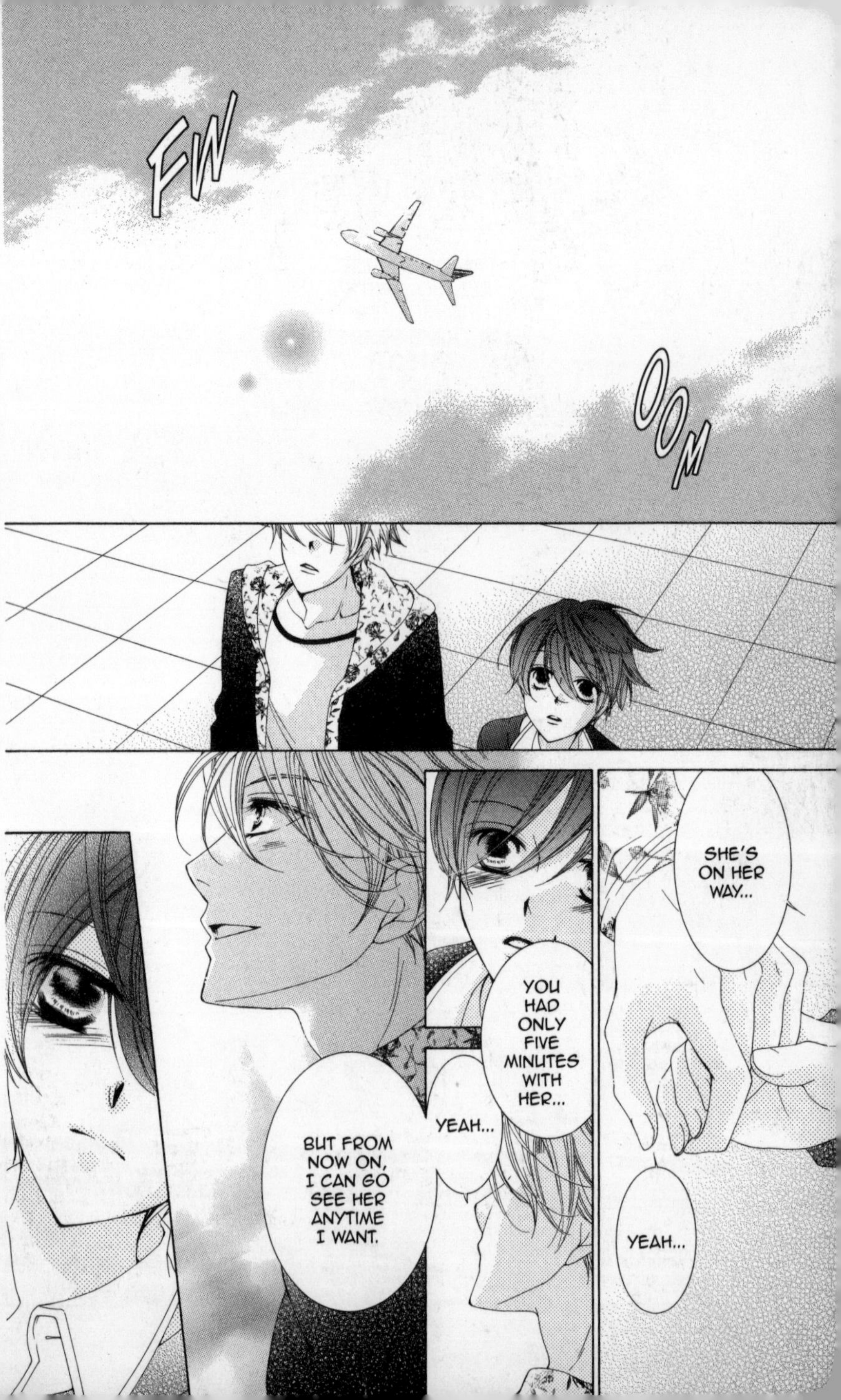
FWOOM
SHE'S ON HER WAY...
YEAH...
YOU HAD ONLY FIVE MINUTES WITH HER...
YEAH...
BUT FROM NOW ON, I CAN GO SEE HER ANYTIME I WANT.

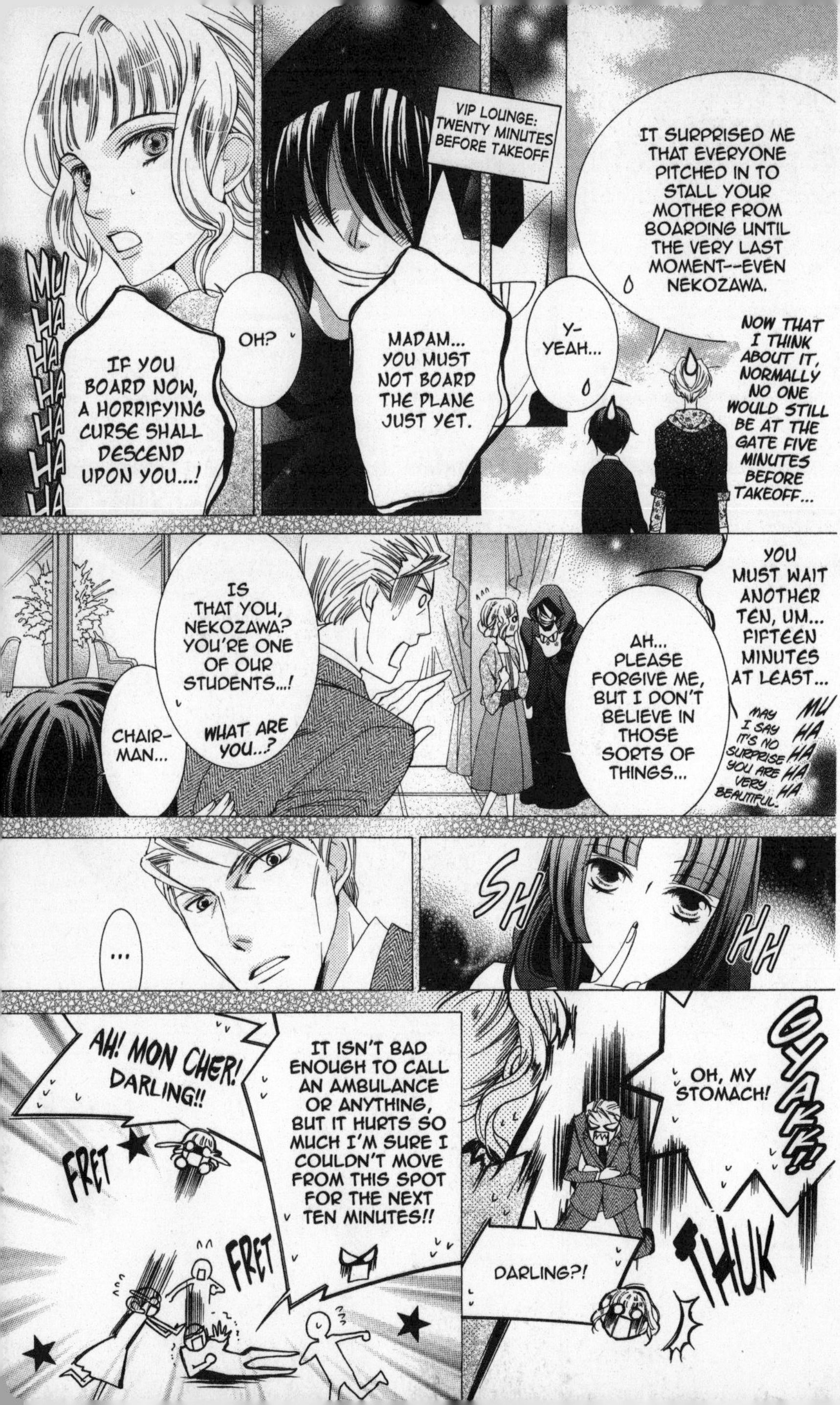
IT SURPRISED ME THAT EVERYONE PITCHED IN TO STALL YOUR MOTHER FROM BOARDING UNTIL THE VERY LAST MOMENT--EVEN NEKOZAWA.
NOW THAT I THINK ABOUT IT, NORMALLY NO ONE WOULD STILL BE AT THE GATE FIVE MINUTES BEFORE TAKEOFF...
Y-YEAH...
VIP LOUNGE: TWENTY MINUTES BEFORE TAKEOFF
MADAM... YOU MUST NOT BOARD THE PLANE JUST YET.
OH?
IF YOU BOARD NOW, A HORRIFYING CURSE SHALL DESCEND UPON YOU...!
MU HA HA HA HA HA HA HA
YOU MUST WAIT ANOTHER TEN, UM... FIFTEEN MINUTES AT LEAST...
MU HA HA HA HA
MAY I SAY IT'S NO SURPRISE YOU ARE VERY BEAUTIFUL.
AH... PLEASE FORGIVE ME, BUT I DON'T BELIEVE IN THOSE SORTS OF THINGS...
IS THAT YOU, NEKOZAWA? YOU'RE ONE OF OUR STUDENTS...!
WHAT ARE YOU...?
CHAIR-MAN...
SHHH
...
OH, MY STOMACH!
THUK
DARLING?!
IT ISN'T BAD ENOUGH TO CALL AN AMBULANCE OR ANYTHING, BUT IT HURTS SO MUCH I'M SURE I COULDN'T MOVE FROM THIS SPOT FOR THE NEXT TEN MINUTES!!
AH! MON CHER! DARLING!!
FRET
FRET

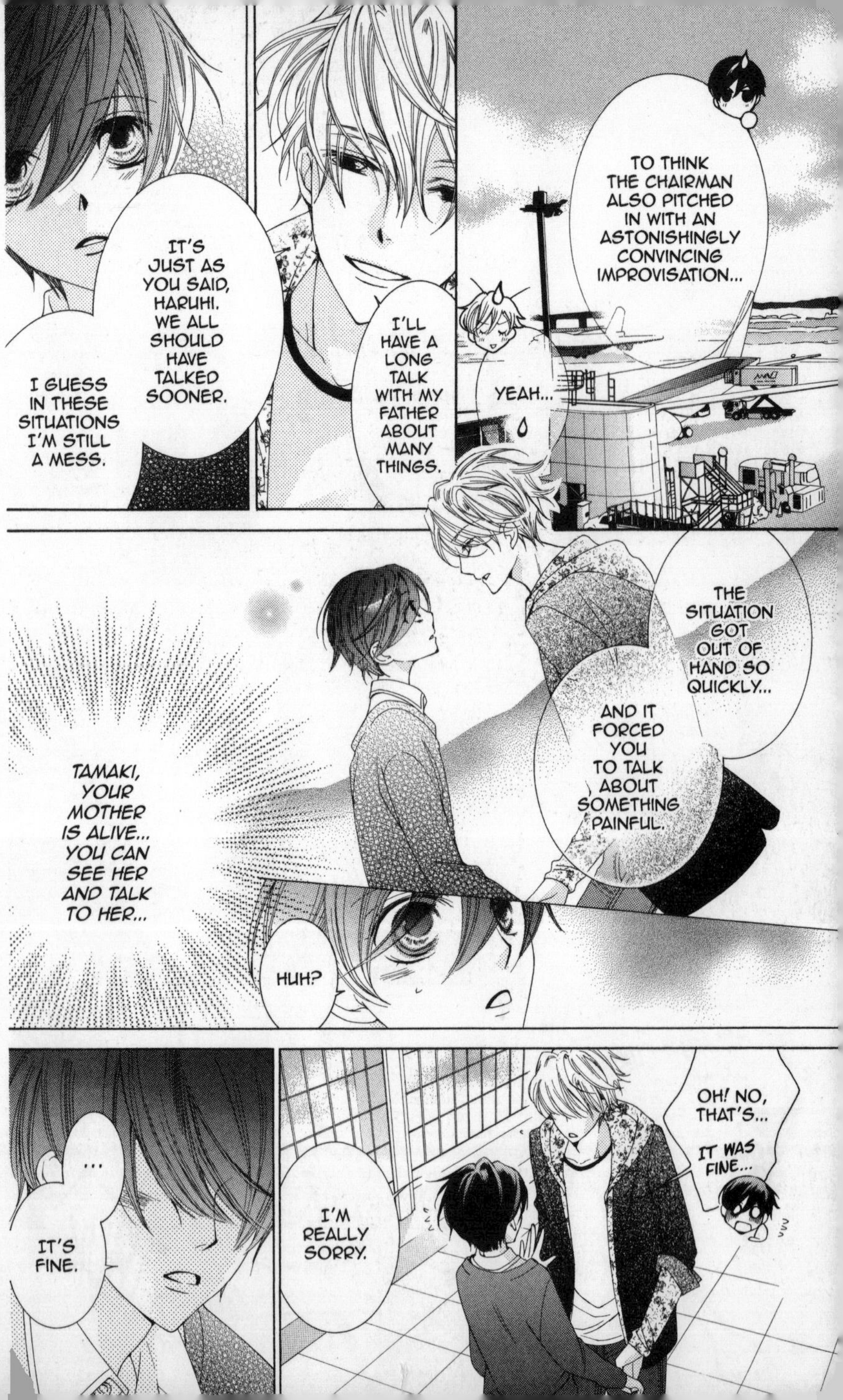
TO THINK THE CHAIRMAN ALSO PITCHED IN WITH AN ASTONISHINGLY CONVINCING IMPROVISATION...
YEAH...
I'LL HAVE A LONG TALK WITH MY FATHER ABOUT MANY THINGS.
IT'S JUST AS YOU SAID, HARUHI. WE ALL SHOULD HAVE TALKED SOONER.
I GUESS IN THESE SITUATIONS I'M STILL A MESS.
THE SITUATION GOT OUT OF HAND SO QUICKLY...
AND IT FORCED YOU TO TALK ABOUT SOMETHING PAINFUL.
TAMAKI, YOUR MOTHER IS ALIVE... YOU CAN SEE HER AND TALK TO HER...
HUH?
OH! NO, THAT'S...
IT WAS FINE...
I'M REALLY SORRY.
...
IT'S FINE.

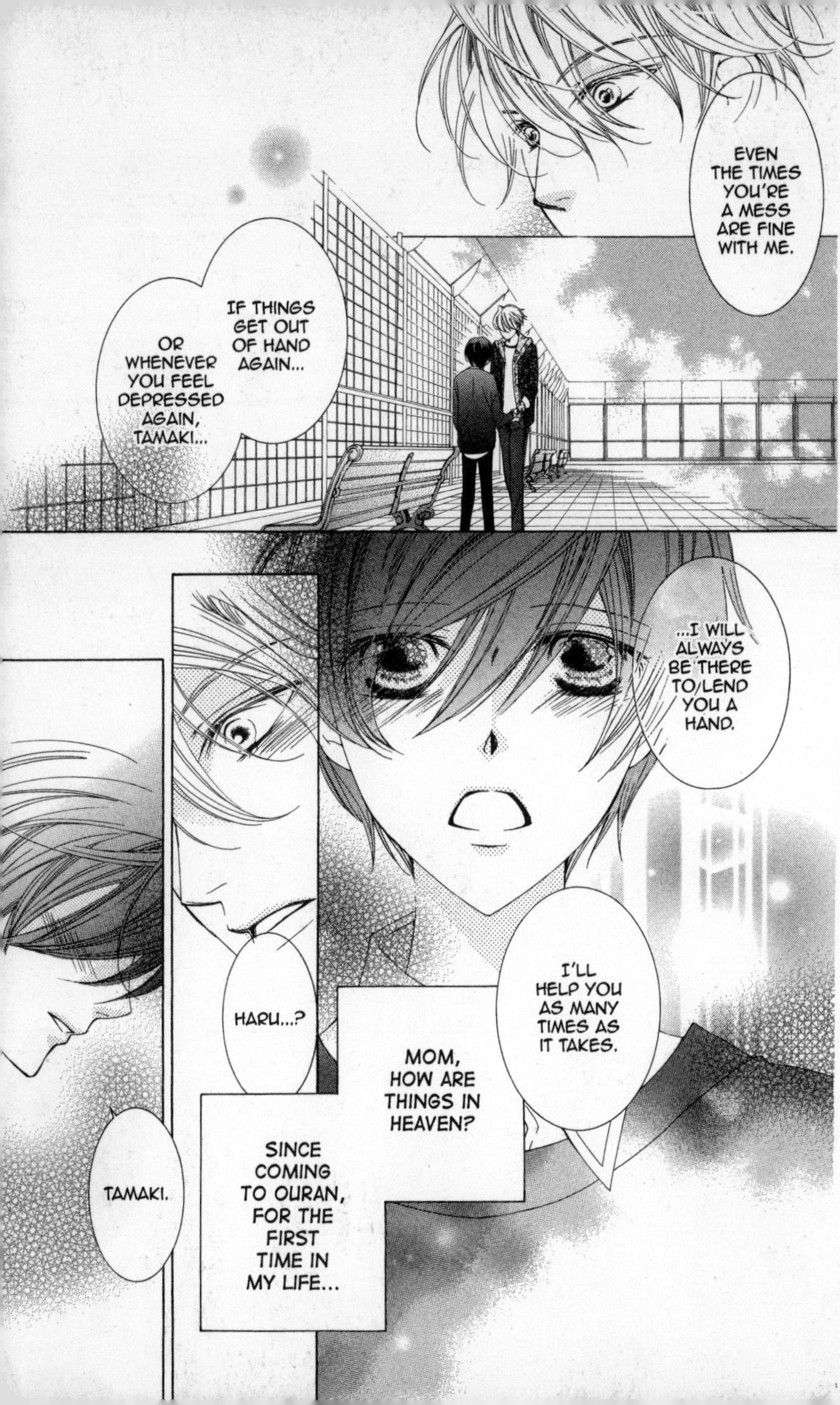
EVEN THE TIMES YOU'RE A MESS ARE FINE WITH ME.
IF THINGS GET OUT OF HAND AGAIN...
OR WHENEVER YOU FEEL DEPRESSED AGAIN, TAMAKI...
...I WILL ALWAYS BE THERE TO LEND YOU A HAND.
I'LL HELP YOU AS MANY TIMES AS IT TAKES.
HARU...?
TAMAKI.
MOM, HOW ARE THINGS IN HEAVEN?
SINCE COMING TO OURAN, FOR THE FIRST TIME IN MY LIFE...

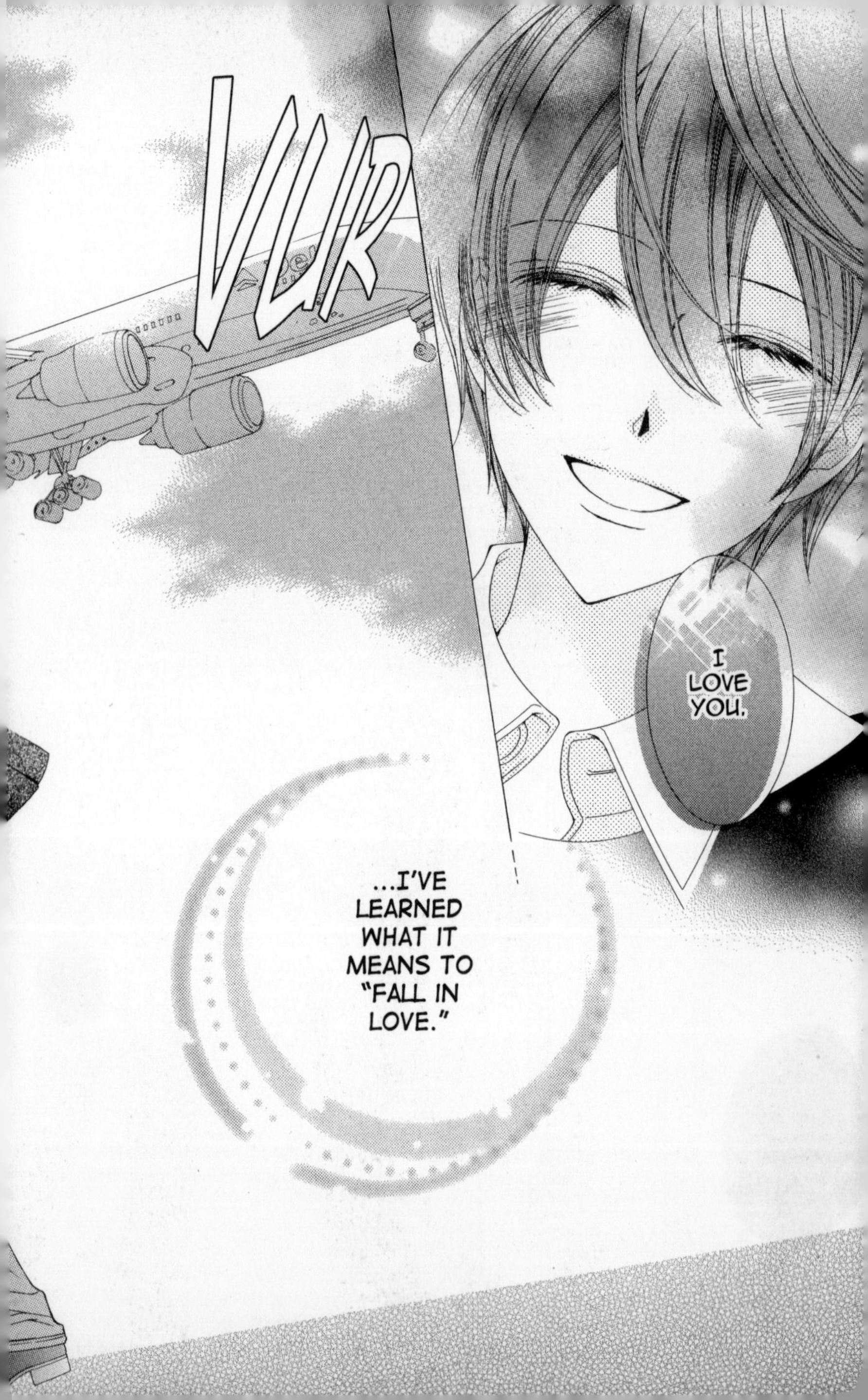
I LOVE YOU.
VUR
...I'VE LEARNED WHAT IT MEANS TO "FALL IN LOVE."

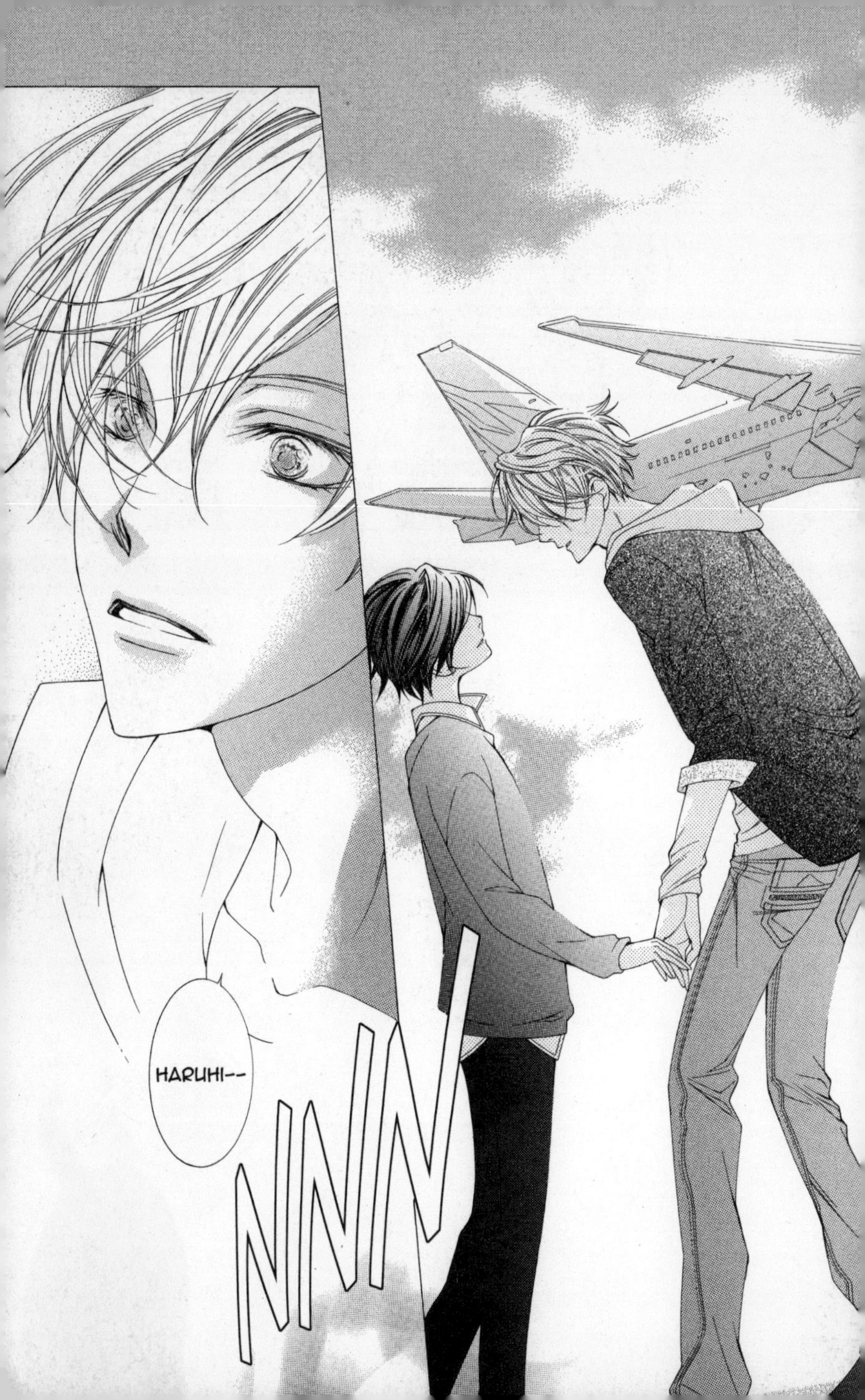
HARUHI--
NNNN

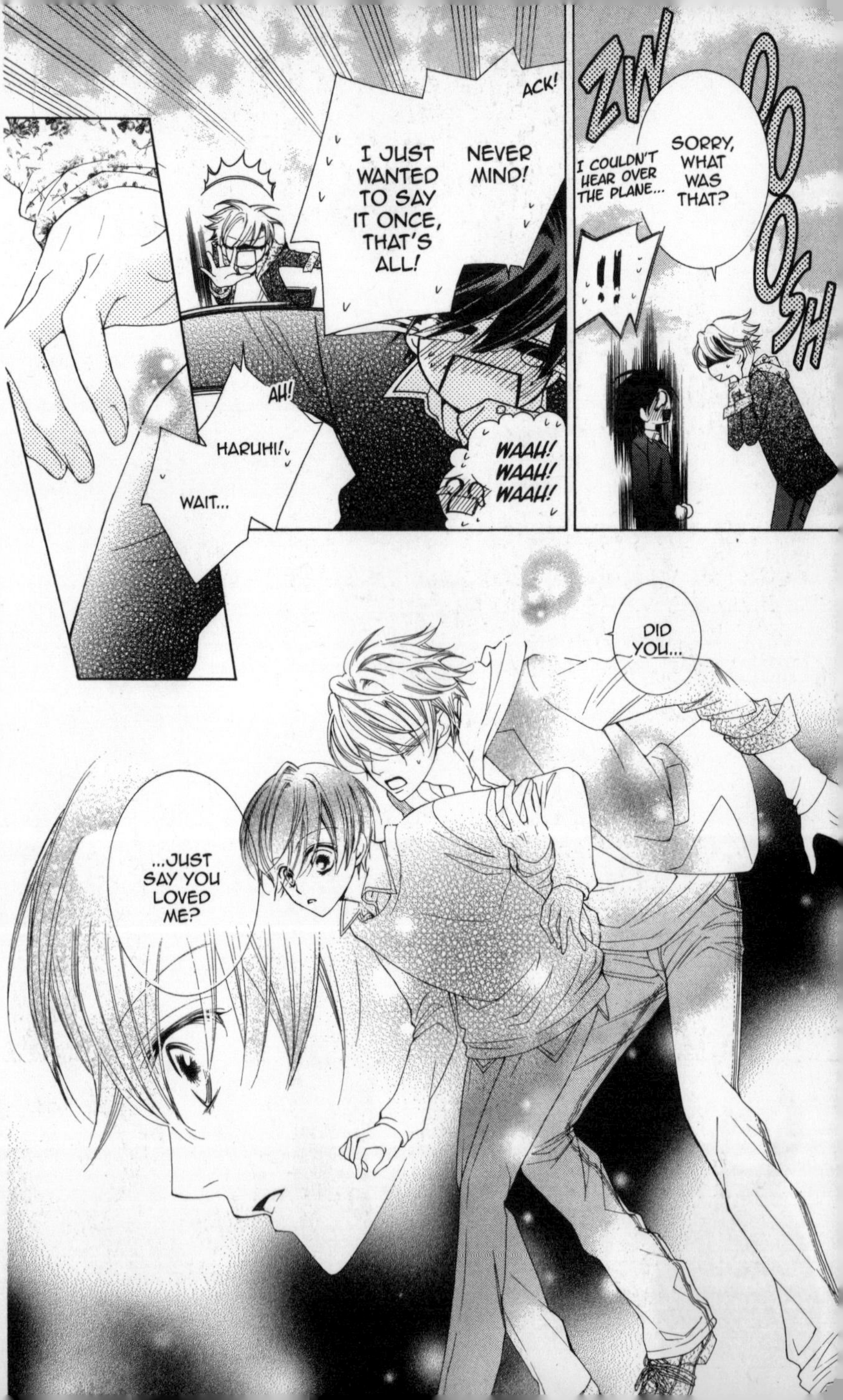
ZWOOOOSH
SORRY, WHAT WAS THAT?
I COULDN'T HEAR OVER THE PLANE...
!!
ACK!
NEVER MIND!
I JUST WANTED TO SAY IT ONCE, THAT'S ALL!
WAAH! WAAH! WAAH!
AH!
HARUHI!
WAIT...
DID YOU...
...JUST SAY YOU LOVED ME?

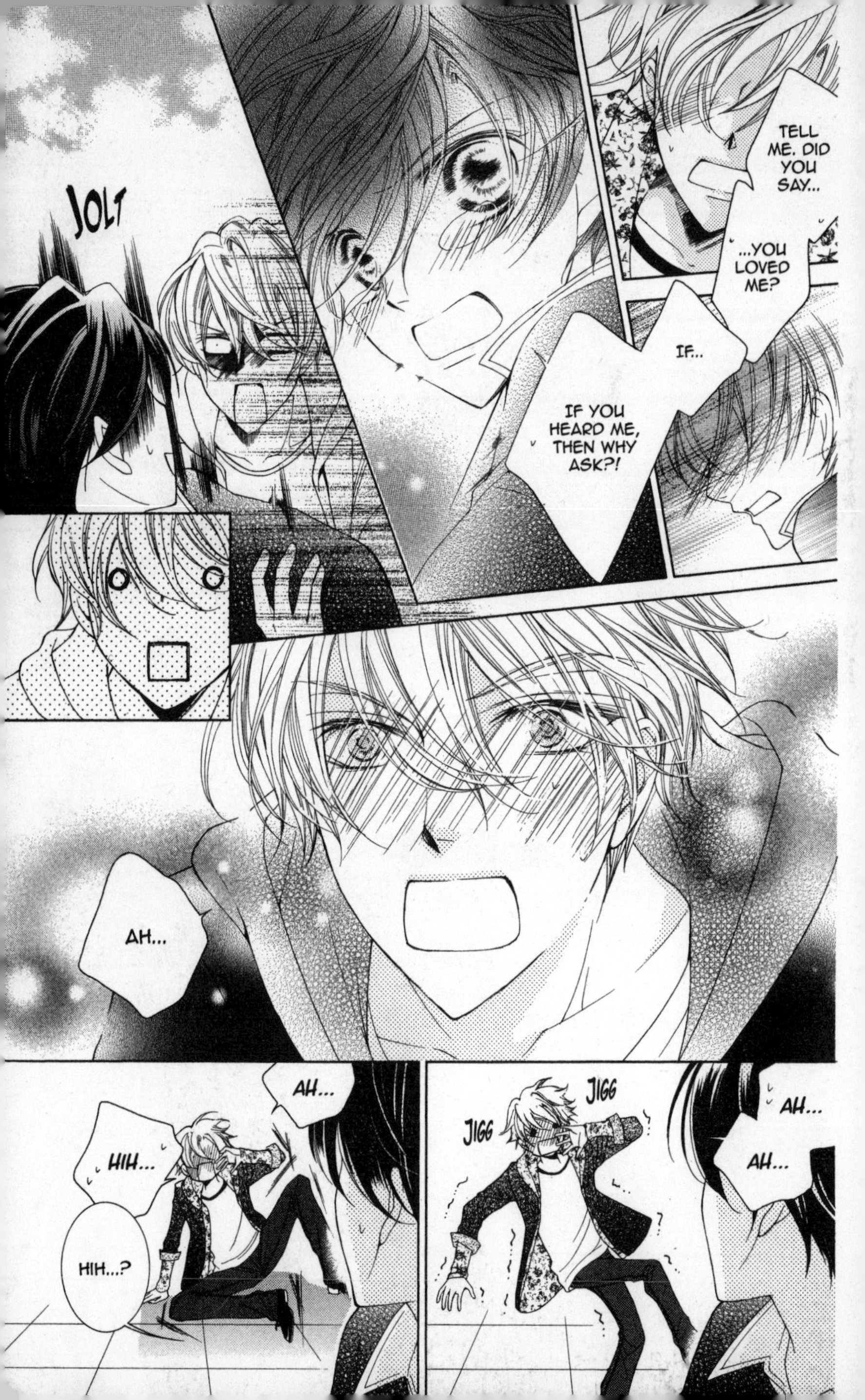
TELL ME. DID YOU SAY...
...YOU LOVED ME?
IF...
IF YOU HEARD ME, THEN WHY ASK?!
JOLT
AH...
AH...
AH...
JIGG
JIGG
AH...
HIH...
HIH...?

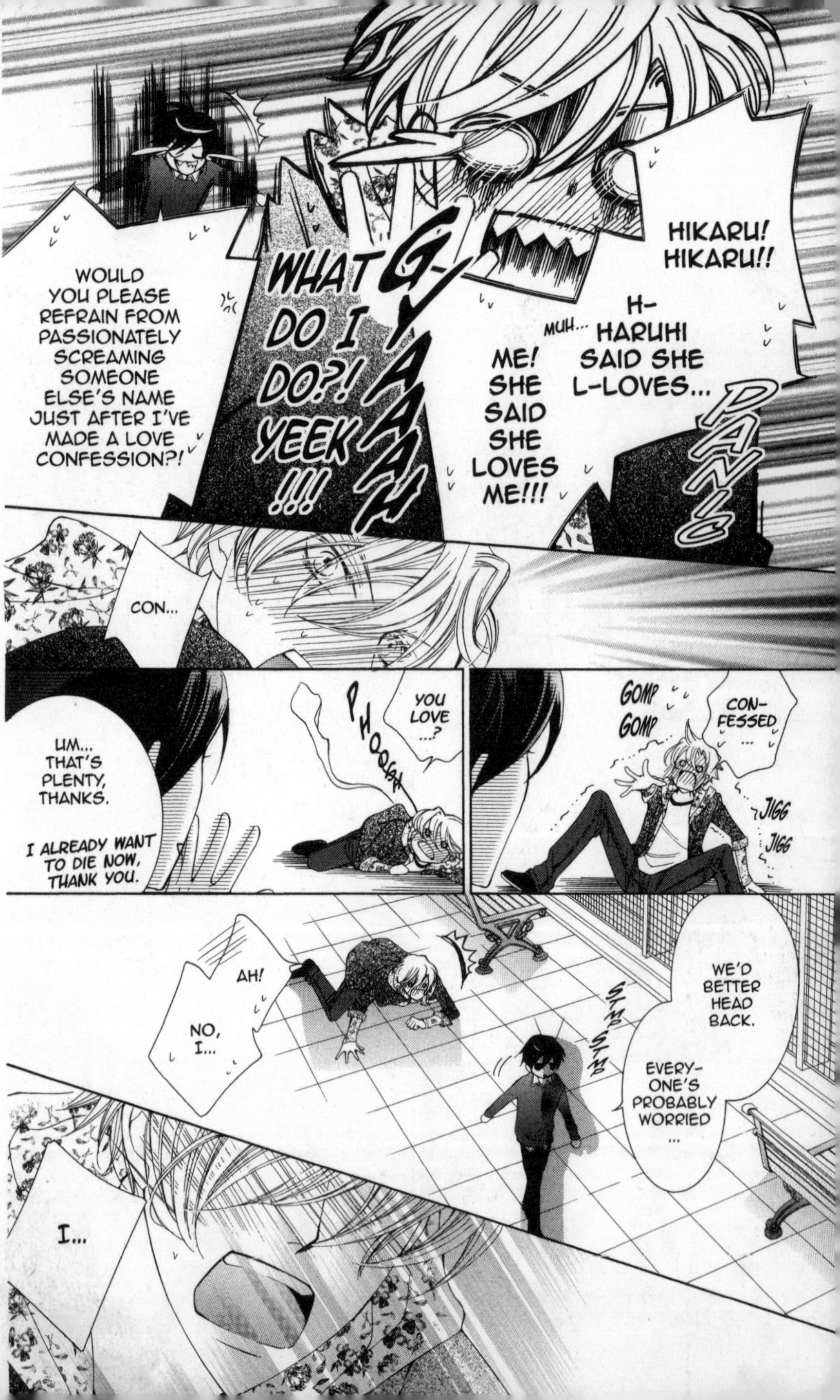
HIKARU! HIKARU!!
PANIC
H- HARUHI SAID SHE L-LOVES...
MUH...
ME! SHE SAID SHE LOVES ME!!!
GYAAAHH
WHAT DO I DO?! YEEK!!!
WOULD YOU PLEASE REFRAIN FROM PASSIONATELY SCREAMING SOMEONE ELSE'S NAME JUST AFTER I'VE MADE A LOVE CONFESSION?!
CON...
CON-FESSED...
GOMP GOMP
JIGG JIGG
YOU LOVE...?
PHOOSH
UM... THAT'S PLENTY, THANKS.
I ALREADY WANT TO DIE NOW, THANK YOU.
WE'D BETTER HEAD BACK.
EVERY-ONE'S PROBABLY WORRIED...
STMP STMP
AH!
NO, I...
I...

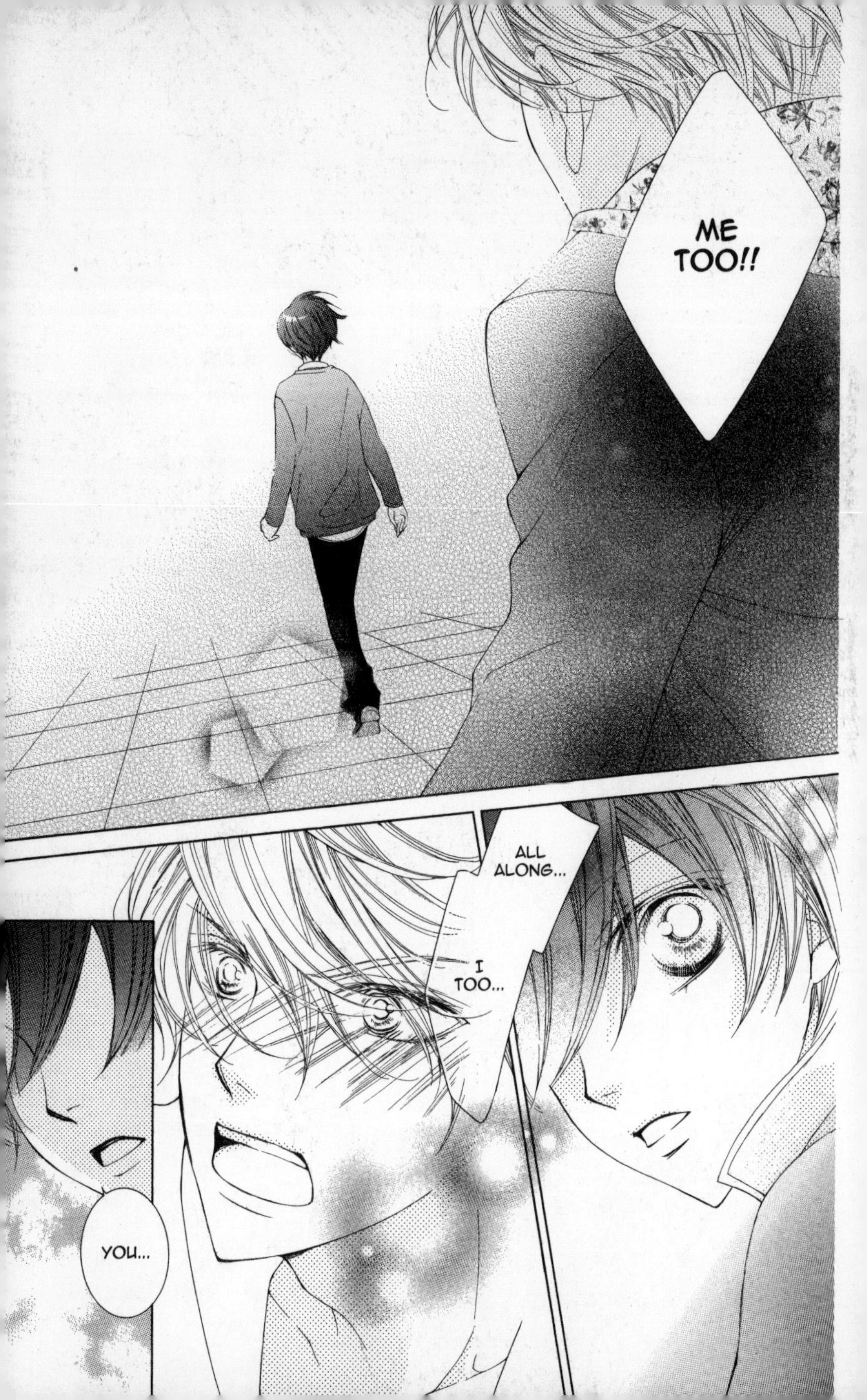
ME TOO!!
ALL ALONG...
I TOO...
YOU...

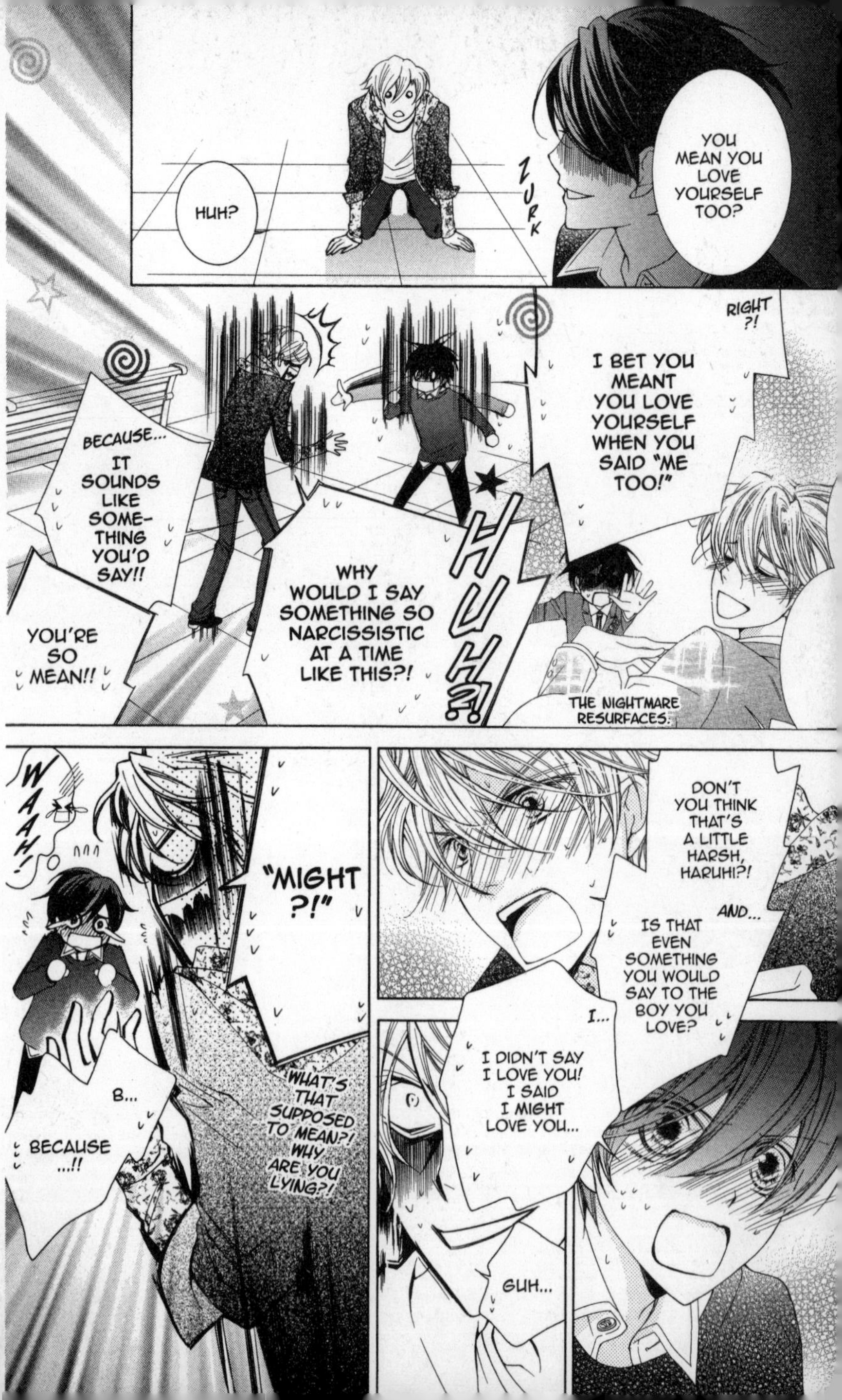
YOU MEAN YOU LOVE YOURSELF TOO?
ZURK
HUH?
RIGHT?!
I BET YOU MEANT YOU LOVE YOURSELF WHEN YOU SAID "ME TOO!"
THE NIGHTMARE RESURFACES.
HUH?!
WHY WOULD I SAY SOMETHING SO NARCISSISTIC AT A TIME LIKE THIS?!
BECAUSE... IT SOUNDS LIKE SOMETHING YOU'D SAY!!
YOU'RE SO MEAN!!
DON'T YOU THINK THAT'S A LITTLE HARSH, HARUHI?!
AND... IS THAT EVEN SOMETHING YOU WOULD SAY TO THE BOY YOU LOVE?
I...
I DIDN'T SAY I LOVE YOU! I SAID I MIGHT LOVE YOU...
GUH...
"MIGHT?!"
WHAT'S THAT SUPPOSED TO MEAN?! WHY ARE YOU LYING?!
WAAAH!
B...
BECAUSE...!!

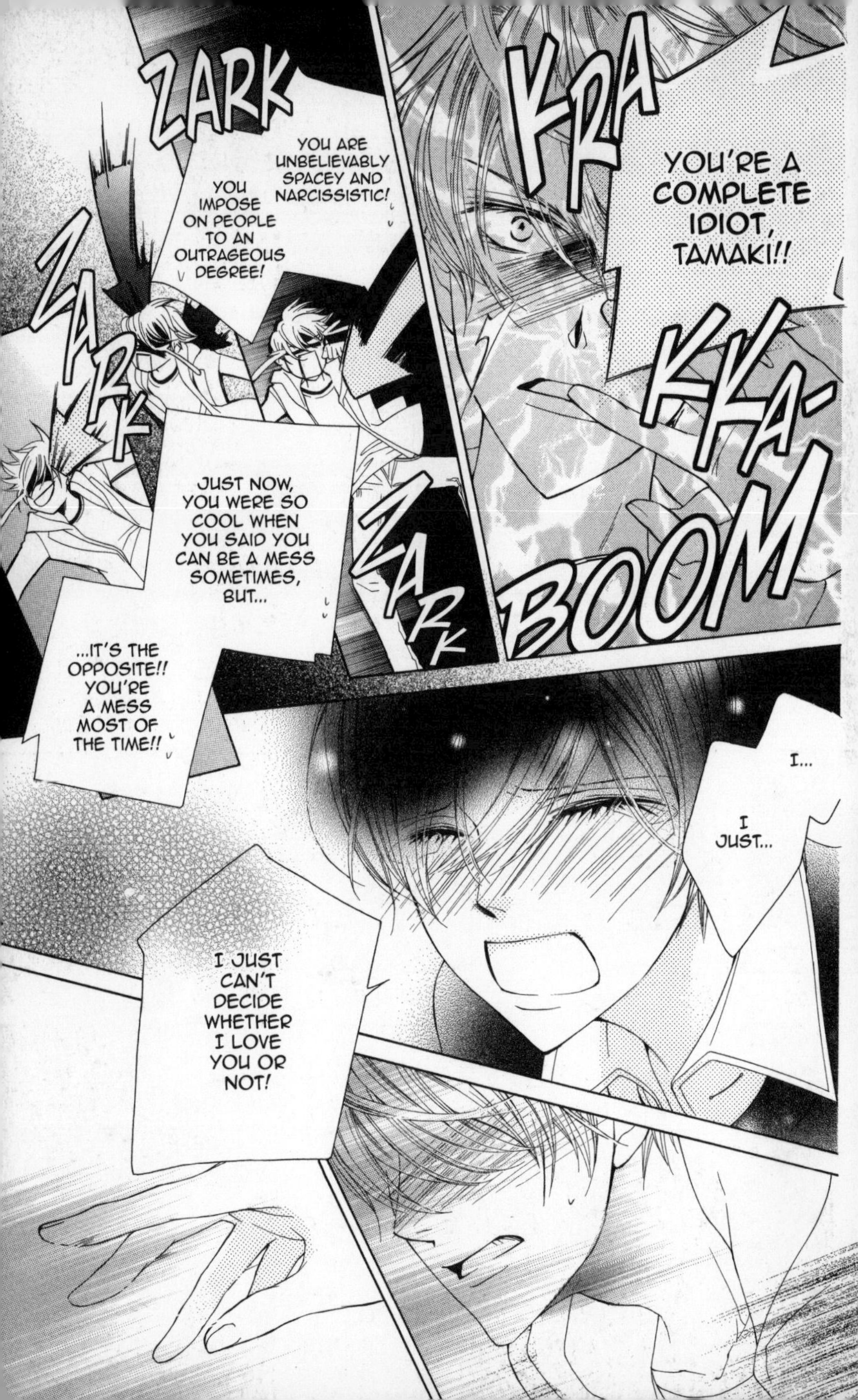
KRA
YOU'RE A COMPLETE IDIOT, TAMAKI!!
KKA-BOOM
ZARK
YOU ARE UNBELIEVABLY SPACEY AND NARCISSISTIC!
YOU IMPOSE ON PEOPLE TO AN OUTRAGEOUS DEGREE!
ZARK
ZARK
JUST NOW, YOU WERE SO COOL WHEN YOU SAID YOU CAN BE A MESS SOMETIMES, BUT...
...IT'S THE OPPOSITE!! YOU'RE A MESS MOST OF THE TIME!!
I...
I JUST...
I JUST CAN'T DECIDE WHETHER I LOVE YOU OR NOT!

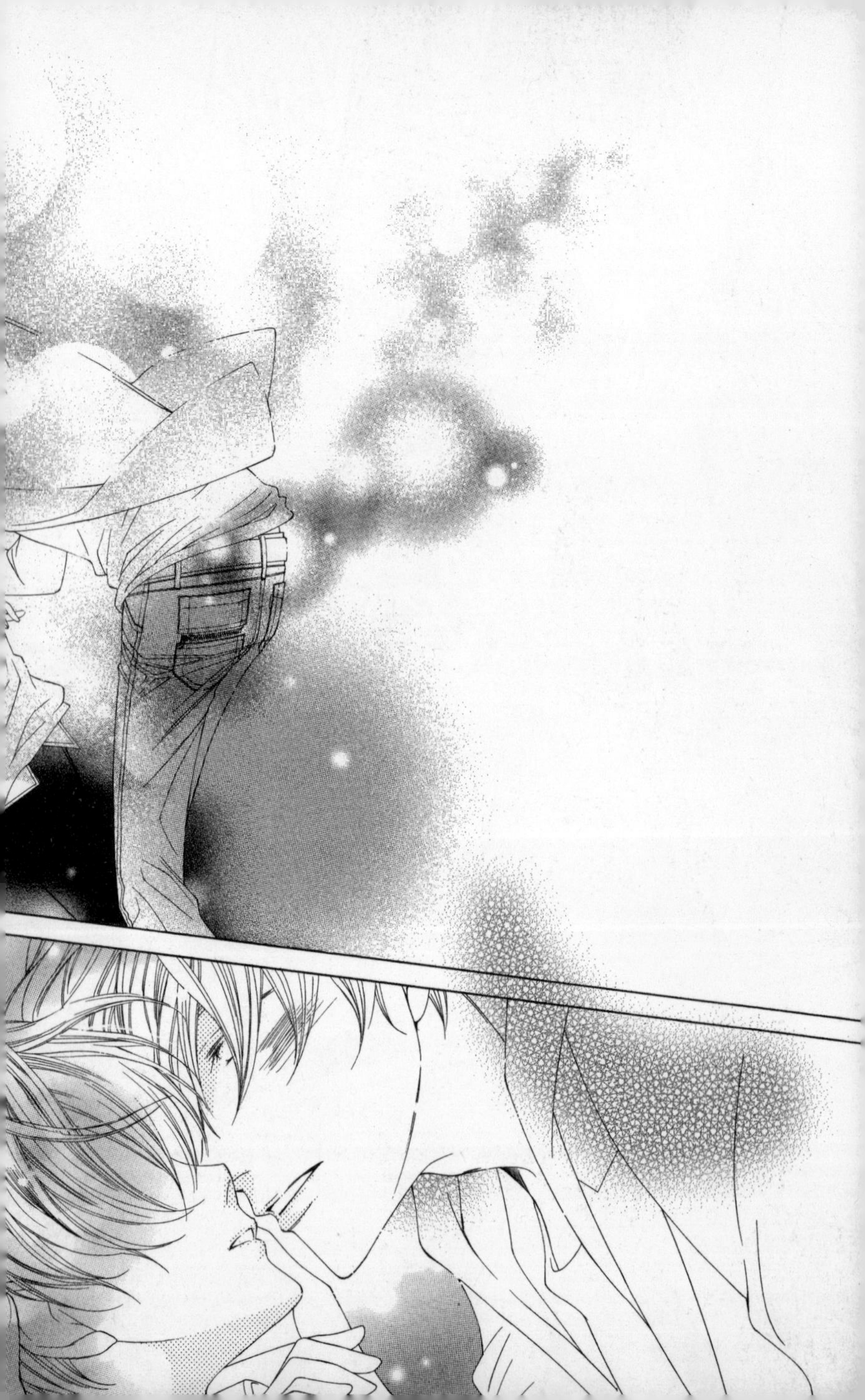

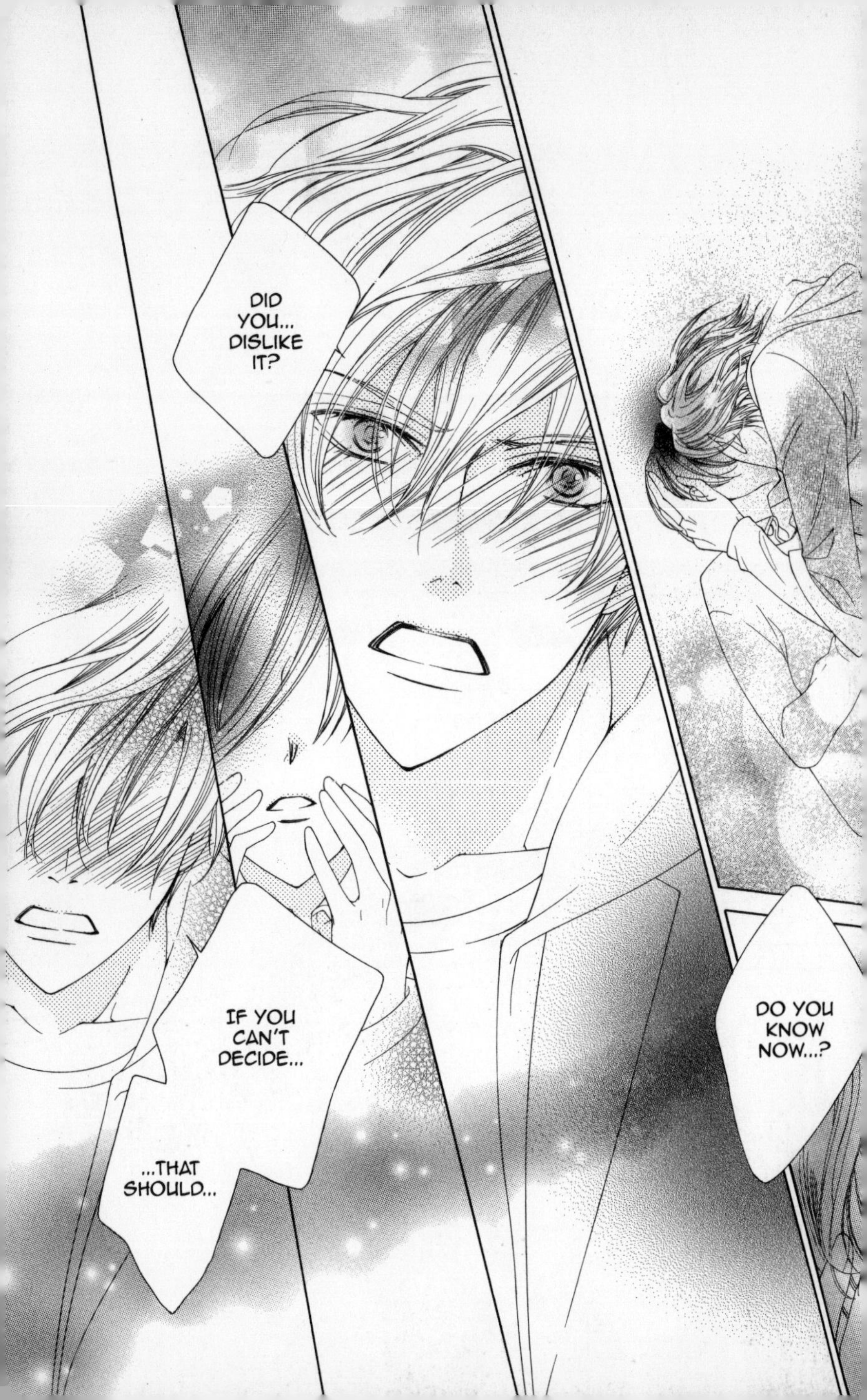
DO YOU KNOW NOW...?
DID YOU... DISLIKE IT?
IF YOU CAN'T DECIDE...
...THAT SHOULD...

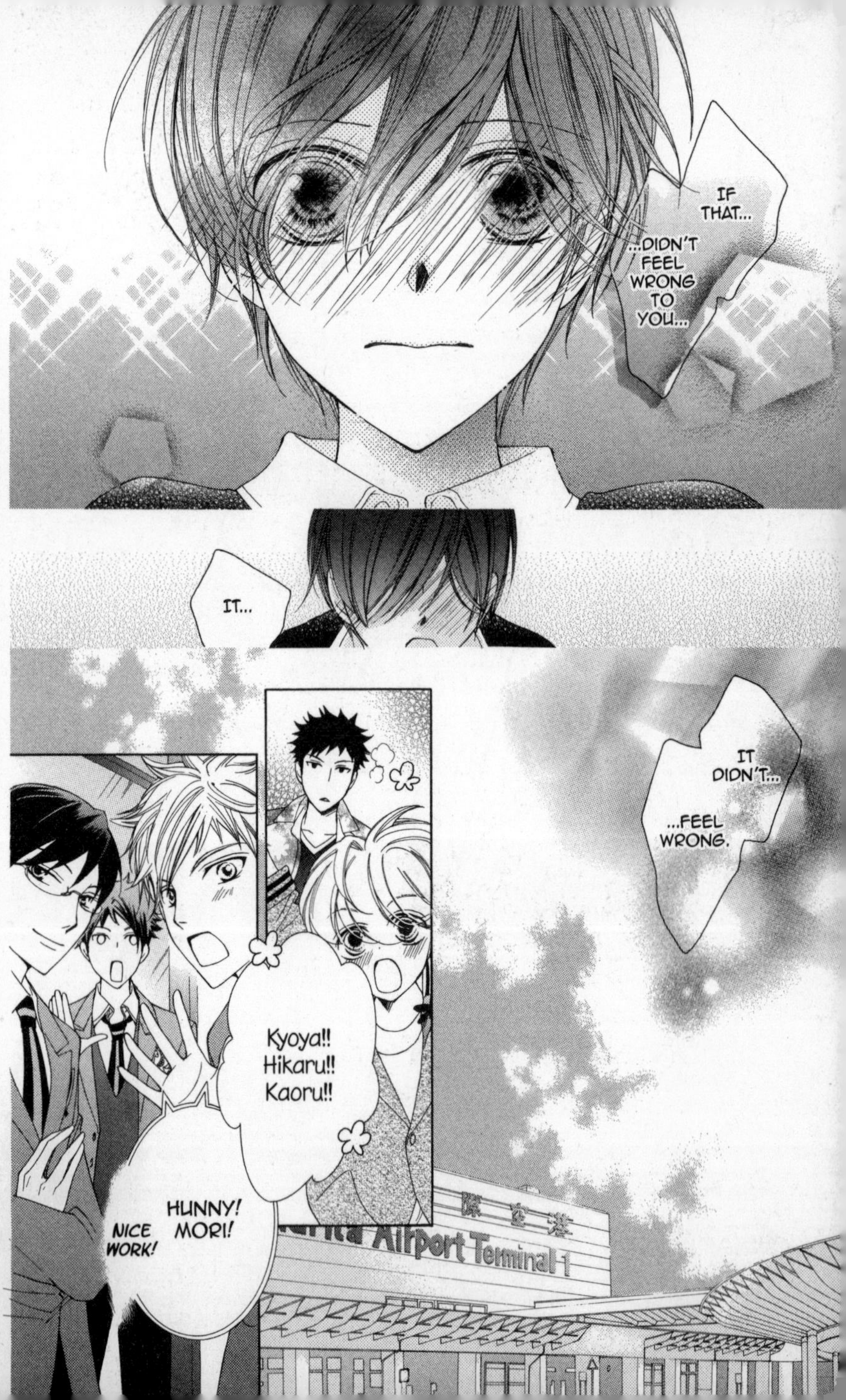
IF THAT...
...DIDN'T FEEL WRONG TO YOU...
IT...
IT DIDN'T...
...FEEL WRONG.
Kyoya!! Hikaru!! Kaoru!!
HUNNY! MORI!
NICE WORK!
Airport Terminal 1

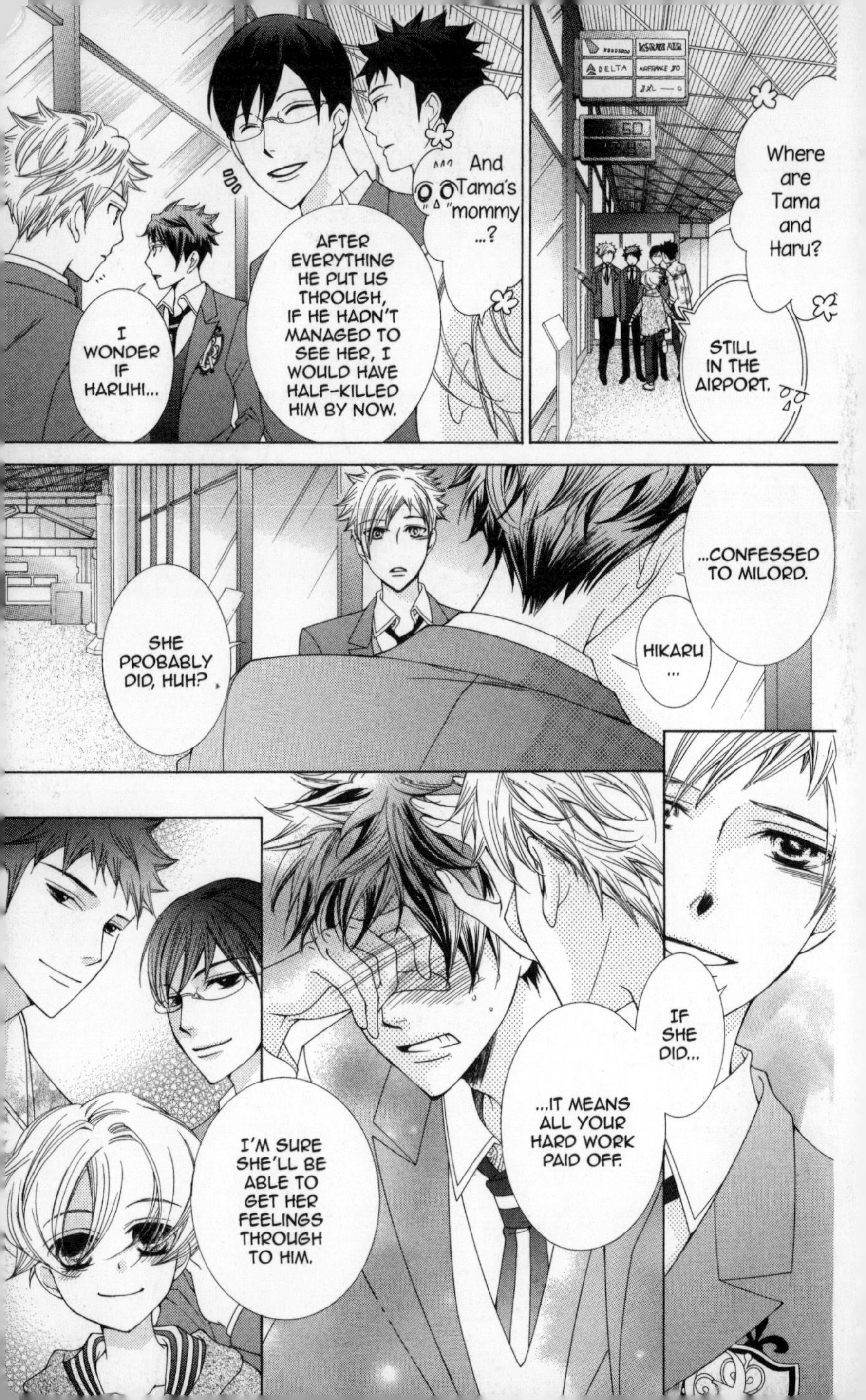
Where are Tama and Haru?
STILL IN THE AIRPORT.
And Tama's "mommy" ...?
AFTER EVERYTHING HE PUT US THROUGH, IF HE HADN'T MANAGED TO SEE HER, I WOULD HAVE HALF-KILLED HIM BY NOW.
I WONDER IF HARUHI...
...CONFESSED TO MILORD.
HIKARU ...
SHE PROBABLY DID, HUH?
IF SHE DID...
...IT MEANS ALL YOUR HARD WORK PAID OFF.
I'M SURE SHE'LL BE ABLE TO GET HER FEELINGS THROUGH TO HIM.

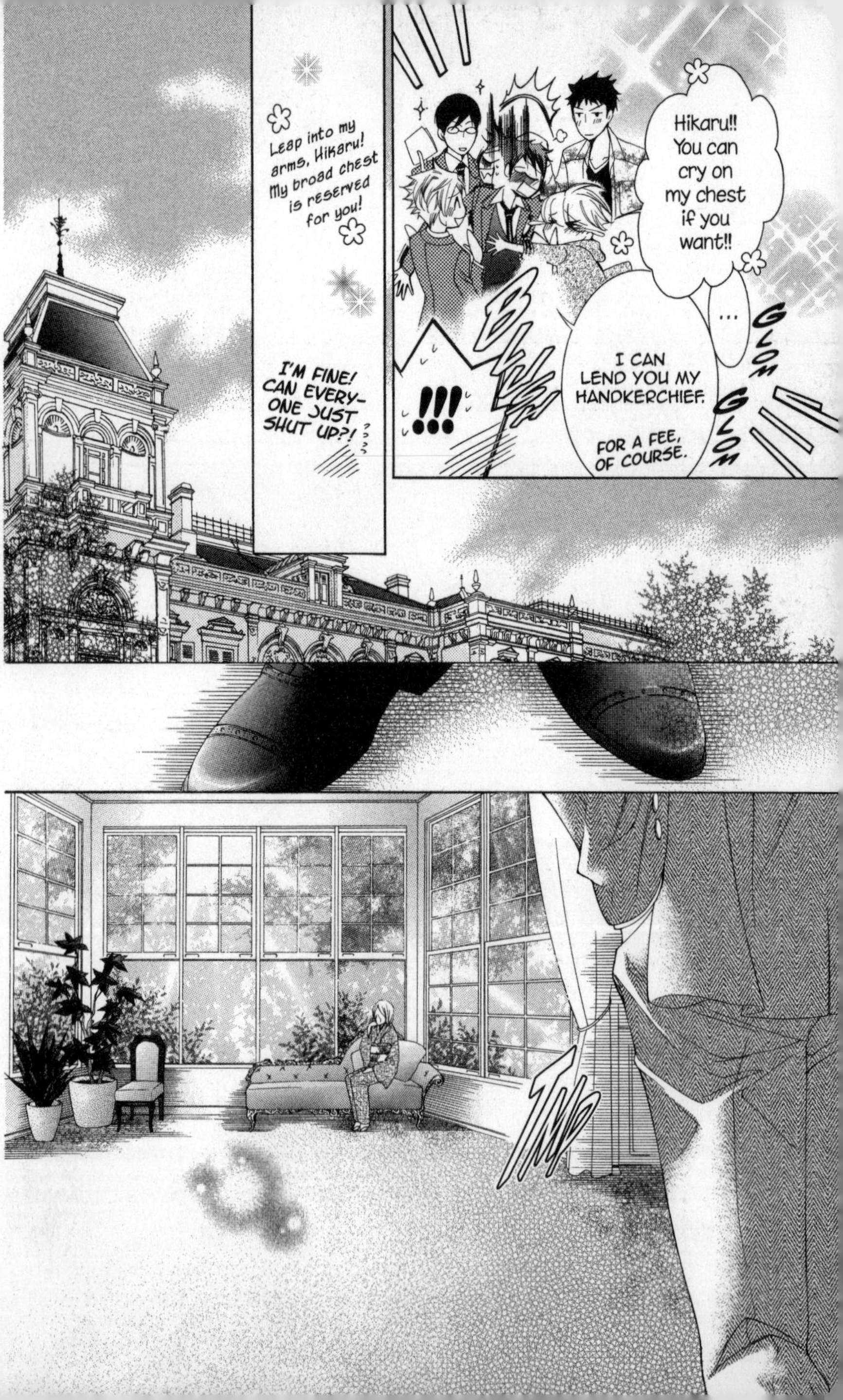
Hikaru!! You can cry on my chest if you want!!
...
I CAN LEND YOU MY HANDKERCHIEF.
FOR A FEE, OF COURSE.
GLOM GLOM
BLUSH
!!!
Leap into my arms, Hikaru! My broad chest is reserved for you!
I'M FINE! CAN EVERYONE JUST SHUT UP?!
TMP

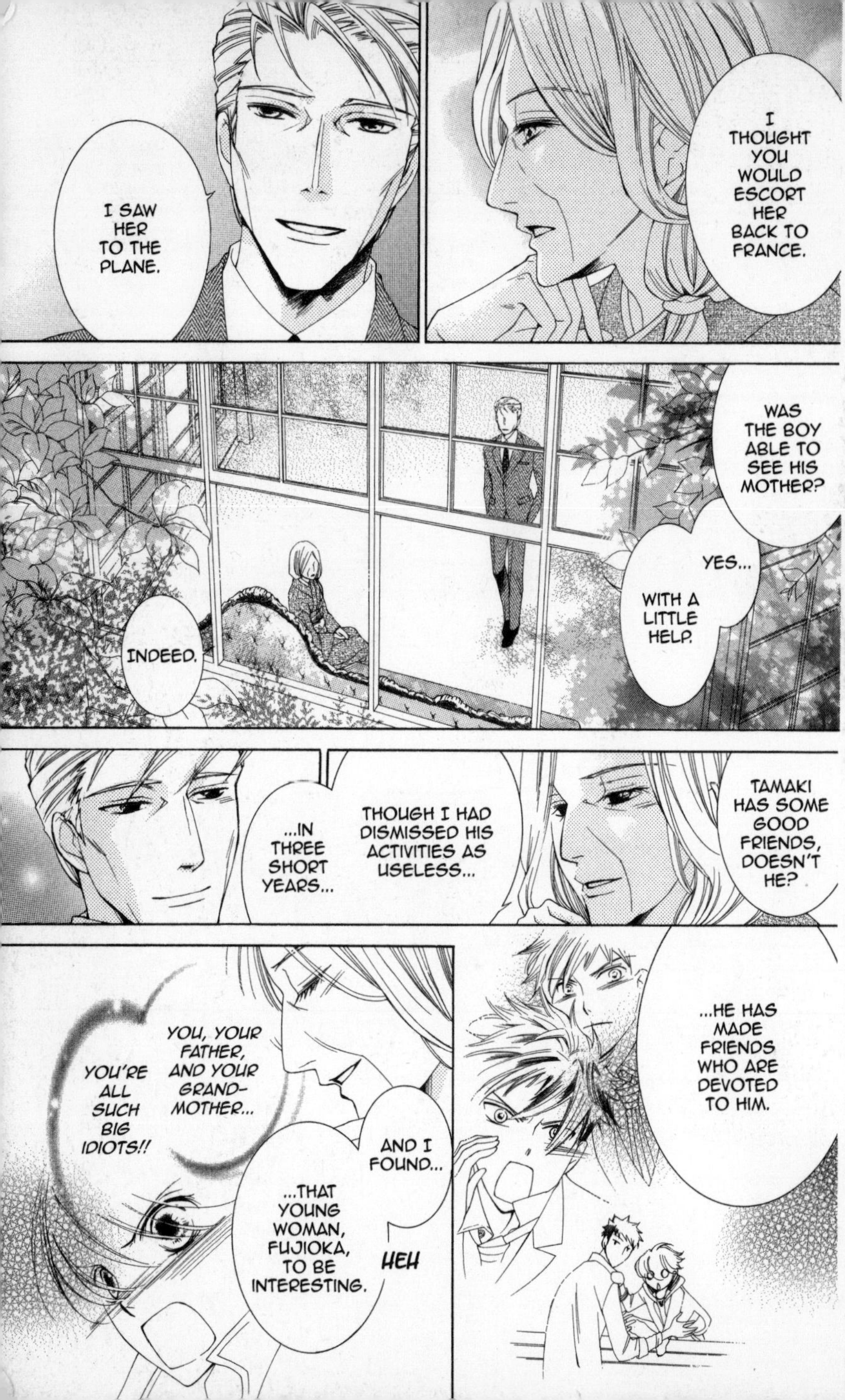

I THOUGHT YOU WOULD ESCORT HER BACK TO FRANCE.
I SAW HER TO THE PLANE.
WAS THE BOY ABLE TO SEE HIS MOTHER?
YES... WITH A LITTLE HELP.
INDEED.
TAMAKI HAS SOME GOOD FRIENDS, DOESN'T HE?
THOUGH I HAD DISMISSED HIS ACTIVITIES AS USELESS...
...IN THREE SHORT YEARS...
...HE HAS MADE FRIENDS WHO ARE DEVOTED TO HIM.
AND I FOUND...
...THAT YOUNG WOMAN, FUJIOKA, TO BE INTERESTING.
HEH
YOU, YOUR FATHER, AND YOUR GRANDMOTHER...
YOU'RE ALL SUCH BIG IDIOTS!!

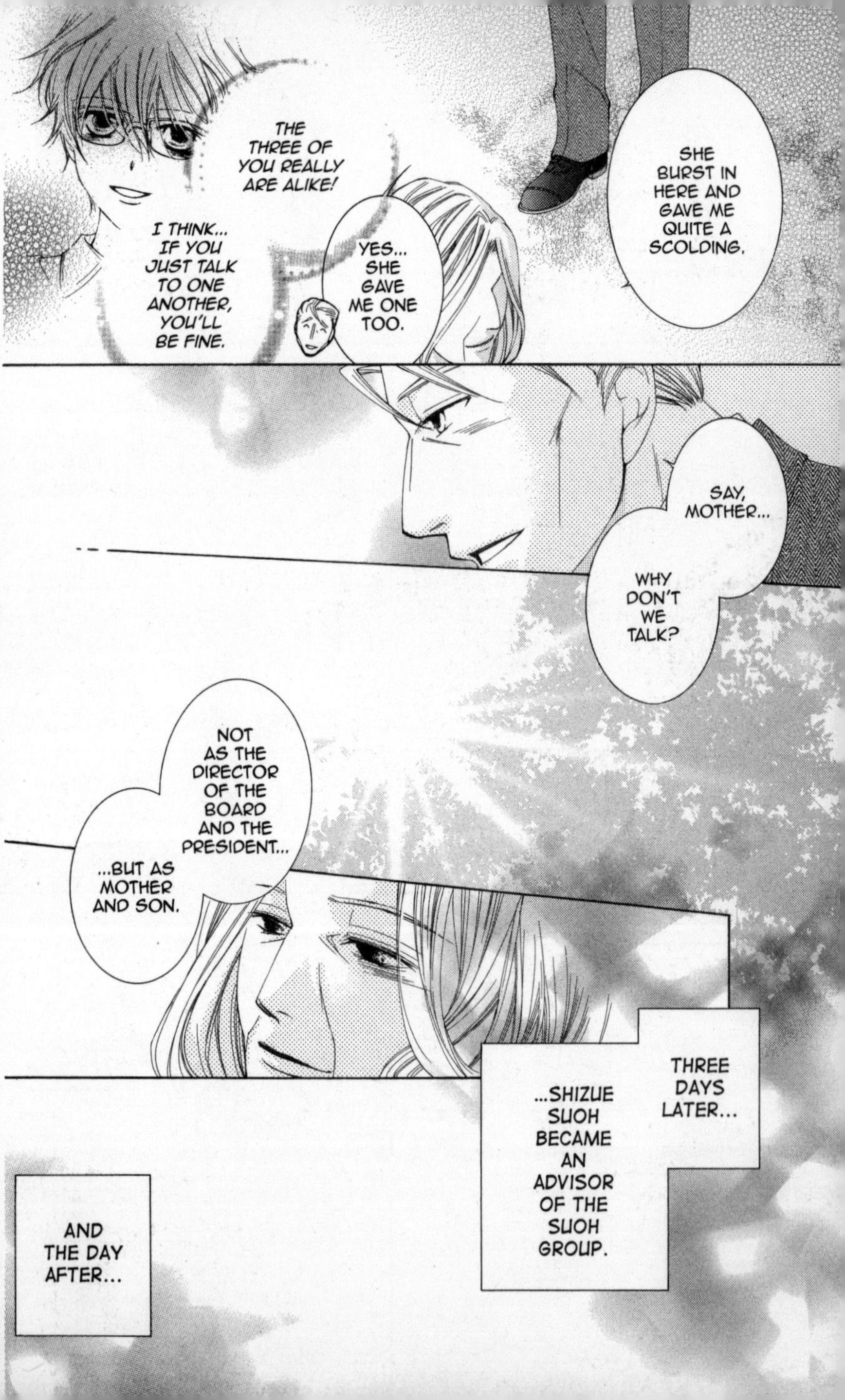
SHE BURST IN HERE AND GAVE ME QUITE A SCOLDING.
YES... SHE GAVE ME ONE TOO.
THE THREE OF YOU REALLY ARE ALIKE!
I THINK... IF YOU JUST TALK TO ONE ANOTHER, YOU'LL BE FINE.
SAY, MOTHER...
WHY DON'T WE TALK?
NOT AS THE DIRECTOR OF THE BOARD AND THE PRESIDENT...
...BUT AS MOTHER AND SON.
THREE DAYS LATER...
...SHIZUE SUOH BECAME AN ADVISOR OF THE SUOH GROUP.
AND THE DAY AFTER...

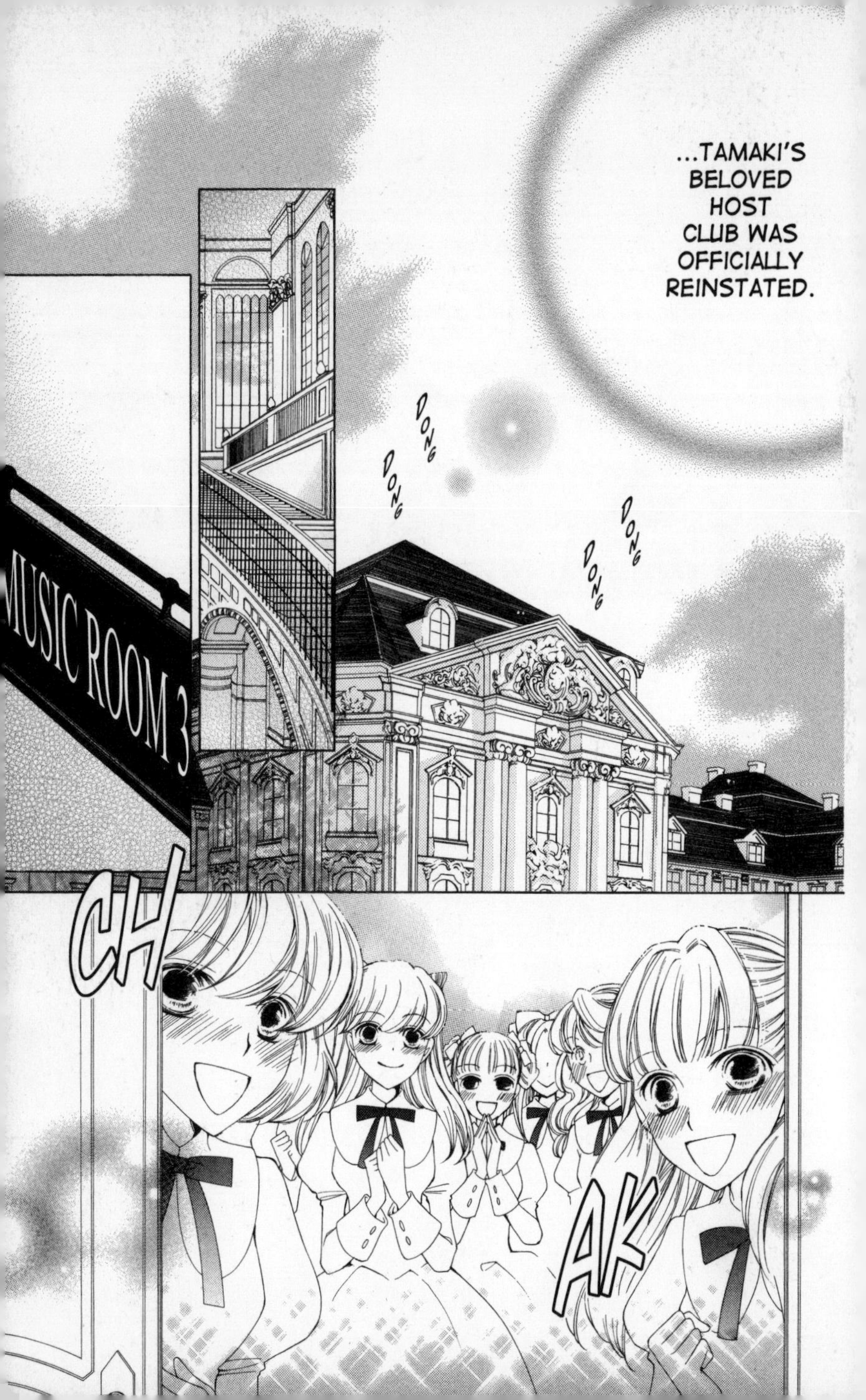
...TAMAKI'S BELOVED HOST CLUB WAS OFFICIALLY REINSTATED.
DONG DONG
DONG DONG
MUSIC ROOM 3
CH
AK

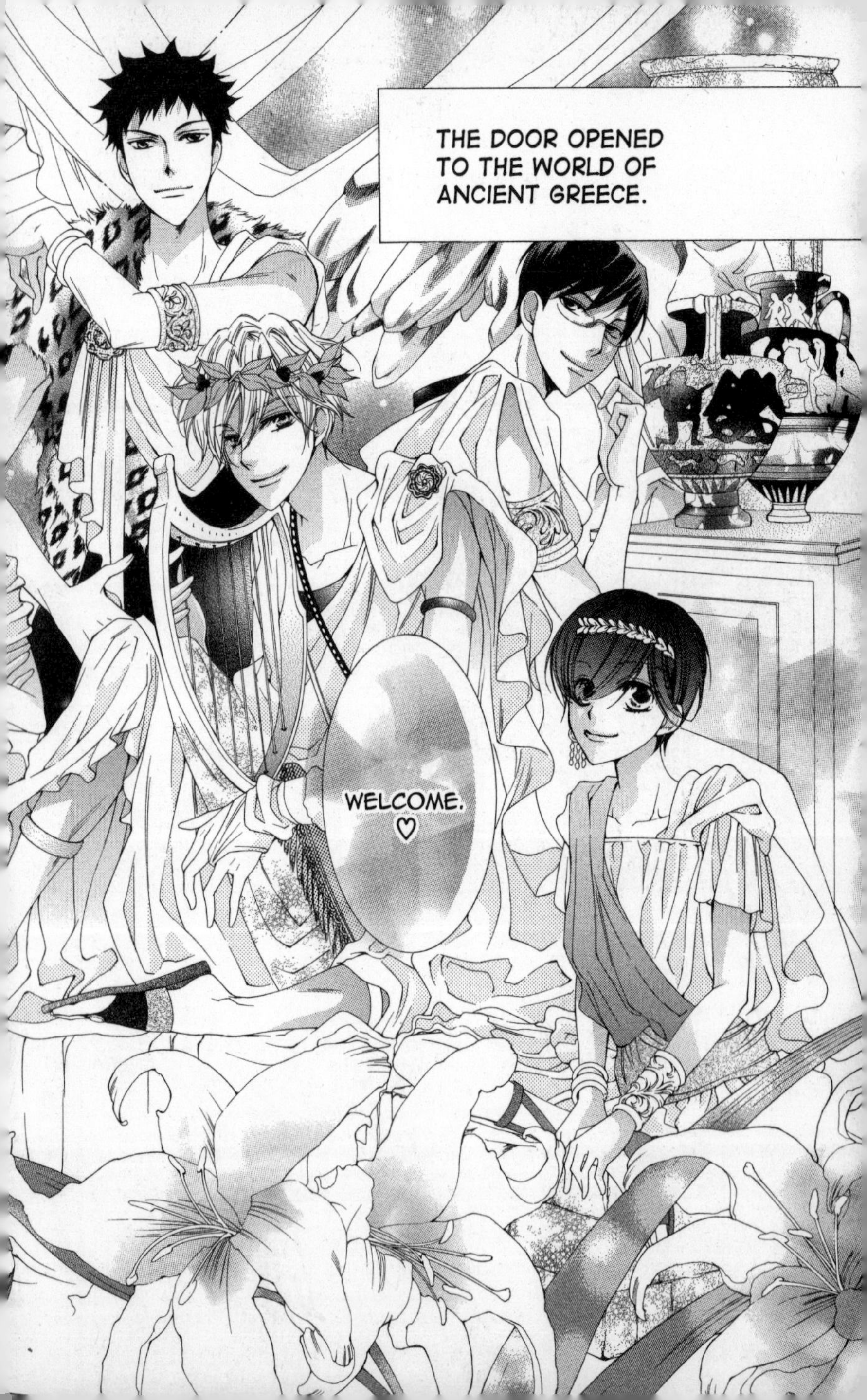
THE DOOR OPENED TO THE WORLD OF ANCIENT GREECE.
WELCOME. ♡

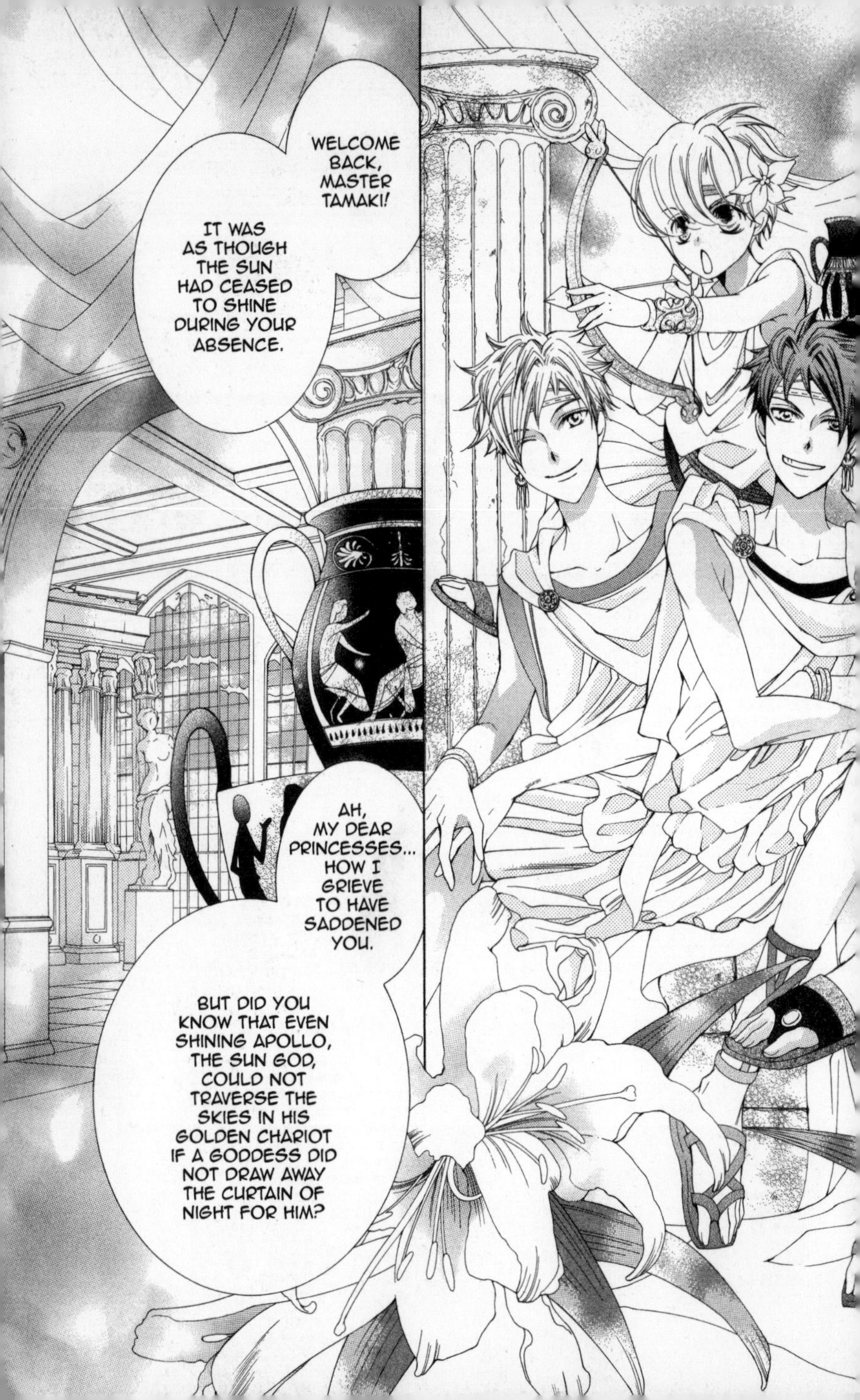
WELCOME BACK, MASTER TAMAKI!
IT WAS AS THOUGH THE SUN HAD CEASED TO SHINE DURING YOUR ABSENCE.
AH, MY DEAR PRINCESSES... HOW I GRIEVE TO HAVE SADDENED YOU.
BUT DID YOU KNOW THAT EVEN SHINING APOLLO, THE SUN GOD, COULD NOT TRAVERSE THE SKIES IN HIS GOLDEN CHARIOT IF A GODDESS DID NOT DRAW AWAY THE CURTAIN OF NIGHT FOR HIM?

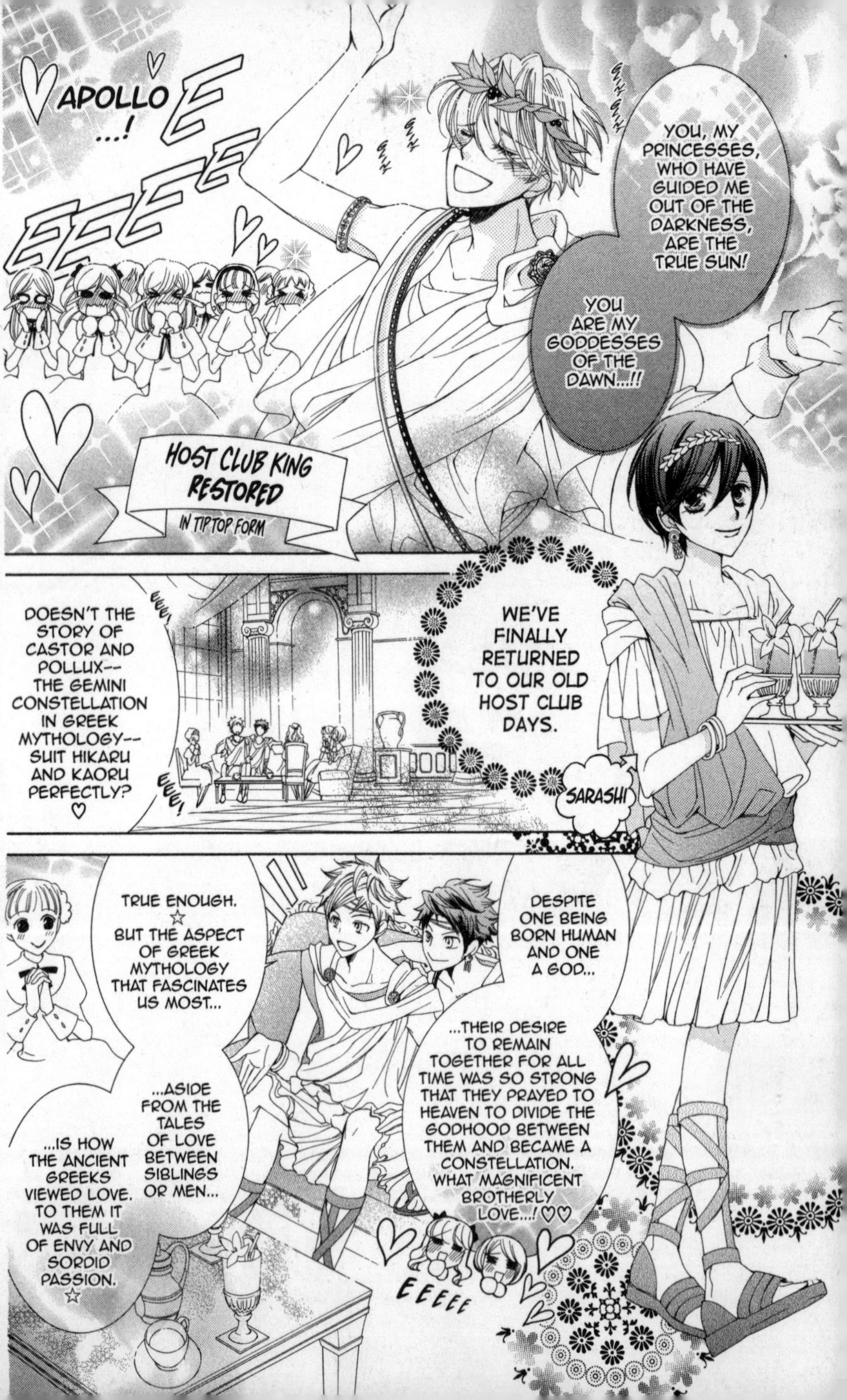
YOU, MY PRINCESSES, WHO HAVE GUIDED ME OUT OF THE DARKNESS, ARE THE TRUE SUN!
YOU ARE MY GODDESSES OF THE DAWN...!!
APOLLO ...!
EEEEEE
HOST CLUB KING RESTORED
IN TIPTOP FORM
WE'VE FINALLY RETURNED TO OUR OLD HOST CLUB DAYS.
SARASHI
DOESN'T THE STORY OF CASTOR AND POLLUX-- THE GEMINI CONSTELLATION IN GREEK MYTHOLOGY-- SUIT HIKARU AND KAORU PERFECTLY? ♡
EEE!
EEE!
DESPITE ONE BEING BORN HUMAN AND ONE A GOD...
...THEIR DESIRE TO REMAIN TOGETHER FOR ALL TIME WAS SO STRONG THAT THEY PRAYED TO HEAVEN TO DIVIDE THE GODHOOD BETWEEN THEM AND BECAME A CONSTELLATION. WHAT MAGNIFICENT BROTHERLY LOVE...! ♡♡
TRUE ENOUGH. ☆ BUT THE ASPECT OF GREEK MYTHOLOGY THAT FASCINATES US MOST...
...ASIDE FROM THE TALES OF LOVE BETWEEN SIBLINGS OR MEN...
...IS HOW THE ANCIENT GREEKS VIEWED LOVE. TO THEM IT WAS FULL OF ENVY AND SORDID PASSION. ☆
EEEEE

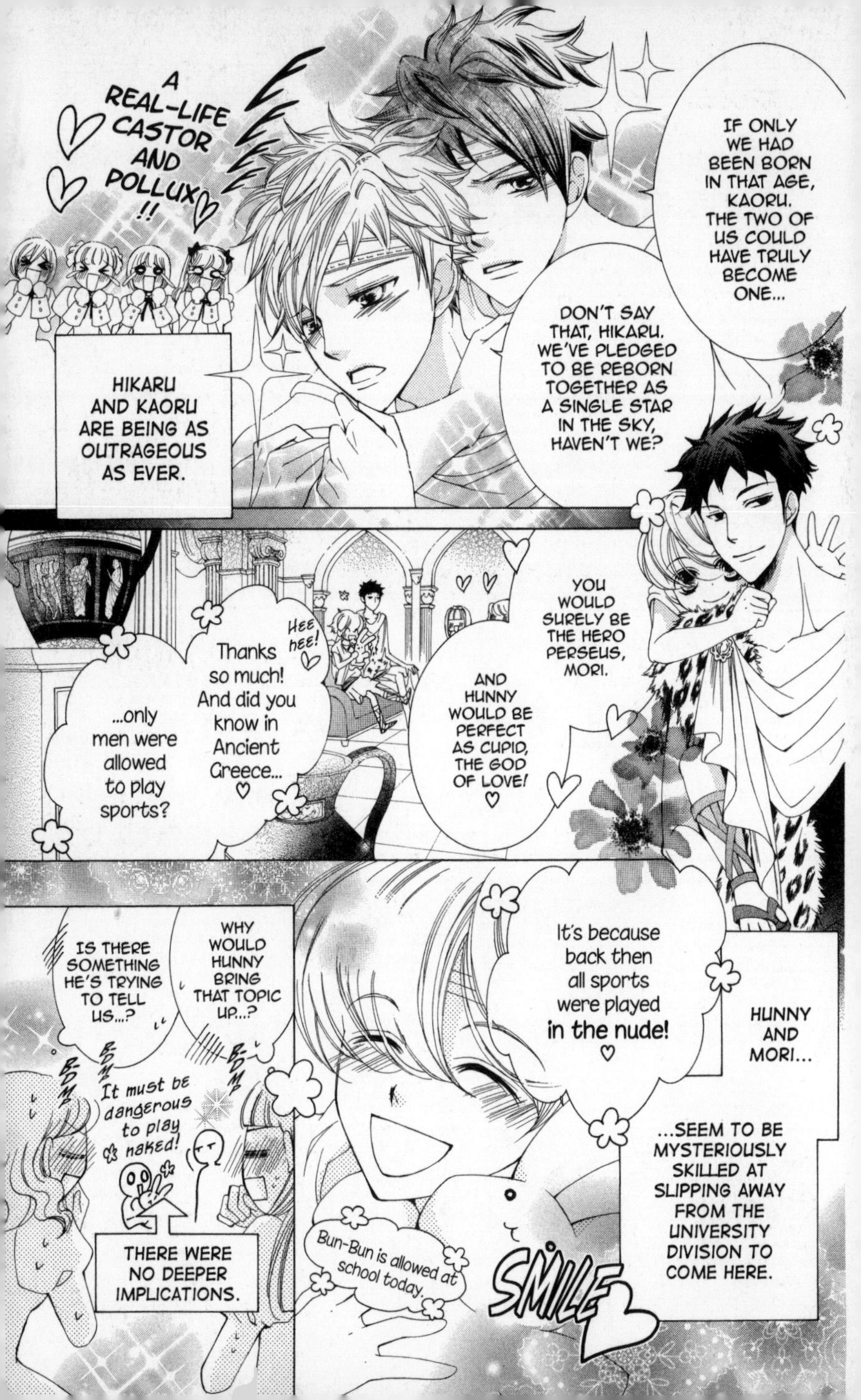
IF ONLY WE HAD BEEN BORN IN THAT AGE, KAORU. THE TWO OF US COULD HAVE TRULY BECOME ONE...
DON'T SAY THAT, HIKARU. WE'VE PLEDGED TO BE REBORN TOGETHER AS A SINGLE STAR IN THE SKY, HAVEN'T WE?
A REAL-LIFE CASTOR AND POLLUX!!
HIKARU AND KAORU ARE BEING AS OUTRAGEOUS AS EVER.
YOU WOULD SURELY BE THE HERO PERSEUS, MORI.
AND HUNNY WOULD BE PERFECT AS CUPID, THE GOD OF LOVE!
HEE HEE!
Thanks so much! And did you know in Ancient Greece...
...only men were allowed to play sports?
HUNNY AND MORI...
It's because back then all sports were played in the nude!
...SEEM TO BE MYSTERIOUSLY SKILLED AT SLIPPING AWAY FROM THE UNIVERSITY DIVISION TO COME HERE.
SMILE
Bun-Bun is allowed at school today.
WHY WOULD HUNNY BRING THAT TOPIC UP...?
IS THERE SOMETHING HE'S TRYING TO TELL US...?
BDMP
BDMP
It must be dangerous to play naked!
THERE WERE NO DEEPER IMPLICATIONS.

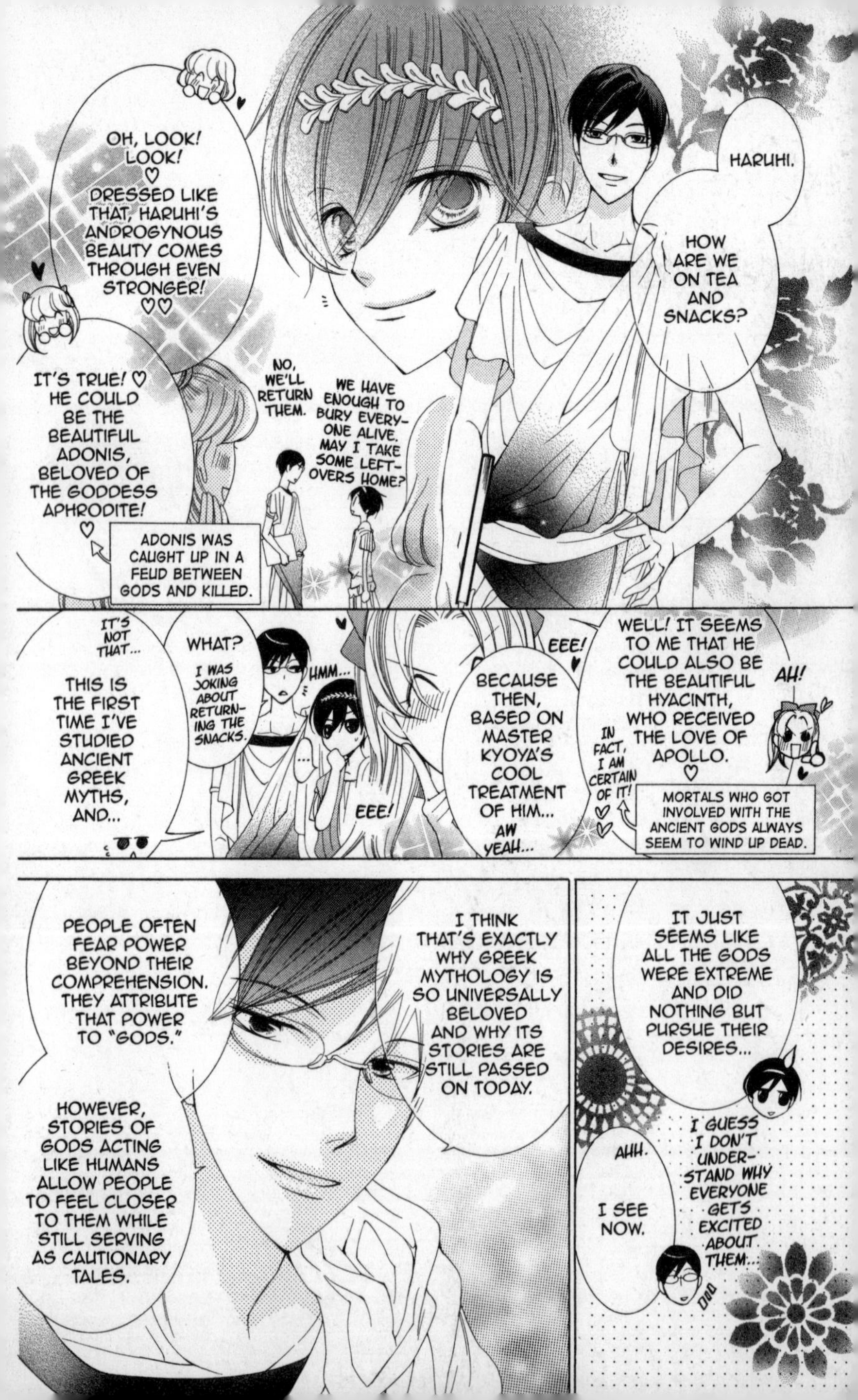
HARUHI.
HOW ARE WE ON TEA AND SNACKS?
OH, LOOK! LOOK! ♡ DRESSED LIKE THAT, HARUHI'S ANDROGYNOUS BEAUTY COMES THROUGH EVEN STRONGER! ♡♡
IT'S TRUE! ♡ HE COULD BE THE BEAUTIFUL ADONIS, BELOVED OF THE GODDESS APHRODITE! ♡
ADONIS WAS CAUGHT UP IN A FEUD BETWEEN GODS AND KILLED.
WE HAVE ENOUGH TO BURY EVERY-ONE ALIVE. MAY I TAKE SOME LEFT-OVERS HOME?
NO, WE'LL RETURN THEM.
AH!
WELL! IT SEEMS TO ME THAT HE COULD ALSO BE THE BEAUTIFUL HYACINTH, WHO RECEIVED THE LOVE OF APOLLO. ♡
IN FACT, I AM CERTAIN OF IT! ♡♡
MORTALS WHO GOT INVOLVED WITH THE ANCIENT GODS ALWAYS SEEM TO WIND UP DEAD.
EEE!
BECAUSE THEN, BASED ON MASTER KYOYA'S COOL TREATMENT OF HIM...
AW YEAH...
EEE!
HMM...
...
WHAT?
I WAS JOKING ABOUT RETURNING THE SNACKS.
IT'S NOT THAT...
THIS IS THE FIRST TIME I'VE STUDIED ANCIENT GREEK MYTHS, AND...
IT JUST SEEMS LIKE ALL THE GODS WERE EXTREME AND DID NOTHING BUT PURSUE THEIR DESIRES...
I GUESS I DON'T UNDER-STAND WHY EVERYONE GETS EXCITED ABOUT THEM...
AHH.
I SEE NOW.
PEOPLE OFTEN FEAR POWER BEYOND THEIR COMPREHENSION. THEY ATTRIBUTE THAT POWER TO "GODS."
HOWEVER, STORIES OF GODS ACTING LIKE HUMANS ALLOW PEOPLE TO FEEL CLOSER TO THEM WHILE STILL SERVING AS CAUTIONARY TALES.
I THINK THAT'S EXACTLY WHY GREEK MYTHOLOGY IS SO UNIVERSALLY BELOVED AND WHY ITS STORIES ARE STILL PASSED ON TODAY.

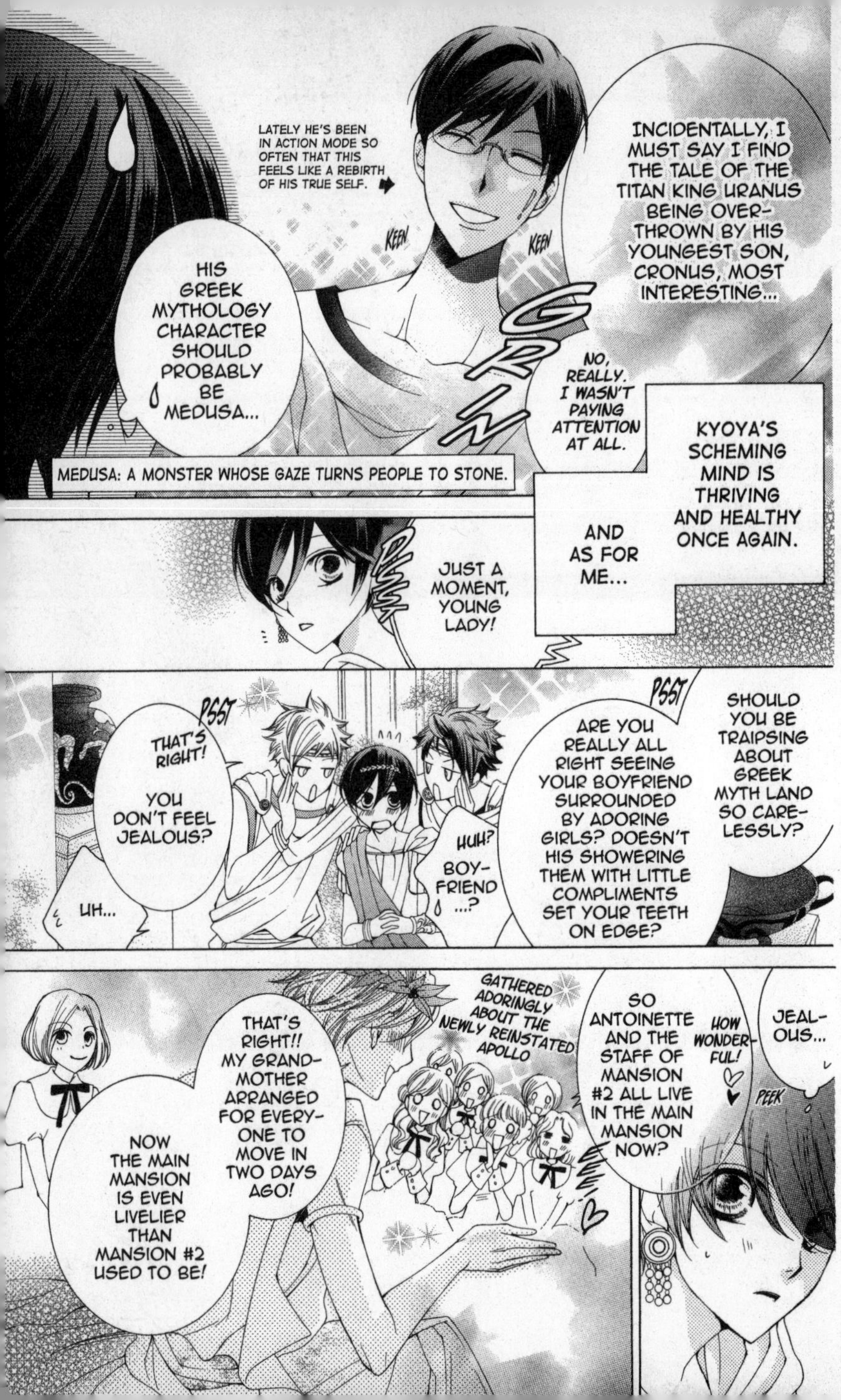
INCIDENTALLY, I MUST SAY I FIND THE TALE OF THE TITAN KING URANUS BEING OVER-THROWN BY HIS YOUNGEST SON, CRONUS, MOST INTERESTING...
KEEN
KEEN
GRIN
LATELY HE'S BEEN IN ACTION MODE SO OFTEN THAT THIS FEELS LIKE A REBIRTH OF HIS TRUE SELF.
HIS GREEK MYTHOLOGY CHARACTER SHOULD PROBABLY BE MEDUSA...
NO, REALLY. I WASN'T PAYING ATTENTION AT ALL.
MEDUSA: A MONSTER WHOSE GAZE TURNS PEOPLE TO STONE.
KYOYA'S SCHEMING MIND IS THRIVING AND HEALTHY ONCE AGAIN.
AND AS FOR ME...
JUST A MOMENT, YOUNG LADY!
SHOULD YOU BE TRAIPSING ABOUT GREEK MYTH LAND SO CARE-LESSLY?
PSST
ARE YOU REALLY ALL RIGHT SEEING YOUR BOYFRIEND SURROUNDED BY ADORING GIRLS? DOESN'T HIS SHOWERING THEM WITH LITTLE COMPLIMENTS SET YOUR TEETH ON EDGE?
HUH? BOY-FRIEND ...?
PSST
THAT'S RIGHT!
YOU DON'T FEEL JEALOUS?
UH...
JEAL-OUS...
PEEK
HOW WONDER-FUL!
SO ANTOINETTE AND THE STAFF OF MANSION #2 ALL LIVE IN THE MAIN MANSION NOW?
GATHERED ADORINGLY ABOUT THE NEWLY REINSTATED APOLLO
THAT'S RIGHT!! MY GRAND-MOTHER ARRANGED FOR EVERY-ONE TO MOVE IN TWO DAYS AGO!
NOW THE MAIN MANSION IS EVEN LIVELIER THAN MANSION #2 USED TO BE!

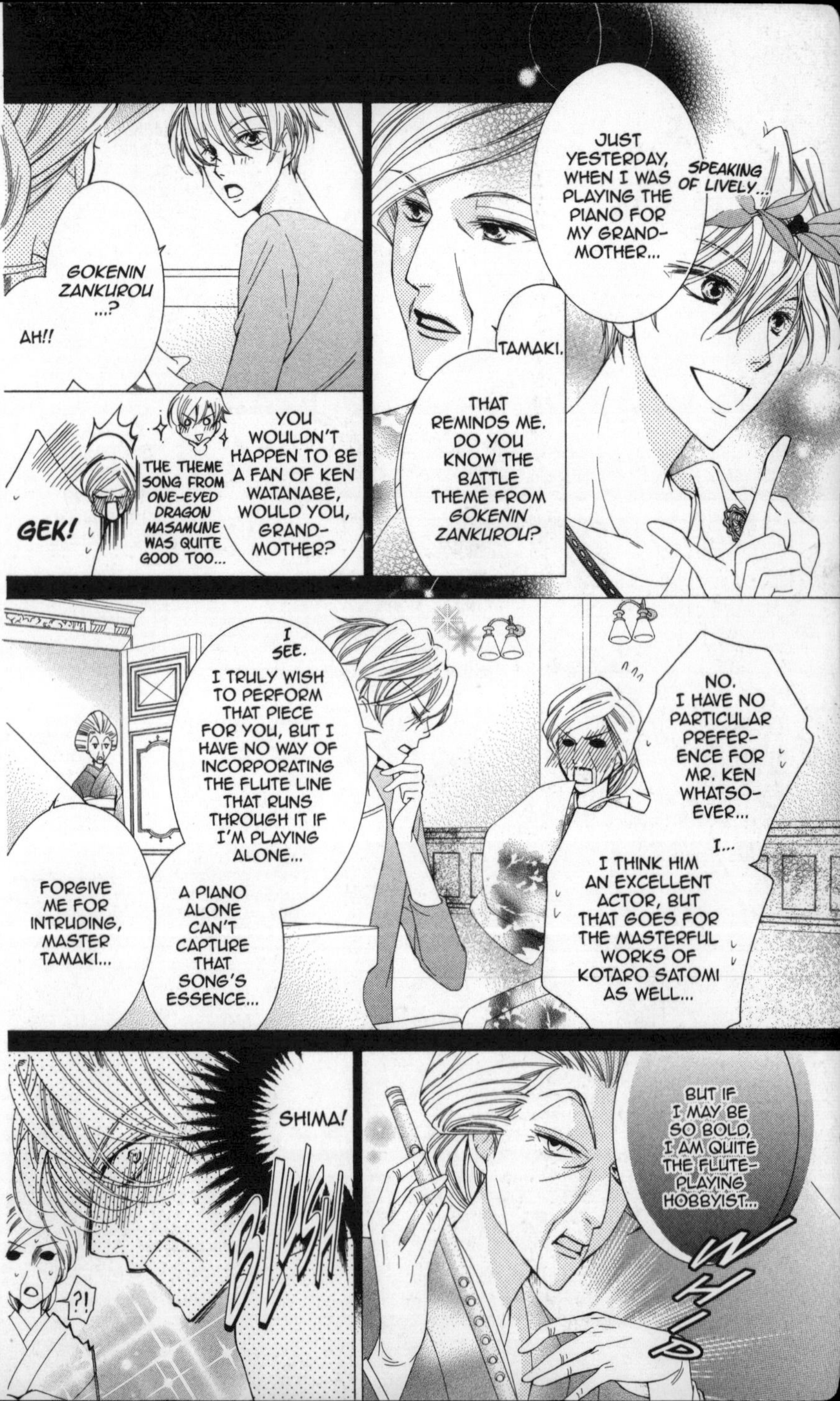
SPEAKING OF LIVELY...
JUST YESTERDAY, WHEN I WAS PLAYING THE PIANO FOR MY GRAND-MOTHER...
TAMAKI.
THAT REMINDS ME. DO YOU KNOW THE BATTLE THEME FROM GOKENIN ZANKUROU?
GOKENIN ZANKUROU ...?
AH!!
YOU WOULDN'T HAPPEN TO BE A FAN OF KEN WATANABE, WOULD YOU, GRAND-MOTHER?
THE THEME SONG FROM ONE-EYED DRAGON MASAMUNE WAS QUITE GOOD TOO...
GEK!
NO. I HAVE NO PARTICULAR PREFER-ENCE FOR MR. KEN WHATSO-EVER...
I...
I THINK HIM AN EXCELLENT ACTOR, BUT THAT GOES FOR THE MASTERFUL WORKS OF KOTARO SATOMI AS WELL...
I SEE.
I TRULY WISH TO PERFORM THAT PIECE FOR YOU, BUT I HAVE NO WAY OF INCORPORATING THE FLUTE LINE THAT RUNS THROUGH IT IF I'M PLAYING ALONE...
A PIANO ALONE CAN'T CAPTURE THAT SONG'S ESSENCE...
FORGIVE ME FOR INTRUDING, MASTER TAMAKI...
BUT IF I MAY BE SO BOLD, I AM QUITE THE FLUTE-PLAYING HOBBYIST...
WHIP
SHIMA!
BLUSH
?!

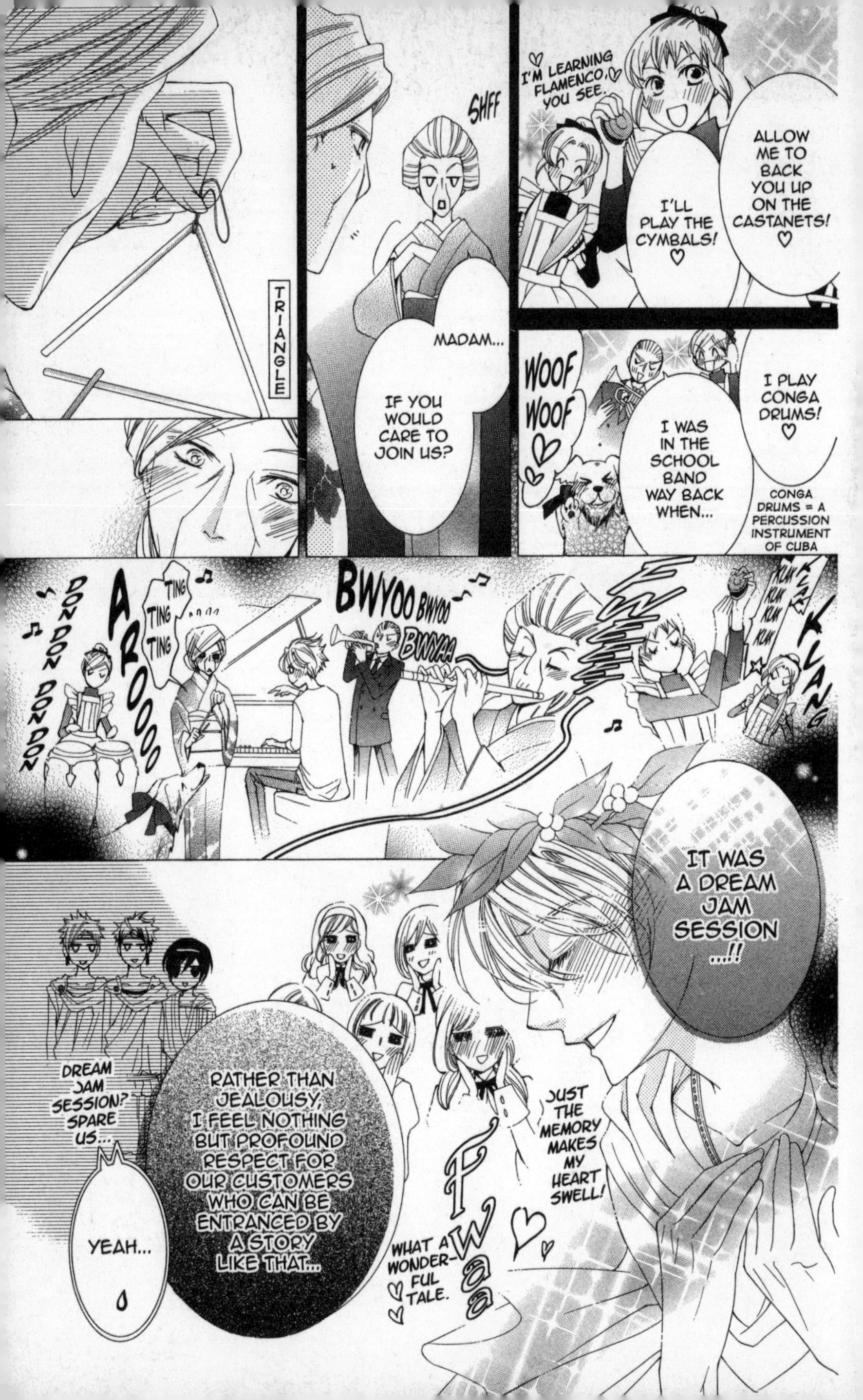
ALLOW ME TO BACK YOU UP ON THE CASTANETS!
I'LL PLAY THE CYMBALS!
I'M LEARNING FLAMENCO, YOU SEE.
I PLAY CONGA DRUMS!
CONGA DRUMS = A PERCUSSION INSTRUMENT OF CUBA
I WAS IN THE SCHOOL BAND WAY BACK WHEN...
WOOF WOOF
SHFF
MADAM...
IF YOU WOULD CARE TO JOIN US?
TRIANGLE
KUAK KUAK KUAK KUAK KUAK
KVANG
BWYOO BWYOO BWYAA
TING TING TING
AROOOOO
DON DON DON DON DON DON
IT WAS A DREAM JAM SESSION ...!!
JUST THE MEMORY MAKES MY HEART SWELL!
FWaa
WHAT A WONDERFUL TALE.
RATHER THAN JEALOUSY, I FEEL NOTHING BUT PROFOUND RESPECT FOR OUR CUSTOMERS WHO CAN BE ENTRANCED BY A STORY LIKE THAT...
DREAM JAM SESSION? SPARE US...
YEAH...

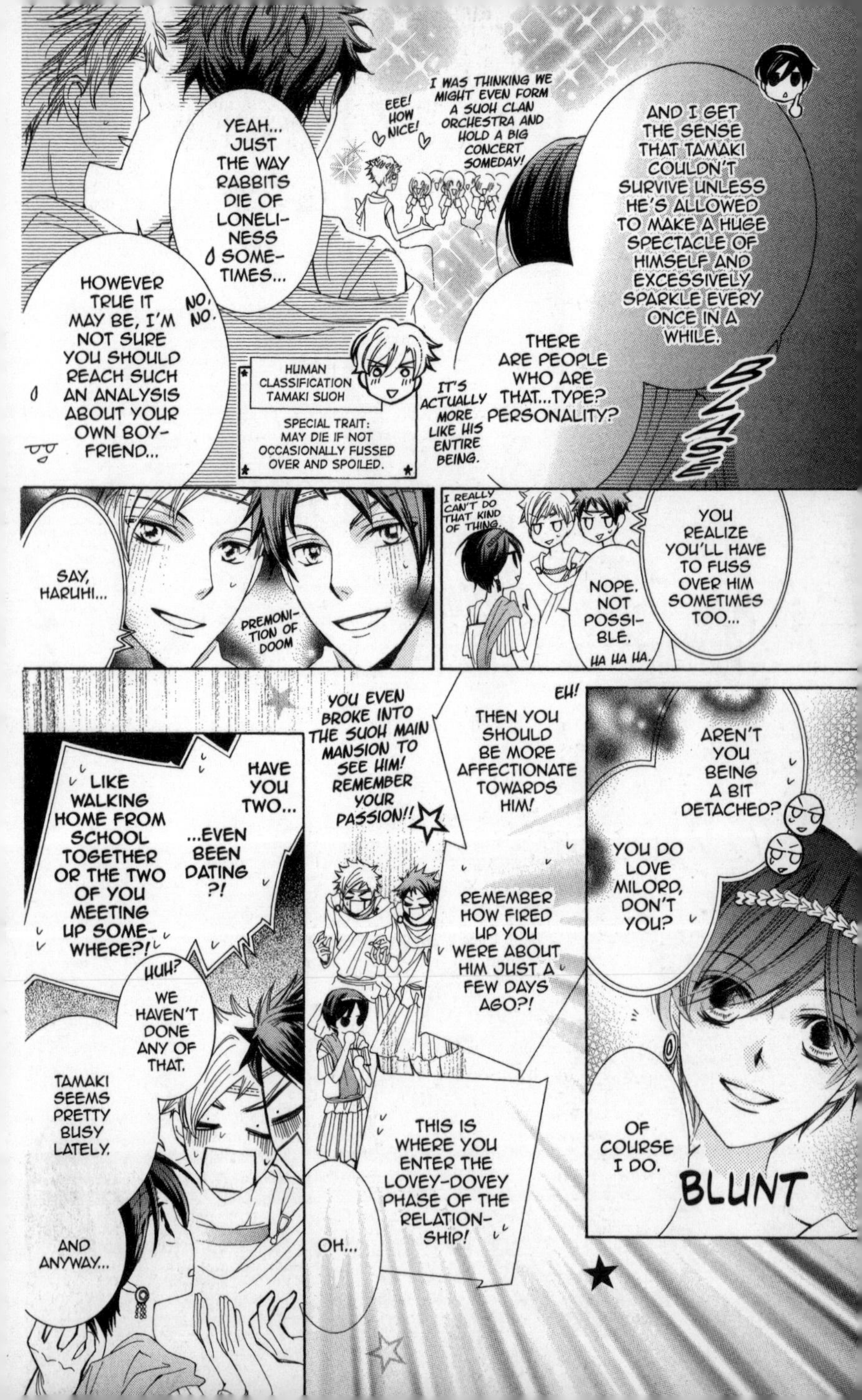
AND I GET THE SENSE THAT TAMAKI COULDN'T SURVIVE UNLESS HE'S ALLOWED TO MAKE A HUGE SPECTACLE OF HIMSELF AND EXCESSIVELY SPARKLE EVERY ONCE IN A WHILE.
BLASE
I WAS THINKING WE MIGHT EVEN FORM A SUOH CLAN ORCHESTRA AND HOLD A BIG CONCERT SOMEDAY!
EEE! HOW NICE!
THERE ARE PEOPLE WHO ARE THAT...TYPE? PERSONALITY?
IT'S ACTUALLY MORE LIKE HIS ENTIRE BEING.
HUMAN CLASSIFICATION TAMAKI SUOH
SPECIAL TRAIT: MAY DIE IF NOT OCCASIONALLY FUSSED OVER AND SPOILED.
YEAH... JUST THE WAY RABBITS DIE OF LONELI-NESS SOME-TIMES...
NO, NO.
HOWEVER TRUE IT MAY BE, I'M NOT SURE YOU SHOULD REACH SUCH AN ANALYSIS ABOUT YOUR OWN BOY-FRIEND...
YOU REALIZE YOU'LL HAVE TO FUSS OVER HIM SOMETIMES TOO...
NOPE. NOT POSSI-BLE.
HA HA HA.
I REALLY CAN'T DO THAT KIND OF THING.
SAY, HARUHI...
PREMONI-TION OF DOOM
AREN'T YOU BEING A BIT DETACHED?
YOU DO LOVE MILORD, DON'T YOU?
OF COURSE I DO.
BLUNT
EH!
THEN YOU SHOULD BE MORE AFFECTIONATE TOWARDS HIM!
YOU EVEN BROKE INTO THE SUOH MAIN MANSION TO SEE HIM! REMEMBER YOUR PASSION!!
REMEMBER HOW FIRED UP YOU WERE ABOUT HIM JUST A FEW DAYS AGO?!
THIS IS WHERE YOU ENTER THE LOVEY-DOVEY PHASE OF THE RELATION-SHIP!
OH...
HAVE YOU TWO...
...EVEN BEEN DATING ?!
LIKE WALKING HOME FROM SCHOOL TOGETHER OR THE TWO OF YOU MEETING UP SOME-WHERE?!
HUH?
WE HAVEN'T DONE ANY OF THAT.
TAMAKI SEEMS PRETTY BUSY LATELY.
AND ANYWAY...

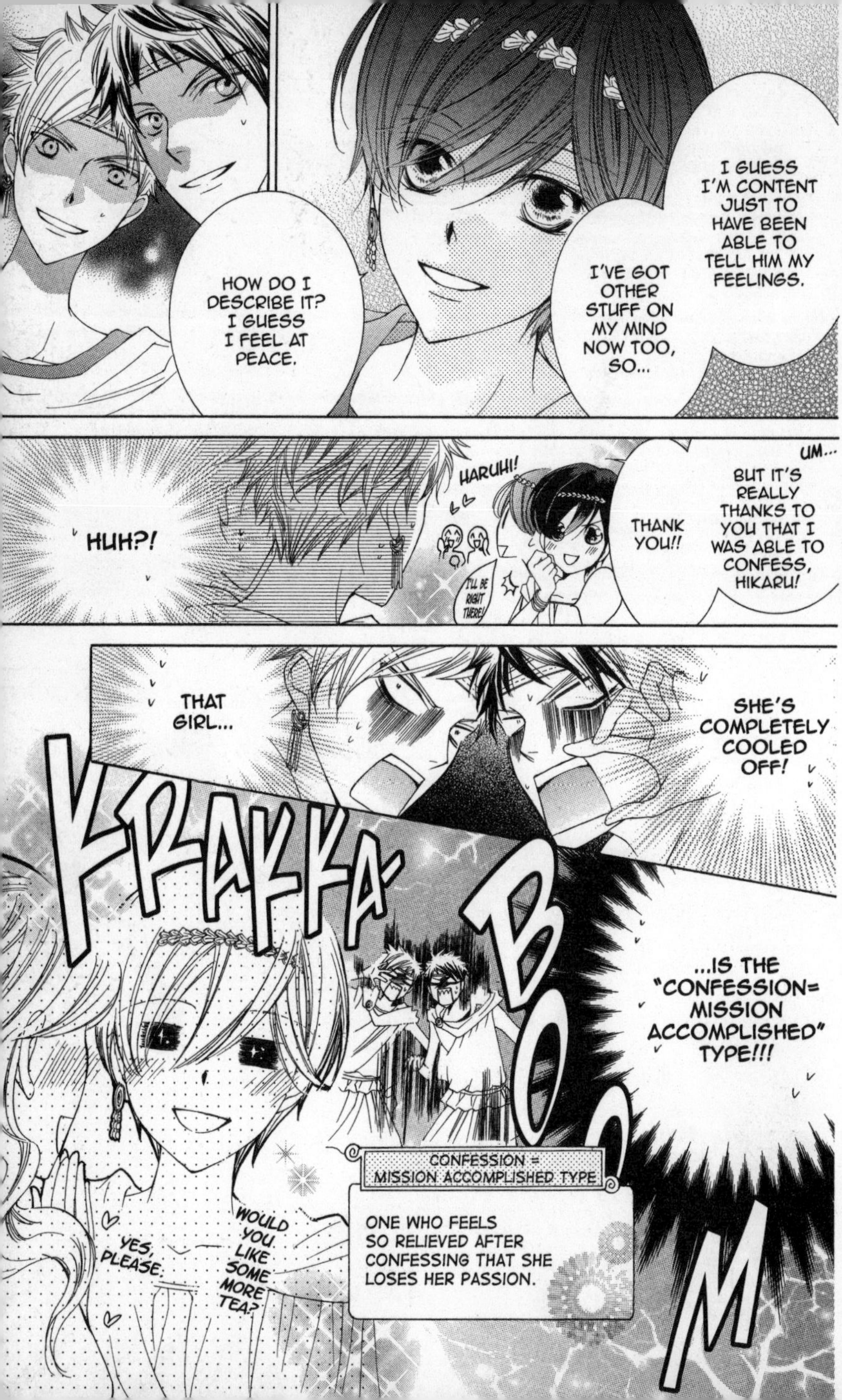
I GUESS I'M CONTENT JUST TO HAVE BEEN ABLE TO TELL HIM MY FEELINGS.
I'VE GOT OTHER STUFF ON MY MIND NOW TOO, SO...
HOW DO I DESCRIBE IT? I GUESS I FEEL AT PEACE.
UM...
BUT IT'S REALLY THANKS TO YOU THAT I WAS ABLE TO CONFESS, HIKARU!
THANK YOU!!
HARUHI!
I'LL BE RIGHT THERE!
HUH?!
SHE'S COMPLETELY COOLED OFF!
THAT GIRL...
KRAKKA-BOOM
...IS THE "CONFESSION= MISSION ACCOMPLISHED" TYPE!!!
CONFESSION = MISSION ACCOMPLISHED TYPE
ONE WHO FEELS SO RELIEVED AFTER CONFESSING THAT SHE LOSES HER PASSION.
WOULD YOU LIKE SOME MORE TEA?
YES, PLEASE.

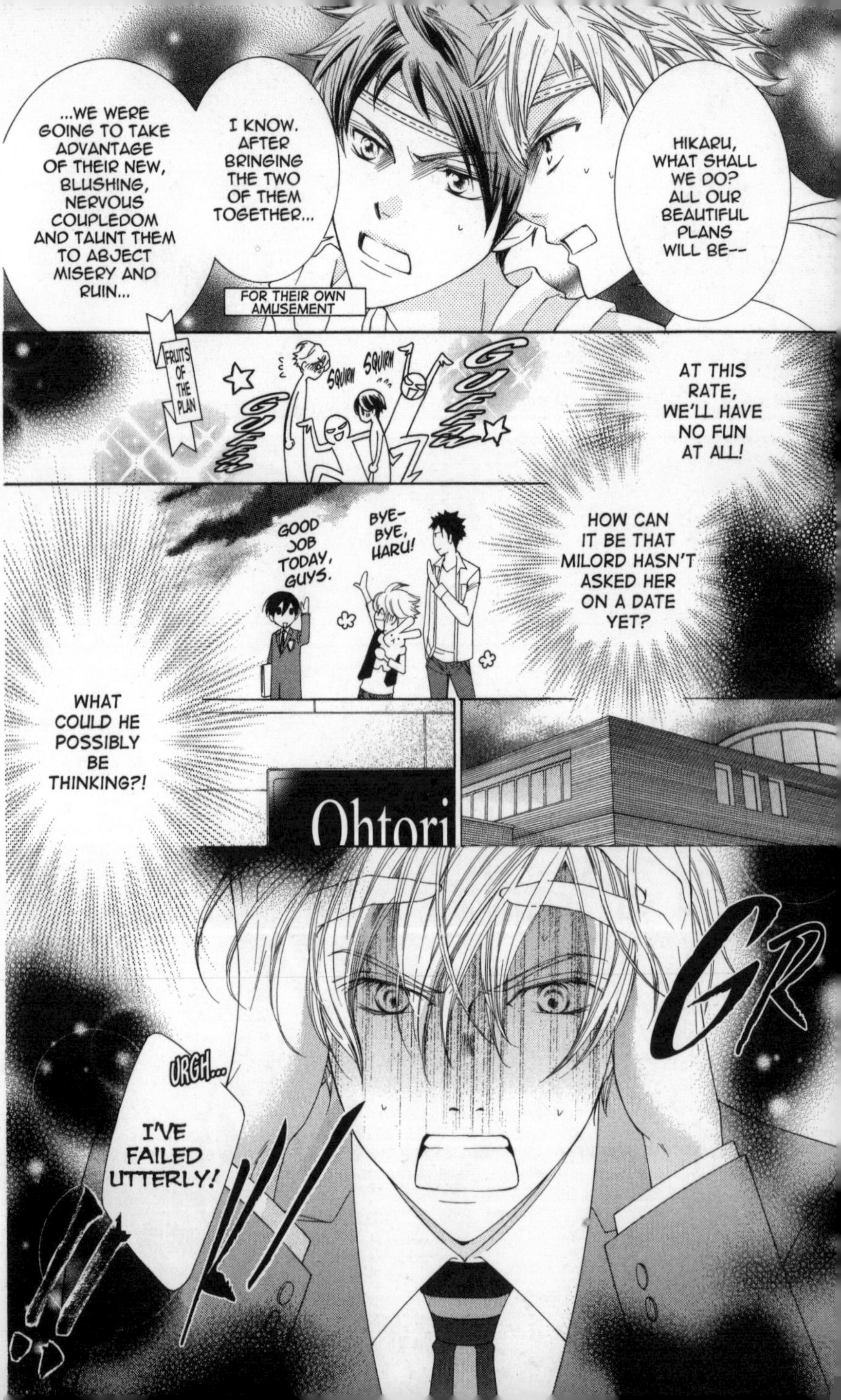
HIKARU, WHAT SHALL WE DO? ALL OUR BEAUTIFUL PLANS WILL BE--
I KNOW. AFTER BRINGING THE TWO OF THEM TOGETHER...
...WE WERE GOING TO TAKE ADVANTAGE OF THEIR NEW, BLUSHING, NERVOUS COUPLEDOM AND TAUNT THEM TO ABJECT MISERY AND RUIN...
FOR THEIR OWN AMUSEMENT
AT THIS RATE, WE'LL HAVE NO FUN AT ALL!
GUFFAW
SQUIRM
SQUIRM
GUFFAW
FRUITS OF THE PLAN
HOW CAN IT BE THAT MILORD HASN'T ASKED HER ON A DATE YET?
BYE-BYE, HARU!
GOOD JOB TODAY, GUYS.
WHAT COULD HE POSSIBLY BE THINKING?!
Ohtori
GR
URGH...
I'VE FAILED UTTERLY!

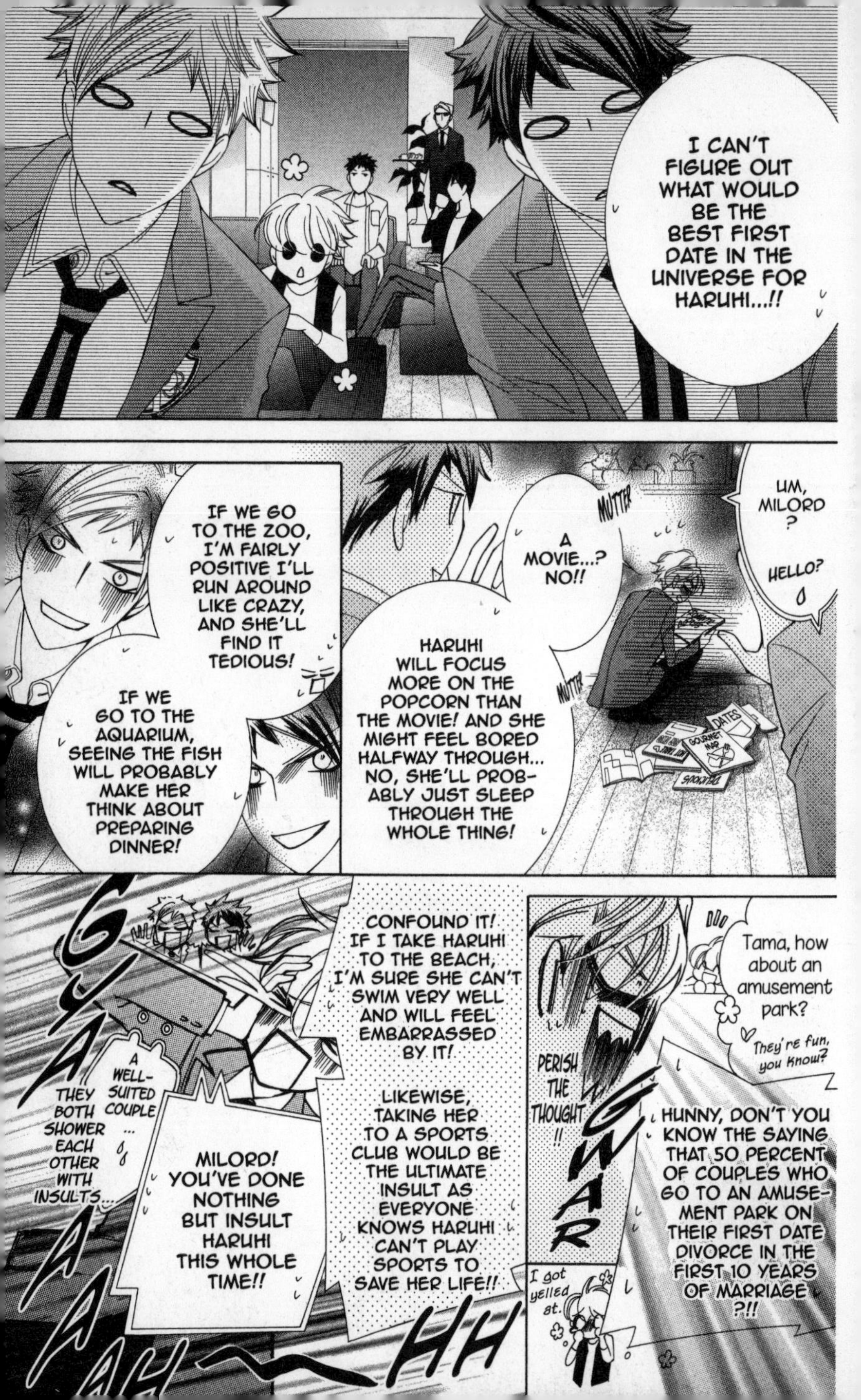

I CAN'T FIGURE OUT WHAT WOULD BE THE BEST FIRST DATE IN THE UNIVERSE FOR HARUHI...!!
UM, MILORD?
HELLO?
MUTTER
A MOVIE...? NO!!
MUTTER
DATES
GOURMET MAP
HARUHI WILL FOCUS MORE ON THE POPCORN THAN THE MOVIE! AND SHE MIGHT FEEL BORED HALFWAY THROUGH... NO, SHE'LL PROBABLY JUST SLEEP THROUGH THE WHOLE THING!
IF WE GO TO THE ZOO, I'M FAIRLY POSITIVE I'LL RUN AROUND LIKE CRAZY, AND SHE'LL FIND IT TEDIOUS!
IF WE GO TO THE AQUARIUM, SEEING THE FISH WILL PROBABLY MAKE HER THINK ABOUT PREPARING DINNER!
Tama, how about an amusement park?
They're fun, you know?
HUNNY, DON'T YOU KNOW THE SAYING THAT 50 PERCENT OF COUPLES WHO GO TO AN AMUSEMENT PARK ON THEIR FIRST DATE DIVORCE IN THE FIRST 10 YEARS OF MARRIAGE?!!
PERISH THE THOUGHT!!
GWAR
I got yelled at.
CONFOUND IT! IF I TAKE HARUHI TO THE BEACH, I'M SURE SHE CAN'T SWIM VERY WELL AND WILL FEEL EMBARRASSED BY IT!
LIKEWISE, TAKING HER TO A SPORTS CLUB WOULD BE THE ULTIMATE INSULT AS EVERYONE KNOWS HARUHI CAN'T PLAY SPORTS TO SAVE HER LIFE!!
MILORD! YOU'VE DONE NOTHING BUT INSULT HARUHI THIS WHOLE TIME!!
A WELL-SUITED COUPLE...
THEY BOTH SHOWER EACH OTHER WITH INSULTS...
GYAAAAAHH

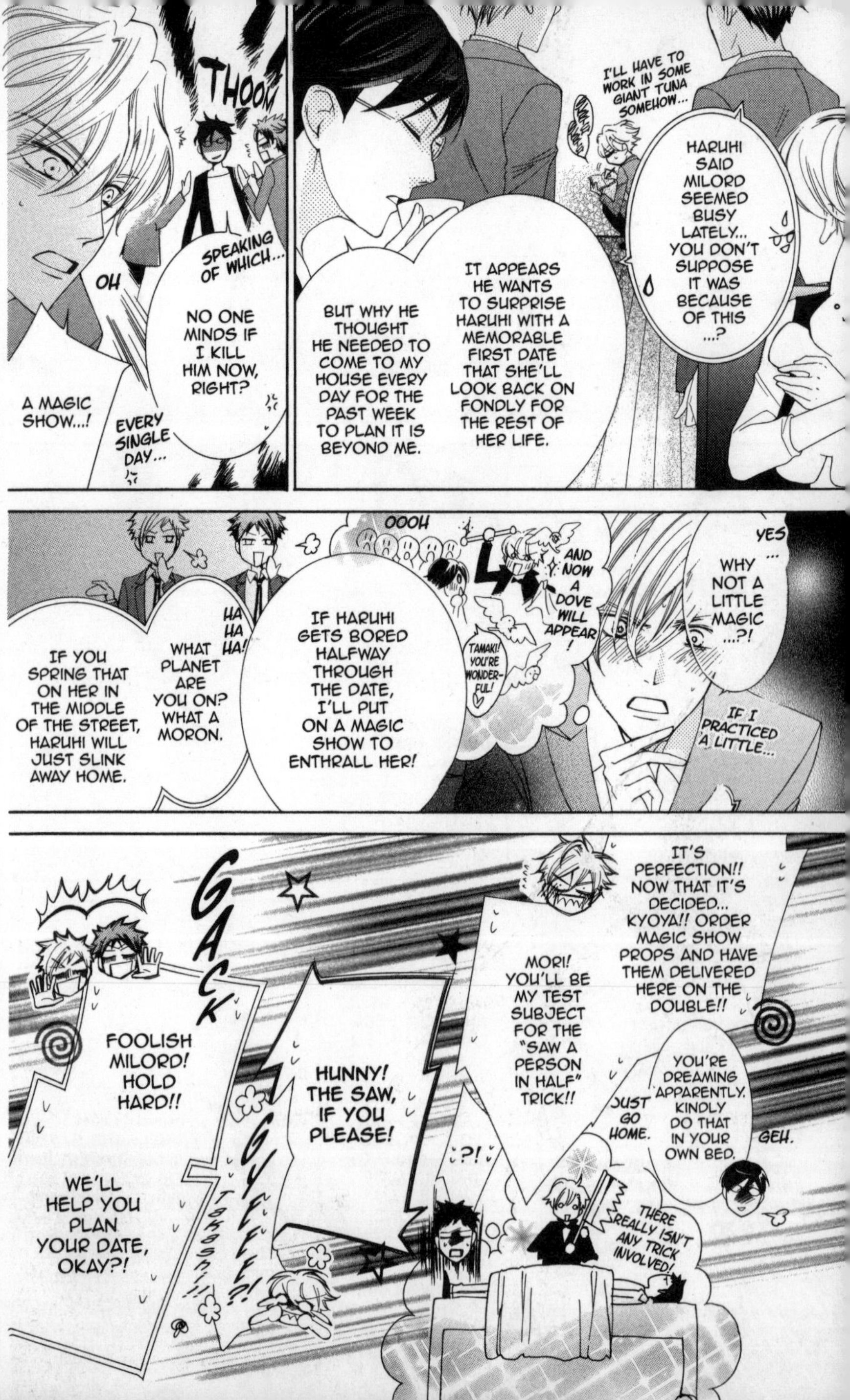
I'LL HAVE TO WORK IN SOME GIANT TUNA SOMEHOW...
HARUHI SAID MILORD SEEMED BUSY LATELY... YOU DON'T SUPPOSE IT WAS BECAUSE OF THIS...?
IT APPEARS HE WANTS TO SURPRISE HARUHI WITH A MEMORABLE FIRST DATE THAT SHE'LL LOOK BACK ON FONDLY FOR THE REST OF HER LIFE.
BUT WHY HE THOUGHT HE NEEDED TO COME TO MY HOUSE EVERY DAY FOR THE PAST WEEK TO PLAN IT IS BEYOND ME.
THOOM
SPEAKING OF WHICH...
NO ONE MINDS IF I KILL HIM NOW, RIGHT?
EVERY SINGLE DAY...
OH
A MAGIC SHOW...!
YES...
WHY NOT A LITTLE MAGIC...?!
IF I PRACTICED A LITTLE...
AND NOW A DOVE WILL APPEAR!
TAMAKI! YOU'RE WONDERFUL!
OOOH
IF HARUHI GETS BORED HALFWAY THROUGH THE DATE, I'LL PUT ON A MAGIC SHOW TO ENTHRALL HER!
HA HA HA!
WHAT PLANET ARE YOU ON? WHAT A MORON.
IF YOU SPRING THAT ON HER IN THE MIDDLE OF THE STREET, HARUHI WILL JUST SLINK AWAY HOME.
IT'S PERFECTION!! NOW THAT IT'S DECIDED... KYOYA!! ORDER MAGIC SHOW PROPS AND HAVE THEM DELIVERED HERE ON THE DOUBLE!!
MORI! YOU'LL BE MY TEST SUBJECT FOR THE "SAW A PERSON IN HALF" TRICK!!
YOU'RE DREAMING APPARENTLY. KINDLY DO THAT IN YOUR OWN BED.
GEH.
JUST GO HOME.
THERE REALLY ISN'T ANY TRICK INVOLVED!
?!
HUNNY! THE SAW, IF YOU PLEASE!
GACK
GYEEEE?!
TAKASHI!!
FOOLISH MILORD! HOLD HARD!!
WE'LL HELP YOU PLAN YOUR DATE, OKAY?!

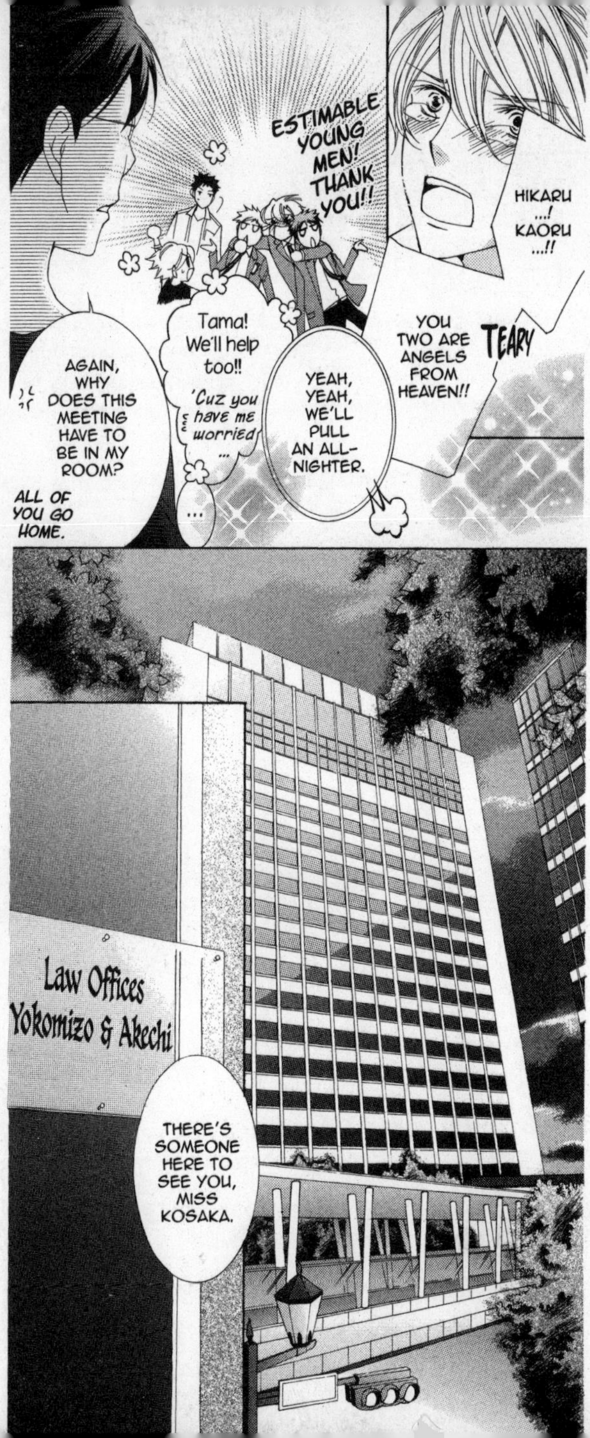
HIKARU ...! KAORU ...!!
TEARY
YOU TWO ARE ANGELS FROM HEAVEN!!
ESTIMABLE YOUNG MEN! THANK YOU!!
YEAH, YEAH, WE'LL PULL AN ALL-NIGHTER.
Tama! We'll help too!!
'Cuz you have me worried ...
...
AGAIN, WHY DOES THIS MEETING HAVE TO BE IN MY ROOM?
ALL OF YOU GO HOME.
Law Offices Yokomizo & Akechi
THERE'S SOMEONE HERE TO SEE YOU, MISS KOSAKA.

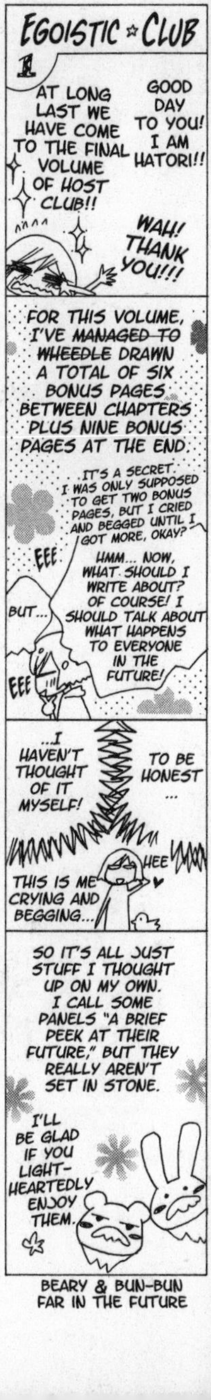
EGOISTIC ☆ CLUB
1
GOOD DAY TO YOU! I AM HATORI!!
AT LONG LAST WE HAVE COME TO THE FINAL VOLUME OF HOST CLUB!!
WAH! THANK YOU!!!
FOR THIS VOLUME, I'VE ~~MANAGED TO WHEEDLE~~ DRAWN A TOTAL OF SIX BONUS PAGES BETWEEN CHAPTERS PLUS NINE BONUS PAGES AT THE END.
IT'S A SECRET. I WAS ONLY SUPPOSED TO GET TWO BONUS PAGES, BUT I CRIED AND BEGGED UNTIL I GOT MORE, OKAY?
EEE
HMM... NOW, WHAT SHOULD I WRITE ABOUT? OF COURSE! I SHOULD TALK ABOUT WHAT HAPPENS TO EVERYONE IN THE FUTURE!
BUT...
EEE
TO BE HONEST ...
...I HAVEN'T THOUGHT OF IT MYSELF!
HEE
THIS IS ME CRYING AND BEGGING...
SO IT'S ALL JUST STUFF I THOUGHT UP ON MY OWN. I CALL SOME PANELS "A BRIEF PEEK AT THEIR FUTURE," BUT THEY REALLY AREN'T SET IN STONE.
I'LL BE GLAD IF YOU LIGHT-HEARTEDLY ENJOY THEM.
BEARY & BUN-BUN FAR IN THE FUTURE

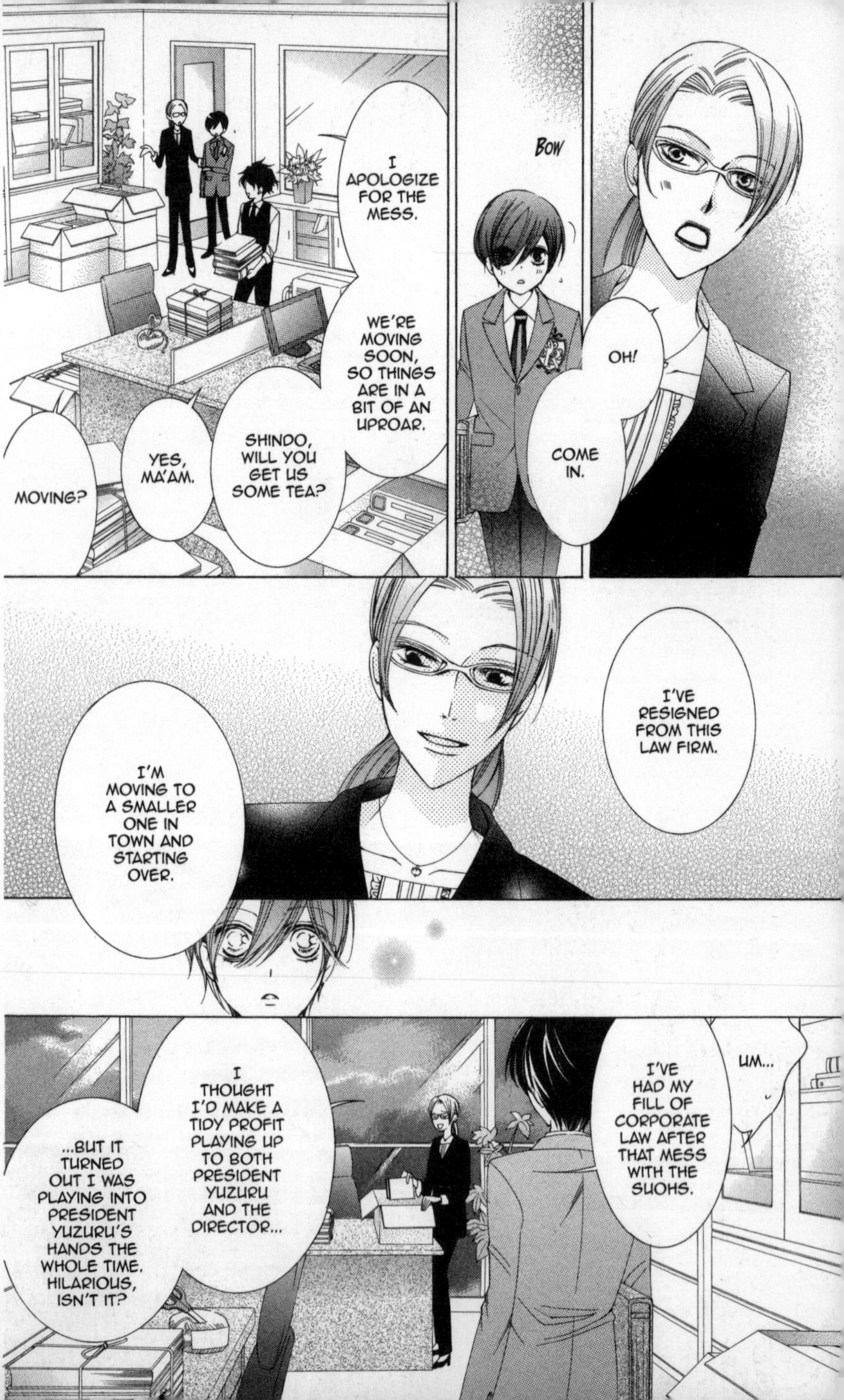
BOW
OH!
COME IN.
I APOLOGIZE FOR THE MESS.
WE'RE MOVING SOON, SO THINGS ARE IN A BIT OF AN UPROAR.
SHINDO, WILL YOU GET US SOME TEA?
YES, MA'AM.
MOVING?
I'VE RESIGNED FROM THIS LAW FIRM.
I'M MOVING TO A SMALLER ONE IN TOWN AND STARTING OVER.
UM...
I'VE HAD MY FILL OF CORPORATE LAW AFTER THAT MESS WITH THE SUOHS.
I THOUGHT I'D MAKE A TIDY PROFIT PLAYING UP TO BOTH PRESIDENT YUZURU AND THE DIRECTOR...
...BUT IT TURNED OUT I WAS PLAYING INTO PRESIDENT YUZURU'S HANDS THE WHOLE TIME. HILARIOUS, ISN'T IT?

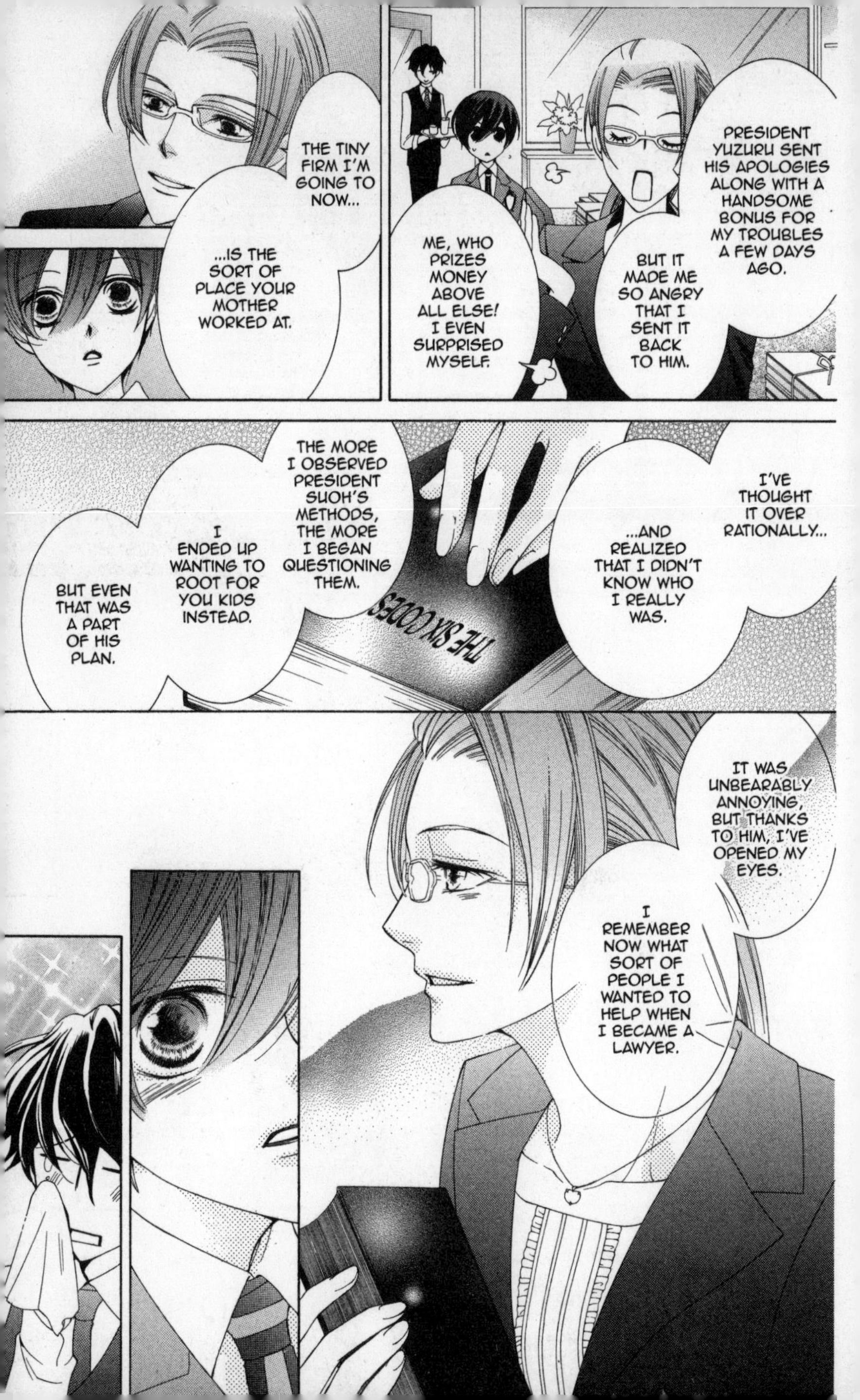
PRESIDENT YUZURU SENT HIS APOLOGIES ALONG WITH A HANDSOME BONUS FOR MY TROUBLES A FEW DAYS AGO.
BUT IT MADE ME SO ANGRY THAT I SENT IT BACK TO HIM.
ME, WHO PRIZES MONEY ABOVE ALL ELSE! I EVEN SURPRISED MYSELF.
THE TINY FIRM I'M GOING TO NOW...
...IS THE SORT OF PLACE YOUR MOTHER WORKED AT.
I'VE THOUGHT IT OVER RATIONALLY...
...AND REALIZED THAT I DIDN'T KNOW WHO I REALLY WAS.
THE SIX CODES
THE MORE I OBSERVED PRESIDENT SUOH'S METHODS, THE MORE I BEGAN QUESTIONING THEM.
I ENDED UP WANTING TO ROOT FOR YOU KIDS INSTEAD.
BUT EVEN THAT WAS A PART OF HIS PLAN.
IT WAS UNBEARABLY ANNOYING, BUT THANKS TO HIM, I'VE OPENED MY EYES.
I REMEMBER NOW WHAT SORT OF PEOPLE I WANTED TO HELP WHEN I BECAME A LAWYER.

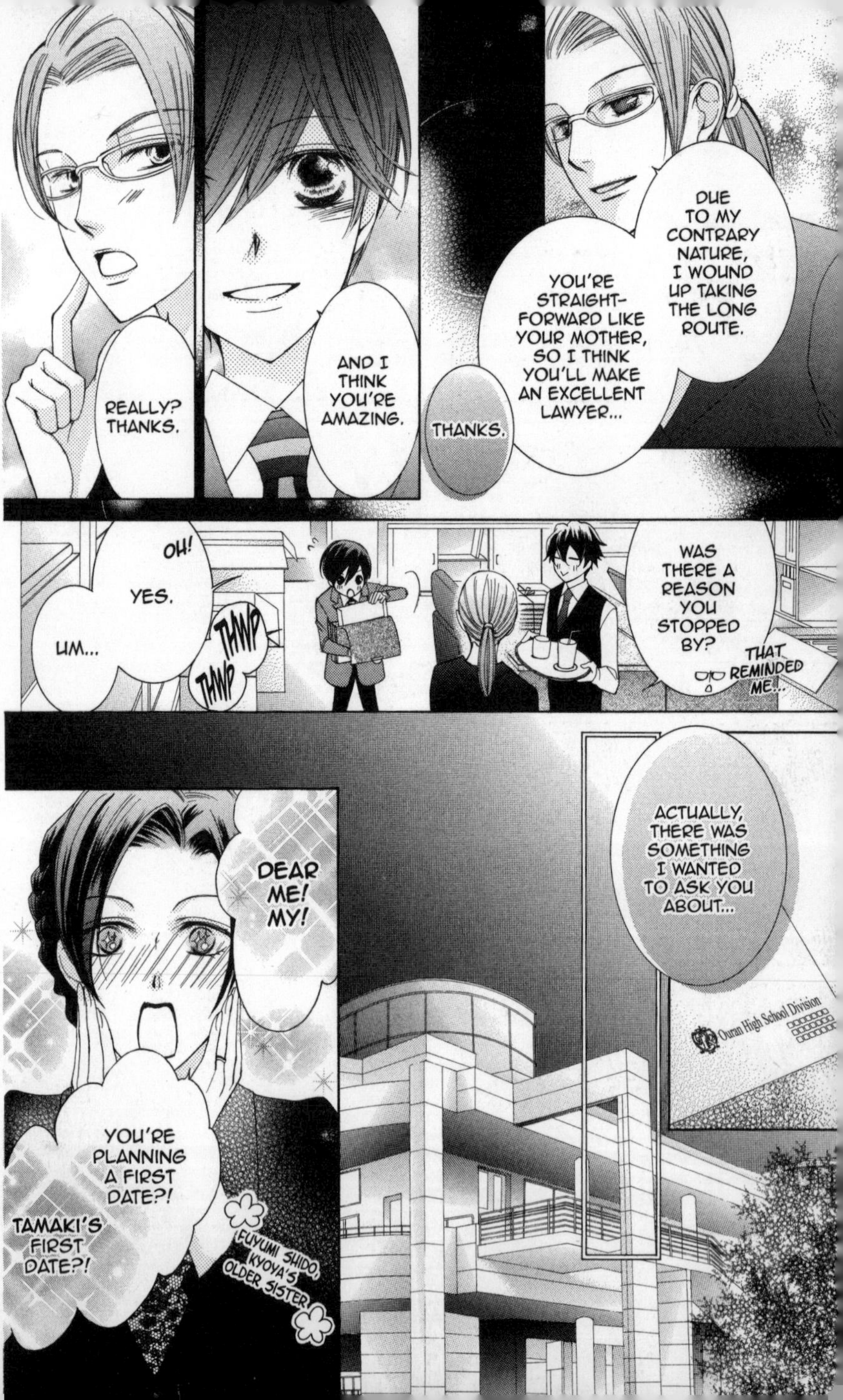
DUE TO MY CONTRARY NATURE, I WOUND UP TAKING THE LONG ROUTE.
YOU'RE STRAIGHT-FORWARD LIKE YOUR MOTHER, SO I THINK YOU'LL MAKE AN EXCELLENT LAWYER...
THANKS.
AND I THINK YOU'RE AMAZING.
REALLY? THANKS.
WAS THERE A REASON YOU STOPPED BY?
THAT REMINDED ME...
THWP THWP
OH! YES. UM...
ACTUALLY, THERE WAS SOMETHING I WANTED TO ASK YOU ABOUT...
Ouran High School Division
DEAR ME! MY!
YOU'RE PLANNING A FIRST DATE?!
TAMAKI'S FIRST DATE?!
FUYUMI SHIDO, KYOYA'S OLDER SISTER

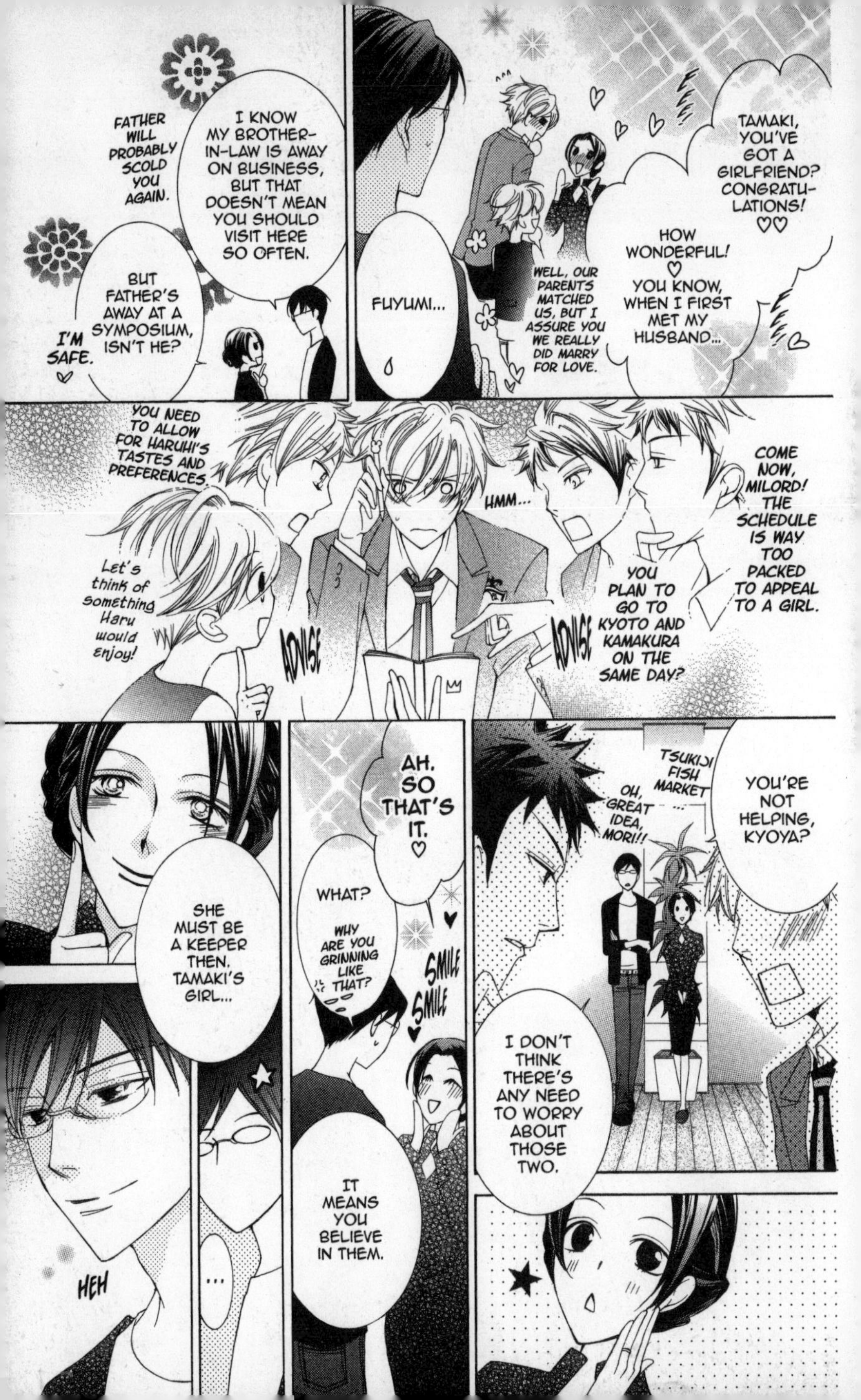
TAMAKI, YOU'VE GOT A GIRLFRIEND? CONGRATULATIONS! ♡♡
HOW WONDERFUL! ♡ YOU KNOW, WHEN I FIRST MET MY HUSBAND...
WELL, OUR PARENTS MATCHED US, BUT I ASSURE YOU WE REALLY DID MARRY FOR LOVE.
FUYUMI...
I KNOW MY BROTHER-IN-LAW IS AWAY ON BUSINESS, BUT THAT DOESN'T MEAN YOU SHOULD VISIT HERE SO OFTEN.
FATHER WILL PROBABLY SCOLD YOU AGAIN.
BUT FATHER'S AWAY AT A SYMPOSIUM, ISN'T HE?
I'M SAFE. ♡
COME NOW, MILORD! THE SCHEDULE IS WAY TOO PACKED TO APPEAL TO A GIRL.
YOU PLAN TO GO TO KYOTO AND KAMAKURA ON THE SAME DAY?
ADVISE
HMM...
YOU NEED TO ALLOW FOR HARUHI'S TASTES AND PREFERENCES.
Let's think of something Haru would enjoy!
ADVISE
TSUKIJI FISH MARKET...
OH, GREAT IDEA, MORI!!
YOU'RE NOT HELPING, KYOYA?
I DON'T THINK THERE'S ANY NEED TO WORRY ABOUT THOSE TWO.
AH. SO THAT'S IT. ♡
WHAT?
WHY ARE YOU GRINNING LIKE THAT?
SMILE SMILE
IT MEANS YOU BELIEVE IN THEM.
SHE MUST BE A KEEPER THEN. TAMAKI'S GIRL...
HEH
...

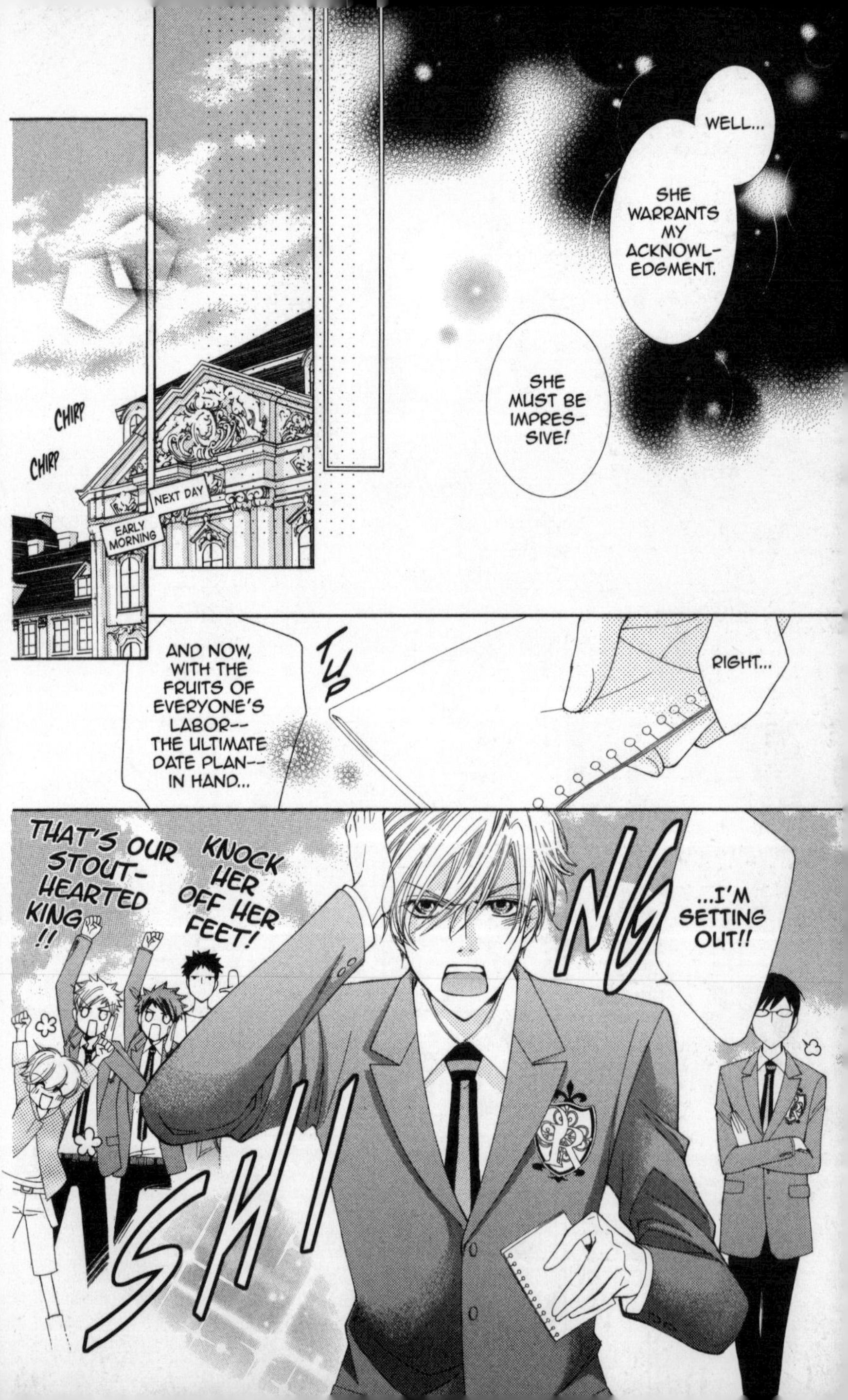
WELL...
SHE WARRANTS MY ACKNOWL-EDGMENT.
SHE MUST BE IMPRES-SIVE!
NEXT DAY
EARLY MORNING
CHIRP
CHIRP
RIGHT...
TUP
AND NOW, WITH THE FRUITS OF EVERYONE'S LABOR-- THE ULTIMATE DATE PLAN-- IN HAND...
...I'M SETTING OUT!!
SHI
NG
KNOCK HER OFF HER FEET!
THAT'S OUR STOUT-HEARTED KING!!

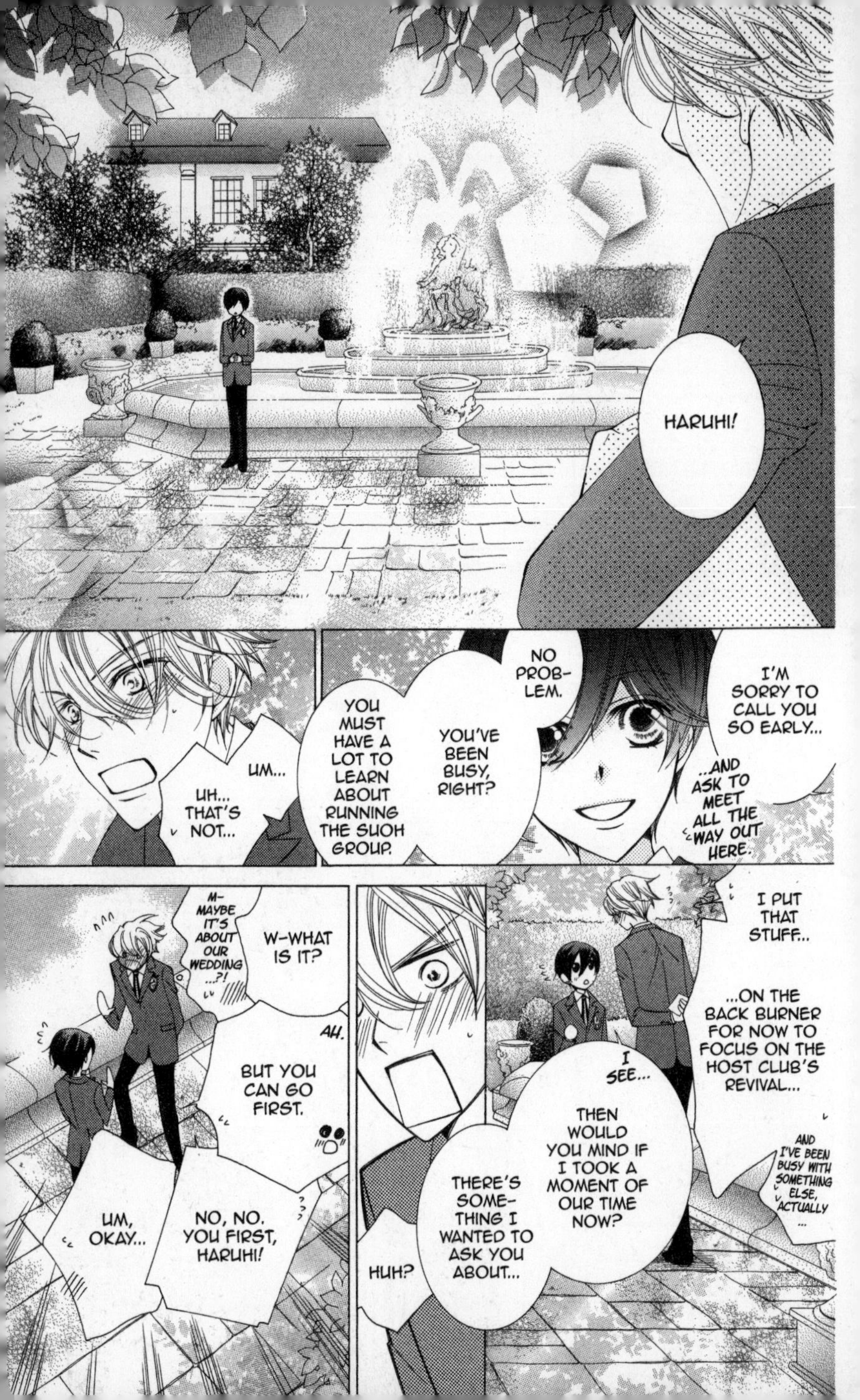
HARUHI!
I'M SORRY TO CALL YOU SO EARLY...
...AND ASK TO MEET ALL THE WAY OUT HERE.
NO PROBLEM.
YOU'VE BEEN BUSY, RIGHT?
YOU MUST HAVE A LOT TO LEARN ABOUT RUNNING THE SUOH GROUP.
UM...
UH... THAT'S NOT...
I PUT THAT STUFF...
...ON THE BACK BURNER FOR NOW TO FOCUS ON THE HOST CLUB'S REVIVAL...
AND I'VE BEEN BUSY WITH SOMETHING ELSE, ACTUALLY...
I SEE...
THEN WOULD YOU MIND IF I TOOK A MOMENT OF OUR TIME NOW?
THERE'S SOMETHING I WANTED TO ASK YOU ABOUT...
HUH?
W-WHAT IS IT?
M-MAYBE IT'S ABOUT OUR WEDDING...?!
AH.
BUT YOU CAN GO FIRST.
NO, NO. YOU FIRST, HARUHI!
UM, OKAY...

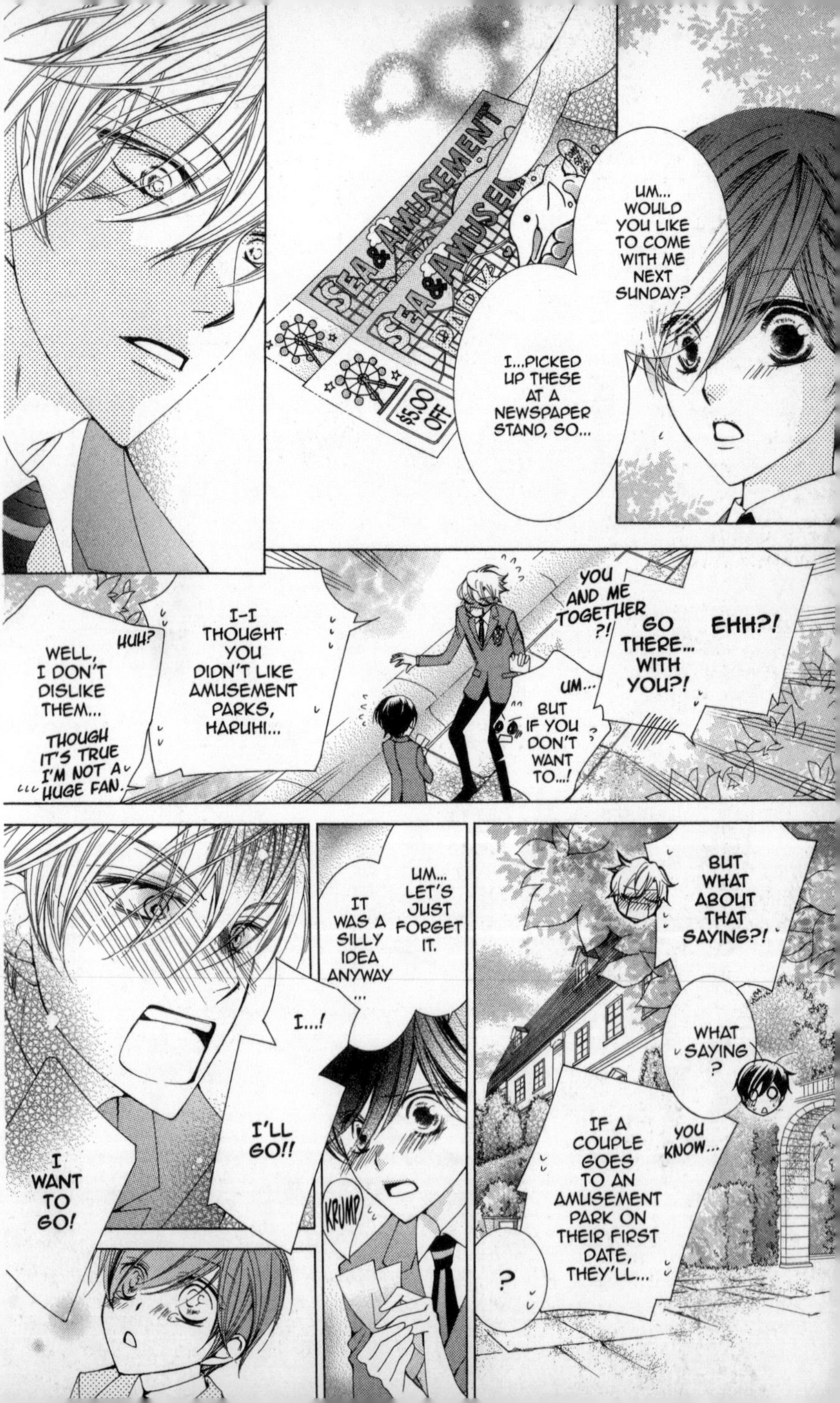
UM... WOULD YOU LIKE TO COME WITH ME NEXT SUNDAY?
I...PICKED UP THESE AT A NEWSPAPER STAND, SO...
SEA & AMUSEMENT
$5.00 OFF
EHH?!
GO THERE... WITH YOU?!
YOU AND ME TOGETHER?!
UM... BUT IF YOU DON'T WANT TO...!
I-I THOUGHT YOU DIDN'T LIKE AMUSEMENT PARKS, HARUHI...
HUH?
WELL, I DON'T DISLIKE THEM...
THOUGH IT'S TRUE I'M NOT A HUGE FAN.
BUT WHAT ABOUT THAT SAYING?!
WHAT SAYING?
YOU KNOW...
IF A COUPLE GOES TO AN AMUSEMENT PARK ON THEIR FIRST DATE, THEY'LL...
?
UM... LET'S JUST FORGET IT.
IT WAS A SILLY IDEA ANYWAY...
KRUMP
I...!
I'LL GO!!
I WANT TO GO!

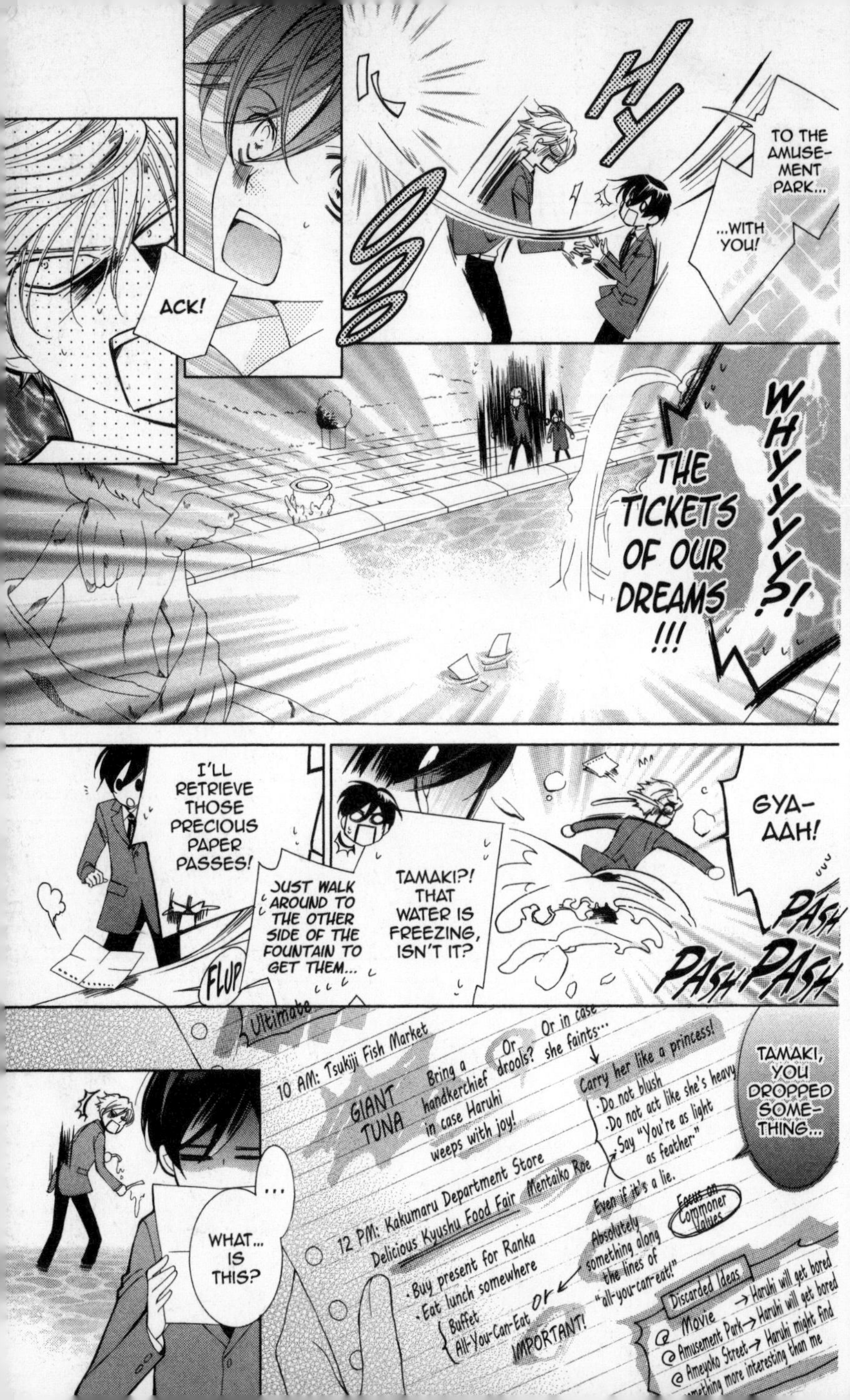

WHY
TO THE AMUSEMENT PARK...
...WITH YOU!
ACK!
WHYYYYY?!
THE TICKETS OF OUR DREAMS !!!
GYA-AAH!
PASH PASH PASH
TAMAKI?! THAT WATER IS FREEZING, ISN'T IT?
JUST WALK AROUND TO THE OTHER SIDE OF THE FOUNTAIN TO GET THEM...
FLUP
I'LL RETRIEVE THOSE PRECIOUS PAPER PASSES!
TAMAKI, YOU DROPPED SOMETHING...
Ultimate
10 AM: Tsukiji Fish Market
GIANT TUNA
Bring a handkerchief in case Haruhi weeps with joy!
Or drools?
Or in case she faints...
Carry her like a princess!
·Do not blush
·Do not act like she's heavy
·Say "You're as light as feather."
Even if it's a lie.
12 PM: Kakumaru Department Store
Delicious Kyushu Food Fair
Mentaiko Roe
·Buy present for Ranka
·Eat lunch somewhere
Buffet
All-You-Can-Eat
or
IMPORTANT!
Absolutely something along the lines of "all-you-can-eat!"
Focus on Commoner Values
Discarded Ideas
Movie → Haruhi will get bored
Amusement Park → Haruhi will get bored
Ameyoko Street → Haruhi might find something more interesting than me
...
WHAT... IS THIS?

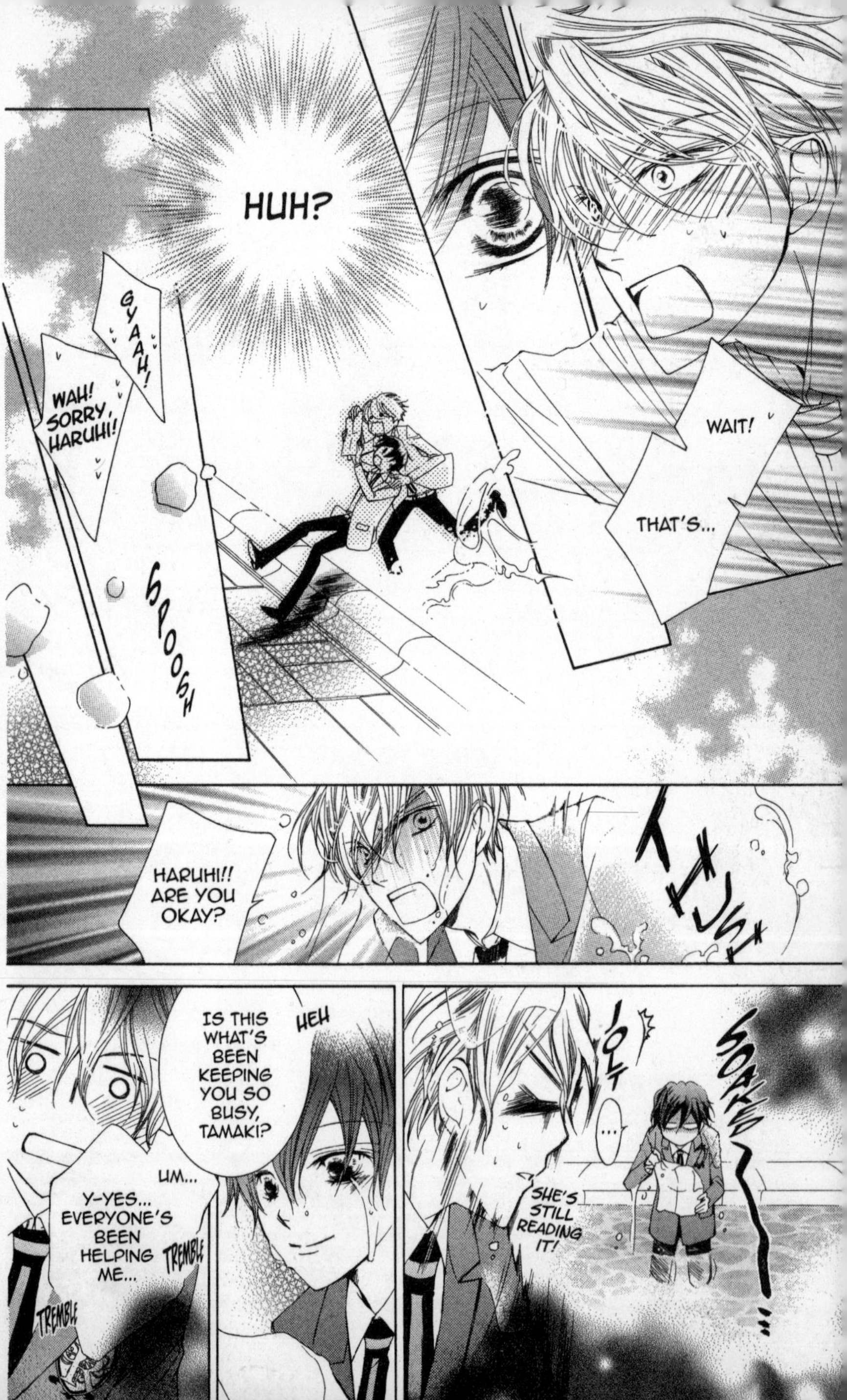
WAIT!
THAT'S...
HUH?
GYAAH!
WAH! SORRY, HARUHI!
SPOOSH
RUSH
HARUHI!! ARE YOU OKAY?
SOAK...!!
JOLT
...
SHE'S STILL READING IT!
HEH
IS THIS WHAT'S BEEN KEEPING YOU SO BUSY, TAMAKI?
UM...
Y-YES... EVERYONE'S BEEN HELPING ME...
TREMBLE
TREMBLE

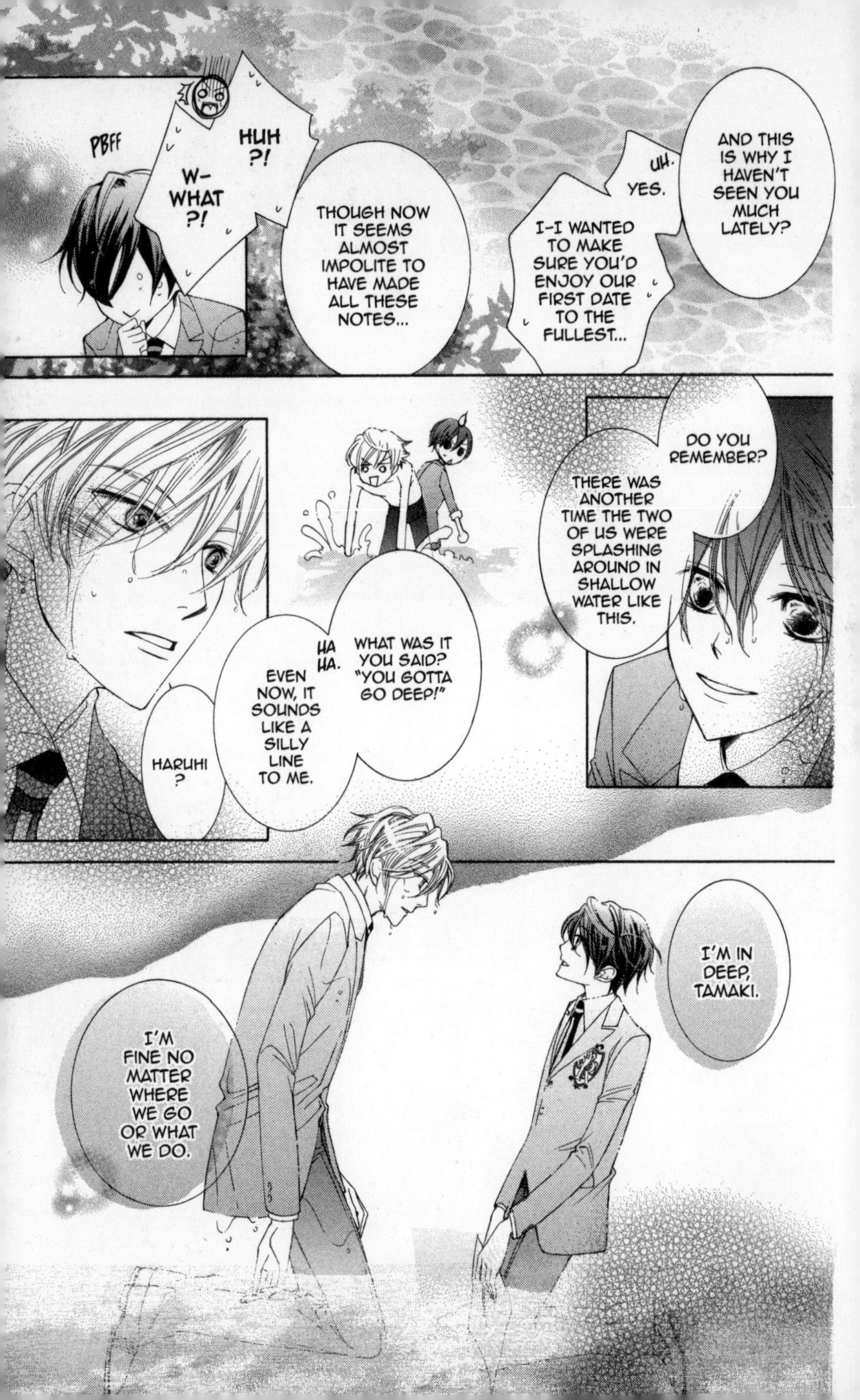
AND THIS IS WHY I HAVEN'T SEEN YOU MUCH LATELY?
UH. YES.
I-I WANTED TO MAKE SURE YOU'D ENJOY OUR FIRST DATE TO THE FULLEST...
THOUGH NOW IT SEEMS ALMOST IMPOLITE TO HAVE MADE ALL THESE NOTES...
HUH ?!
W-WHAT ?!
PBFF
DO YOU REMEMBER?
THERE WAS ANOTHER TIME THE TWO OF US WERE SPLASHING AROUND IN SHALLOW WATER LIKE THIS.
WHAT WAS IT YOU SAID? "YOU GOTTA GO DEEP!"
HA HA.
EVEN NOW, IT SOUNDS LIKE A SILLY LINE TO ME.
HARUHI ?
I'M IN DEEP, TAMAKI.
I'M FINE NO MATTER WHERE WE GO OR WHAT WE DO.

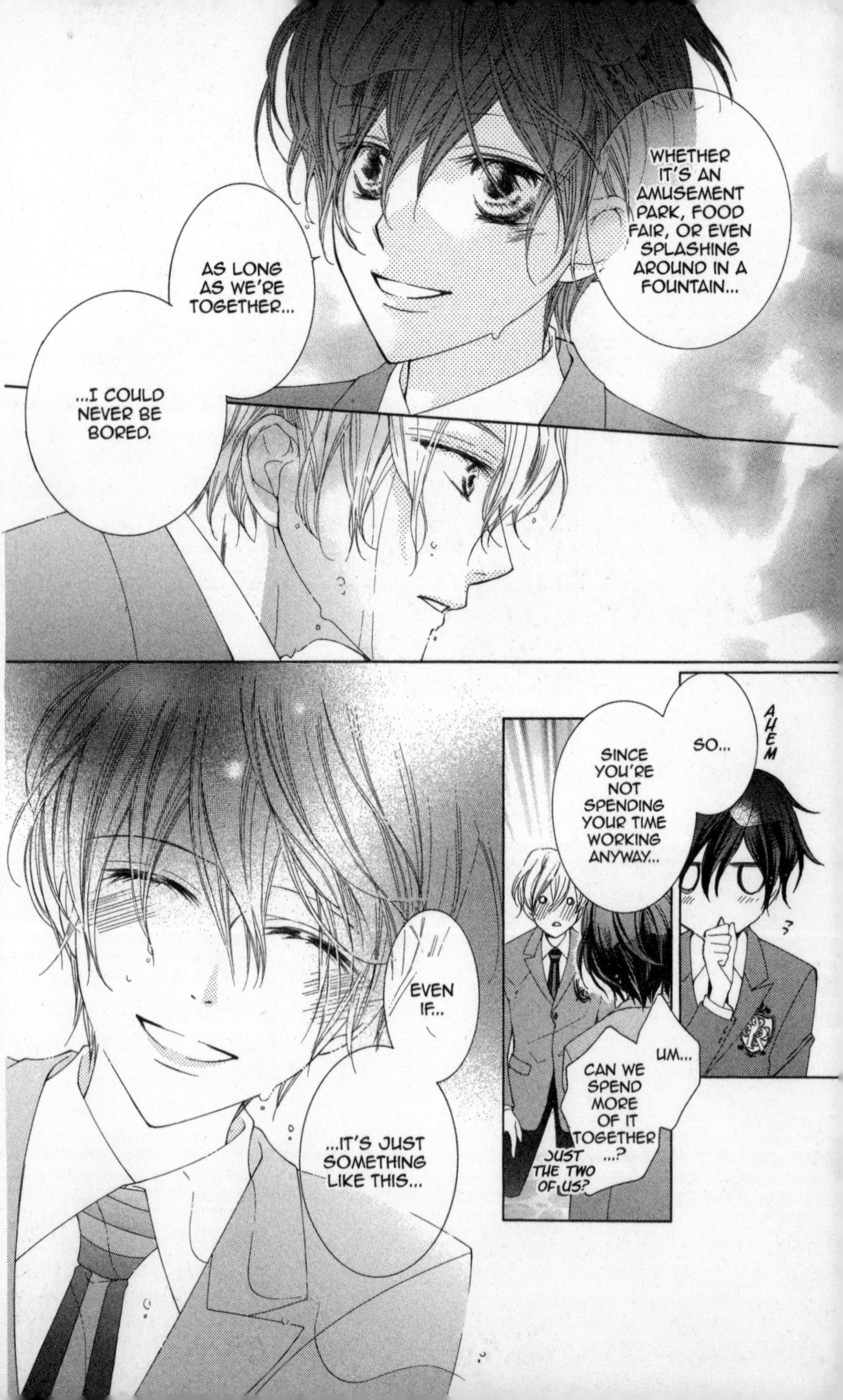
WHETHER IT'S AN AMUSEMENT PARK, FOOD FAIR, OR EVEN SPLASHING AROUND IN A FOUNTAIN...
AS LONG AS WE'RE TOGETHER...
...I COULD NEVER BE BORED.
AHEM
SO...
SINCE YOU'RE NOT SPENDING YOUR TIME WORKING ANYWAY...
UM...
CAN WE SPEND MORE OF IT TOGETHER ...?
JUST THE TWO OF US?
EVEN IF...
...IT'S JUST SOMETHING LIKE THIS...

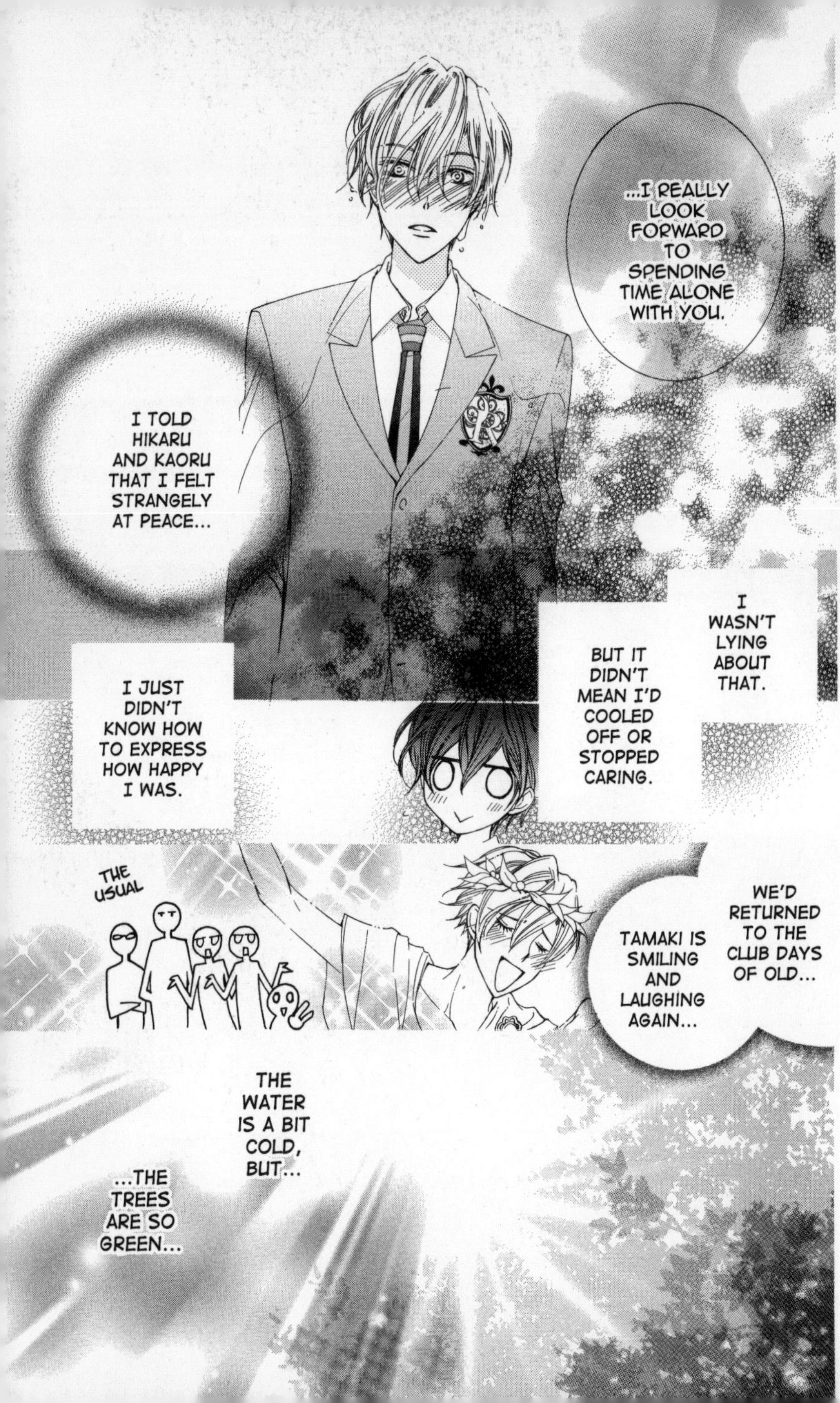
...I REALLY LOOK FORWARD TO SPENDING TIME ALONE WITH YOU.
I TOLD HIKARU AND KAORU THAT I FELT STRANGELY AT PEACE...
I WASN'T LYING ABOUT THAT.
BUT IT DIDN'T MEAN I'D COOLED OFF OR STOPPED CARING.
I JUST DIDN'T KNOW HOW TO EXPRESS HOW HAPPY I WAS.
WE'D RETURNED TO THE CLUB DAYS OF OLD...
TAMAKI IS SMILING AND LAUGHING AGAIN...
THE USUAL
THE WATER IS A BIT COLD, BUT...
...THE TREES ARE SO GREEN...

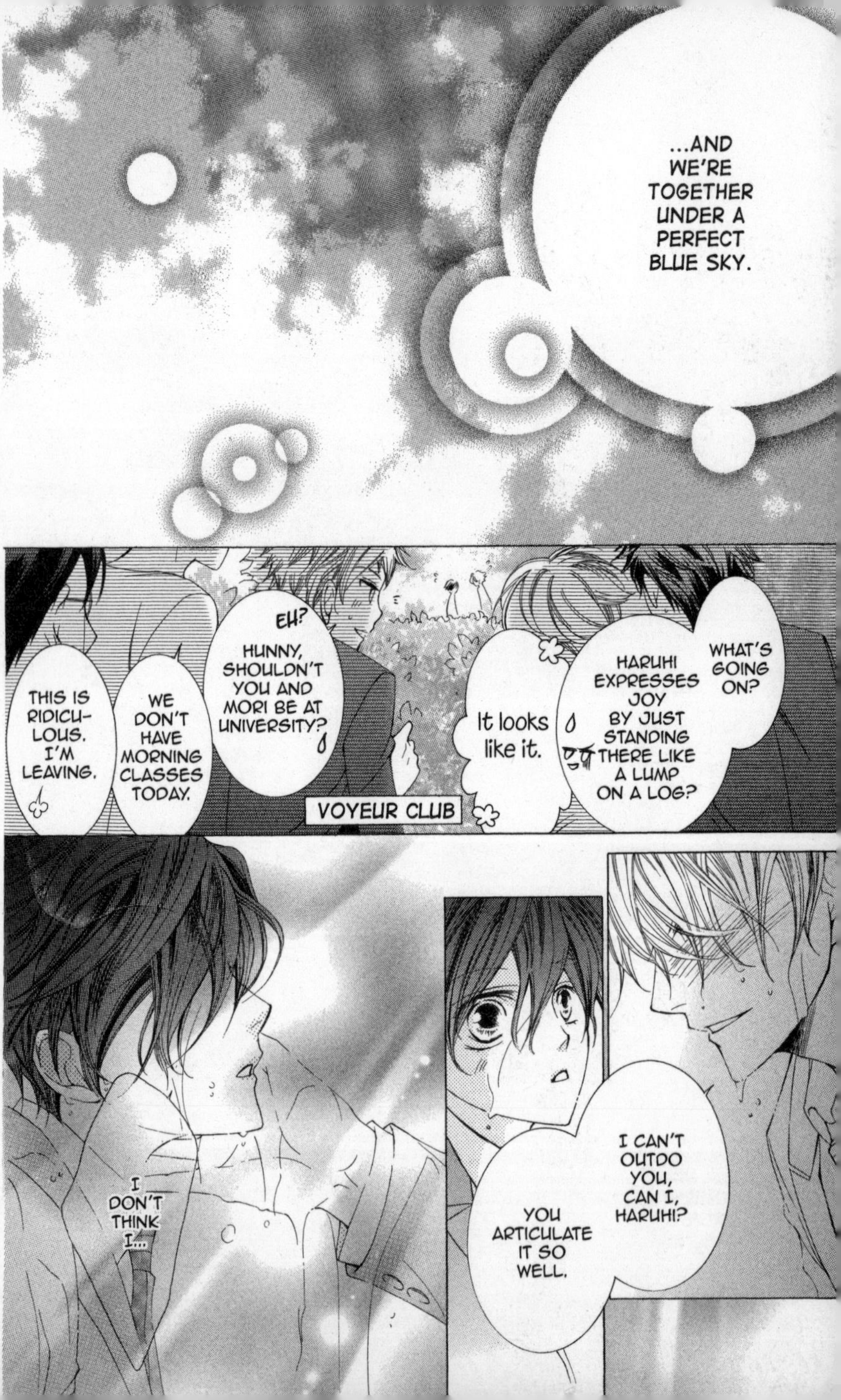
...AND WE'RE TOGETHER UNDER A PERFECT BLUE SKY.
WHAT'S GOING ON?
HARUHI EXPRESSES JOY BY JUST STANDING THERE LIKE A LUMP ON A LOG?
It looks like it.
EH?
HUNNY, SHOULDN'T YOU AND MORI BE AT UNIVERSITY?
WE DON'T HAVE MORNING CLASSES TODAY.
THIS IS RIDICULOUS. I'M LEAVING.
VOYEUR CLUB
I CAN'T OUTDO YOU, CAN I, HARUHI?
YOU ARTICULATE IT SO WELL.
I DON'T THINK I...

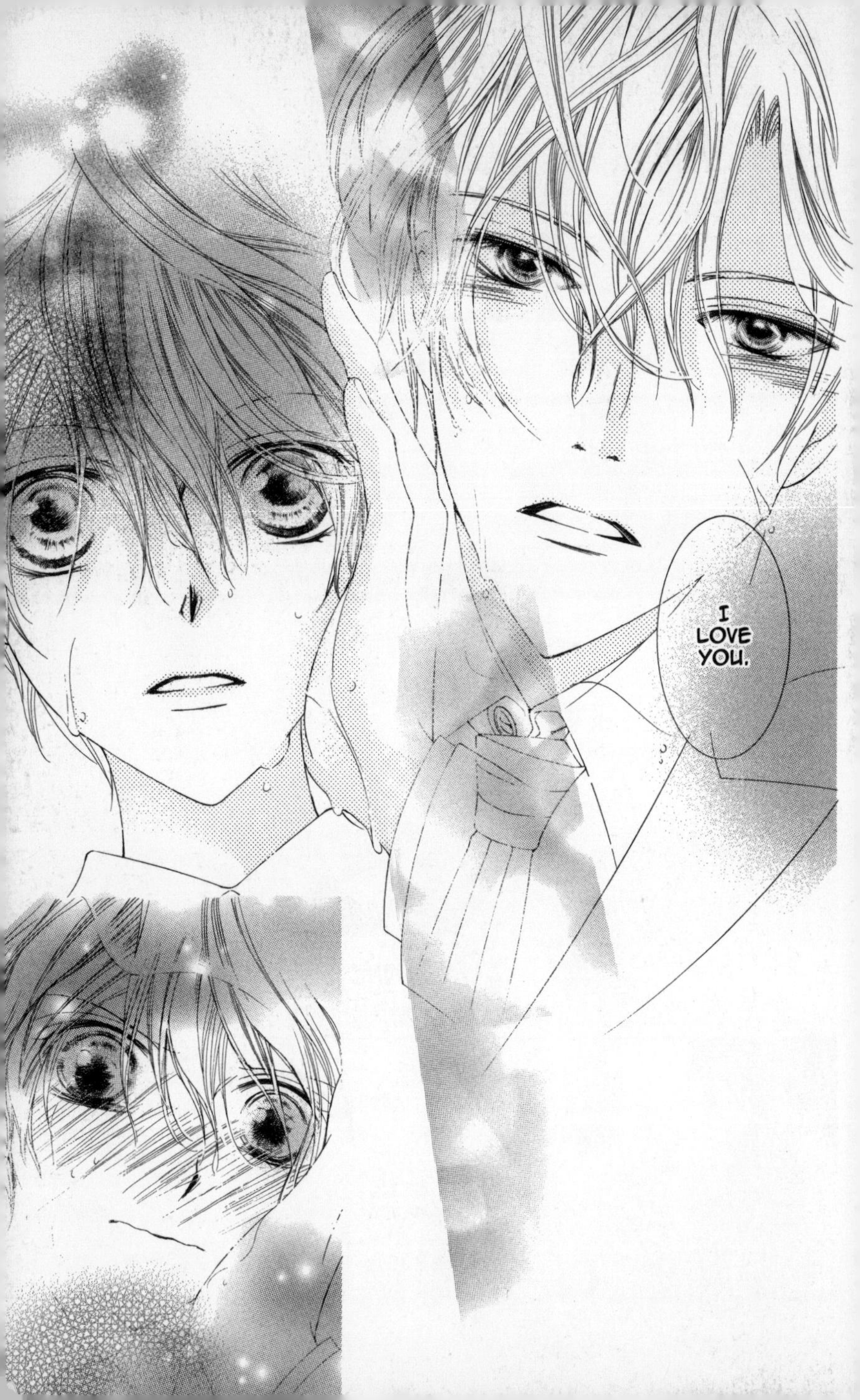
I LOVE YOU.

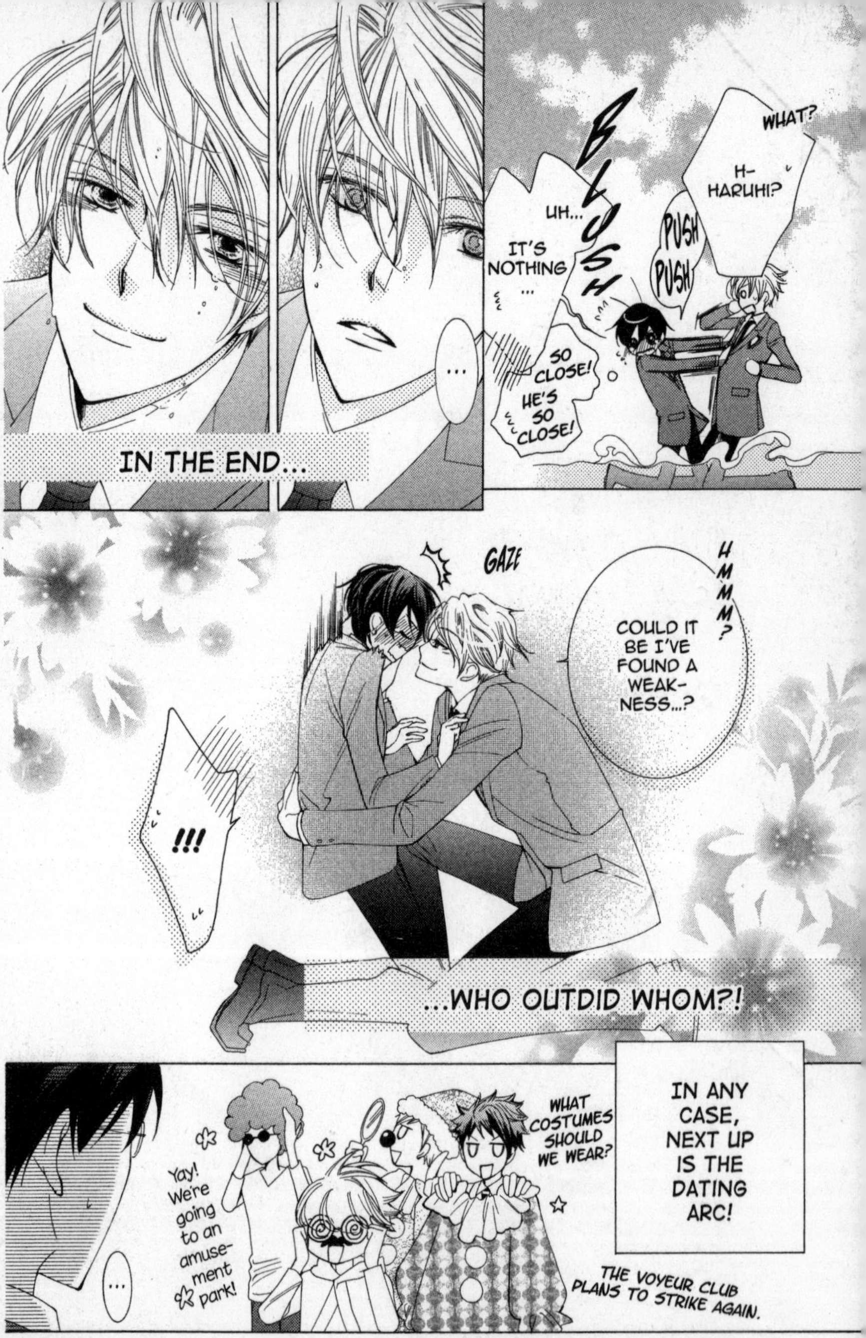
WHAT?
H-HARUHI?
PUSH PUSH
BLUSH
UH... IT'S NOTHING ...
SO CLOSE! HE'S SO CLOSE!
...
IN THE END...
HMMMM?
COULD IT BE I'VE FOUND A WEAKNESS...?
GAZE
!!!
...WHO OUTDID WHOM?!
IN ANY CASE, NEXT UP IS THE DATING ARC!
WHAT COSTUMES SHOULD WE WEAR?
THE VOYEUR CLUB PLANS TO STRIKE AGAIN.
Yay! We're going to an amusement park!
...

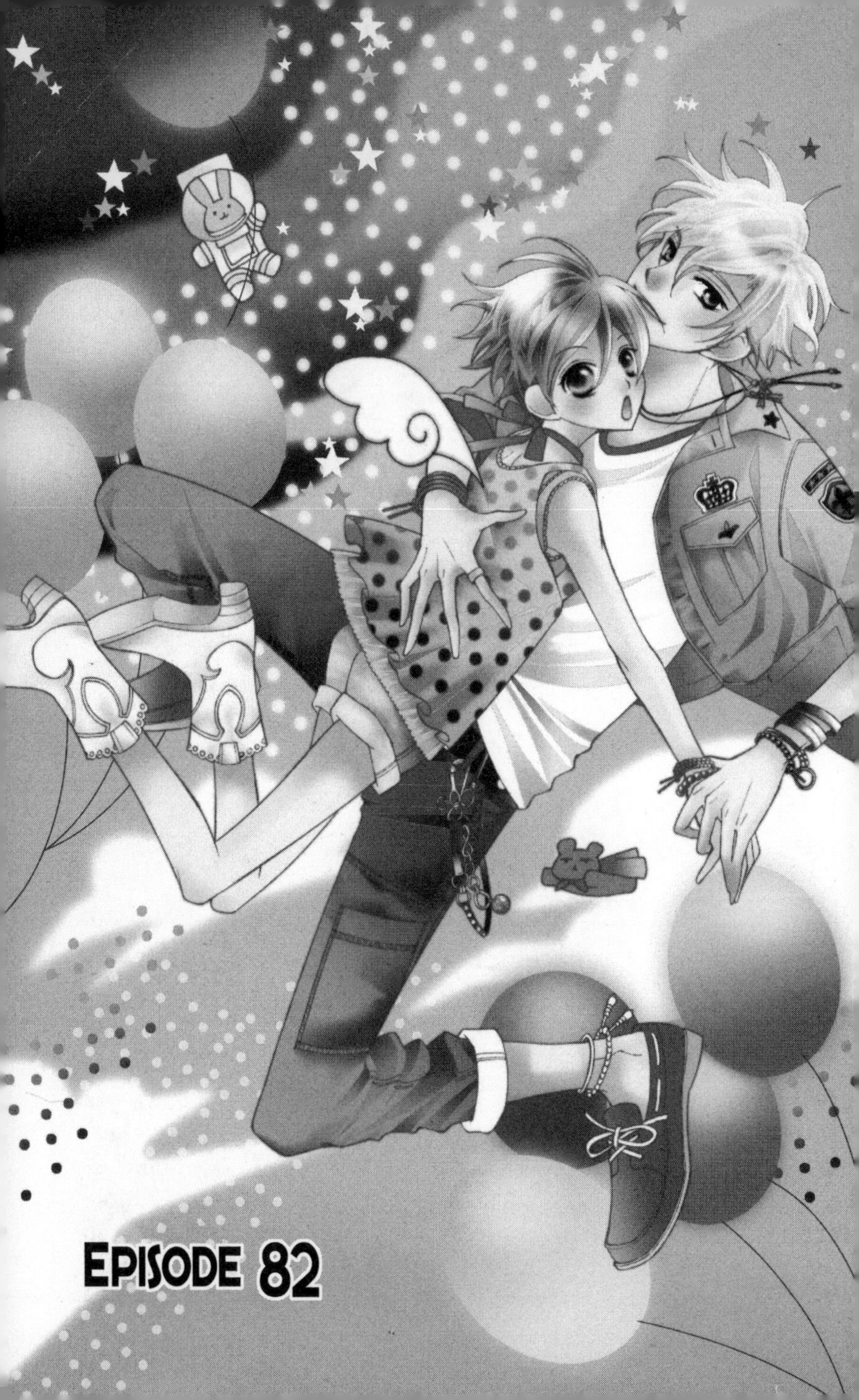
EPISODE 82

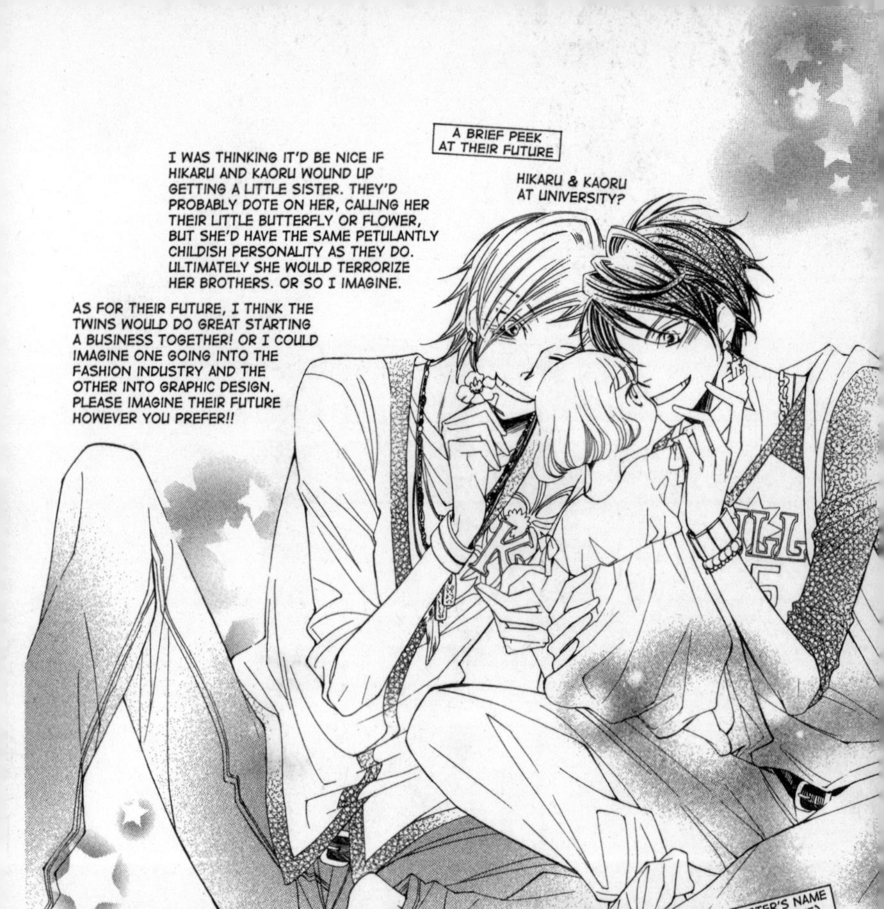
A BRIEF PEEK AT THEIR FUTURE
HIKARU & KAORU AT UNIVERSITY?
I WAS THINKING IT'D BE NICE IF HIKARU AND KAORU WOUND UP GETTING A LITTLE SISTER. THEY'D PROBABLY DOTE ON HER, CALLING HER THEIR LITTLE BUTTERFLY OR FLOWER, BUT SHE'D HAVE THE SAME PETULANTLY CHILDISH PERSONALITY AS THEY DO. ULTIMATELY SHE WOULD TERRORIZE HER BROTHERS. OR SO I IMAGINE.
AS FOR THEIR FUTURE, I THINK THE TWINS WOULD DO GREAT STARTING A BUSINESS TOGETHER! OR I COULD IMAGINE ONE GOING INTO THE FASHION INDUSTRY AND THE OTHER INTO GRAPHIC DESIGN. PLEASE IMAGINE THEIR FUTURE HOWEVER YOU PREFER!!

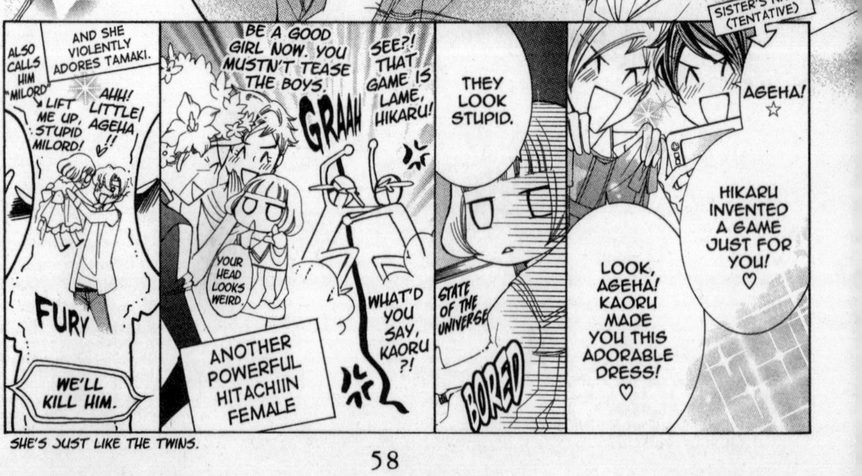
SISTER'S NAME (TENTATIVE)
AGEHA! ☆
HIKARU INVENTED A GAME JUST FOR YOU! ♡
LOOK, AGEHA! KAORU MADE YOU THIS ADORABLE DRESS! ♡
THEY LOOK STUPID.
STATE OF THE UNIVERSE
BORED
SEE?! THAT GAME IS LAME, HIKARU!
BE A GOOD GIRL NOW. YOU MUSTN'T TEASE THE BOYS.
GRAAH
YOUR HEAD LOOKS WEIRD.
WHAT'D YOU SAY, KAORU?!
ANOTHER POWERFUL HITACHIIN FEMALE
AND SHE VIOLENTLY ADORES TAMAKI.
ALSO CALLS HIM "MILORD"
AHH! LITTLE! AGEHA!!
LIFT ME UP, STUPID MILORD!
FURY
WE'LL KILL HIM.

SHE'S JUST LIKE THE TWINS.

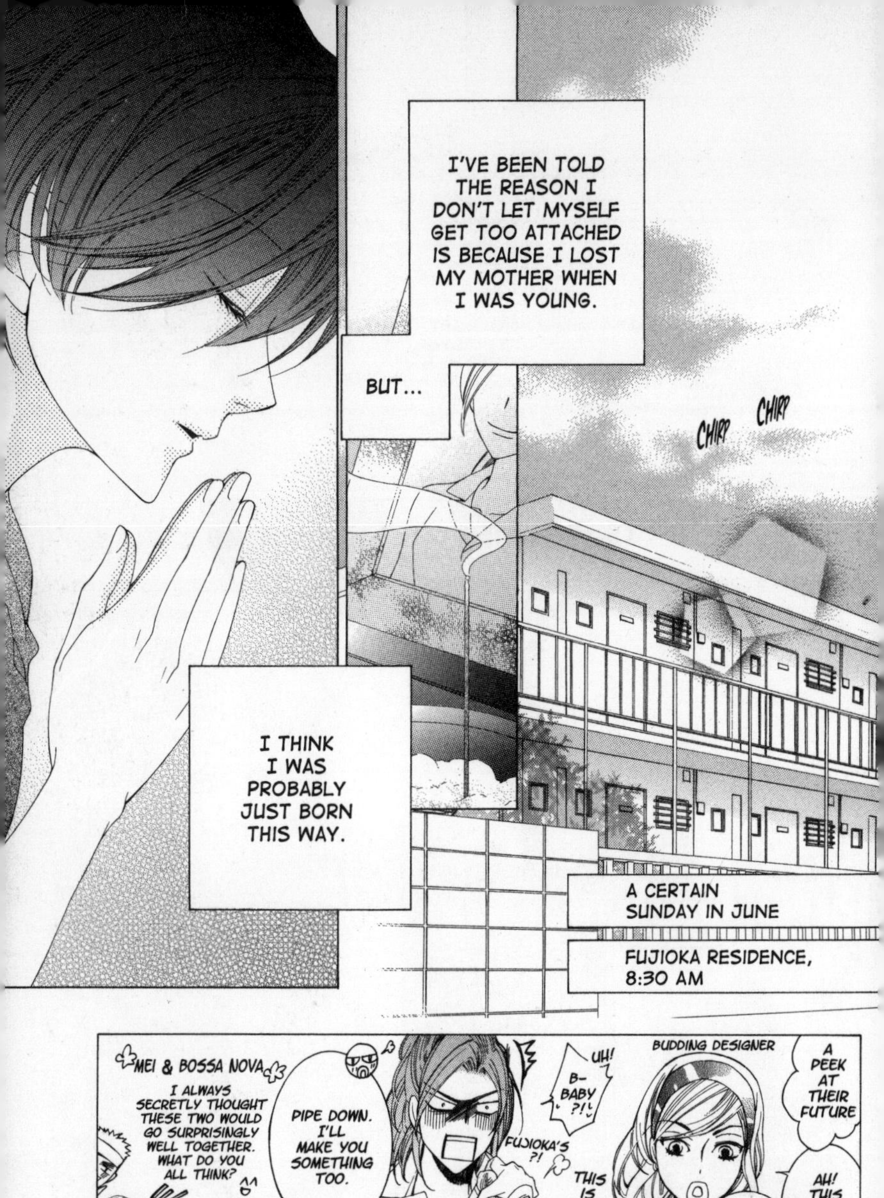
I'VE BEEN TOLD THE REASON I DON'T LET MYSELF GET TOO ATTACHED IS BECAUSE I LOST MY MOTHER WHEN I WAS YOUNG.
BUT...
I THINK I WAS PROBABLY JUST BORN THIS WAY.
CHIRP
CHIRP
A CERTAIN SUNDAY IN JUNE
FUJIOKA RESIDENCE, 8:30 AM

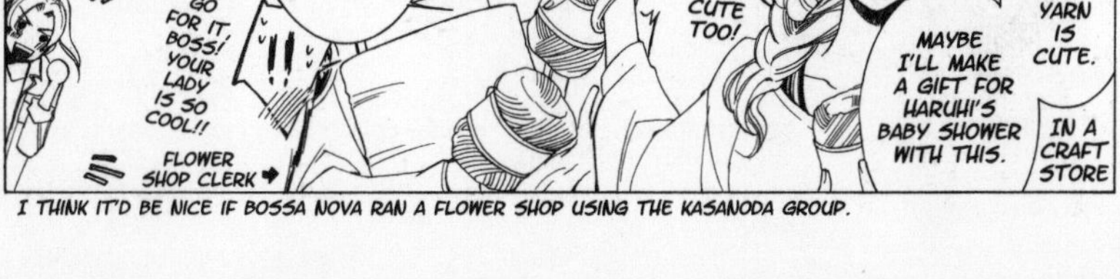
IN A CRAFT STORE
A PEEK AT THEIR FUTURE
BUDDING DESIGNER
AH! THIS YARN IS CUTE.
MAYBE I'LL MAKE A GIFT FOR HARUHI'S BABY SHOWER WITH THIS.
UH!
B-BABY?!
FUJIOKA'S?!
THIS IS CUTE TOO!
PIPE DOWN. I'LL MAKE YOU SOMETHING TOO.
MEI & BOSSA NOVA
I ALWAYS SECRETLY THOUGHT THESE TWO WOULD GO SURPRISINGLY WELL TOGETHER. WHAT DO YOU ALL THINK?
GO FOR IT, BOSS! YOUR LADY IS SO COOL!!
FLOWER SHOP CLERK
I THINK IT'D BE NICE IF BOSSA NOVA RAN A FLOWER SHOP USING THE KASANODA GROUP.

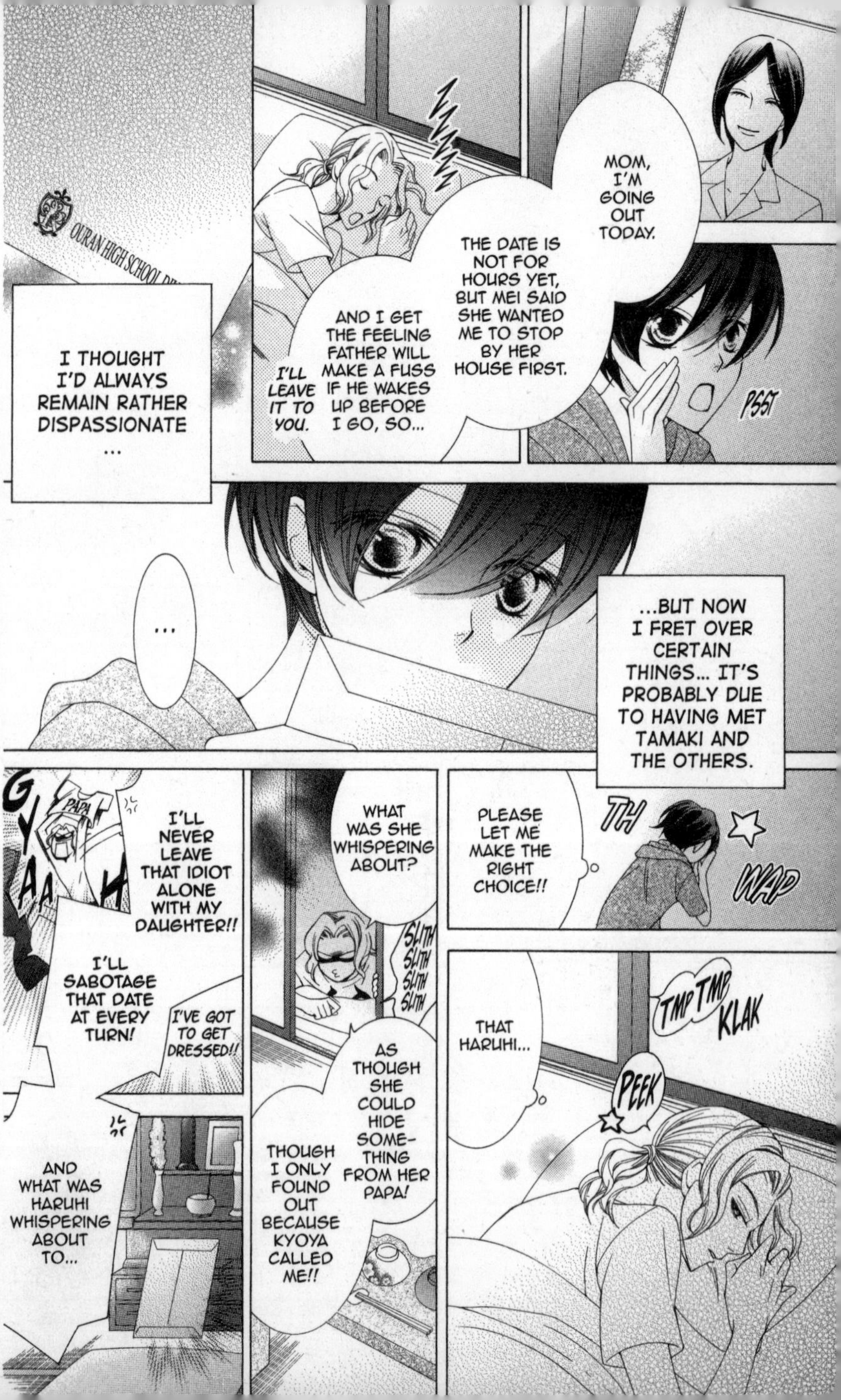
MOM, I'M GOING OUT TODAY.
THE DATE IS NOT FOR HOURS YET, BUT MEI SAID SHE WANTED ME TO STOP BY HER HOUSE FIRST.
AND I GET THE FEELING FATHER WILL MAKE A FUSS IF HE WAKES UP BEFORE I GO, SO...
I'LL LEAVE IT TO YOU.
PSST
OURAN HIGH SCHOOL
I THOUGHT I'D ALWAYS REMAIN RATHER DISPASSIONATE ...
...BUT NOW I FRET OVER CERTAIN THINGS... IT'S PROBABLY DUE TO HAVING MET TAMAKI AND THE OTHERS.
...
PLEASE LET ME MAKE THE RIGHT CHOICE!!
TH
WAP
THAT HARUHI...
TMP TMP
KLAK
PEEK
WHAT WAS SHE WHISPERING ABOUT?
SLITH SLITH SLITH SLITH
AS THOUGH SHE COULD HIDE SOME-THING FROM HER PAPA!
THOUGH I ONLY FOUND OUT BECAUSE KYOYA CALLED ME!!
GYAAH
PAPA
I'LL NEVER LEAVE THAT IDIOT ALONE WITH MY DAUGHTER!!
I'LL SABOTAGE THAT DATE AT EVERY TURN!
I'VE GOT TO GET DRESSED!!
AND WHAT WAS HARUHI WHISPERING ABOUT TO...

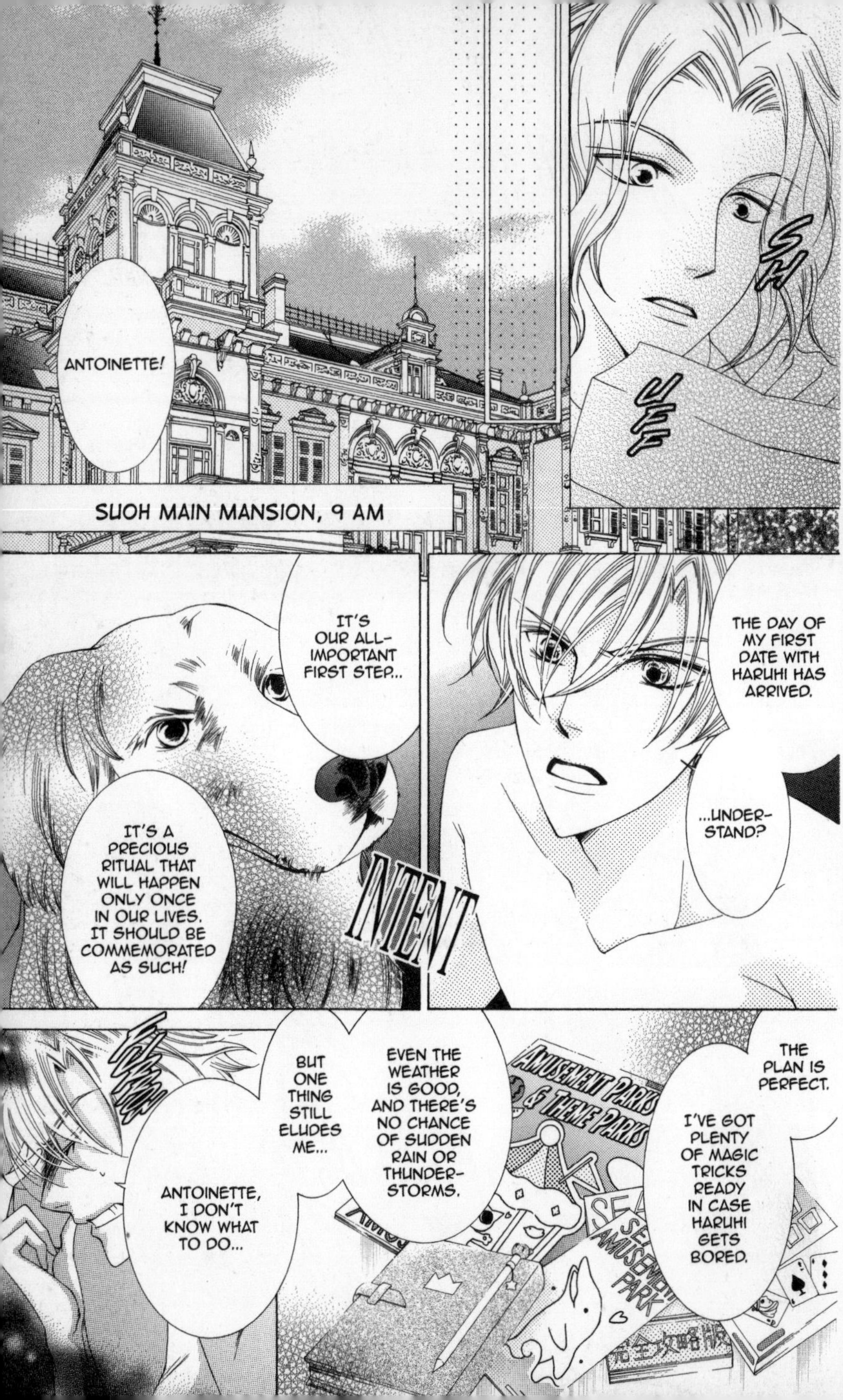
ANTOINETTE!
SUOH MAIN MANSION, 9 AM
THE DAY OF MY FIRST DATE WITH HARUHI HAS ARRIVED.
...UNDERSTAND?
IT'S OUR ALL-IMPORTANT FIRST STEP...
INTENT
IT'S A PRECIOUS RITUAL THAT WILL HAPPEN ONLY ONCE IN OUR LIVES. IT SHOULD BE COMMEMORATED AS SUCH!
THE PLAN IS PERFECT.
I'VE GOT PLENTY OF MAGIC TRICKS READY IN CASE HARUHI GETS BORED.
AMUSEMENT PARKS & THEME PARKS
完全攻略版
EVEN THE WEATHER IS GOOD, AND THERE'S NO CHANCE OF SUDDEN RAIN OR THUNDER-STORMS.
BUT ONE THING STILL ELUDES ME...
ANTOINETTE, I DON'T KNOW WHAT TO DO...

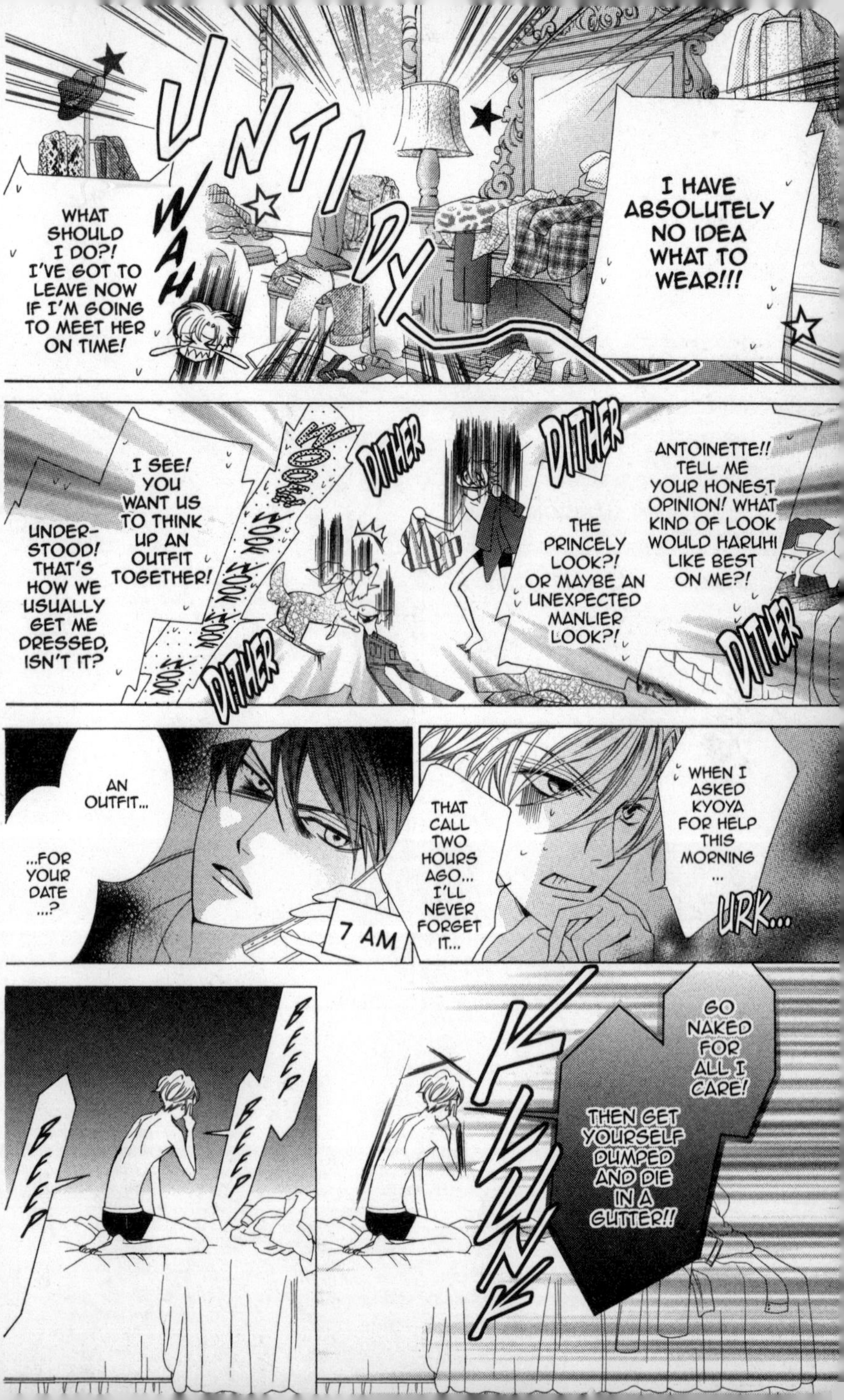

I HAVE ABSOLUTELY NO IDEA WHAT TO WEAR!!!
UNTIDY
WAH
WHAT SHOULD I DO?! I'VE GOT TO LEAVE NOW IF I'M GOING TO MEET HER ON TIME!
ANTOINETTE!! TELL ME YOUR HONEST OPINION! WHAT KIND OF LOOK WOULD HARUHI LIKE BEST ON ME?!
DITHER
THE PRINCELY LOOK?! OR MAYBE AN UNEXPECTED MANLIER LOOK?!
DITHER
DITHER
I SEE! YOU WANT US TO THINK UP AN OUTFIT TOGETHER!
UNDER-STOOD! THAT'S HOW WE USUALLY GET ME DRESSED, ISN'T IT?
DITHER
WHEN I ASKED KYOYA FOR HELP THIS MORNING...
URK...
THAT CALL TWO HOURS AGO... I'LL NEVER FORGET IT...
7 AM
AN OUTFIT...
...FOR YOUR DATE...?
GO NAKED FOR ALL I CARE!
THEN GET YOURSELF DUMPED AND DIE IN A GUTTER!!
BEEP BEEP
BEEP

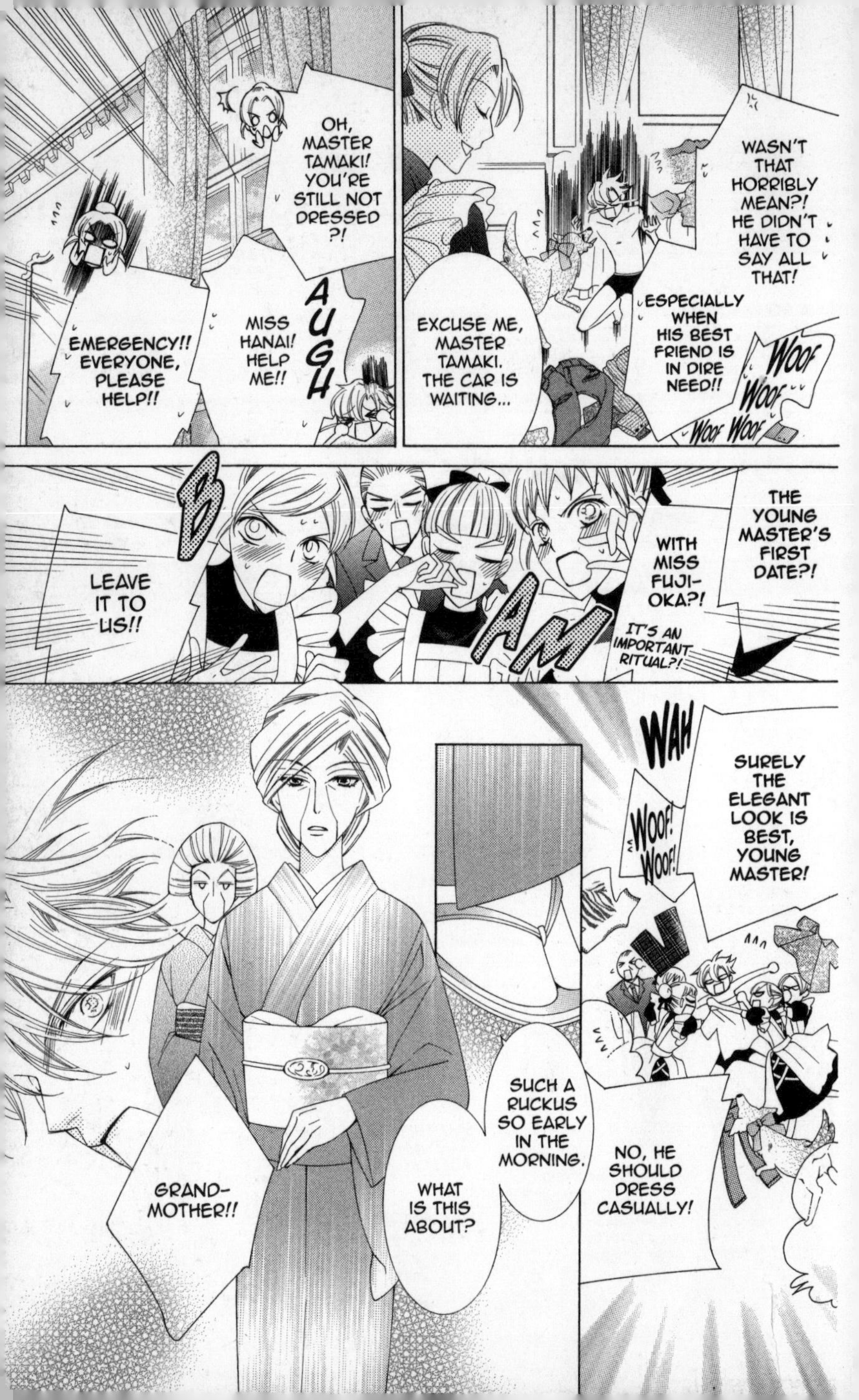
WASN'T THAT HORRIBLY MEAN?! HE DIDN'T HAVE TO SAY ALL THAT!
ESPECIALLY WHEN HIS BEST FRIEND IS IN DIRE NEED!!
WOOF WOOF WOOF WOOF
EXCUSE ME, MASTER TAMAKI. THE CAR IS WAITING...
OH, MASTER TAMAKI! YOU'RE STILL NOT DRESSED?!
AUGH
MISS HANAI! HELP ME!!
EMERGENCY!! EVERYONE, PLEASE HELP!!
THE YOUNG MASTER'S FIRST DATE?!
WITH MISS FUJI-OKA?!
IT'S AN IMPORTANT RITUAL?!
BAM
LEAVE IT TO US!!
WAH
SURELY THE ELEGANT LOOK IS BEST, YOUNG MASTER!
WOOF! WOOF!
NO, HE SHOULD DRESS CASUALLY!
SUCH A RUCKUS SO EARLY IN THE MORNING.
WHAT IS THIS ABOUT?
GRAND-MOTHER!!

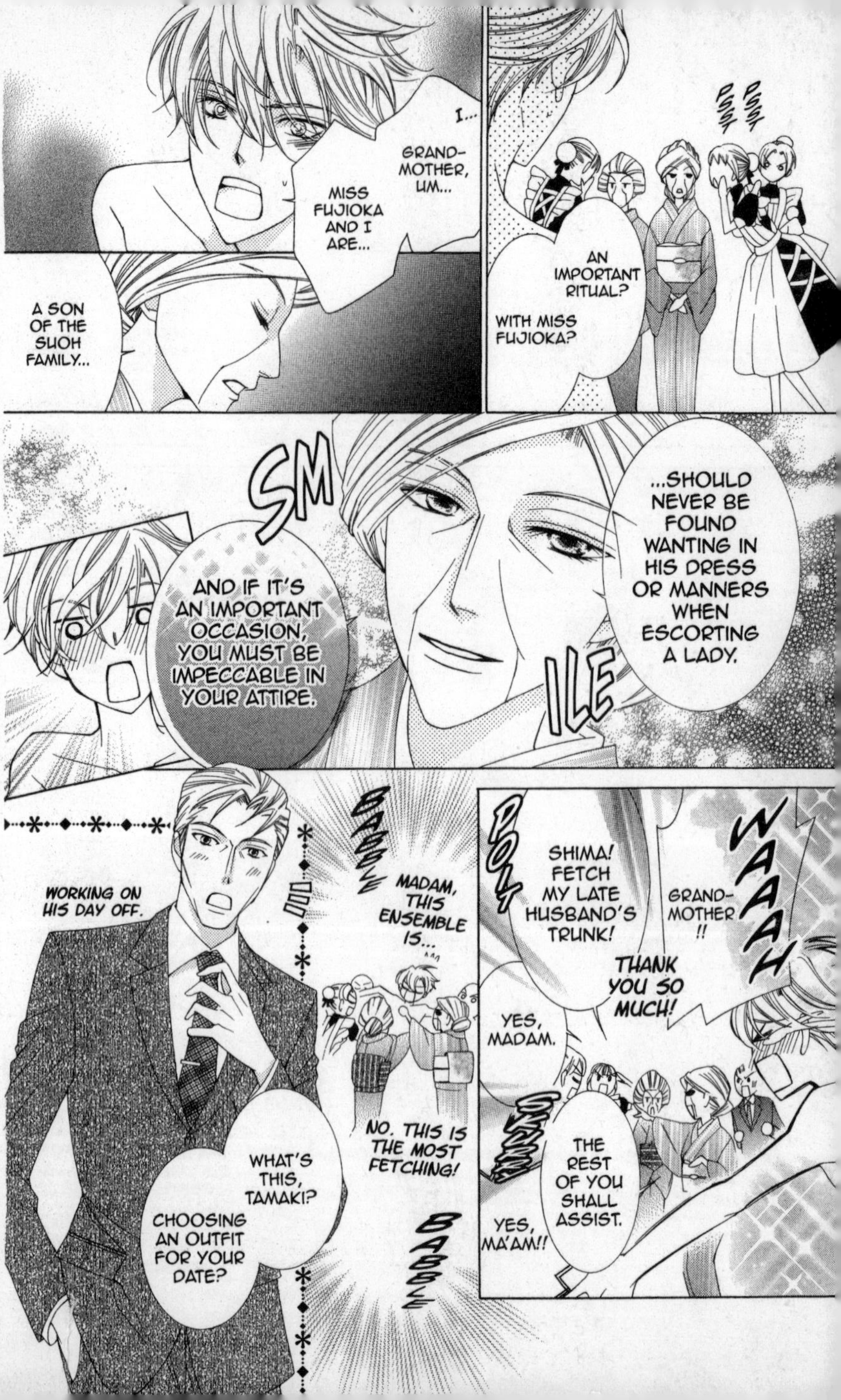
PSST PSST
AN IMPORTANT RITUAL?
WITH MISS FUJIOKA?
I...
GRANDMOTHER, UM...
MISS FUJIOKA AND I ARE...
A SON OF THE SUOH FAMILY...
...SHOULD NEVER BE FOUND WANTING IN HIS DRESS OR MANNERS WHEN ESCORTING A LADY.
SM ILE
AND IF IT'S AN IMPORTANT OCCASION, YOU MUST BE IMPECCABLE IN YOUR ATTIRE.
WAAAH
GRANDMOTHER!!
POK
SHIMA! FETCH MY LATE HUSBAND'S TRUNK!
THANK YOU SO MUCH!
YES, MADAM.
THE REST OF YOU SHALL ASSIST.
YES, MA'AM!!
BABBLE
MADAM, THIS ENSEMBLE IS...
NO. THIS IS THE MOST FETCHING!
BABBLE
WORKING ON HIS DAY OFF.
WHAT'S THIS, TAMAKI?
CHOOSING AN OUTFIT FOR YOUR DATE?

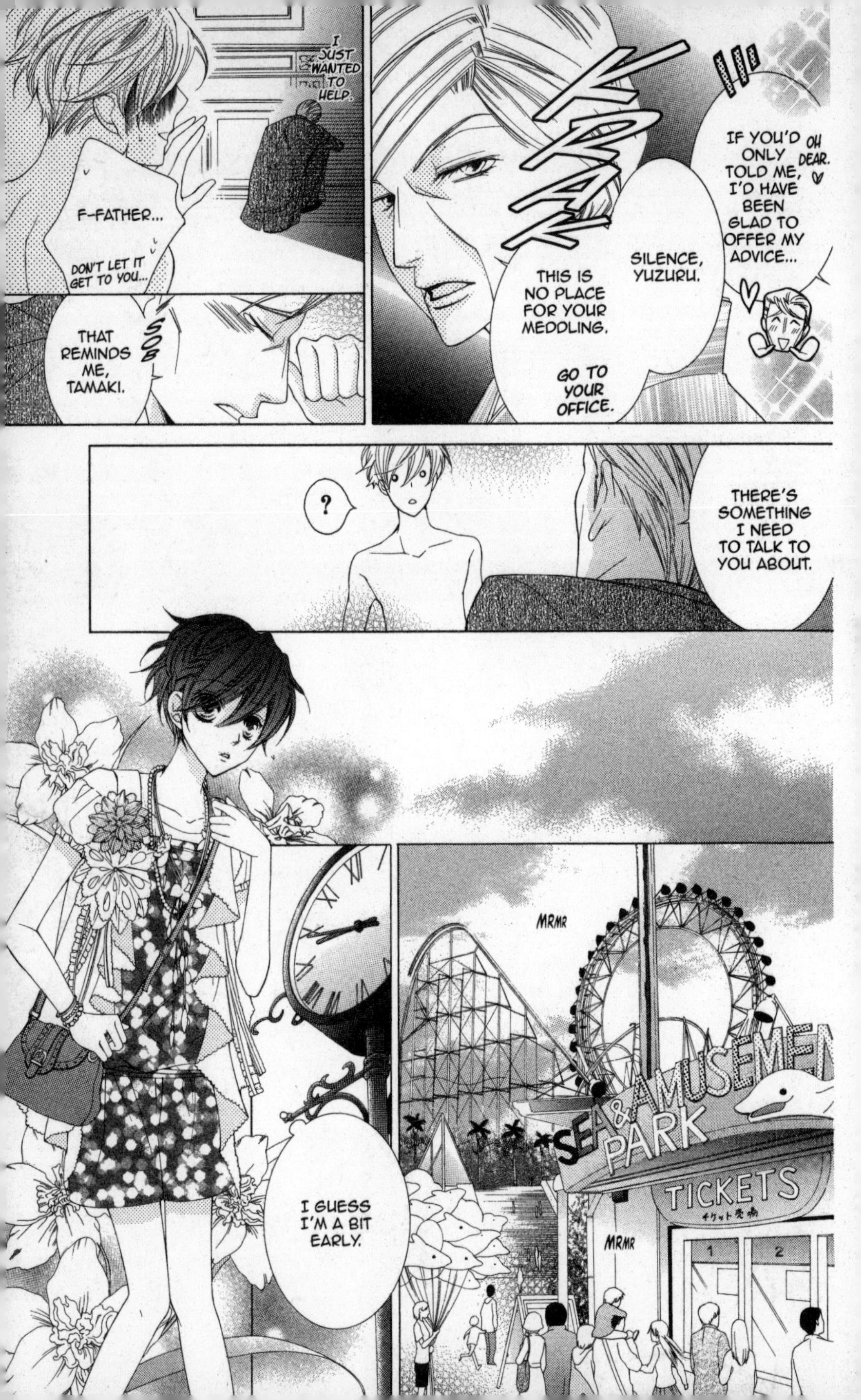
IF YOU'D ONLY TOLD ME, I'D HAVE BEEN GLAD TO OFFER MY ADVICE...
OH DEAR. ♥
SILENCE, YUZURU.
THIS IS NO PLACE FOR YOUR MEDDLING.
GO TO YOUR OFFICE.
I JUST WANTED TO HELP.
F-FATHER...
DON'T LET IT GET TO YOU...
SOB
THAT REMINDS ME, TAMAKI.
THERE'S SOMETHING I NEED TO TALK TO YOU ABOUT.
?
MRMR
SEA & AMUSEMENT PARK
TICKETS
MRMR
I GUESS I'M A BIT EARLY.

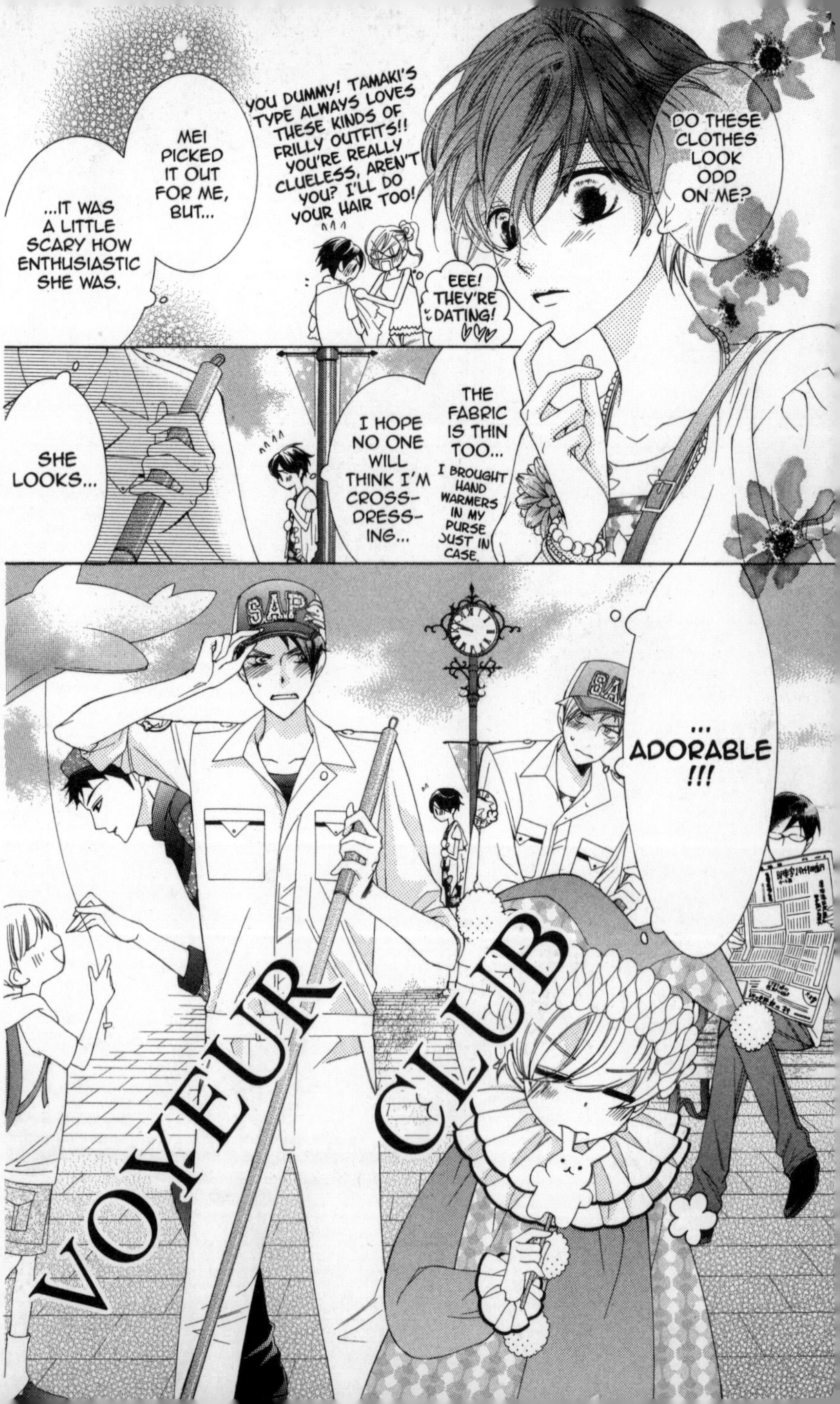
DO THESE CLOTHES LOOK ODD ON ME?
THE FABRIC IS THIN TOO...
I BROUGHT HAND WARMERS IN MY PURSE JUST IN CASE.
EEE! THEY'RE DATING!
YOU DUMMY! TAMAKI'S TYPE ALWAYS LOVES THESE KINDS OF FRILLY OUTFITS!! YOU'RE REALLY CLUELESS, AREN'T YOU? I'LL DO YOUR HAIR TOO!
MEI PICKED IT OUT FOR ME, BUT...
...IT WAS A LITTLE SCARY HOW ENTHUSIASTIC SHE WAS.
I HOPE NO ONE WILL THINK I'M CROSS-DRESSING...
SHE LOOKS...
... ADORABLE !!!
VOYEUR CLUB

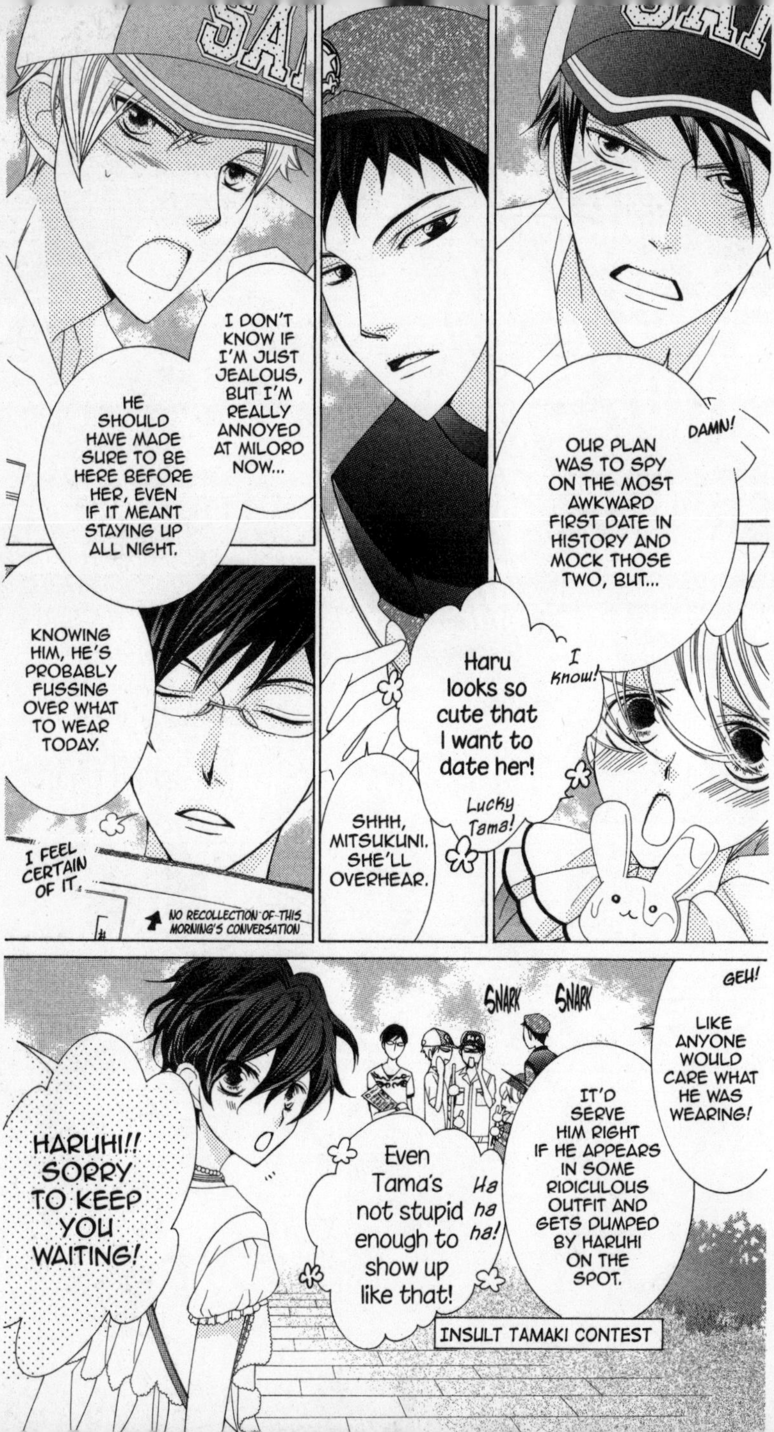
DAMN!
OUR PLAN WAS TO SPY ON THE MOST AWKWARD FIRST DATE IN HISTORY AND MOCK THOSE TWO, BUT...
I Know!
Haru looks so cute that I want to date her!
Lucky Tama!
SHHH, MITSUKUNI. SHE'LL OVERHEAR.
I DON'T KNOW IF I'M JUST JEALOUS, BUT I'M REALLY ANNOYED AT MILORD NOW...
HE SHOULD HAVE MADE SURE TO BE HERE BEFORE HER, EVEN IF IT MEANT STAYING UP ALL NIGHT.
KNOWING HIM, HE'S PROBABLY FUSSING OVER WHAT TO WEAR TODAY.
I FEEL CERTAIN OF IT.
NO RECOLLECTION OF THIS MORNING'S CONVERSATION
GEH!
LIKE ANYONE WOULD CARE WHAT HE WAS WEARING!
IT'D SERVE HIM RIGHT IF HE APPEARS IN SOME RIDICULOUS OUTFIT AND GETS DUMPED BY HARUHI ON THE SPOT.
SNARK SNARK
Ha ha ha!
Even Tama's not stupid enough to show up like that!
INSULT TAMAKI CONTEST
HARUHI!! SORRY TO KEEP YOU WAITING!

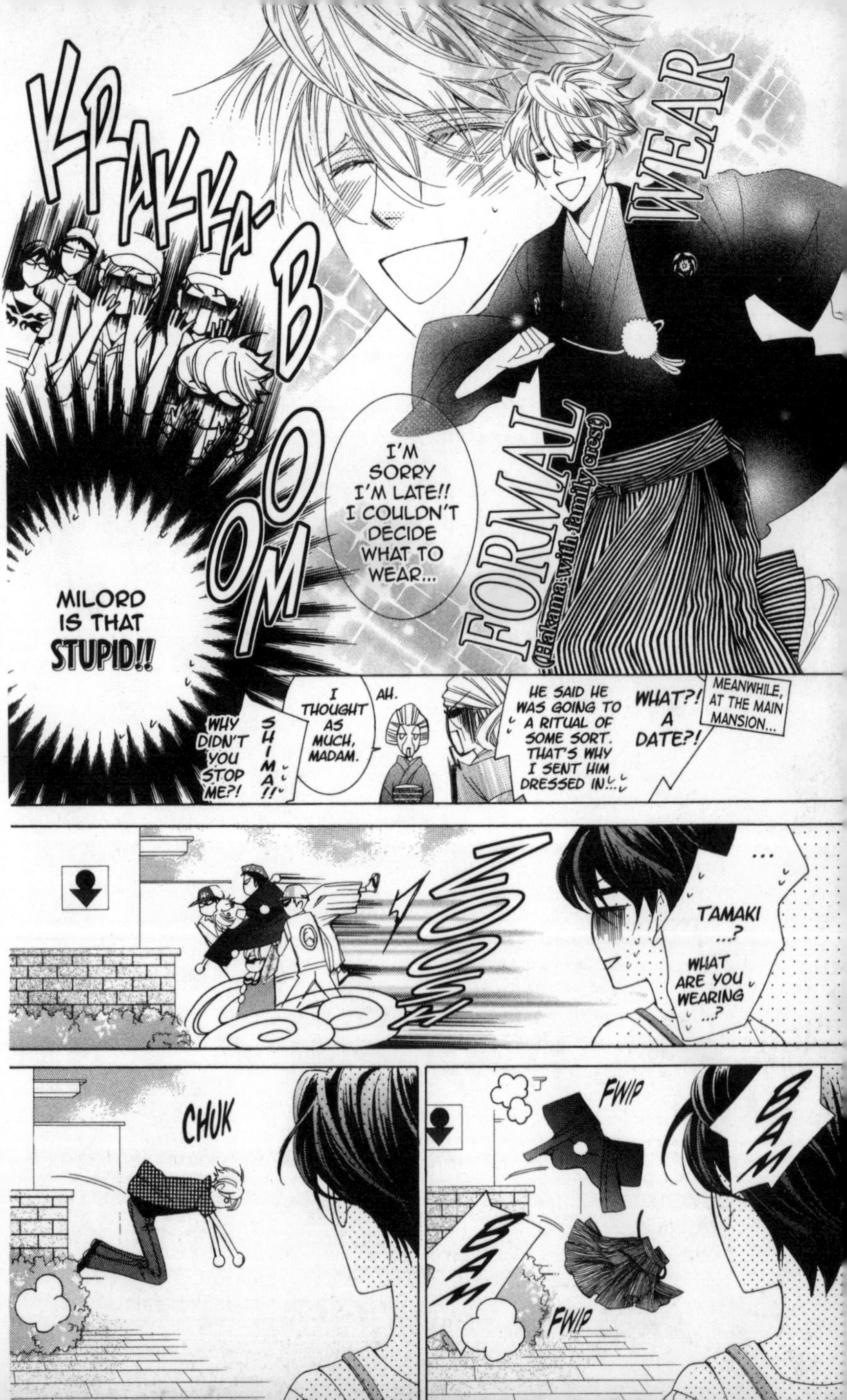
KRAKKA-BOOOM
FORMAL WEAR
(Hakama with family crest)
I'M SORRY I'M LATE!! I COULDN'T DECIDE WHAT TO WEAR...
MILORD IS THAT STUPID!!
MEANWHILE, AT THE MAIN MANSION...
WHAT?! A DATE?!
HE SAID HE WAS GOING TO A RITUAL OF SOME SORT. THAT'S WHY I SENT HIM DRESSED IN...
AH.
I THOUGHT AS MUCH, MADAM.
SHIMA!!
WHY DIDN'T YOU STOP ME?!
...
TAMAKI ...?
WHAT ARE YOU WEARING ...?
WOOOOSSH
FWIP
BAM
BAM
FWIP
CHUK

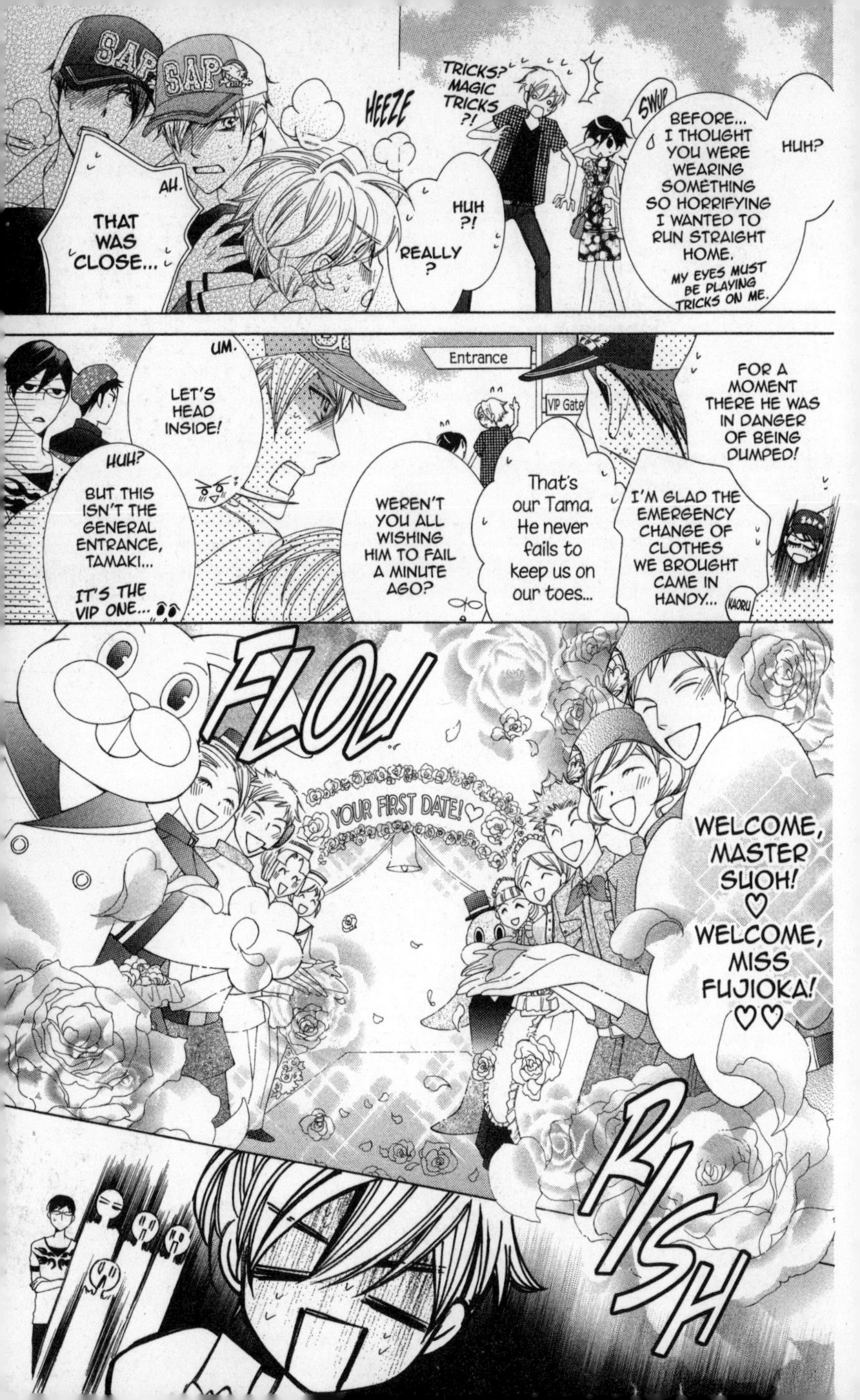
HUH?
BEFORE... I THOUGHT YOU WERE WEARING SOMETHING SO HORRIFYING I WANTED TO RUN STRAIGHT HOME.
MY EYES MUST BE PLAYING TRICKS ON ME.
SWUP
TRICKS? MAGIC TRICKS ?!
HUH ?!
REALLY ?
HEEZE
AH.
THAT WAS CLOSE...
FOR A MOMENT THERE HE WAS IN DANGER OF BEING DUMPED!
I'M GLAD THE EMERGENCY CHANGE OF CLOTHES WE BROUGHT CAME IN HANDY...
KAORU
That's our Tama. He never fails to keep us on our toes...
WEREN'T YOU ALL WISHING HIM TO FAIL A MINUTE AGO?
Entrance
VIP Gate
UM.
LET'S HEAD INSIDE!
HUH?
BUT THIS ISN'T THE GENERAL ENTRANCE, TAMAKI...
IT'S THE VIP ONE...
WELCOME, MASTER SUOH! ♡ WELCOME, MISS FUJIOKA! ♡♡
YOUR FIRST DATE! ♡
FLOW
RISH

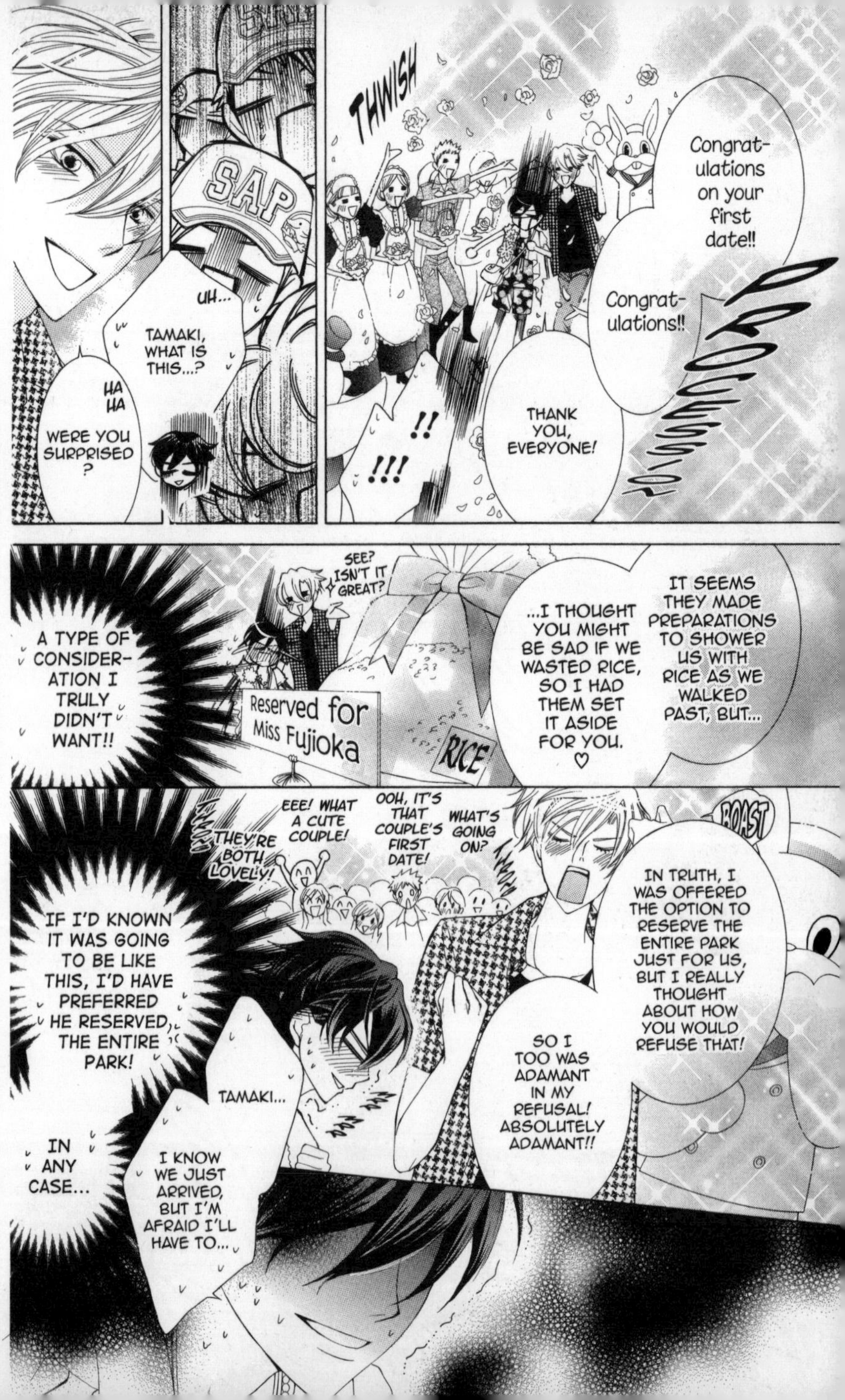
THWISH
Congrat-ulations on your first date!!
Congrat-ulations!!
THANK YOU, EVERYONE!
!!
!!!
SAP
UH...
TAMAKI, WHAT IS THIS...?
HA HA
WERE YOU SURPRISED?
IT SEEMS THEY MADE PREPARATIONS TO SHOWER US WITH RICE AS WE WALKED PAST, BUT...
...I THOUGHT YOU MIGHT BE SAD IF WE WASTED RICE, SO I HAD THEM SET IT ASIDE FOR YOU. ♡
SEE? ISN'T IT GREAT?
Reserved for Miss Fujioka
RICE
A TYPE OF CONSIDER-ATION I TRULY DIDN'T WANT!!
BOAST
IN TRUTH, I WAS OFFERED THE OPTION TO RESERVE THE ENTIRE PARK JUST FOR US, BUT I REALLY THOUGHT ABOUT HOW YOU WOULD REFUSE THAT!
SO I TOO WAS ADAMANT IN MY REFUSAL! ABSOLUTELY ADAMANT!!
WHAT'S GOING ON?
OOH, IT'S THAT COUPLE'S FIRST DATE!
EEE! WHAT A CUTE COUPLE!
THEY'RE BOTH LOVELY!
TAMAKI...
IF I'D KNOWN IT WAS GOING TO BE LIKE THIS, I'D HAVE PREFERRED HE RESERVED THE ENTIRE PARK!
I KNOW WE JUST ARRIVED, BUT I'M AFRAID I'LL HAVE TO...
IN ANY CASE...

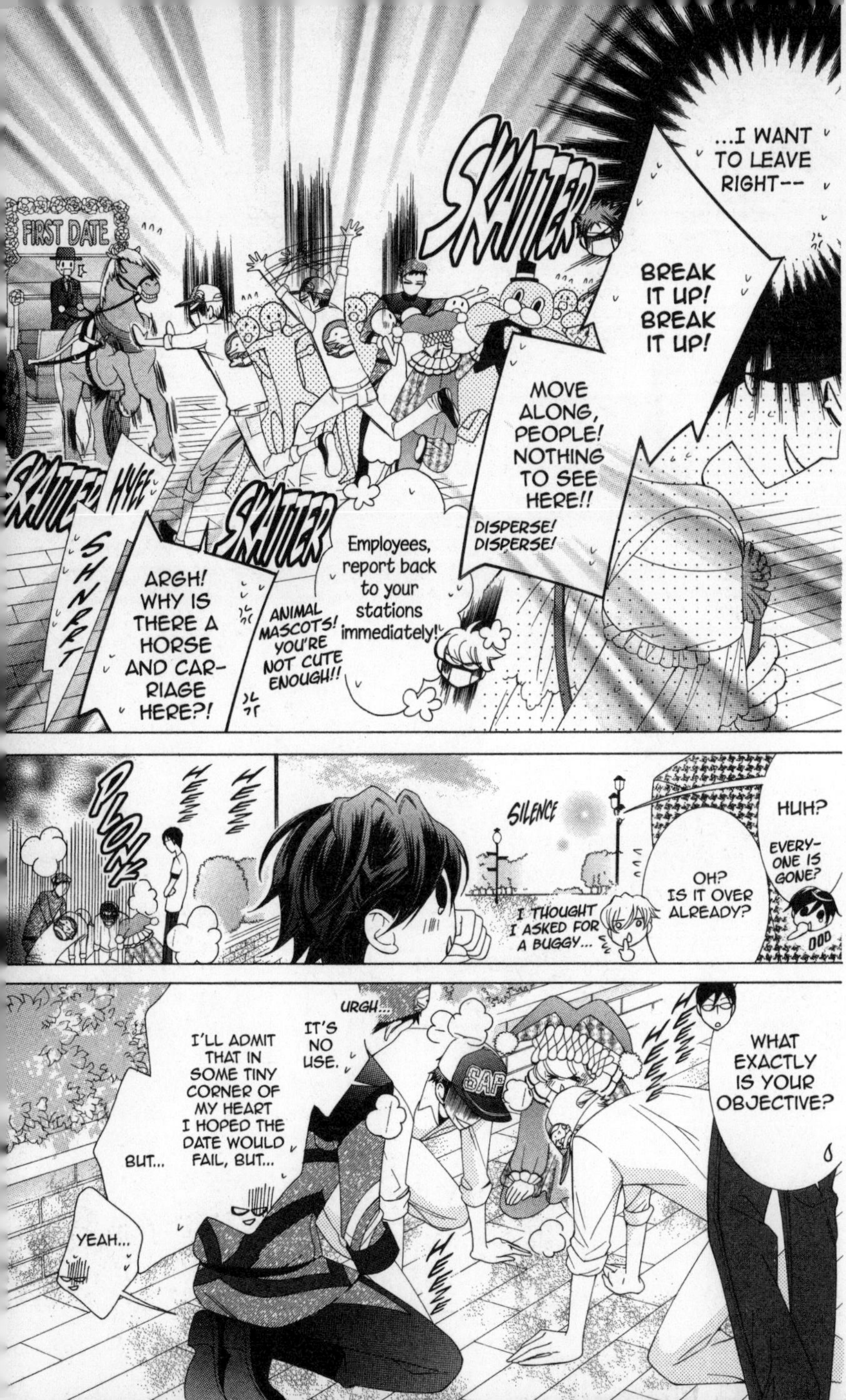
...I WANT TO LEAVE RIGHT--
BREAK IT UP! BREAK IT UP!
SKATTER
MOVE ALONG, PEOPLE! NOTHING TO SEE HERE!!
DISPERSE! DISPERSE!
Employees, report back to your stations immediately!
ANIMAL MASCOTS! YOU'RE NOT CUTE ENOUGH!!
SKATTER
ARGH! WHY IS THERE A HORSE AND CARRIAGE HERE?!
SHNRRT
HYEE
SKATTER
FIRST DATE
HUH?
EVERYONE IS GONE?
OH? IS IT OVER ALREADY?
I THOUGHT I ASKED FOR A BUGGY...
SILENCE
PLOMP
WHAT EXACTLY IS YOUR OBJECTIVE?
URGH...
IT'S NO USE.
I'LL ADMIT THAT IN SOME TINY CORNER OF MY HEART I HOPED THE DATE WOULD FAIL, BUT...
BUT...
YEAH...

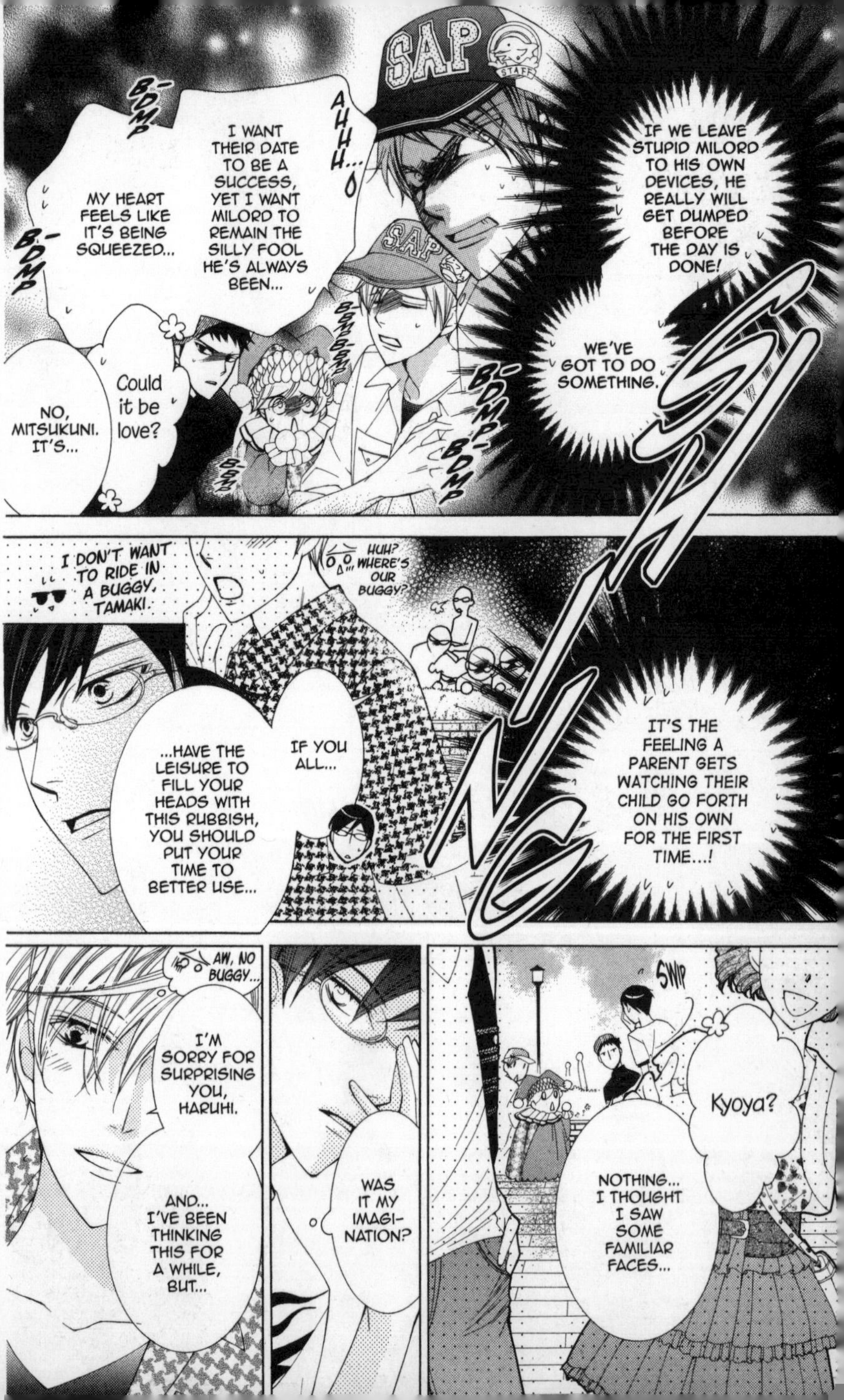
IF WE LEAVE STUPID MILORD TO HIS OWN DEVICES, HE REALLY WILL GET DUMPED BEFORE THE DAY IS DONE!
WE'VE GOT TO DO SOMETHING.
AHHH...
B-DOMP
I WANT THEIR DATE TO BE A SUCCESS, YET I WANT MILORD TO REMAIN THE SILLY FOOL HE'S ALWAYS BEEN...
B-DOMP
MY HEART FEELS LIKE IT'S BEING SQUEEZED...
B-DOMP
Could it be love?
NO, MITSUKUNI. IT'S...
SHING
IT'S THE FEELING A PARENT GETS WATCHING THEIR CHILD GO FORTH ON HIS OWN FOR THE FIRST TIME...!
HUH? WHERE'S OUR BUGGY?
I DON'T WANT TO RIDE IN A BUGGY, TAMAKI.
IF YOU ALL...
...HAVE THE LEISURE TO FILL YOUR HEADS WITH THIS RUBBISH, YOU SHOULD PUT YOUR TIME TO BETTER USE...
SWIP
Kyoya?
NOTHING... I THOUGHT I SAW SOME FAMILIAR FACES...
WAS IT MY IMAGINATION?
AW, NO BUGGY...
I'M SORRY FOR SURPRISING YOU, HARUHI.
AND... I'VE BEEN THINKING THIS FOR A WHILE, BUT...

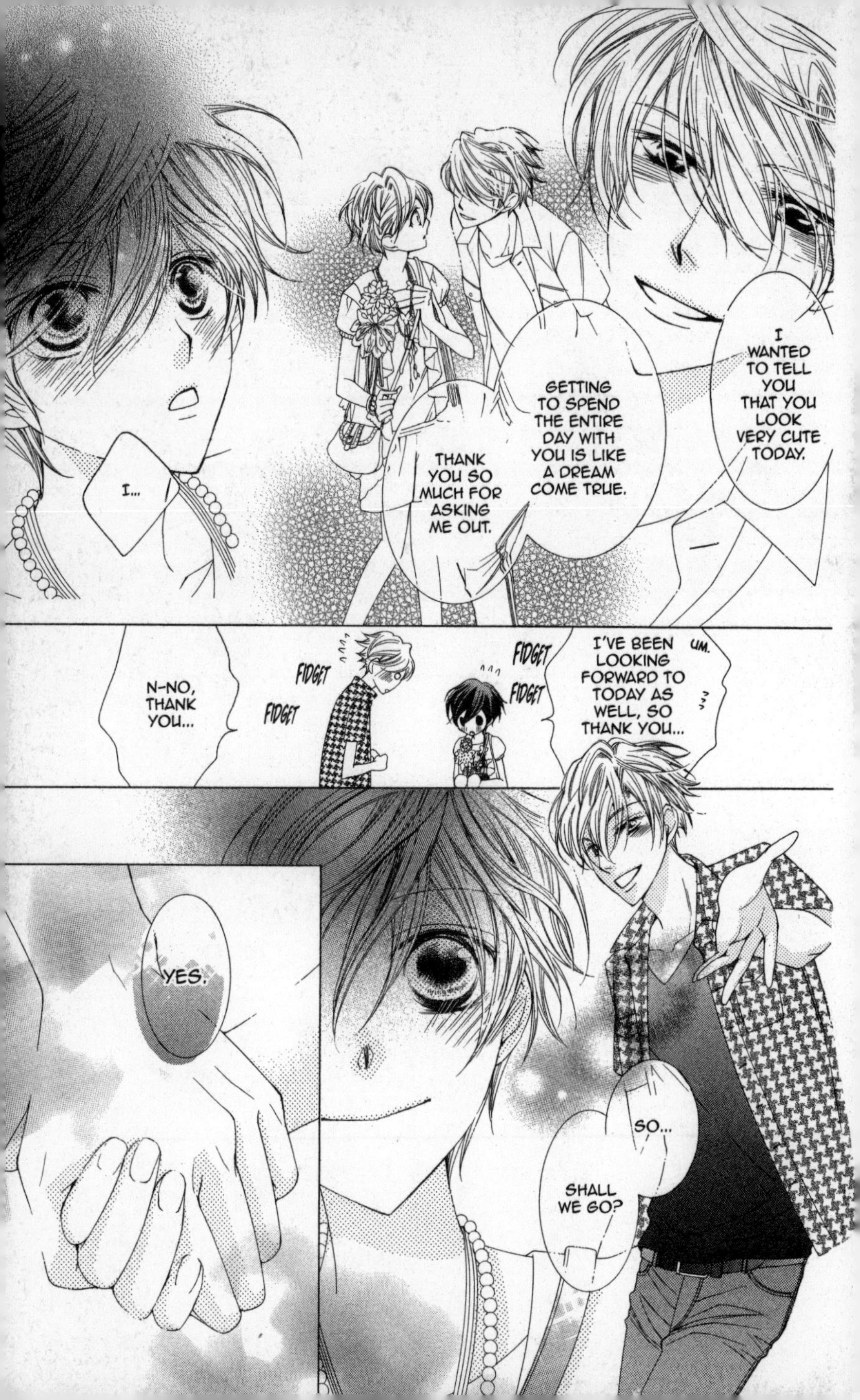
I WANTED TO TELL YOU THAT YOU LOOK VERY CUTE TODAY.
GETTING TO SPEND THE ENTIRE DAY WITH YOU IS LIKE A DREAM COME TRUE.
THANK YOU SO MUCH FOR ASKING ME OUT.
I...
UM.
I'VE BEEN LOOKING FORWARD TO TODAY AS WELL, SO THANK YOU...
FIDGET
FIDGET
FIDGET
FIDGET
N-NO, THANK YOU...
SO...
SHALL WE GO?
YES.

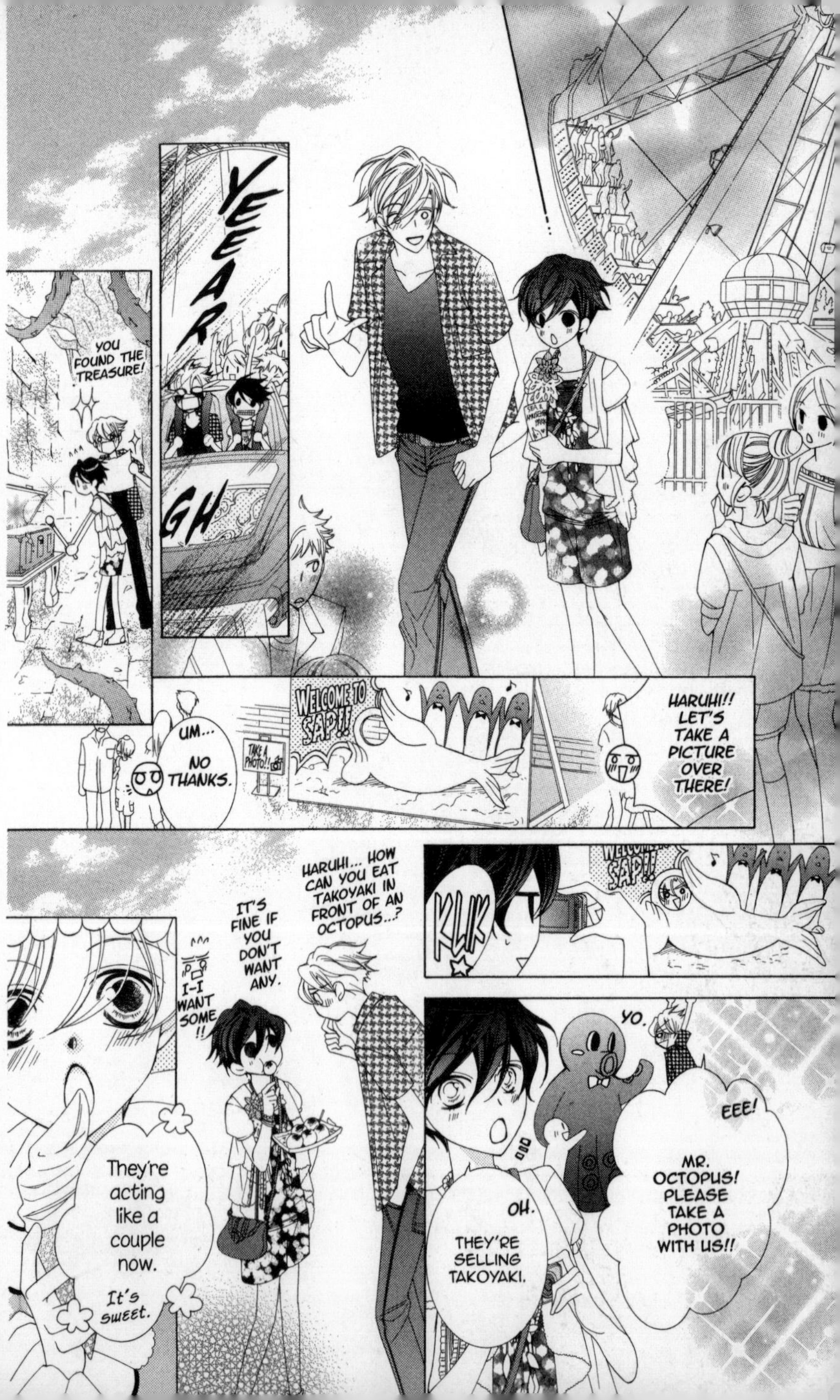
YEEARGH
YOU FOUND THE TREASURE!
HARUHI!! LET'S TAKE A PICTURE OVER THERE!
WELCOME TO SAP!!
TAKE A PHOTO!!
UM... NO THANKS.
WELCOME TO SAP!!
KLIK
YO.
EEE!
MR. OCTOPUS! PLEASE TAKE A PHOTO WITH US!!
OH.
THEY'RE SELLING TAKOYAKI.
HARUHI... HOW CAN YOU EAT TAKOYAKI IN FRONT OF AN OCTOPUS...?
IT'S FINE IF YOU DON'T WANT ANY.
I-I WANT SOME!!
They're acting like a couple now.
It's sweet.

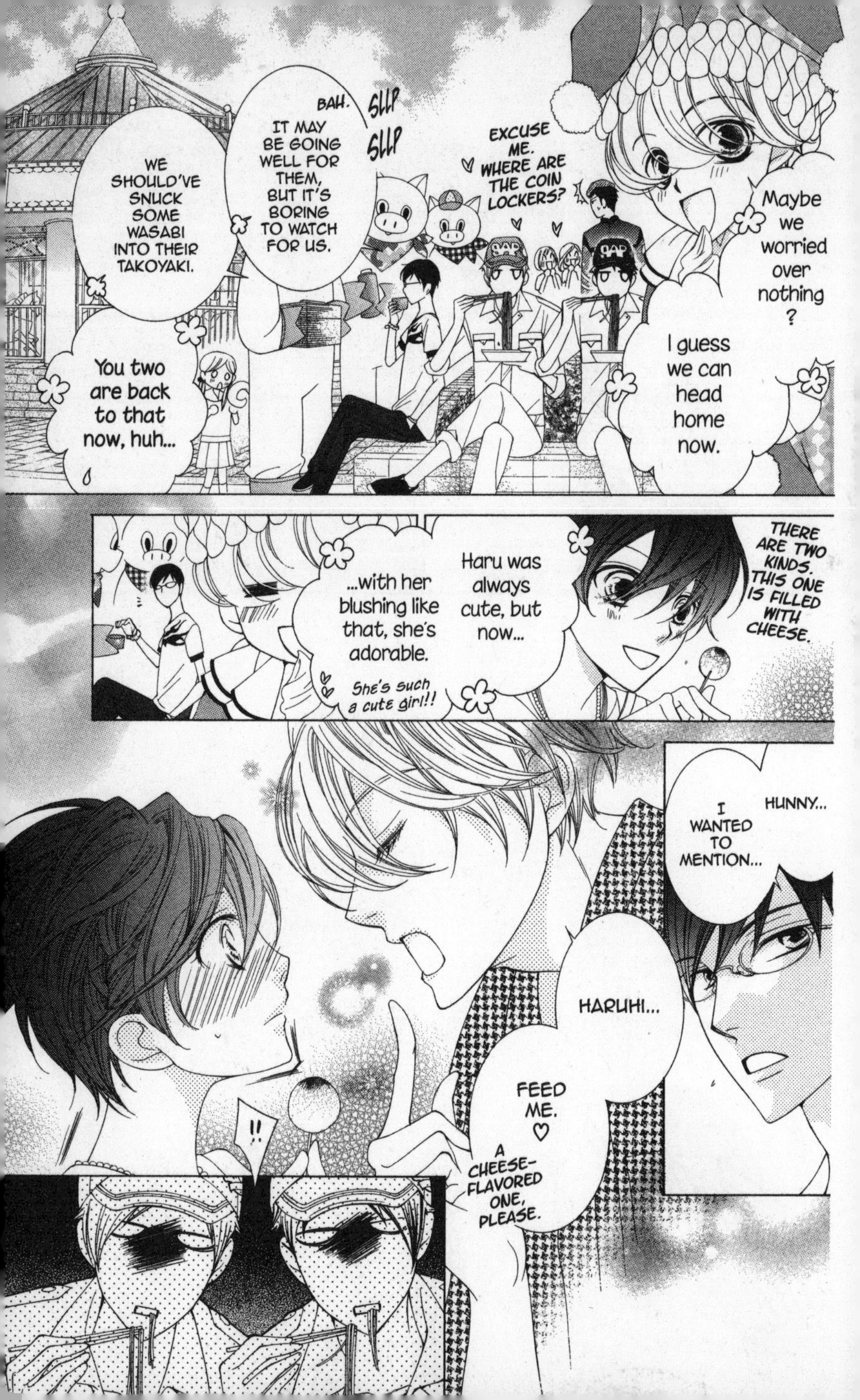
Maybe we worried over nothing?
I guess we can head home now.
EXCUSE ME. WHERE ARE THE COIN LOCKERS?
BAH.
SLLP
SLLP
IT MAY BE GOING WELL FOR THEM, BUT IT'S BORING TO WATCH FOR US.
WE SHOULD'VE SNUCK SOME WASABI INTO THEIR TAKOYAKI.
You two are back to that now, huh...
THERE ARE TWO KINDS. THIS ONE IS FILLED WITH CHEESE.
Haru was always cute, but now...
...with her blushing like that, she's adorable.
She's such a cute girl!!
HUNNY...
I WANTED TO MENTION...
HARUHI...
FEED ME.
A CHEESE-FLAVORED ONE, PLEASE.
!!

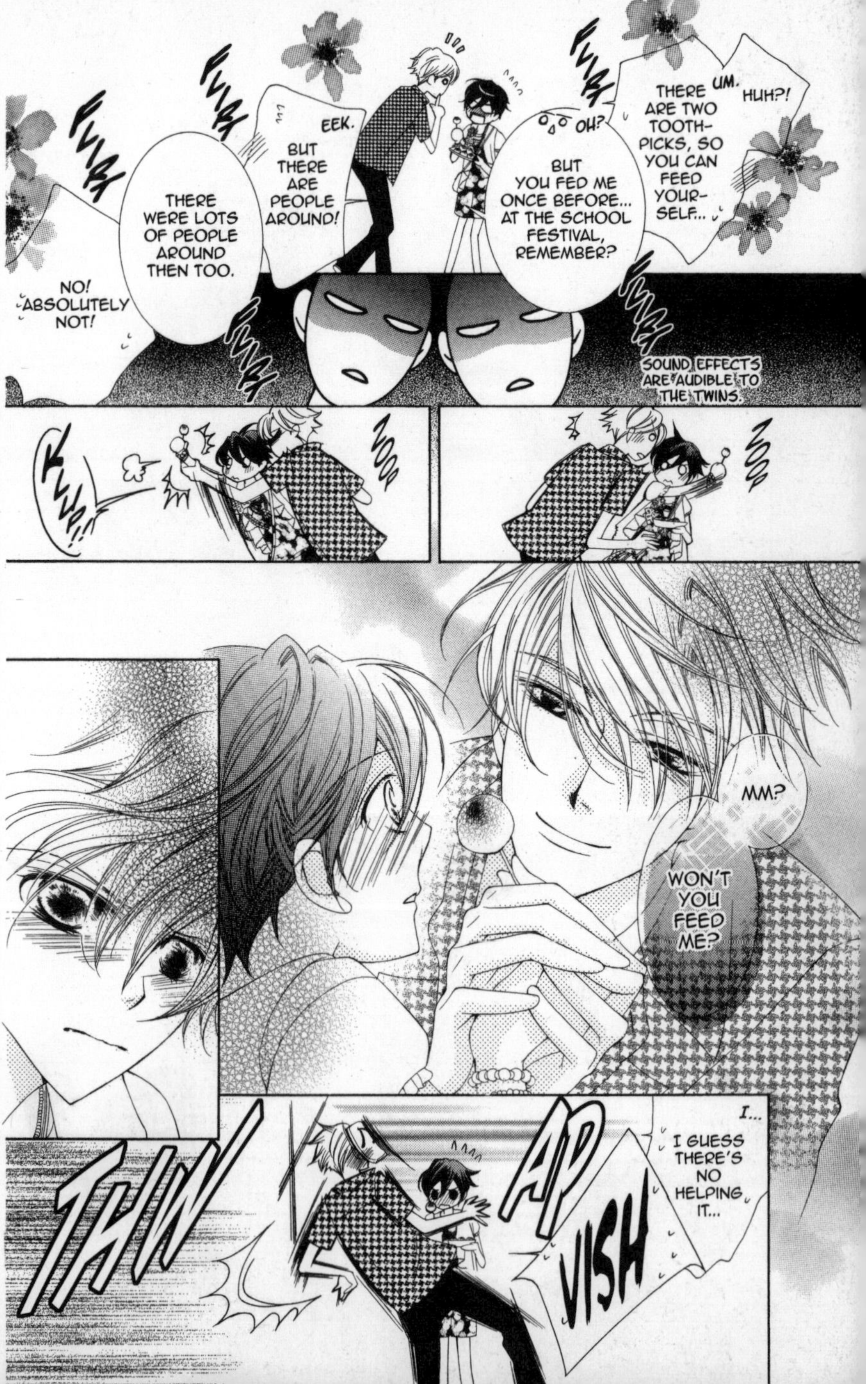
HUH?!
UM.
THERE ARE TWO TOOTH-PICKS, SO YOU CAN FEED YOUR-SELF...
OH?
BUT YOU FED ME ONCE BEFORE... AT THE SCHOOL FESTIVAL, REMEMBER?
EEK.
BUT THERE ARE PEOPLE AROUND!
THERE WERE LOTS OF PEOPLE AROUND THEN TOO.
NO! ABSOLUTELY NOT!
SOUND EFFECTS ARE AUDIBLE TO THE TWINS.
MM?
WON'T YOU FEED ME?
I...
I GUESS THERE'S NO HELPING IT...
AP
VISH
THW

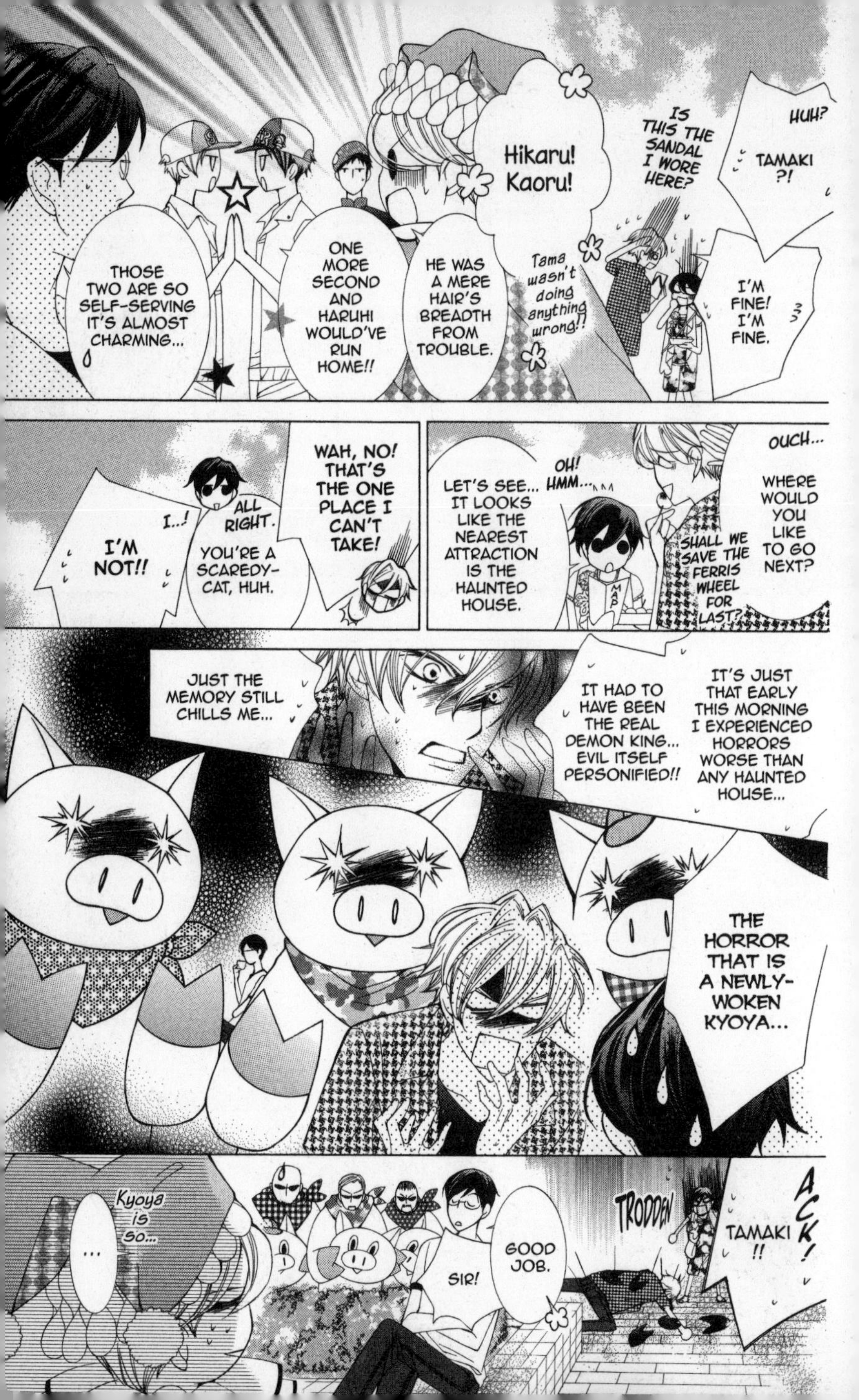

HUH?
TAMAKI ?!
I'M FINE! I'M FINE.
IS THIS THE SANDAL I WORE HERE?
Hikaru! Kaoru!
Tama wasn't doing anything wrong!!
HE WAS A MERE HAIR'S BREADTH FROM TROUBLE.
ONE MORE SECOND AND HARUHI WOULD'VE RUN HOME!!
THOSE TWO ARE SO SELF-SERVING IT'S ALMOST CHARMING...
OUCH...
WHERE WOULD YOU LIKE TO GO NEXT?
SHALL WE SAVE THE FERRIS WHEEL FOR LAST?
OH! HMM...
LET'S SEE... IT LOOKS LIKE THE NEAREST ATTRACTION IS THE HAUNTED HOUSE.
MAP
WAH, NO! THAT'S THE ONE PLACE I CAN'T TAKE!
ALL RIGHT.
YOU'RE A SCAREDY-CAT, HUH.
I...!
I'M NOT!!
IT'S JUST THAT EARLY THIS MORNING I EXPERIENCED HORRORS WORSE THAN ANY HAUNTED HOUSE...
IT HAD TO HAVE BEEN THE REAL DEMON KING... EVIL ITSELF PERSONIFIED!!
JUST THE MEMORY STILL CHILLS ME...
THE HORROR THAT IS A NEWLY-WOKEN KYOYA...
ACK!
TAMAKI !!
TRODDEN
GOOD JOB.
SIR!
Kyoya is so...
...

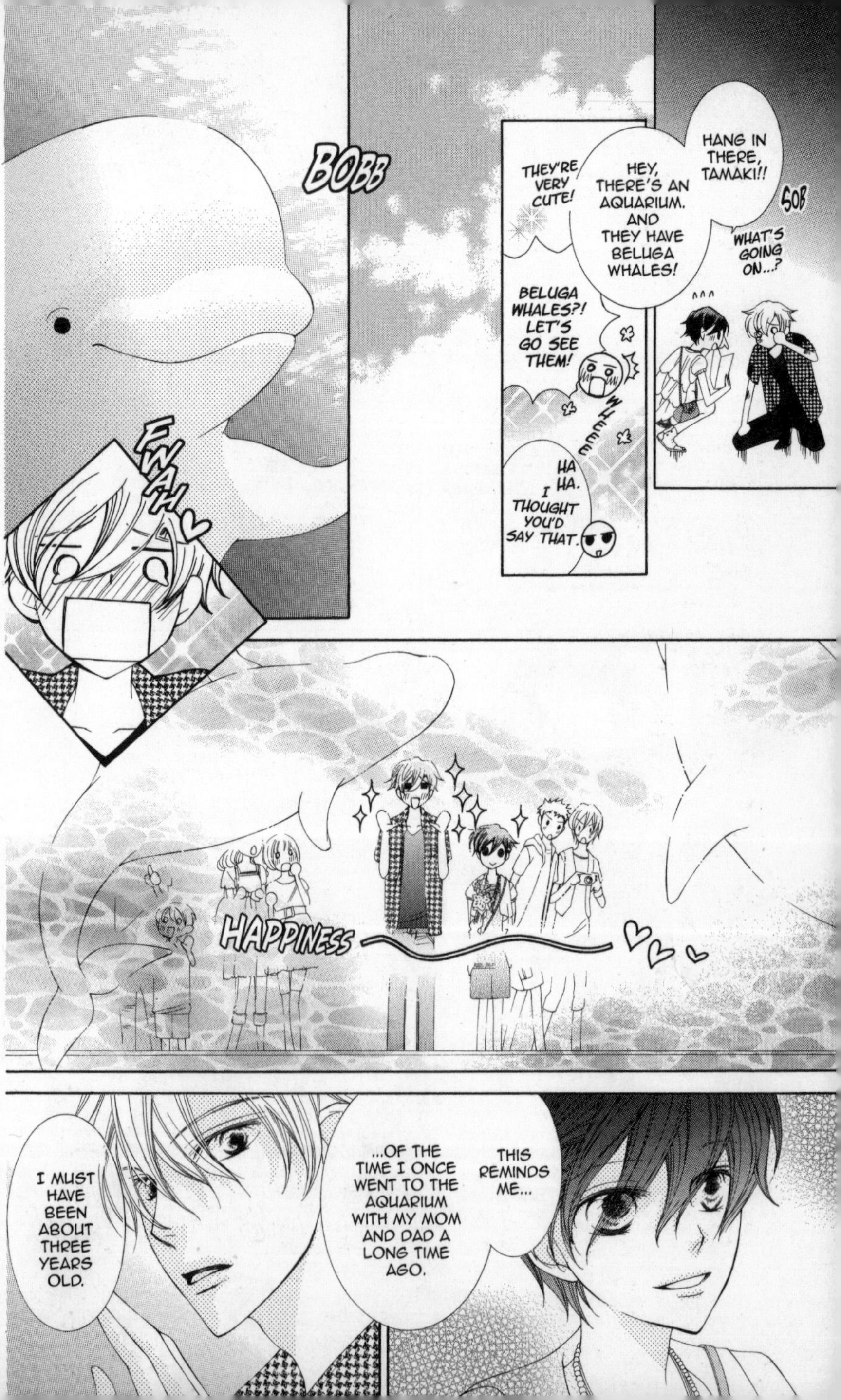
HANG IN THERE, TAMAKI!!
SOB
WHAT'S GOING ON...?
HEY, THERE'S AN AQUARIUM. AND THEY HAVE BELUGA WHALES!
THEY'RE VERY CUTE!
BELUGA WHALES?! LET'S GO SEE THEM!
WHEEE
HA HA. I THOUGHT YOU'D SAY THAT.
BOBB
FWAH
HAPPINESS
THIS REMINDS ME...
...OF THE TIME I ONCE WENT TO THE AQUARIUM WITH MY MOM AND DAD A LONG TIME AGO.
I MUST HAVE BEEN ABOUT THREE YEARS OLD.

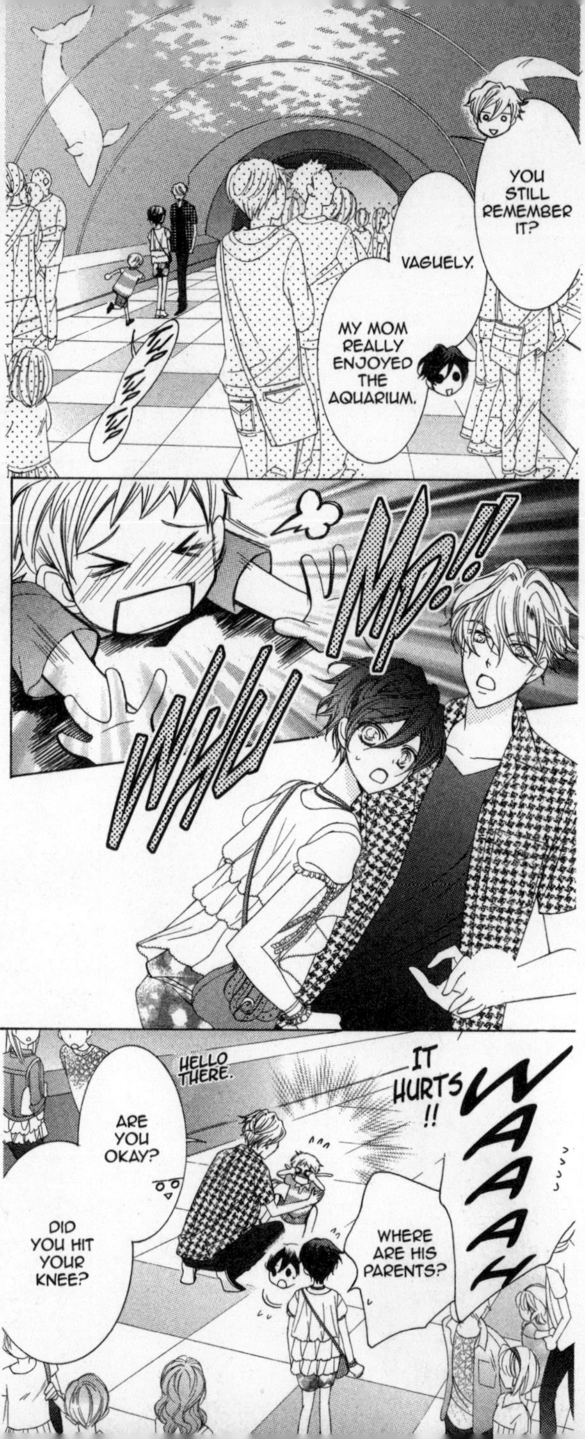
YOU STILL REMEMBER IT?
VAGUELY.
MY MOM REALLY ENJOYED THE AQUARIUM.
WHUMP!!
WAAAH
IT HURTS!!
HELLO THERE.
WHERE ARE HIS PARENTS?
ARE YOU OKAY?
DID YOU HIT YOUR KNEE?

EGOISTIC ☆ CLUB 2

TEXT-ONLY VERSION!!

✿ IN VOLUME 18 WE'VE COMPILED EPISODES 81-83, WHICH WERE ADVERTISED IN *LALA* MAGAZINE AS "THE FINAL ARC." ALSO INCLUDED IS THE SPECIAL SIDE STORY THAT CAME OUT FOUR MONTHS AFTER THE SERIES ENDED.

✿ SINCE VOLUME 17 WAS SO SERIOUS THROUGHOUT, I DID MY BEST TO PACK VOLUME 18 WITH AS MUCH FUN AS POSSIBLE!! AT LEAST, THAT WAS MY INTENTION AS I DREW IT. I REALLY HOPE A LOT OF PEOPLE WILL BE ABLE TO ENJOY THEMSELVES READING THIS ENDING!

✿ I HAD WANTED TO INCLUDE THE PLOT FROM THE SPECIAL SIDE STORY IN THE SERIES ITSELF, BUT SINCE I COULDN'T, I DECIDED TO MAKE IT INTO ITS OWN STORY. THE IDEA WAS SOMETHING LIKE "A FUN TRIP OVERSEAS WITH THE HOST CLUB!"

EVEN THOUGH THEY'RE ALL MILLIONAIRES, KYOYA IS THE ONLY ONE WHO IS SEEN OVERSEAS DURING THE SERIES. I WAS THINKING HOW FUN IT'D BE TO DRAW THE HOST CLUB ACTING LIKE THEIR USUAL CRAZY SELVES IN A FOREIGN COUNTRY. I HOPE ALL OF YOU WILL FIND IT FUN AS WELL. ✿

I ALSO WANTED TO DRAW THE HOST CLUB EXPLORING ANCIENT CASTLES IN GERMANY, OR MAYBE SOMEWHERE IN THE SOUTHERN HEMISPHERE. I HAD A LOT OF IDEAS, BUT IN THE END, THIS WAS THE ONE I ENDED UP CHOOSING.

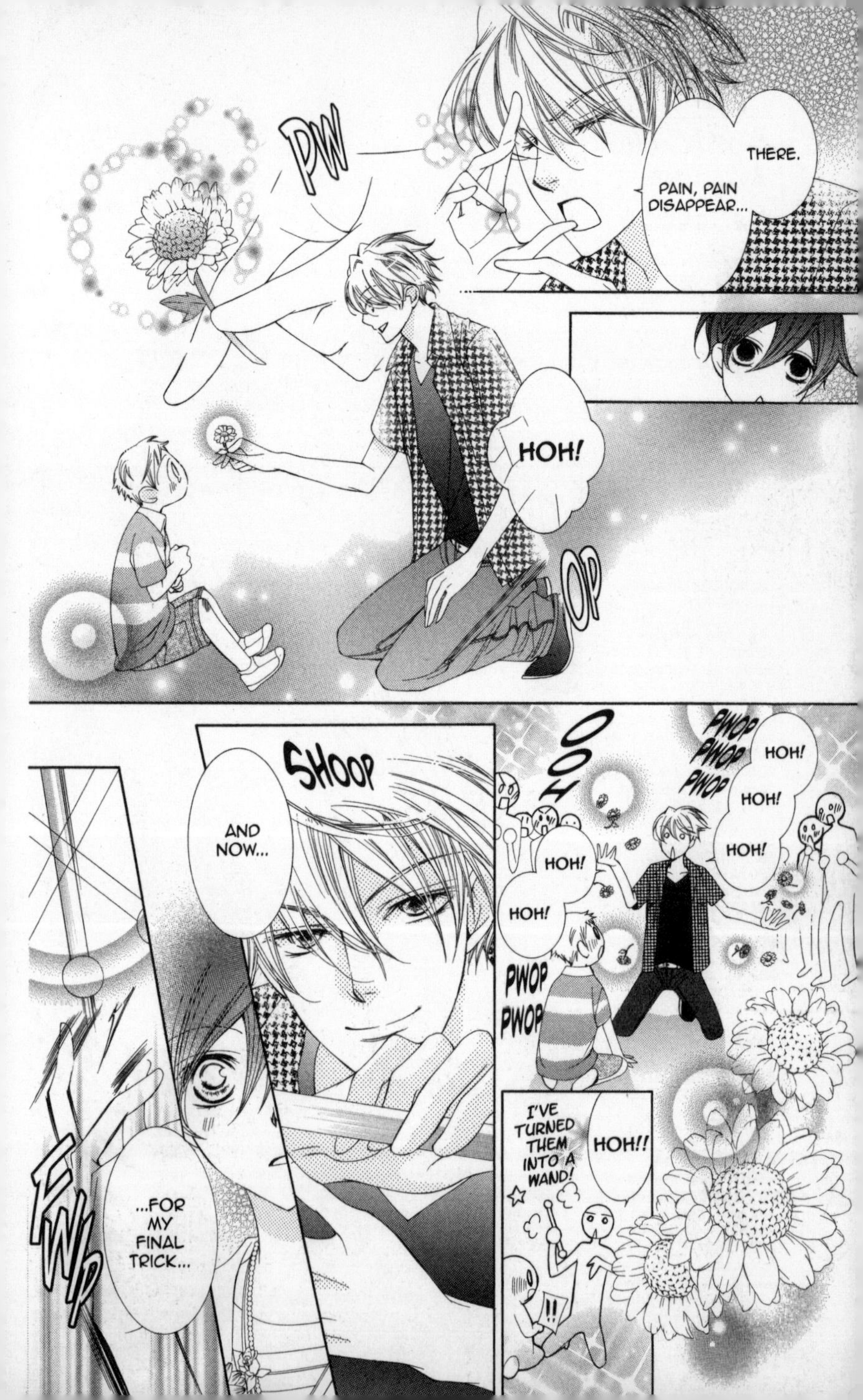
THERE.
PAIN, PAIN DISAPPEAR...
PW
HOH!
OP
PWOP PWOP PWOP
HOH!
HOH!
HOH!
OOH
HOH!
HOH!
PWOP PWOP
HOH!!
I'VE TURNED THEM INTO A WAND!
!!
SHOOP
AND NOW...
...FOR MY FINAL TRICK...
FWIP

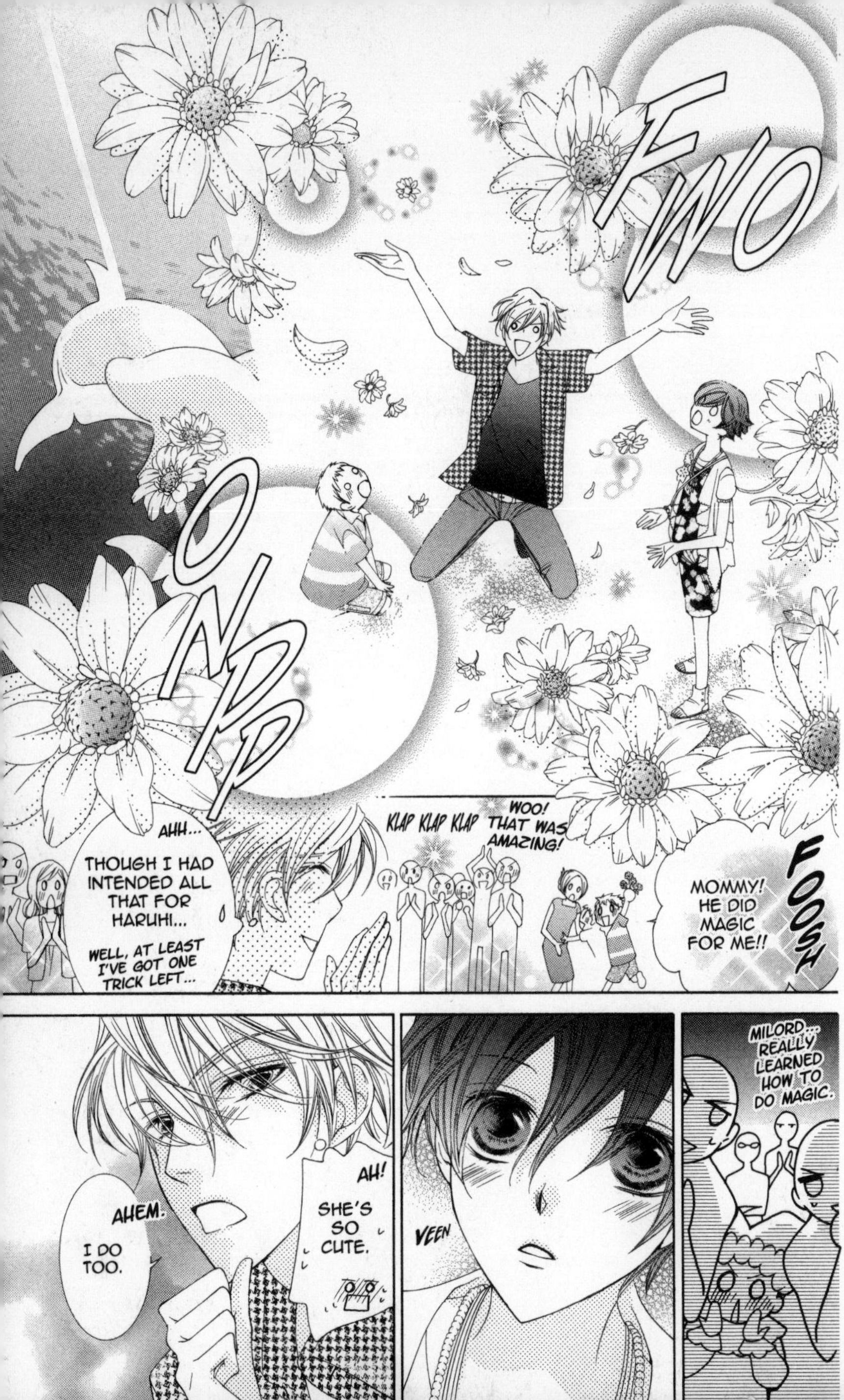
FWO
ONPP
FOOSH
MOMMY! HE DID MAGIC FOR ME!!
WOO! THAT WAS AMAZING!
KLAP KLAP KLAP
AHH...
THOUGH I HAD INTENDED ALL THAT FOR HARUHI...
WELL, AT LEAST I'VE GOT ONE TRICK LEFT...
MILORD... REALLY LEARNED HOW TO DO MAGIC.
VEEN
AH!
SHE'S SO CUTE.
AHEM.
I DO TOO.

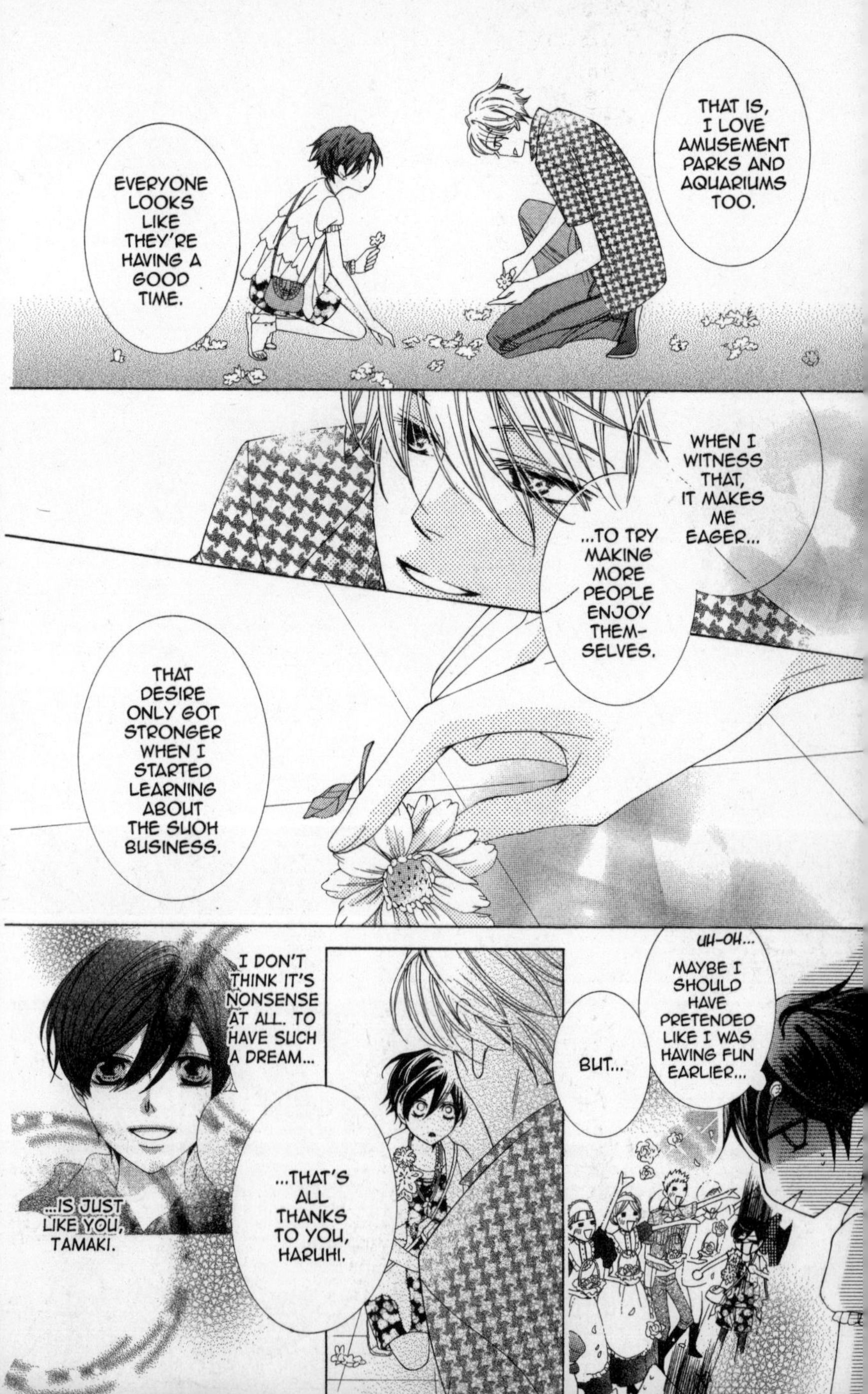
THAT IS, I LOVE AMUSEMENT PARKS AND AQUARIUMS TOO.
EVERYONE LOOKS LIKE THEY'RE HAVING A GOOD TIME.
WHEN I WITNESS THAT, IT MAKES ME EAGER...
...TO TRY MAKING MORE PEOPLE ENJOY THEM-SELVES.
THAT DESIRE ONLY GOT STRONGER WHEN I STARTED LEARNING ABOUT THE SUOH BUSINESS.
UH-OH...
MAYBE I SHOULD HAVE PRETENDED LIKE I WAS HAVING FUN EARLIER...
BUT...
...THAT'S ALL THANKS TO YOU, HARUHI.
I DON'T THINK IT'S NONSENSE AT ALL. TO HAVE SUCH A DREAM...
...IS JUST LIKE YOU, TAMAKI.

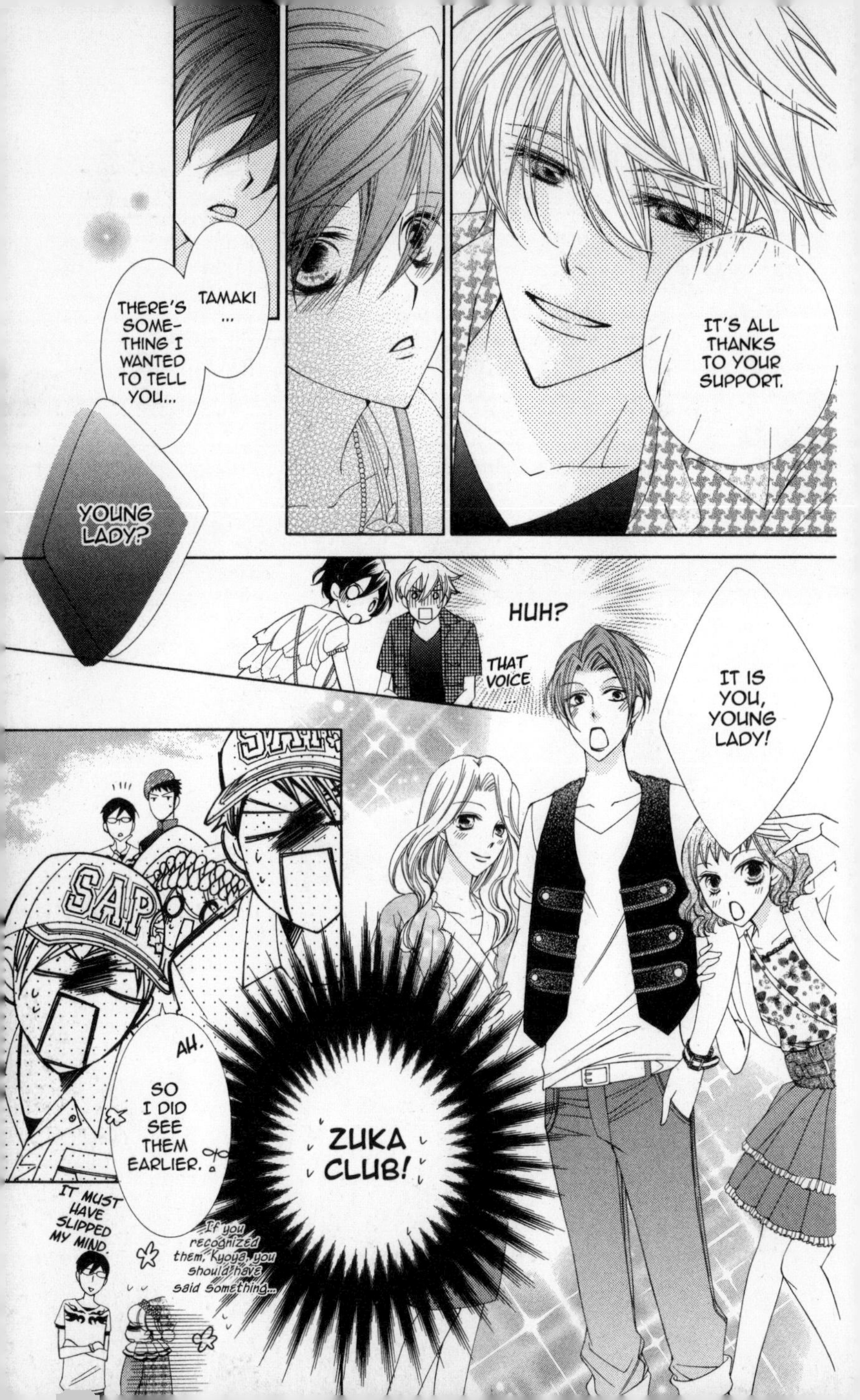
IT'S ALL THANKS TO YOUR SUPPORT.
TAMAKI ...
THERE'S SOME-THING I WANTED TO TELL YOU...
YOUNG LADY?
HUH?
THAT VOICE ...
IT IS YOU, YOUNG LADY!
ZUKA CLUB!
AH.
SO I DID SEE THEM EARLIER.
If you recognized them, Kyoya, you should have said something...
IT MUST HAVE SLIPPED MY MIND.

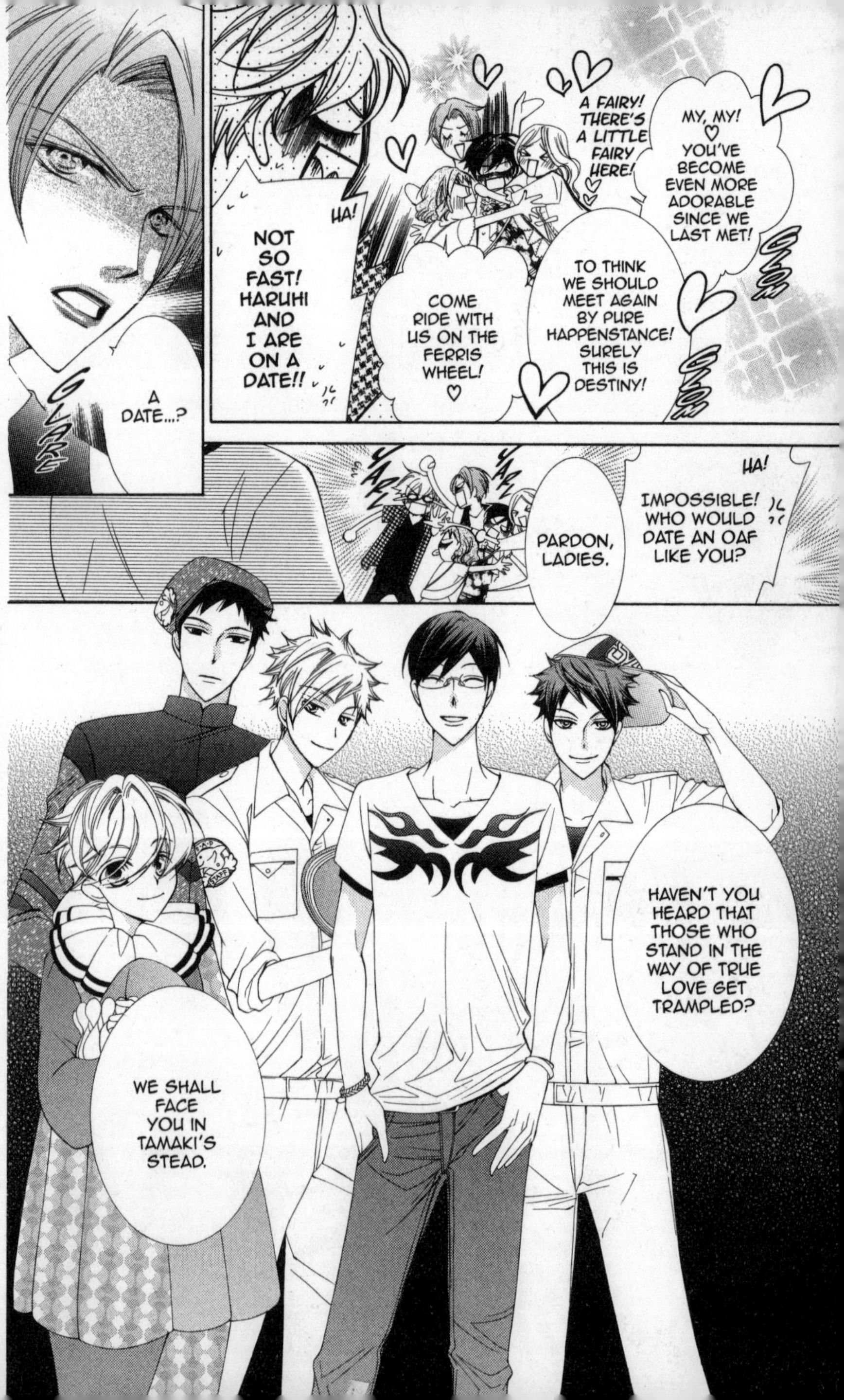
MY, MY! ♡ YOU'VE BECOME EVEN MORE ADORABLE SINCE WE LAST MET!
A FAIRY! THERE'S A LITTLE FAIRY HERE!
TO THINK WE SHOULD MEET AGAIN BY PURE HAPPENSTANCE! SURELY THIS IS DESTINY!
COME RIDE WITH US ON THE FERRIS WHEEL! ♡
HA!
NOT SO FAST! HARUHI AND I ARE ON A DATE!!
A DATE...?
GLARE
HA!
IMPOSSIBLE! WHO WOULD DATE AN OAF LIKE YOU?
PARDON, LADIES.
HAVEN'T YOU HEARD THAT THOSE WHO STAND IN THE WAY OF TRUE LOVE GET TRAMPLED?
WE SHALL FACE YOU IN TAMAKI'S STEAD.

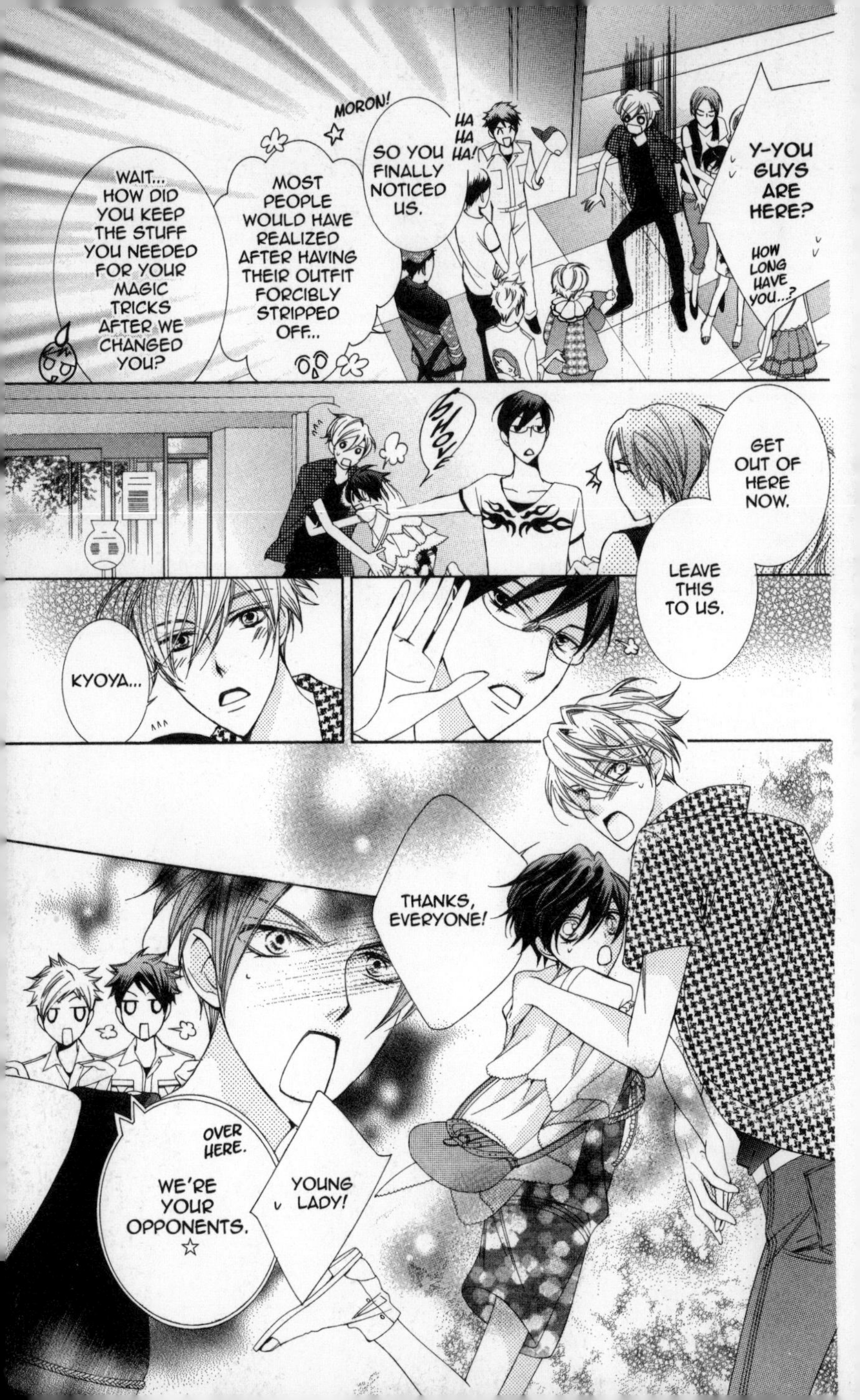
Y-YOU GUYS ARE HERE?
HOW LONG HAVE YOU...?
SO YOU FINALLY NOTICED US.
HA HA HA!
MORON!
MOST PEOPLE WOULD HAVE REALIZED AFTER HAVING THEIR OUTFIT FORCIBLY STRIPPED OFF...
WAIT... HOW DID YOU KEEP THE STUFF YOU NEEDED FOR YOUR MAGIC TRICKS AFTER WE CHANGED YOU?
GET OUT OF HERE NOW.
SHOVE
LEAVE THIS TO US.
KYOYA...
THANKS, EVERYONE!
YOUNG LADY!
OVER HERE.
WE'RE YOUR OPPONENTS. ☆

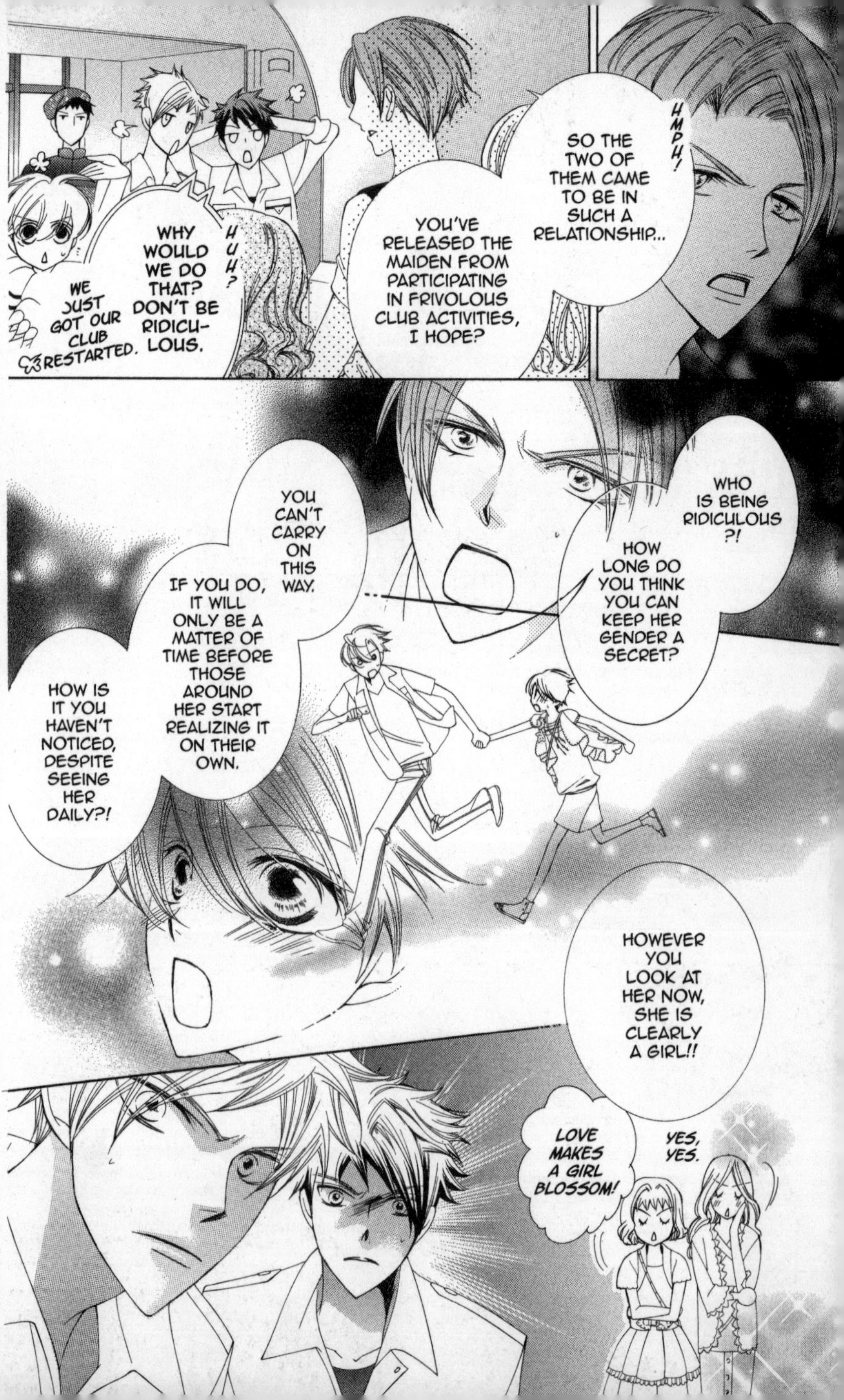
HMPH!
SO THE TWO OF THEM CAME TO BE IN SUCH A RELATIONSHIP...
YOU'VE RELEASED THE MAIDEN FROM PARTICIPATING IN FRIVOLOUS CLUB ACTIVITIES, I HOPE?
HUH?
WHY WOULD WE DO THAT? DON'T BE RIDICULOUS.
WE JUST GOT OUR CLUB RESTARTED.
WHO IS BEING RIDICULOUS?!
HOW LONG DO YOU THINK YOU CAN KEEP HER GENDER A SECRET?
YOU CAN'T CARRY ON THIS WAY.
IF YOU DO, IT WILL ONLY BE A MATTER OF TIME BEFORE THOSE AROUND HER START REALIZING IT ON THEIR OWN.
HOW IS IT YOU HAVEN'T NOTICED, DESPITE SEEING HER DAILY?!
HOWEVER YOU LOOK AT HER NOW, SHE IS CLEARLY A GIRL!!
YES, YES.
LOVE MAKES A GIRL BLOSSOM!

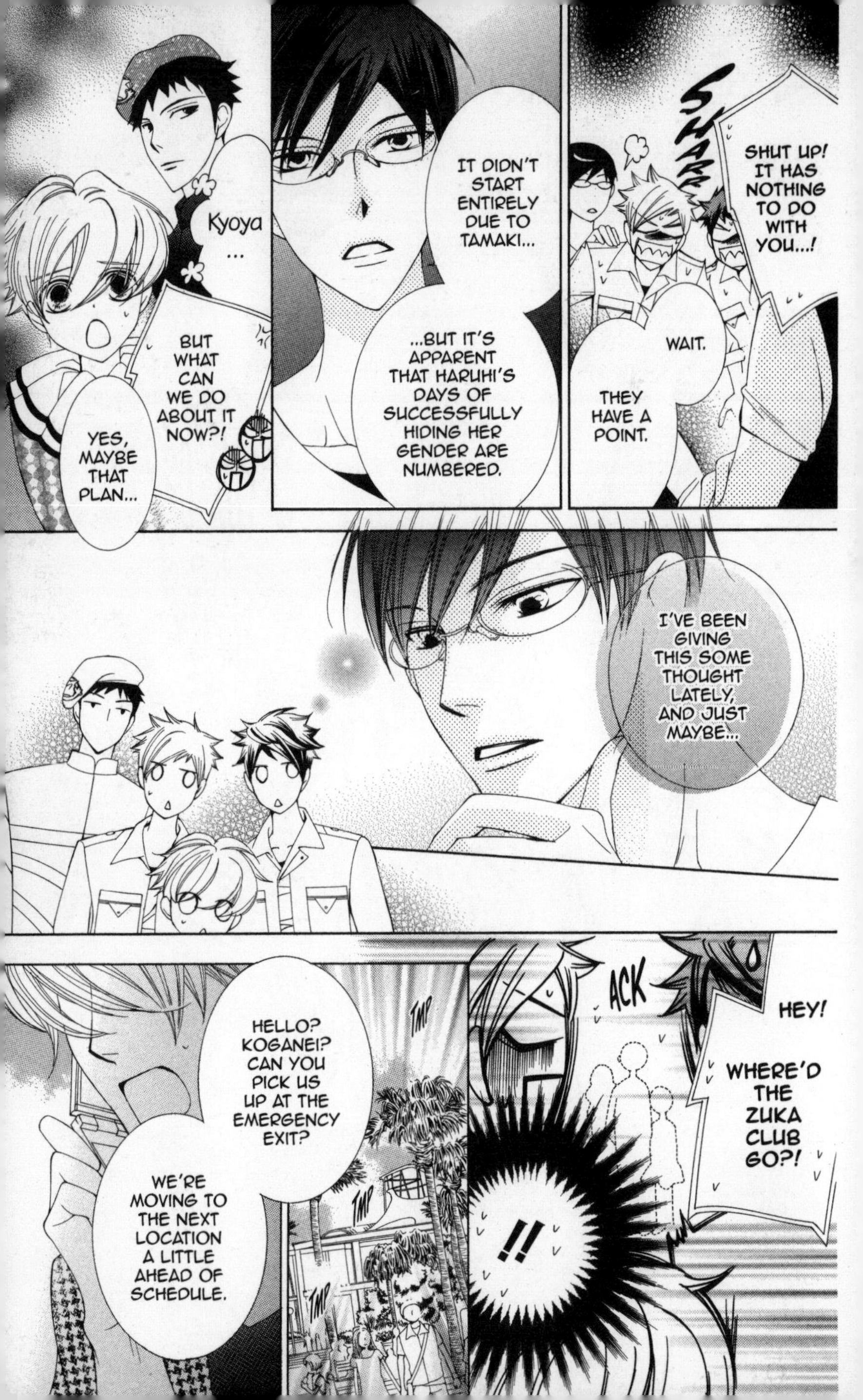
SHUT UP! IT HAS NOTHING TO DO WITH YOU...!
WAIT.
THEY HAVE A POINT.
IT DIDN'T START ENTIRELY DUE TO TAMAKI...
...BUT IT'S APPARENT THAT HARUHI'S DAYS OF SUCCESSFULLY HIDING HER GENDER ARE NUMBERED.
Kyoya ...
BUT WHAT CAN WE DO ABOUT IT NOW?!
YES, MAYBE THAT PLAN...
I'VE BEEN GIVING THIS SOME THOUGHT LATELY, AND JUST MAYBE...
ACK
HEY!
WHERE'D THE ZUKA CLUB GO?!
!!
TMP
TMP
TMP
HELLO? KOGANEI? CAN YOU PICK US UP AT THE EMERGENCY EXIT?
WE'RE MOVING TO THE NEXT LOCATION A LITTLE AHEAD OF SCHEDULE.

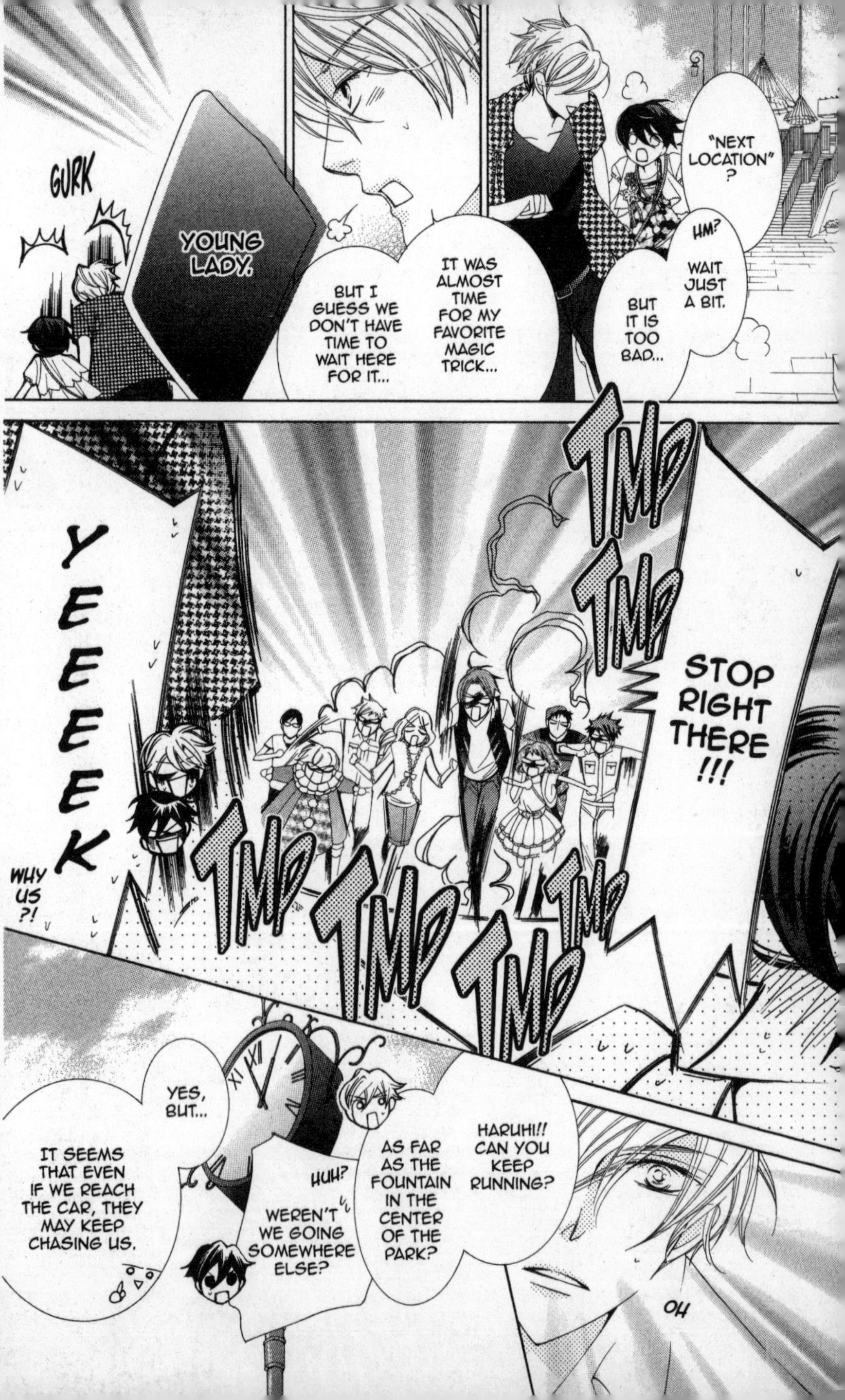
"NEXT LOCATION"?
HM? WAIT JUST A BIT.
BUT IT IS TOO BAD...
IT WAS ALMOST TIME FOR MY FAVORITE MAGIC TRICK...
BUT I GUESS WE DON'T HAVE TIME TO WAIT HERE FOR IT...
YOUNG LADY.
GURK
TMP TMP
STOP RIGHT THERE!!!
TMP TMP TMP TMP TMP
YEEEEK
WHY US?!
OH
HARUHI!! CAN YOU KEEP RUNNING?
AS FAR AS THE FOUNTAIN IN THE CENTER OF THE PARK?
HUH? WEREN'T WE GOING SOMEWHERE ELSE?
YES, BUT...
IT SEEMS THAT EVEN IF WE REACH THE CAR, THEY MAY KEEP CHASING US.

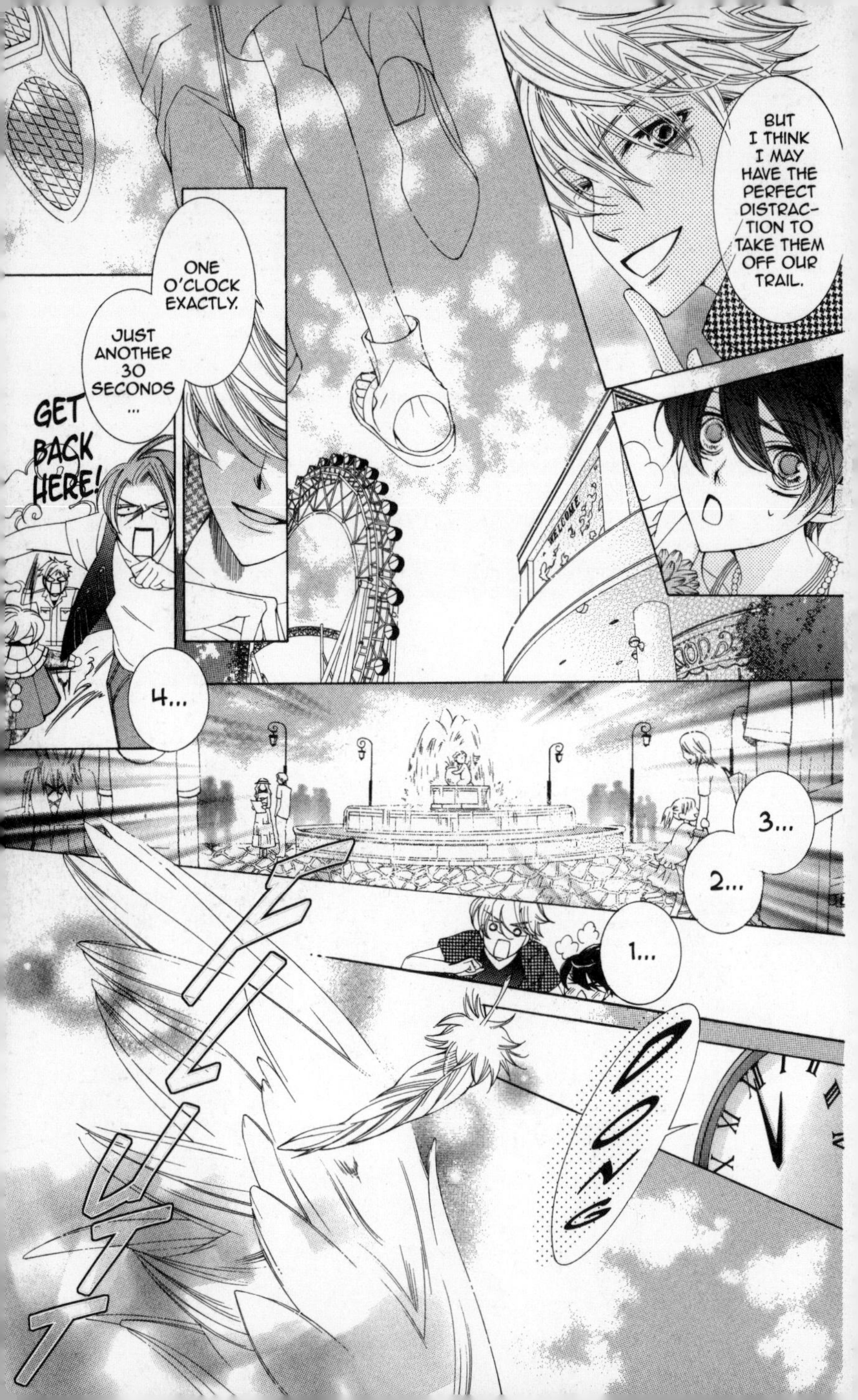
BUT I THINK I MAY HAVE THE PERFECT DISTRAC-TION TO TAKE THEM OFF OUR TRAIL.
ONE O'CLOCK EXACTLY.
JUST ANOTHER 30 SECONDS ...
GET BACK HERE!
4...
3...
2...
1...
DONG

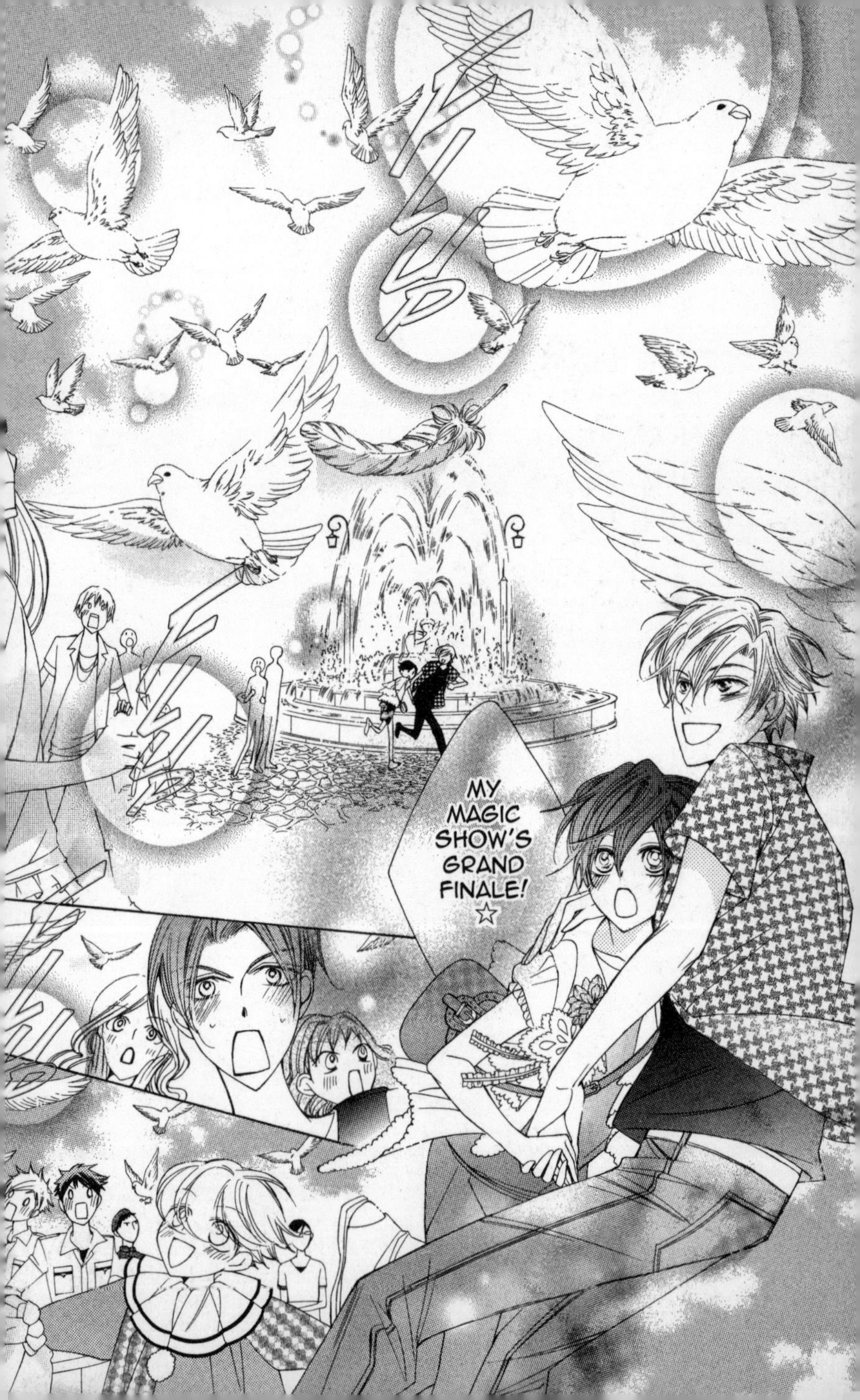
MY MAGIC SHOW'S GRAND FINALE! ☆

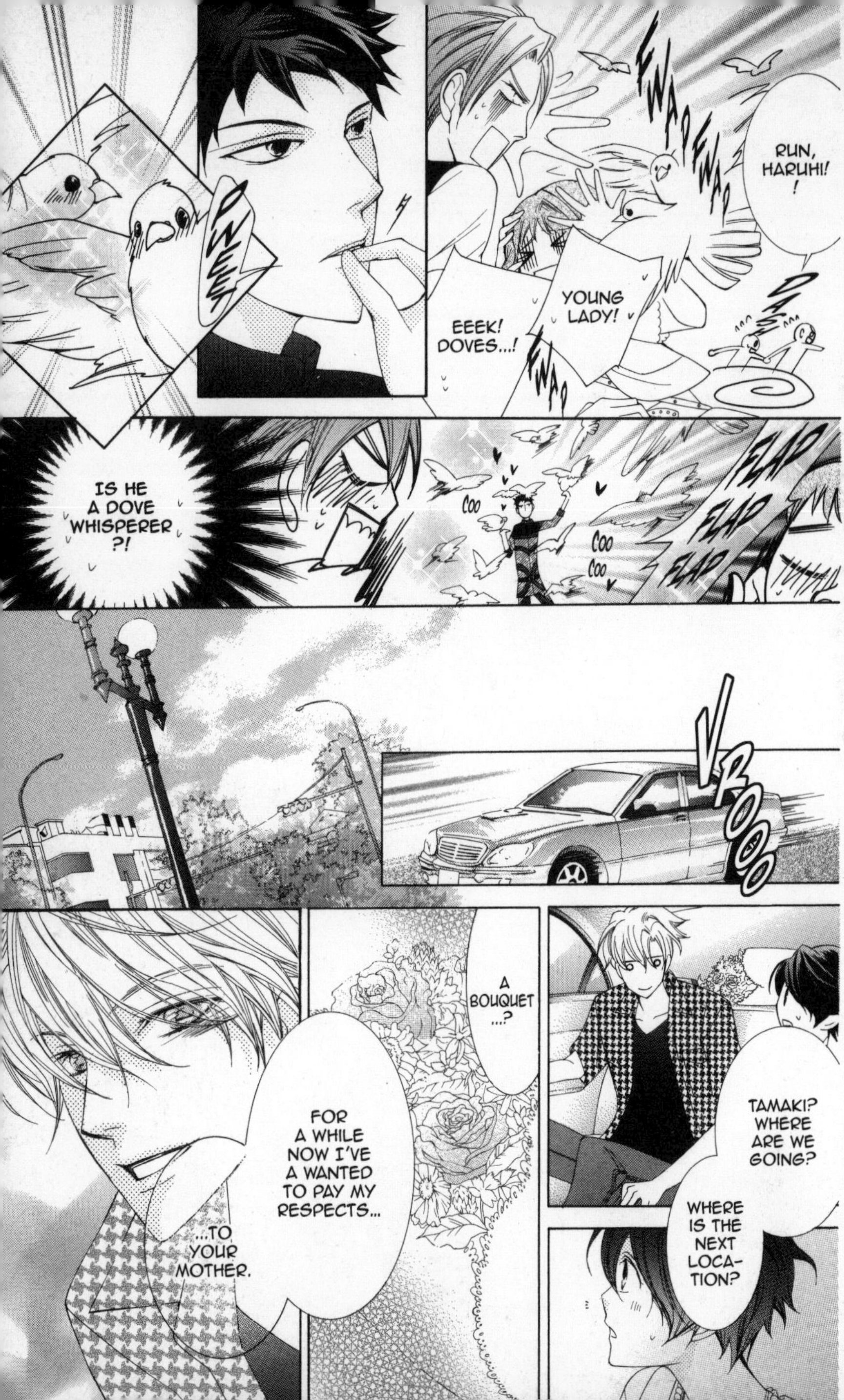

RUN, HARUHI!!
FWAP FWAP
YOUNG LADY!
EEEK! DOVES...!
FWAP
DASH
FLAP FLAP FLAP
COO
COO COO
IS HE A DOVE WHISPERER?!
VROOOO
TAMAKI? WHERE ARE WE GOING?
WHERE IS THE NEXT LOCATION?
A BOUQUET...?
FOR A WHILE NOW I'VE A WANTED TO PAY MY RESPECTS...
...TO YOUR MOTHER.

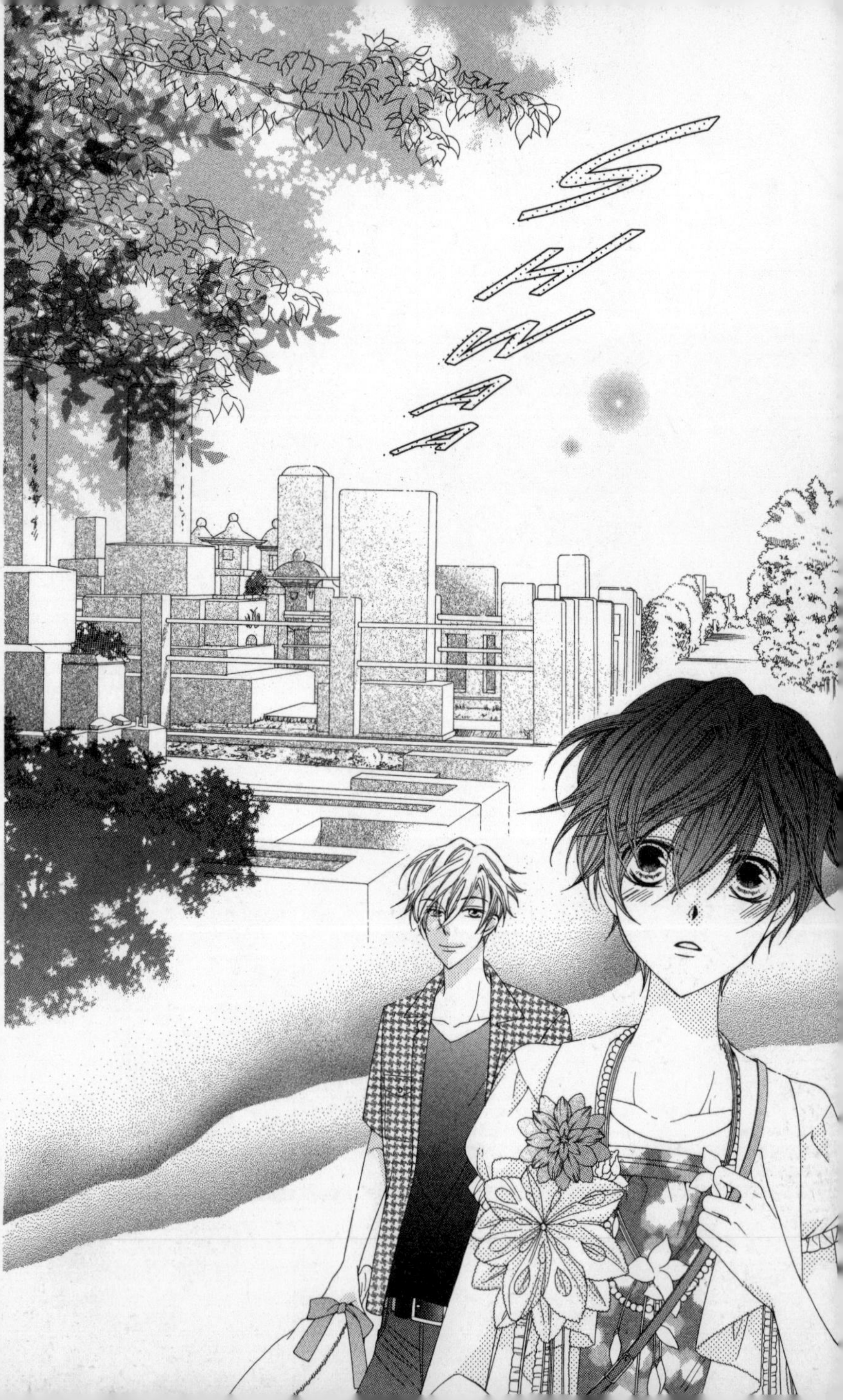
SHWAAA

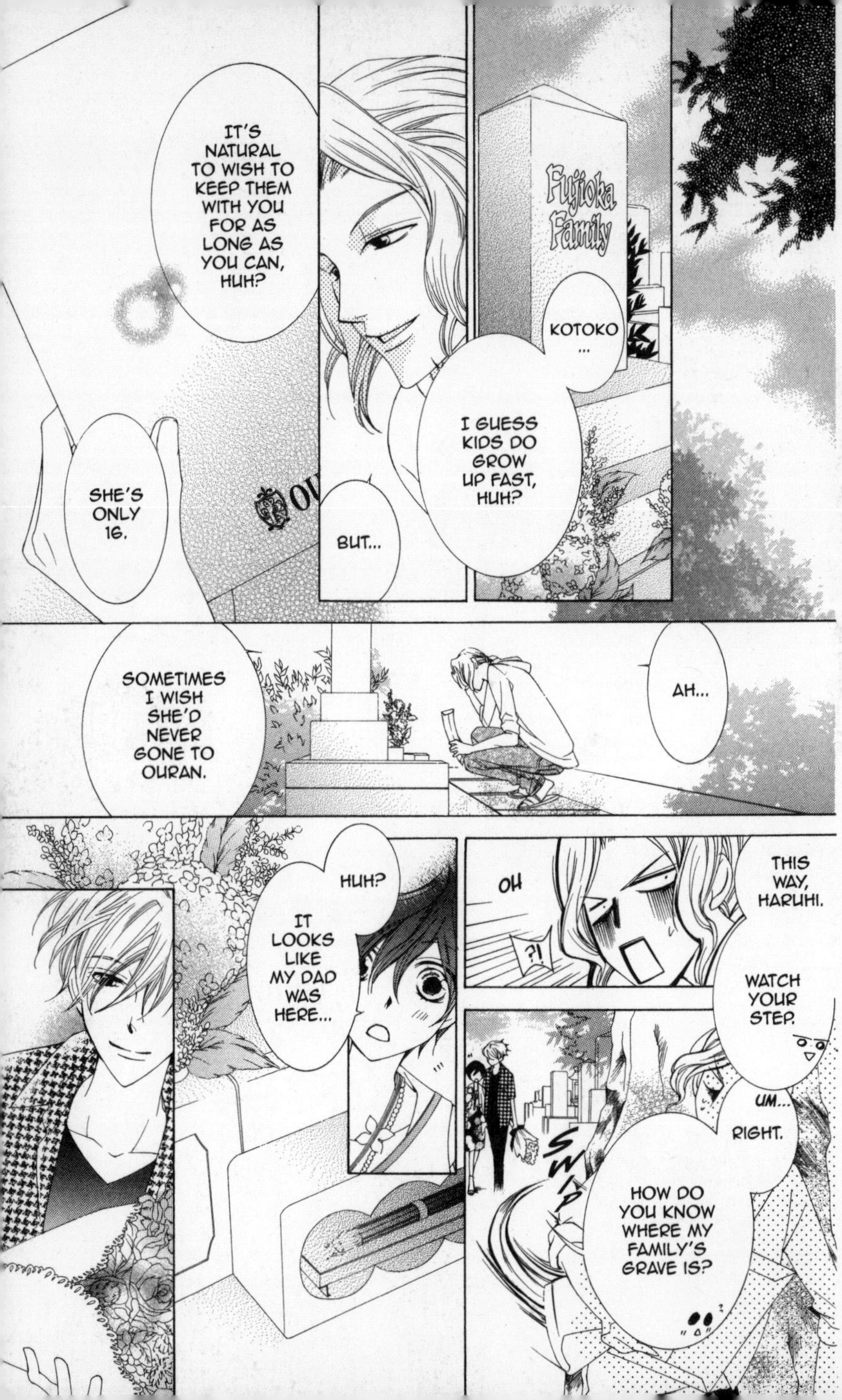
Fujioka Family
KOTOKO...
I GUESS KIDS DO GROW UP FAST, HUH?
BUT...
IT'S NATURAL TO WISH TO KEEP THEM WITH YOU FOR AS LONG AS YOU CAN, HUH?
SHE'S ONLY 16.
AH...
SOMETIMES I WISH SHE'D NEVER GONE TO OURAN.
THIS WAY, HARUHI.
OH
?!
WATCH YOUR STEP.
UM...
RIGHT.
SWIP
HOW DO YOU KNOW WHERE MY FAMILY'S GRAVE IS?
HUH?
IT LOOKS LIKE MY DAD WAS HERE...

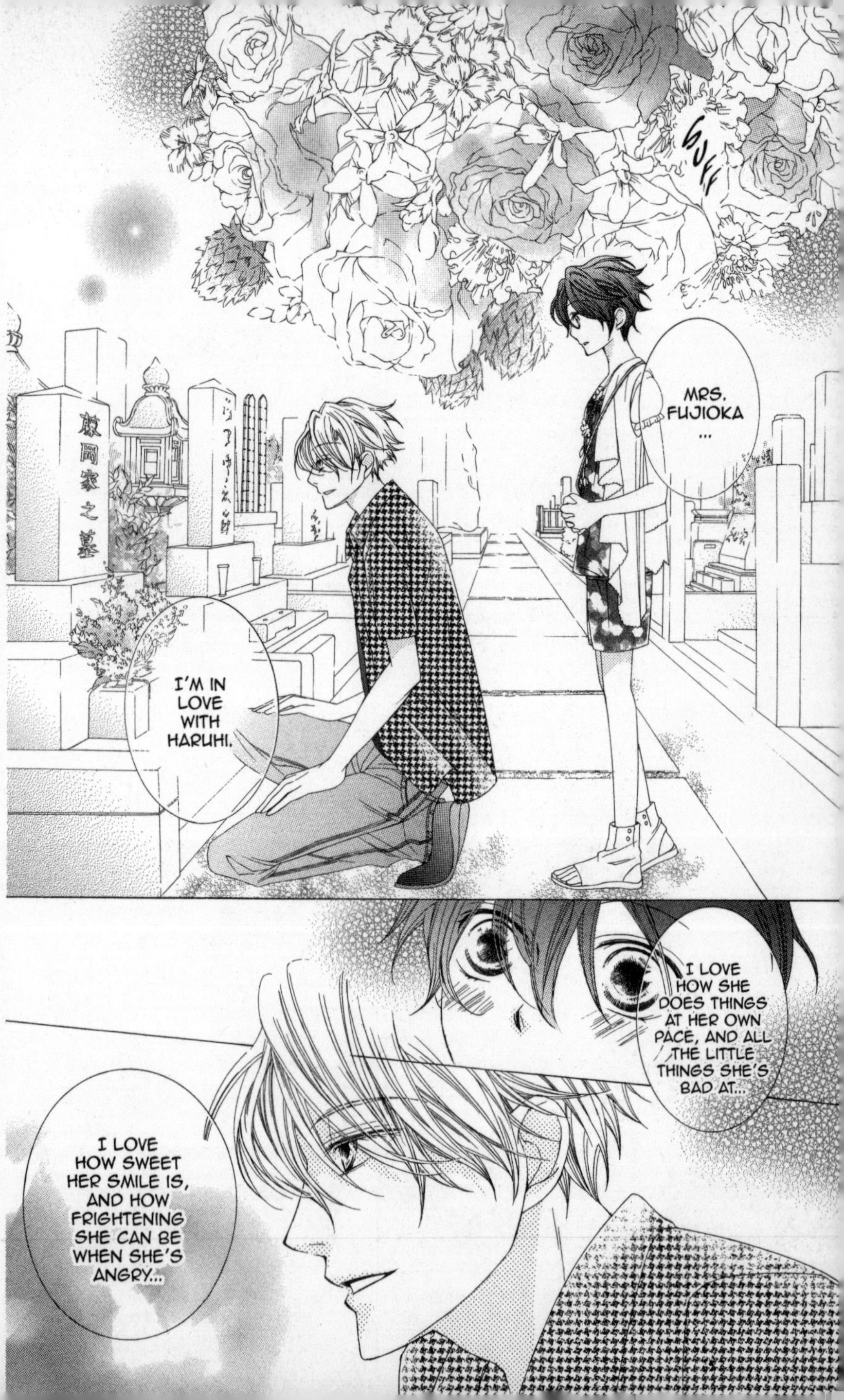
SUFF
MRS. FUJIOKA ...
藤岡家之墓
I'M IN LOVE WITH HARUHI.
I LOVE HOW SHE DOES THINGS AT HER OWN PACE, AND ALL THE LITTLE THINGS SHE'S BAD AT...
I LOVE HOW SWEET HER SMILE IS, AND HOW FRIGHTENING SHE CAN BE WHEN SHE'S ANGRY...

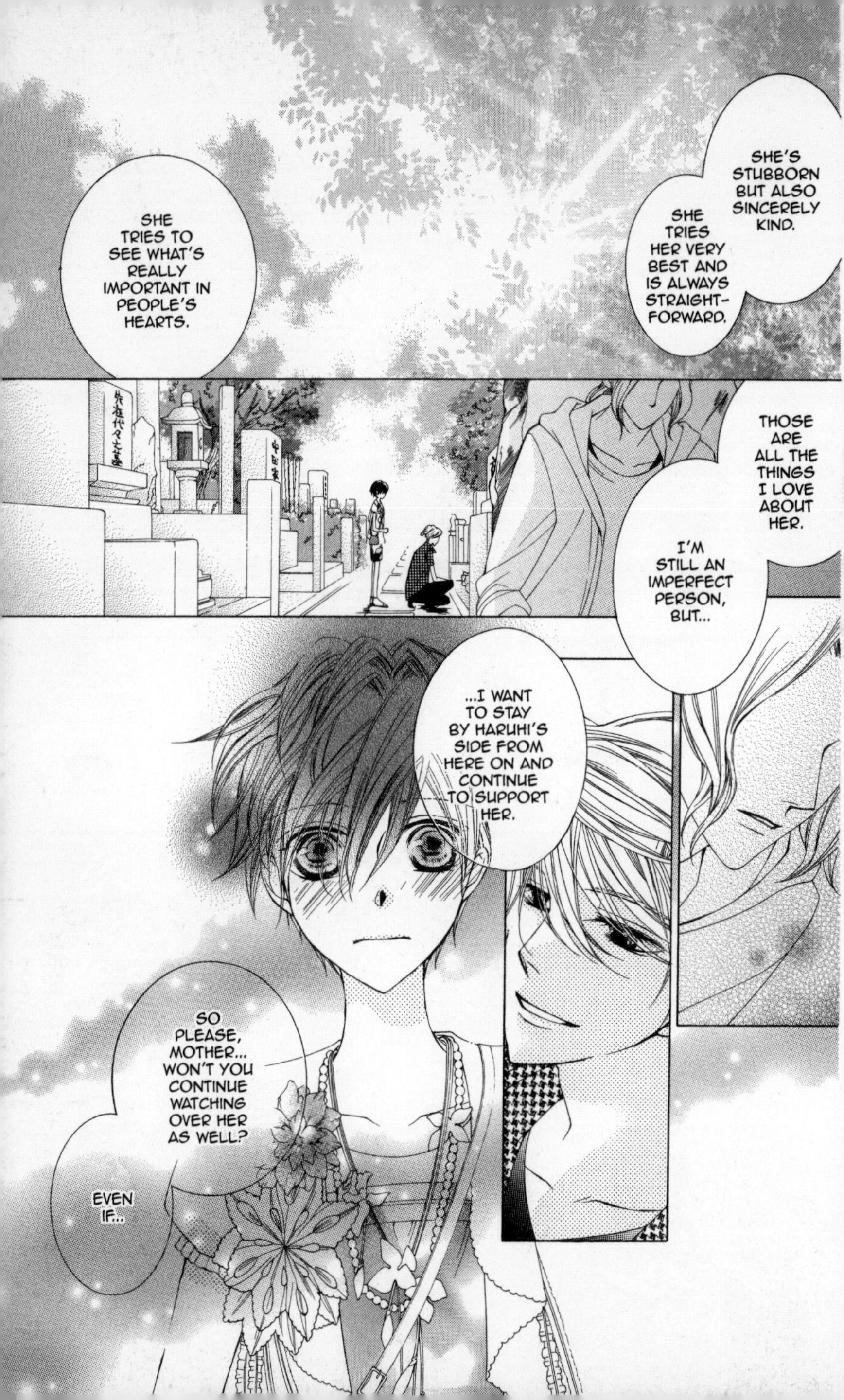
SHE'S STUBBORN BUT ALSO SINCERELY KIND.
SHE TRIES HER VERY BEST AND IS ALWAYS STRAIGHT-FORWARD.
SHE TRIES TO SEE WHAT'S REALLY IMPORTANT IN PEOPLE'S HEARTS.
THOSE ARE ALL THE THINGS I LOVE ABOUT HER.
I'M STILL AN IMPERFECT PERSON, BUT...
...I WANT TO STAY BY HARUHI'S SIDE FROM HERE ON AND CONTINUE TO SUPPORT HER.
SO PLEASE, MOTHER... WON'T YOU CONTINUE WATCHING OVER HER AS WELL?
EVEN IF...

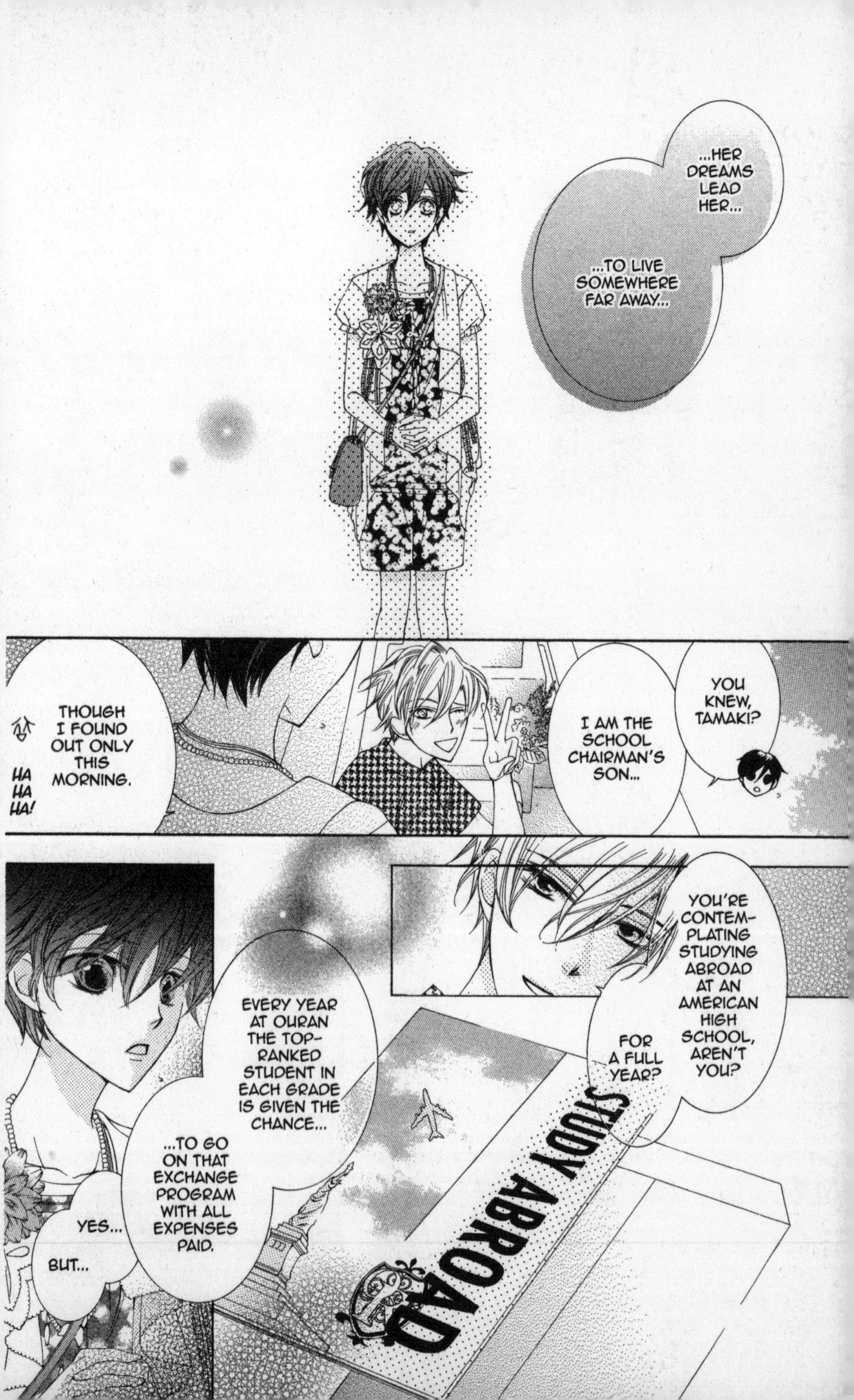

...HER DREAMS LEAD HER...
...TO LIVE SOMEWHERE FAR AWAY...
YOU KNEW, TAMAKI?
I AM THE SCHOOL CHAIRMAN'S SON...
THOUGH I FOUND OUT ONLY THIS MORNING.
HA HA HA!
YOU'RE CONTEM-PLATING STUDYING ABROAD AT AN AMERICAN HIGH SCHOOL, AREN'T YOU?
FOR A FULL YEAR?
STUDY ABROAD
EVERY YEAR AT OURAN THE TOP-RANKED STUDENT IN EACH GRADE IS GIVEN THE CHANCE...
...TO GO ON THAT EXCHANGE PROGRAM WITH ALL EXPENSES PAID.
YES...
BUT...

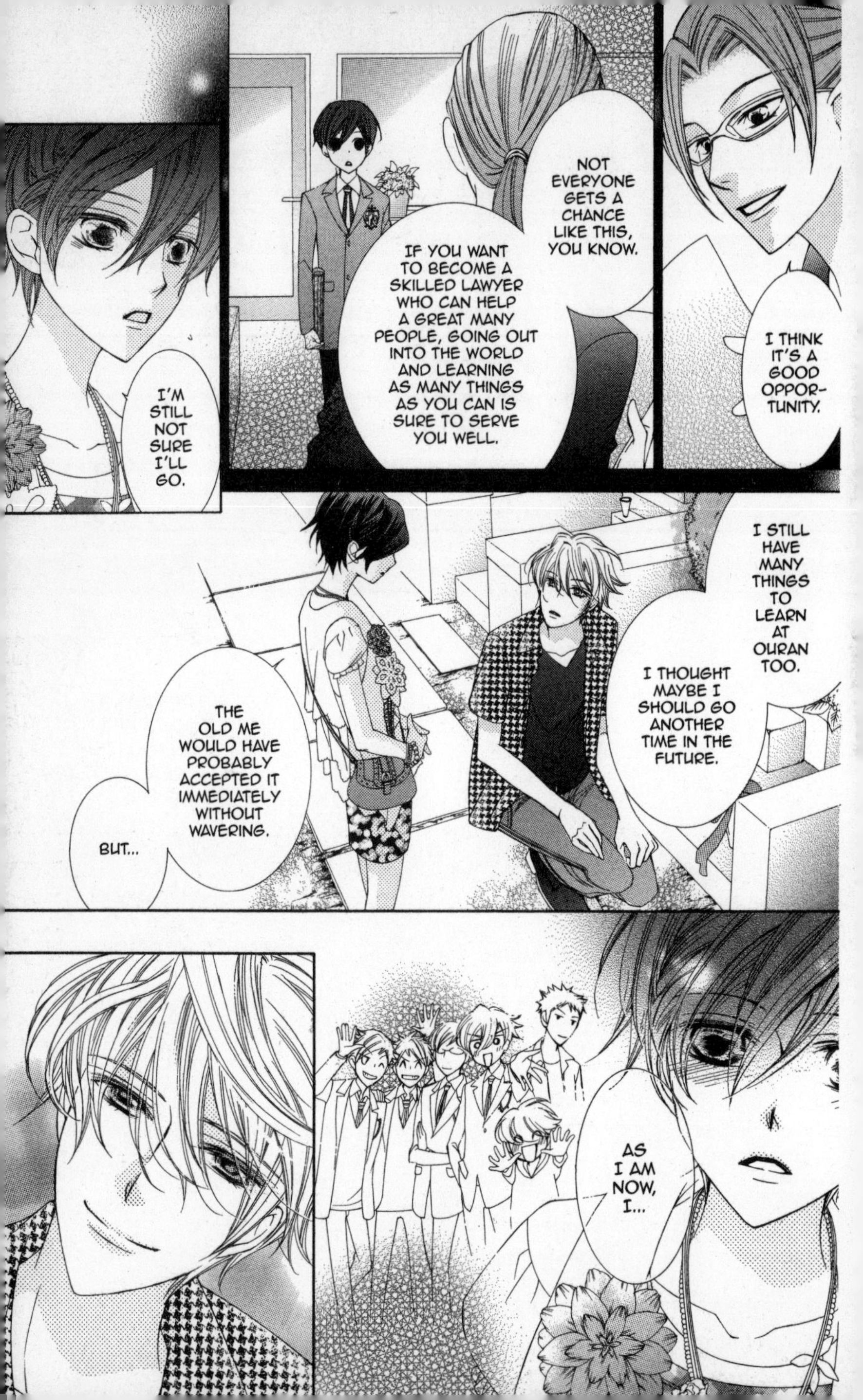

I THINK IT'S A GOOD OPPORTUNITY.
NOT EVERYONE GETS A CHANCE LIKE THIS, YOU KNOW.
IF YOU WANT TO BECOME A SKILLED LAWYER WHO CAN HELP A GREAT MANY PEOPLE, GOING OUT INTO THE WORLD AND LEARNING AS MANY THINGS AS YOU CAN IS SURE TO SERVE YOU WELL.
I'M STILL NOT SURE I'LL GO.
I STILL HAVE MANY THINGS TO LEARN AT OURAN TOO.
I THOUGHT MAYBE I SHOULD GO ANOTHER TIME IN THE FUTURE.
THE OLD ME WOULD HAVE PROBABLY ACCEPTED IT IMMEDIATELY WITHOUT WAVERING.
BUT...
AS I AM NOW, I...

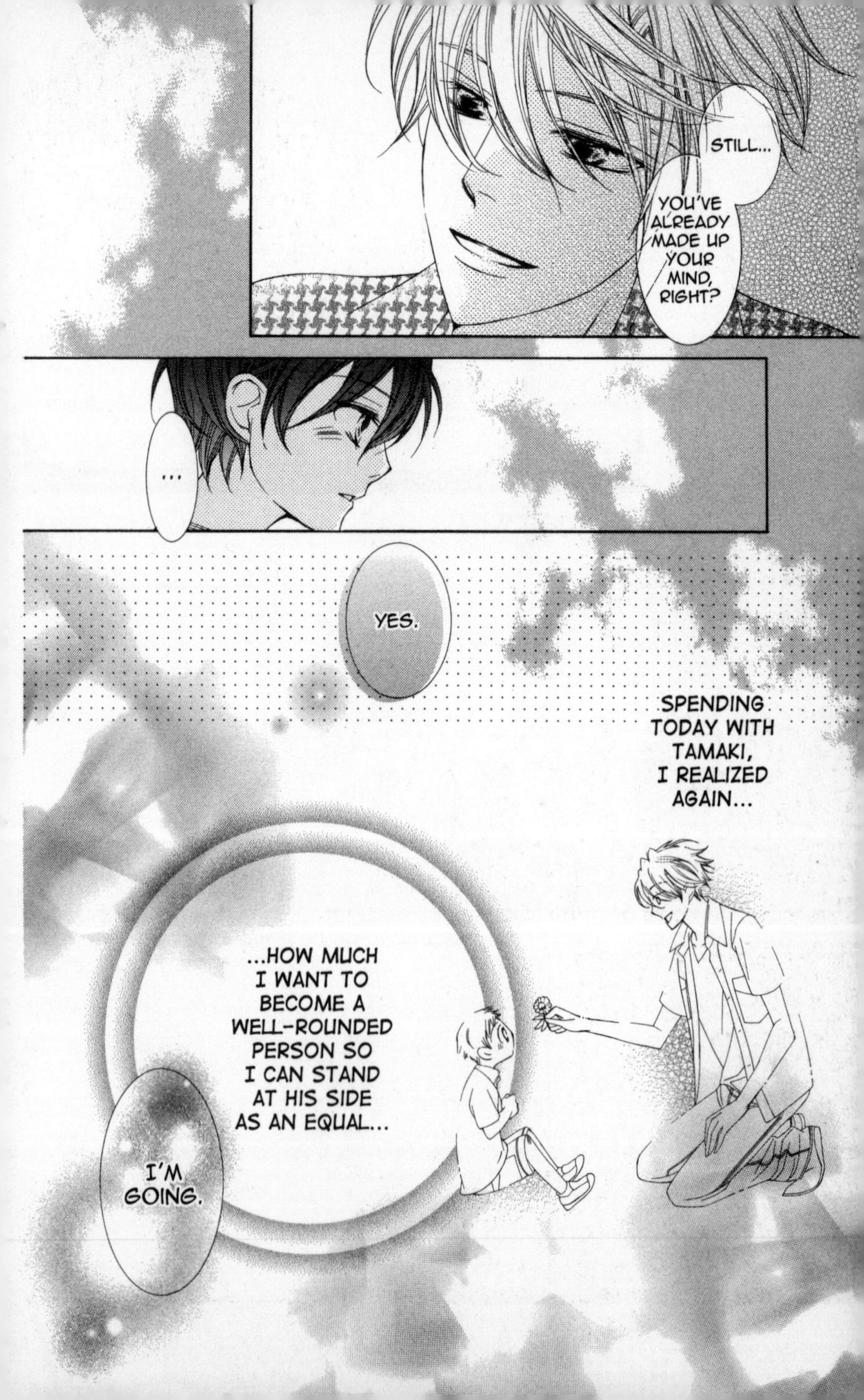
STILL...
YOU'VE ALREADY MADE UP YOUR MIND, RIGHT?
...
YES.
SPENDING TODAY WITH TAMAKI, I REALIZED AGAIN...
...HOW MUCH I WANT TO BECOME A WELL-ROUNDED PERSON SO I CAN STAND AT HIS SIDE AS AN EQUAL...
I'M GOING.

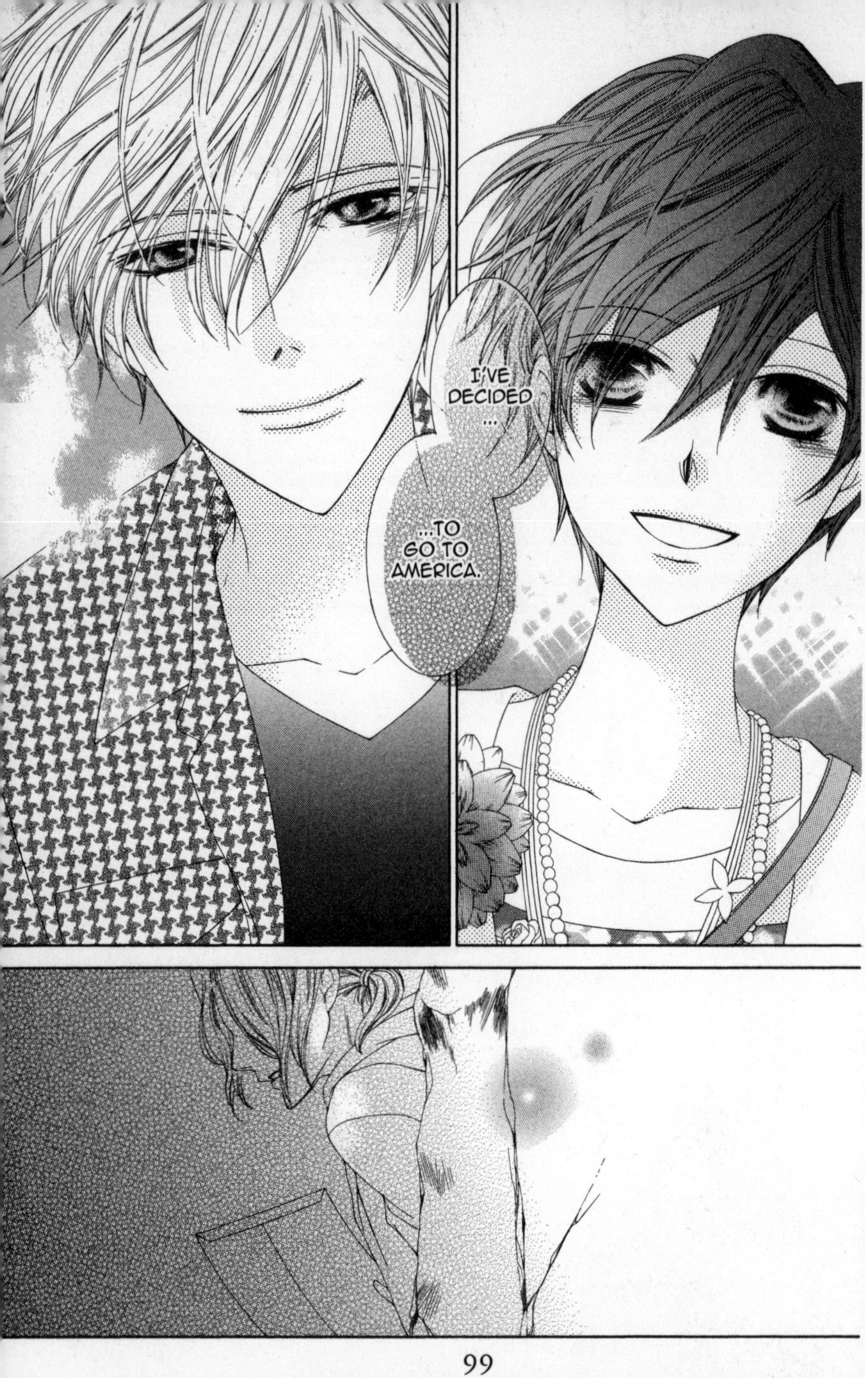
I'VE DECIDED ...
...TO GO TO AMERICA.

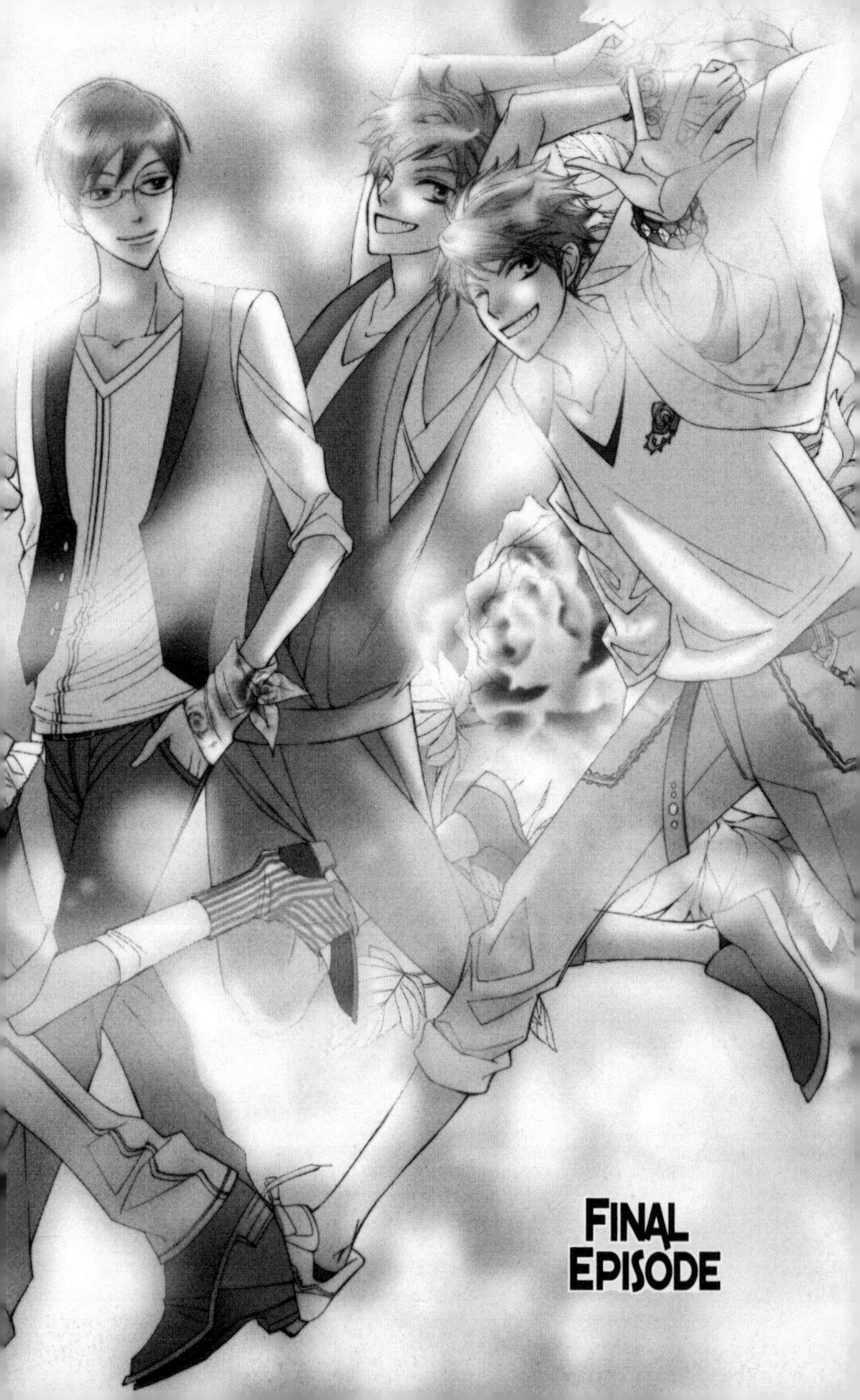

FINAL EPISODE

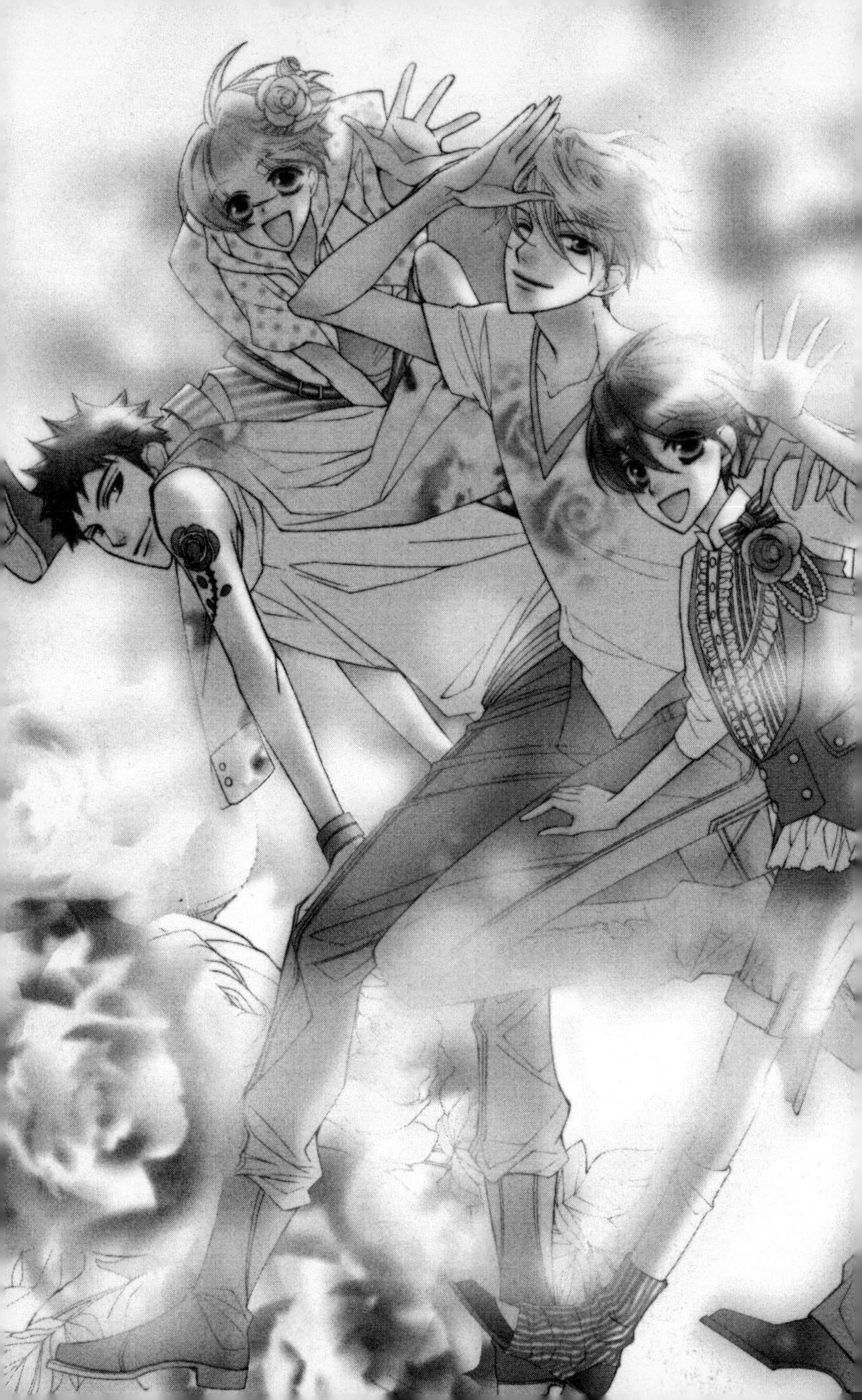

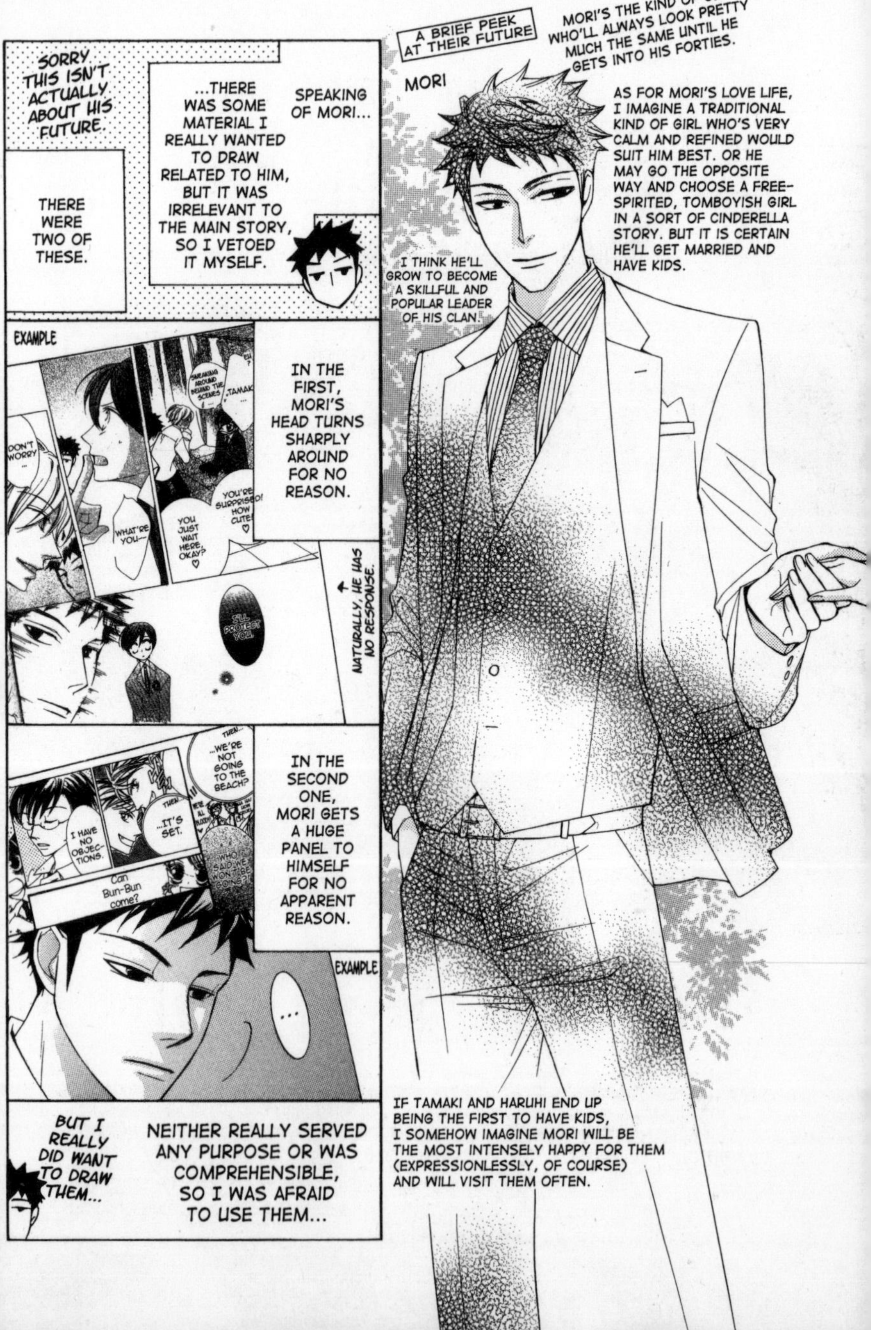
A BRIEF PEEK AT THEIR FUTURE
MORI'S THE KIND OF GUY WHO'LL ALWAYS LOOK PRETTY MUCH THE SAME UNTIL HE GETS INTO HIS FORTIES.
MORI
AS FOR MORI'S LOVE LIFE, I IMAGINE A TRADITIONAL KIND OF GIRL WHO'S VERY CALM AND REFINED WOULD SUIT HIM BEST. OR HE MAY GO THE OPPOSITE WAY AND CHOOSE A FREE-SPIRITED, TOMBOYISH GIRL IN A SORT OF CINDERELLA STORY. BUT IT IS CERTAIN HE'LL GET MARRIED AND HAVE KIDS.
I THINK HE'LL GROW TO BECOME A SKILLFUL AND POPULAR LEADER OF HIS CLAN.
IF TAMAKI AND HARUHI END UP BEING THE FIRST TO HAVE KIDS, I SOMEHOW IMAGINE MORI WILL BE THE MOST INTENSELY HAPPY FOR THEM (EXPRESSIONLESSLY, OF COURSE) AND WILL VISIT THEM OFTEN.
SPEAKING OF MORI...
...THERE WAS SOME MATERIAL I REALLY WANTED TO DRAW RELATED TO HIM, BUT IT WAS IRRELEVANT TO THE MAIN STORY, SO I VETOED IT MYSELF.
SORRY. THIS ISN'T ACTUALLY ABOUT HIS FUTURE.
THERE WERE TWO OF THESE.
NATURALLY, HE HAS NO RESPONSE.
IN THE FIRST, MORI'S HEAD TURNS SHARPLY AROUND FOR NO REASON.
EXAMPLE
SNEAKING AROUND BEHIND THE SCENES...
EH?
TAMAKI...
YOU'RE SURPRISED! HOW CUTE! ♡
YOU JUST WAIT HERE, OKAY? ♡
WHAT'RE YOU--
DON'T WORRY...
I'LL PROTECT YOU.
IN THE SECOND ONE, MORI GETS A HUGE PANEL TO HIMSELF FOR NO APPARENT REASON.
THEN... ...WE'RE NOT GOING TO THE BEACH?
THEN ...IT'S SET.
WHO SAID WE WON'T BE GOING?
I HAVE NO OBJECTIONS.
Can Bun-Bun come?
EXAMPLE
...
NEITHER REALLY SERVED ANY PURPOSE OR WAS COMPREHENSIBLE, SO I WAS AFRAID TO USE THEM...
BUT I REALLY DID WANT TO DRAW THEM...

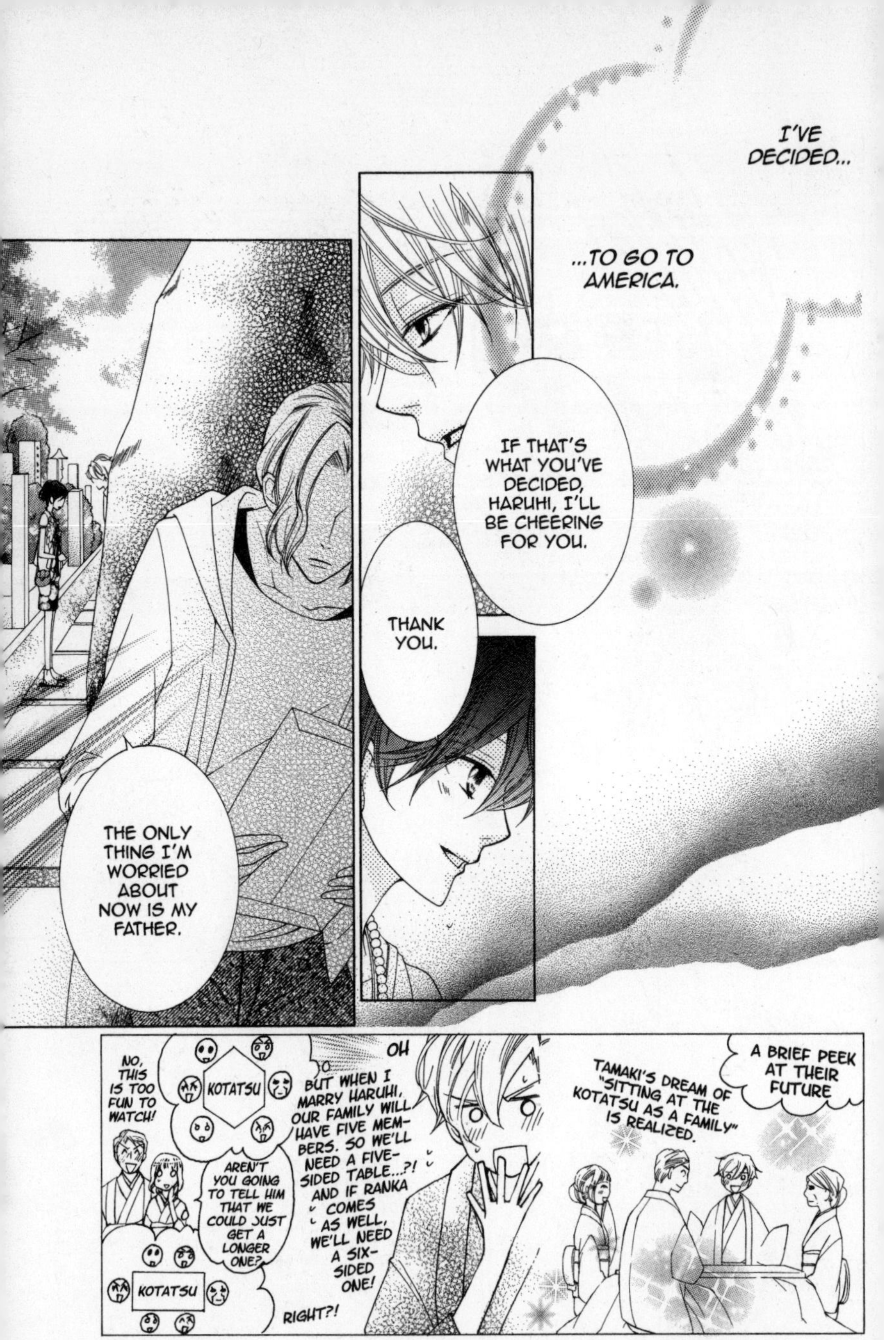
I'VE DECIDED...
...TO GO TO AMERICA.
IF THAT'S WHAT YOU'VE DECIDED, HARUHI, I'LL BE CHEERING FOR YOU.
THANK YOU.
THE ONLY THING I'M WORRIED ABOUT NOW IS MY FATHER.
A BRIEF PEEK AT THEIR FUTURE
TAMAKI'S DREAM OF "SITTING AT THE KOTATSU AS A FAMILY" IS REALIZED.
OH
BUT WHEN I MARRY HARUHI, OUR FAMILY WILL HAVE FIVE MEMBERS. SO WE'LL NEED A FIVE-SIDED TABLE...?! AND IF RANKA COMES AS WELL, WE'LL NEED A SIX-SIDED ONE!
RIGHT?!
KOTATSU
KOTATSU
AREN'T YOU GOING TO TELL HIM THAT WE COULD JUST GET A LONGER ONE?
NO, THIS IS TOO FUN TO WATCH!

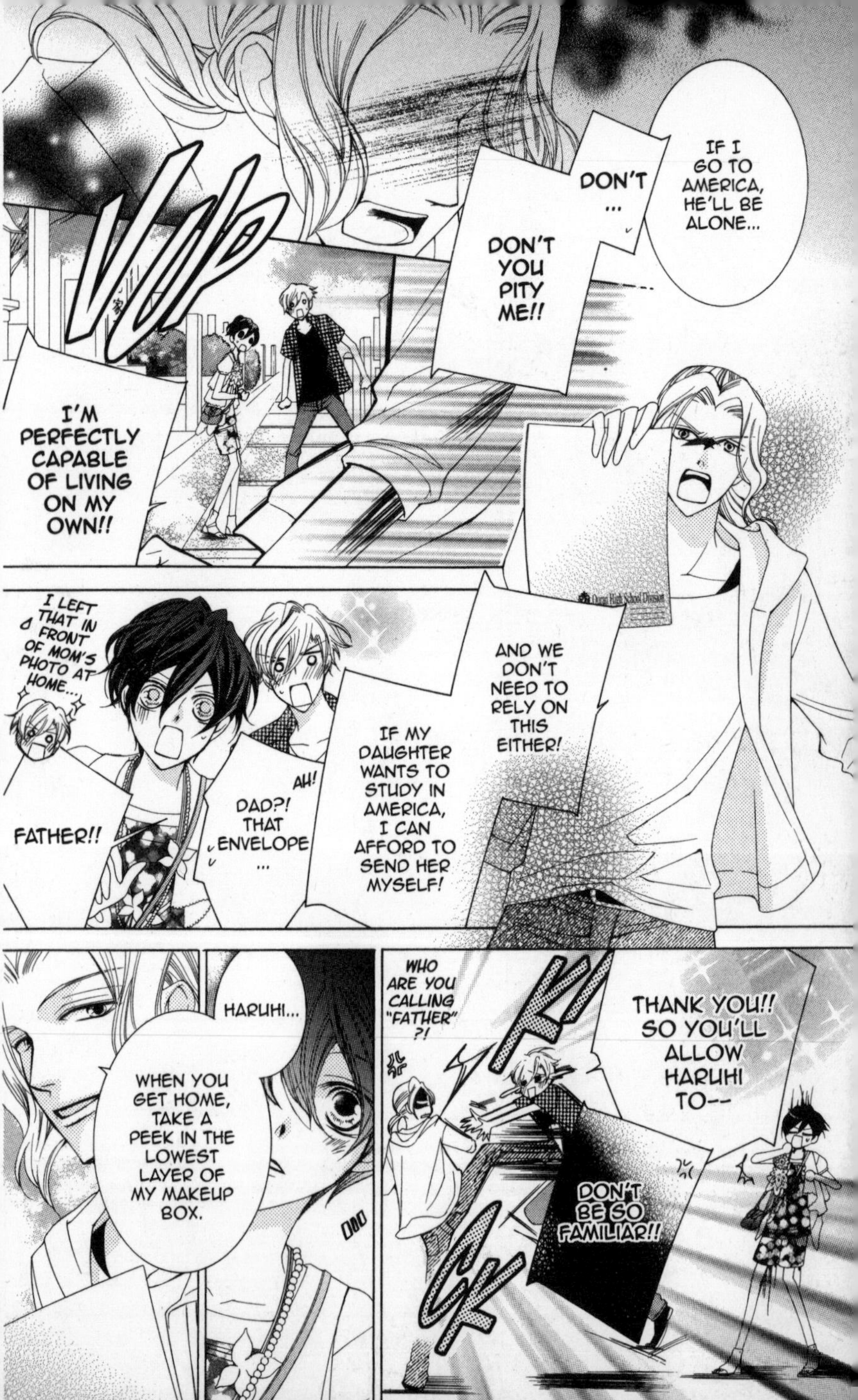

IF I GO TO AMERICA, HE'LL BE ALONE...
DON'T ...
DON'T YOU PITY ME!!
I'M PERFECTLY CAPABLE OF LIVING ON MY OWN!!
AND WE DON'T NEED TO RELY ON THIS EITHER!
Ouran High School Division
IF MY DAUGHTER WANTS TO STUDY IN AMERICA, I CAN AFFORD TO SEND HER MYSELF!
AH!
DAD?! THAT ENVELOPE ...
FATHER!!
I LEFT THAT IN FRONT OF MOM'S PHOTO AT HOME...
THANK YOU!! SO YOU'LL ALLOW HARUHI TO--
WHO ARE YOU CALLING "FATHER"?!
DON'T BE SO FAMILIAR!!
HARUHI...
WHEN YOU GET HOME, TAKE A PEEK IN THE LOWEST LAYER OF MY MAKEUP BOX.

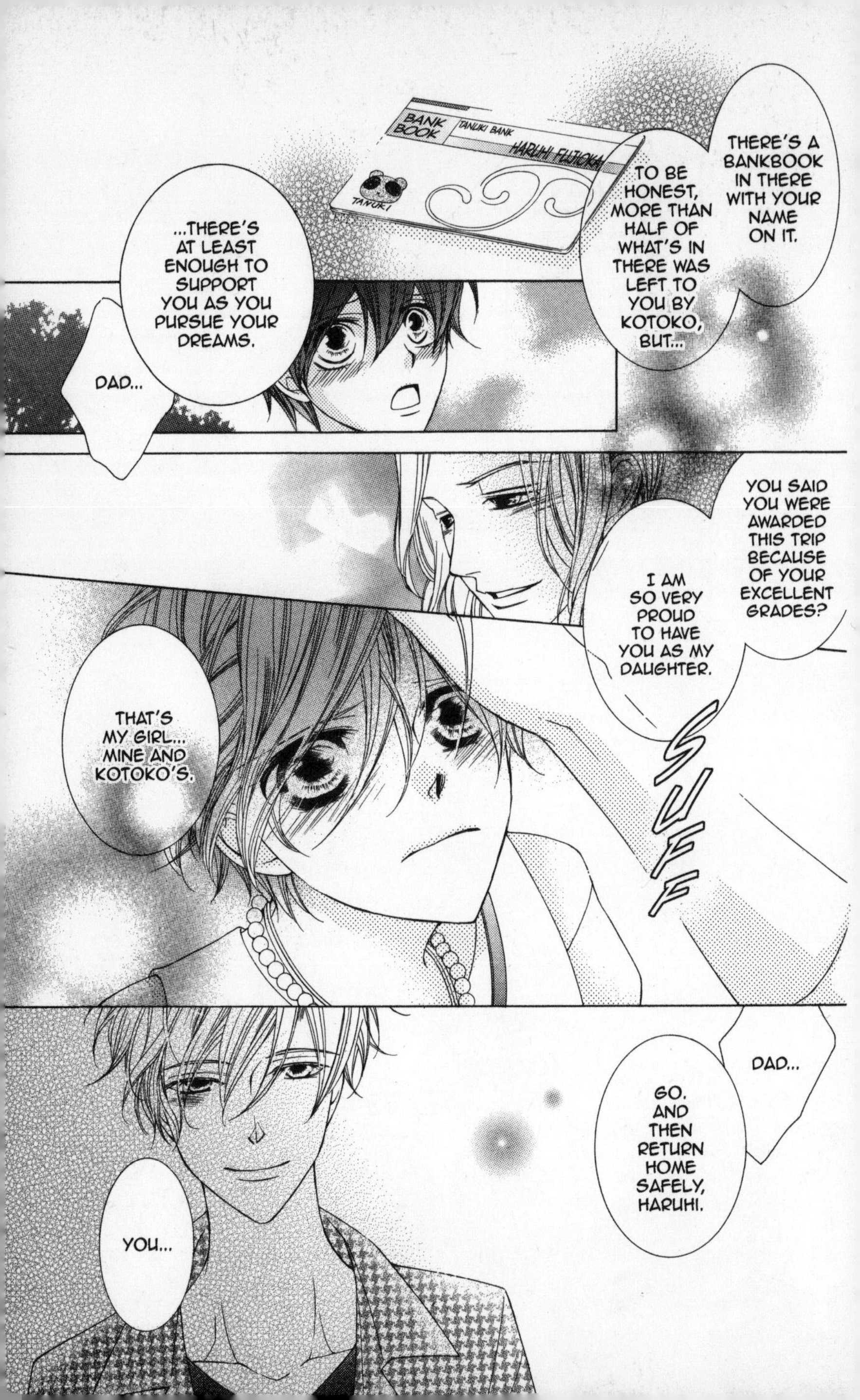
THERE'S A BANKBOOK IN THERE WITH YOUR NAME ON IT.
BANK BOOK
TANUKI BANK
HARUHI FUJIOKA
TANUKI
TO BE HONEST, MORE THAN HALF OF WHAT'S IN THERE WAS LEFT TO YOU BY KOTOKO, BUT...
...THERE'S AT LEAST ENOUGH TO SUPPORT YOU AS YOU PURSUE YOUR DREAMS.
DAD...
YOU SAID YOU WERE AWARDED THIS TRIP BECAUSE OF YOUR EXCELLENT GRADES?
I AM SO VERY PROUD TO HAVE YOU AS MY DAUGHTER.
SUFF
THAT'S MY GIRL... MINE AND KOTOKO'S.
DAD...
GO. AND THEN RETURN HOME SAFELY, HARUHI.
YOU...

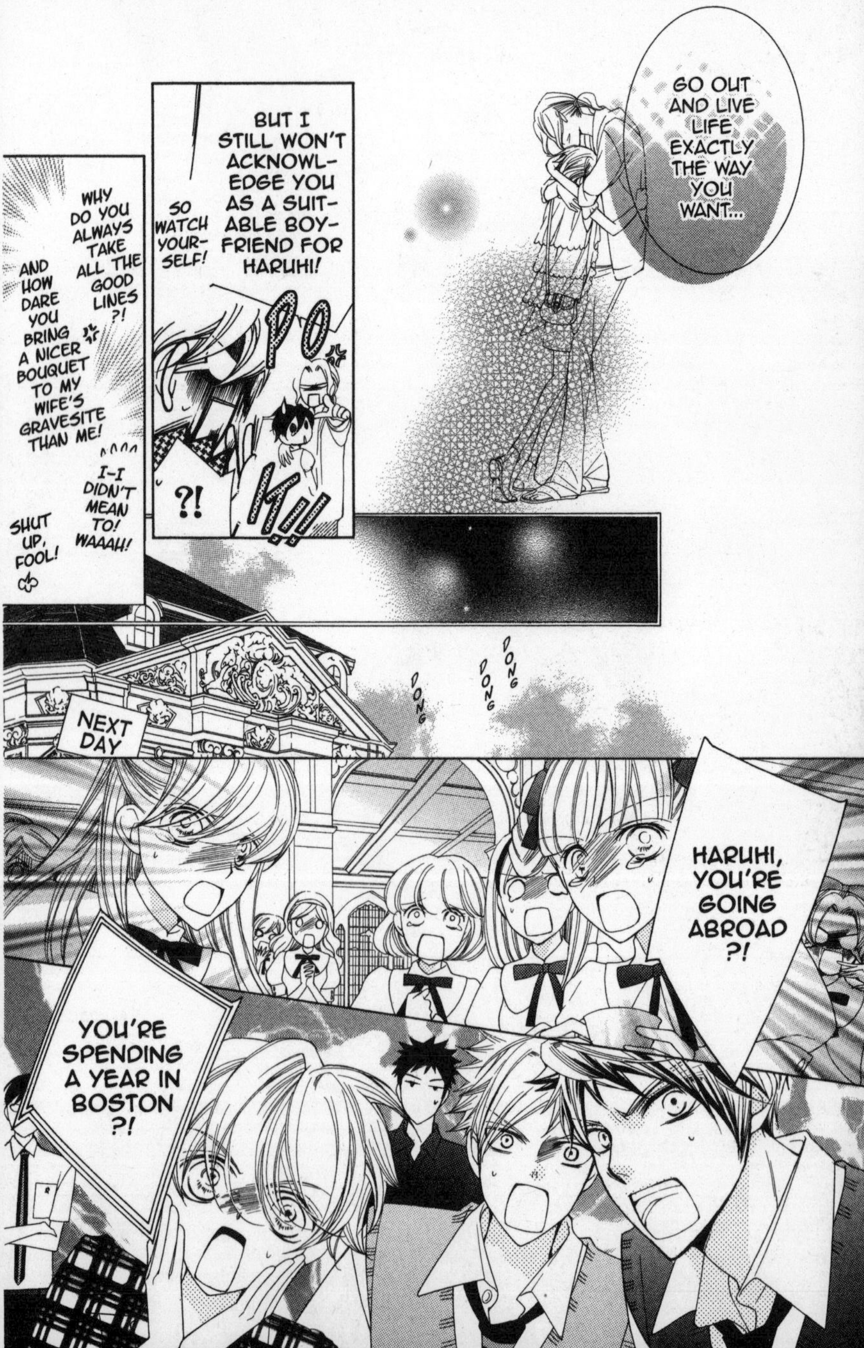
GO OUT AND LIVE LIFE EXACTLY THE WAY YOU WANT...
BUT I STILL WON'T ACKNOWLEDGE YOU AS A SUITABLE BOYFRIEND FOR HARUHI!
SO WATCH YOURSELF!
POKI!!
?!
WHY DO YOU ALWAYS TAKE ALL THE GOOD LINES ?!
AND HOW DARE YOU BRING A NICER BOUQUET TO MY WIFE'S GRAVESITE THAN ME!
I-I DIDN'T MEAN TO! WAAAH!
SHUT UP, FOOL!
DONG
DONG
DONG
NEXT DAY
HARUHI, YOU'RE GOING ABROAD ?!
YOU'RE SPENDING A YEAR IN BOSTON ?!

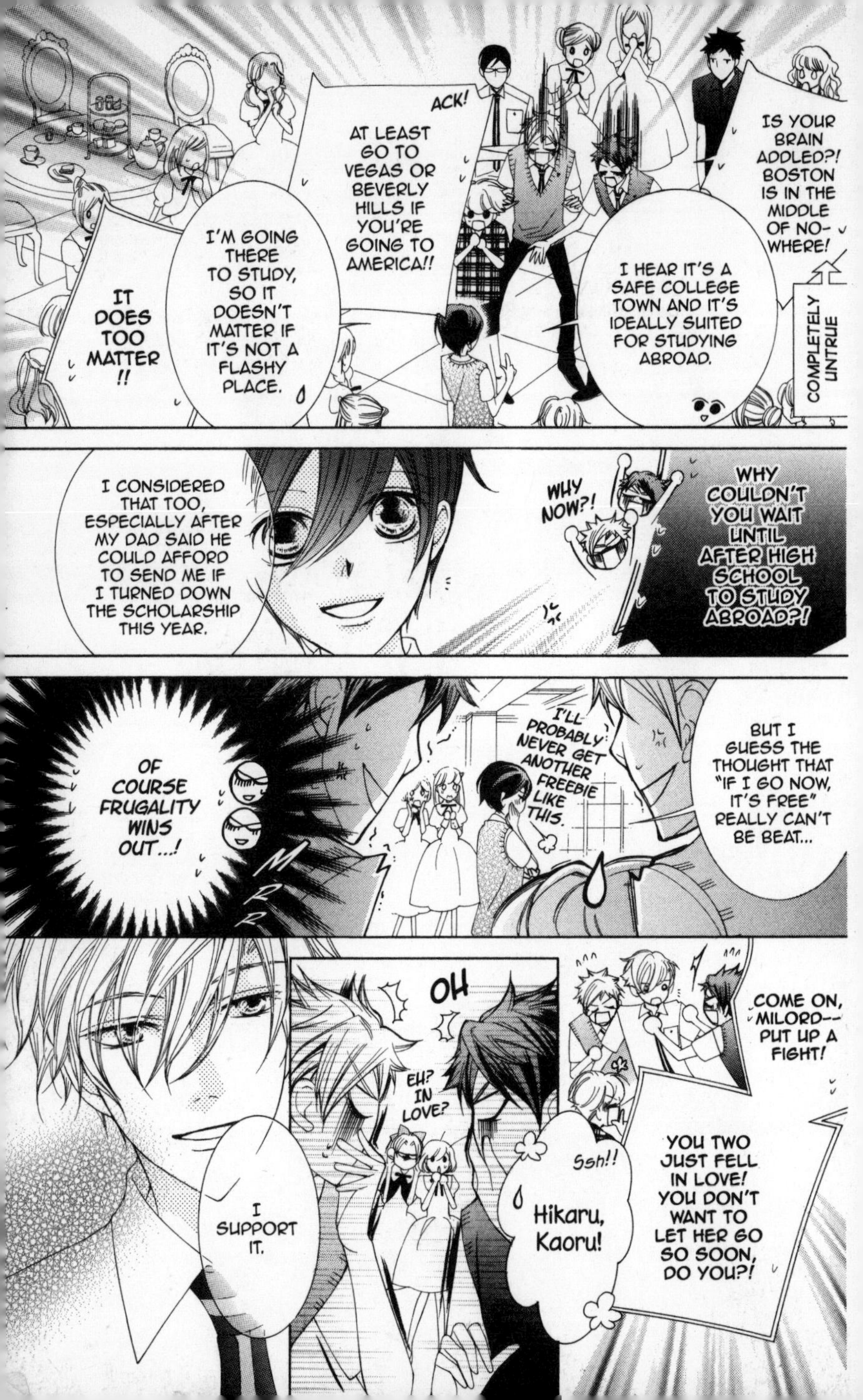
IS YOUR BRAIN ADDLED?! BOSTON IS IN THE MIDDLE OF NO-WHERE!
COMPLETELY UNTRUE
I HEAR IT'S A SAFE COLLEGE TOWN AND IT'S IDEALLY SUITED FOR STUDYING ABROAD.
ACK!
AT LEAST GO TO VEGAS OR BEVERLY HILLS IF YOU'RE GOING TO AMERICA!!
I'M GOING THERE TO STUDY, SO IT DOESN'T MATTER IF IT'S NOT A FLASHY PLACE.
IT DOES TOO MATTER!!
WHY COULDN'T YOU WAIT UNTIL AFTER HIGH SCHOOL TO STUDY ABROAD?!
WHY NOW?!
I CONSIDERED THAT TOO, ESPECIALLY AFTER MY DAD SAID HE COULD AFFORD TO SEND ME IF I TURNED DOWN THE SCHOLARSHIP THIS YEAR.
BUT I GUESS THE THOUGHT THAT "IF I GO NOW, IT'S FREE" REALLY CAN'T BE BEAT...
I'LL PROBABLY NEVER GET ANOTHER FREEBIE LIKE THIS.
OF COURSE FRUGALITY WINS OUT...!
MRRR
COME ON, MILORD--PUT UP A FIGHT!
YOU TWO JUST FELL IN LOVE! YOU DON'T WANT TO LET HER GO SO SOON, DO YOU?!
Ssh!! Hikaru, Kaoru!
OH
EH? IN LOVE?
I SUPPORT IT.

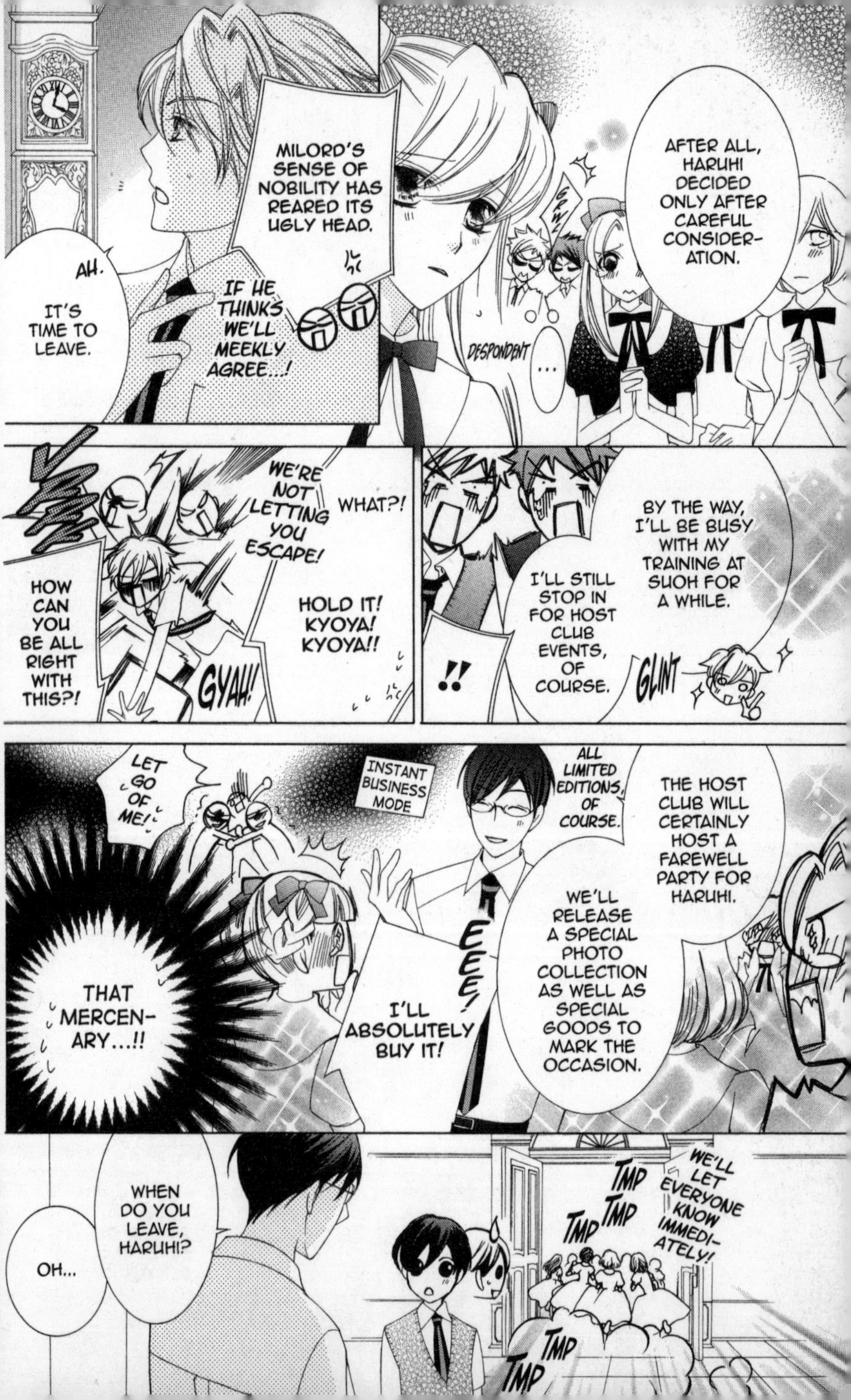
AFTER ALL, HARUHI DECIDED ONLY AFTER CAREFUL CONSIDERATION.
DESPONDENT
...
MILORD'S SENSE OF NOBILITY HAS REARED ITS UGLY HEAD.
IF HE THINKS WE'LL MEEKLY AGREE...!
AH.
IT'S TIME TO LEAVE.
BY THE WAY, I'LL BE BUSY WITH MY TRAINING AT SUOH FOR A WHILE.
GLINT
I'LL STILL STOP IN FOR HOST CLUB EVENTS, OF COURSE.
!!
WHAT?!
WE'RE NOT LETTING YOU ESCAPE!
HOLD IT! KYOYA! KYOYA!!
GYAH!
HOW CAN YOU BE ALL RIGHT WITH THIS?!
THE HOST CLUB WILL CERTAINLY HOST A FAREWELL PARTY FOR HARUHI.
ALL LIMITED EDITIONS, OF COURSE.
WE'LL RELEASE A SPECIAL PHOTO COLLECTION AS WELL AS SPECIAL GOODS TO MARK THE OCCASION.
INSTANT BUSINESS MODE
EEE!
I'LL ABSOLUTELY BUY IT!
LET GO OF ME!
THAT MERCENARY...!!
WE'LL LET EVERYONE KNOW IMMEDIATELY!
TMP TMP
TMP
TMP TMP
WHEN DO YOU LEAVE, HARUHI?
OH...

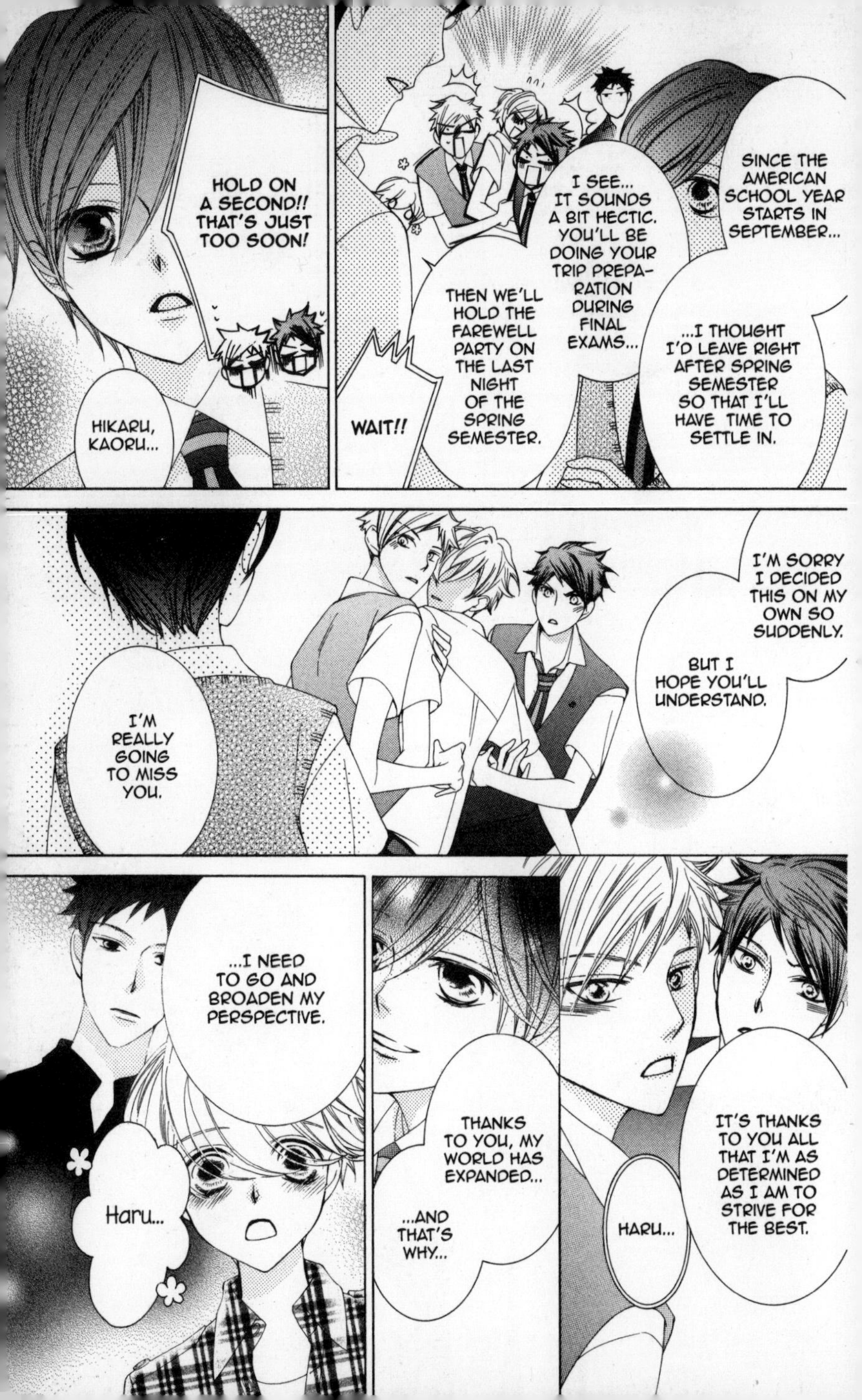
SINCE THE AMERICAN SCHOOL YEAR STARTS IN SEPTEMBER...
...I THOUGHT I'D LEAVE RIGHT AFTER SPRING SEMESTER SO THAT I'LL HAVE TIME TO SETTLE IN.
I SEE... IT SOUNDS A BIT HECTIC. YOU'LL BE DOING YOUR TRIP PREPA-RATION DURING FINAL EXAMS...
THEN WE'LL HOLD THE FAREWELL PARTY ON THE LAST NIGHT OF THE SPRING SEMESTER.
WAIT!!
HOLD ON A SECOND!! THAT'S JUST TOO SOON!
HIKARU, KAORU...
I'M SORRY I DECIDED THIS ON MY OWN SO SUDDENLY.
BUT I HOPE YOU'LL UNDERSTAND.
I'M REALLY GOING TO MISS YOU.
IT'S THANKS TO YOU ALL THAT I'M AS DETERMINED AS I AM TO STRIVE FOR THE BEST.
HARU...
THANKS TO YOU, MY WORLD HAS EXPANDED...
...AND THAT'S WHY...
...I NEED TO GO AND BROADEN MY PERSPECTIVE.
Haru...

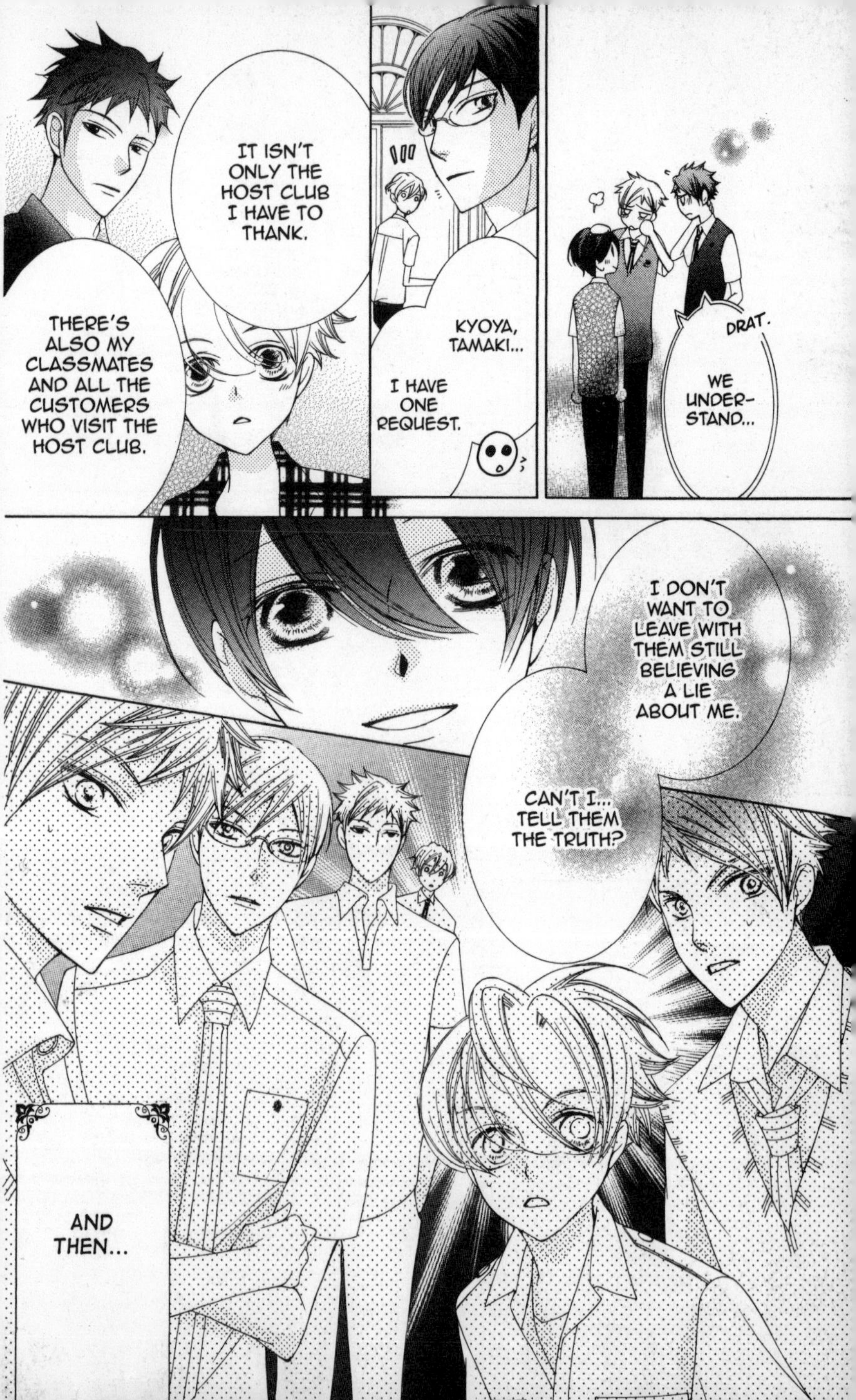
DRAT.
WE UNDERSTAND...
KYOYA, TAMAKI...
I HAVE ONE REQUEST.
IT ISN'T ONLY THE HOST CLUB I HAVE TO THANK.
THERE'S ALSO MY CLASSMATES AND ALL THE CUSTOMERS WHO VISIT THE HOST CLUB.
I DON'T WANT TO LEAVE WITH THEM STILL BELIEVING A LIE ABOUT ME.
CAN'T I... TELL THEM THE TRUTH?
AND THEN...

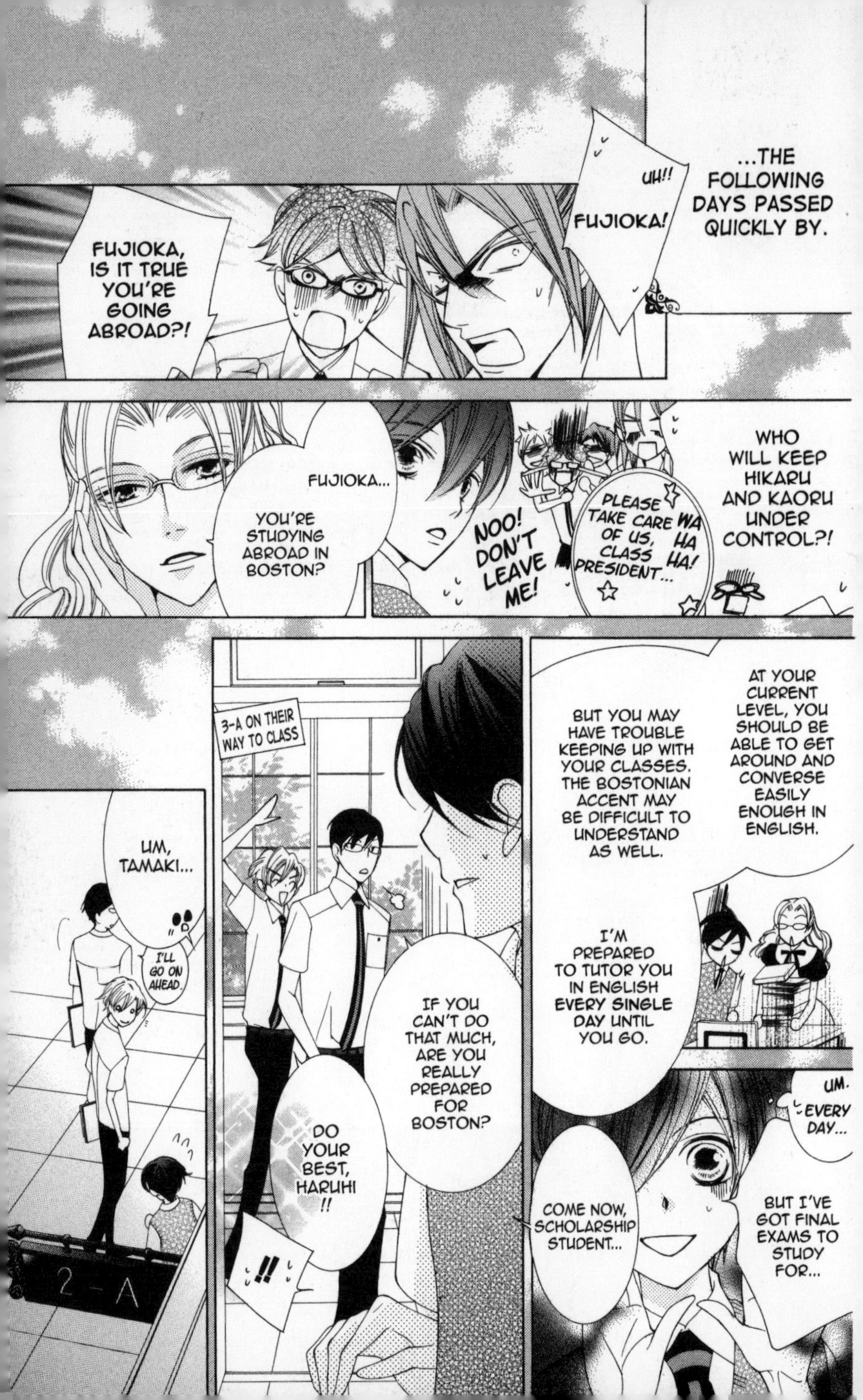
...THE FOLLOWING DAYS PASSED QUICKLY BY.
UH!!
FUJIOKA!
FUJIOKA, IS IT TRUE YOU'RE GOING ABROAD?!
WHO WILL KEEP HIKARU AND KAORU UNDER CONTROL?!
WA HA HA!
PLEASE TAKE CARE OF US, CLASS PRESIDENT...
NOO! DON'T LEAVE ME!
FUJIOKA...
YOU'RE STUDYING ABROAD IN BOSTON?
AT YOUR CURRENT LEVEL, YOU SHOULD BE ABLE TO GET AROUND AND CONVERSE EASILY ENOUGH IN ENGLISH.
BUT YOU MAY HAVE TROUBLE KEEPING UP WITH YOUR CLASSES. THE BOSTONIAN ACCENT MAY BE DIFFICULT TO UNDERSTAND AS WELL.
I'M PREPARED TO TUTOR YOU IN ENGLISH EVERY SINGLE DAY UNTIL YOU GO.
UM.
EVERY DAY...
BUT I'VE GOT FINAL EXAMS TO STUDY FOR...
COME NOW, SCHOLARSHIP STUDENT...
IF YOU CAN'T DO THAT MUCH, ARE YOU REALLY PREPARED FOR BOSTON?
3-A ON THEIR WAY TO CLASS
DO YOUR BEST, HARUHI!!
!!
UM, TAMAKI...
I'LL GO ON AHEAD.
2-A

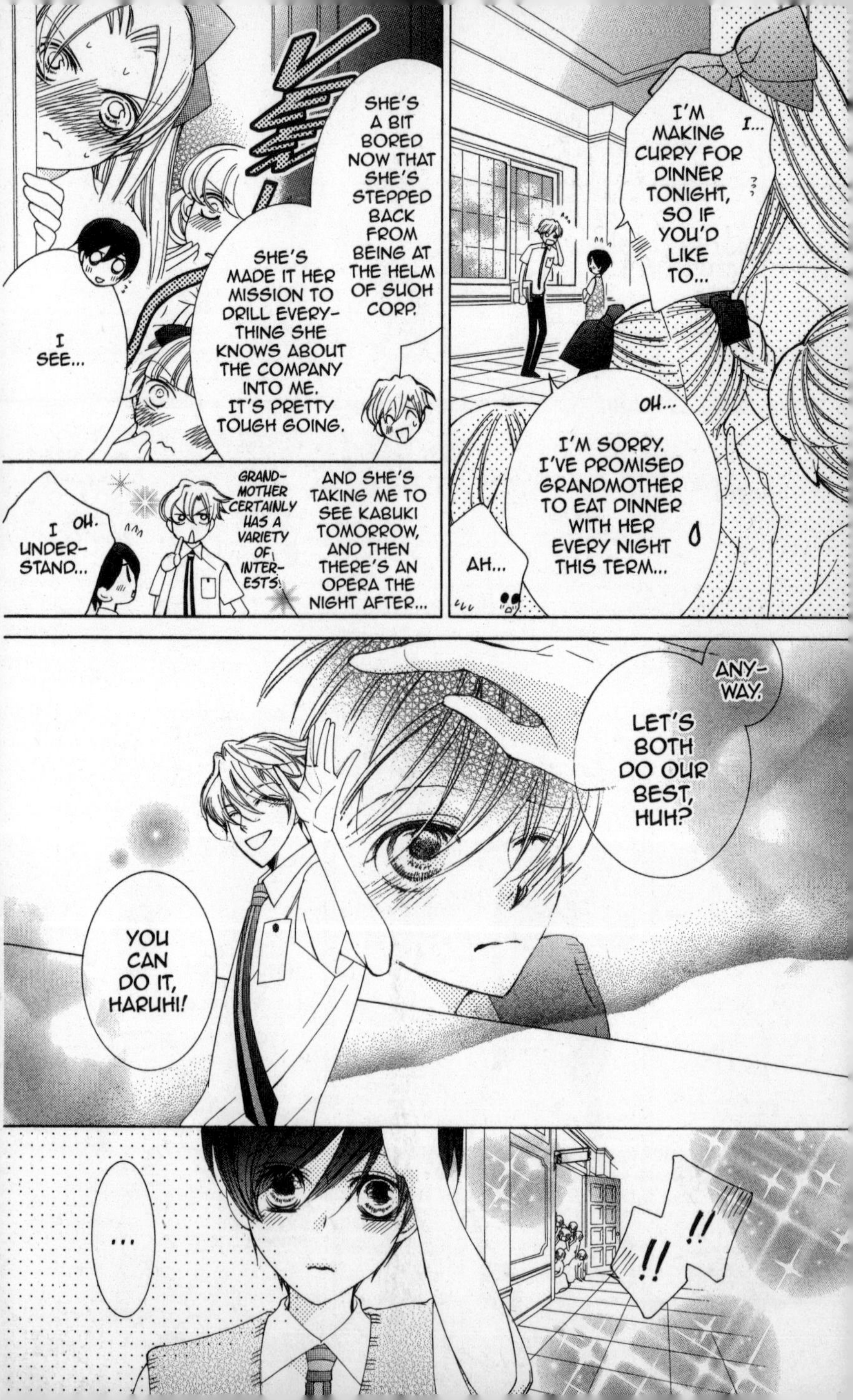

I...
I'M MAKING CURRY FOR DINNER TONIGHT, SO IF YOU'D LIKE TO...
OH...
I'M SORRY. I'VE PROMISED GRANDMOTHER TO EAT DINNER WITH HER EVERY NIGHT THIS TERM...
AH...
SHE'S A BIT BORED NOW THAT SHE'S STEPPED BACK FROM BEING AT THE HELM OF SUOH CORP.
SHE'S MADE IT HER MISSION TO DRILL EVERYTHING SHE KNOWS ABOUT THE COMPANY INTO ME. IT'S PRETTY TOUGH GOING.
I SEE...
AND SHE'S TAKING ME TO SEE KABUKI TOMORROW, AND THEN THERE'S AN OPERA THE NIGHT AFTER...
GRANDMOTHER CERTAINLY HAS A VARIETY OF INTERESTS.
OH. I UNDERSTAND...
ANYWAY.
LET'S BOTH DO OUR BEST, HUH?
YOU CAN DO IT, HARUHI!
!!
!!
...

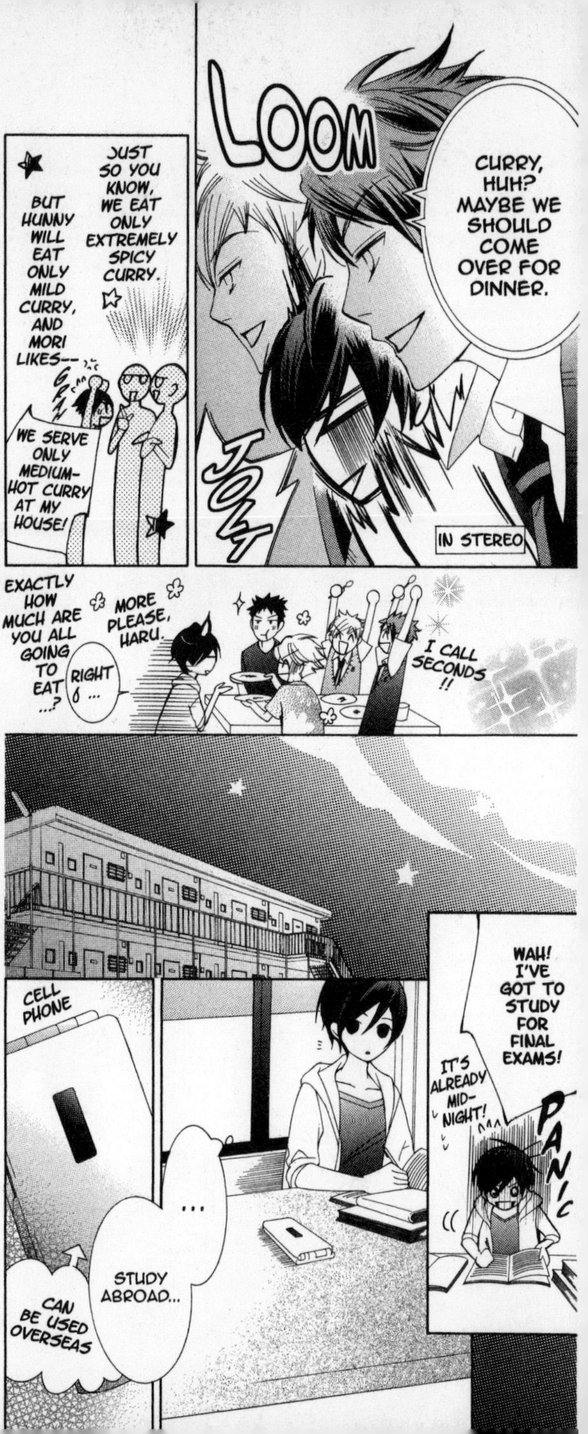
LOOM
CURRY, HUH? MAYBE WE SHOULD COME OVER FOR DINNER.
JOWL
IN STEREO
JUST SO YOU KNOW, WE EAT ONLY EXTREMELY SPICY CURRY.
BUT HUNNY WILL EAT ONLY MILD CURRY, AND MORI LIKES--
GRAAH
WE SERVE ONLY MEDIUM-HOT CURRY AT MY HOUSE!
I CALL SECONDS!!
MORE PLEASE, HARU.
RIGHT...
EXACTLY HOW MUCH ARE YOU ALL GOING TO EAT...?
WAH! I'VE GOT TO STUDY FOR FINAL EXAMS!
IT'S ALREADY MID-NIGHT!
PANIC
...
STUDY ABROAD...
CELL PHONE
CAN BE USED OVERSEAS

A BRIEF PEEK AT THEIR FUTURE

RENGE SEEMS LIKE SHE'D OPEN HER OWN BUSINESS WHILE IN UNIVERSITY. IT WOULD BE AN OTAKU BUSINESS, OF COURSE. GO FORTH AND GRANT THE DREAMS OF FUJOSHI EVERYWHERE, RENGE!!

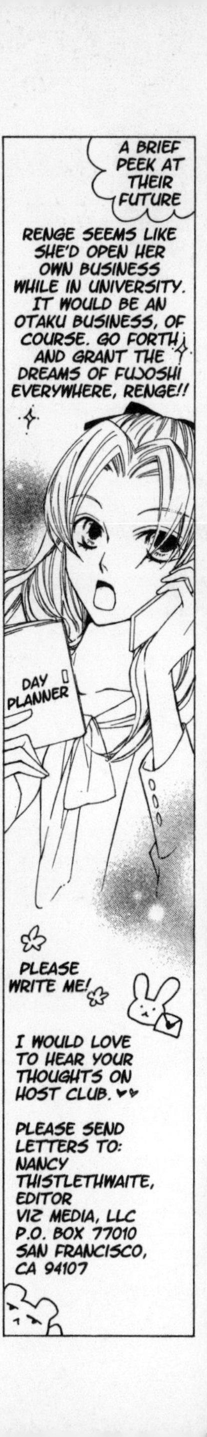
DAY PLANNER

PLEASE WRITE ME!

I WOULD LOVE TO HEAR YOUR THOUGHTS ON HOST CLUB.

PLEASE SEND LETTERS TO:
NANCY THISTLETHWAITE, EDITOR
VIZ MEDIA, LLC
P.O. BOX 77010
SAN FRANCISCO, CA 94107

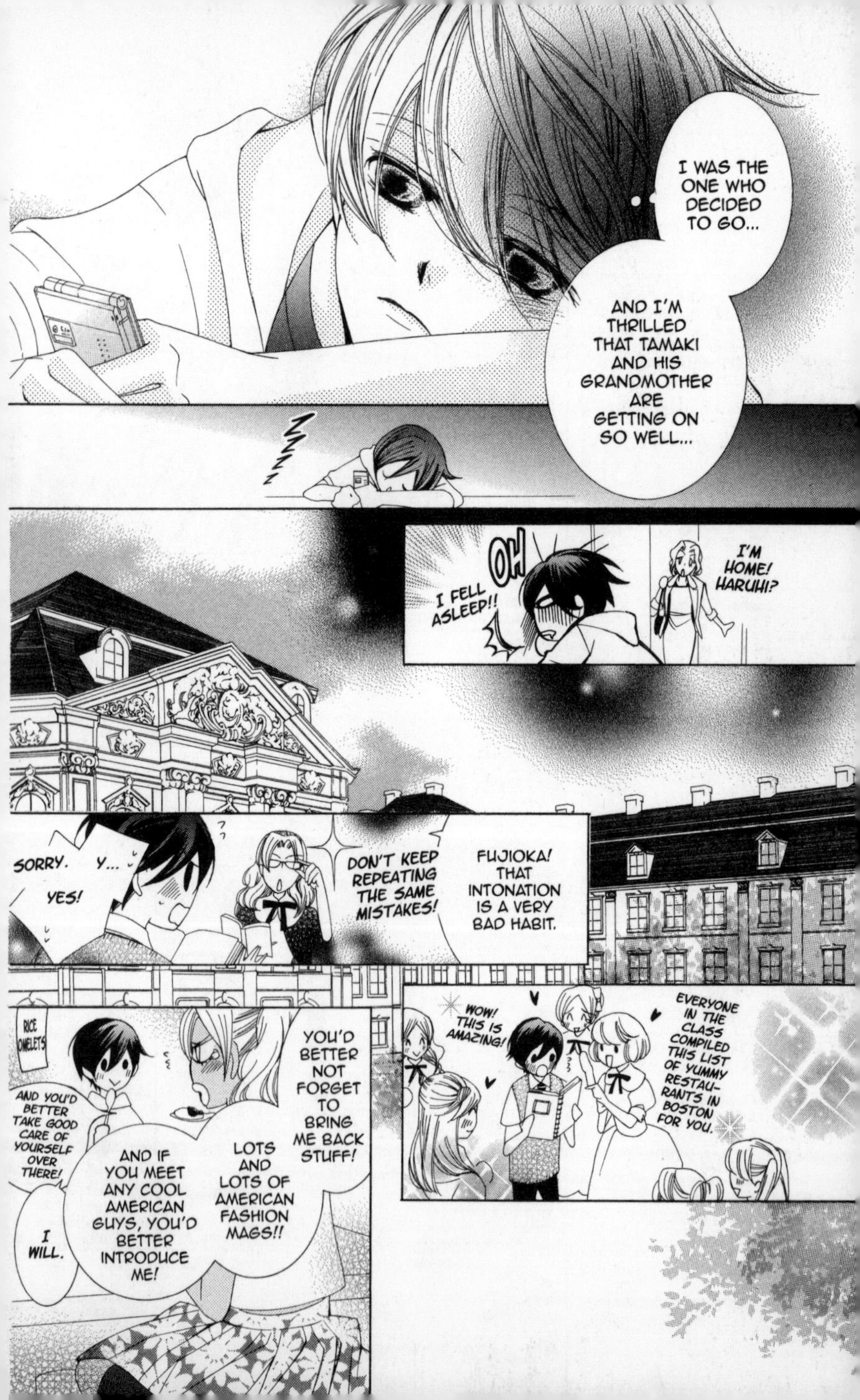
I WAS THE ONE WHO DECIDED TO GO...
AND I'M THRILLED THAT TAMAKI AND HIS GRANDMOTHER ARE GETTING ON SO WELL...
ZZZZ
I'M HOME! HARUHI?
OH
I FELL ASLEEP!!
FUJIOKA! THAT INTONATION IS A VERY BAD HABIT.
DON'T KEEP REPEATING THE SAME MISTAKES!
Y...
YES!
SORRY.
EVERYONE IN THE CLASS COMPILED THIS LIST OF YUMMY RESTAURANTS IN BOSTON FOR YOU.
WOW! THIS IS AMAZING!
YOU'D BETTER NOT FORGET TO BRING ME BACK STUFF!
LOTS AND LOTS OF AMERICAN FASHION MAGS!!
AND IF YOU MEET ANY COOL AMERICAN GUYS, YOU'D BETTER INTRODUCE ME!
RICE OMELETS
AND YOU'D BETTER TAKE GOOD CARE OF YOURSELF OVER THERE!
I WILL.

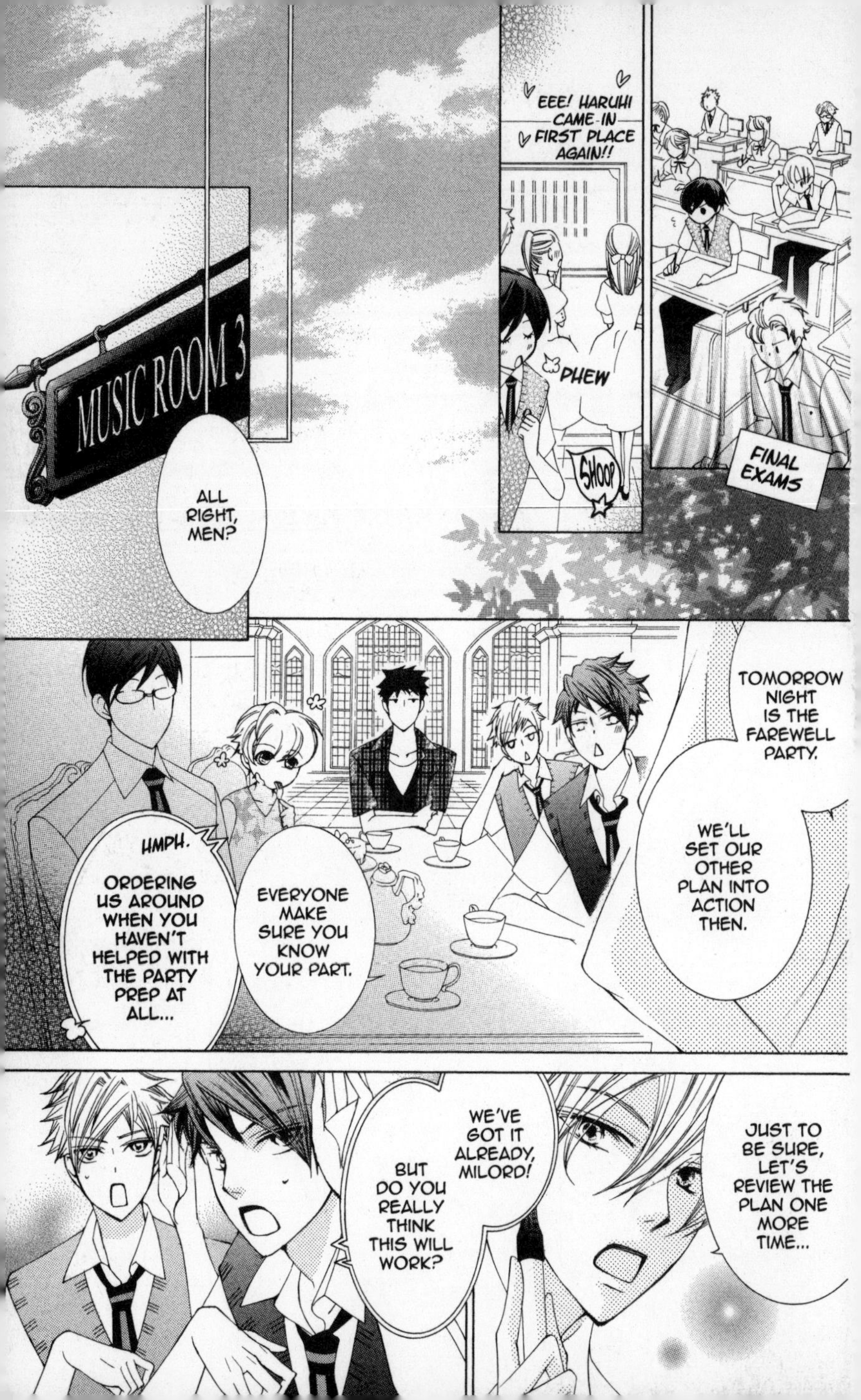
FINAL EXAMS
EEE! HARUHI CAME IN FIRST PLACE AGAIN!!
PHEW
SHOOP
MUSIC ROOM 3
ALL RIGHT, MEN?
TOMORROW NIGHT IS THE FAREWELL PARTY.
WE'LL SET OUR OTHER PLAN INTO ACTION THEN.
EVERYONE MAKE SURE YOU KNOW YOUR PART.
HMPH.
ORDERING US AROUND WHEN YOU HAVEN'T HELPED WITH THE PARTY PREP AT ALL...
JUST TO BE SURE, LET'S REVIEW THE PLAN ONE MORE TIME...
WE'VE GOT IT ALREADY, MILORD!
BUT DO YOU REALLY THINK THIS WILL WORK?

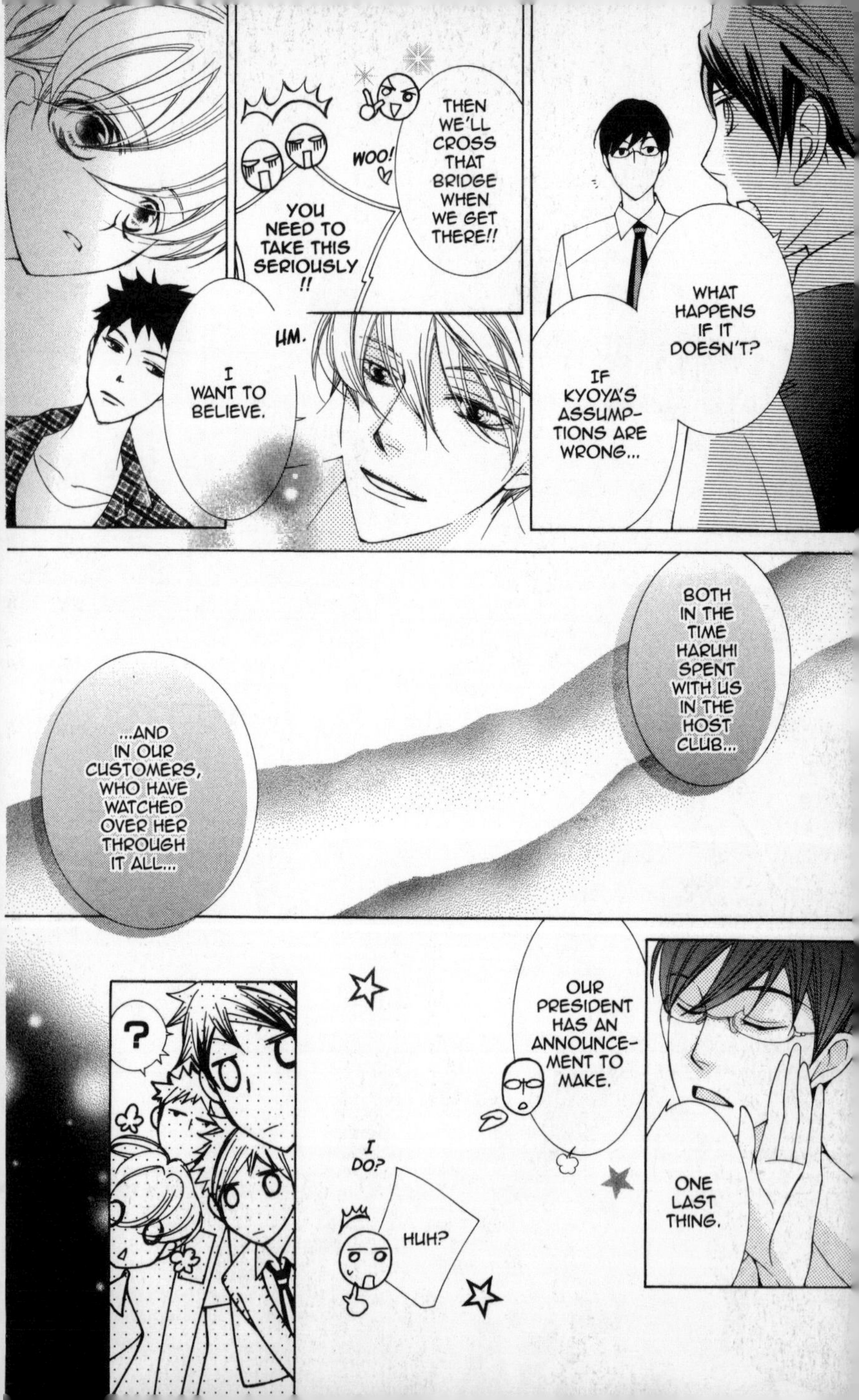
WHAT HAPPENS IF IT DOESN'T?
IF KYOYA'S ASSUMPTIONS ARE WRONG...
THEN WE'LL CROSS THAT BRIDGE WHEN WE GET THERE!!
WOO!
YOU NEED TO TAKE THIS SERIOUSLY!!
HM.
I WANT TO BELIEVE.
BOTH IN THE TIME HARUHI SPENT WITH US IN THE HOST CLUB...
...AND IN OUR CUSTOMERS, WHO HAVE WATCHED OVER HER THROUGH IT ALL...
ONE LAST THING.
OUR PRESIDENT HAS AN ANNOUNCEMENT TO MAKE.
I DO?
HUH?
?

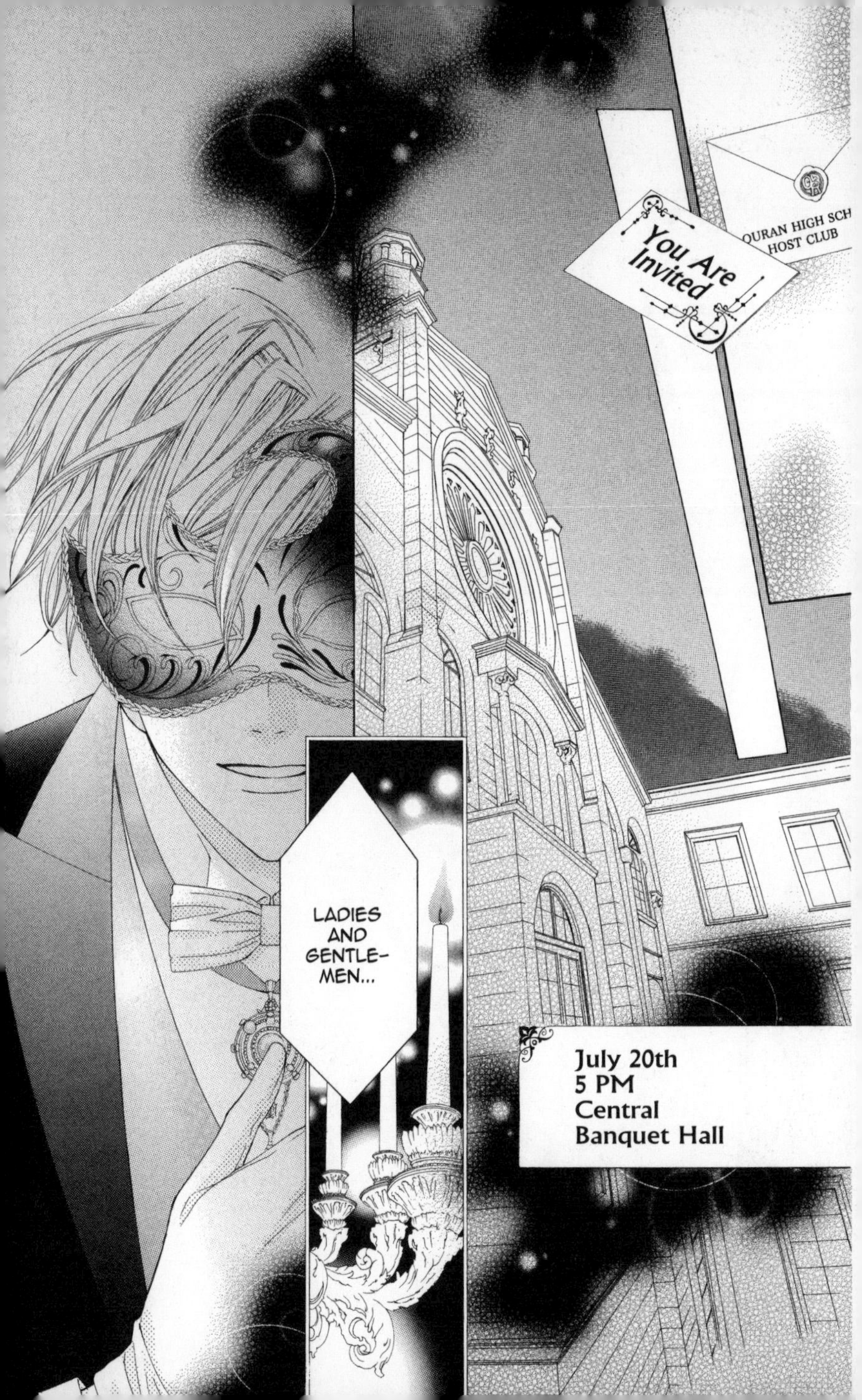
OURAN HIGH SCH
HOST CLUB
You Are Invited
July 20th
5 PM
Central
Banquet Hall
LADIES AND GENTLEMEN...

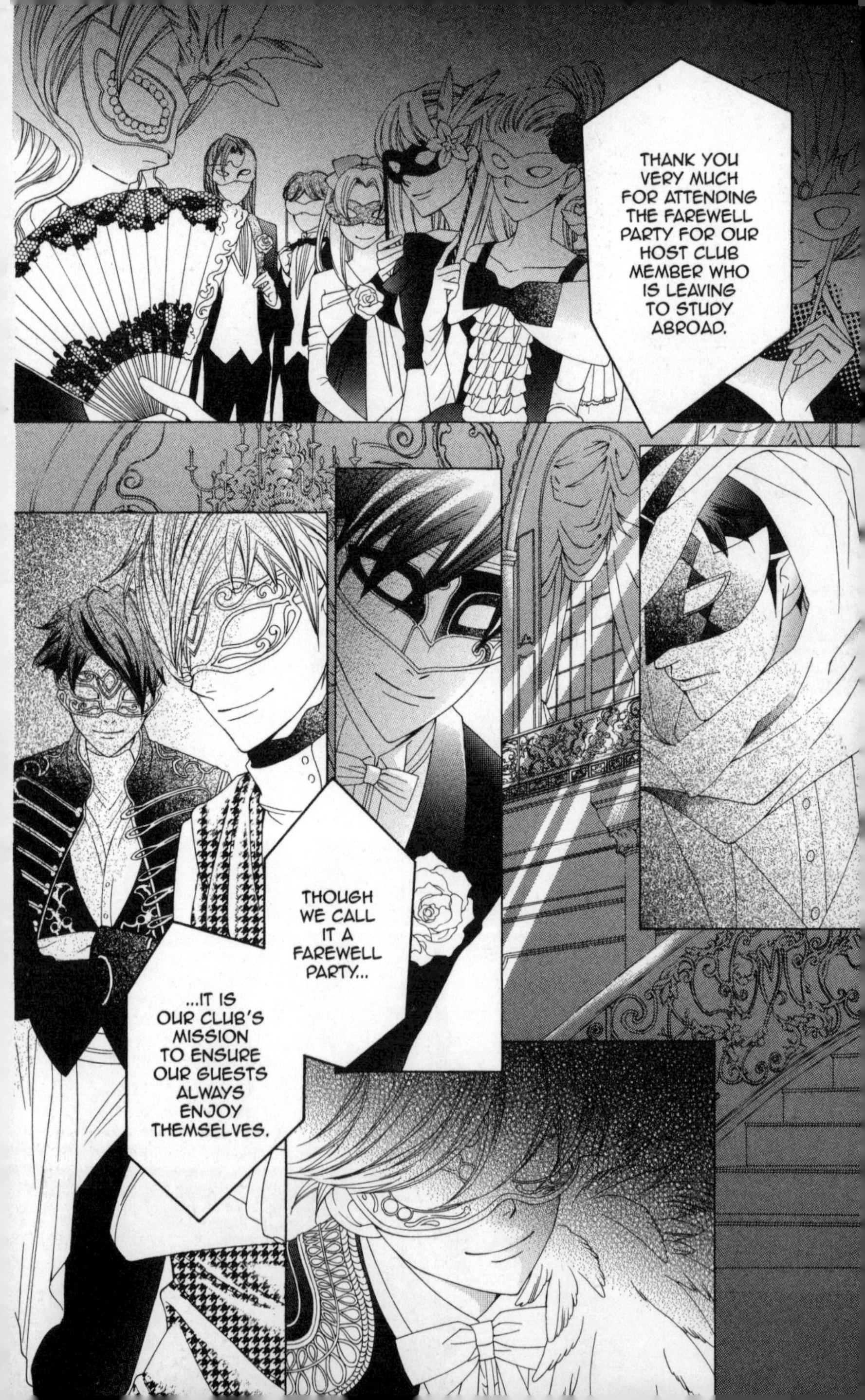
THANK YOU VERY MUCH FOR ATTENDING THE FAREWELL PARTY FOR OUR HOST CLUB MEMBER WHO IS LEAVING TO STUDY ABROAD.
THOUGH WE CALL IT A FAREWELL PARTY...
...IT IS OUR CLUB'S MISSION TO ENSURE OUR GUESTS ALWAYS ENJOY THEMSELVES.

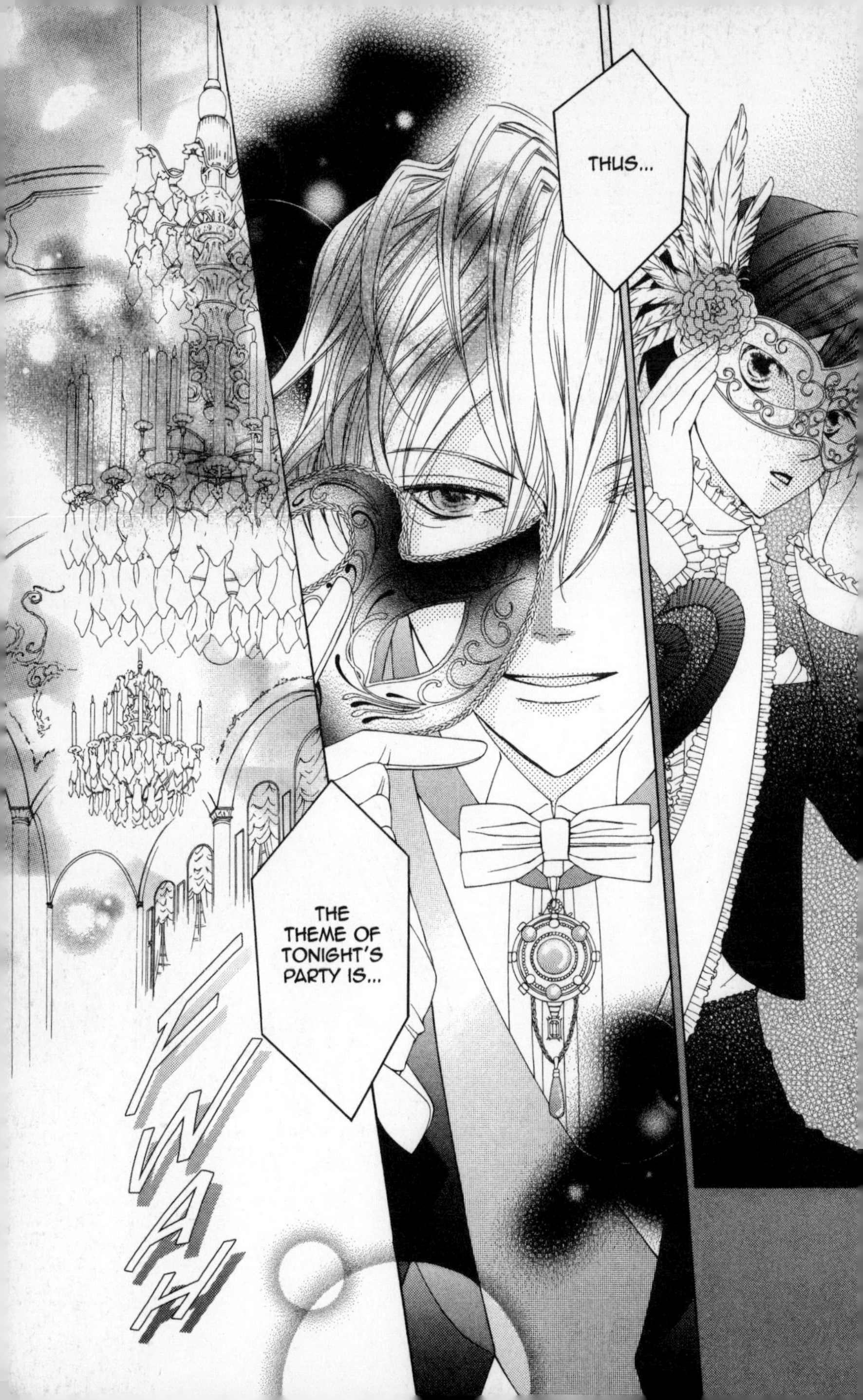
THUS...
THE THEME OF TONIGHT'S PARTY IS...
FWAH

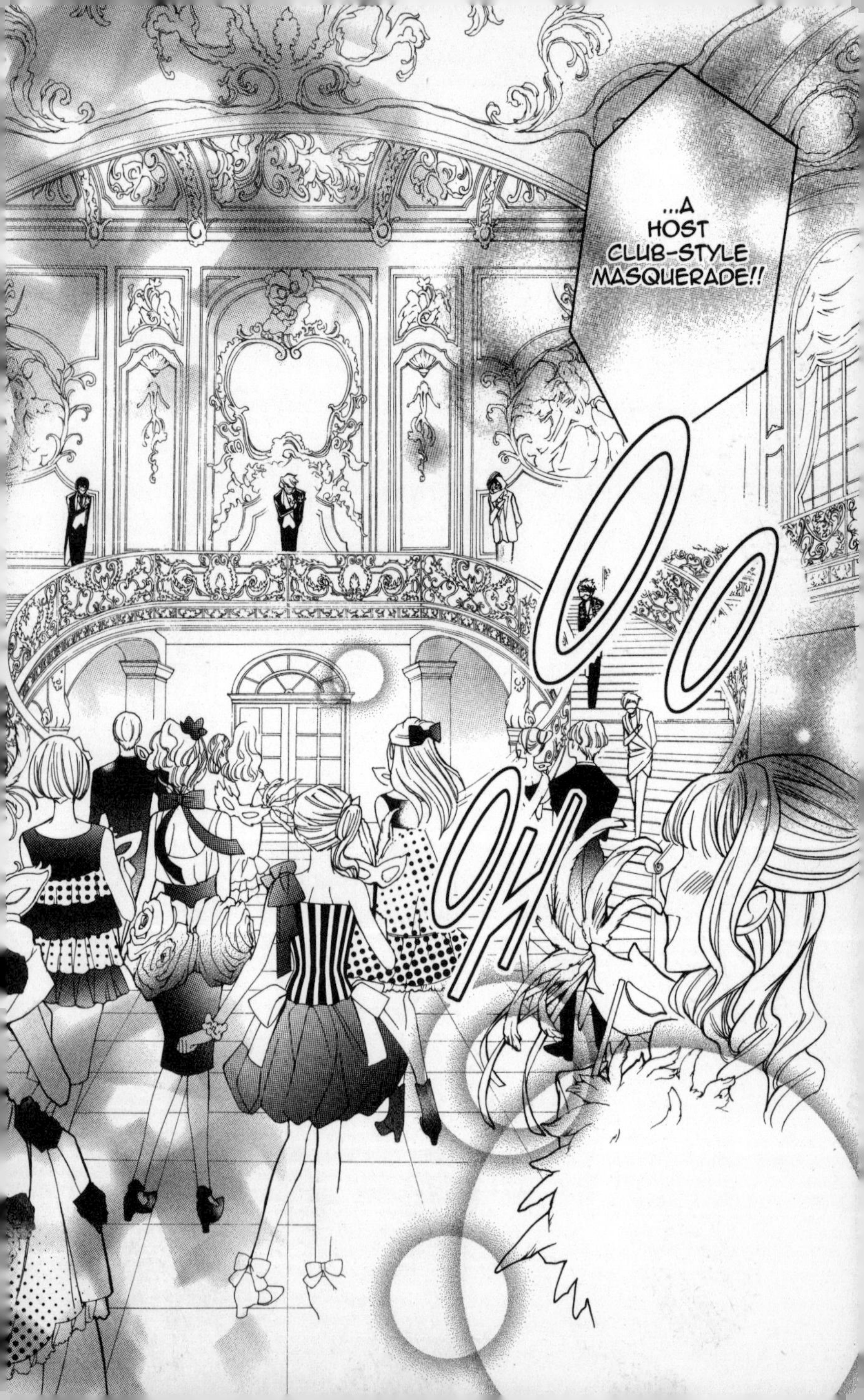
...A HOST CLUB-STYLE MASQUERADE!!
OOOH

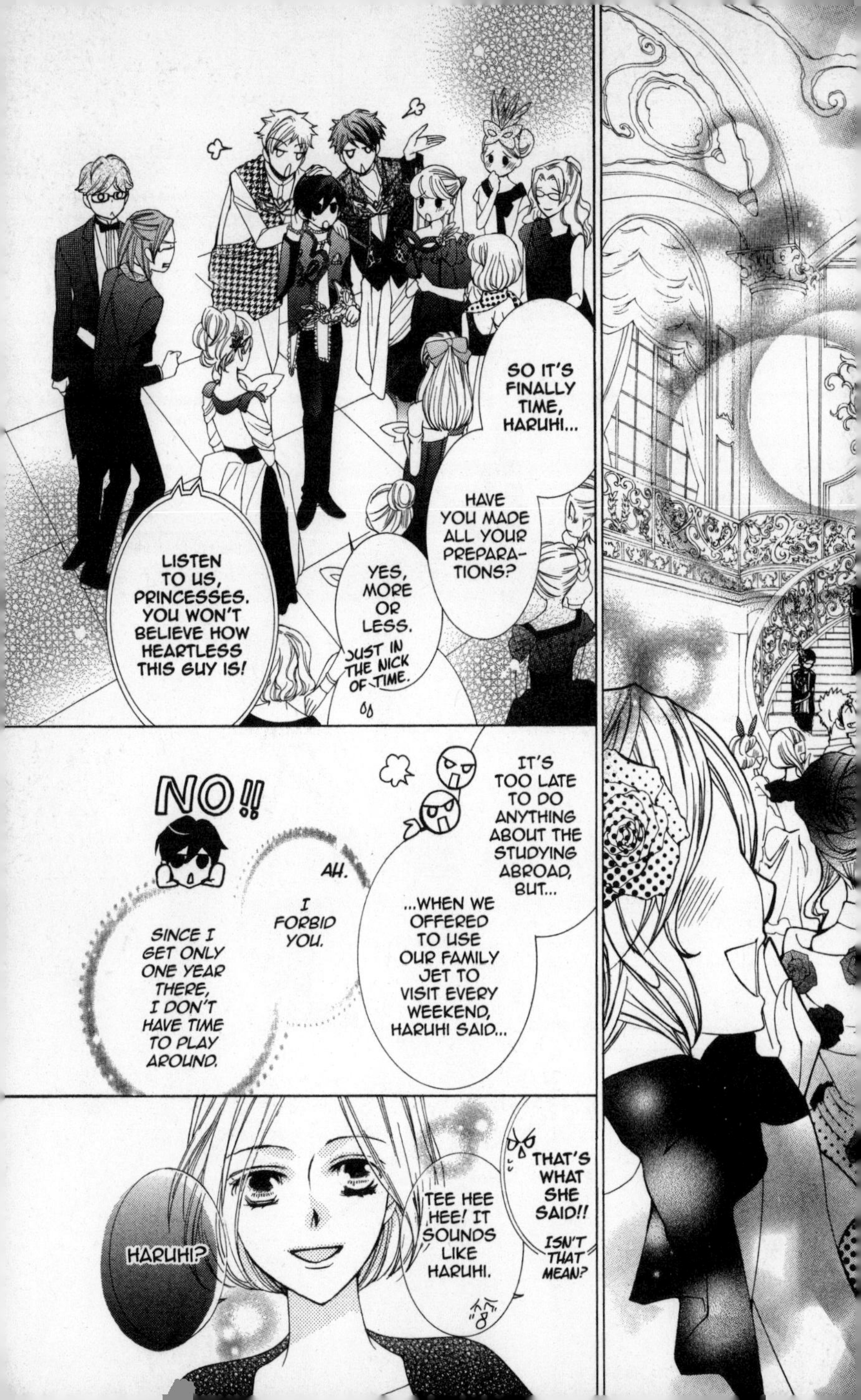
SO IT'S FINALLY TIME, HARUHI...
HAVE YOU MADE ALL YOUR PREPARATIONS?
YES, MORE OR LESS.
JUST IN THE NICK OF TIME.
LISTEN TO US, PRINCESSES. YOU WON'T BELIEVE HOW HEARTLESS THIS GUY IS!
IT'S TOO LATE TO DO ANYTHING ABOUT THE STUDYING ABROAD, BUT...
...WHEN WE OFFERED TO USE OUR FAMILY JET TO VISIT EVERY WEEKEND, HARUHI SAID...
AH.
I FORBID YOU.
SINCE I GET ONLY ONE YEAR THERE, I DON'T HAVE TIME TO PLAY AROUND.
NO!!
THAT'S WHAT SHE SAID!!
ISN'T THAT MEAN?
TEE HEE HEE! IT SOUNDS LIKE HARUHI.
HARUHI?

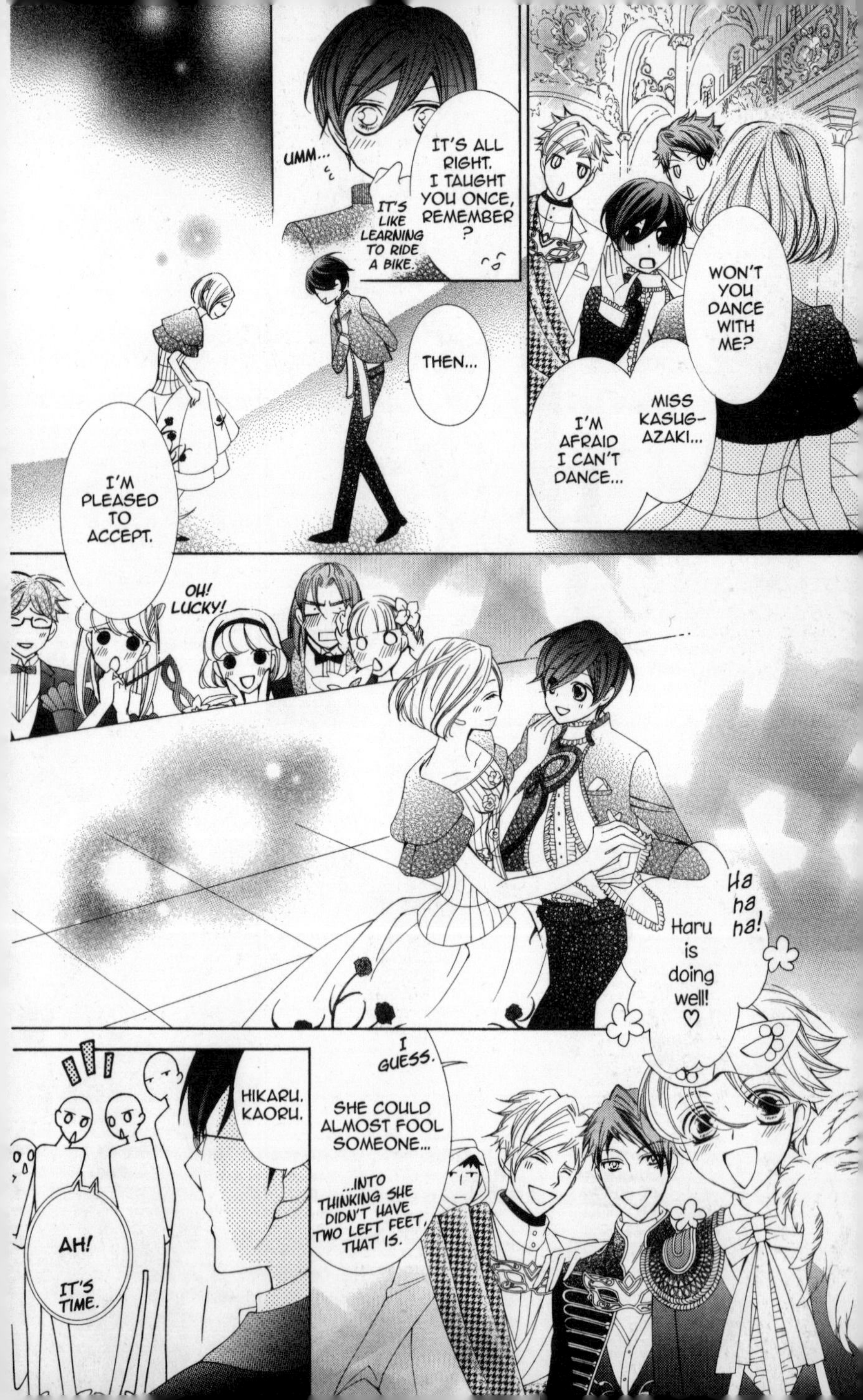
WON'T YOU DANCE WITH ME?
MISS KASUGAZAKI...
I'M AFRAID I CAN'T DANCE...
UMM...
IT'S ALL RIGHT. I TAUGHT YOU ONCE, REMEMBER?
IT'S LIKE LEARNING TO RIDE A BIKE.
THEN...
I'M PLEASED TO ACCEPT.
OH! LUCKY!
Ha ha ha!
Haru is doing well! ♡
I GUESS.
SHE COULD ALMOST FOOL SOMEONE...
...INTO THINKING SHE DIDN'T HAVE TWO LEFT FEET, THAT IS.
HIKARU. KAORU.
AH! IT'S TIME.

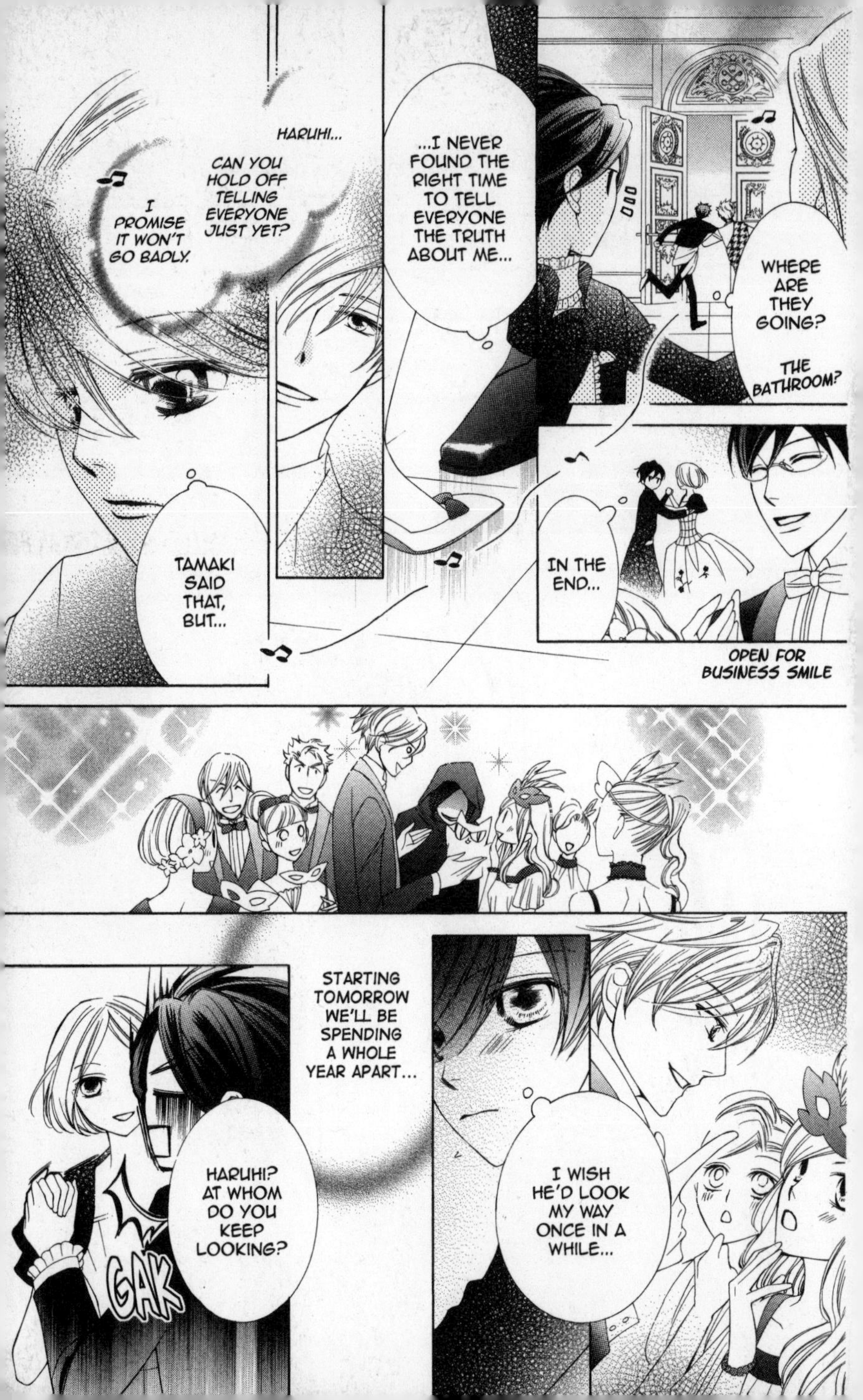
WHERE ARE THEY GOING?
THE BATHROOM?
IN THE END...
OPEN FOR BUSINESS SMILE
...I NEVER FOUND THE RIGHT TIME TO TELL EVERYONE THE TRUTH ABOUT ME...
HARUHI...
CAN YOU HOLD OFF TELLING EVERYONE JUST YET?
I PROMISE IT WON'T GO BADLY.
TAMAKI SAID THAT, BUT...
STARTING TOMORROW WE'LL BE SPENDING A WHOLE YEAR APART...
I WISH HE'D LOOK MY WAY ONCE IN A WHILE...
HARUHI? AT WHOM DO YOU KEEP LOOKING?
GAK

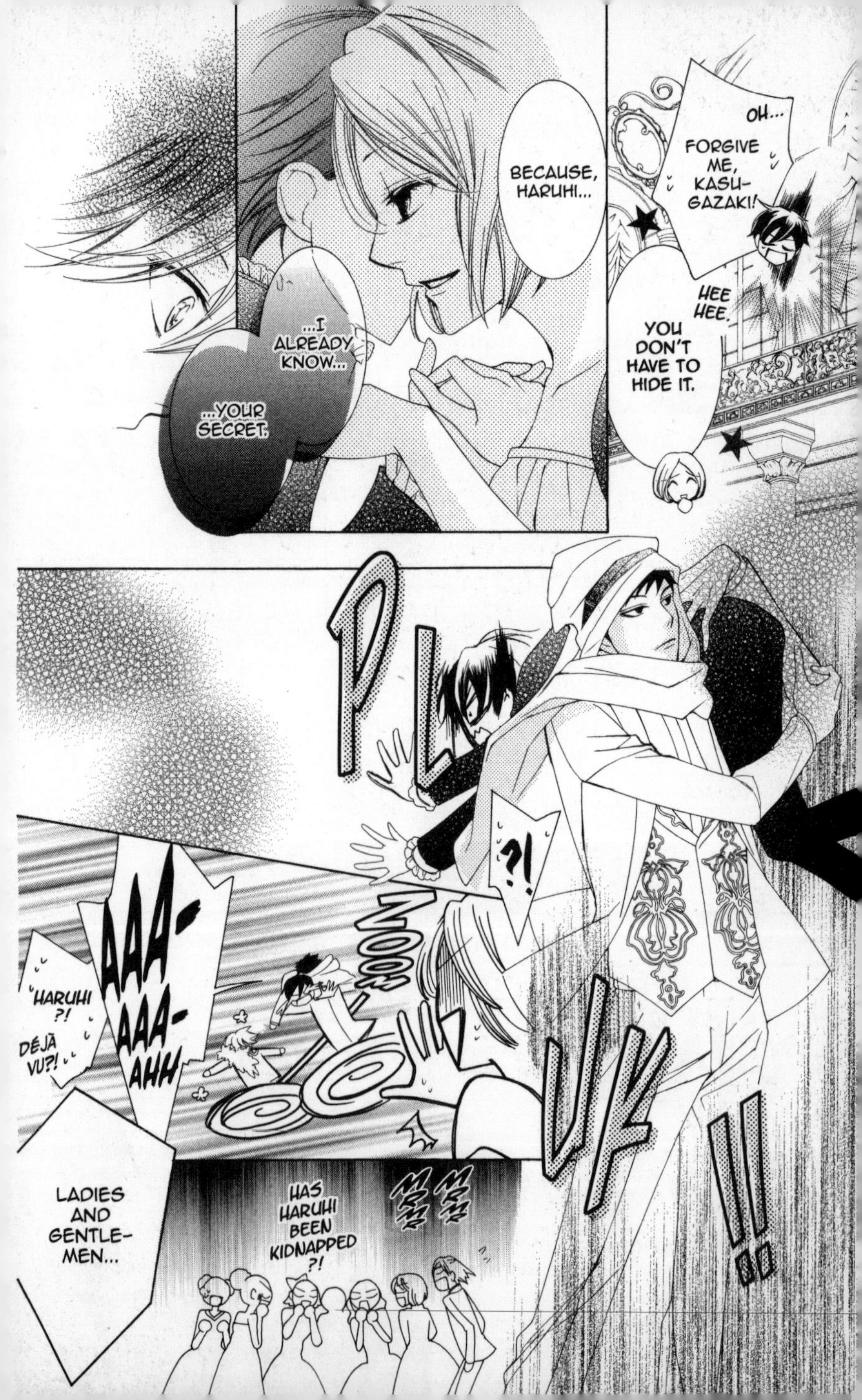
OH...
FORGIVE ME, KASU-GAZAKI!
HEE HEE.
YOU DON'T HAVE TO HIDE IT.
BECAUSE, HARUHI...
...I ALREADY KNOW...
...YOUR SECRET.
PLUK!!
?!
ZWOOM
AAA-AAA-AHH
HARUHI?!
DÉJÀ VU?!
HAS HARUHI BEEN KIDNAPPED?!
LADIES AND GENTLE-MEN...

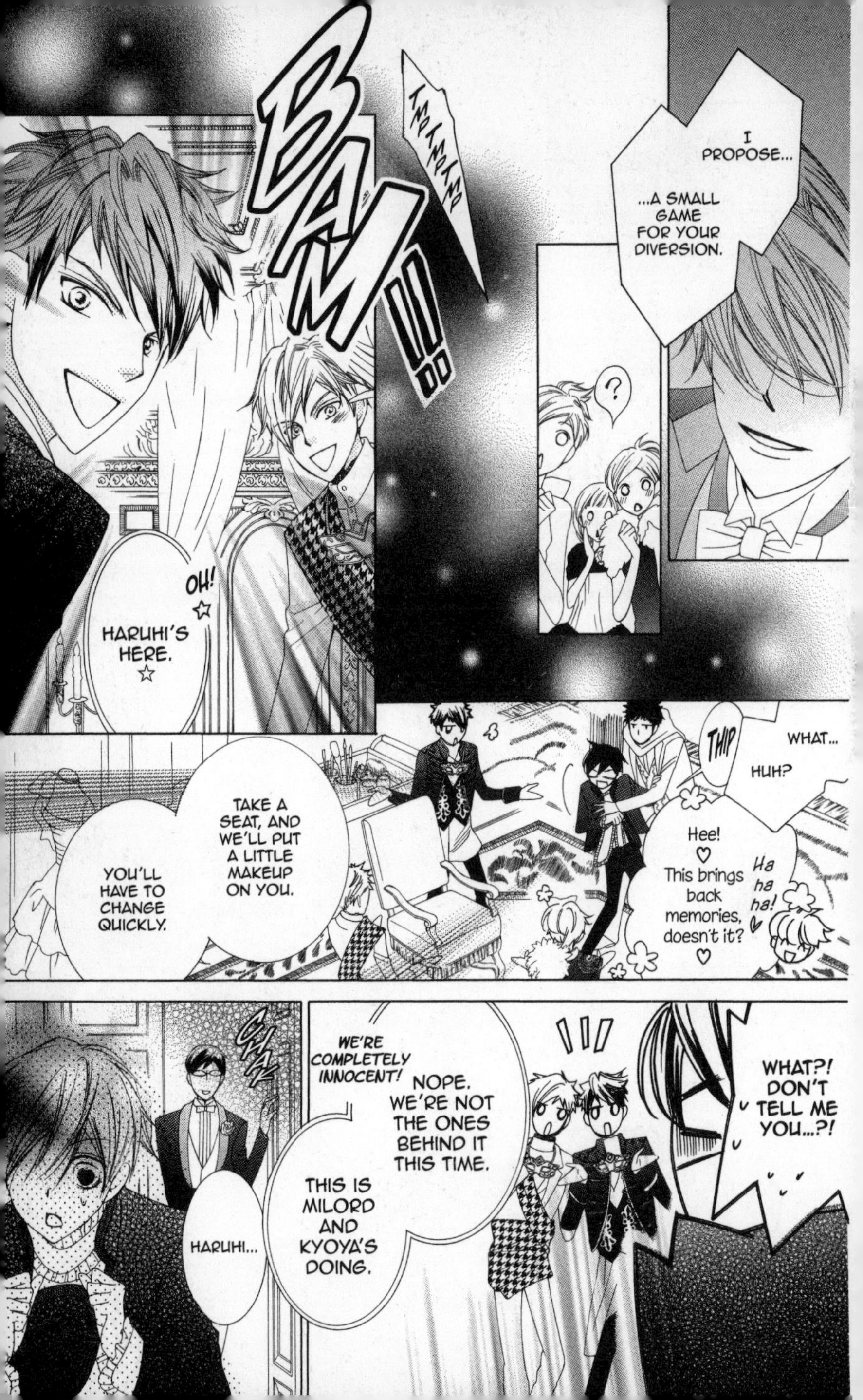
I PROPOSE...
...A SMALL GAME FOR YOUR DIVERSION.
?
BAM!!
OH! ☆
HARUHI'S HERE. ☆
WHAT...
HUH?
THIP
Hee! ♡ This brings back memories, doesn't it? ♡
Ha ha ha! ♡
TAKE A SEAT, AND WE'LL PUT A LITTLE MAKEUP ON YOU.
YOU'LL HAVE TO CHANGE QUICKLY.
WHAT?! DON'T TELL ME YOU...?!
WE'RE COMPLETELY INNOCENT!
NOPE. WE'RE NOT THE ONES BEHIND IT THIS TIME.
THIS IS MILORD AND KYOYA'S DOING.
CHAK
HARUHI...

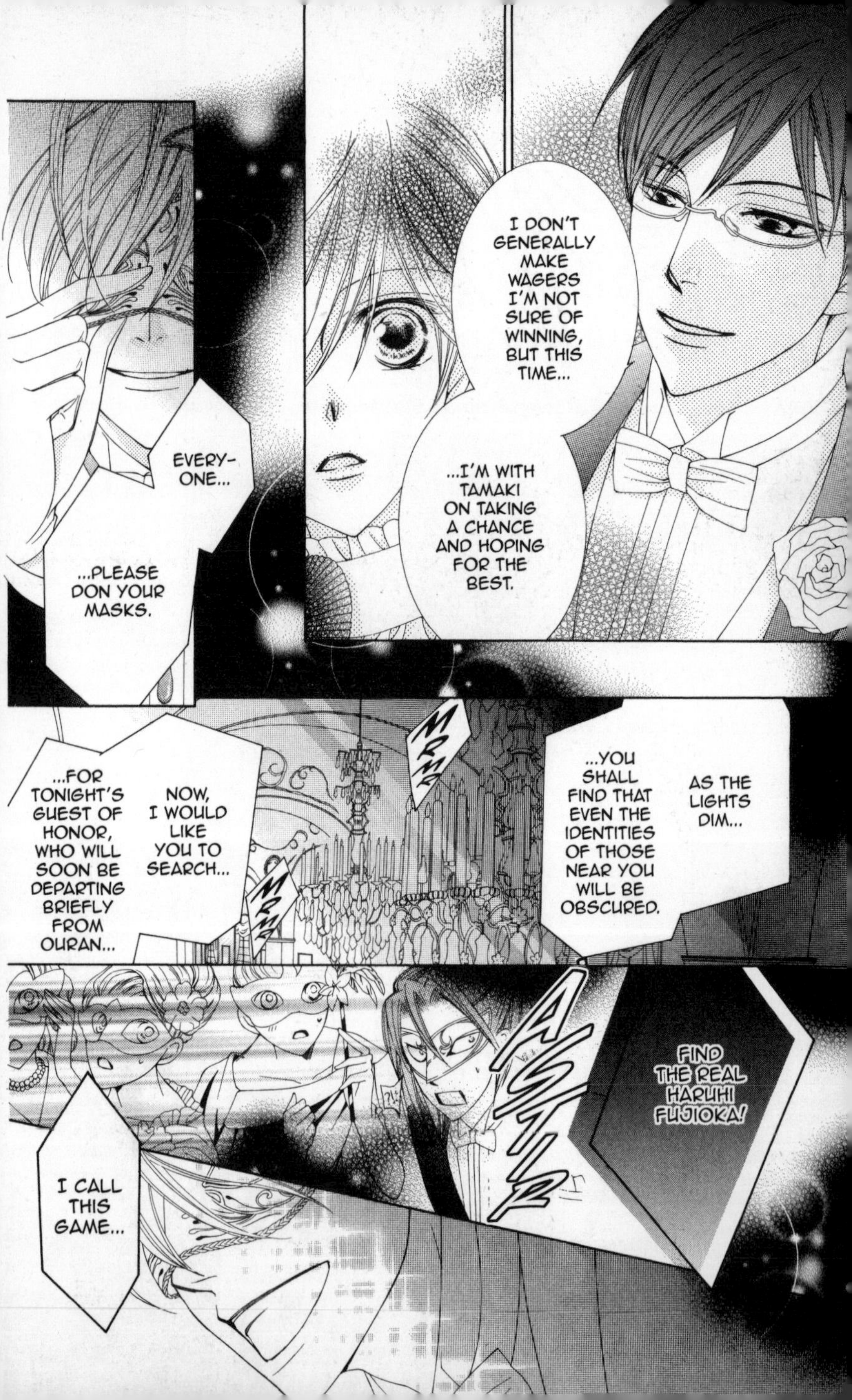
I DON'T GENERALLY MAKE WAGERS I'M NOT SURE OF WINNING, BUT THIS TIME...
...I'M WITH TAMAKI ON TAKING A CHANCE AND HOPING FOR THE BEST.
EVERY-ONE...
...PLEASE DON YOUR MASKS.
AS THE LIGHTS DIM...
...YOU SHALL FIND THAT EVEN THE IDENTITIES OF THOSE NEAR YOU WILL BE OBSCURED.
MRMR
MRMR
NOW, I WOULD LIKE YOU TO SEARCH...
...FOR TONIGHT'S GUEST OF HONOR, WHO WILL SOON BE DEPARTING BRIEFLY FROM OURAN...
I CALL THIS GAME...
FIND THE REAL HARUHI FUJIOKA!

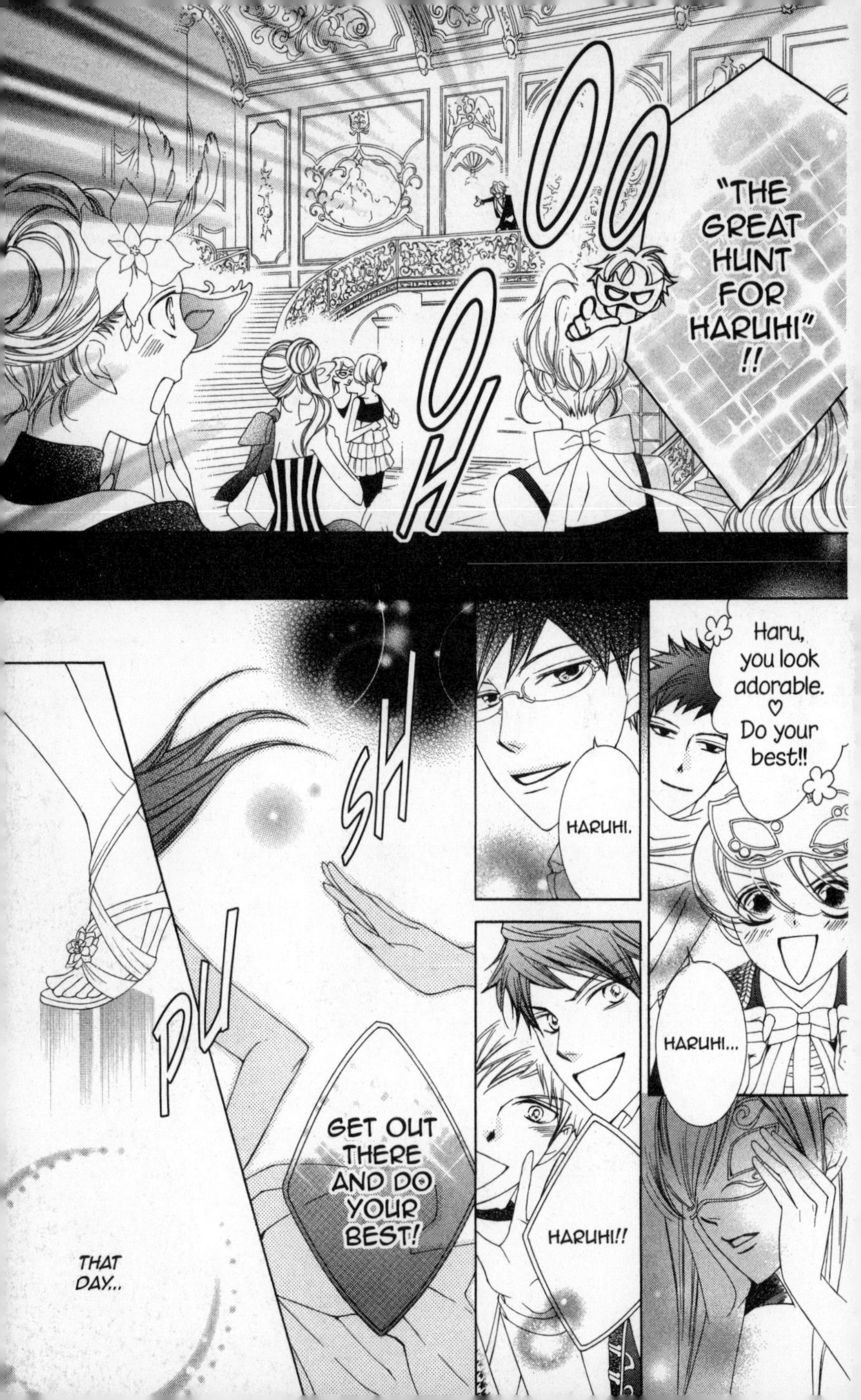
"THE GREAT HUNT FOR HARUHI" !!
Haru, you look adorable. ♡ Do your best!!
HARUHI...
HARUHI.
HARUHI!!
GET OUT THERE AND DO YOUR BEST!
SH
PU
THAT DAY...

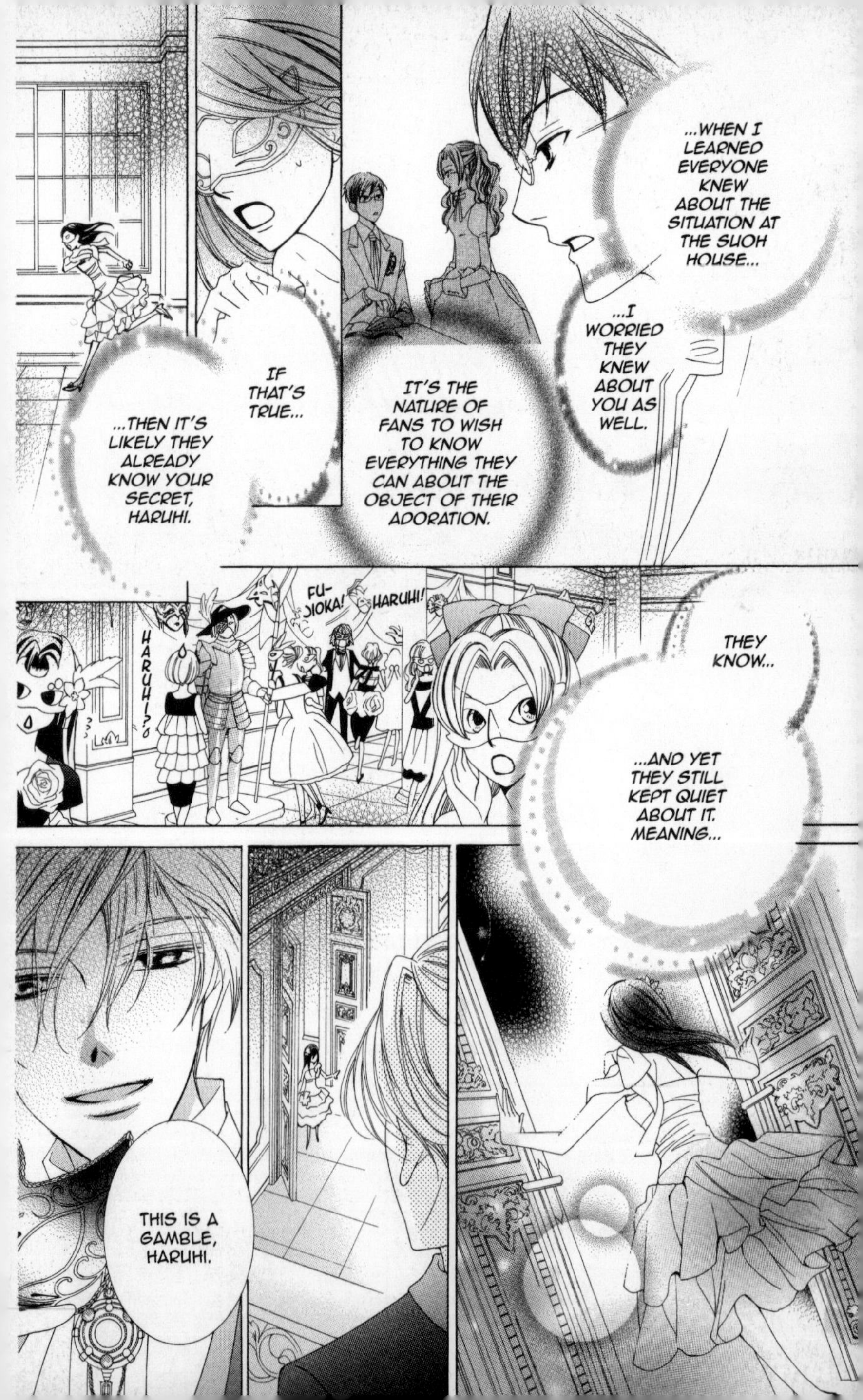
...WHEN I LEARNED EVERYONE KNEW ABOUT THE SITUATION AT THE SUOH HOUSE...
...I WORRIED THEY KNEW ABOUT YOU AS WELL.
IT'S THE NATURE OF FANS TO WISH TO KNOW EVERYTHING THEY CAN ABOUT THE OBJECT OF THEIR ADORATION.
IF THAT'S TRUE...
...THEN IT'S LIKELY THEY ALREADY KNOW YOUR SECRET, HARUHI.
THEY KNOW...
...AND YET THEY STILL KEPT QUIET ABOUT IT. MEANING...
HARUHI!
FU-IOKA!
HARUHI!?
THIS IS A GAMBLE, HARUHI.

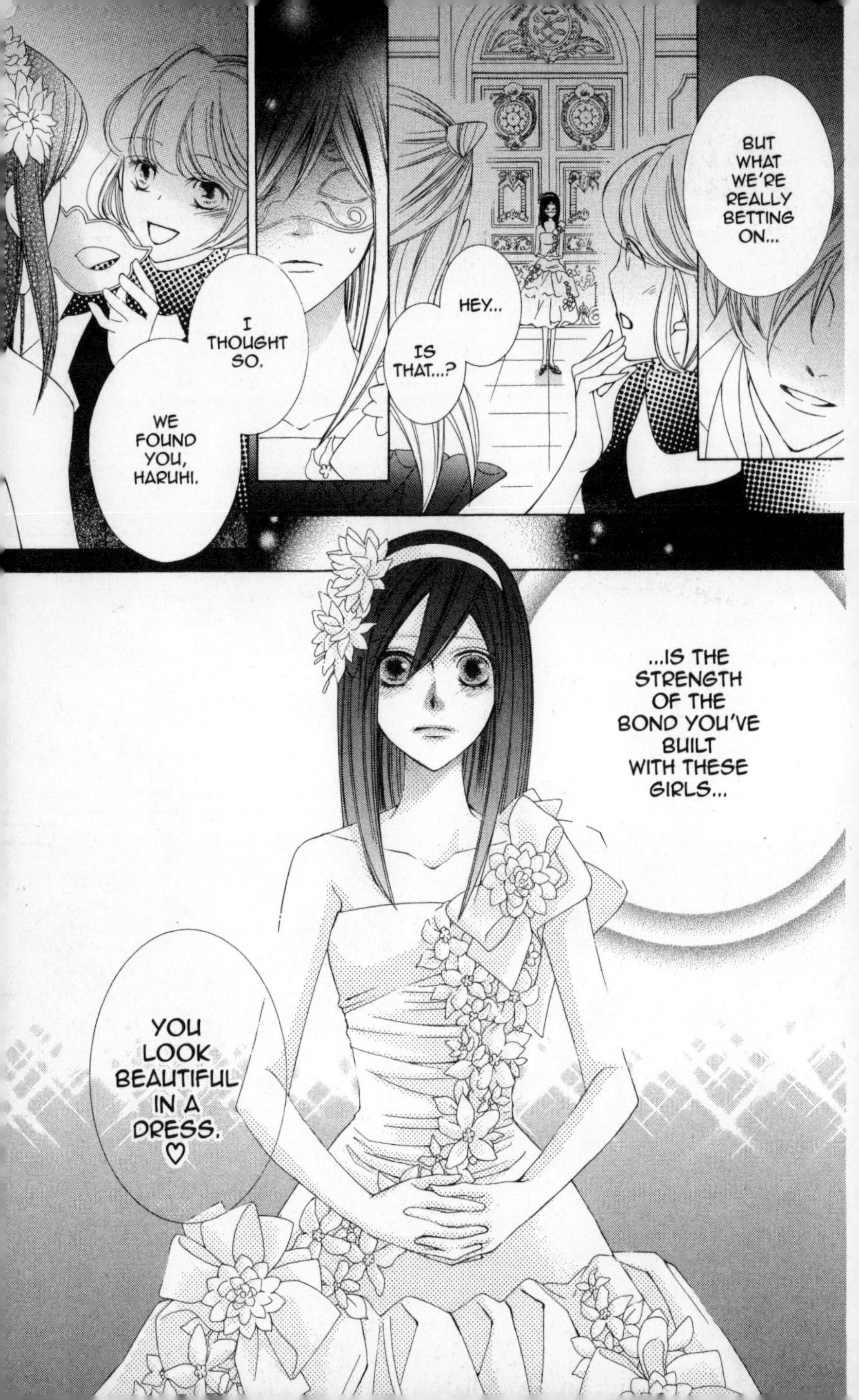
BUT WHAT WE'RE REALLY BETTING ON...
HEY...
IS THAT...?
I THOUGHT SO.
WE FOUND YOU, HARUHI.
...IS THE STRENGTH OF THE BOND YOU'VE BUILT WITH THESE GIRLS...
YOU LOOK BEAUTIFUL IN A DRESS. ♡

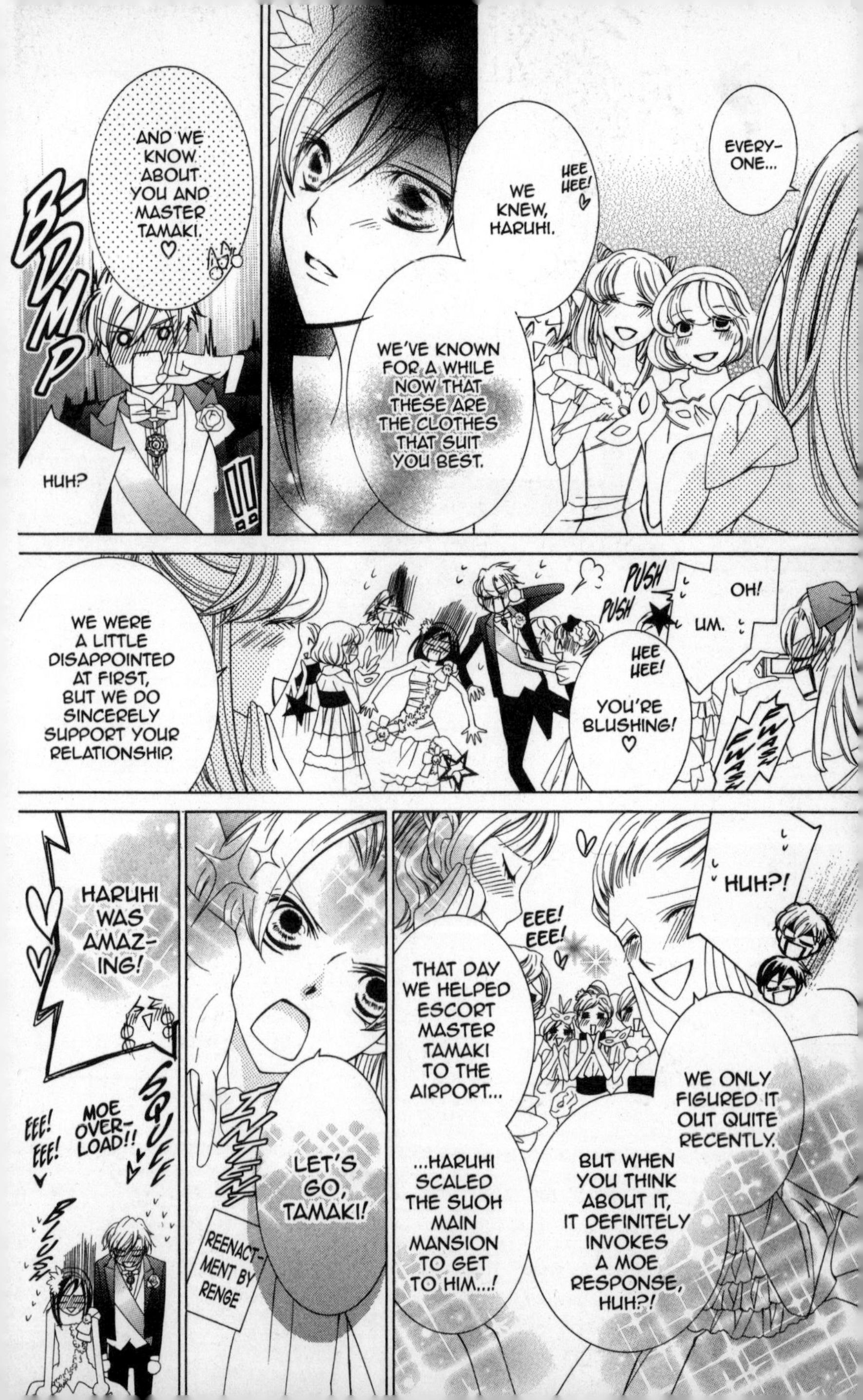
EVERY-ONE...
HEE HEE! ♥
WE KNEW, HARUHI.
WE'VE KNOWN FOR A WHILE NOW THAT THESE ARE THE CLOTHES THAT SUIT YOU BEST.
AND WE KNOW ABOUT YOU AND MASTER TAMAKI. ♥
B-DUMP
!!
HUH?
OH!
UM.
PUSH
PUSH
HEE HEE!
YOU'RE BLUSHING! ♥
FWASH FWASH
WE WERE A LITTLE DISAPPOINTED AT FIRST, BUT WE DO SINCERELY SUPPORT YOUR RELATIONSHIP.
HUH?!
EEE! EEE!
WE ONLY FIGURED IT OUT QUITE RECENTLY.
BUT WHEN YOU THINK ABOUT IT, IT DEFINITELY INVOKES A MOE RESPONSE, HUH?!
THAT DAY WE HELPED ESCORT MASTER TAMAKI TO THE AIRPORT...
...HARUHI SCALED THE SUOH MAIN MANSION TO GET TO HIM...!
LET'S GO, TAMAKI!
REENACT-MENT BY RENGE
HARUHI WAS AMAZ-ING!
SQUEE
MOE OVER-LOAD!!
EEE! EEE!
BLUSH

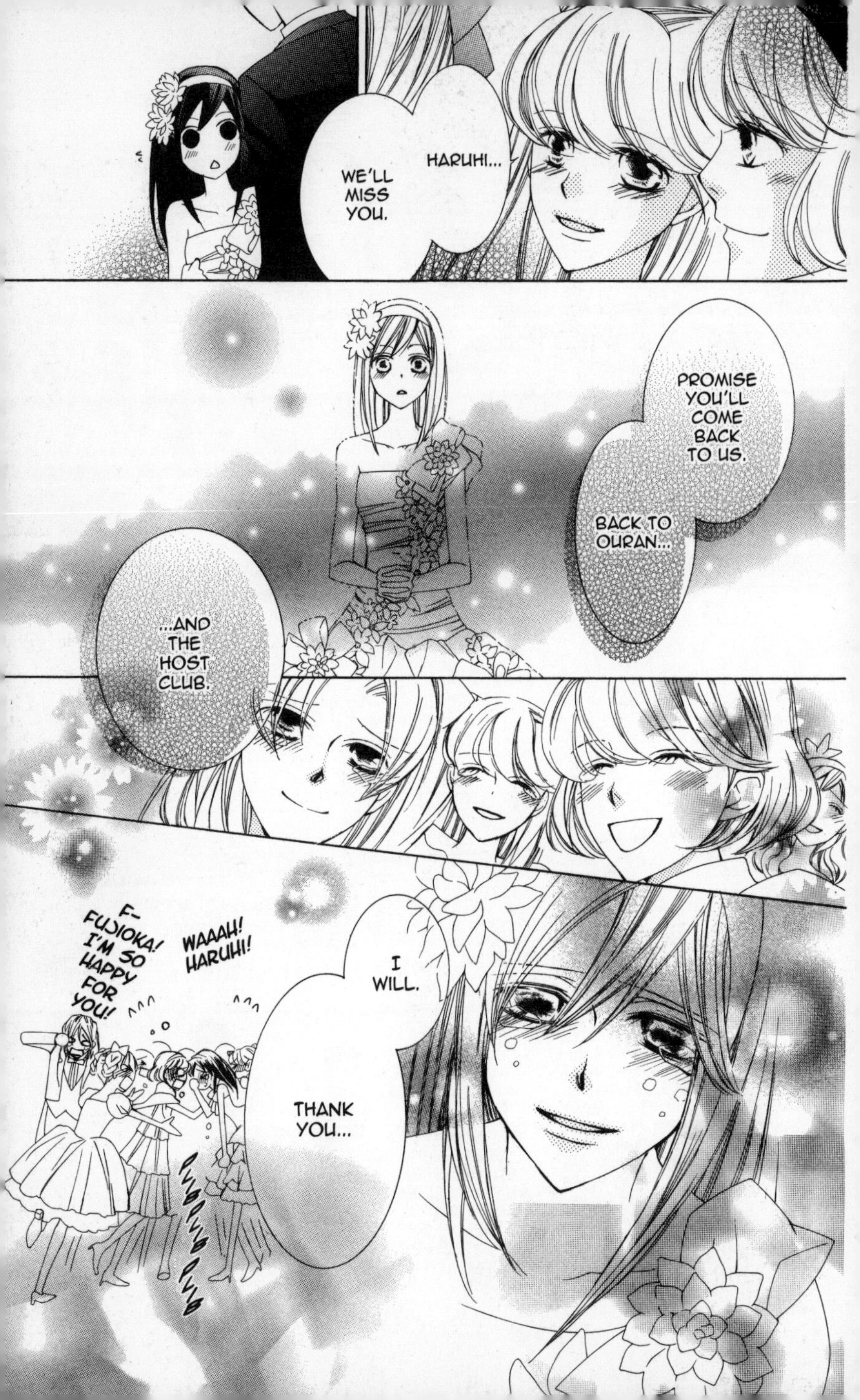
HARUHI...
WE'LL MISS YOU.
PROMISE YOU'LL COME BACK TO US.
BACK TO OURAN...
...AND THE HOST CLUB.
I WILL.
THANK YOU...
WAAAH! HARUHI!
F-FUJIOKA! I'M SO HAPPY FOR YOU!

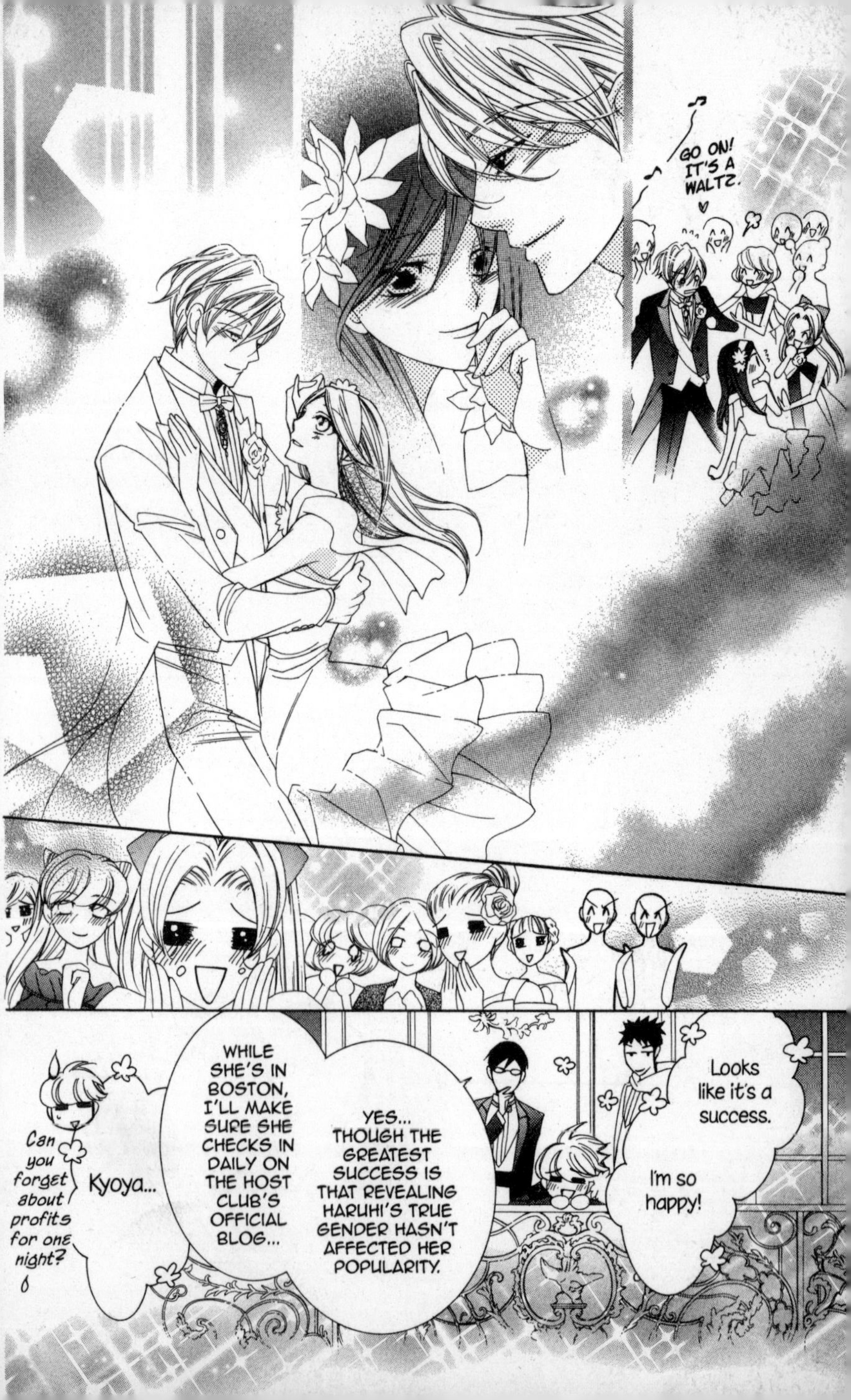
GO ON! IT'S A WALTZ.
Looks like it's a success.
I'm so happy!
YES... THOUGH THE GREATEST SUCCESS IS THAT REVEALING HARUHI'S TRUE GENDER HASN'T AFFECTED HER POPULARITY.
WHILE SHE'S IN BOSTON, I'LL MAKE SURE SHE CHECKS IN DAILY ON THE HOST CLUB'S OFFICIAL BLOG...
Kyoya...
Can you forget about profits for one night?

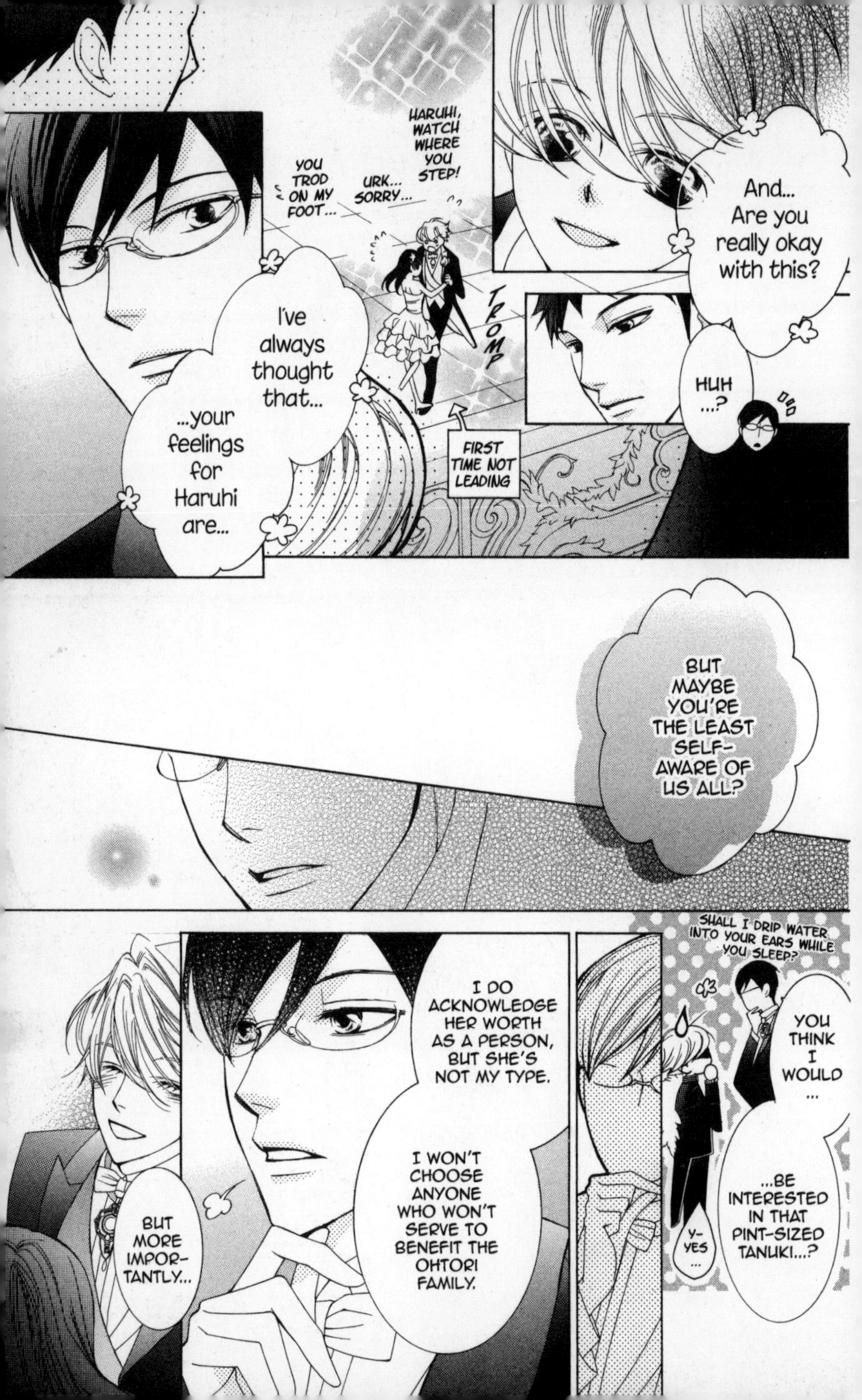
And... Are you really okay with this?
HUH ...?
HARUHI, WATCH WHERE YOU STEP!
URK... SORRY...
YOU TROD ON MY FOOT...
TROMP
FIRST TIME NOT LEADING
I've always thought that...
...your feelings for Haruhi are...
BUT MAYBE YOU'RE THE LEAST SELF-AWARE OF US ALL?
SHALL I DRIP WATER INTO YOUR EARS WHILE YOU SLEEP?
YOU THINK I WOULD ...
...BE INTERESTED IN THAT PINT-SIZED TANUKI...?
Y-YES ...
I DO ACKNOWLEDGE HER WORTH AS A PERSON, BUT SHE'S NOT MY TYPE.
I WON'T CHOOSE ANYONE WHO WON'T SERVE TO BENEFIT THE OHTORI FAMILY.
BUT MORE IMPORTANTLY...

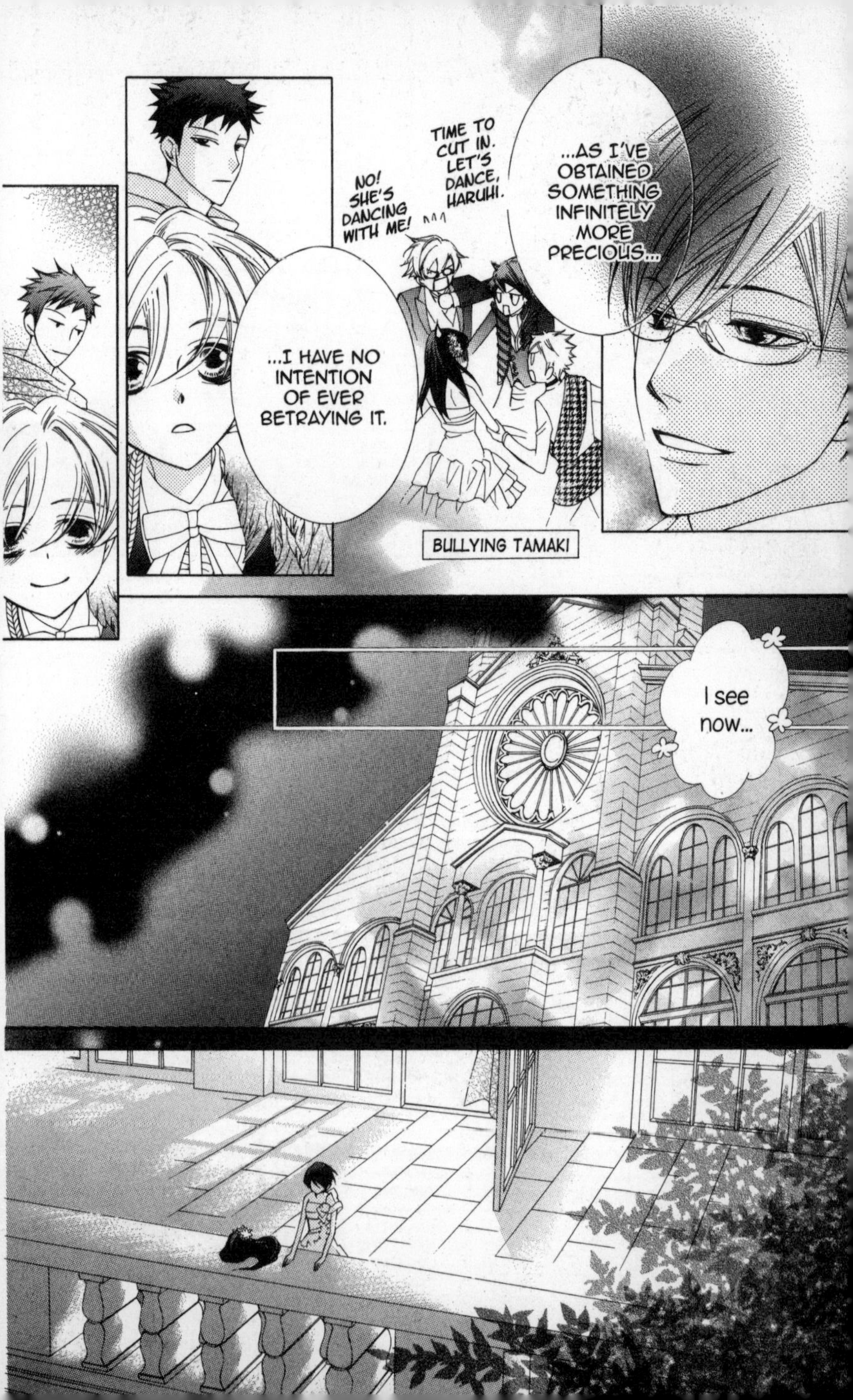
...AS I'VE OBTAINED SOMETHING INFINITELY MORE PRECIOUS...
TIME TO CUT IN. LET'S DANCE, HARUHI.
NO! SHE'S DANCING WITH ME!
...I HAVE NO INTENTION OF EVER BETRAYING IT.
BULLYING TAMAKI
I see now...

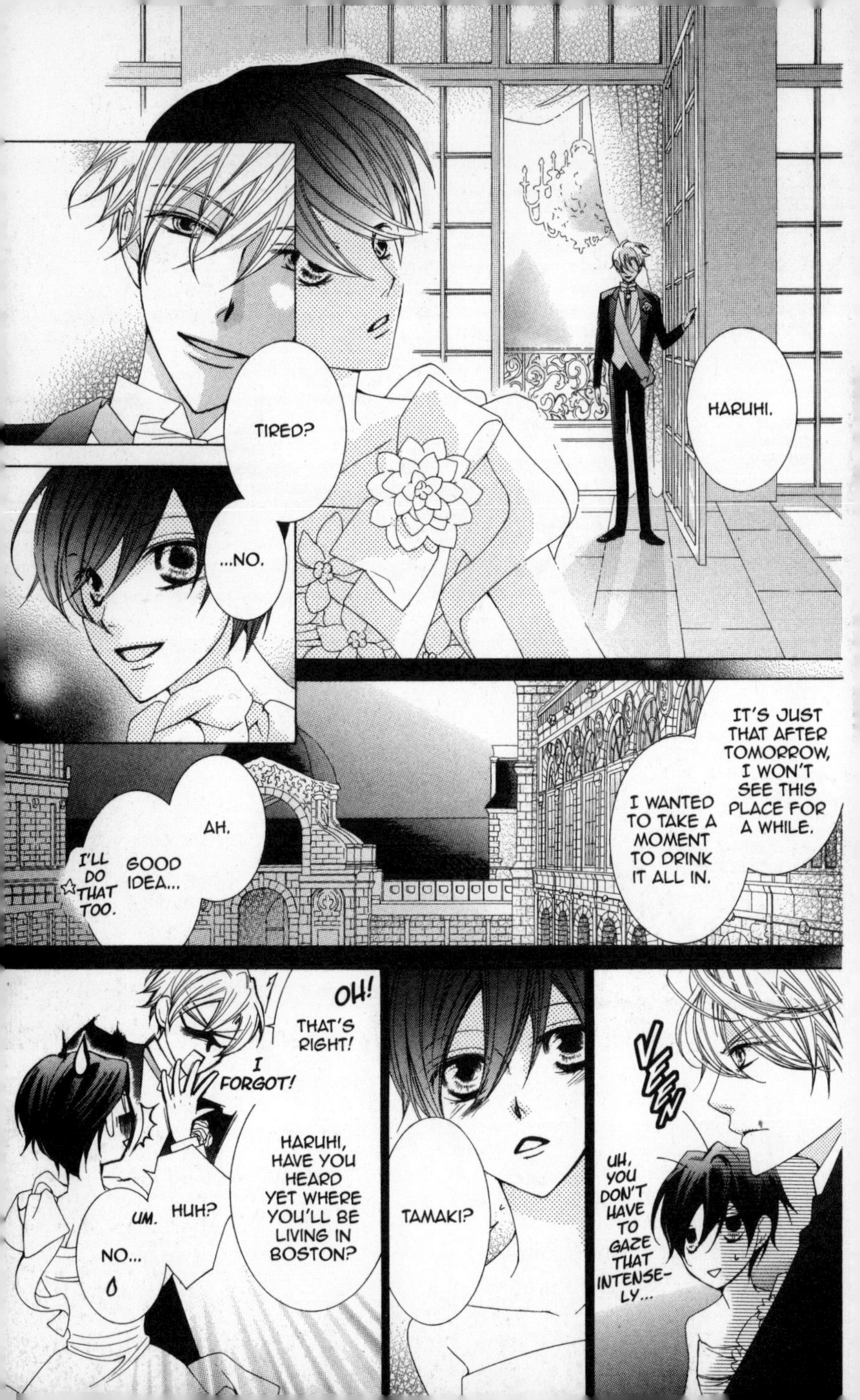
HARUHI.
TIRED?
...NO.
IT'S JUST THAT AFTER TOMORROW, I WON'T SEE THIS PLACE FOR A WHILE.
I WANTED TO TAKE A MOMENT TO DRINK IT ALL IN.
AH.
GOOD IDEA...
I'LL DO THAT TOO. ☆
UH, YOU DON'T HAVE TO GAZE THAT INTENSE-LY...
TAMAKI?
OH! THAT'S RIGHT! I FORGOT!
HARUHI, HAVE YOU HEARD YET WHERE YOU'LL BE LIVING IN BOSTON?
HUH?
UM.
NO...

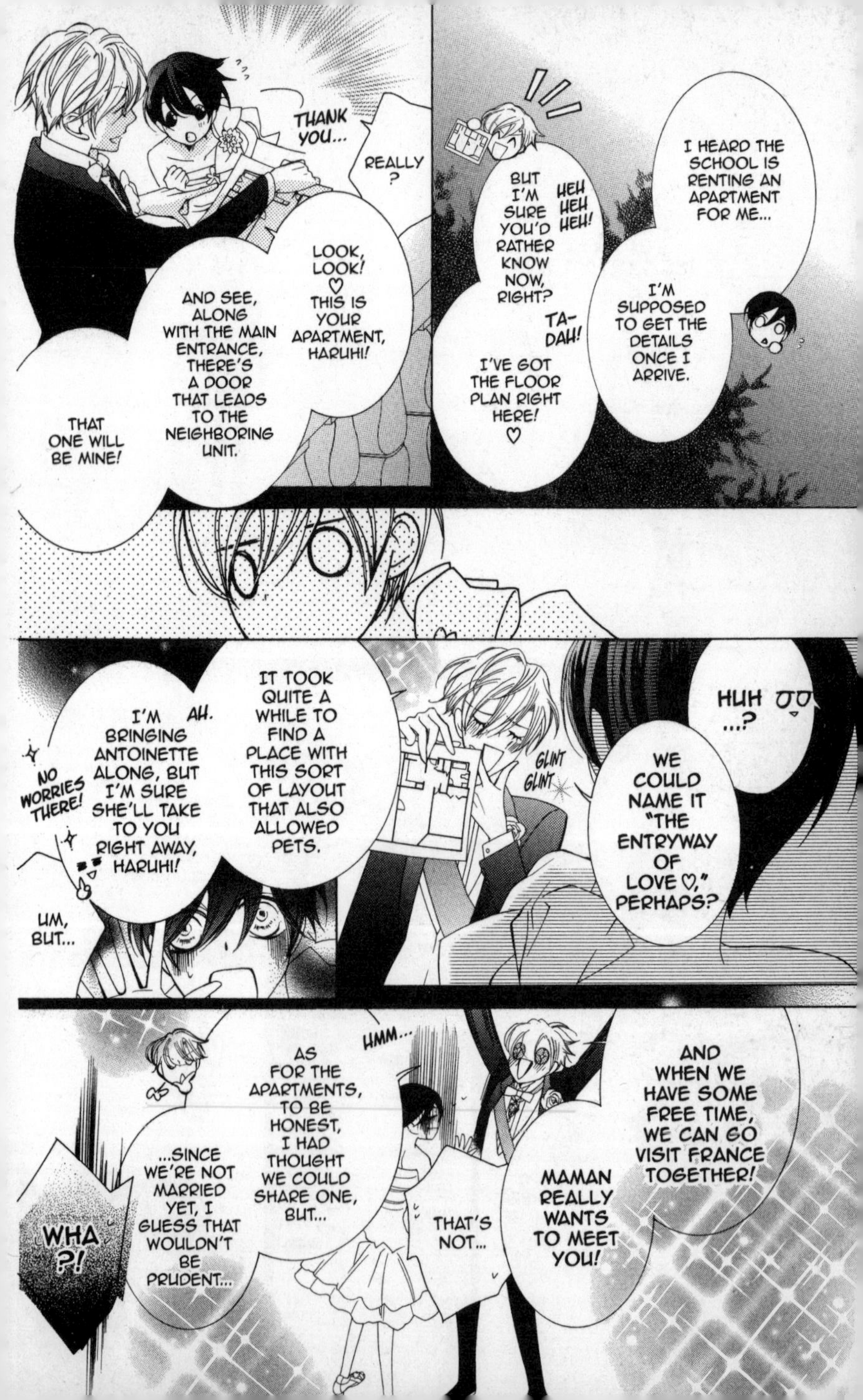
I HEARD THE SCHOOL IS RENTING AN APARTMENT FOR ME...
I'M SUPPOSED TO GET THE DETAILS ONCE I ARRIVE.
BUT I'M SURE YOU'D RATHER KNOW NOW, RIGHT?
HEH HEH HEH!
TA-DAH!
I'VE GOT THE FLOOR PLAN RIGHT HERE! ♡
THANK YOU...
REALLY?
LOOK, LOOK! ♡ THIS IS YOUR APARTMENT, HARUHI!
AND SEE, ALONG WITH THE MAIN ENTRANCE, THERE'S A DOOR THAT LEADS TO THE NEIGHBORING UNIT.
THAT ONE WILL BE MINE!
HUH ...?
WE COULD NAME IT "THE ENTRYWAY OF LOVE ♡," PERHAPS?
GLINT GLINT
IT TOOK QUITE A WHILE TO FIND A PLACE WITH THIS SORT OF LAYOUT THAT ALSO ALLOWED PETS.
AH.
I'M BRINGING ANTOINETTE ALONG, BUT I'M SURE SHE'LL TAKE TO YOU RIGHT AWAY, HARUHI!
NO WORRIES THERE!
UM, BUT...
AND WHEN WE HAVE SOME FREE TIME, WE CAN GO VISIT FRANCE TOGETHER!
MAMAN REALLY WANTS TO MEET YOU!
THAT'S NOT...
HMM...
AS FOR THE APARTMENTS, TO BE HONEST, I HAD THOUGHT WE COULD SHARE ONE, BUT...
...SINCE WE'RE NOT MARRIED YET, I GUESS THAT WOULDN'T BE PRUDENT...
WHA ?!

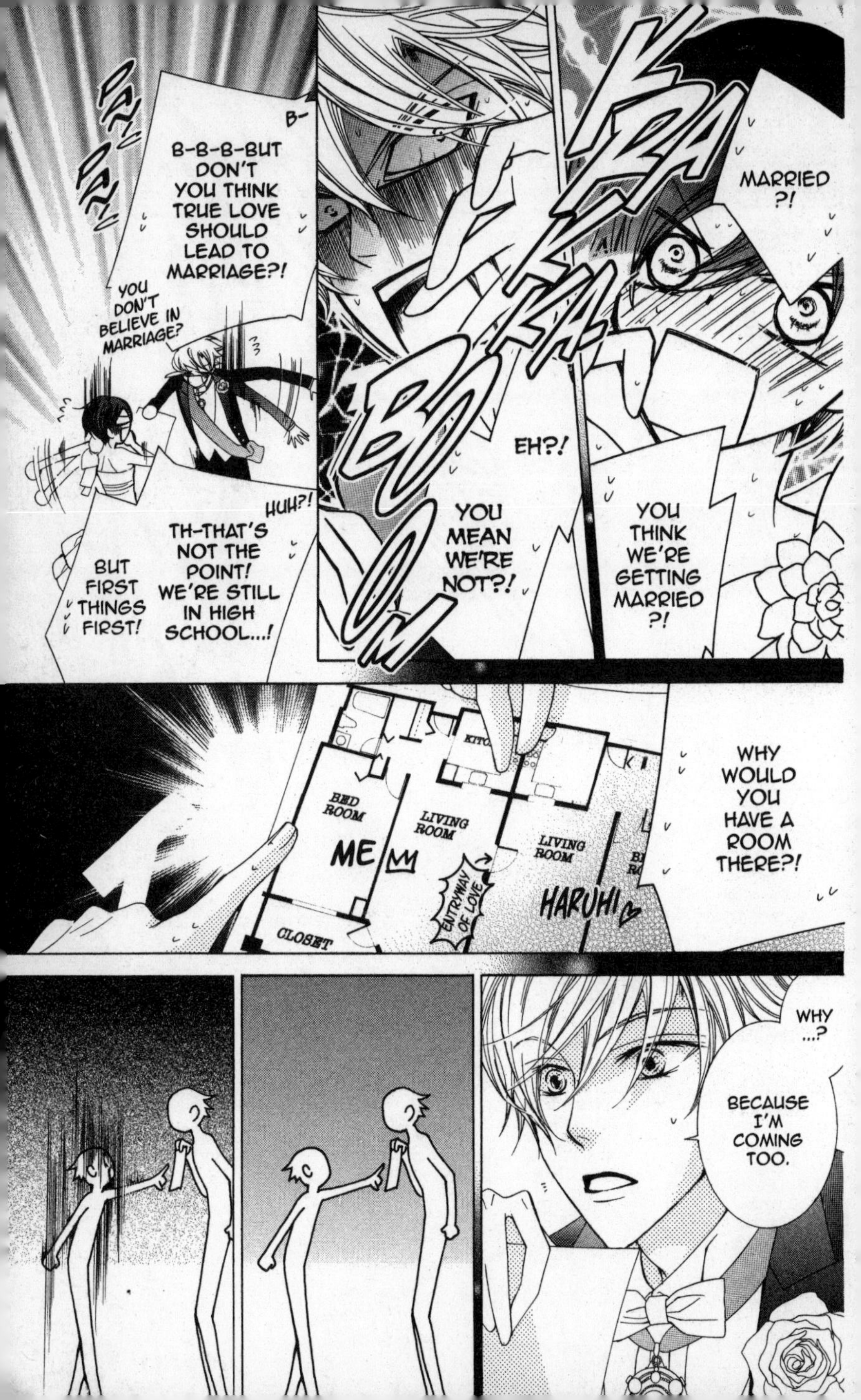
MARRIED ?!
KAKABOOM
YOU THINK WE'RE GETTING MARRIED ?!
EH?!
YOU MEAN WE'RE NOT?!
B-
B-B-B-BUT DON'T YOU THINK TRUE LOVE SHOULD LEAD TO MARRIAGE?!
YOU DON'T BELIEVE IN MARRIAGE?
HUH?!
TH-THAT'S NOT THE POINT! WE'RE STILL IN HIGH SCHOOL...!
BUT FIRST THINGS FIRST!
WHY WOULD YOU HAVE A ROOM THERE?!
BED ROOM
LIVING ROOM
ME
LIVING ROOM
HARUHI
ENTRYWAY OF LOVE
CLOSET
WHY ...?
BECAUSE I'M COMING TOO.

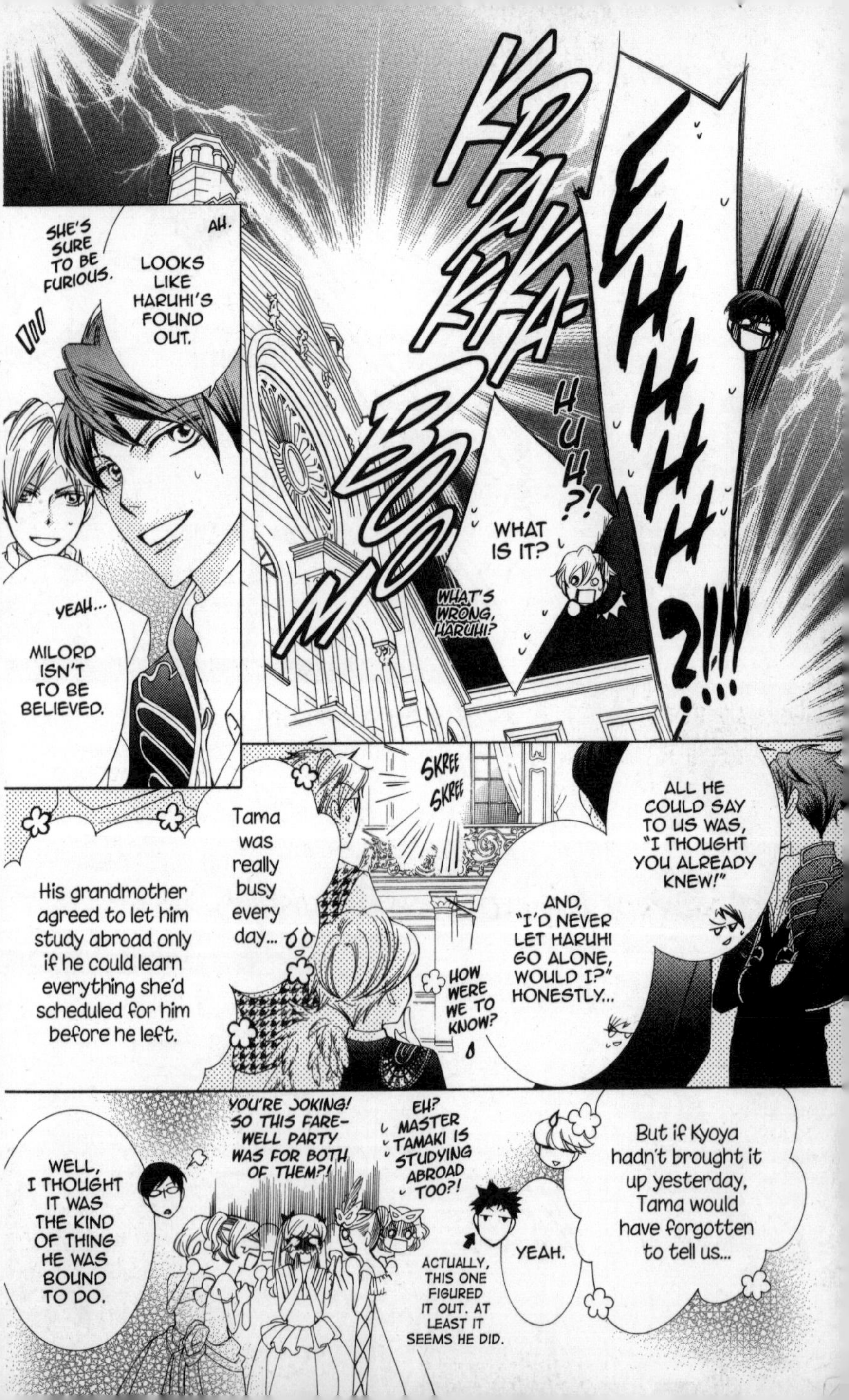
EHHHHH?!!!
KRAKKA-BOOM
HUH?!
WHAT IS IT?
WHAT'S WRONG, HARUHI?
AH.
LOOKS LIKE HARUHI'S FOUND OUT.
SHE'S SURE TO BE FURIOUS.
YEAH...
MILORD ISN'T TO BE BELIEVED.
ALL HE COULD SAY TO US WAS, "I THOUGHT YOU ALREADY KNEW!"
AND, "I'D NEVER LET HARUHI GO ALONE, WOULD I?" HONESTLY...
HOW WERE WE TO KNOW?
SKREE SKREE
Tama was really busy every day...
His grandmother agreed to let him study abroad only if he could learn everything she'd scheduled for him before he left.
But if Kyoya hadn't brought it up yesterday, Tama would have forgotten to tell us...
YEAH.
ACTUALLY, THIS ONE FIGURED IT OUT. AT LEAST IT SEEMS HE DID.
EH? MASTER TAMAKI IS STUDYING ABROAD TOO?!
YOU'RE JOKING! SO THIS FAREWELL PARTY WAS FOR BOTH OF THEM?!
WELL, I THOUGHT IT WAS THE KIND OF THING HE WAS BOUND TO DO.

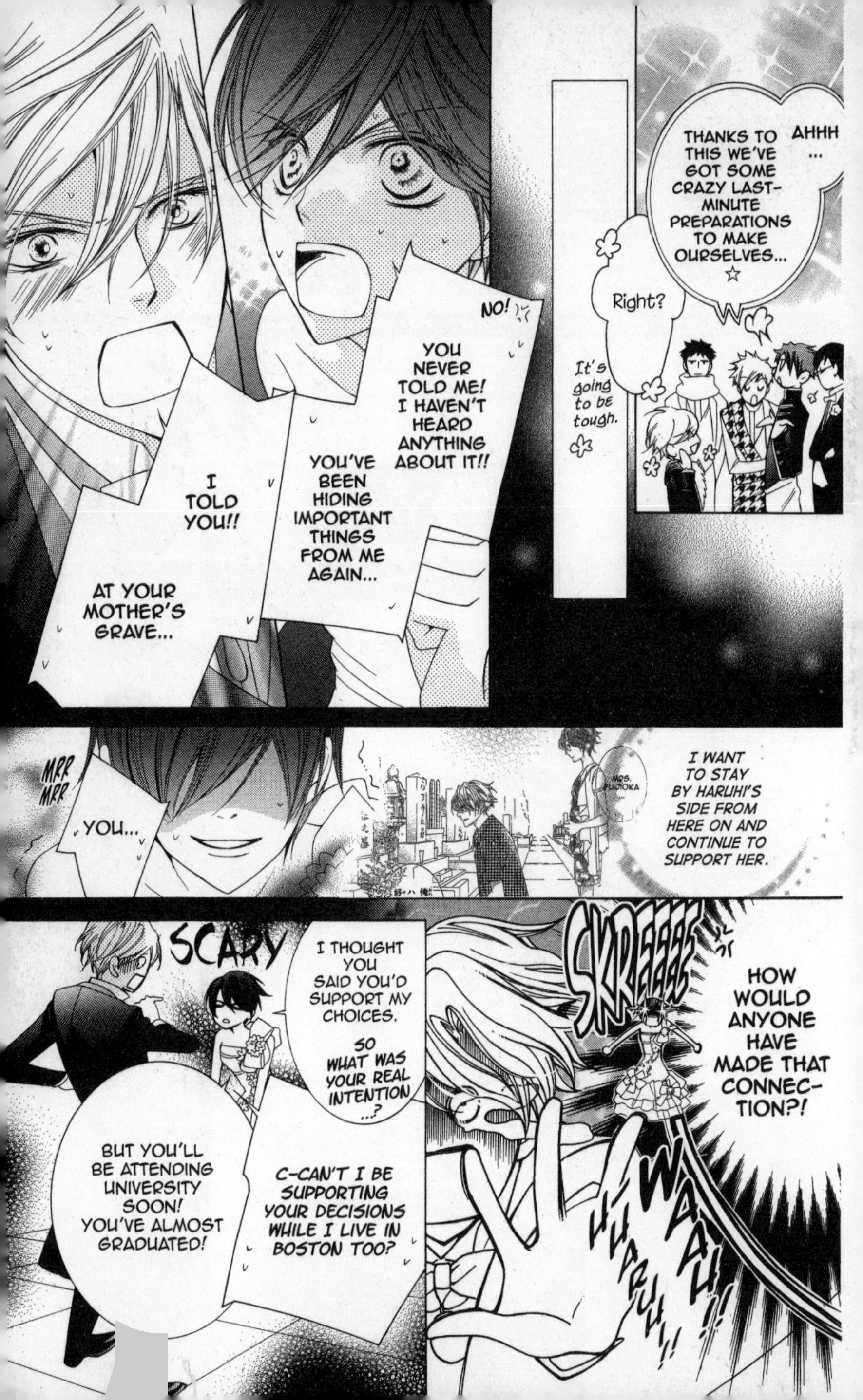
THANKS TO THIS WE'VE GOT SOME CRAZY LAST-MINUTE PREPARATIONS TO MAKE OURSELVES... ☆
AHHH ...
Right?
It's going to be tough.
NO!
YOU NEVER TOLD ME! I HAVEN'T HEARD ANYTHING ABOUT IT!!
YOU'VE BEEN HIDING IMPORTANT THINGS FROM ME AGAIN...
I TOLD YOU!!
AT YOUR MOTHER'S GRAVE...
I WANT TO STAY BY HARUHI'S SIDE FROM HERE ON AND CONTINUE TO SUPPORT HER.
MRS. FUJIOKA
MRR MRR
YOU...
HOW WOULD ANYONE HAVE MADE THAT CONNECTION?!
WAAH!!
H-HARUHI!!
SCARY
I THOUGHT YOU SAID YOU'D SUPPORT MY CHOICES.
SO WHAT WAS YOUR REAL INTENTION ...?
C-CAN'T I BE SUPPORTING YOUR DECISIONS WHILE I LIVE IN BOSTON TOO?
BUT YOU'LL BE ATTENDING UNIVERSITY SOON! YOU'VE ALMOST GRADUATED!

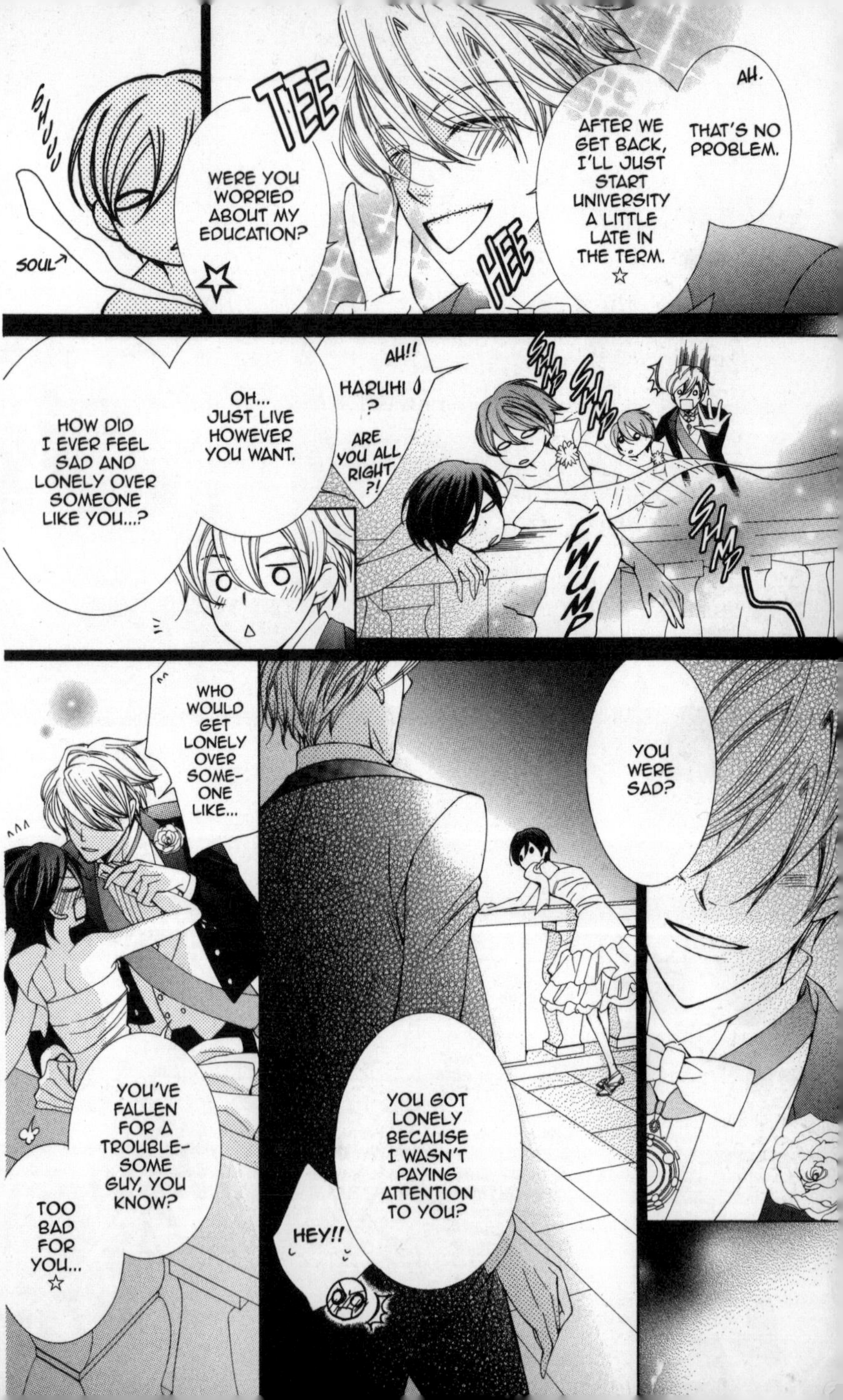
AH.
THAT'S NO PROBLEM.
AFTER WE GET BACK, I'LL JUST START UNIVERSITY A LITTLE LATE IN THE TERM. ☆
HEE
TEE
WERE YOU WORRIED ABOUT MY EDUCATION? ☆
SHUUU
SOUL
AH!!
HARUHI?
ARE YOU ALL RIGHT?!
OH... JUST LIVE HOWEVER YOU WANT.
HOW DID I EVER FEEL SAD AND LONELY OVER SOMEONE LIKE YOU...?
FWUMP
YOU WERE SAD?
YOU GOT LONELY BECAUSE I WASN'T PAYING ATTENTION TO YOU?
HEY!!
WHO WOULD GET LONELY OVER SOME-ONE LIKE...
YOU'VE FALLEN FOR A TROUBLE-SOME GUY, YOU KNOW?
TOO BAD FOR YOU... ☆

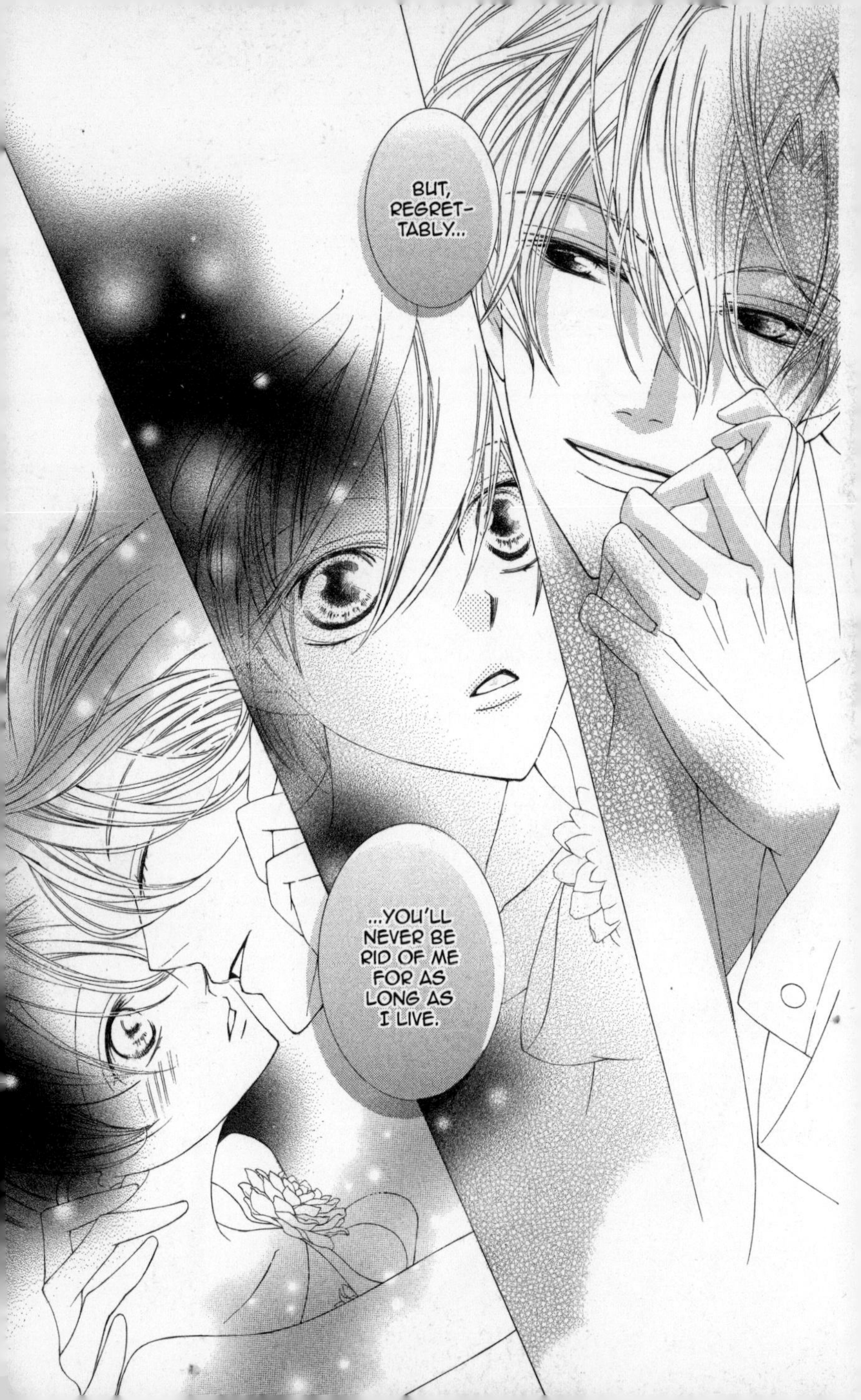
BUT, REGRET-TABLY...
...YOU'LL NEVER BE RID OF ME FOR AS LONG AS I LIVE.

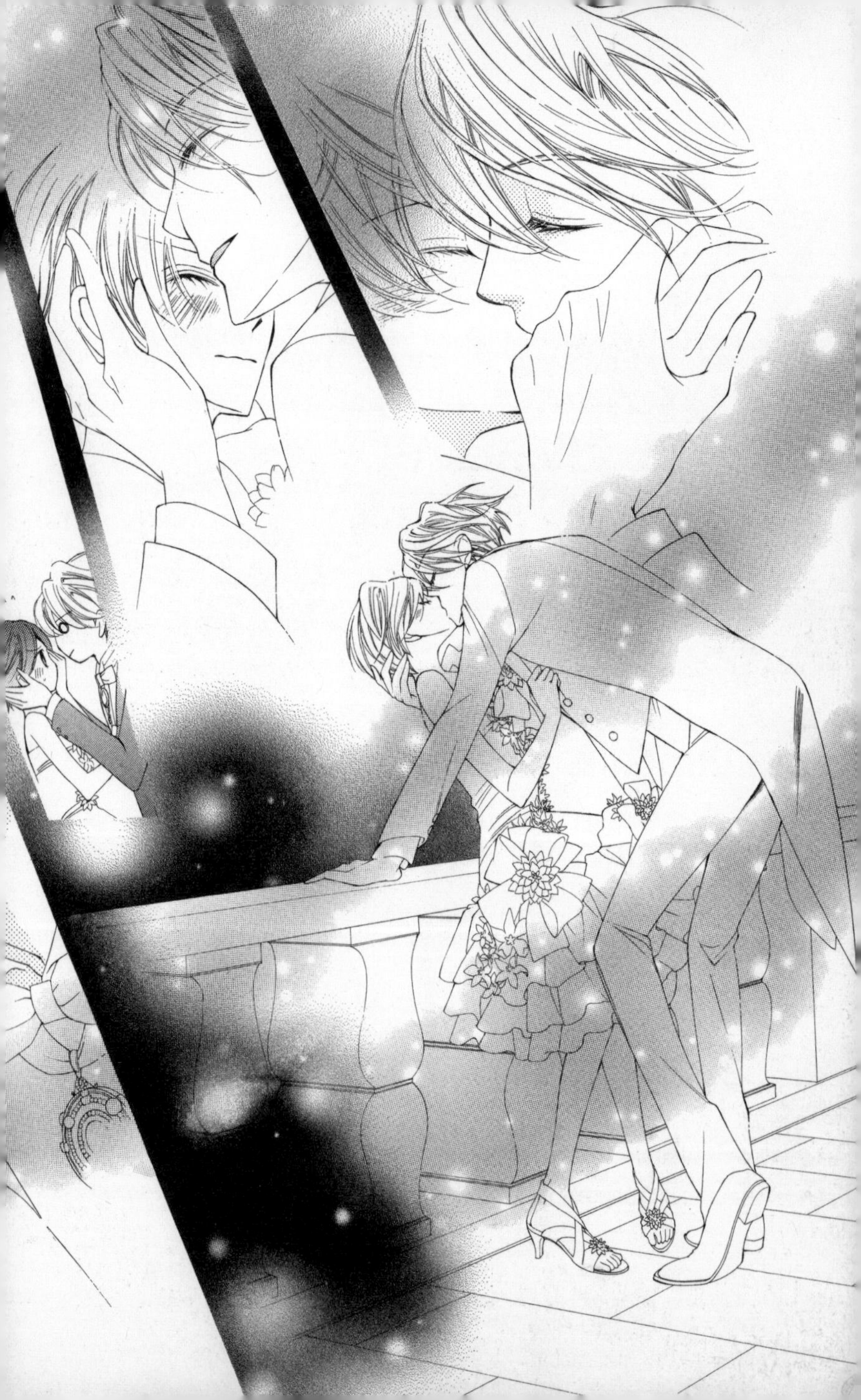

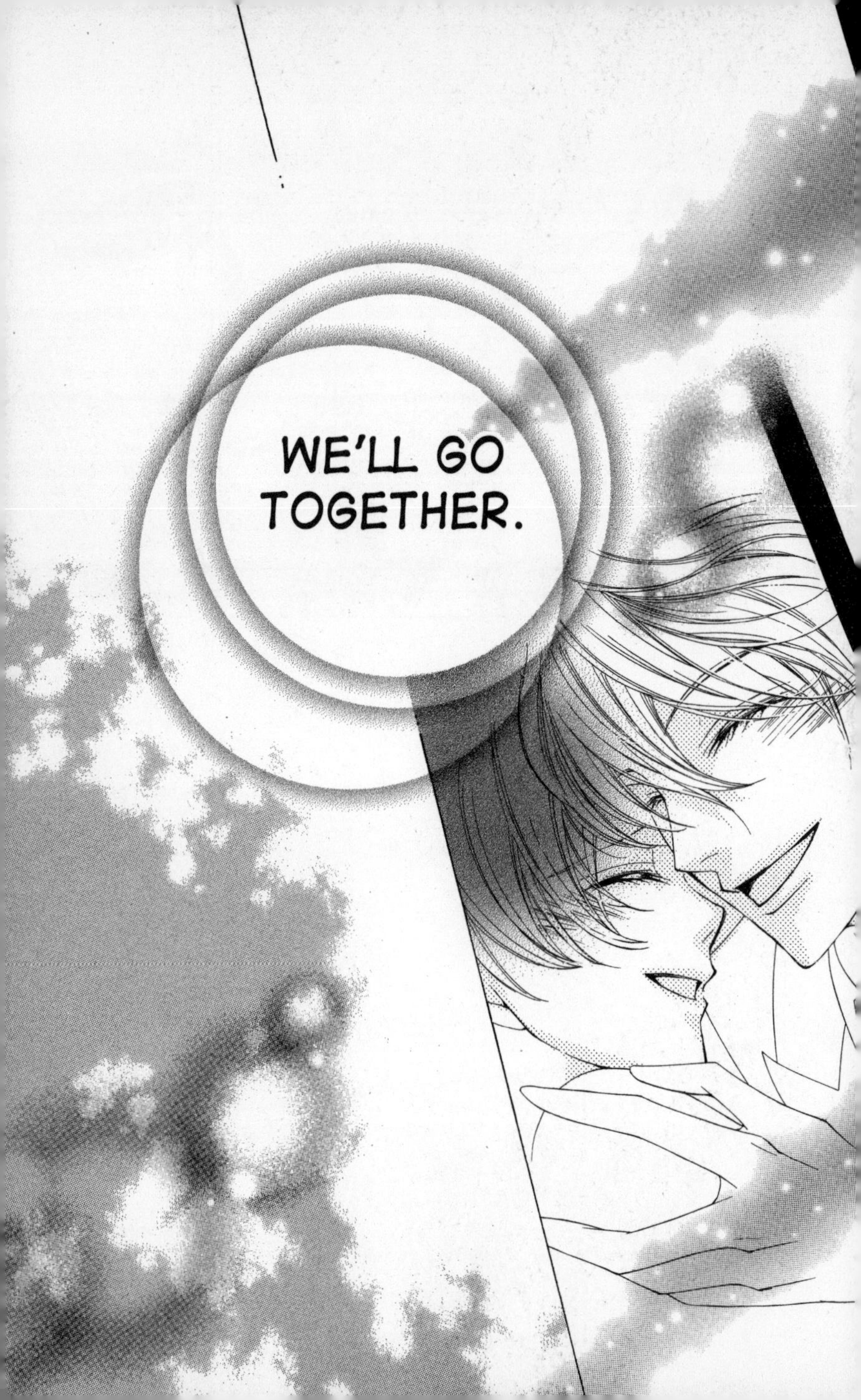
WE'LL GO TOGETHER.

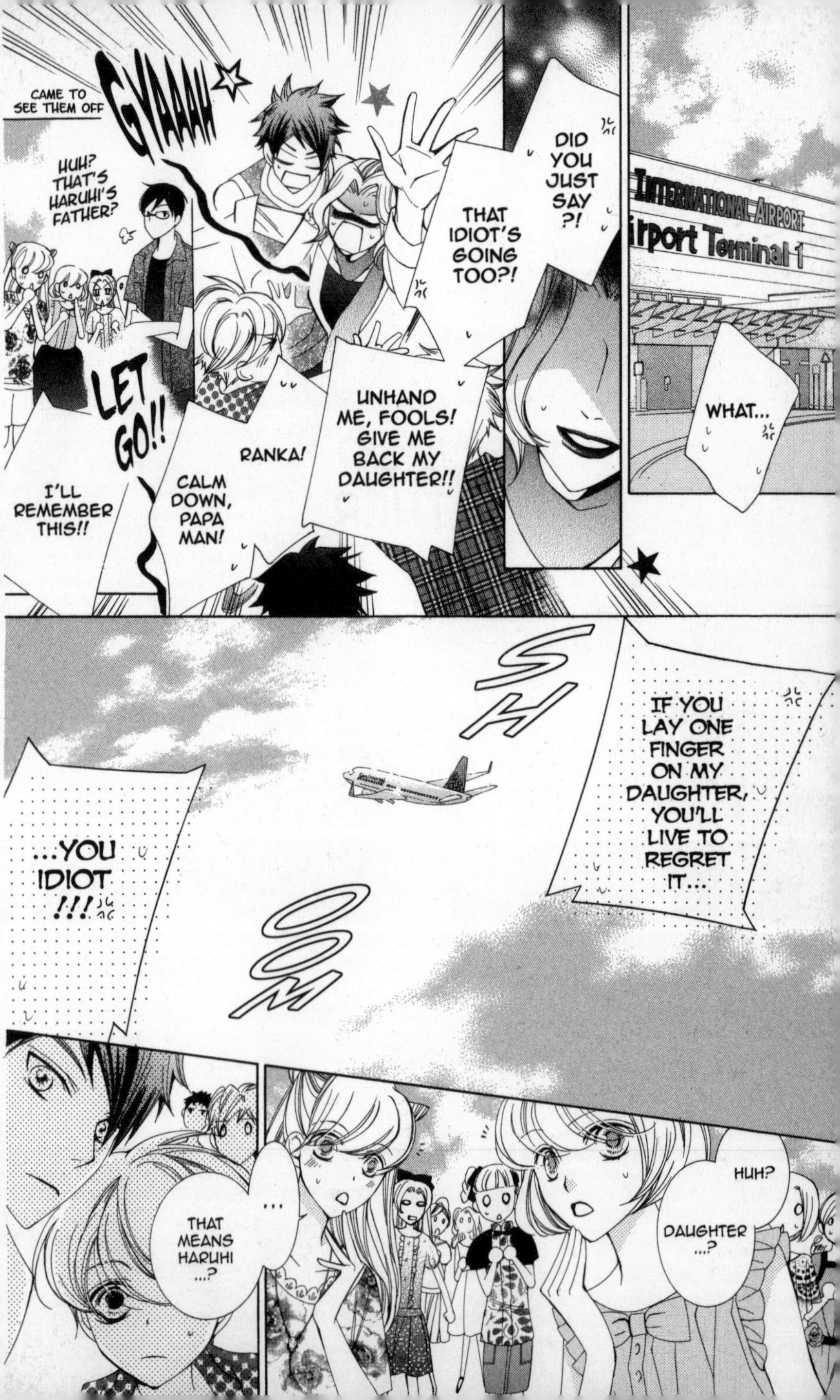
INTERNATIONAL AIRPORT
irport Terminal 1
WHAT...
DID YOU JUST SAY?!
THAT IDIOT'S GOING TOO?!
GYAAAH
CAME TO SEE THEM OFF
HUH? THAT'S HARUHI'S FATHER?
UNHAND ME, FOOLS! GIVE ME BACK MY DAUGHTER!!
RANKA!
LET GO!!
CALM DOWN, PAPA MAN!
I'LL REMEMBER THIS!!
IF YOU LAY ONE FINGER ON MY DAUGHTER, YOU'LL LIVE TO REGRET IT...
SHOOM
...YOU IDIOT!!!
HUH?
DAUGHTER...?
...
THAT MEANS HARUHI...?

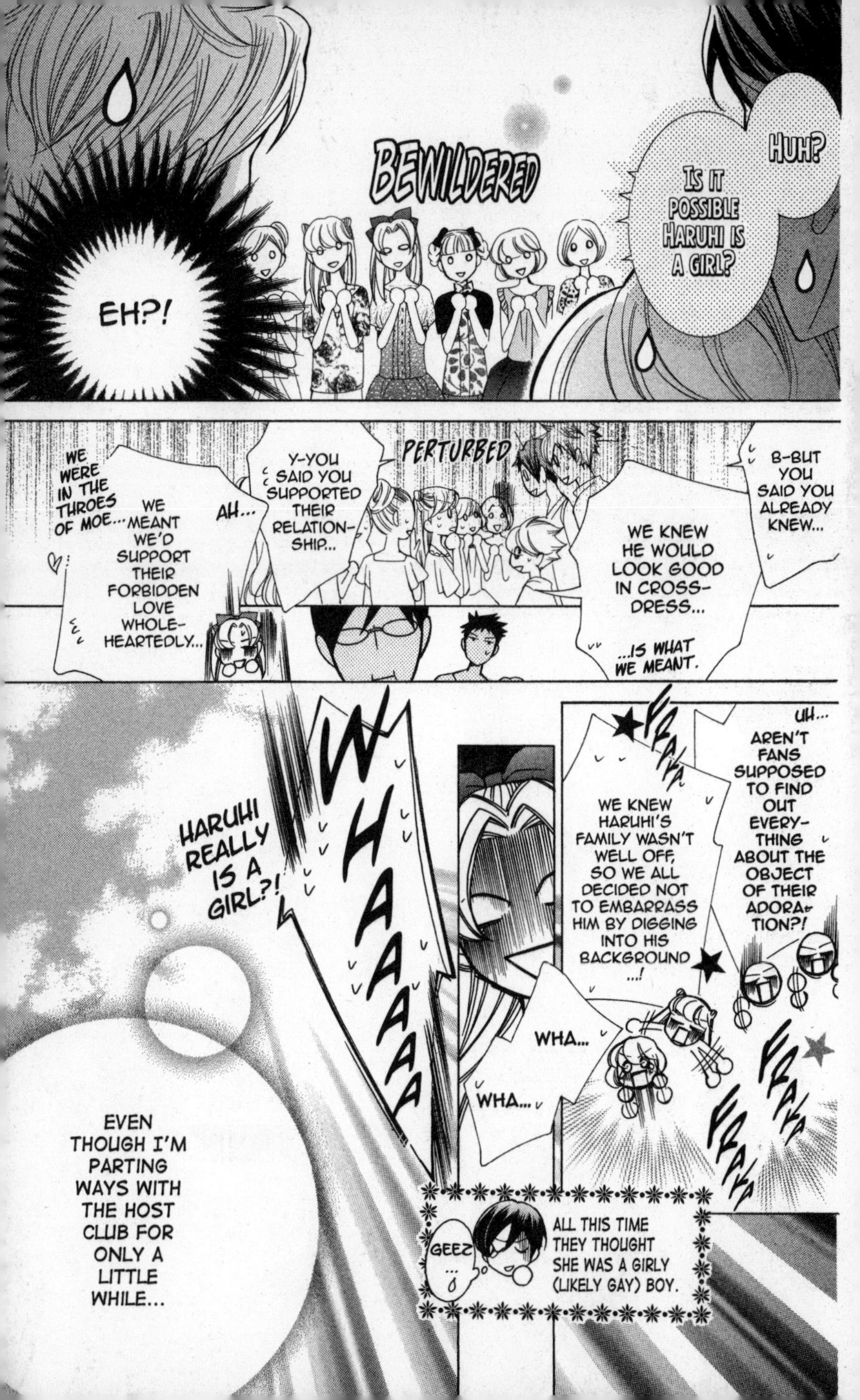
HUH?
IS IT POSSIBLE HARUHI IS A GIRL?
BEWILDERED
EH?!
B-BUT YOU SAID YOU ALREADY KNEW...
WE KNEW HE WOULD LOOK GOOD IN CROSS-DRESS...
...IS WHAT WE MEANT.
PERTURBED
Y-YOU SAID YOU SUPPORTED THEIR RELATIONSHIP...
AH...
WE WERE IN THE THROES OF MOE...
WE MEANT WE'D SUPPORT THEIR FORBIDDEN LOVE WHOLEHEARTEDLY...
UH... AREN'T FANS SUPPOSED TO FIND OUT EVERYTHING ABOUT THE OBJECT OF THEIR ADORATION?!
WE KNEW HARUHI'S FAMILY WASN'T WELL OFF, SO WE ALL DECIDED NOT TO EMBARRASS HIM BY DIGGING INTO HIS BACKGROUND...!
WHA...
WHA...
ALL THIS TIME THEY THOUGHT SHE WAS A GIRLY (LIKELY GAY) BOY.
GEEZ...
WHAAAAAA
HARUHI REALLY IS A GIRL?!
EVEN THOUGH I'M PARTING WAYS WITH THE HOST CLUB FOR ONLY A LITTLE WHILE...

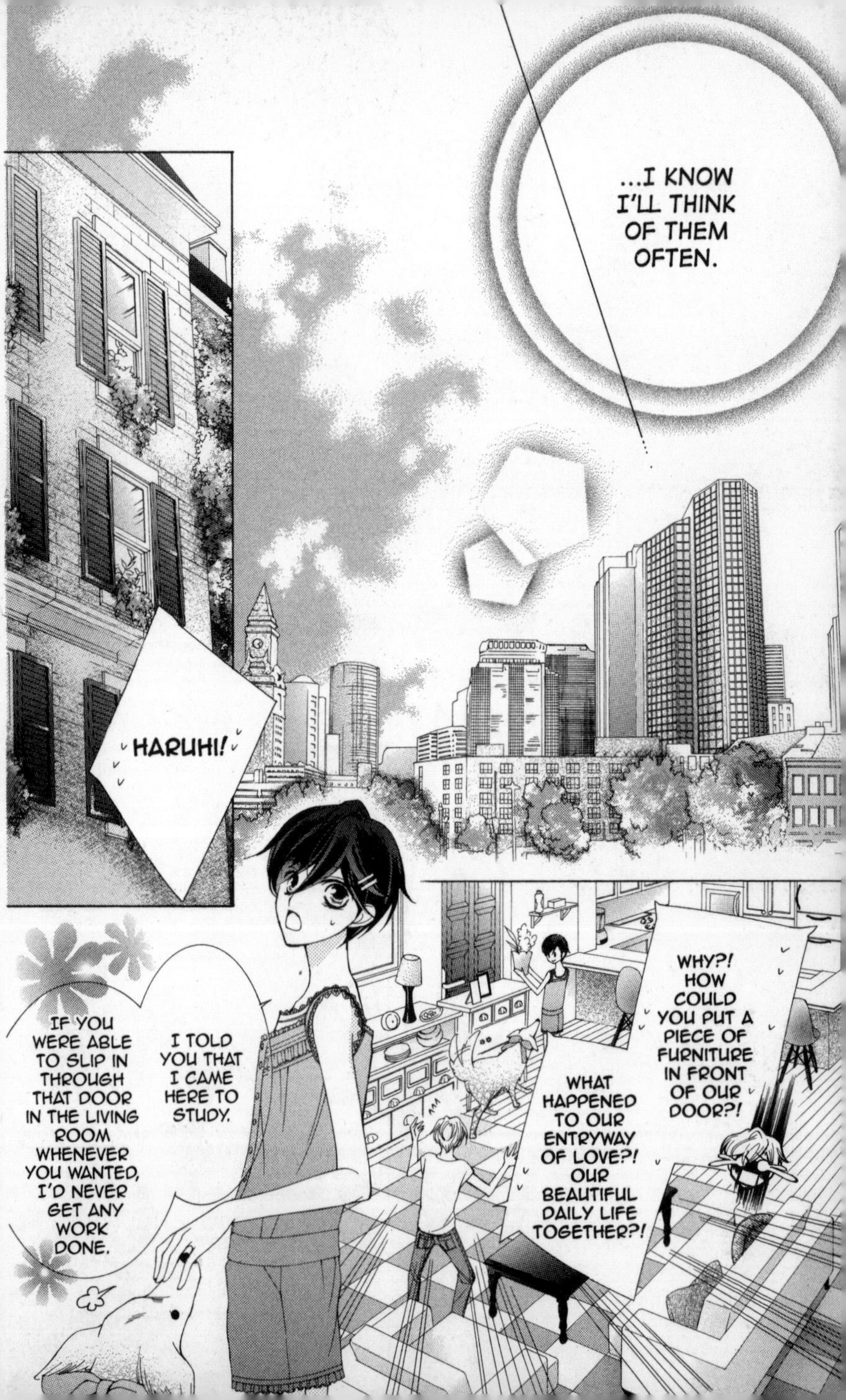
...I KNOW I'LL THINK OF THEM OFTEN.
HARUHI!
WHY?! HOW COULD YOU PUT A PIECE OF FURNITURE IN FRONT OF OUR DOOR?!
WHAT HAPPENED TO OUR ENTRYWAY OF LOVE?! OUR BEAUTIFUL DAILY LIFE TOGETHER?!
I TOLD YOU THAT I CAME HERE TO STUDY.
IF YOU WERE ABLE TO SLIP IN THROUGH THAT DOOR IN THE LIVING ROOM WHENEVER YOU WANTED, I'D NEVER GET ANY WORK DONE.

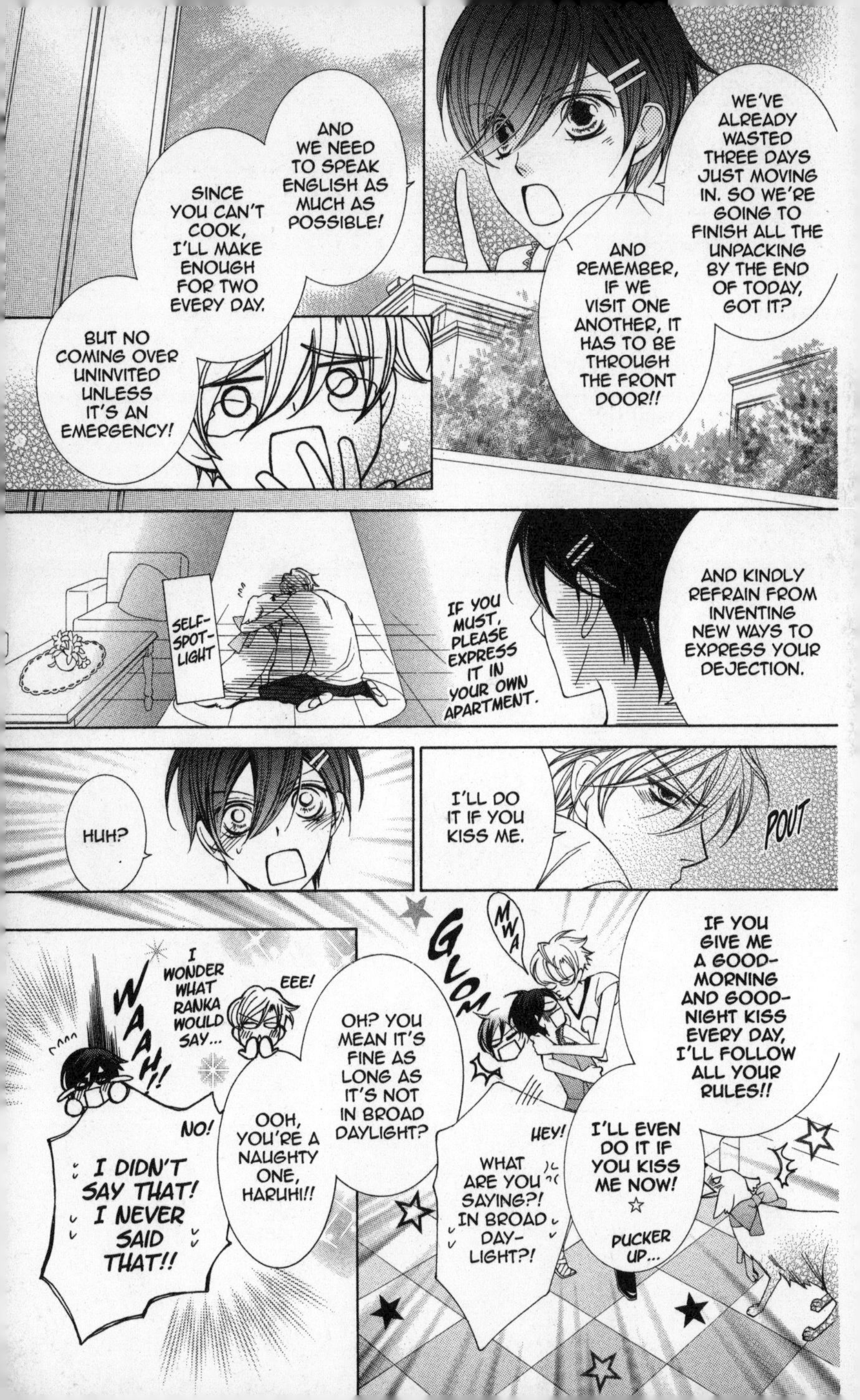
WE'VE ALREADY WASTED THREE DAYS JUST MOVING IN. SO WE'RE GOING TO FINISH ALL THE UNPACKING BY THE END OF TODAY, GOT IT?
AND REMEMBER, IF WE VISIT ONE ANOTHER, IT HAS TO BE THROUGH THE FRONT DOOR!!
AND WE NEED TO SPEAK ENGLISH AS MUCH AS POSSIBLE!
SINCE YOU CAN'T COOK, I'LL MAKE ENOUGH FOR TWO EVERY DAY.
BUT NO COMING OVER UNINVITED UNLESS IT'S AN EMERGENCY!
AND KINDLY REFRAIN FROM INVENTING NEW WAYS TO EXPRESS YOUR DEJECTION.
IF YOU MUST, PLEASE EXPRESS IT IN YOUR OWN APARTMENT.
SELF-SPOTLIGHT
POUT
I'LL DO IT IF YOU KISS ME.
HUH?
IF YOU GIVE ME A GOOD-MORNING AND GOOD-NIGHT KISS EVERY DAY, I'LL FOLLOW ALL YOUR RULES!!
MWA
I'LL EVEN DO IT IF YOU KISS ME NOW! ☆
PUCKER UP...
HEY!
WHAT ARE YOU SAYING?! IN BROAD DAYLIGHT?!
OH? YOU MEAN IT'S FINE AS LONG AS IT'S NOT IN BROAD DAYLIGHT?
OOH, YOU'RE A NAUGHTY ONE, HARUHI!!
EEE!
I WONDER WHAT RANKA WOULD SAY...
WAAAH!
NO!
I DIDN'T SAY THAT! I NEVER SAID THAT!!

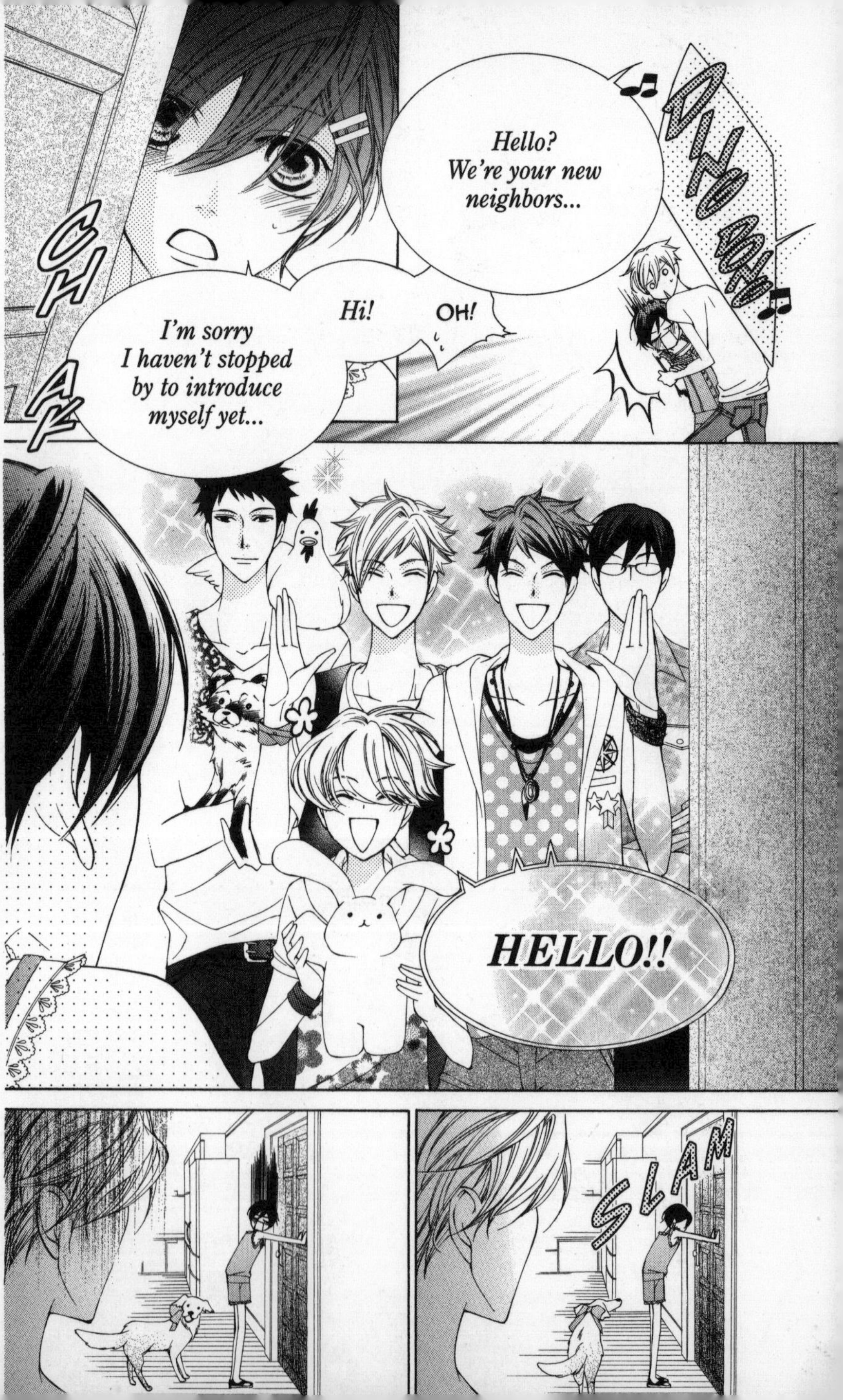
Hello? We're your new neighbors...
OH!
Hi!
I'm sorry I haven't stopped by to introduce myself yet...
CHAK
HELLO!!
SLAM

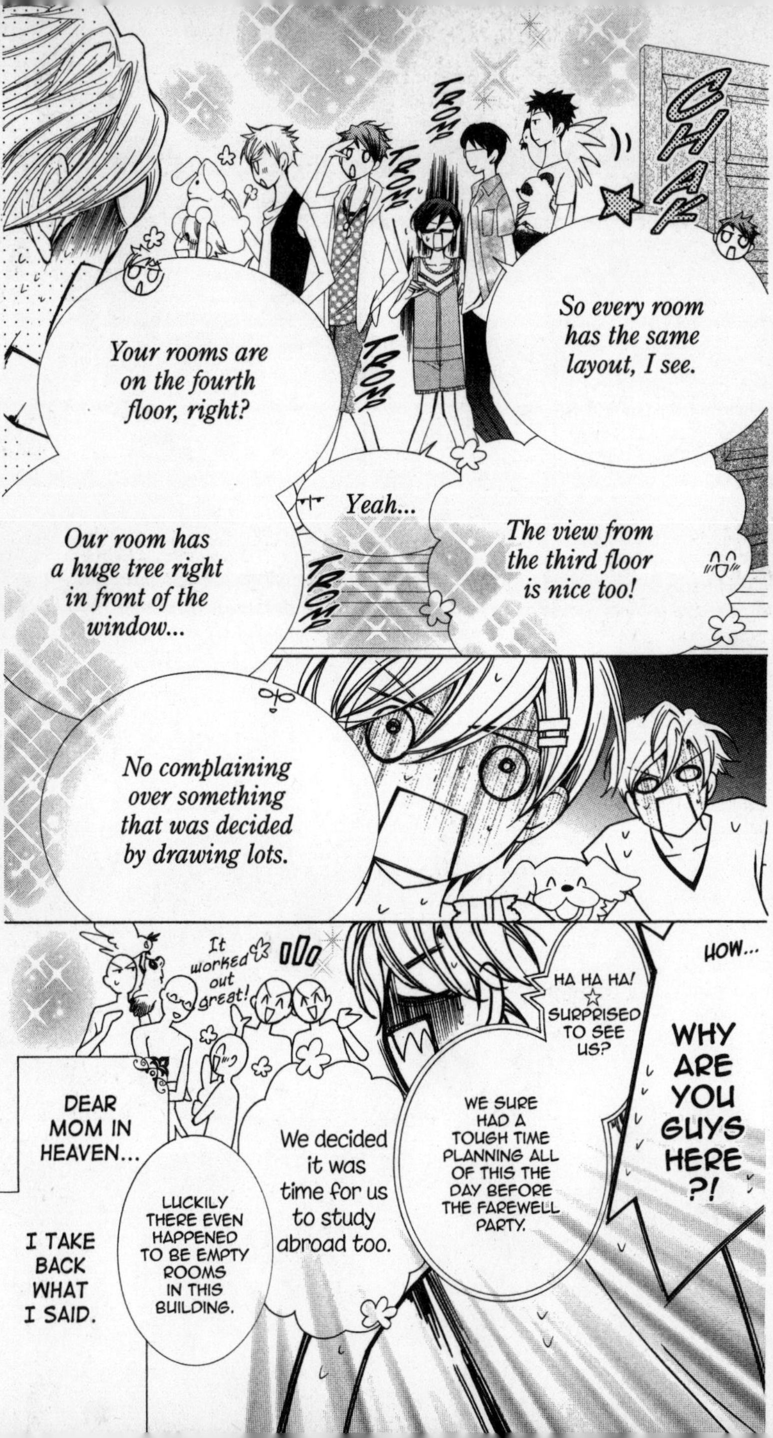
CHAK
So every room has the same layout, I see.
TROMP
TROMP
TROMP
Your rooms are on the fourth floor, right?
Yeah...
The view from the third floor is nice too!
TROMP
Our room has a huge tree right in front of the window...
No complaining over something that was decided by drawing lots.
HOW...
WHY ARE YOU GUYS HERE?!
HA HA HA! ☆ SURPRISED TO SEE US?
WE SURE HAD A TOUGH TIME PLANNING ALL OF THIS THE DAY BEFORE THE FAREWELL PARTY.
It worked out great!
We decided it was time for us to study abroad too.
LUCKILY THERE EVEN HAPPENED TO BE EMPTY ROOMS IN THIS BUILDING.
DEAR MOM IN HEAVEN...
I TAKE BACK WHAT I SAID.

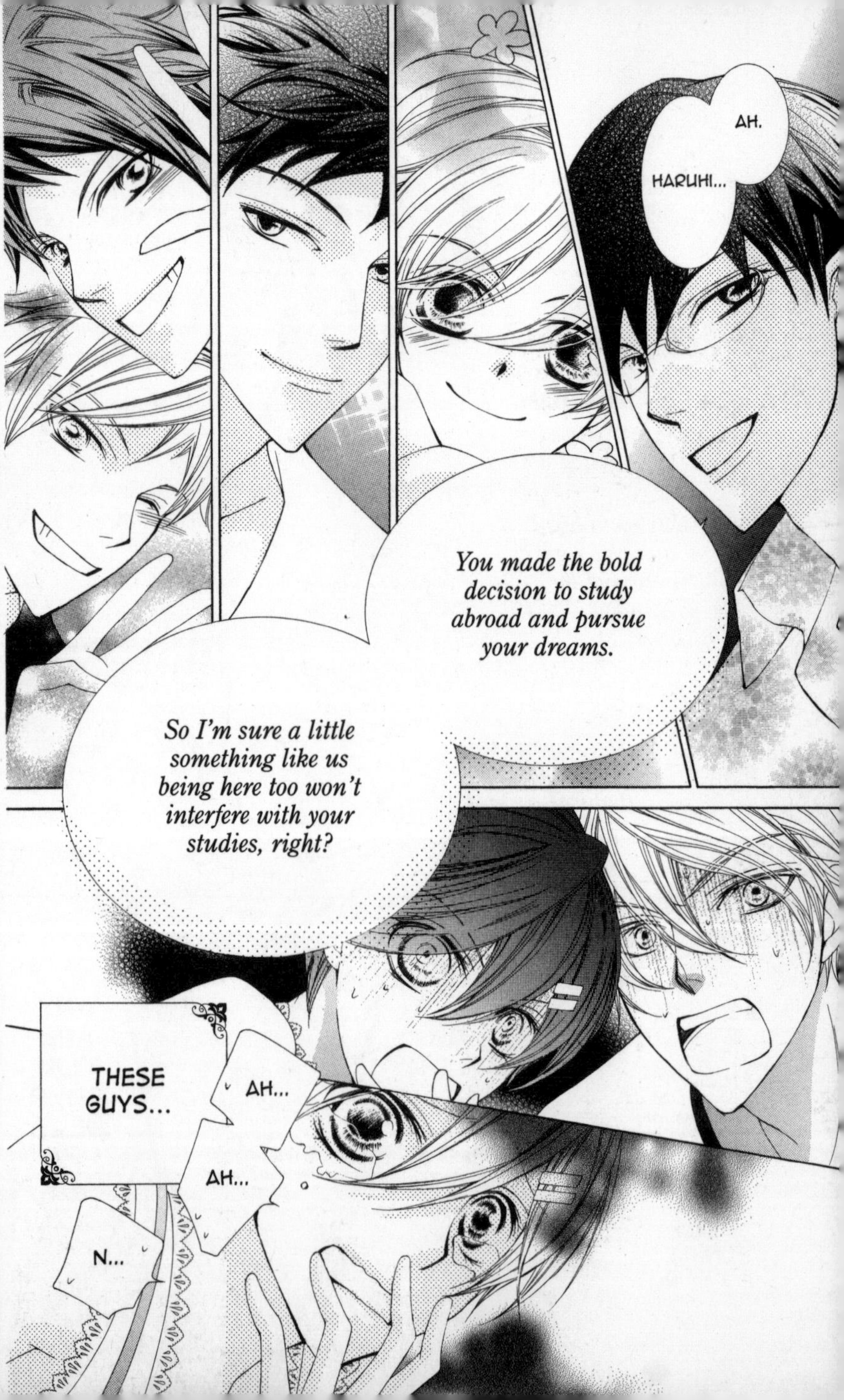
AH.
HARUHI...
You made the bold decision to study abroad and pursue your dreams.
So I'm sure a little something like us being here too won't interfere with your studies, right?
AH...
AH...
N...
THESE GUYS...

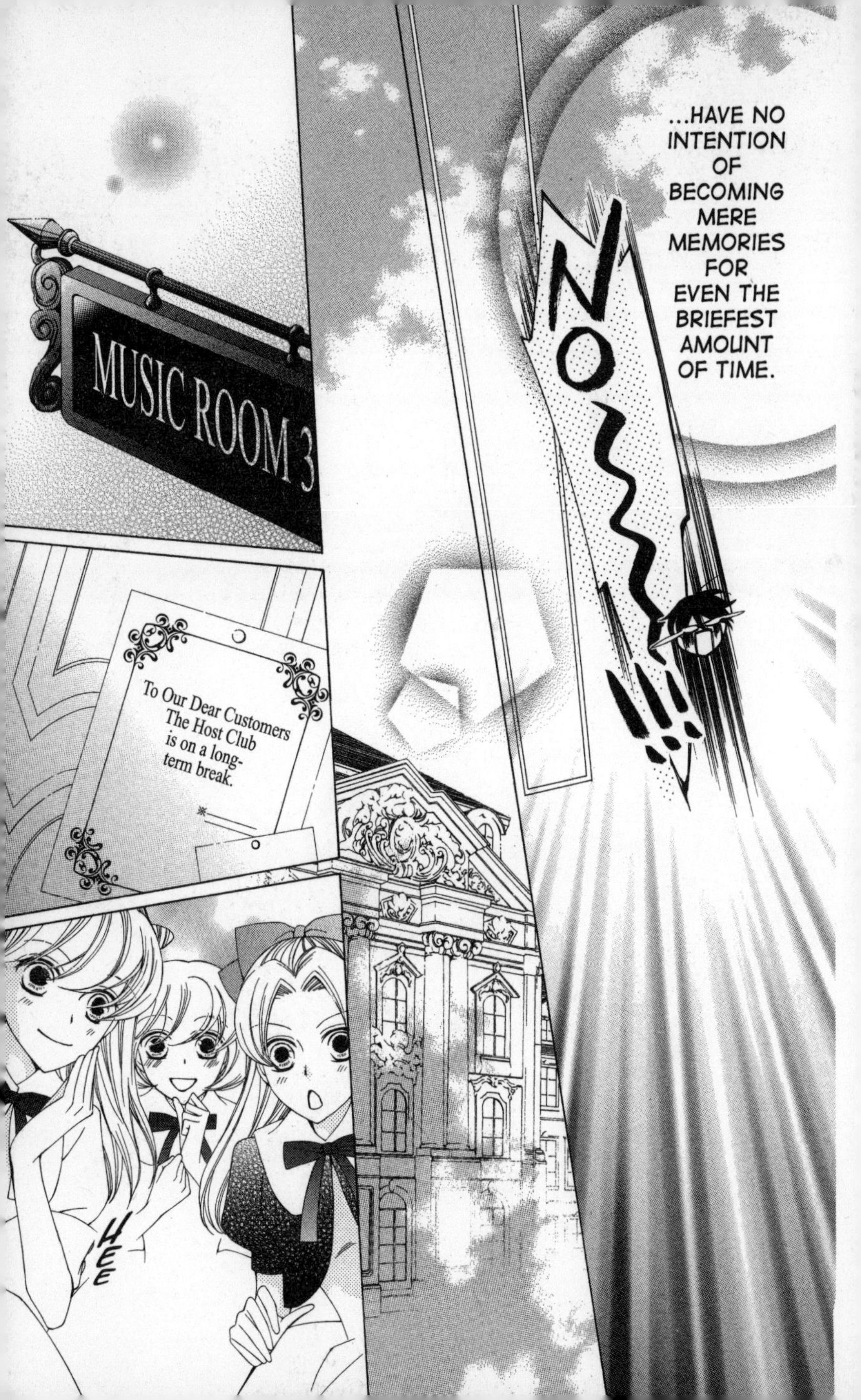
...HAVE NO INTENTION OF BECOMING MERE MEMORIES FOR EVEN THE BRIEFEST AMOUNT OF TIME.
NO!!!
MUSIC ROOM 3
To Our Dear Customers
The Host Club is on a long-term break.
HEE

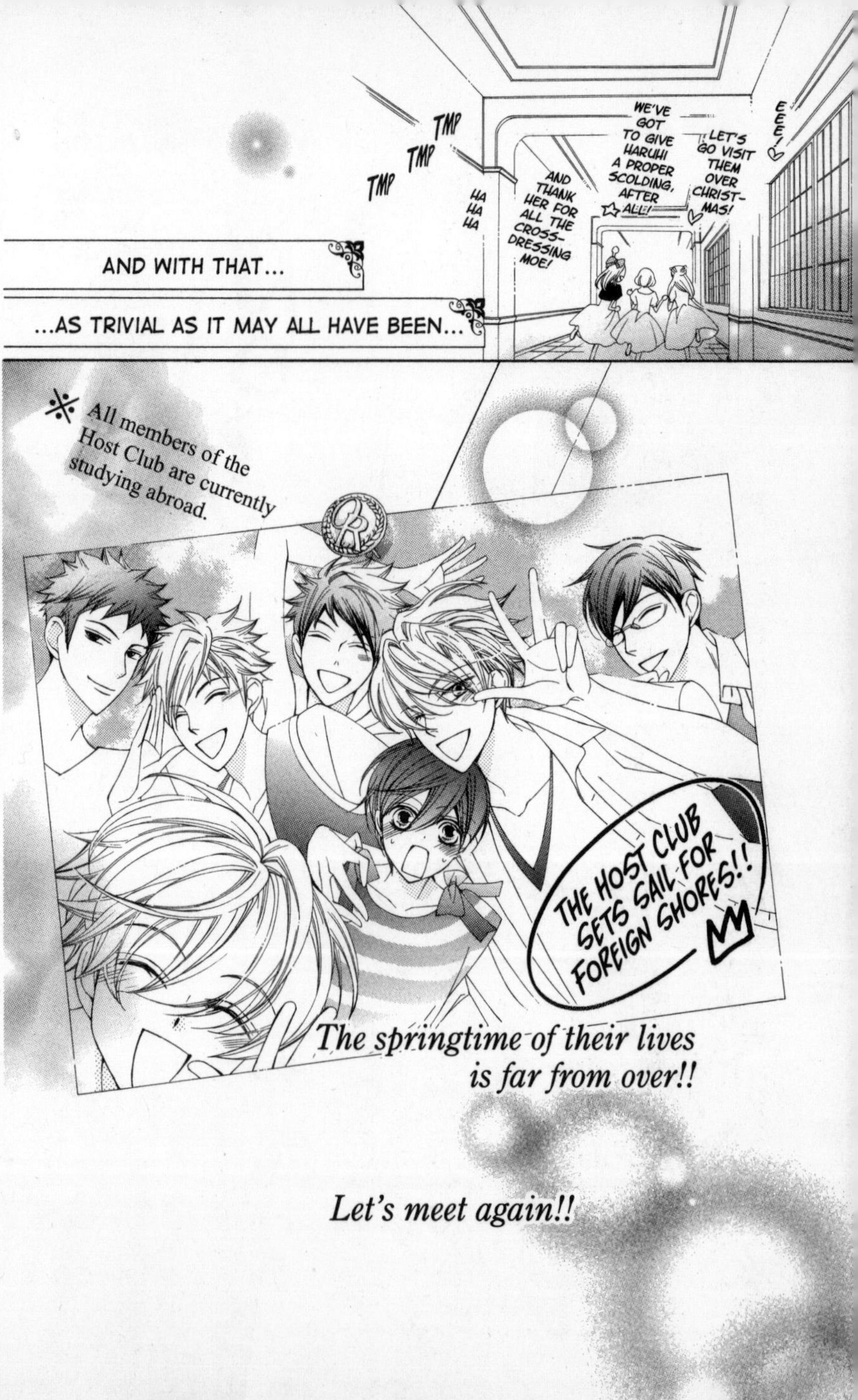
EEE!
LET'S GO VISIT THEM OVER CHRIST-MAS!
WE'VE GOT TO GIVE HARUHI A PROPER SCOLDING, AFTER ALL!
AND THANK HER FOR ALL THE CROSS-DRESSING MOE!
HA HA HA
TMP TMP TMP
AND WITH THAT...
...AS TRIVIAL AS IT MAY ALL HAVE BEEN...
※ All members of the Host Club are currently studying abroad.
THE HOST CLUB SETS SAIL FOR FOREIGN SHORES!!
The springtime of their lives is far from over!!
Let's meet again!!

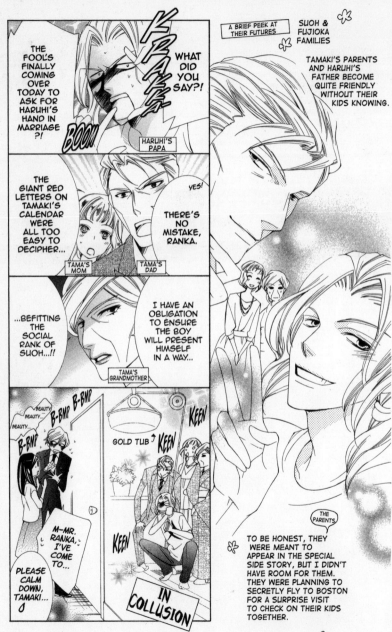

A BRIEF PEEK AT THEIR FUTURES

SUOH & FUJIOKA FAMILIES

TAMAKI'S PARENTS AND HARUHI'S FATHER BECOME QUITE FRIENDLY WITHOUT THEIR KIDS KNOWING.

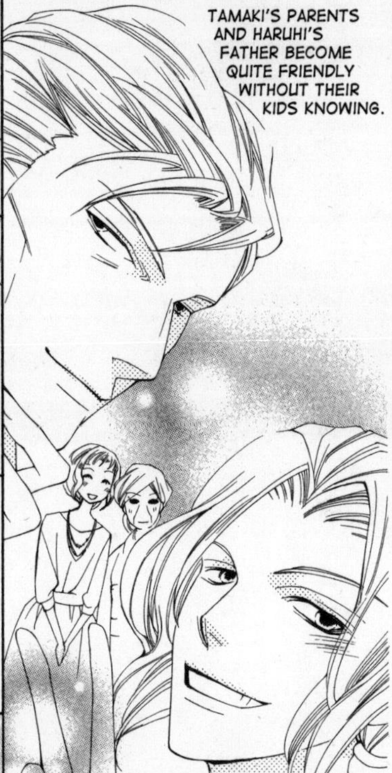
THE PARENTS

TO BE HONEST, THEY WERE MEANT TO APPEAR IN THE SPECIAL SIDE STORY, BUT I DIDN'T HAVE ROOM FOR THEM. THEY WERE PLANNING TO SECRETLY FLY TO BOSTON FOR A SURPRISE VISIT TO CHECK ON THEIR KIDS TOGETHER.

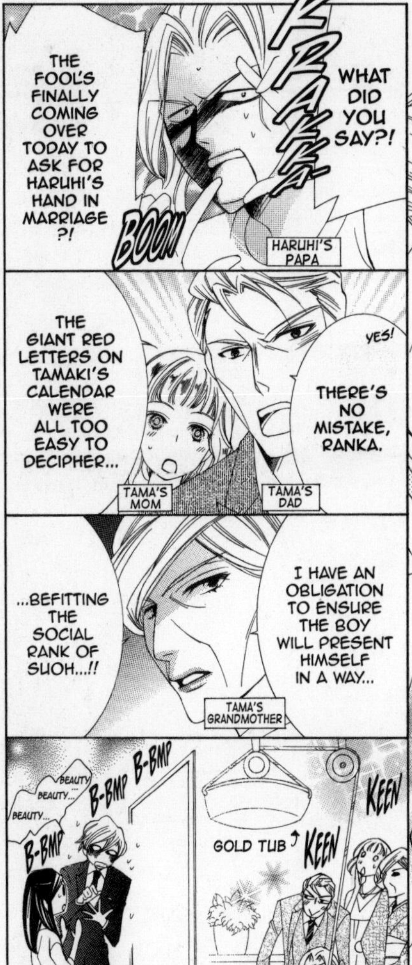
KRAKKA
WHAT DID YOU SAY?!
THE FOOL'S FINALLY COMING OVER TODAY TO ASK FOR HARUHI'S HAND IN MARRIAGE?!
BOOM
HARUHI'S PAPA
YES!
THERE'S NO MISTAKE, RANKA.
THE GIANT RED LETTERS ON TAMAKI'S CALENDAR WERE ALL TOO EASY TO DECIPHER...
TAMA'S DAD
TAMA'S MOM
I HAVE AN OBLIGATION TO ENSURE THE BOY WILL PRESENT HIMSELF IN A WAY...
...BEFITTING THE SOCIAL RANK OF SUOH...!!
TAMA'S GRANDMOTHER
KEEN
GOLD TUB
KEEN
KEEN
IN COLLUSION
B-BMP B-BMP
BEAUTY... BEAUTY... BEAUTY...
B-BMP
M-MR. RANKA, I'VE COME TO...
PLEASE CALM DOWN, TAMAKI...

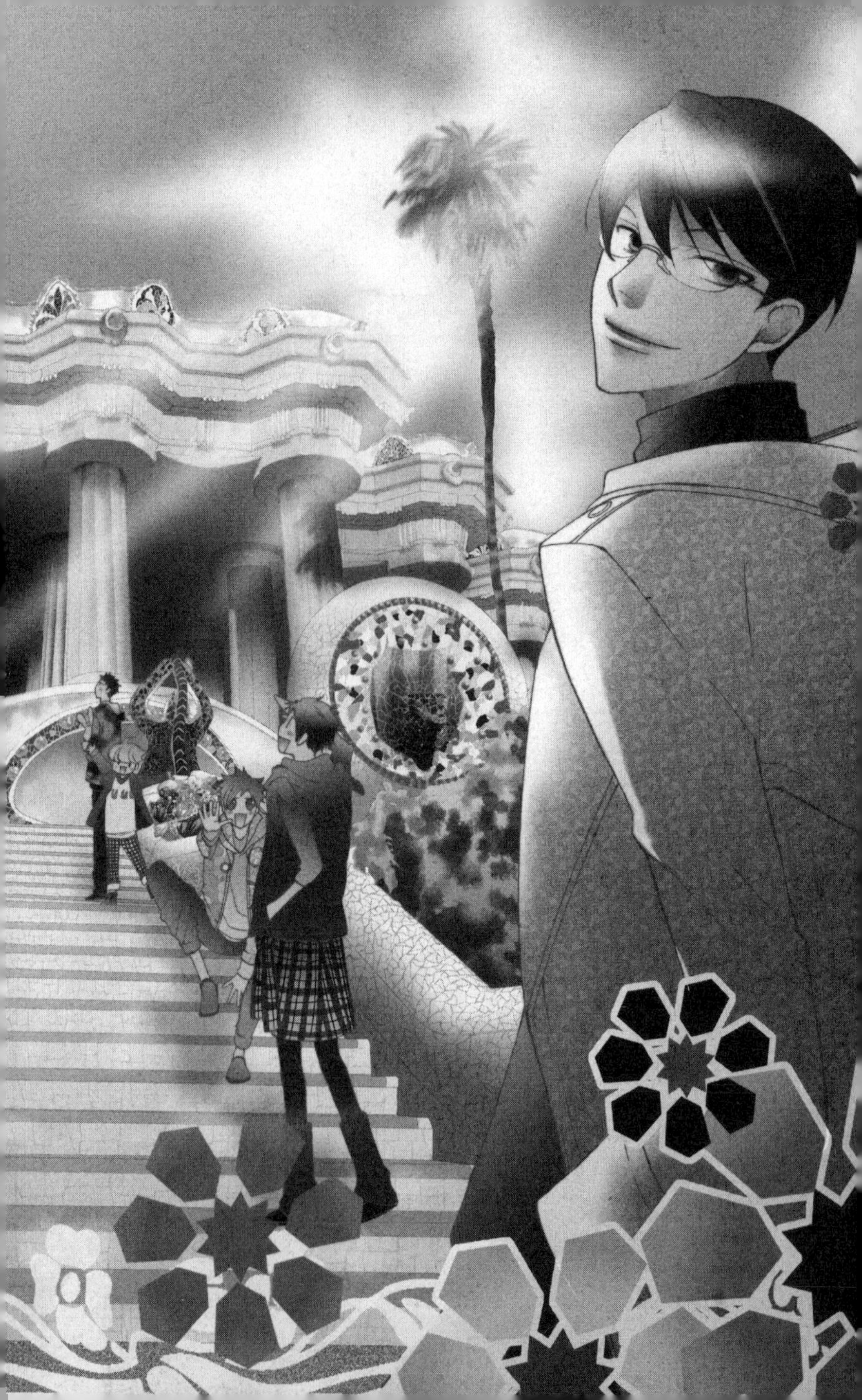

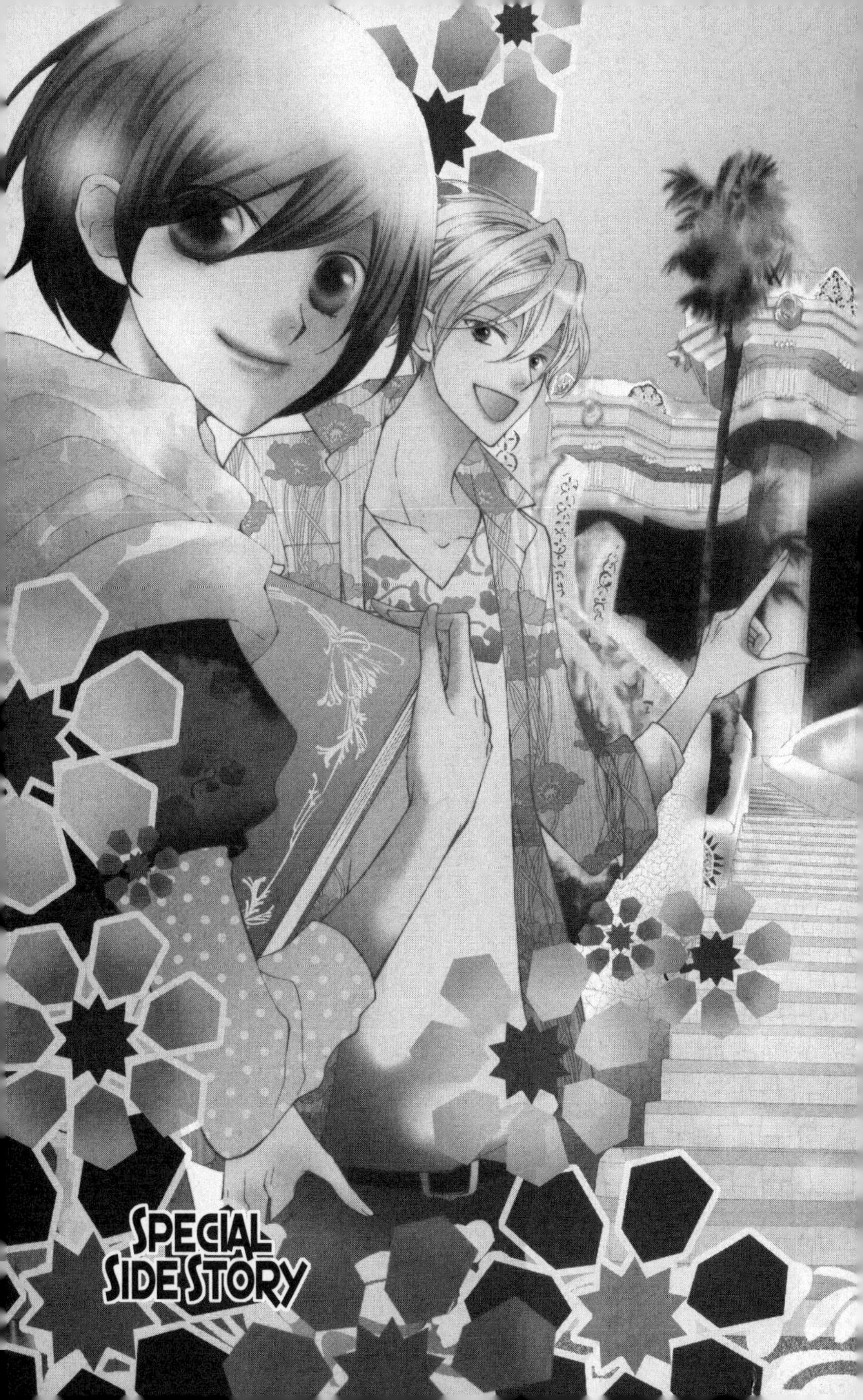
SPECIAL
SIDE STORY

A BRIEF PEEK AT THEIR FUTURES

KYOYA

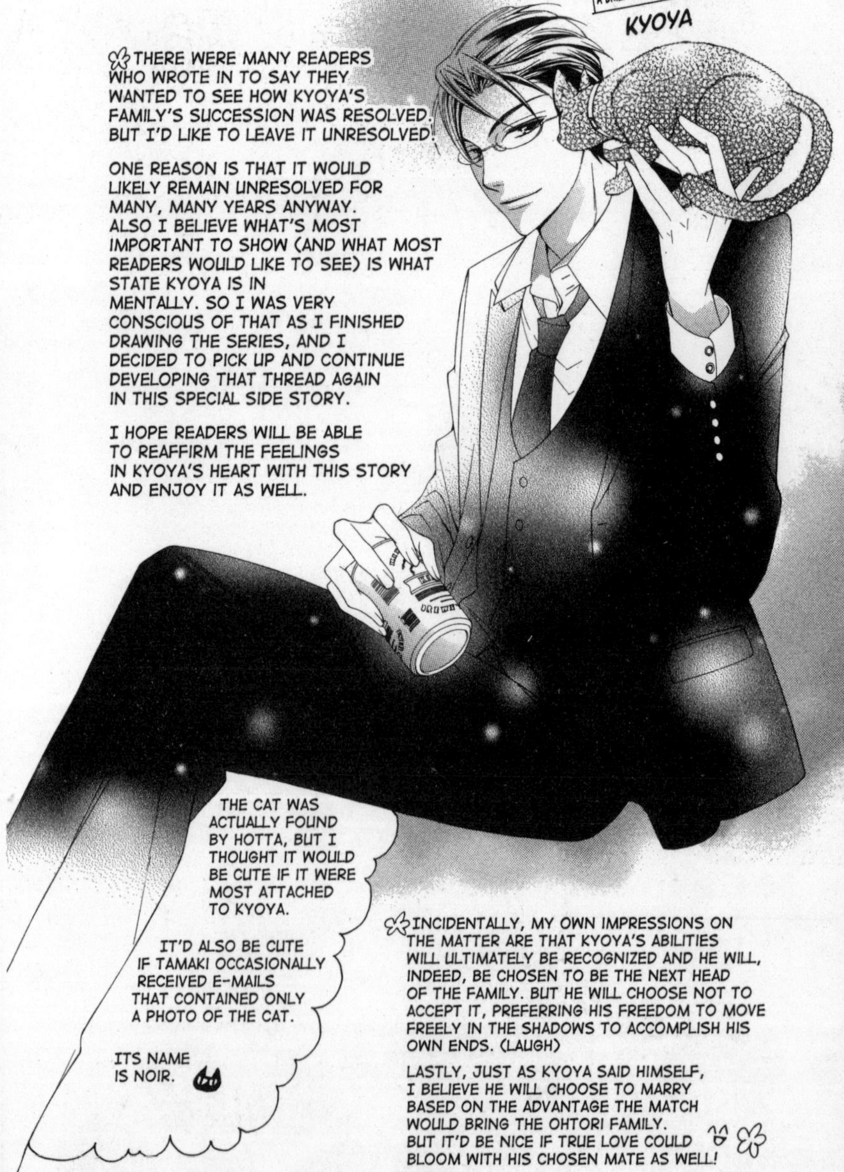

THERE WERE MANY READERS WHO WROTE IN TO SAY THEY WANTED TO SEE HOW KYOYA'S FAMILY'S SUCCESSION WAS RESOLVED. BUT I'D LIKE TO LEAVE IT UNRESOLVED.

ONE REASON IS THAT IT WOULD LIKELY REMAIN UNRESOLVED FOR MANY, MANY YEARS ANYWAY. ALSO I BELIEVE WHAT'S MOST IMPORTANT TO SHOW (AND WHAT MOST READERS WOULD LIKE TO SEE) IS WHAT STATE KYOYA IS IN MENTALLY. SO I WAS VERY CONSCIOUS OF THAT AS I FINISHED DRAWING THE SERIES, AND I DECIDED TO PICK UP AND CONTINUE DEVELOPING THAT THREAD AGAIN IN THIS SPECIAL SIDE STORY.

I HOPE READERS WILL BE ABLE TO REAFFIRM THE FEELINGS IN KYOYA'S HEART WITH THIS STORY AND ENJOY IT AS WELL.

INCIDENTALLY, MY OWN IMPRESSIONS ON THE MATTER ARE THAT KYOYA'S ABILITIES WILL ULTIMATELY BE RECOGNIZED AND HE WILL, INDEED, BE CHOSEN TO BE THE NEXT HEAD OF THE FAMILY. BUT HE WILL CHOOSE NOT TO ACCEPT IT, PREFERRING HIS FREEDOM TO MOVE FREELY IN THE SHADOWS TO ACCOMPLISH HIS OWN ENDS. (LAUGH)

LASTLY, JUST AS KYOYA SAID HIMSELF, I BELIEVE HE WILL CHOOSE TO MARRY BASED ON THE ADVANTAGE THE MATCH WOULD BRING THE OHTORI FAMILY. BUT IT'D BE NICE IF TRUE LOVE COULD BLOOM WITH HIS CHOSEN MATE AS WELL!

THE CAT WAS ACTUALLY FOUND BY HOTTA, BUT I THOUGHT IT WOULD BE CUTE IF IT WERE MOST ATTACHED TO KYOYA.

IT'D ALSO BE CUTE IF TAMAKI OCCASIONALLY RECEIVED E-MAILS THAT CONTAINED ONLY A PHOTO OF THE CAT.

ITS NAME IS NOIR.

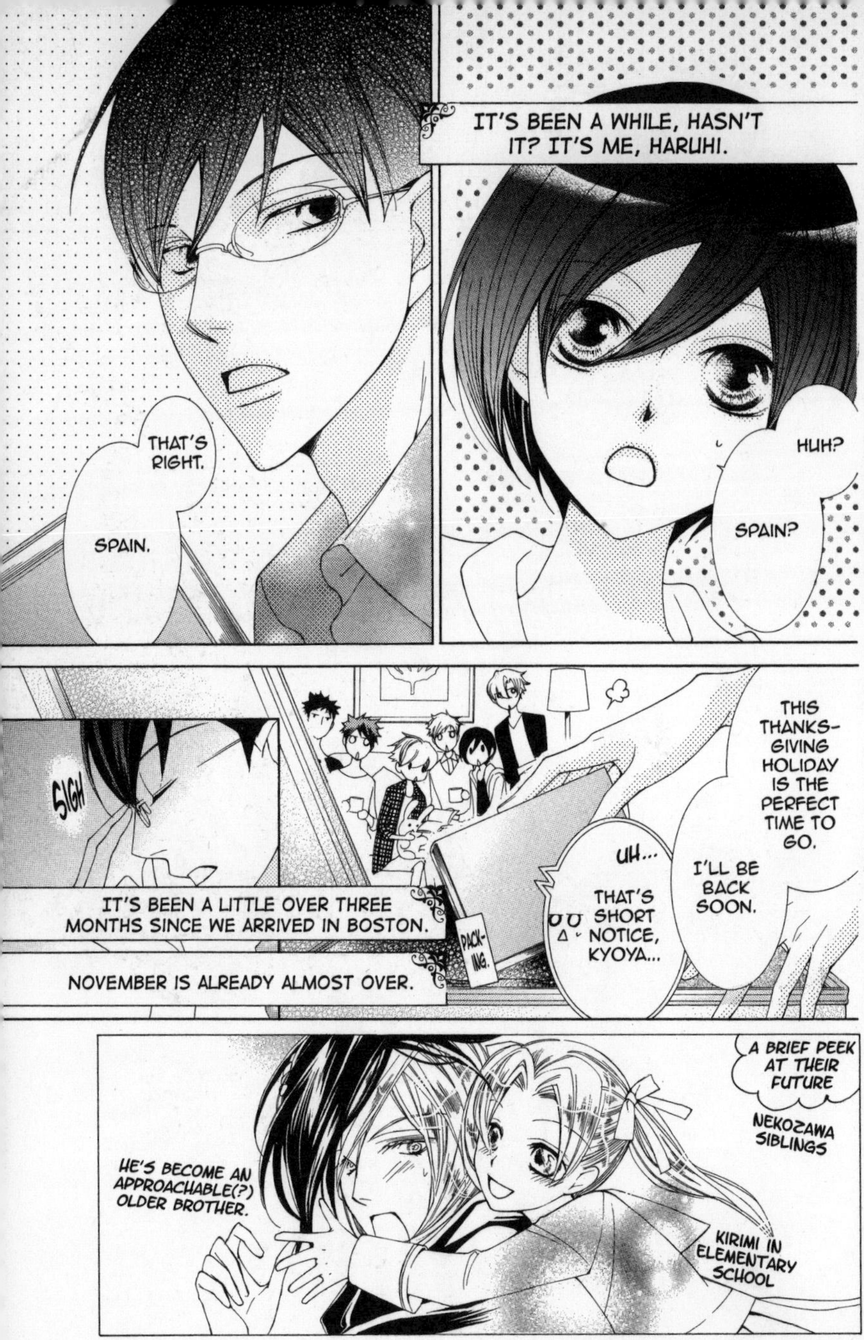
IT'S BEEN A WHILE, HASN'T IT? IT'S ME, HARUHI.
HUH? SPAIN?
THAT'S RIGHT. SPAIN.
THIS THANKSGIVING HOLIDAY IS THE PERFECT TIME TO GO. I'LL BE BACK SOON.
UH... THAT'S SHORT NOTICE, KYOYA...
PACKING.
SIGH
IT'S BEEN A LITTLE OVER THREE MONTHS SINCE WE ARRIVED IN BOSTON.
NOVEMBER IS ALREADY ALMOST OVER.
A BRIEF PEEK AT THEIR FUTURE
NEKOZAWA SIBLINGS
KIRIMI IN ELEMENTARY SCHOOL
HE'S BECOME AN APPROACHABLE(?) OLDER BROTHER.

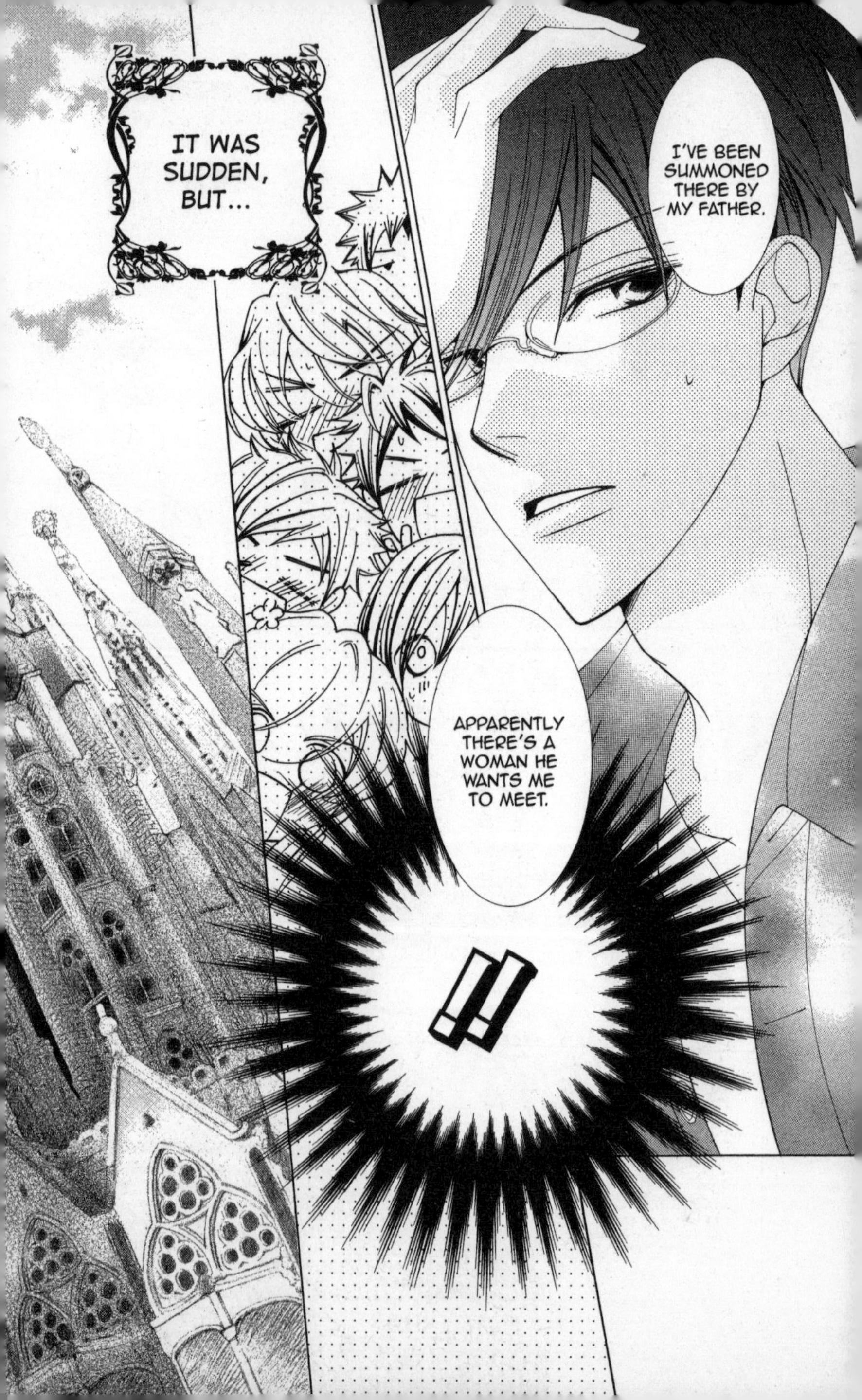
I'VE BEEN SUMMONED THERE BY MY FATHER.
APPARENTLY THERE'S A WOMAN HE WANTS ME TO MEET.
!!
IT WAS SUDDEN, BUT...

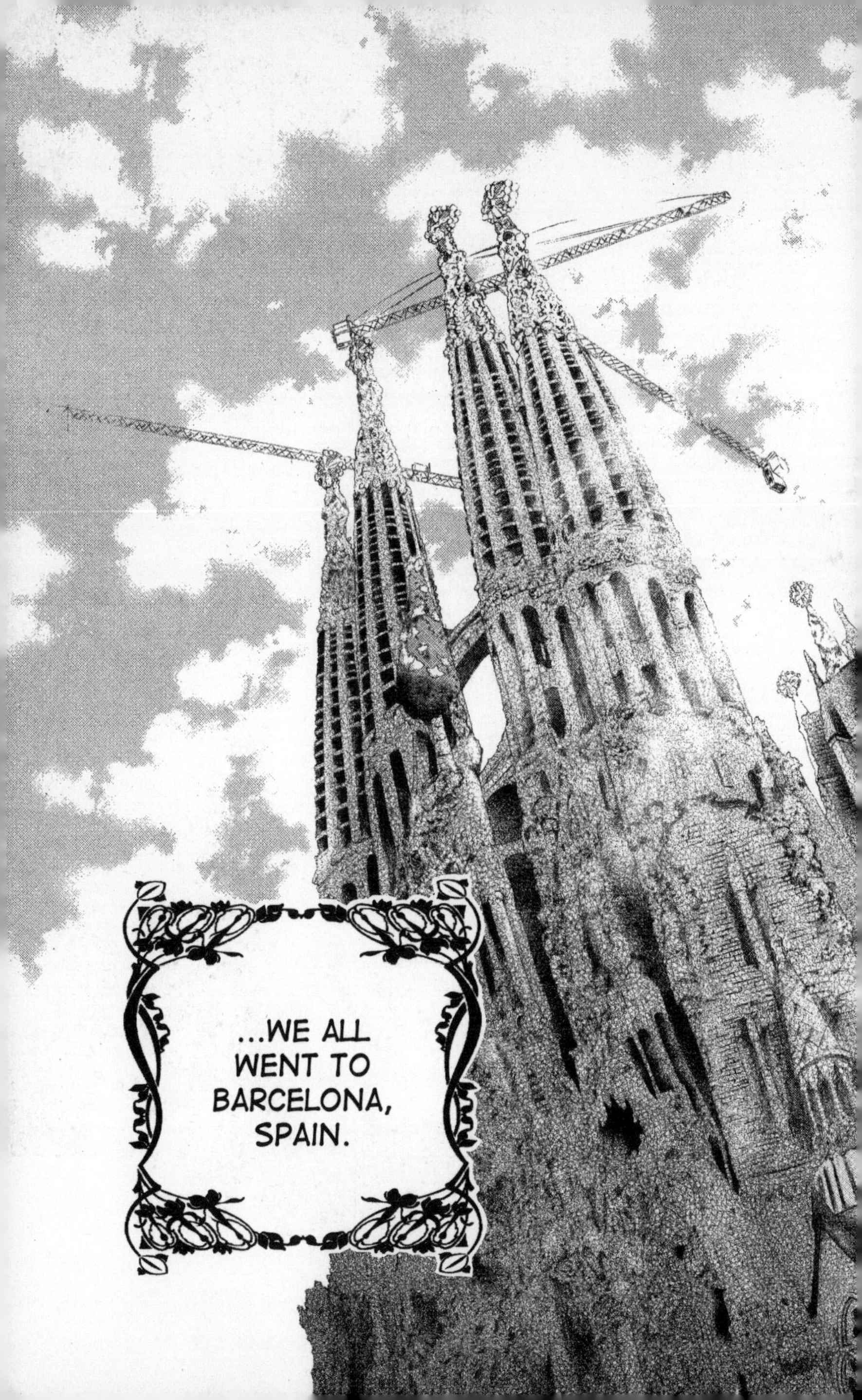
...WE ALL WENT TO BARCELONA, SPAIN.

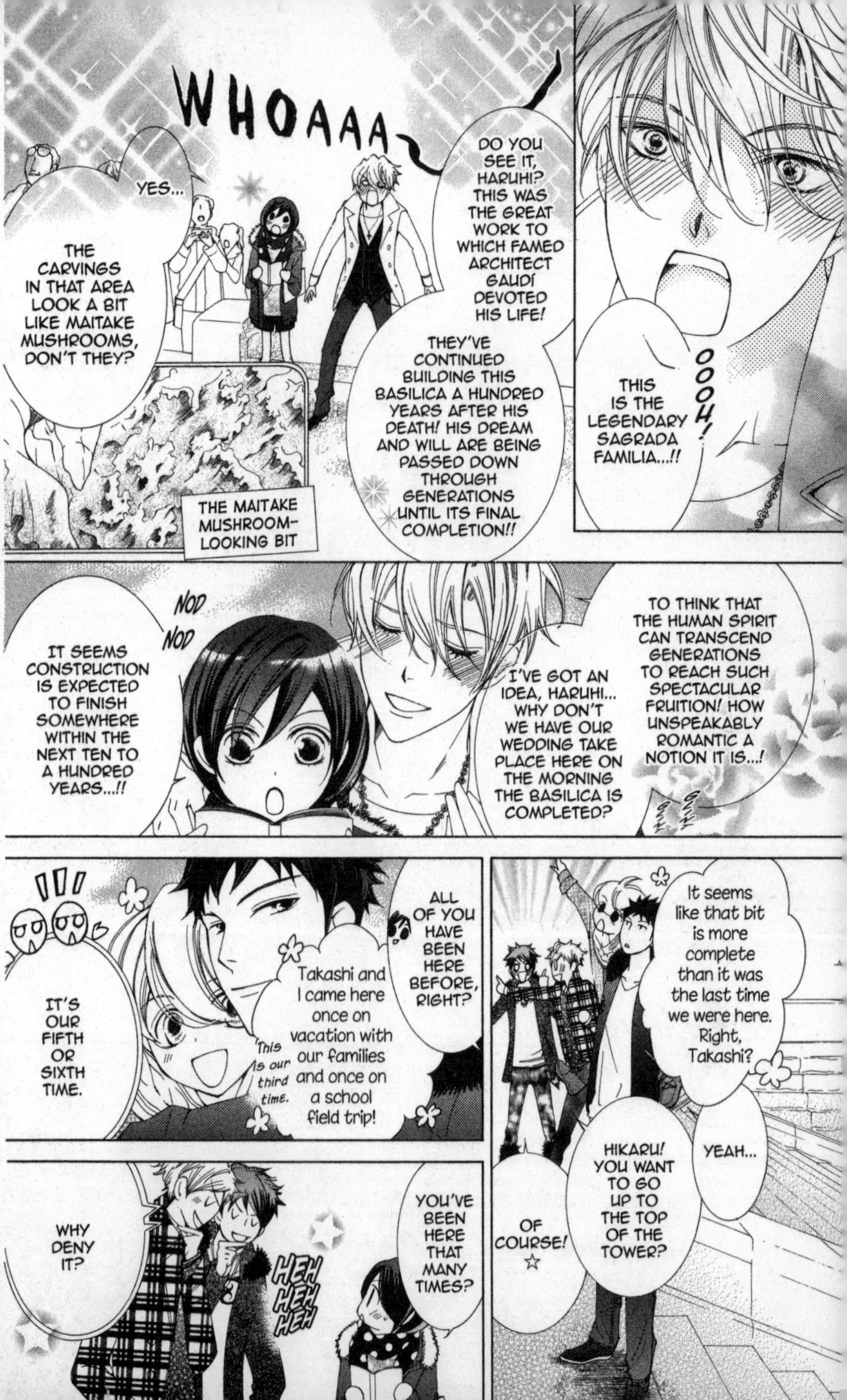
THIS IS THE LEGENDARY SAGRADA FAMILIA...!!
OOOH!
WHOAAA~
DO YOU SEE IT, HARUHI? THIS WAS THE GREAT WORK TO WHICH FAMED ARCHITECT GAUDÍ DEVOTED HIS LIFE!
THEY'VE CONTINUED BUILDING THIS BASILICA A HUNDRED YEARS AFTER HIS DEATH! HIS DREAM AND WILL ARE BEING PASSED DOWN THROUGH GENERATIONS UNTIL ITS FINAL COMPLETION!!
YES...
THE CARVINGS IN THAT AREA LOOK A BIT LIKE MAITAKE MUSHROOMS, DON'T THEY?
THE MAITAKE MUSHROOM-LOOKING BIT
TO THINK THAT THE HUMAN SPIRIT CAN TRANSCEND GENERATIONS TO REACH SUCH SPECTACULAR FRUITION! HOW UNSPEAKABLY ROMANTIC A NOTION IT IS...!
I'VE GOT AN IDEA, HARUHI... WHY DON'T WE HAVE OUR WEDDING TAKE PLACE HERE ON THE MORNING THE BASILICA IS COMPLETED?
NOD NOD
IT SEEMS CONSTRUCTION IS EXPECTED TO FINISH SOMEWHERE WITHIN THE NEXT TEN TO A HUNDRED YEARS...!!
It seems like that bit is more complete than it was the last time we were here. Right, Takashi?
YEAH...
ALL OF YOU HAVE BEEN HERE BEFORE, RIGHT?
Takashi and I came here once on vacation with our families and once on a school field trip!
This is our third time.
IT'S OUR FIFTH OR SIXTH TIME.
HIKARU! YOU WANT TO GO UP TO THE TOP OF THE TOWER?
OF COURSE! ☆
YOU'VE BEEN HERE THAT MANY TIMES?
HEH HEH HEH
WHY DENY IT?

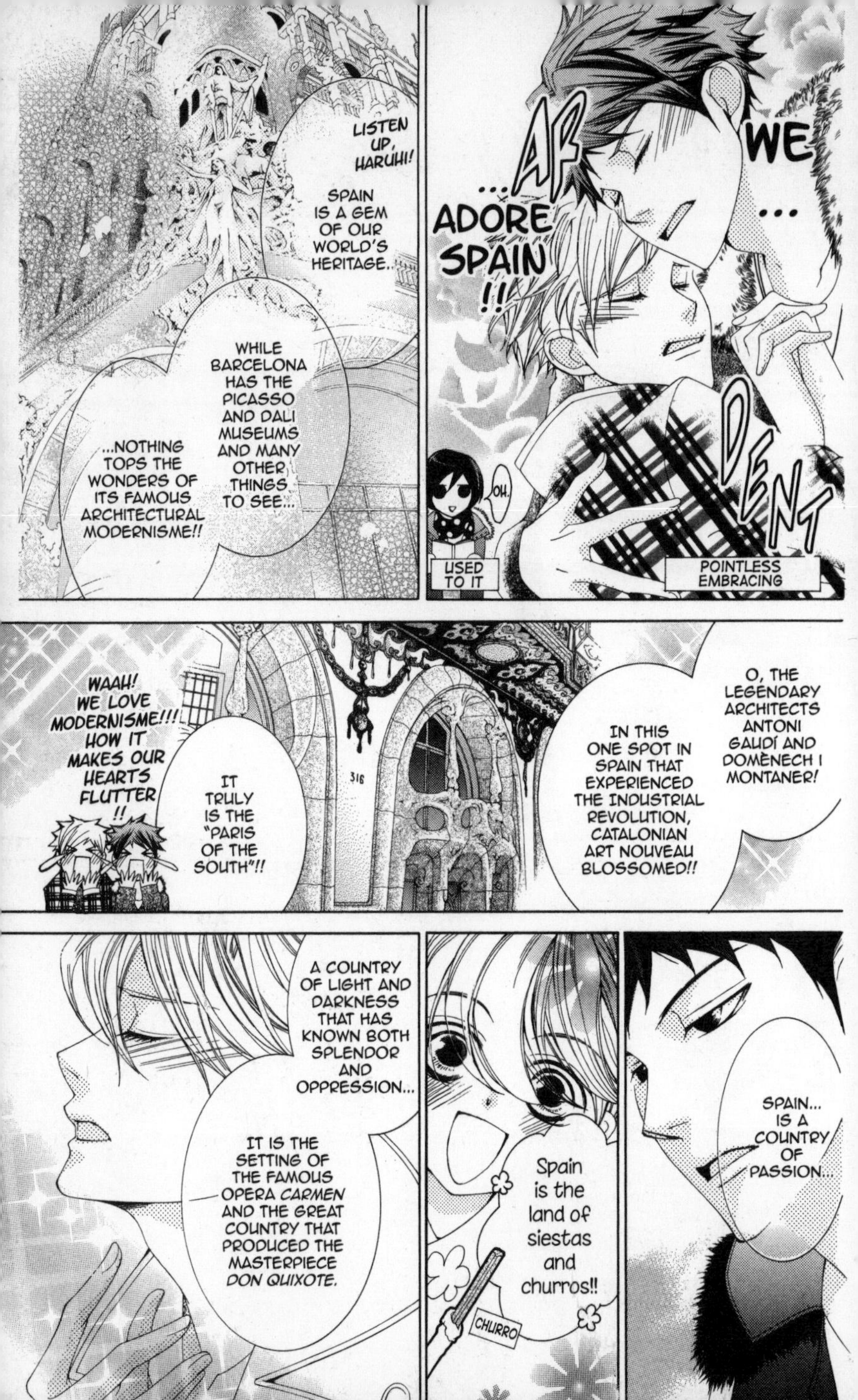
WE...
AH
...ADORE SPAIN!!
DENT
POINTLESS EMBRACING
OH.
USED TO IT
LISTEN UP, HARUHI!
SPAIN IS A GEM OF OUR WORLD'S HERITAGE...
WHILE BARCELONA HAS THE PICASSO AND DALI MUSEUMS AND MANY OTHER THINGS TO SEE...
...NOTHING TOPS THE WONDERS OF ITS FAMOUS ARCHITECTURAL MODERNISME!!
IN THIS ONE SPOT IN SPAIN THAT EXPERIENCED THE INDUSTRIAL REVOLUTION, CATALONIAN ART NOUVEAU BLOSSOMED!!
O, THE LEGENDARY ARCHITECTS ANTONI GAUDÍ AND DOMÈNECH I MONTANER!
IT TRULY IS THE "PARIS OF THE SOUTH"!!
WAAH! WE LOVE MODERNISME!!! HOW IT MAKES OUR HEARTS FLUTTER!!
SPAIN... IS A COUNTRY OF PASSION...
Spain is the land of siestas and churros!!
CHURRO
A COUNTRY OF LIGHT AND DARKNESS THAT HAS KNOWN BOTH SPLENDOR AND OPPRESSION...
IT IS THE SETTING OF THE FAMOUS OPERA CARMEN AND THE GREAT COUNTRY THAT PRODUCED THE MASTERPIECE DON QUIXOTE.

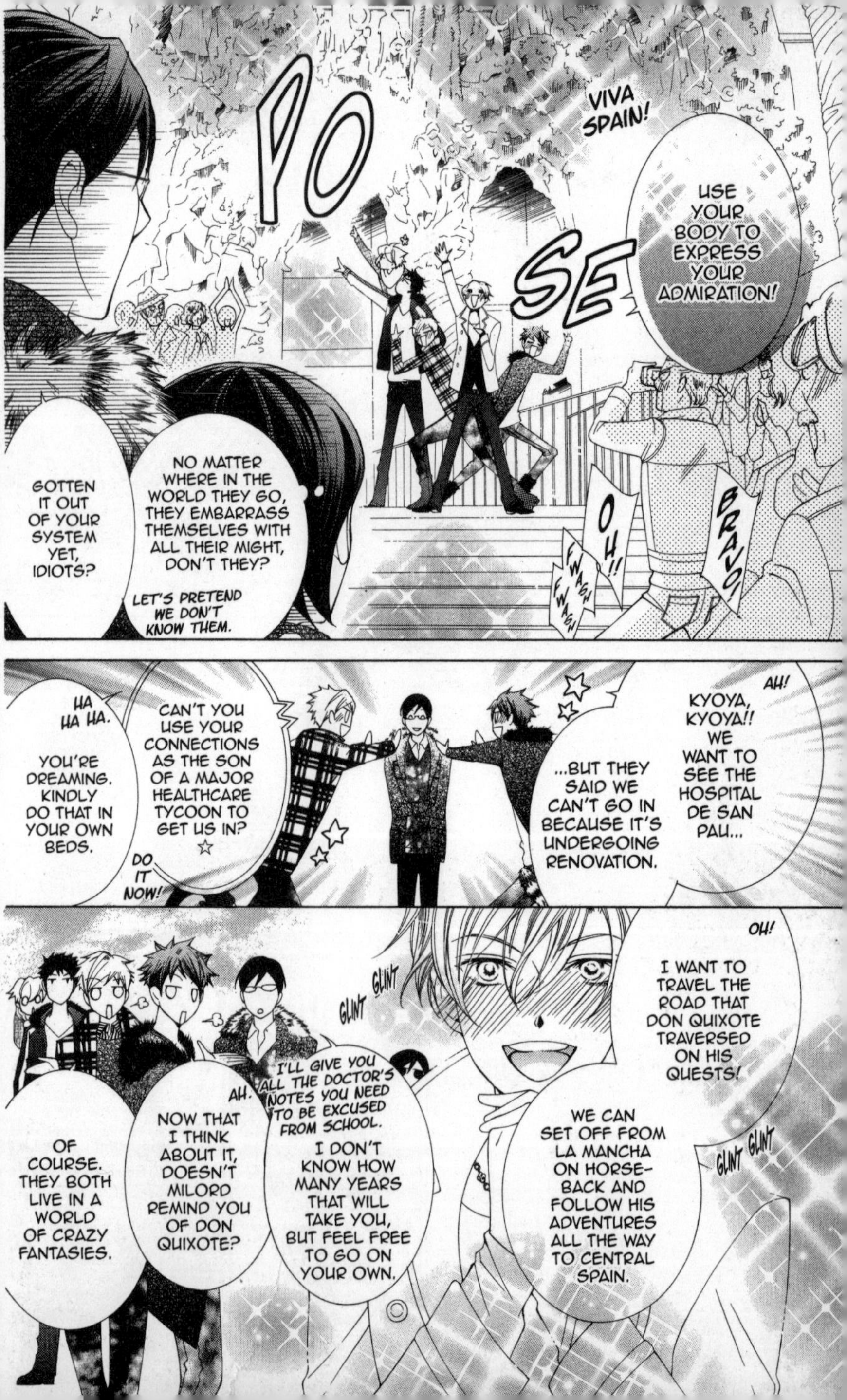
USE YOUR BODY TO EXPRESS YOUR ADMIRATION!
VIVA SPAIN!
PO
SE
BRAVO!
OH!!
FWASH FWASH
NO MATTER WHERE IN THE WORLD THEY GO, THEY EMBARRASS THEMSELVES WITH ALL THEIR MIGHT, DON'T THEY?
LET'S PRETEND WE DON'T KNOW THEM.
GOTTEN IT OUT OF YOUR SYSTEM YET, IDIOTS?
AH!
KYOYA, KYOYA!! WE WANT TO SEE THE HOSPITAL DE SAN PAU...
...BUT THEY SAID WE CAN'T GO IN BECAUSE IT'S UNDERGOING RENOVATION.
CAN'T YOU USE YOUR CONNECTIONS AS THE SON OF A MAJOR HEALTHCARE TYCOON TO GET US IN? ☆
DO IT NOW!
HA HA HA.
YOU'RE DREAMING. KINDLY DO THAT IN YOUR OWN BEDS.
OH!
I WANT TO TRAVEL THE ROAD THAT DON QUIXOTE TRAVERSED ON HIS QUESTS!
WE CAN SET OFF FROM LA MANCHA ON HORSE-BACK AND FOLLOW HIS ADVENTURES ALL THE WAY TO CENTRAL SPAIN.
GLINT GLINT
GLINT GLINT
I'LL GIVE YOU ALL THE DOCTOR'S NOTES YOU NEED TO BE EXCUSED FROM SCHOOL.
I DON'T KNOW HOW MANY YEARS THAT WILL TAKE YOU, BUT FEEL FREE TO GO ON YOUR OWN.
AH.
NOW THAT I THINK ABOUT IT, DOESN'T MILORD REMIND YOU OF DON QUIXOTE?
OF COURSE. THEY BOTH LIVE IN A WORLD OF CRAZY FANTASIES.

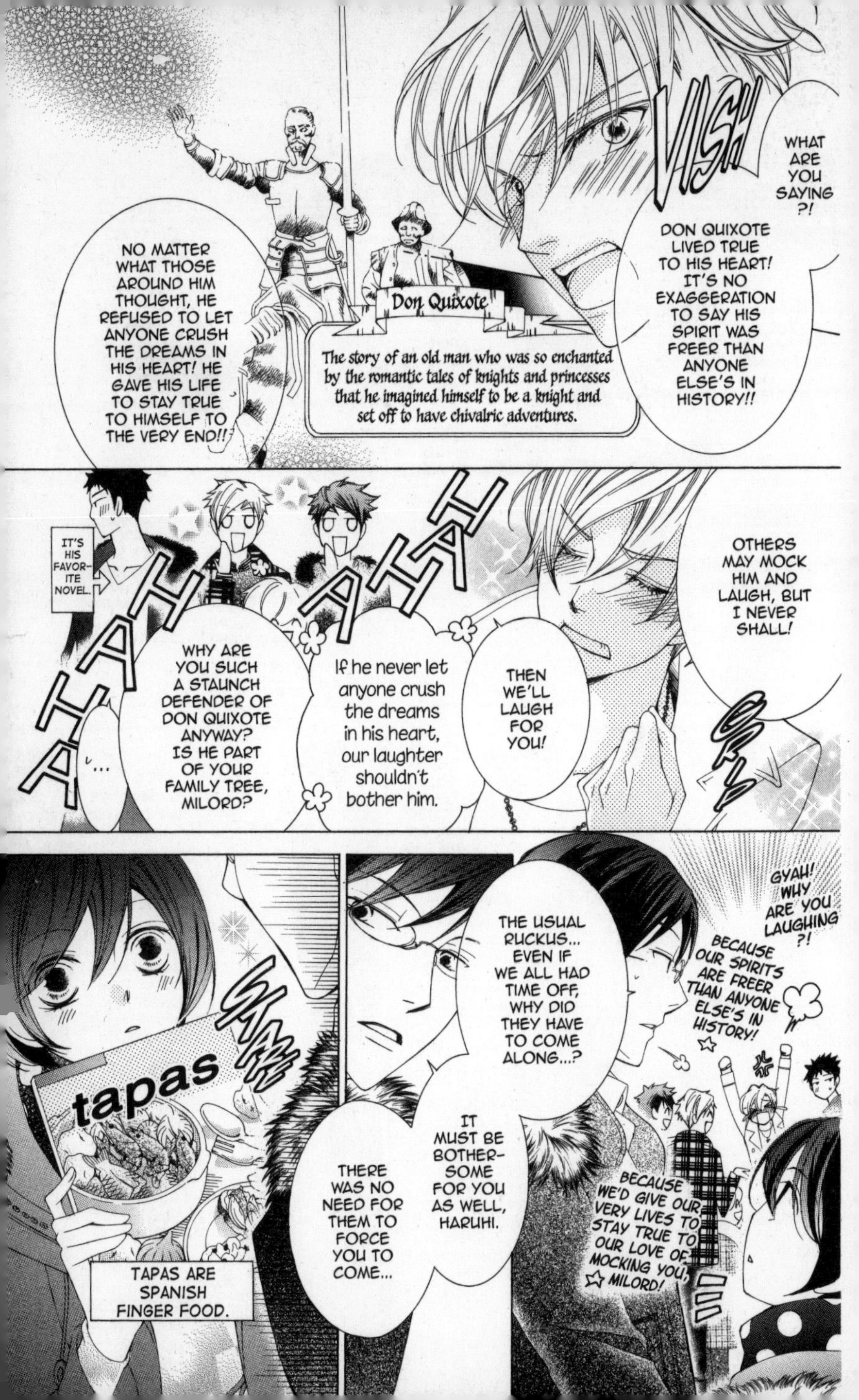
VISH
WHAT ARE YOU SAYING ?!
DON QUIXOTE LIVED TRUE TO HIS HEART! IT'S NO EXAGGERATION TO SAY HIS SPIRIT WAS FREER THAN ANYONE ELSE'S IN HISTORY!!
Don Quixote
The story of an old man who was so enchanted by the romantic tales of knights and princesses that he imagined himself to be a knight and set off to have chivalric adventures.
NO MATTER WHAT THOSE AROUND HIM THOUGHT, HE REFUSED TO LET ANYONE CRUSH THE DREAMS IN HIS HEART! HE GAVE HIS LIFE TO STAY TRUE TO HIMSELF TO THE VERY END!!
OTHERS MAY MOCK HIM AND LAUGH, BUT I NEVER SHALL!
THEN WE'LL LAUGH FOR YOU!
If he never let anyone crush the dreams in his heart, our laughter shouldn't bother him.
WHY ARE YOU SUCH A STAUNCH DEFENDER OF DON QUIXOTE ANYWAY? IS HE PART OF YOUR FAMILY TREE, MILORD?
...
AHAHAHAHAHA
IT'S HIS FAVORITE NOVEL.
GYAH! WHY ARE YOU LAUGHING ?!
BECAUSE OUR SPIRITS ARE FREER THAN ANYONE ELSE'S IN HISTORY! ☆
THE USUAL RUCKUS... EVEN IF WE ALL HAD TIME OFF, WHY DID THEY HAVE TO COME ALONG...?
IT MUST BE BOTHERSOME FOR YOU AS WELL, HARUHI.
BECAUSE WE'D GIVE OUR VERY LIVES TO STAY TRUE TO OUR LOVE OF MOCKING YOU, ☆ MILORD!
THERE WAS NO NEED FOR THEM TO FORCE YOU TO COME...
tapas
TAPAS ARE SPANISH FINGER FOOD.

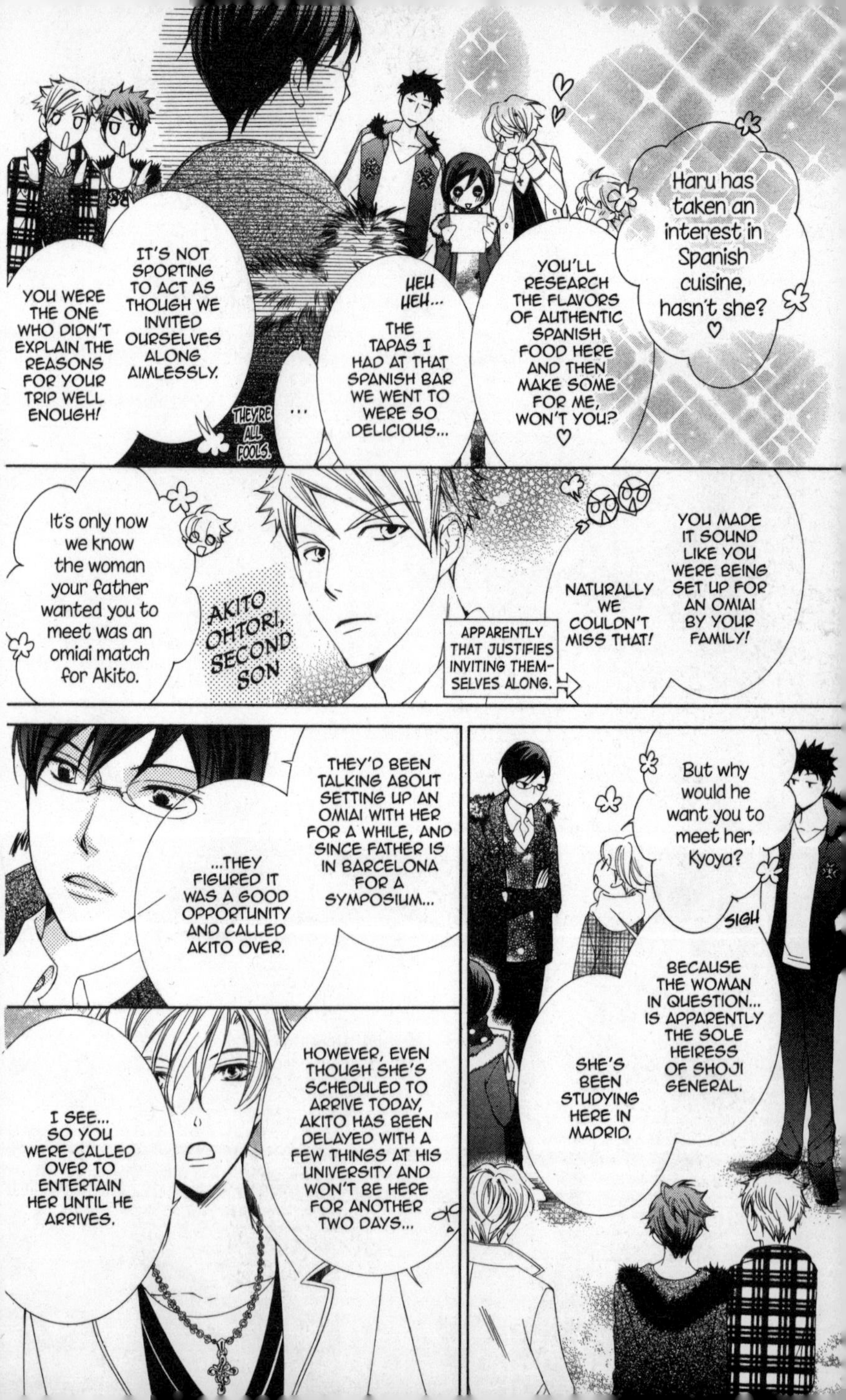

Haru has taken an interest in Spanish cuisine, hasn't she? ♡
YOU'LL RESEARCH THE FLAVORS OF AUTHENTIC SPANISH FOOD HERE AND THEN MAKE SOME FOR ME, WON'T YOU? ♡
HEH HEH... THE TAPAS I HAD AT THAT SPANISH BAR WE WENT TO WERE SO DELICIOUS...
...
THEY'RE ALL FOOLS.
IT'S NOT SPORTING TO ACT AS THOUGH WE INVITED OURSELVES ALONG AIMLESSLY.
YOU WERE THE ONE WHO DIDN'T EXPLAIN THE REASONS FOR YOUR TRIP WELL ENOUGH!
YOU MADE IT SOUND LIKE YOU WERE BEING SET UP FOR AN OMIAI BY YOUR FAMILY!
NATURALLY WE COULDN'T MISS THAT!
APPARENTLY THAT JUSTIFIES INVITING THEMSELVES ALONG.
AKITO OHTORI, SECOND SON
It's only now we know the woman your father wanted you to meet was an omiai match for Akito.
But why would he want you to meet her, Kyoya?
SIGH
BECAUSE THE WOMAN IN QUESTION... IS APPARENTLY THE SOLE HEIRESS OF SHOJI GENERAL.
SHE'S BEEN STUDYING HERE IN MADRID.
THEY'D BEEN TALKING ABOUT SETTING UP AN OMIAI WITH HER FOR A WHILE, AND SINCE FATHER IS IN BARCELONA FOR A SYMPOSIUM...
...THEY FIGURED IT WAS A GOOD OPPORTUNITY AND CALLED AKITO OVER.
HOWEVER, EVEN THOUGH SHE'S SCHEDULED TO ARRIVE TODAY, AKITO HAS BEEN DELAYED WITH A FEW THINGS AT HIS UNIVERSITY AND WON'T BE HERE FOR ANOTHER TWO DAYS...
I SEE... SO YOU WERE CALLED OVER TO ENTERTAIN HER UNTIL HE ARRIVES.

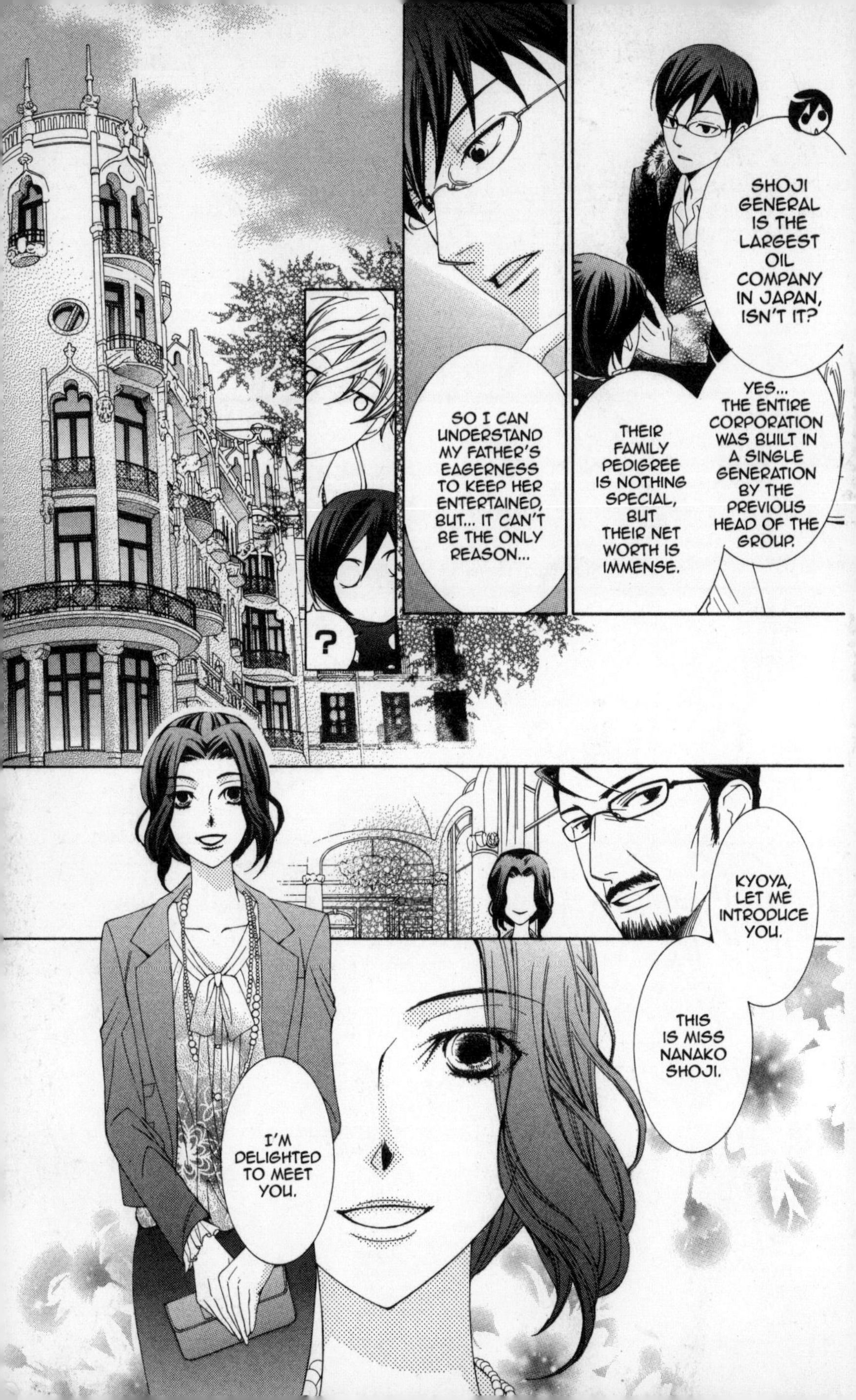
SHOJI GENERAL IS THE LARGEST OIL COMPANY IN JAPAN, ISN'T IT?
YES... THE ENTIRE CORPORATION WAS BUILT IN A SINGLE GENERATION BY THE PREVIOUS HEAD OF THE GROUP.
THEIR FAMILY PEDIGREE IS NOTHING SPECIAL, BUT THEIR NET WORTH IS IMMENSE.
SO I CAN UNDERSTAND MY FATHER'S EAGERNESS TO KEEP HER ENTERTAINED, BUT... IT CAN'T BE THE ONLY REASON...
?
KYOYA, LET ME INTRODUCE YOU.
THIS IS MISS NANAKO SHOJI.
I'M DELIGHTED TO MEET YOU.

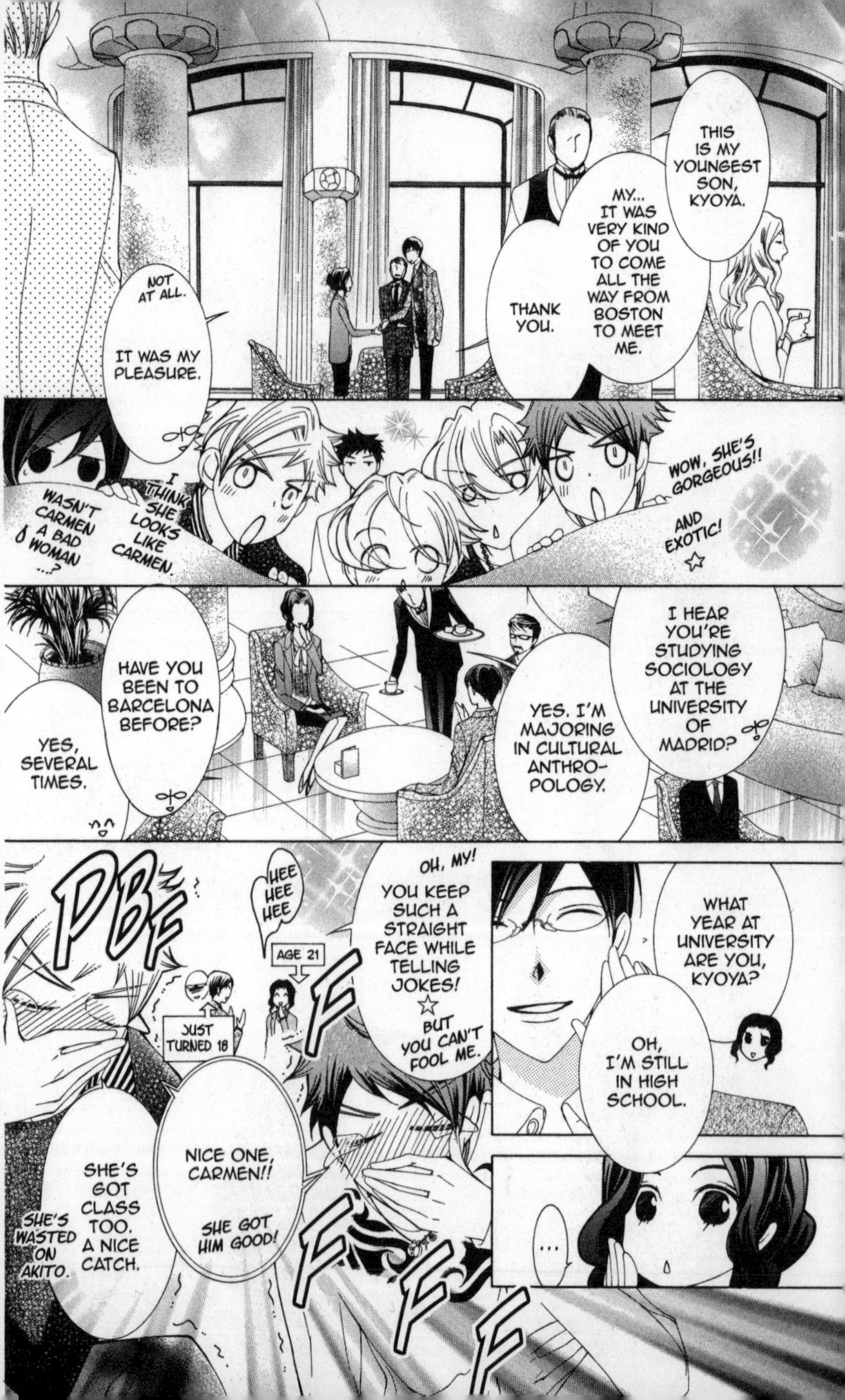
THIS IS MY YOUNGEST SON, KYOYA.
MY... IT WAS VERY KIND OF YOU TO COME ALL THE WAY FROM BOSTON TO MEET ME.
THANK YOU.
NOT AT ALL.
IT WAS MY PLEASURE.
WOW, SHE'S GORGEOUS!!
AND EXOTIC! ☆
I THINK SHE LOOKS LIKE CARMEN.
WASN'T CARMEN A BAD WOMAN ...?
I HEAR YOU'RE STUDYING SOCIOLOGY AT THE UNIVERSITY OF MADRID?
YES. I'M MAJORING IN CULTURAL ANTHRO-POLOGY.
HAVE YOU BEEN TO BARCELONA BEFORE?
YES, SEVERAL TIMES.
WHAT YEAR AT UNIVERSITY ARE YOU, KYOYA?
OH, I'M STILL IN HIGH SCHOOL.
...
OH, MY!
YOU KEEP SUCH A STRAIGHT FACE WHILE TELLING JOKES! ☆
BUT YOU CAN'T FOOL ME.
HEE HEE HEE
AGE 21
JUST TURNED 18
PBF
FFFF
NICE ONE, CARMEN!!
SHE GOT HIM GOOD!
SHE'S GOT CLASS TOO. A NICE CATCH.
SHE'S WASTED ON AKITO.

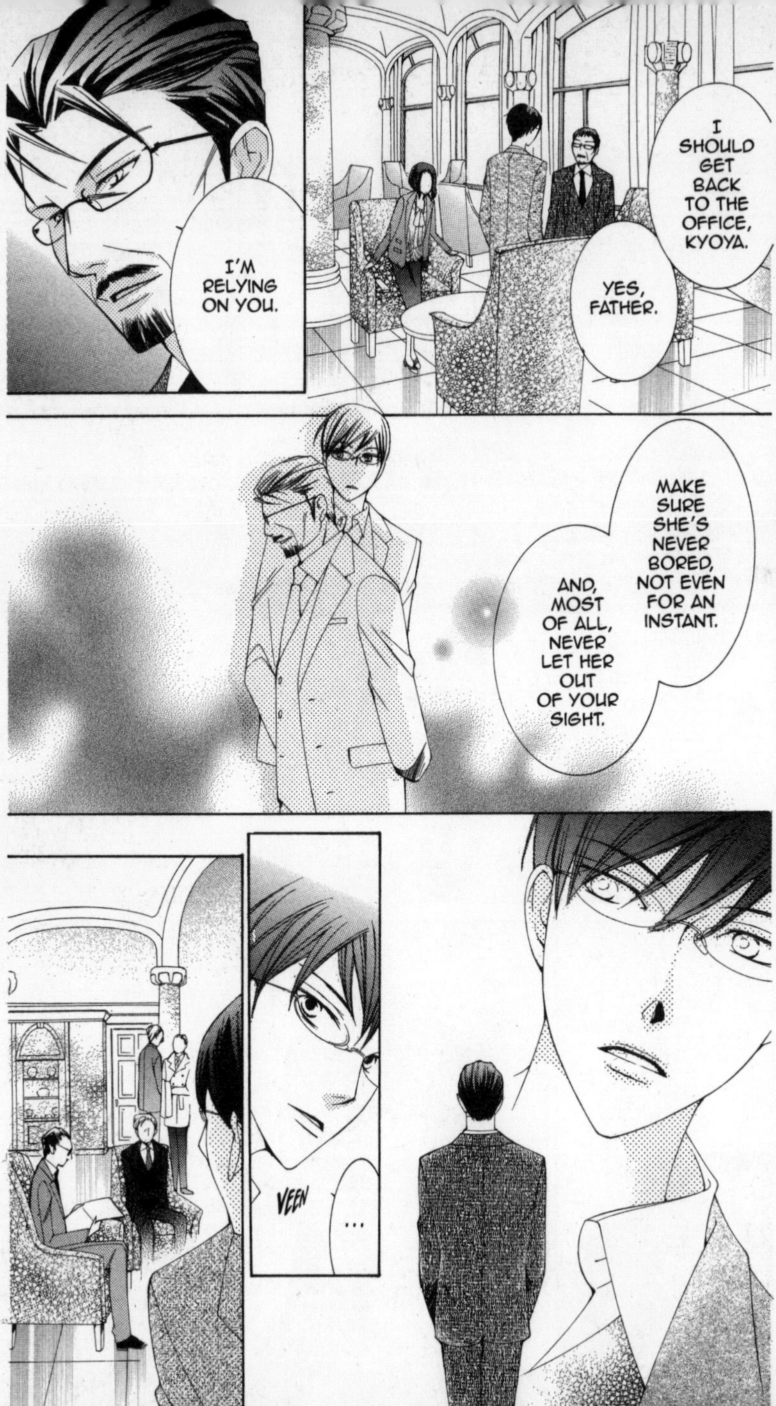
I SHOULD GET BACK TO THE OFFICE, KYOYA.
YES, FATHER.
I'M RELYING ON YOU.
MAKE SURE SHE'S NEVER BORED, NOT EVEN FOR AN INSTANT.
AND, MOST OF ALL, NEVER LET HER OUT OF YOUR SIGHT.
VEEN
...

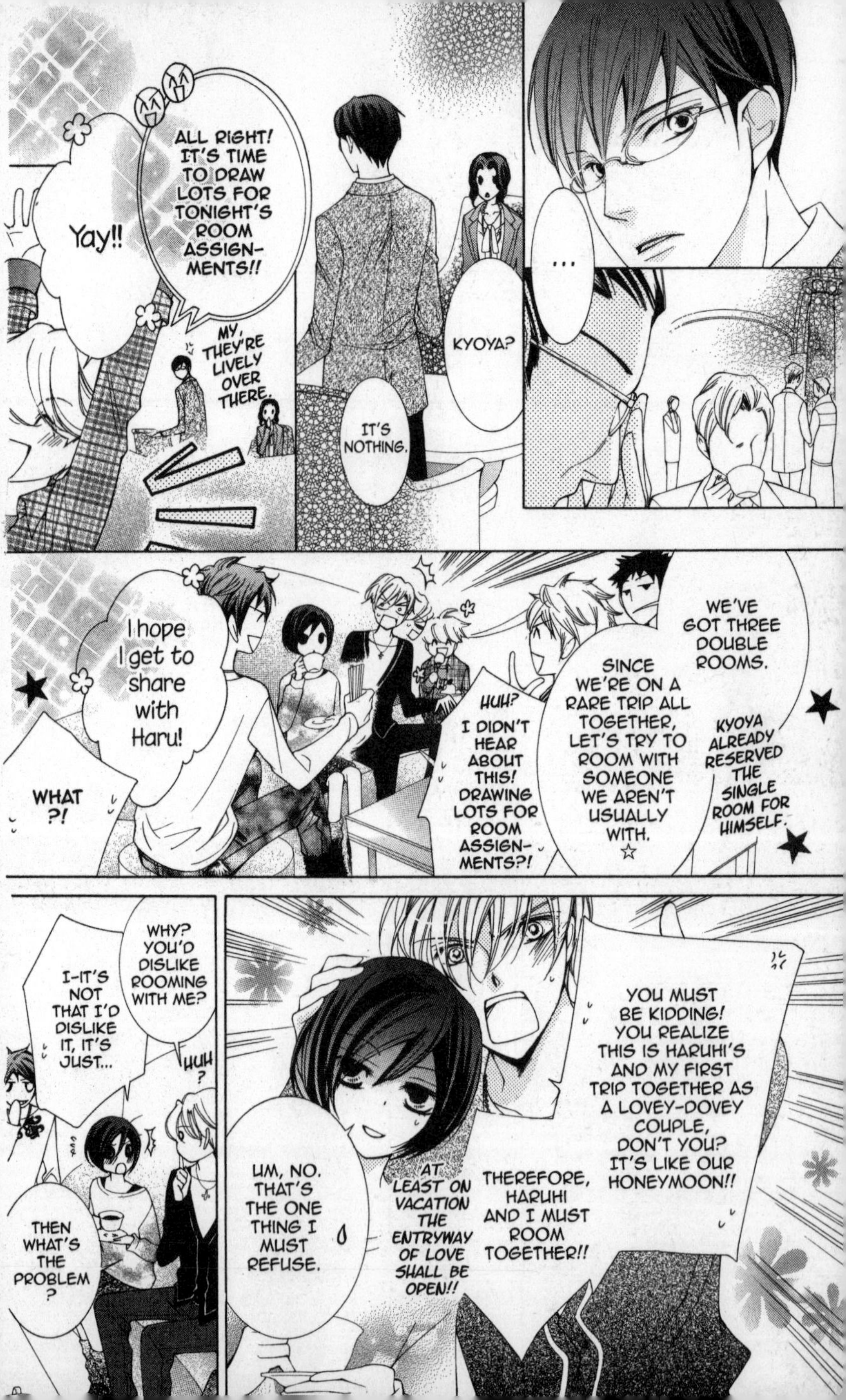
...
KYOYA?
IT'S NOTHING.
ALL RIGHT! IT'S TIME TO DRAW LOTS FOR TONIGHT'S ROOM ASSIGNMENTS!!
Yay!!
MY, THEY'RE LIVELY OVER THERE.
WE'VE GOT THREE DOUBLE ROOMS.
KYOYA ALREADY RESERVED THE SINGLE ROOM FOR HIMSELF.
SINCE WE'RE ON A RARE TRIP ALL TOGETHER, LET'S TRY TO ROOM WITH SOMEONE WE AREN'T USUALLY WITH. ☆
HUH? I DIDN'T HEAR ABOUT THIS! DRAWING LOTS FOR ROOM ASSIGNMENTS?!
I hope I get to share with Haru!
WHAT?!
YOU MUST BE KIDDING! YOU REALIZE THIS IS HARUHI'S AND MY FIRST TRIP TOGETHER AS A LOVEY-DOVEY COUPLE, DON'T YOU? IT'S LIKE OUR HONEYMOON!!
THEREFORE, HARUHI AND I MUST ROOM TOGETHER!!
AT LEAST ON VACATION THE ENTRYWAY OF LOVE SHALL BE OPEN!!
UM, NO. THAT'S THE ONE THING I MUST REFUSE.
WHY? YOU'D DISLIKE ROOMING WITH ME?
I-IT'S NOT THAT I'D DISLIKE IT, IT'S JUST...
HUH?
THEN WHAT'S THE PROBLEM?

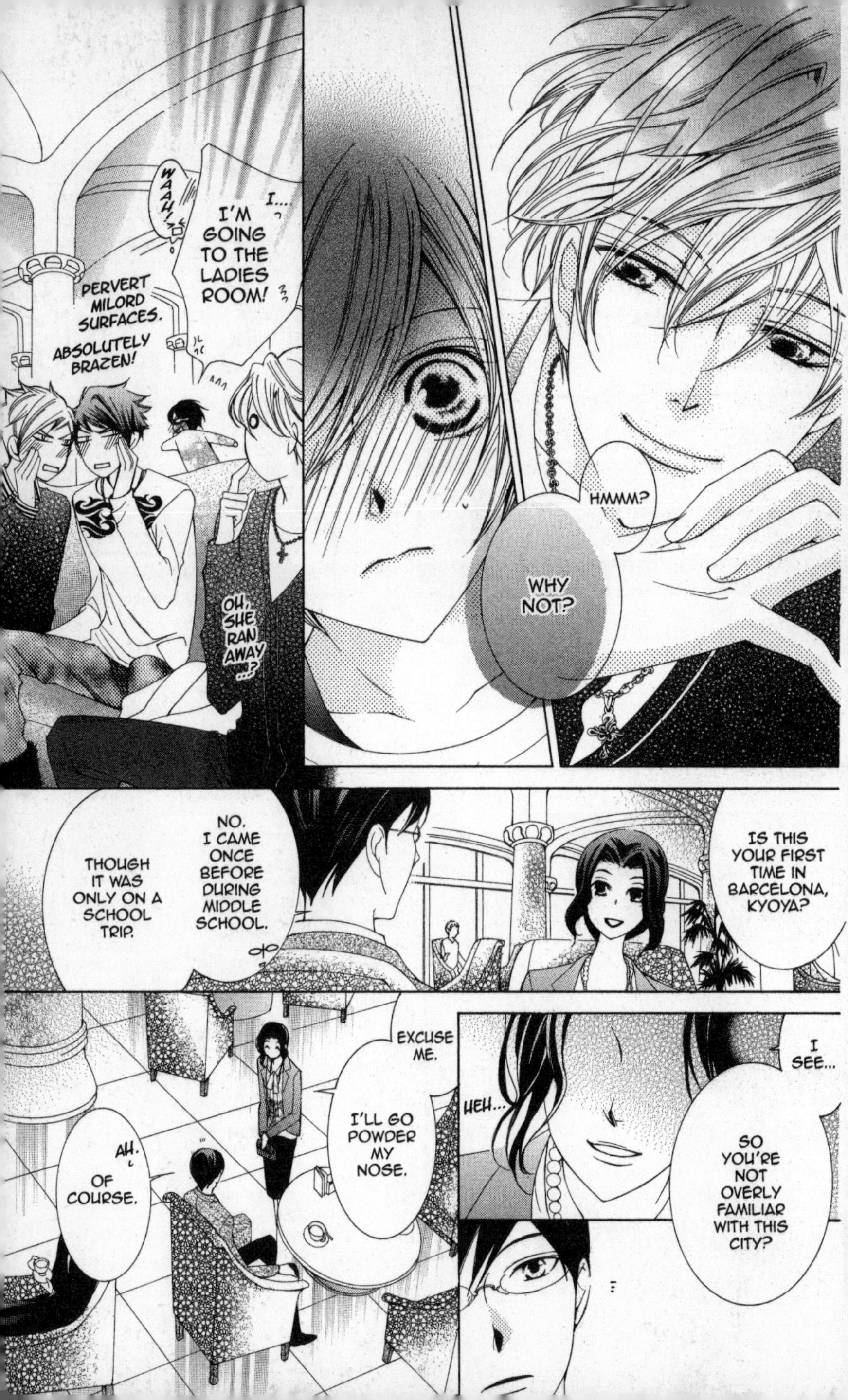
HMMM?
WHY NOT?
I...
I'M GOING TO THE LADIES ROOM!
WAAAH!
PERVERT MILORD SURFACES.
ABSOLUTELY BRAZEN!
OH, SHE RAN AWAY...?
IS THIS YOUR FIRST TIME IN BARCELONA, KYOYA?
NO. I CAME ONCE BEFORE DURING MIDDLE SCHOOL.
THOUGH IT WAS ONLY ON A SCHOOL TRIP.
I SEE...
HEH...
SO YOU'RE NOT OVERLY FAMILIAR WITH THIS CITY?
EXCUSE ME.
I'LL GO POWDER MY NOSE.
AH.
OF COURSE.

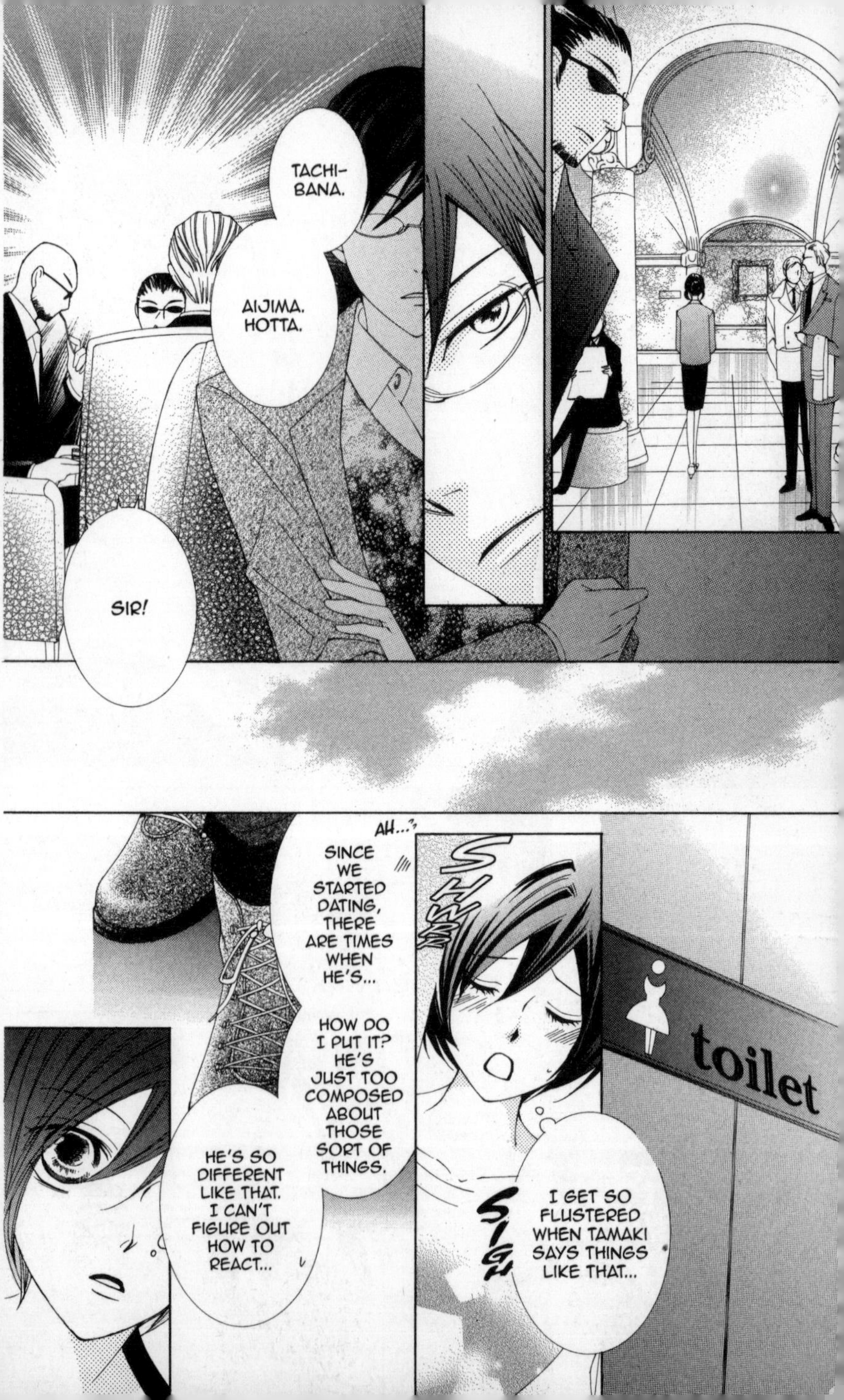
TACHI-BANA.
AIJIMA. HOTTA.
SIR!
SHWM
toilet
I GET SO FLUSTERED WHEN TAMAKI SAYS THINGS LIKE THAT...
SIGH
AH...?
SINCE WE STARTED DATING, THERE ARE TIMES WHEN HE'S...
HOW DO I PUT IT? HE'S JUST TOO COMPOSED ABOUT THOSE SORT OF THINGS.
HE'S SO DIFFERENT LIKE THAT. I CAN'T FIGURE OUT HOW TO REACT...

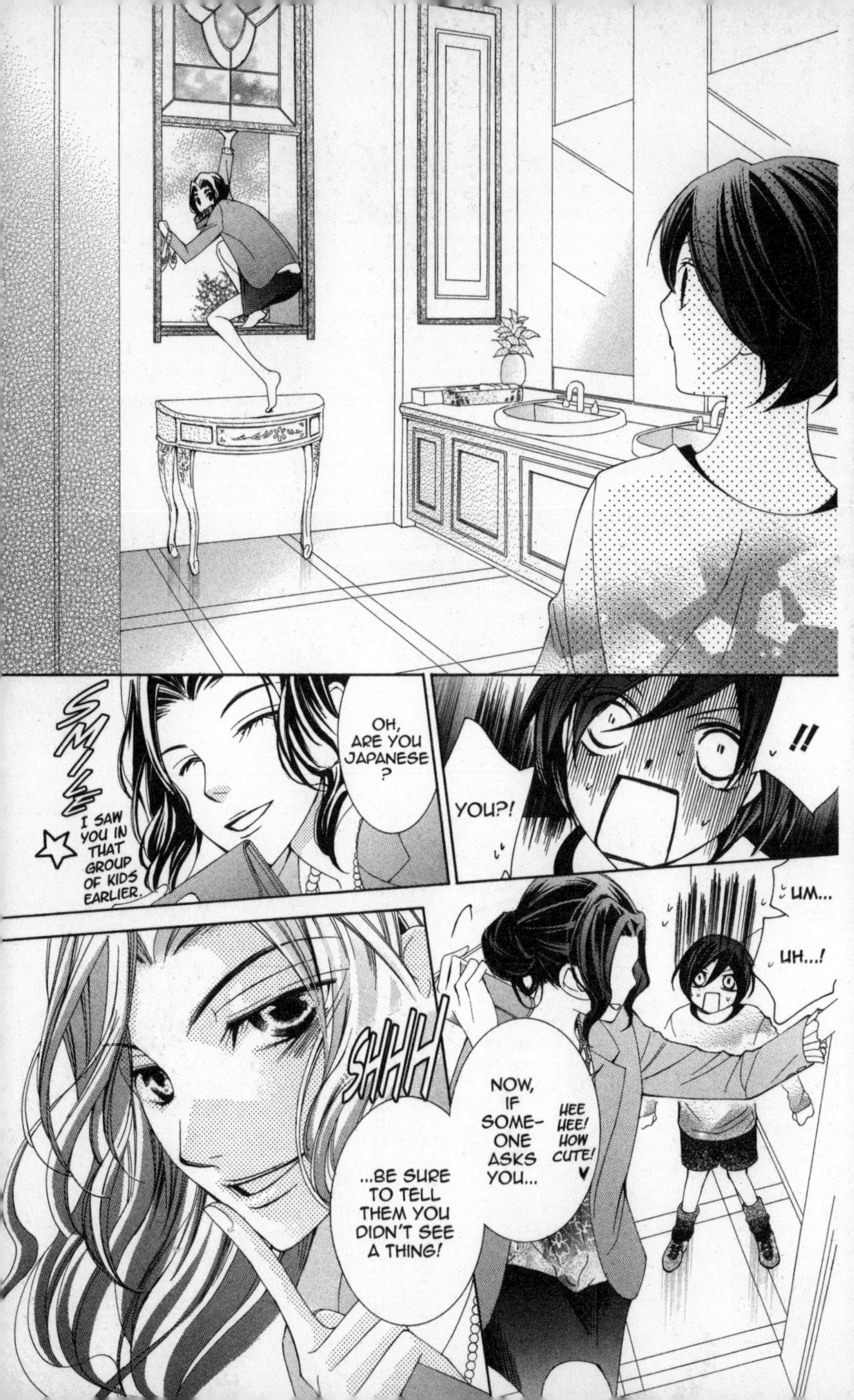
!!
YOU?!
OH, ARE YOU JAPANESE?
SMILE
I SAW YOU IN THAT GROUP OF KIDS EARLIER.
UM...
UH...!
NOW, IF SOME-ONE ASKS YOU...
HEE HEE! HOW CUTE!
SHHH
...BE SURE TO TELL THEM YOU DIDN'T SEE A THING!

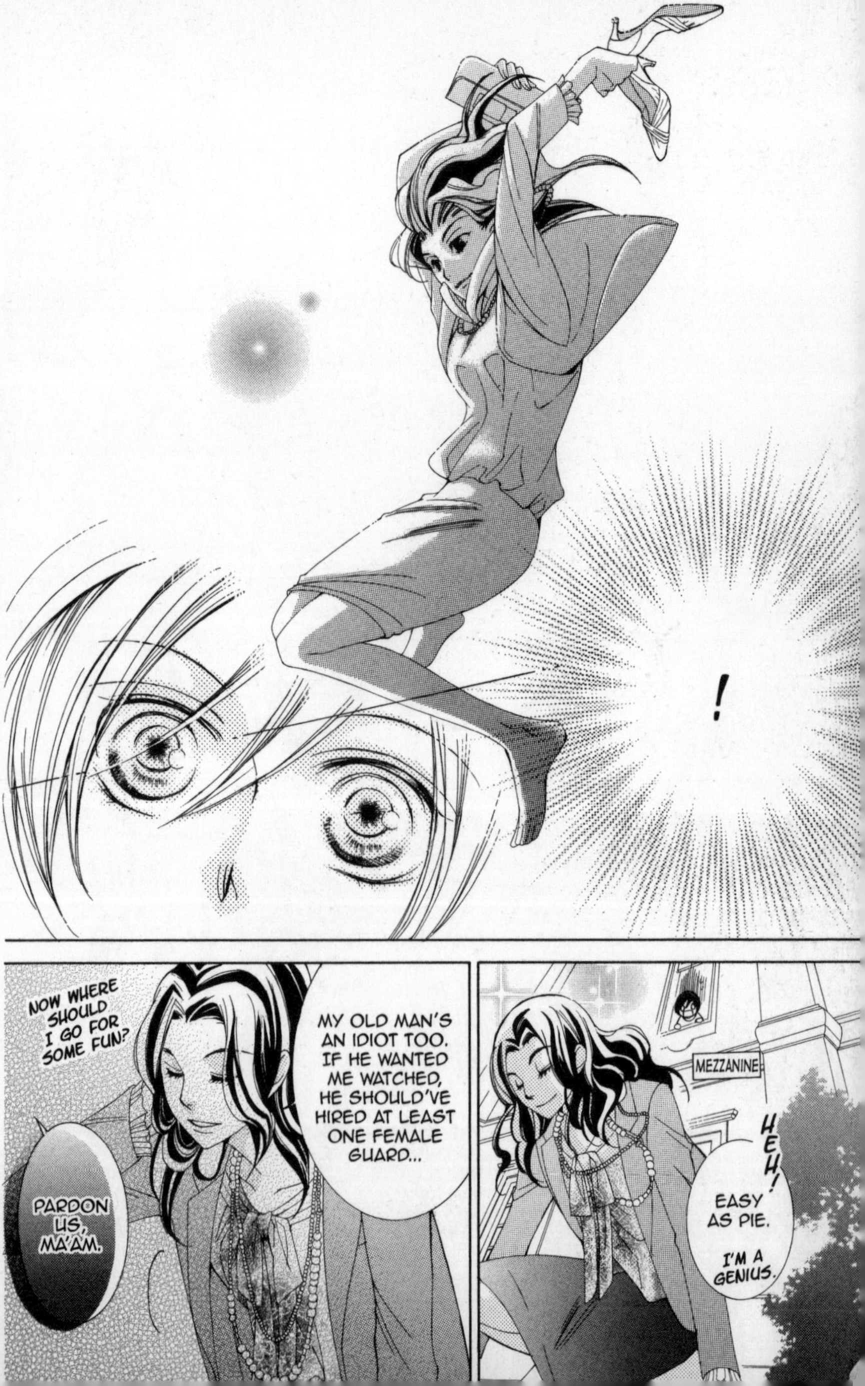
!
MEZZANINE
HEH!
EASY AS PIE.
I'M A GENIUS.
MY OLD MAN'S AN IDIOT TOO. IF HE WANTED ME WATCHED, HE SHOULD'VE HIRED AT LEAST ONE FEMALE GUARD...
NOW WHERE SHOULD I GO FOR SOME FUN?
PARDON US, MA'AM.

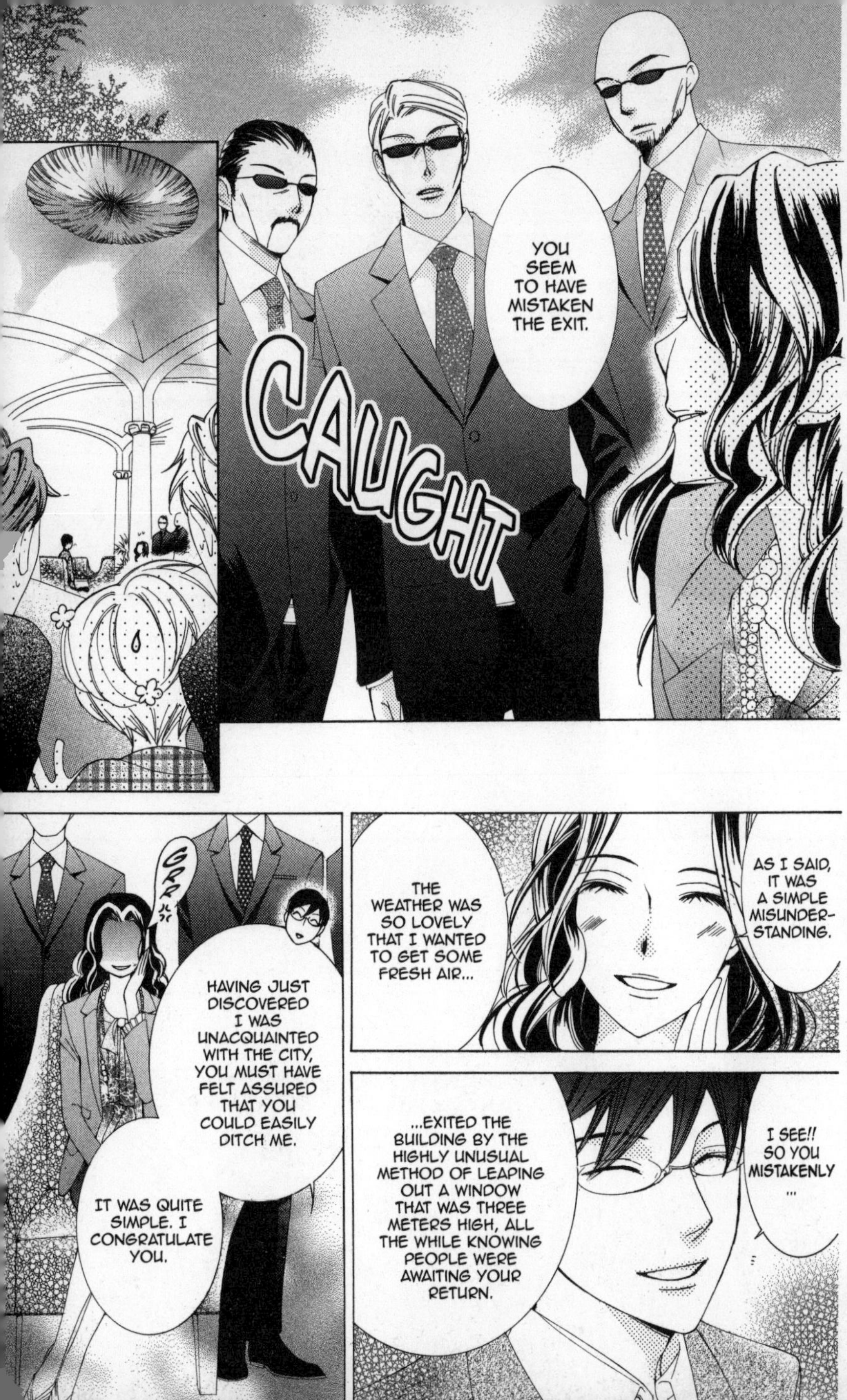
YOU SEEM TO HAVE MISTAKEN THE EXIT.
CAUGHT
AS I SAID, IT WAS A SIMPLE MISUNDERSTANDING.
THE WEATHER WAS SO LOVELY THAT I WANTED TO GET SOME FRESH AIR...
I SEE!! SO YOU MISTAKENLY ...
...EXITED THE BUILDING BY THE HIGHLY UNUSUAL METHOD OF LEAPING OUT A WINDOW THAT WAS THREE METERS HIGH, ALL THE WHILE KNOWING PEOPLE WERE AWAITING YOUR RETURN.
GRR
HAVING JUST DISCOVERED I WAS UNACQUAINTED WITH THE CITY, YOU MUST HAVE FELT ASSURED THAT YOU COULD EASILY DITCH ME.
IT WAS QUITE SIMPLE. I CONGRATULATE YOU.

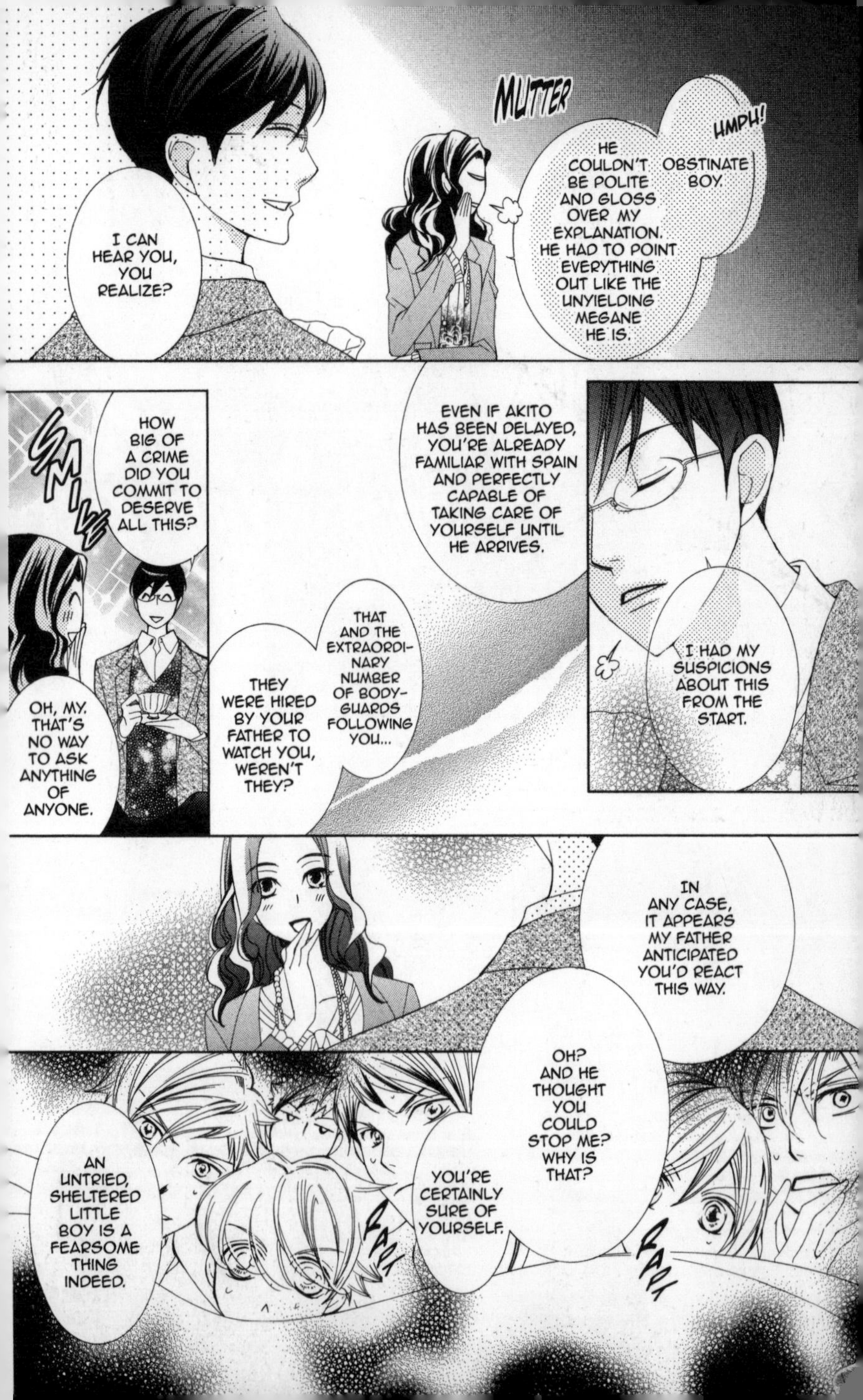
MUTTER
HMPH!
OBSTINATE BOY.
HE COULDN'T BE POLITE AND GLOSS OVER MY EXPLANATION. HE HAD TO POINT EVERYTHING OUT LIKE THE UNYIELDING MEGANE HE IS.
I CAN HEAR YOU, YOU REALIZE?
EVEN IF AKITO HAS BEEN DELAYED, YOU'RE ALREADY FAMILIAR WITH SPAIN AND PERFECTLY CAPABLE OF TAKING CARE OF YOURSELF UNTIL HE ARRIVES.
I HAD MY SUSPICIONS ABOUT THIS FROM THE START.
THAT AND THE EXTRAORDINARY NUMBER OF BODY-GUARDS FOLLOWING YOU...
THEY WERE HIRED BY YOUR FATHER TO WATCH YOU, WEREN'T THEY?
SMILE
HOW BIG OF A CRIME DID YOU COMMIT TO DESERVE ALL THIS?
OH, MY. THAT'S NO WAY TO ASK ANYTHING OF ANYONE.
IN ANY CASE, IT APPEARS MY FATHER ANTICIPATED YOU'D REACT THIS WAY.
OH? AND HE THOUGHT YOU COULD STOP ME? WHY IS THAT?
YOU'RE CERTAINLY SURE OF YOURSELF.
AN UNTRIED, SHELTERED LITTLE BOY IS A FEARSOME THING INDEED.

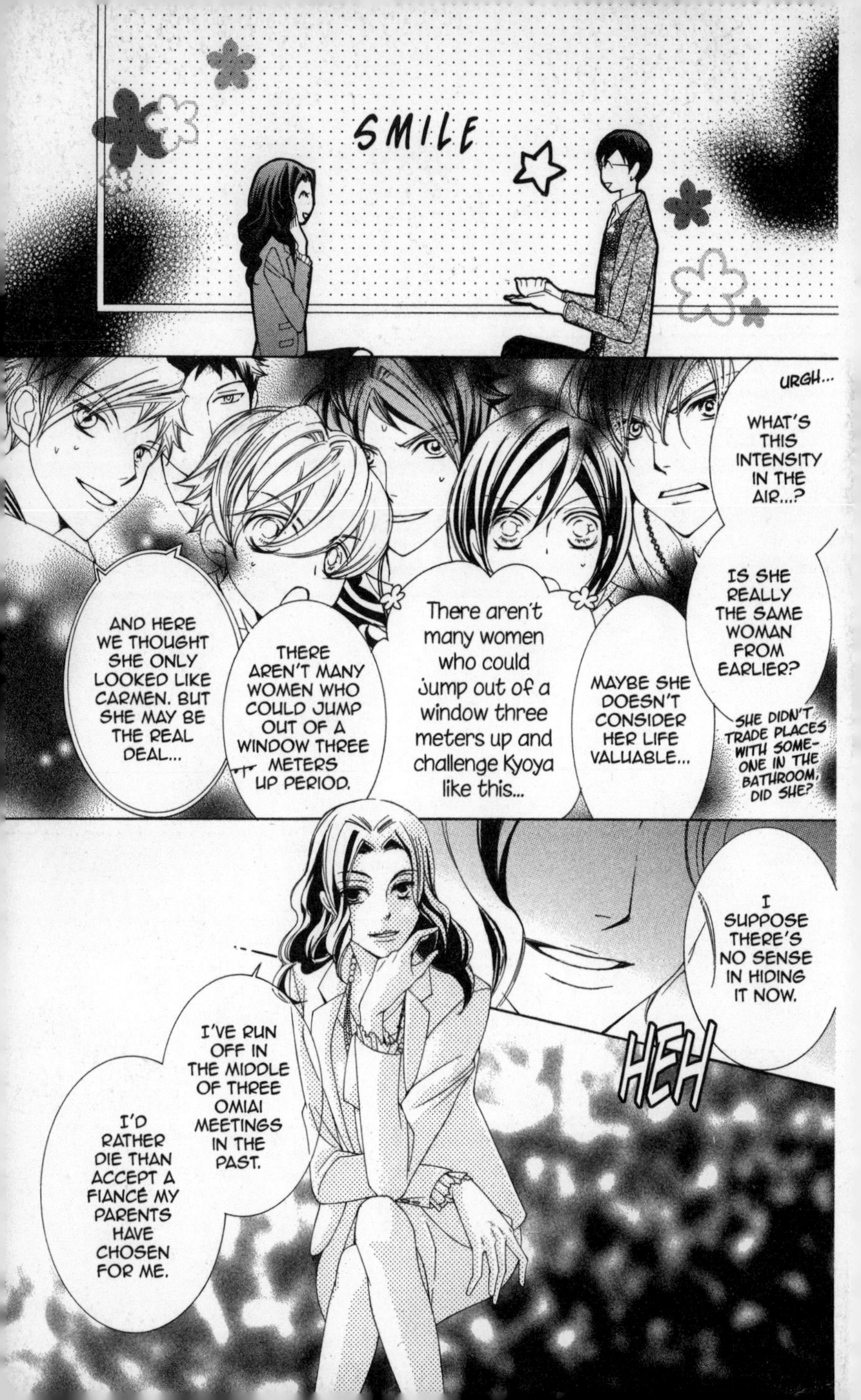
SMILE
URGH...
WHAT'S THIS INTENSITY IN THE AIR...?
IS SHE REALLY THE SAME WOMAN FROM EARLIER?
SHE DIDN'T TRADE PLACES WITH SOME-ONE IN THE BATHROOM, DID SHE?
MAYBE SHE DOESN'T CONSIDER HER LIFE VALUABLE...
There aren't many women who could jump out of a window three meters up and challenge Kyoya like this...
THERE AREN'T MANY WOMEN WHO COULD JUMP OUT OF A WINDOW THREE METERS UP PERIOD.
AND HERE WE THOUGHT SHE ONLY LOOKED LIKE CARMEN. BUT SHE MAY BE THE REAL DEAL...
I SUPPOSE THERE'S NO SENSE IN HIDING IT NOW.
HEH
I'VE RUN OFF IN THE MIDDLE OF THREE OMIAI MEETINGS IN THE PAST.
I'D RATHER DIE THAN ACCEPT A FIANCÉ MY PARENTS HAVE CHOSEN FOR ME.

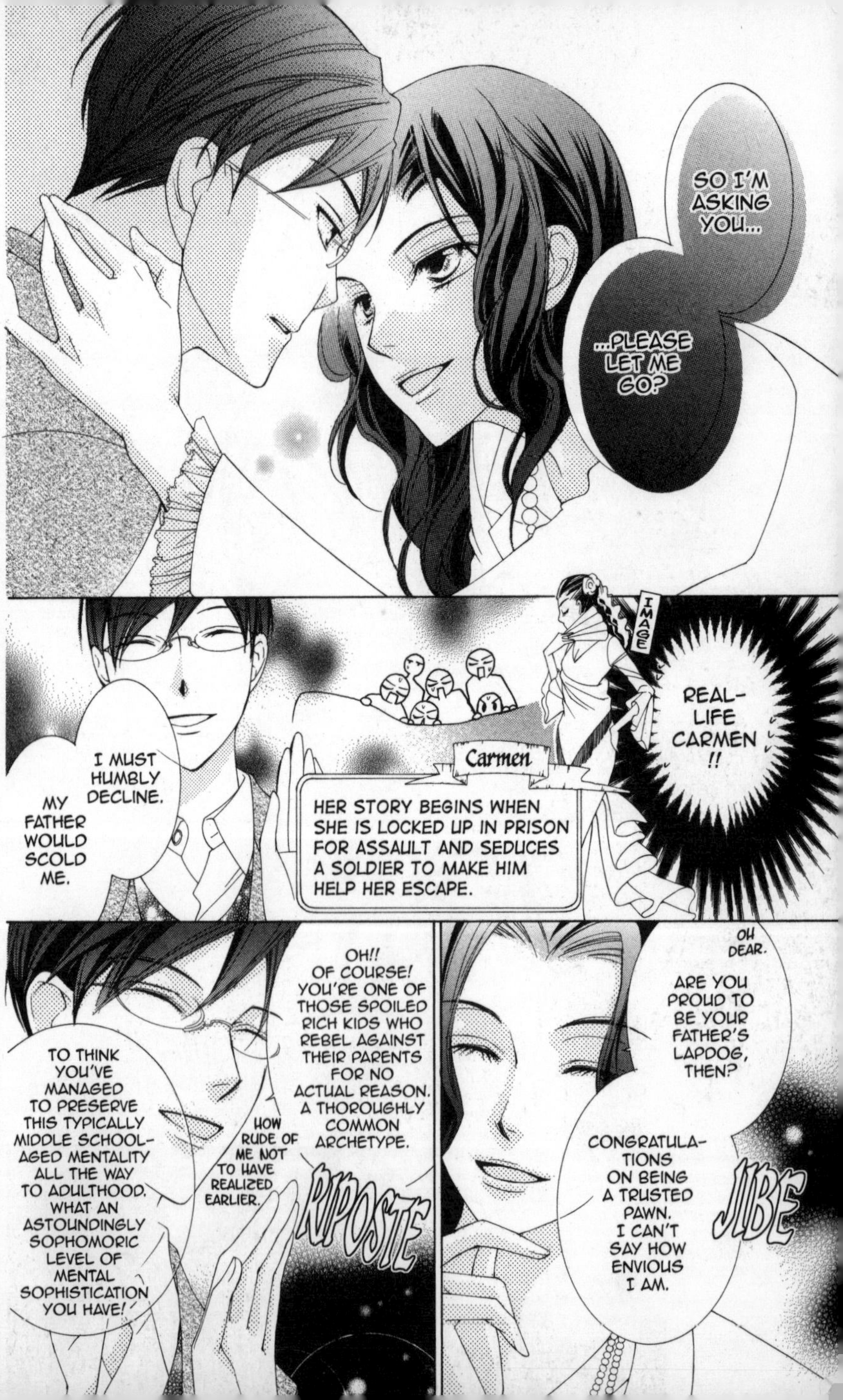
SO I'M ASKING YOU...
...PLEASE LET ME GO?
IMAGE
REAL-LIFE CARMEN !!
Carmen
HER STORY BEGINS WHEN SHE IS LOCKED UP IN PRISON FOR ASSAULT AND SEDUCES A SOLDIER TO MAKE HIM HELP HER ESCAPE.
I MUST HUMBLY DECLINE.
MY FATHER WOULD SCOLD ME.
OH DEAR.
ARE YOU PROUD TO BE YOUR FATHER'S LAPDOG, THEN?
JIBE
CONGRATULA-TIONS ON BEING A TRUSTED PAWN. I CAN'T SAY HOW ENVIOUS I AM.
OH!! OF COURSE! YOU'RE ONE OF THOSE SPOILED RICH KIDS WHO REBEL AGAINST THEIR PARENTS FOR NO ACTUAL REASON. A THOROUGHLY COMMON ARCHETYPE.
HOW RUDE OF ME NOT TO HAVE REALIZED EARLIER.
RIPOSTE
TO THINK YOU'VE MANAGED TO PRESERVE THIS TYPICALLY MIDDLE SCHOOL-AGED MENTALITY ALL THE WAY TO ADULTHOOD. WHAT AN ASTOUNDINGLY SOPHOMORIC LEVEL OF MENTAL SOPHISTICATION YOU HAVE!

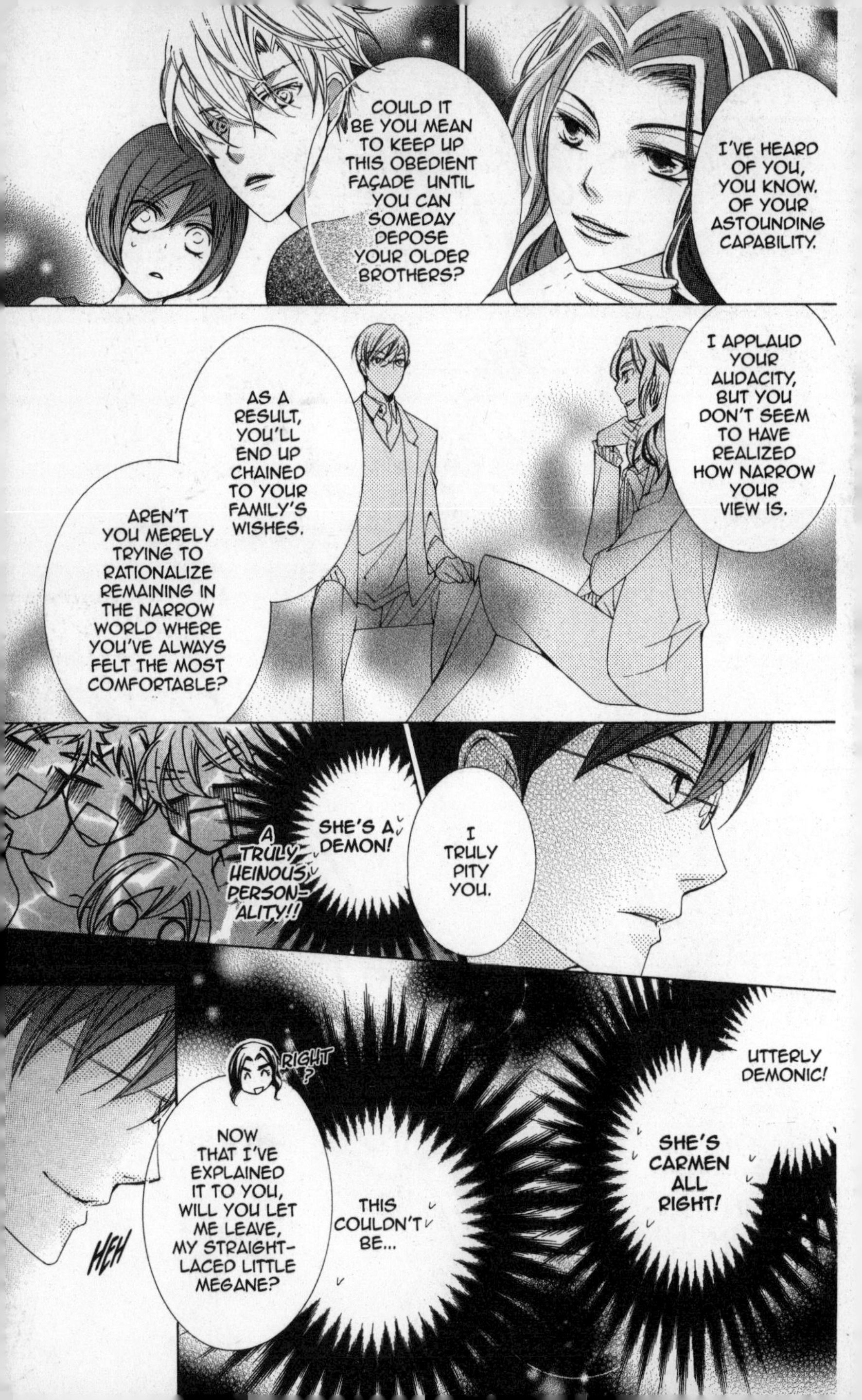
I'VE HEARD OF YOU, YOU KNOW. OF YOUR ASTOUNDING CAPABILITY.
COULD IT BE YOU MEAN TO KEEP UP THIS OBEDIENT FAÇADE UNTIL YOU CAN SOMEDAY DEPOSE YOUR OLDER BROTHERS?
I APPLAUD YOUR AUDACITY, BUT YOU DON'T SEEM TO HAVE REALIZED HOW NARROW YOUR VIEW IS.
AS A RESULT, YOU'LL END UP CHAINED TO YOUR FAMILY'S WISHES.
AREN'T YOU MERELY TRYING TO RATIONALIZE REMAINING IN THE NARROW WORLD WHERE YOU'VE ALWAYS FELT THE MOST COMFORTABLE?
I TRULY PITY YOU.
SHE'S A DEMON!
A TRULY HEINOUS PERSONALITY!!
UTTERLY DEMONIC!
SHE'S CARMEN ALL RIGHT!
THIS COULDN'T BE...
RIGHT?
NOW THAT I'VE EXPLAINED IT TO YOU, WILL YOU LET ME LEAVE, MY STRAIGHT-LACED LITTLE MEGANE?
HEH

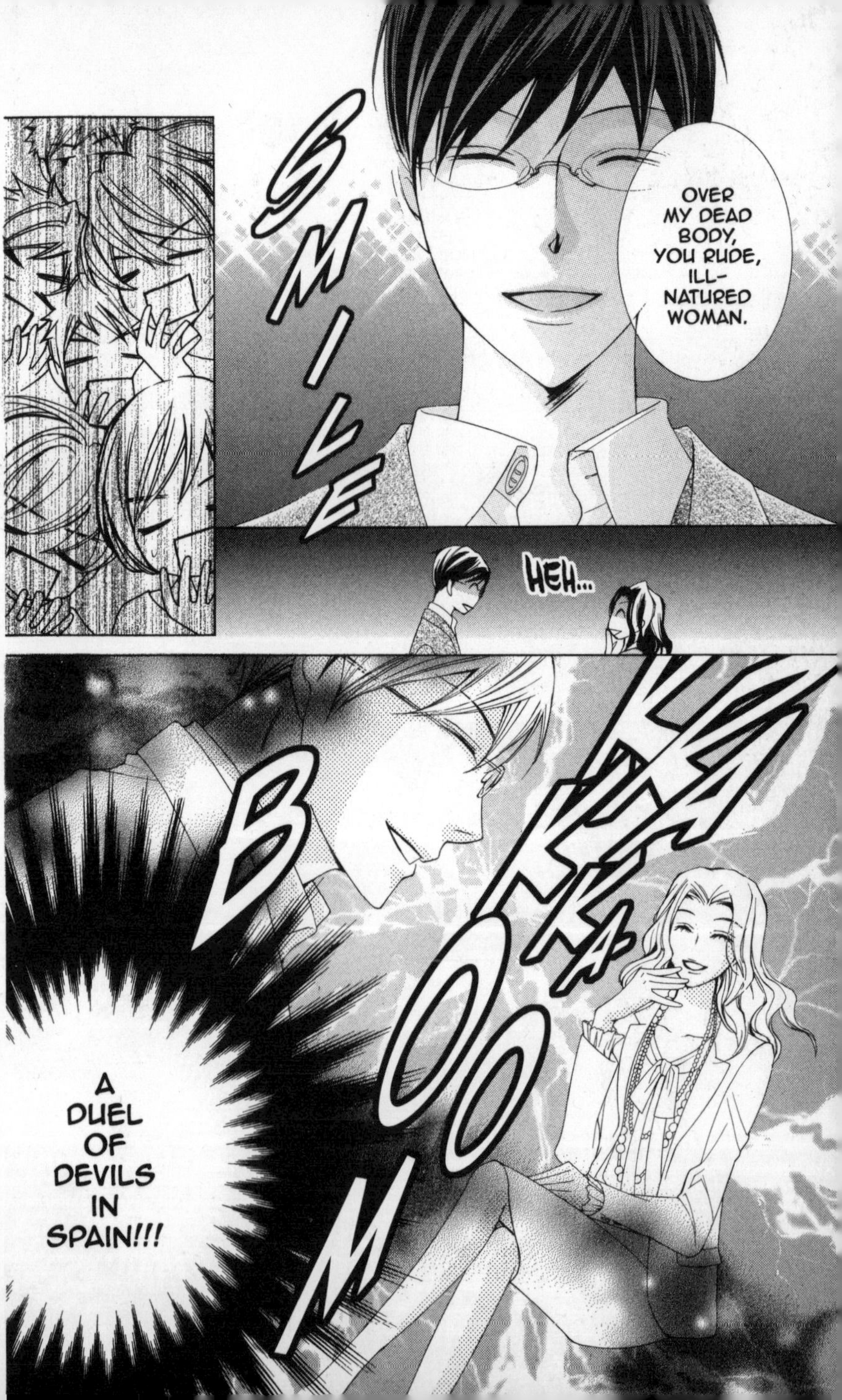
SMILE
OVER MY DEAD BODY, YOU RUDE, ILL-NATURED WOMAN.
HEH...
BOOOM
A DUEL OF DEVILS IN SPAIN!!!

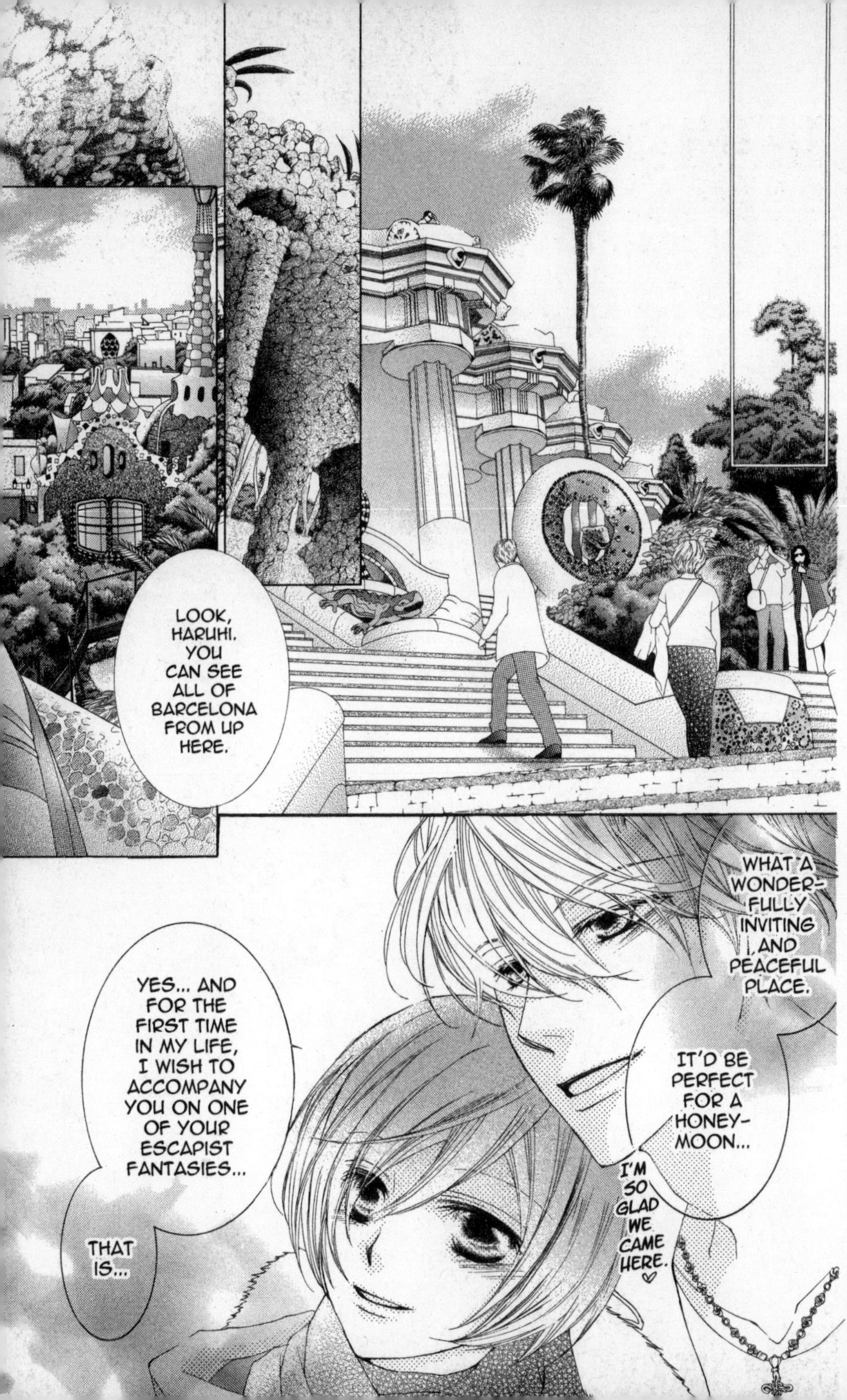
LOOK, HARUHI. YOU CAN SEE ALL OF BARCELONA FROM UP HERE.
WHAT A WONDERFULLY INVITING AND PEACEFUL PLACE.
IT'D BE PERFECT FOR A HONEYMOON...
I'M SO GLAD WE CAME HERE. ♡
YES... AND FOR THE FIRST TIME IN MY LIFE, I WISH TO ACCOMPANY YOU ON ONE OF YOUR ESCAPIST FANTASIES...
THAT IS...

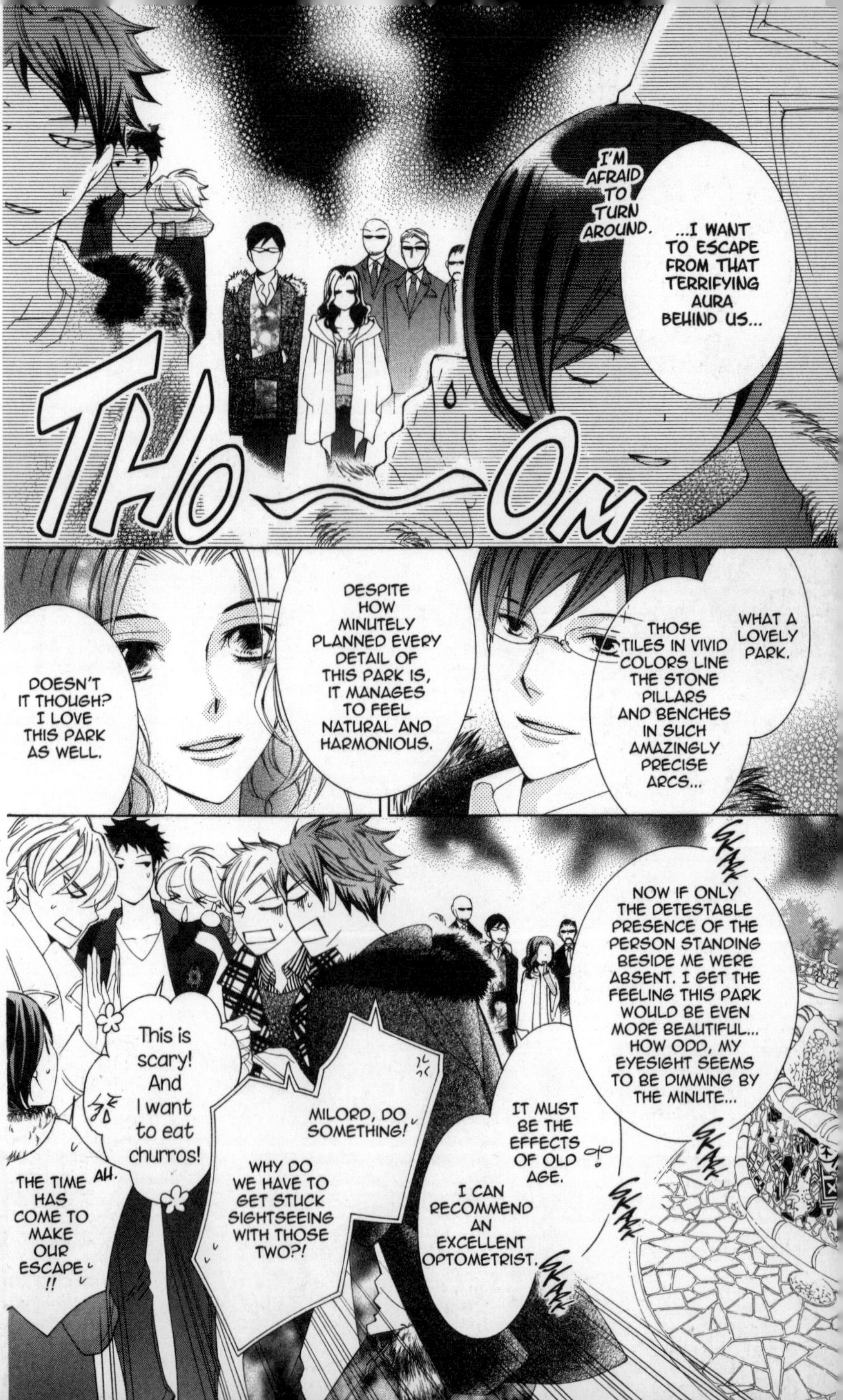
...I WANT TO ESCAPE FROM THAT TERRIFYING AURA BEHIND US...
I'M AFRAID TO TURN AROUND.
THO—OM
WHAT A LOVELY PARK.
THOSE TILES IN VIVID COLORS LINE THE STONE PILLARS AND BENCHES IN SUCH AMAZINGLY PRECISE ARCS...
DESPITE HOW MINUTELY PLANNED EVERY DETAIL OF THIS PARK IS, IT MANAGES TO FEEL NATURAL AND HARMONIOUS.
DOESN'T IT THOUGH? I LOVE THIS PARK AS WELL.
GKAK
NOW IF ONLY THE DETESTABLE PRESENCE OF THE PERSON STANDING BESIDE ME WERE ABSENT. I GET THE FEELING THIS PARK WOULD BE EVEN MORE BEAUTIFUL... HOW ODD, MY EYESIGHT SEEMS TO BE DIMMING BY THE MINUTE...
GKAK
IT MUST BE THE EFFECTS OF OLD AGE.
GKAK
I CAN RECOMMEND AN EXCELLENT OPTOMETRIST.
GKAK
MILORD, DO SOMETHING!
WHY DO WE HAVE TO GET STUCK SIGHTSEEING WITH THOSE TWO?!
This is scary! And I want to eat churros!
AH.
THE TIME HAS COME TO MAKE OUR ESCAPE!!

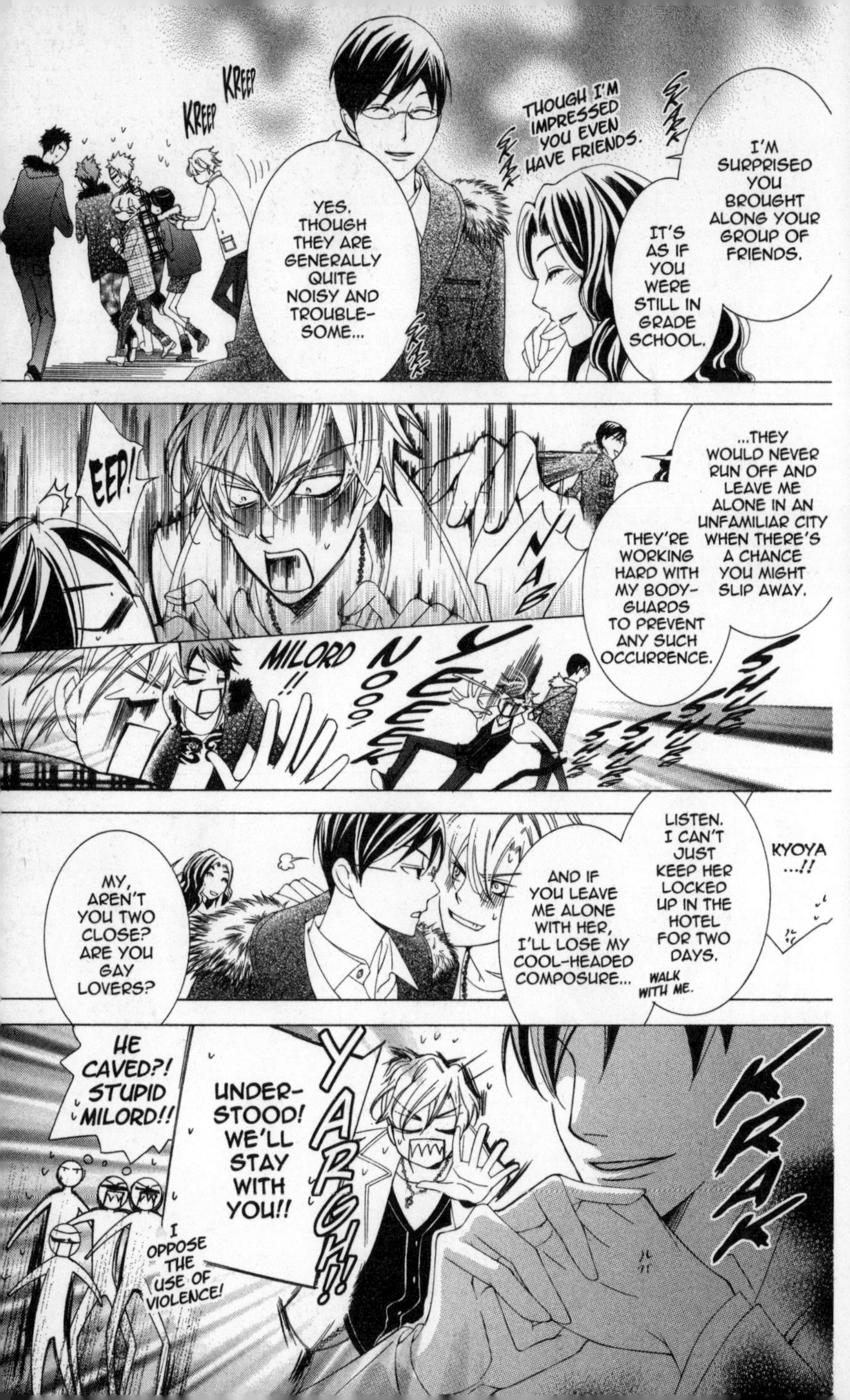
I'M SURPRISED YOU BROUGHT ALONG YOUR GROUP OF FRIENDS.
IT'S AS IF YOU WERE STILL IN GRADE SCHOOL.
SKRAK
THOUGH I'M IMPRESSED YOU EVEN HAVE FRIENDS.
SKRAK
YES. THOUGH THEY ARE GENERALLY QUITE NOISY AND TROUBLE-SOME...
SKRAK
KREEP
KREEP
...THEY WOULD NEVER RUN OFF AND LEAVE ME ALONE IN AN UNFAMILIAR CITY WHEN THERE'S A CHANCE YOU MIGHT SLIP AWAY.
THEY'RE WORKING HARD WITH MY BODY-GUARDS TO PREVENT ANY SUCH OCCURRENCE.
NAB
EEP!
SHUF SHUF SHUF SHUF
YEEEEK
NOOOO
MILORD!!
KYOYA...!!
LISTEN. I CAN'T JUST KEEP HER LOCKED UP IN THE HOTEL FOR TWO DAYS.
AND IF YOU LEAVE ME ALONE WITH HER, I'LL LOSE MY COOL-HEADED COMPOSURE...
WALK WITH ME.
MY, AREN'T YOU TWO CLOSE? ARE YOU GAY LOVERS?
KRAK
YAARGH!!
UNDER-STOOD! WE'LL STAY WITH YOU!!
HE CAVED?! STUPID MILORD!!
I OPPOSE THE USE OF VIOLENCE!

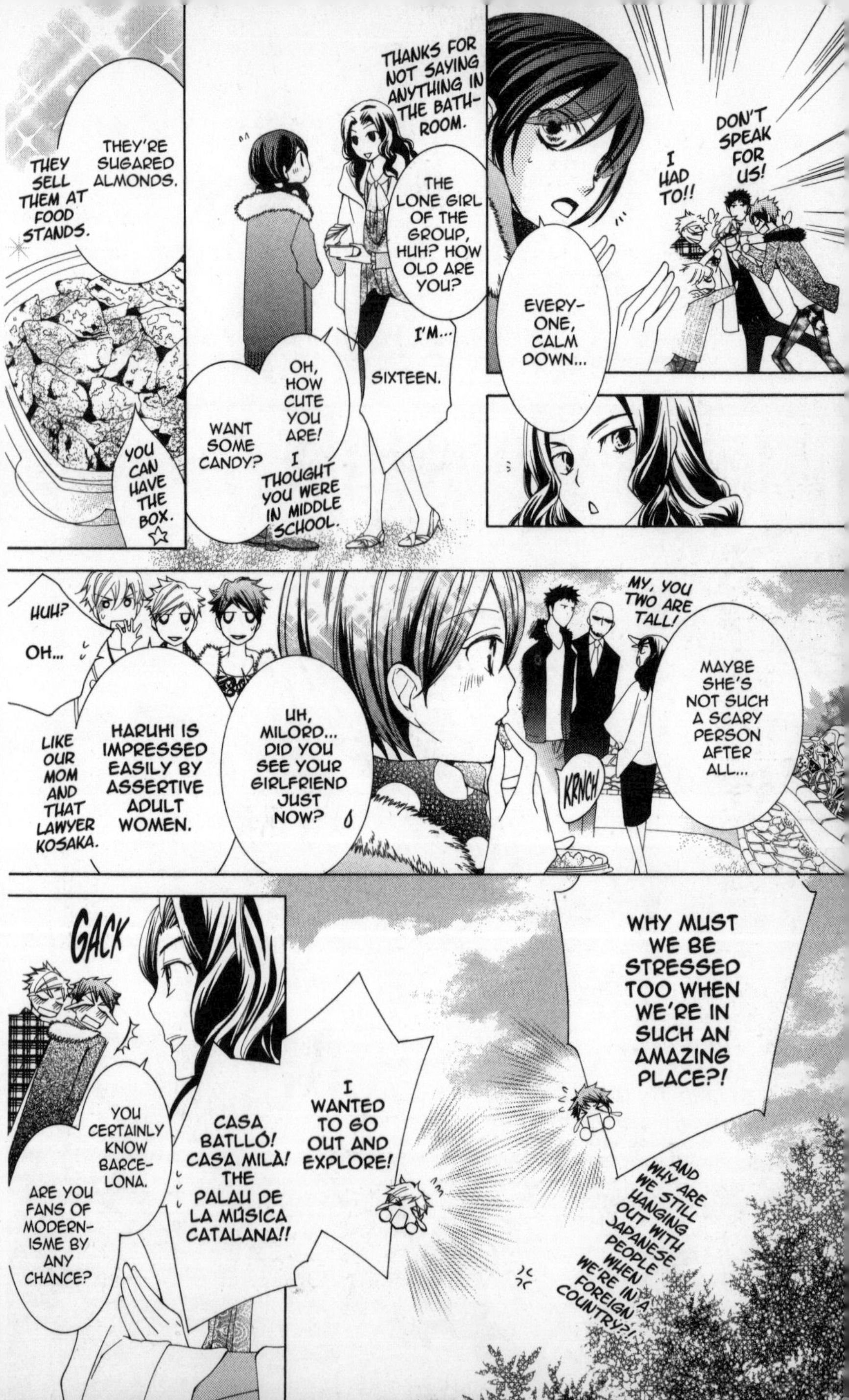
DON'T SPEAK FOR US!
I HAD TO!!
EVERY-ONE, CALM DOWN...
THANKS FOR NOT SAYING ANYTHING IN THE BATH-ROOM.
THE LONE GIRL OF THE GROUP, HUH? HOW OLD ARE YOU?
I'M...
SIXTEEN.
OH, HOW CUTE YOU ARE! I THOUGHT YOU WERE IN MIDDLE SCHOOL.
WANT SOME CANDY?
THEY'RE SUGARED ALMONDS.
THEY SELL THEM AT FOOD STANDS.
YOU CAN HAVE THE BOX. ☆
MY, YOU TWO ARE TALL!
MAYBE SHE'S NOT SUCH A SCARY PERSON AFTER ALL...
KRNCH
UH, MILORD... DID YOU SEE YOUR GIRLFRIEND JUST NOW?
HARUHI IS IMPRESSED EASILY BY ASSERTIVE ADULT WOMEN.
LIKE OUR MOM AND THAT LAWYER KOSAKA.
HUH?
OH...
WHY MUST WE BE STRESSED TOO WHEN WE'RE IN SUCH AN AMAZING PLACE?!
AND WHY ARE WE STILL HANGING OUT WITH JAPANESE PEOPLE WHEN WE'RE IN A FOREIGN COUNTRY?!
I WANTED TO GO OUT AND EXPLORE!
CASA BATLLÓ! CASA MILÀ! THE PALAU DE LA MÚSICA CATALANA!!
YOU CERTAINLY KNOW BARCE-LONA.
ARE YOU FANS OF MODERN-ISME BY ANY CHANCE?
GACK

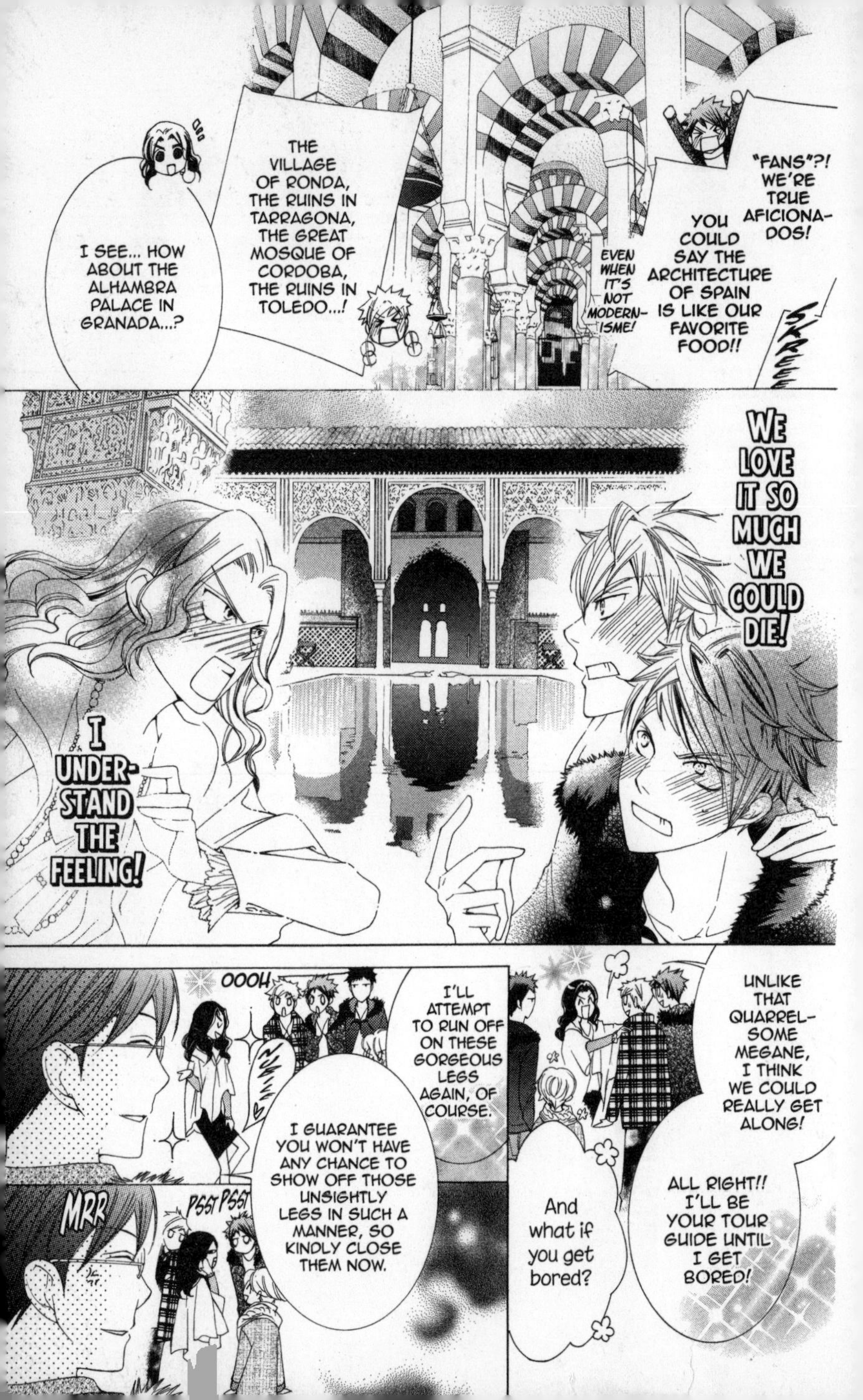
"FANS"?! WE'RE TRUE AFICIONADOS!
YOU COULD SAY THE ARCHITECTURE OF SPAIN IS LIKE OUR FAVORITE FOOD!!
EVEN WHEN IT'S NOT MODERNISME!
SKREEE
THE VILLAGE OF RONDA, THE RUINS IN TARRAGONA, THE GREAT MOSQUE OF CORDOBA, THE RUINS IN TOLEDO...!
I SEE... HOW ABOUT THE ALHAMBRA PALACE IN GRANADA...?
WE LOVE IT SO MUCH WE COULD DIE!
I UNDERSTAND THE FEELING!
UNLIKE THAT QUARRELSOME MEGANE, I THINK WE COULD REALLY GET ALONG!
ALL RIGHT!! I'LL BE YOUR TOUR GUIDE UNTIL I GET BORED!
And what if you get bored?
I'LL ATTEMPT TO RUN OFF ON THESE GORGEOUS LEGS AGAIN, OF COURSE.
OOOH
I GUARANTEE YOU WON'T HAVE ANY CHANCE TO SHOW OFF THOSE UNSIGHTLY LEGS IN SUCH A MANNER, SO KINDLY CLOSE THEM NOW.
PSST PSST
MRR

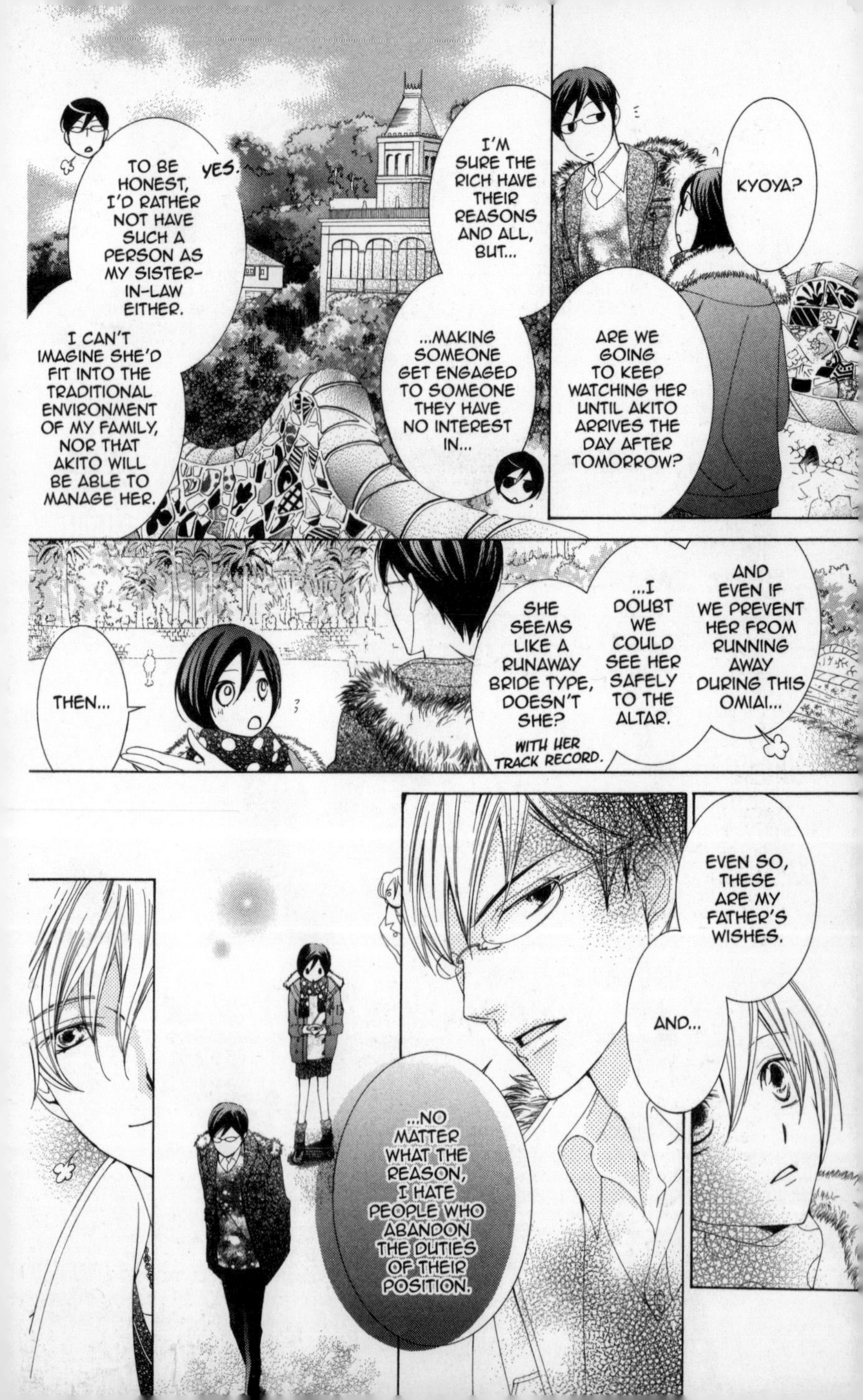
KYOYA?
ARE WE GOING TO KEEP WATCHING HER UNTIL AKITO ARRIVES THE DAY AFTER TOMORROW?
I'M SURE THE RICH HAVE THEIR REASONS AND ALL, BUT...
...MAKING SOMEONE GET ENGAGED TO SOMEONE THEY HAVE NO INTEREST IN...
YES.
TO BE HONEST, I'D RATHER NOT HAVE SUCH A PERSON AS MY SISTER-IN-LAW EITHER.
I CAN'T IMAGINE SHE'D FIT INTO THE TRADITIONAL ENVIRONMENT OF MY FAMILY, NOR THAT AKITO WILL BE ABLE TO MANAGE HER.
AND EVEN IF WE PREVENT HER FROM RUNNING AWAY DURING THIS OMIAI...
...I DOUBT WE COULD SEE HER SAFELY TO THE ALTAR.
SHE SEEMS LIKE A RUNAWAY BRIDE TYPE, DOESN'T SHE?
WITH HER TRACK RECORD.
THEN...
EVEN SO, THESE ARE MY FATHER'S WISHES.
AND...
...NO MATTER WHAT THE REASON, I HATE PEOPLE WHO ABANDON THE DUTIES OF THEIR POSITION.

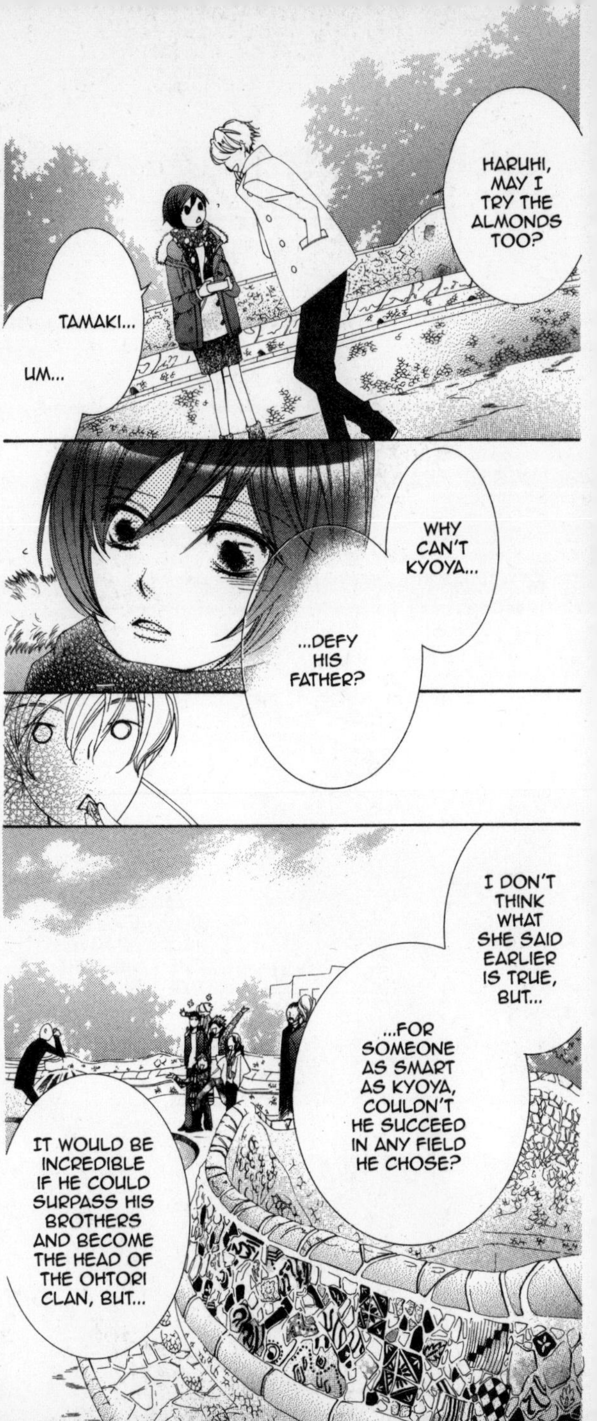
HARUHI, MAY I TRY THE ALMONDS TOO?
TAMAKI...
UM...
WHY CAN'T KYOYA...
...DEFY HIS FATHER?
I DON'T THINK WHAT SHE SAID EARLIER IS TRUE, BUT...
...FOR SOMEONE AS SMART AS KYOYA, COULDN'T HE SUCCEED IN ANY FIELD HE CHOSE?
IT WOULD BE INCREDIBLE IF HE COULD SURPASS HIS BROTHERS AND BECOME THE HEAD OF THE OHTORI CLAN, BUT...

EGOISTIC ☆ CLUB 3

✿ THIS IS THE LAST AUTHOR SIDEBAR. I'D BEEN THINKING OF ALL SORTS OF THINGS I WANTED TO WRITE IN IT, BUT IN THE END, I WASN'T ABLE TO SORT OUT EXACTLY WHAT TO INCLUDE...

RIGHT NOW MY HEART JUST FEELS SO FULL. I'M SO HAPPY THAT I WAS ABLE TO SEE THE FINAL VOLUME SAFELY COMPLETED... I'M SO VERY HAPPY. THOUGH I'M GOING TO MISS *HOST CLUB* VERY MUCH, IT WAS MY GOAL TO FINALLY FINISH A FULL SERIES.

TO MY ENTIRE STAFF AND TO EVERYONE AT THE EDITORIAL OFFICE WHO HAS SUPPORTED ME EVERY STEP OF THE WAY, THANK YOU SO VERY MUCH...!! AND FINALLY, TO ALL YOU READERS WHO STUCK WITH THE SERIES (DESPITE ALL ITS FLAWS AND FRUSTRATING MOMENTS) TO THE VERY END AND CHEERED ME ON THE WHOLE TIME, LET ME JUST SAY THAT IT WAS TRULY THANKS TO YOU THAT I WAS ABLE TO MAKE IT THIS FAR.

TRULY!

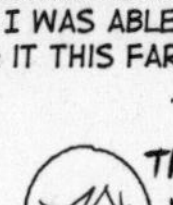
THANK YOU SO VERY MUCH!!

I HOPE SOMEDAY, SOMEWHERE, I'LL BE ABLE TO MEET EACH AND EVERY ONE OF YOU. AT THE END OF THIS VOLUME YOU'LL FIND THE LOVEY-DOVEY TAMAKI X HARUHI BONUS MANGA I'VE ALWAYS WANTED TO DRAW.

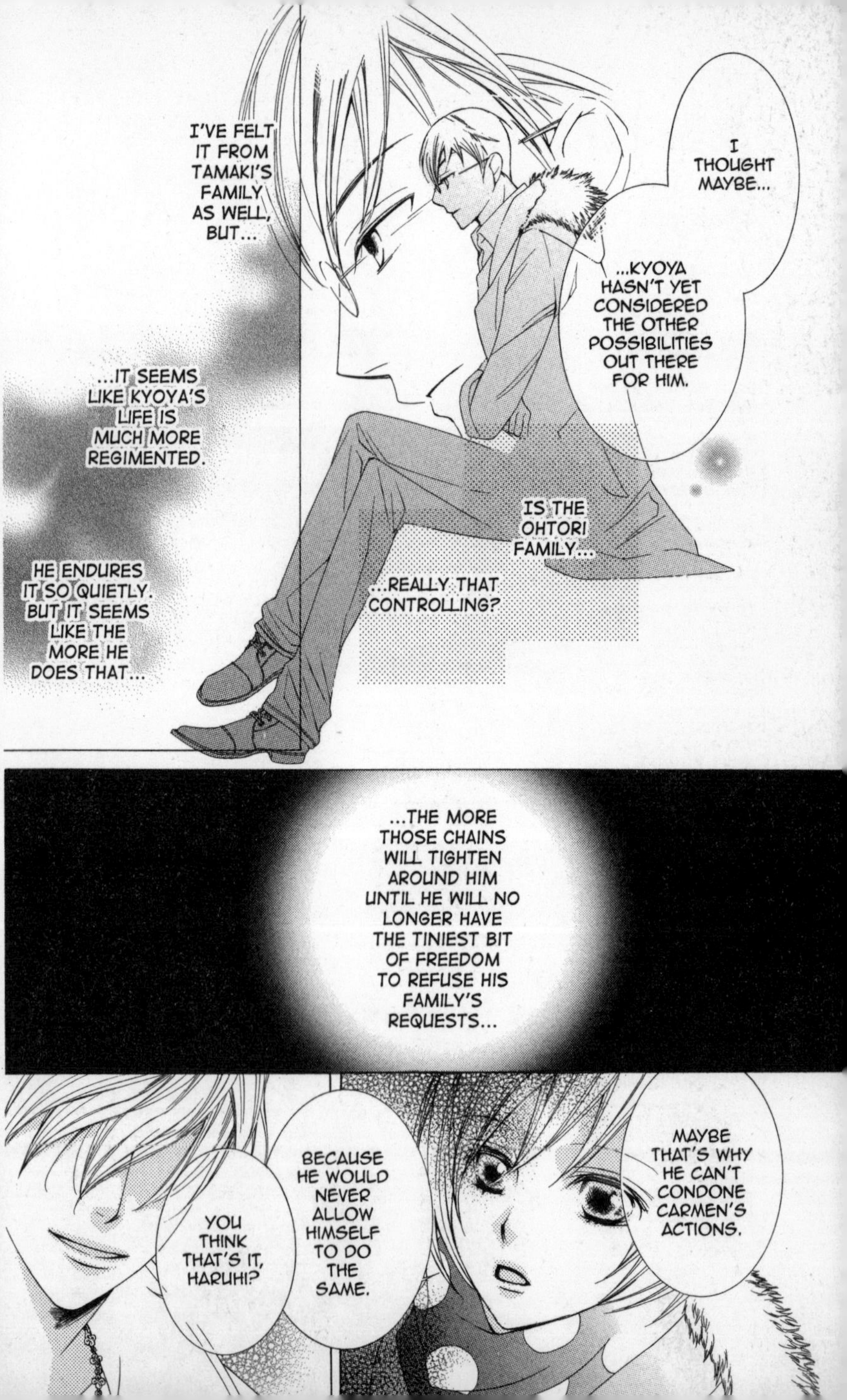
I THOUGHT MAYBE...
...KYOYA HASN'T YET CONSIDERED THE OTHER POSSIBILITIES OUT THERE FOR HIM.
IS THE OHTORI FAMILY...
...REALLY THAT CONTROLLING?
I'VE FELT IT FROM TAMAKI'S FAMILY AS WELL, BUT...
...IT SEEMS LIKE KYOYA'S LIFE IS MUCH MORE REGIMENTED.
HE ENDURES IT SO QUIETLY. BUT IT SEEMS LIKE THE MORE HE DOES THAT...
...THE MORE THOSE CHAINS WILL TIGHTEN AROUND HIM UNTIL HE WILL NO LONGER HAVE THE TINIEST BIT OF FREEDOM TO REFUSE HIS FAMILY'S REQUESTS...
MAYBE THAT'S WHY HE CAN'T CONDONE CARMEN'S ACTIONS.
BECAUSE HE WOULD NEVER ALLOW HIMSELF TO DO THE SAME.
YOU THINK THAT'S IT, HARUHI?

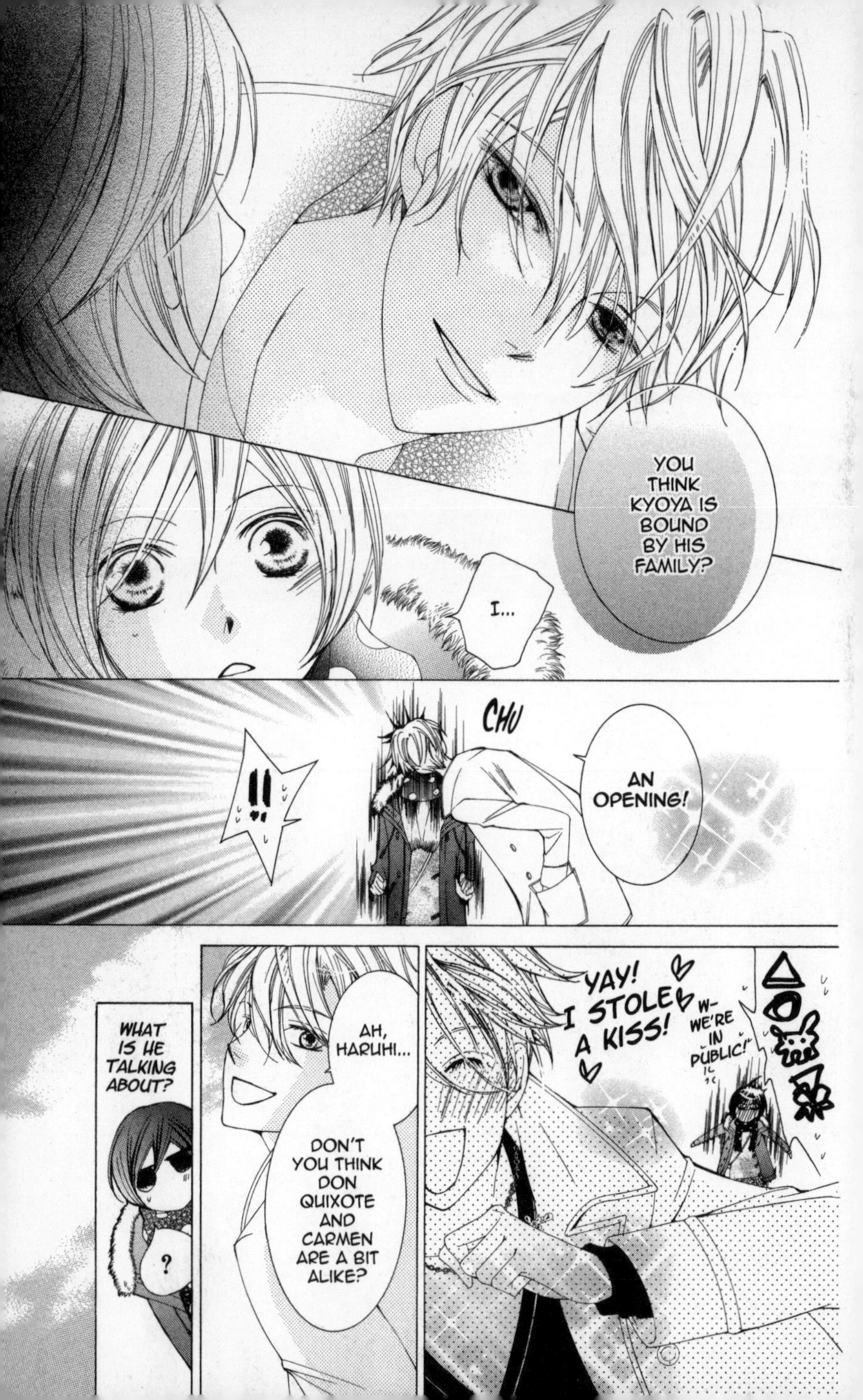
YOU THINK KYOYA IS BOUND BY HIS FAMILY?
I...
AN OPENING!
CHU
!!
W-WE'RE IN PUBLIC!
YAY! I STOLE A KISS!
AH, HARUHI...
DON'T YOU THINK DON QUIXOTE AND CARMEN ARE A BIT ALIKE?
WHAT IS HE TALKING ABOUT?
?

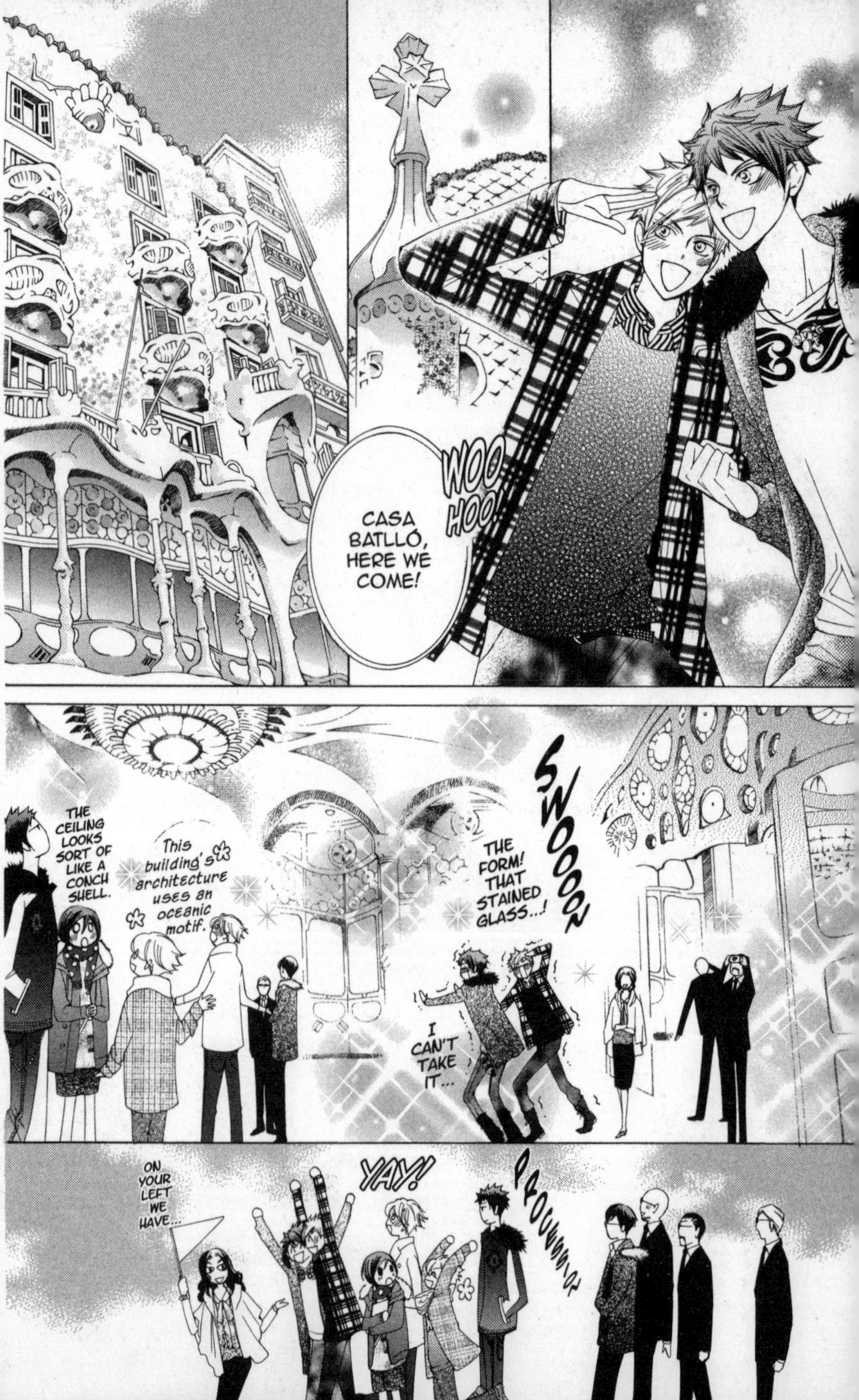
WOO HOO!
CASA BATLLÓ, HERE WE COME!
SWOOOOON
THE FORM! THAT STAINED GLASS...!
I CAN'T TAKE IT...
This building's architecture uses an oceanic motif.
THE CEILING LOOKS SORT OF LIKE A CONCH SHELL.
YAY!
ON YOUR LEFT WE HAVE...

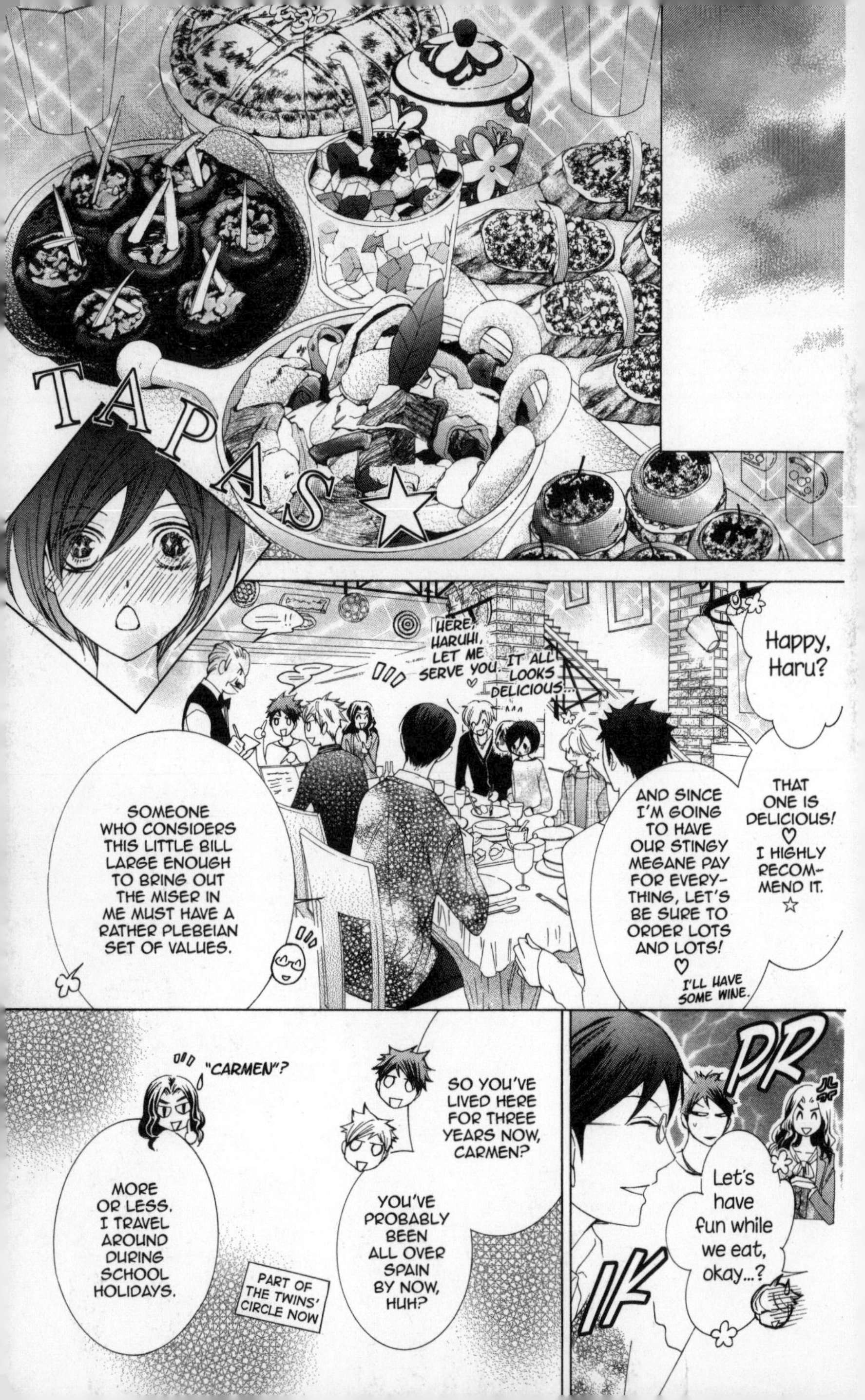
TAPAS☆
Happy, Haru?
THAT ONE IS DELICIOUS! ♡ I HIGHLY RECOMMEND IT. ☆
AND SINCE I'M GOING TO HAVE OUR STINGY MEGANE PAY FOR EVERYTHING, LET'S BE SURE TO ORDER LOTS AND LOTS! ♡
I'LL HAVE SOME WINE.
IT ALL LOOKS DELICIOUS...
HERE, HARUHI, LET ME SERVE YOU. ♡
SOMEONE WHO CONSIDERS THIS LITTLE BILL LARGE ENOUGH TO BRING OUT THE MISER IN ME MUST HAVE A RATHER PLEBEIAN SET OF VALUES.
PR
Let's have fun while we eat, okay...?
IK
SO YOU'VE LIVED HERE FOR THREE YEARS NOW, CARMEN?
YOU'VE PROBABLY BEEN ALL OVER SPAIN BY NOW, HUH?
"CARMEN"?
MORE OR LESS. I TRAVEL AROUND DURING SCHOOL HOLIDAYS.
PART OF THE TWINS' CIRCLE NOW

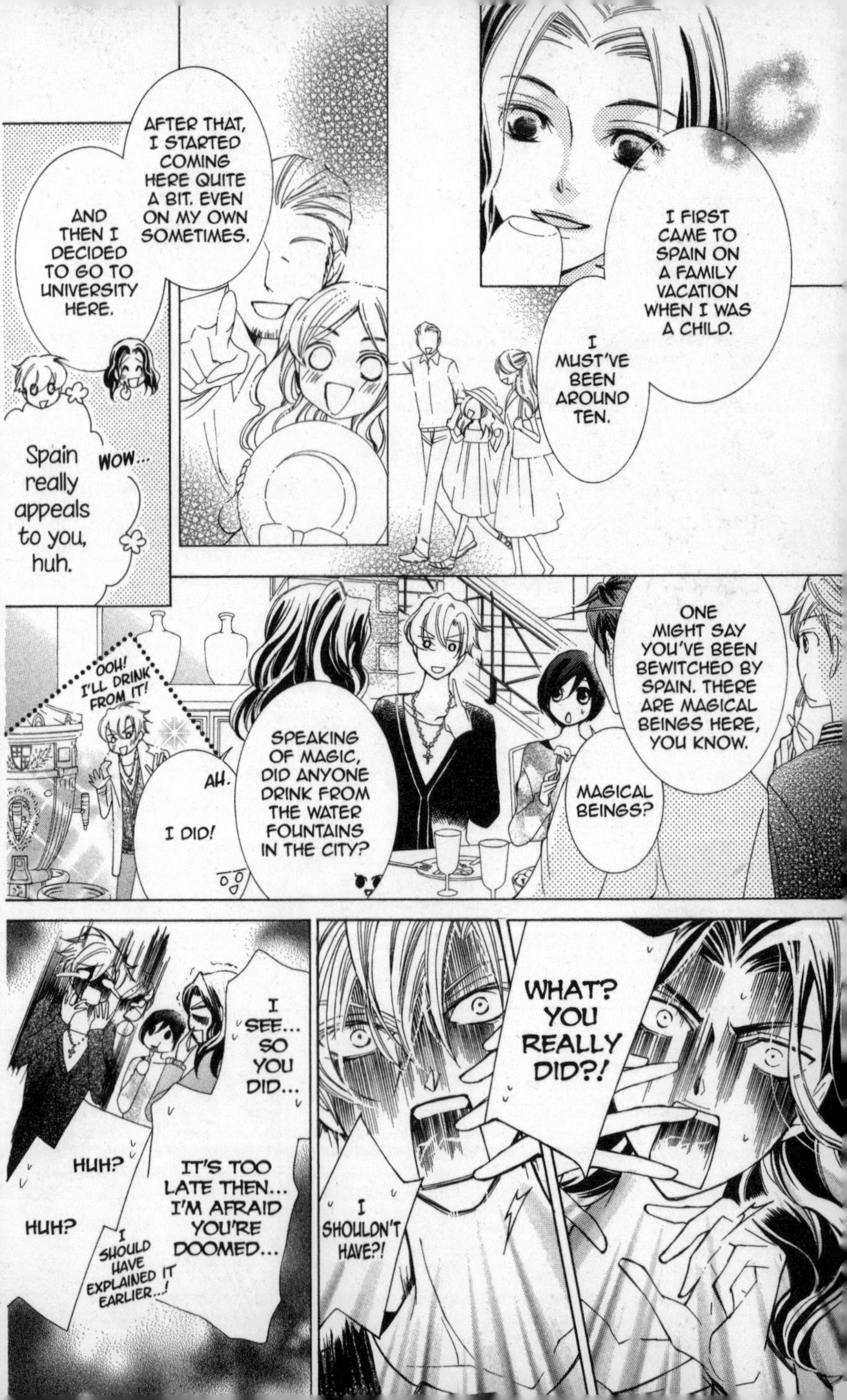
I FIRST CAME TO SPAIN ON A FAMILY VACATION WHEN I WAS A CHILD.
I MUST'VE BEEN AROUND TEN.
AFTER THAT, I STARTED COMING HERE QUITE A BIT. EVEN ON MY OWN SOMETIMES.
AND THEN I DECIDED TO GO TO UNIVERSITY HERE.
WOW...
Spain really appeals to you, huh.
ONE MIGHT SAY YOU'VE BEEN BEWITCHED BY SPAIN. THERE ARE MAGICAL BEINGS HERE, YOU KNOW.
MAGICAL BEINGS?
SPEAKING OF MAGIC, DID ANYONE DRINK FROM THE WATER FOUNTAINS IN THE CITY?
AH.
I DID!
OOH! I'LL DRINK FROM IT!
WHAT? YOU REALLY DID?!
I SHOULDN'T HAVE?!
I SEE... SO YOU DID...
HUH?
HUH?
IT'S TOO LATE THEN... I'M AFRAID YOU'RE DOOMED...
I SHOULD HAVE EXPLAINED IT EARLIER...!

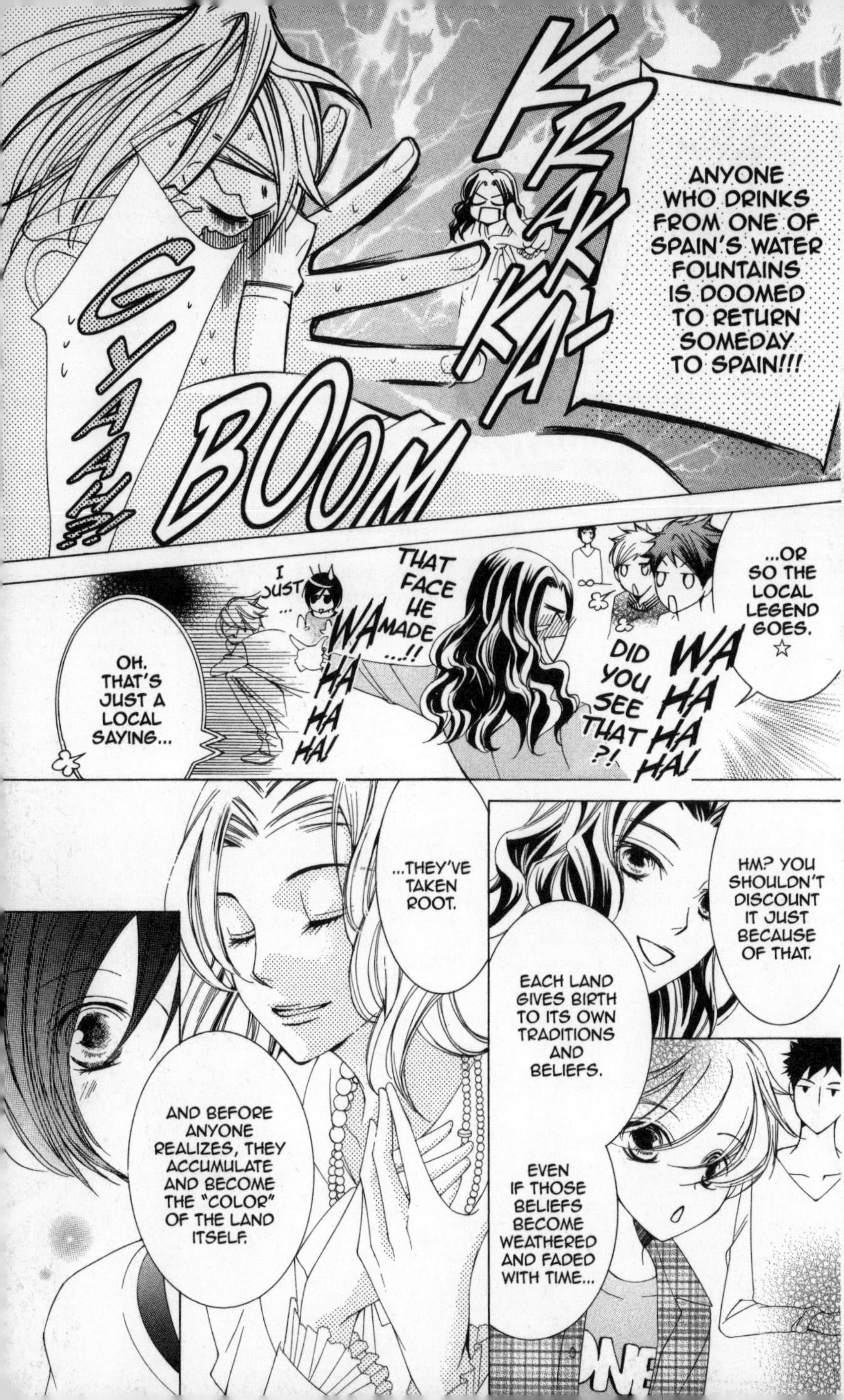
ANYONE WHO DRINKS FROM ONE OF SPAIN'S WATER FOUNTAINS IS DOOMED TO RETURN SOMEDAY TO SPAIN!!!
KRAKAKA-
BOOM
GYAAAH!!
...OR SO THE LOCAL LEGEND GOES. ☆
WA HA HA HA!
DID YOU SEE THAT?!
THAT FACE HE MADE...!!
WA HA HA HA!
I JUST...
OH. THAT'S JUST A LOCAL SAYING...
HM? YOU SHOULDN'T DISCOUNT IT JUST BECAUSE OF THAT.
EACH LAND GIVES BIRTH TO ITS OWN TRADITIONS AND BELIEFS.
EVEN IF THOSE BELIEFS BECOME WEATHERED AND FADED WITH TIME...
...THEY'VE TAKEN ROOT.
AND BEFORE ANYONE REALIZES, THEY ACCUMULATE AND BECOME THE "COLOR" OF THE LAND ITSELF.

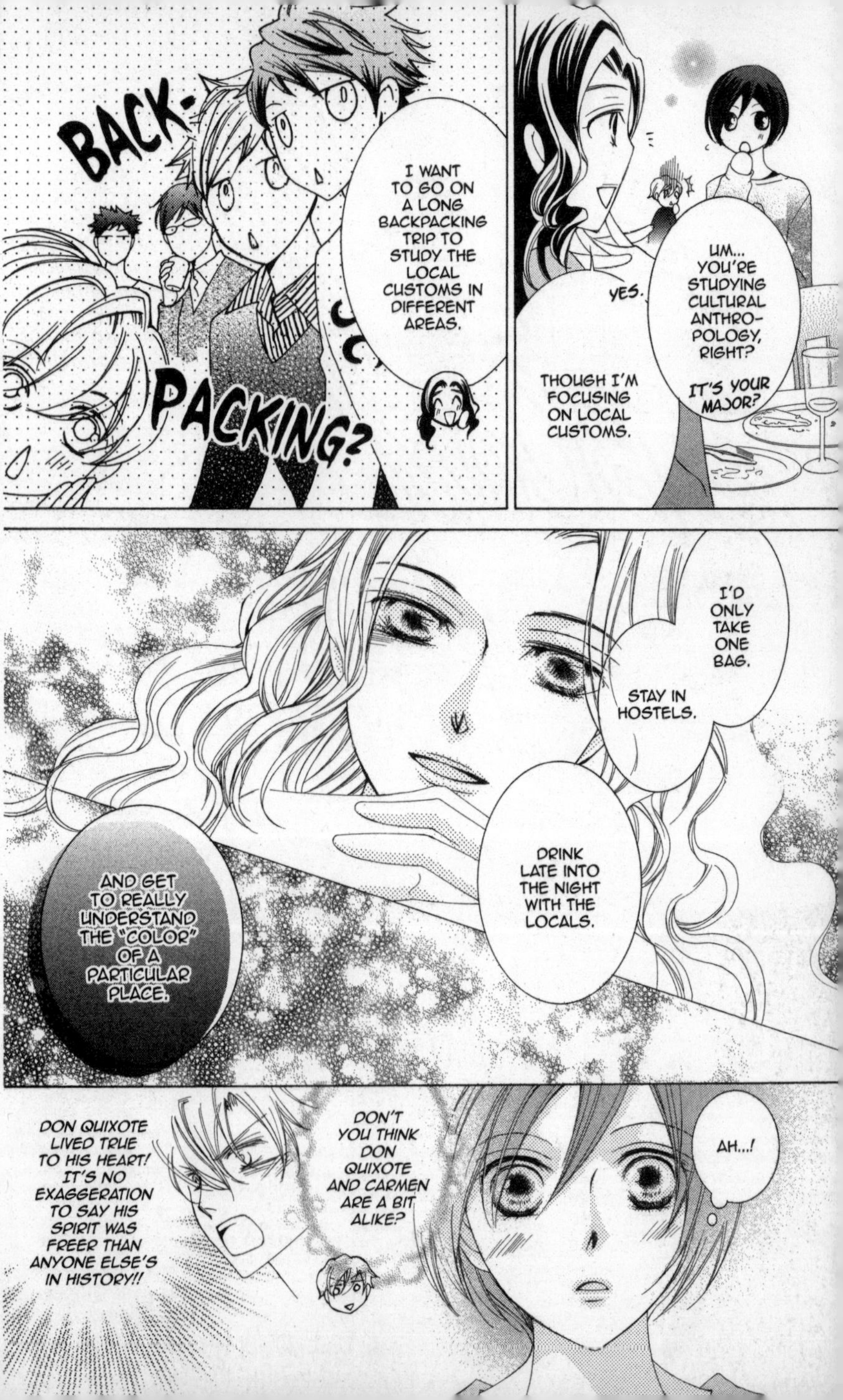
UM... YOU'RE STUDYING CULTURAL ANTHRO-POLOGY, RIGHT?
IT'S YOUR MAJOR?
YES.
THOUGH I'M FOCUSING ON LOCAL CUSTOMS.
I WANT TO GO ON A LONG BACKPACKING TRIP TO STUDY THE LOCAL CUSTOMS IN DIFFERENT AREAS.
BACK-
PACKING?
I'D ONLY TAKE ONE BAG.
STAY IN HOSTELS.
DRINK LATE INTO THE NIGHT WITH THE LOCALS.
AND GET TO REALLY UNDERSTAND THE "COLOR" OF A PARTICULAR PLACE.
AH...!
DON'T YOU THINK DON QUIXOTE AND CARMEN ARE A BIT ALIKE?
DON QUIXOTE LIVED TRUE TO HIS HEART! IT'S NO EXAGGERATION TO SAY HIS SPIRIT WAS FREER THAN ANYONE ELSE'S IN HISTORY!!

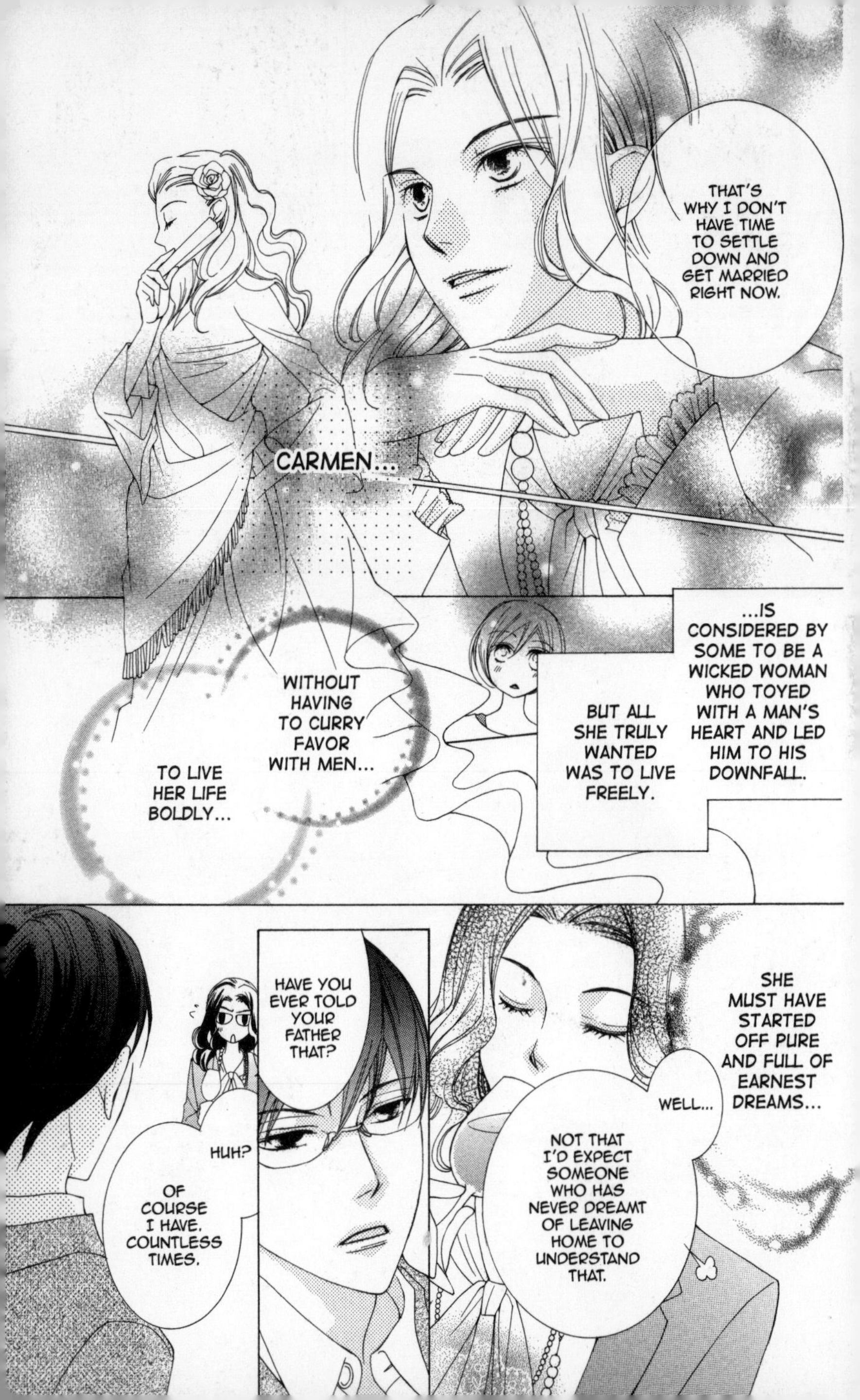
THAT'S WHY I DON'T HAVE TIME TO SETTLE DOWN AND GET MARRIED RIGHT NOW.
CARMEN...
...IS CONSIDERED BY SOME TO BE A WICKED WOMAN WHO TOYED WITH A MAN'S HEART AND LED HIM TO HIS DOWNFALL.
BUT ALL SHE TRULY WANTED WAS TO LIVE FREELY.
WITHOUT HAVING TO CURRY FAVOR WITH MEN...
TO LIVE HER LIFE BOLDLY...
SHE MUST HAVE STARTED OFF PURE AND FULL OF EARNEST DREAMS...
WELL...
NOT THAT I'D EXPECT SOMEONE WHO HAS NEVER DREAMT OF LEAVING HOME TO UNDERSTAND THAT.
HAVE YOU EVER TOLD YOUR FATHER THAT?
HUH?
OF COURSE I HAVE. COUNTLESS TIMES.

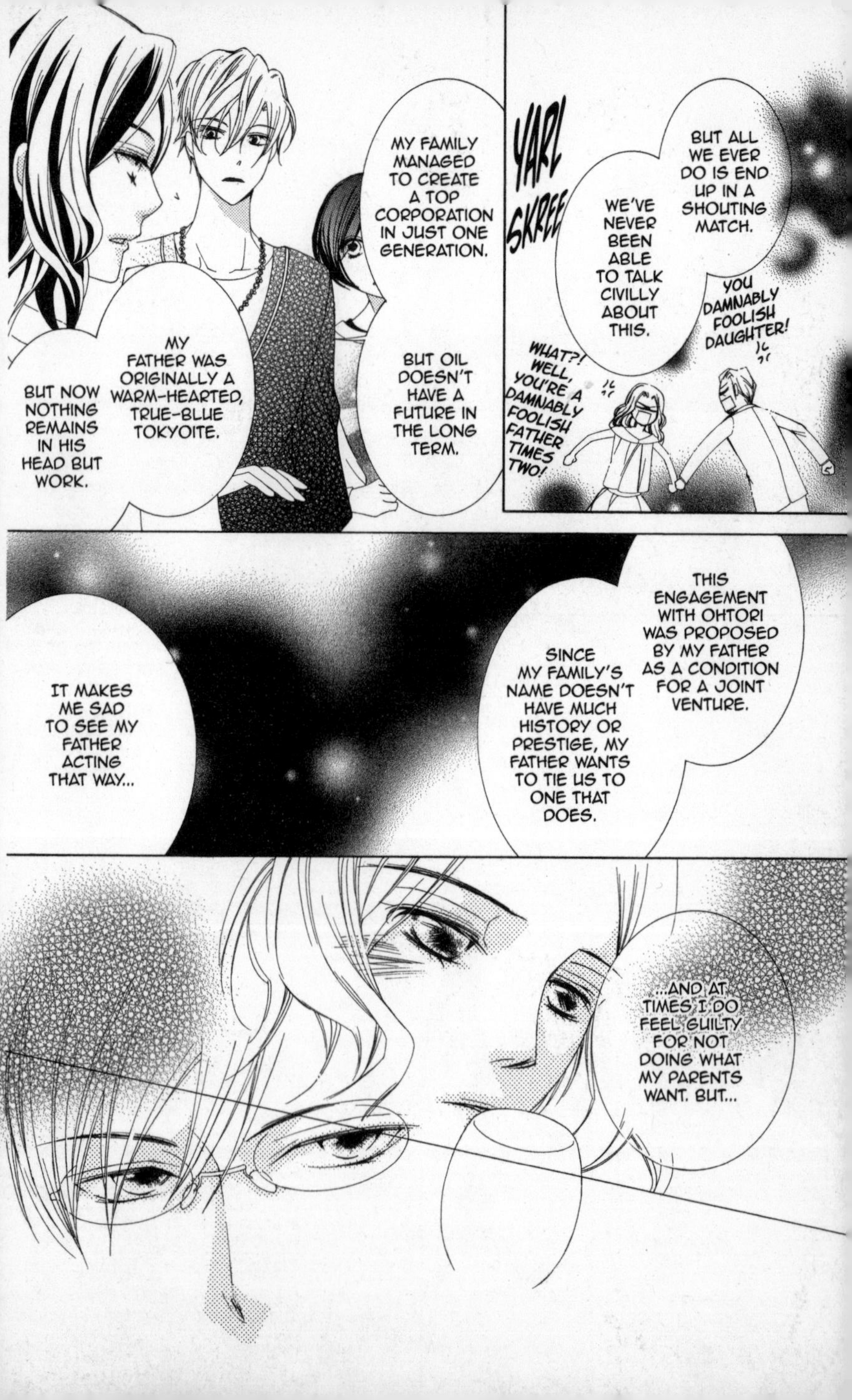

BUT ALL WE EVER DO IS END UP IN A SHOUTING MATCH.
WE'VE NEVER BEEN ABLE TO TALK CIVILLY ABOUT THIS.
YARL
SKREE
YOU DAMNABLY FOOLISH DAUGHTER!
WHAT?! WELL, YOU'RE A DAMNABLY FOOLISH FATHER TIMES TWO!
MY FAMILY MANAGED TO CREATE A TOP CORPORATION IN JUST ONE GENERATION.
BUT OIL DOESN'T HAVE A FUTURE IN THE LONG TERM.
MY FATHER WAS ORIGINALLY A WARM-HEARTED, TRUE-BLUE TOKYOITE.
BUT NOW NOTHING REMAINS IN HIS HEAD BUT WORK.
THIS ENGAGEMENT WITH OHTORI WAS PROPOSED BY MY FATHER AS A CONDITION FOR A JOINT VENTURE.
SINCE MY FAMILY'S NAME DOESN'T HAVE MUCH HISTORY OR PRESTIGE, MY FATHER WANTS TO TIE US TO ONE THAT DOES.
IT MAKES ME SAD TO SEE MY FATHER ACTING THAT WAY...
...AND AT TIMES I DO FEEL GUILTY FOR NOT DOING WHAT MY PARENTS WANT. BUT...

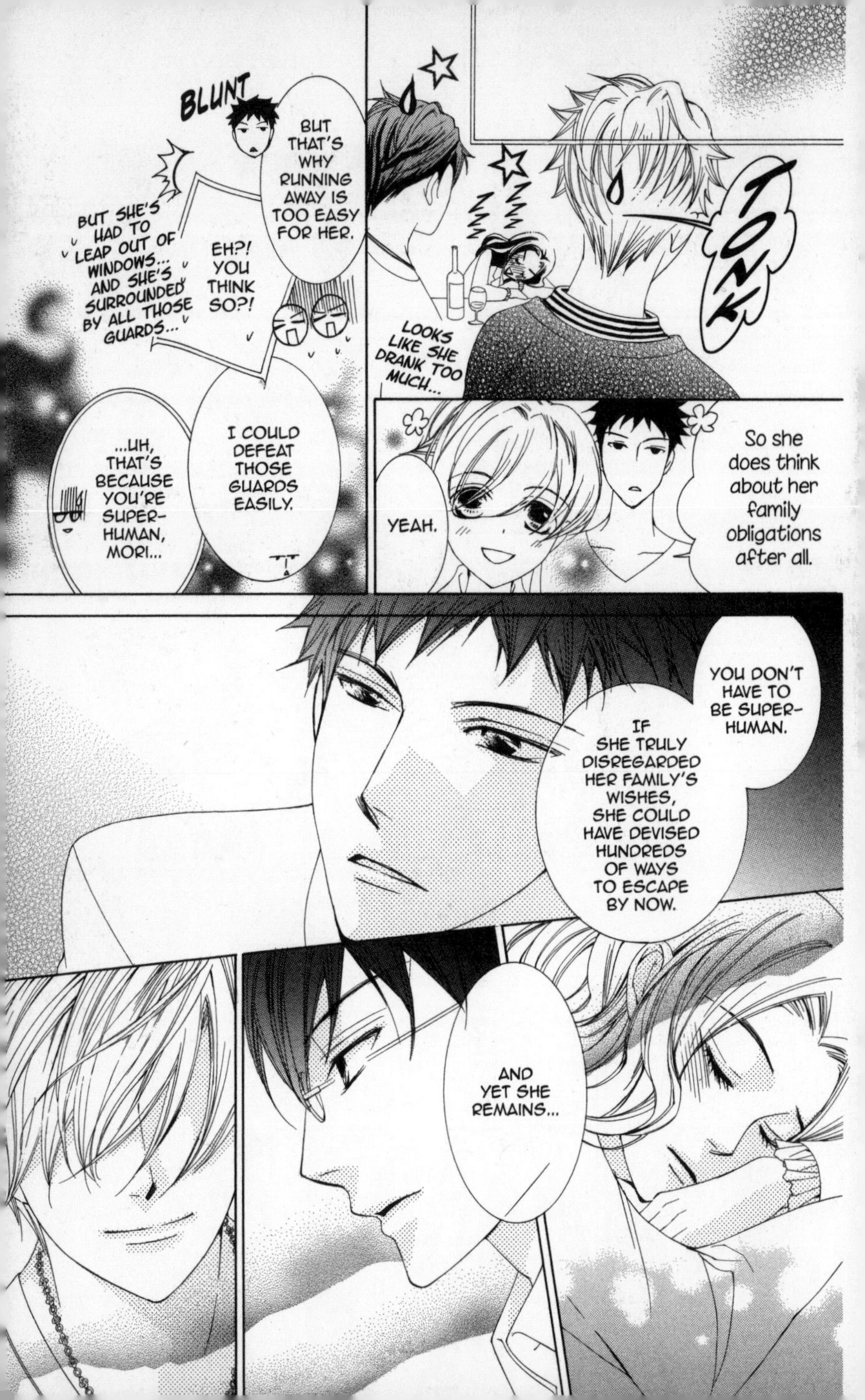
TONK
ZZZ
LOOKS LIKE SHE DRANK TOO MUCH...
So she does think about her family obligations after all.
YEAH.
BUT THAT'S WHY RUNNING AWAY IS TOO EASY FOR HER.
BLUNT
BUT SHE'S HAD TO LEAP OUT OF WINDOWS... AND SHE'S SURROUNDED BY ALL THOSE GUARDS...
EH?! YOU THINK SO?!
I COULD DEFEAT THOSE GUARDS EASILY.
...UH, THAT'S BECAUSE YOU'RE SUPER-HUMAN, MORI...
YOU DON'T HAVE TO BE SUPER-HUMAN.
IF SHE TRULY DISREGARDED HER FAMILY'S WISHES, SHE COULD HAVE DEVISED HUNDREDS OF WAYS TO ESCAPE BY NOW.
AND YET SHE REMAINS...

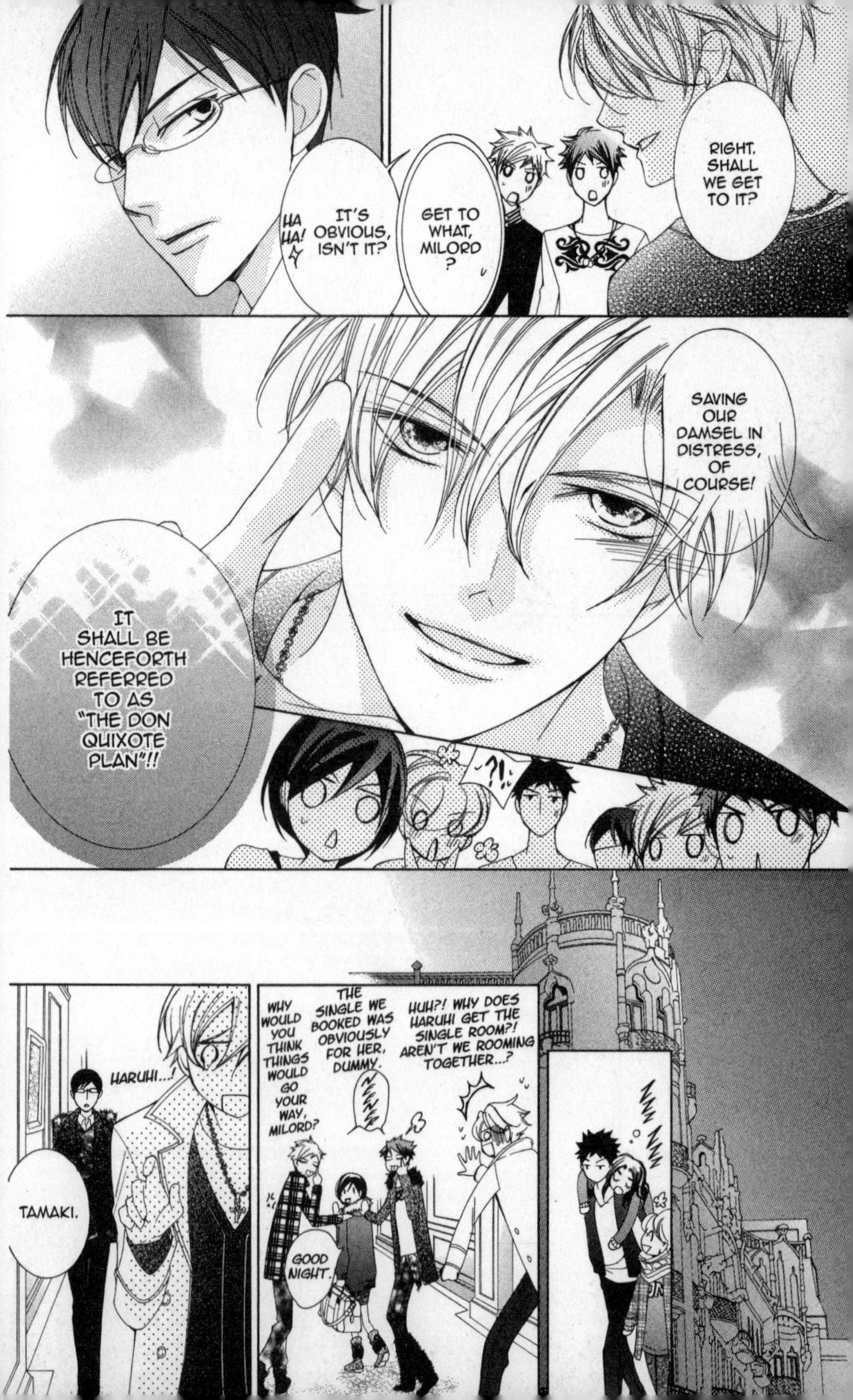
RIGHT. SHALL WE GET TO IT?
GET TO WHAT, MILORD?
IT'S OBVIOUS, ISN'T IT?
HA HA!
SAVING OUR DAMSEL IN DISTRESS, OF COURSE!
IT SHALL BE HENCEFORTH REFERRED TO AS "THE DON QUIXOTE PLAN"!!
?!
HUH?! WHY DOES HARUHI GET THE SINGLE ROOM?! AREN'T WE ROOMING TOGETHER...?
THE SINGLE WE BOOKED WAS OBVIOUSLY FOR HER, DUMMY.
WHY WOULD YOU THINK THINGS WOULD GO YOUR WAY, MILORD?
NEENER
GOOD NIGHT.
HARUHI...!
TAMAKI.

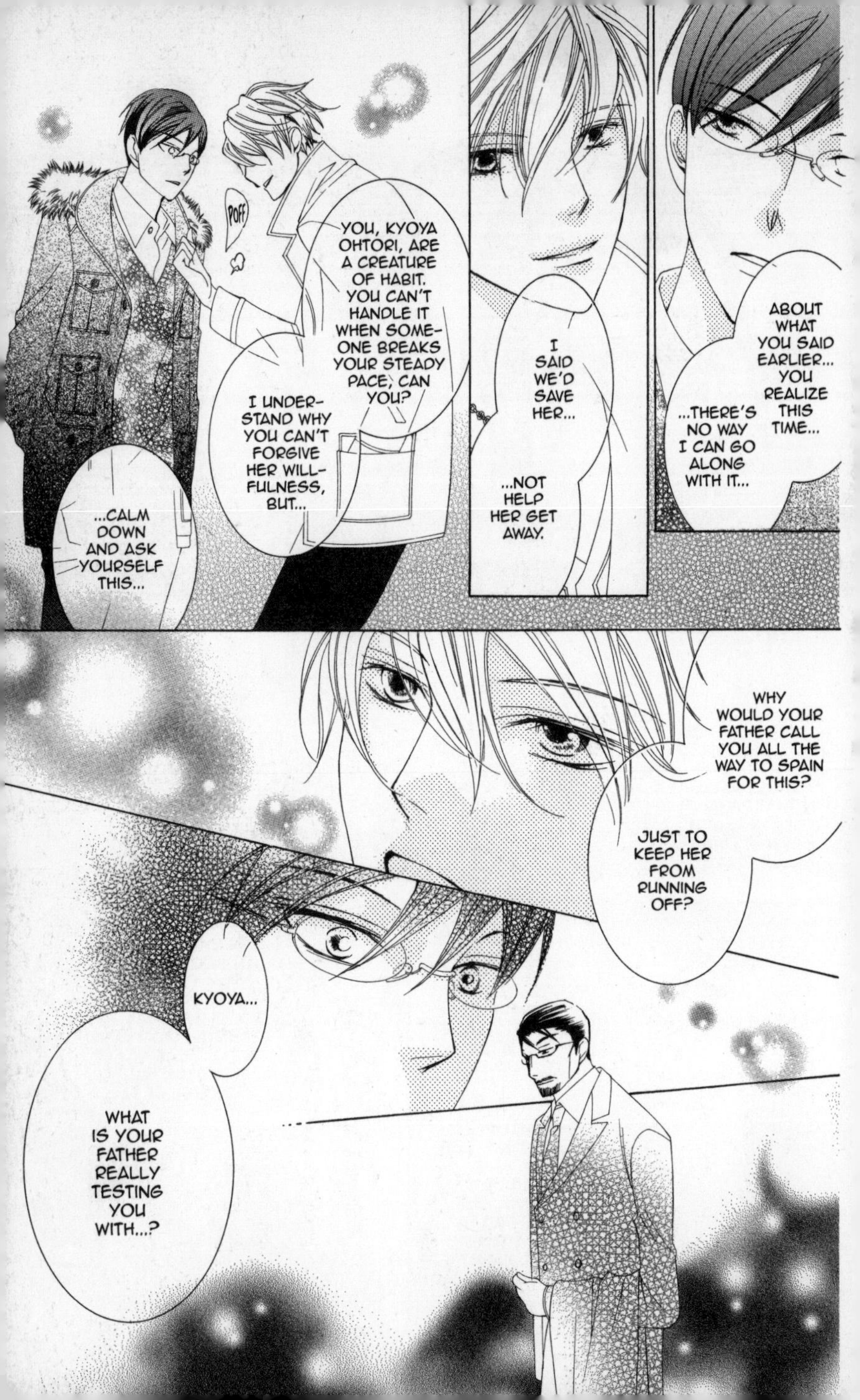
ABOUT WHAT YOU SAID EARLIER... YOU REALIZE THIS TIME...
...THERE'S NO WAY I CAN GO ALONG WITH IT...
I SAID WE'D SAVE HER...
...NOT HELP HER GET AWAY.
YOU, KYOYA OHTORI, ARE A CREATURE OF HABIT. YOU CAN'T HANDLE IT WHEN SOME-ONE BREAKS YOUR STEADY PACE, CAN YOU?
POFF
I UNDER-STAND WHY YOU CAN'T FORGIVE HER WILL-FULNESS, BUT...
...CALM DOWN AND ASK YOURSELF THIS...
WHY WOULD YOUR FATHER CALL YOU ALL THE WAY TO SPAIN FOR THIS?
JUST TO KEEP HER FROM RUNNING OFF?
KYOYA...
WHAT IS YOUR FATHER REALLY TESTING YOU WITH...?

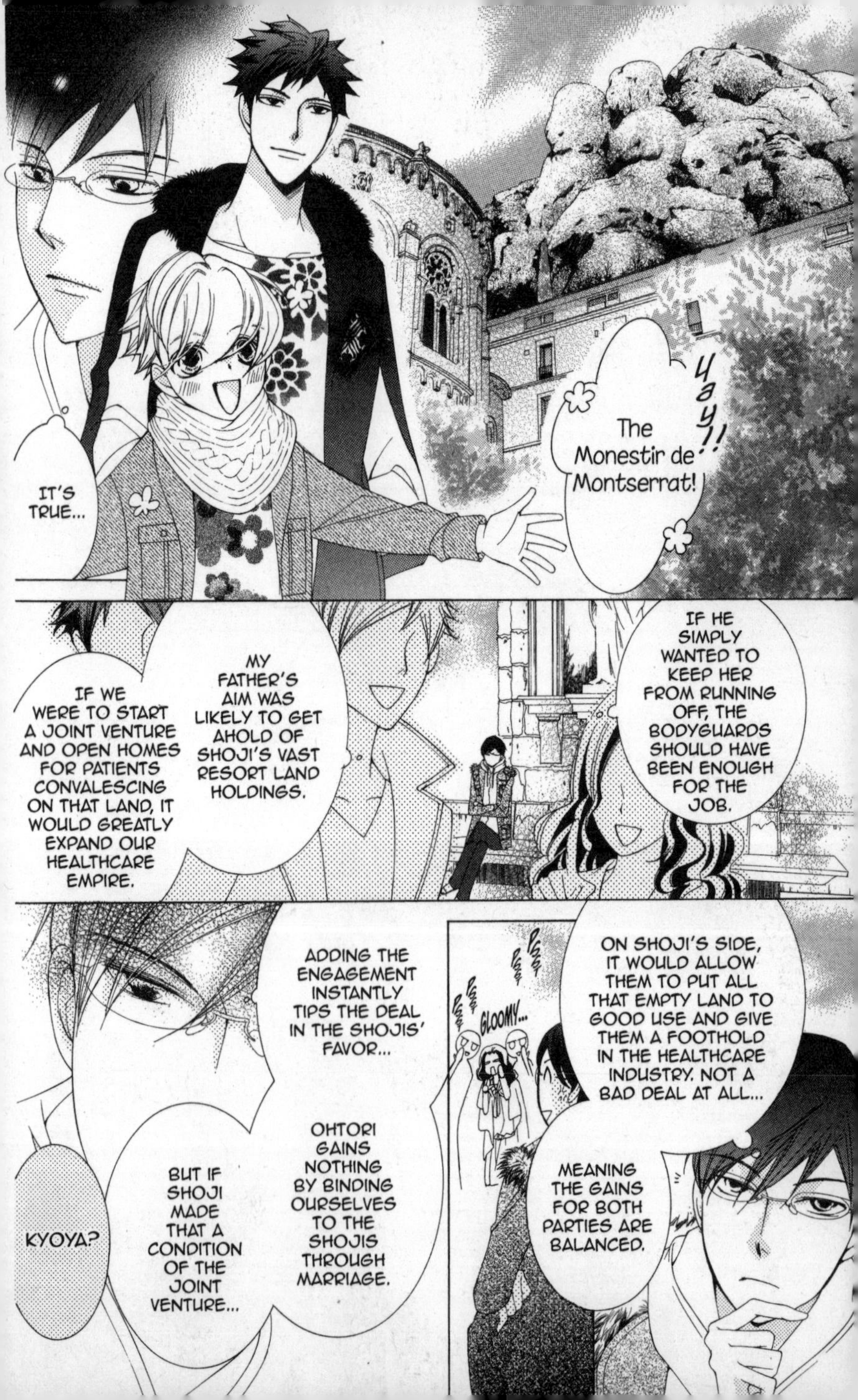
Yay!!
The Monestir de Montserrat!
IT'S TRUE...
IF HE SIMPLY WANTED TO KEEP HER FROM RUNNING OFF, THE BODYGUARDS SHOULD HAVE BEEN ENOUGH FOR THE JOB.
MY FATHER'S AIM WAS LIKELY TO GET AHOLD OF SHOJI'S VAST RESORT LAND HOLDINGS.
IF WE WERE TO START A JOINT VENTURE AND OPEN HOMES FOR PATIENTS CONVALESCING ON THAT LAND, IT WOULD GREATLY EXPAND OUR HEALTHCARE EMPIRE.
ON SHOJI'S SIDE, IT WOULD ALLOW THEM TO PUT ALL THAT EMPTY LAND TO GOOD USE AND GIVE THEM A FOOTHOLD IN THE HEALTHCARE INDUSTRY. NOT A BAD DEAL AT ALL...
GLOOMY...
MEANING THE GAINS FOR BOTH PARTIES ARE BALANCED.
ADDING THE ENGAGEMENT INSTANTLY TIPS THE DEAL IN THE SHOJIS' FAVOR...
OHTORI GAINS NOTHING BY BINDING OURSELVES TO THE SHOJIS THROUGH MARRIAGE.
BUT IF SHOJI MADE THAT A CONDITION OF THE JOINT VENTURE...
KYOYA?

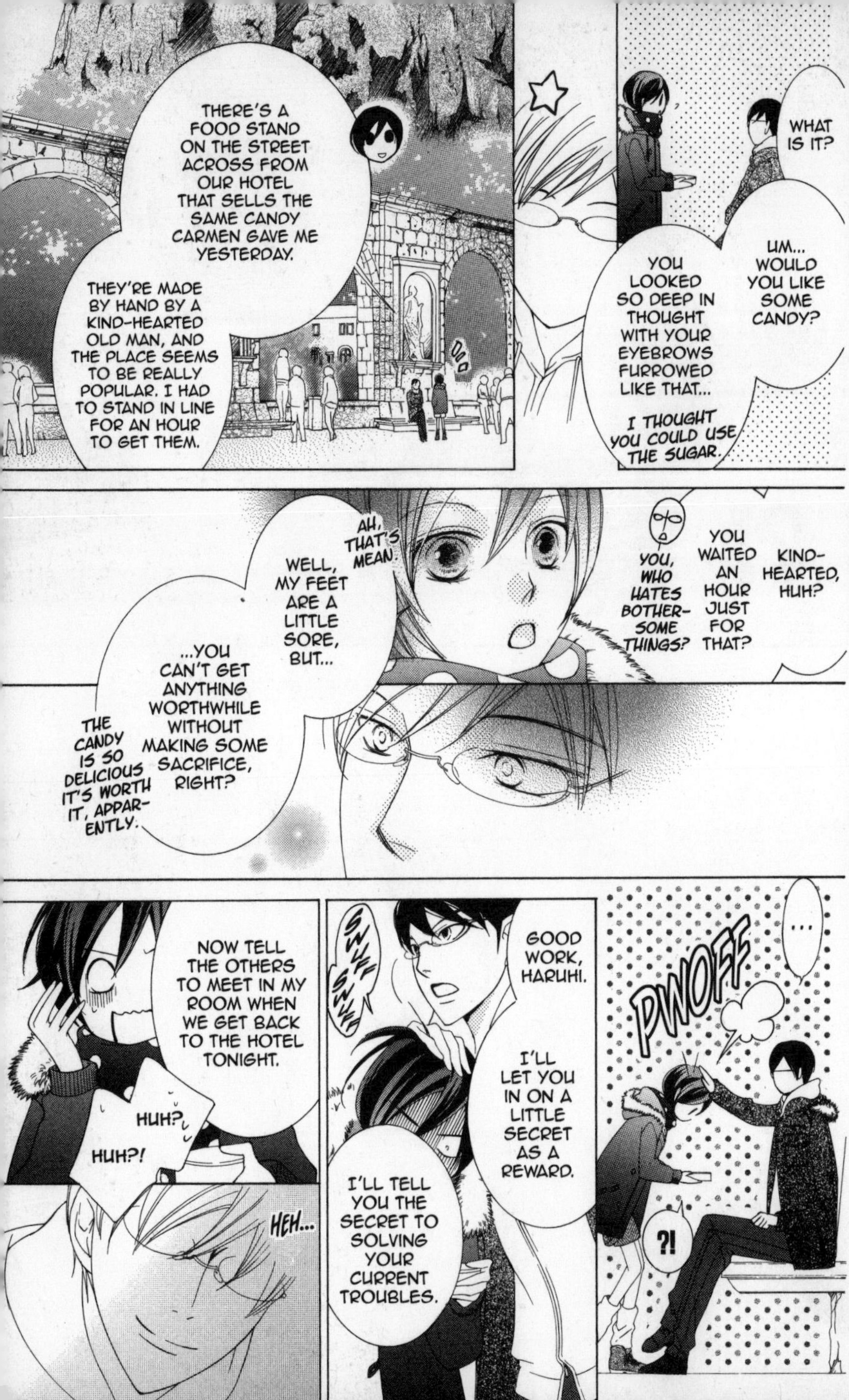
WHAT IS IT?
UM... WOULD YOU LIKE SOME CANDY?
YOU LOOKED SO DEEP IN THOUGHT WITH YOUR EYEBROWS FURROWED LIKE THAT...
I THOUGHT YOU COULD USE THE SUGAR.
THERE'S A FOOD STAND ON THE STREET ACROSS FROM OUR HOTEL THAT SELLS THE SAME CANDY CARMEN GAVE ME YESTERDAY.
THEY'RE MADE BY HAND BY A KIND-HEARTED OLD MAN, AND THE PLACE SEEMS TO BE REALLY POPULAR. I HAD TO STAND IN LINE FOR AN HOUR TO GET THEM.
KIND-HEARTED, HUH?
YOU WAITED AN HOUR JUST FOR THAT?
YOU, WHO HATES BOTHER-SOME THINGS?
AH, THAT'S MEAN.
WELL, MY FEET ARE A LITTLE SORE, BUT...
...YOU CAN'T GET ANYTHING WORTHWHILE WITHOUT MAKING SOME SACRIFICE, RIGHT?
THE CANDY IS SO DELICIOUS IT'S WORTH IT, APPAR-ENTLY.
...
PWOFF
?!
GOOD WORK, HARUHI.
I'LL LET YOU IN ON A LITTLE SECRET AS A REWARD.
SNIFF SNIFF
I'LL TELL YOU THE SECRET TO SOLVING YOUR CURRENT TROUBLES.
NOW TELL THE OTHERS TO MEET IN MY ROOM WHEN WE GET BACK TO THE HOTEL TONIGHT.
HUH?
HUH?!
HEH...

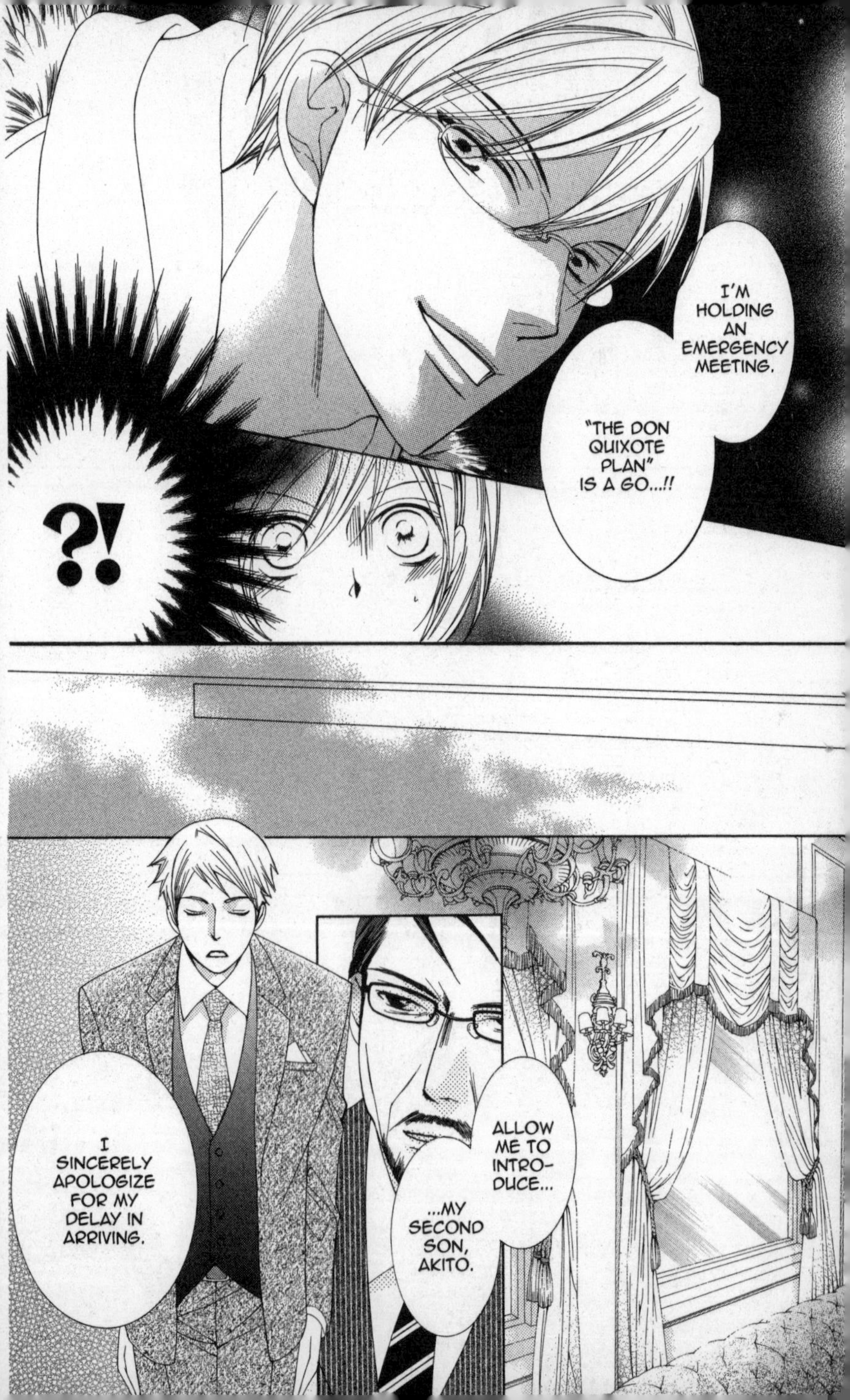
I'M HOLDING AN EMERGENCY MEETING.
"THE DON QUIXOTE PLAN" IS A GO...!!
?!
ALLOW ME TO INTRO-DUCE...
...MY SECOND SON, AKITO.
I SINCERELY APOLOGIZE FOR MY DELAY IN ARRIVING.

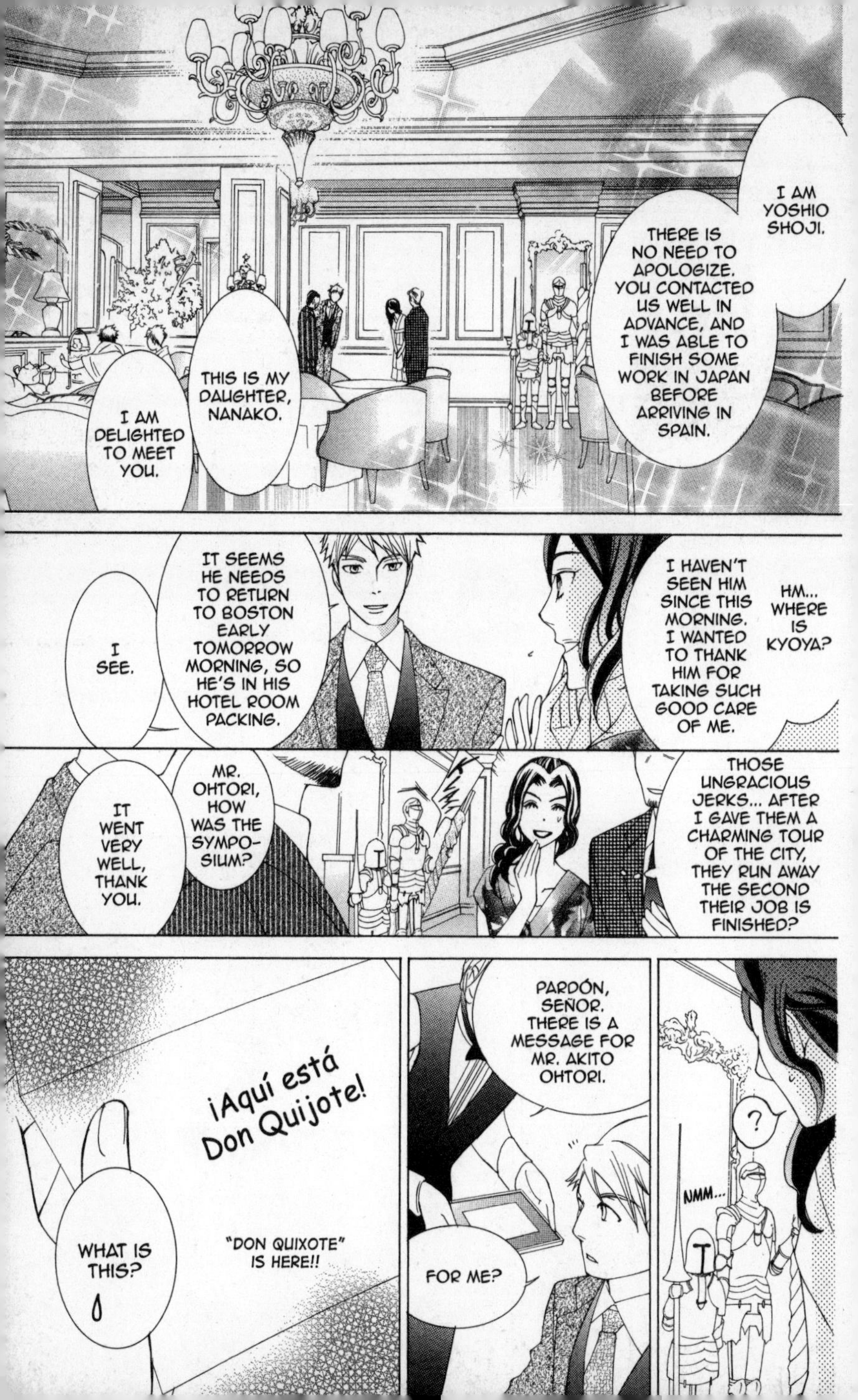
I AM YOSHIO SHOJI.
THERE IS NO NEED TO APOLOGIZE. YOU CONTACTED US WELL IN ADVANCE, AND I WAS ABLE TO FINISH SOME WORK IN JAPAN BEFORE ARRIVING IN SPAIN.
THIS IS MY DAUGHTER, NANAKO.
I AM DELIGHTED TO MEET YOU.
HM... WHERE IS KYOYA?
I HAVEN'T SEEN HIM SINCE THIS MORNING. I WANTED TO THANK HIM FOR TAKING SUCH GOOD CARE OF ME.
IT SEEMS HE NEEDS TO RETURN TO BOSTON EARLY TOMORROW MORNING, SO HE'S IN HIS HOTEL ROOM PACKING.
I SEE.
THOSE UNGRACIOUS JERKS... AFTER I GAVE THEM A CHARMING TOUR OF THE CITY, THEY RUN AWAY THE SECOND THEIR JOB IS FINISHED?
MR. OHTORI, HOW WAS THE SYMPOSIUM?
IT WENT VERY WELL, THANK YOU.
?
NMM...
PARDÓN, SEÑOR. THERE IS A MESSAGE FOR MR. AKITO OHTORI.
FOR ME?
¡Aquí está Don Quijote!
"DON QUIXOTE" IS HERE!!
WHAT IS THIS?

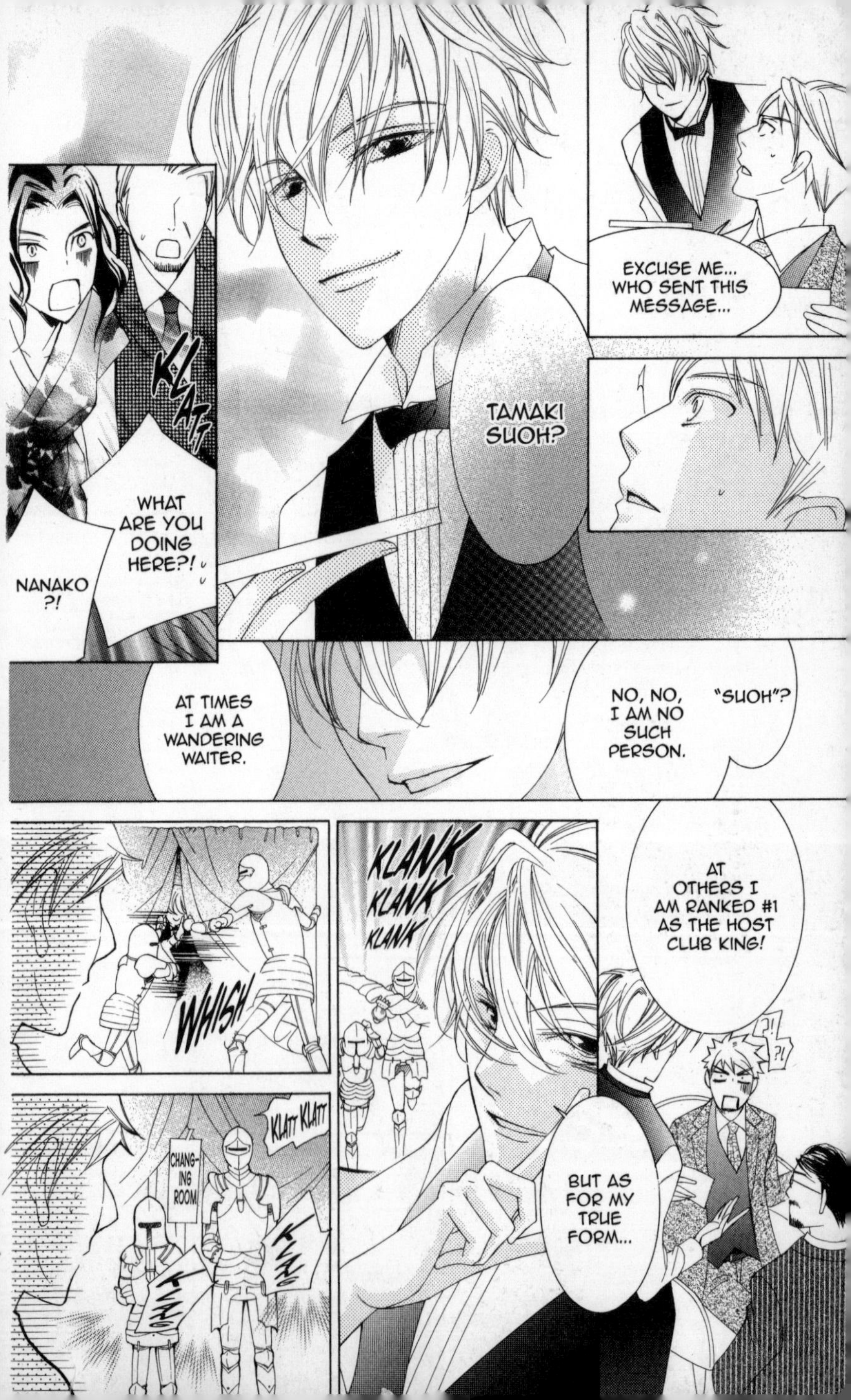
EXCUSE ME... WHO SENT THIS MESSAGE...
TAMAKI SUOH?
KLATT
WHAT ARE YOU DOING HERE?!
NANAKO ?!
"SUOH"?
NO, NO, I AM NO SUCH PERSON.
AT TIMES I AM A WANDERING WAITER.
AT OTHERS I AM RANKED #1 AS THE HOST CLUB KING!
KLANK KLANK KLANK
?! ?!
BUT AS FOR MY TRUE FORM...
WHISH
KLATT KLATT
CHANG-ING ROOM
KLANG
KLANG

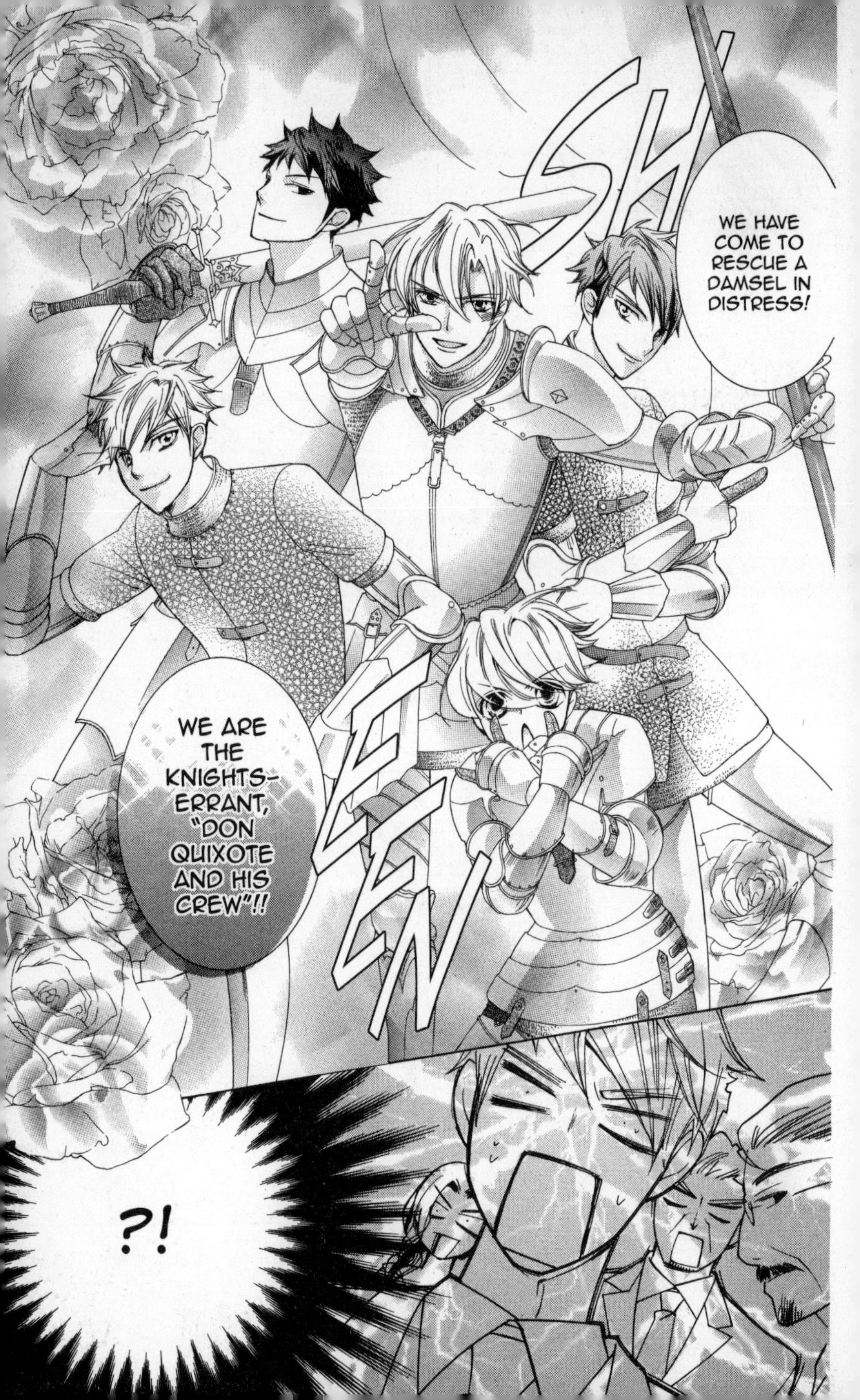
WE HAVE COME TO RESCUE A DAMSEL IN DISTRESS!
WE ARE THE KNIGHTS-ERRANT, "DON QUIXOTE AND HIS CREW"!!
?!

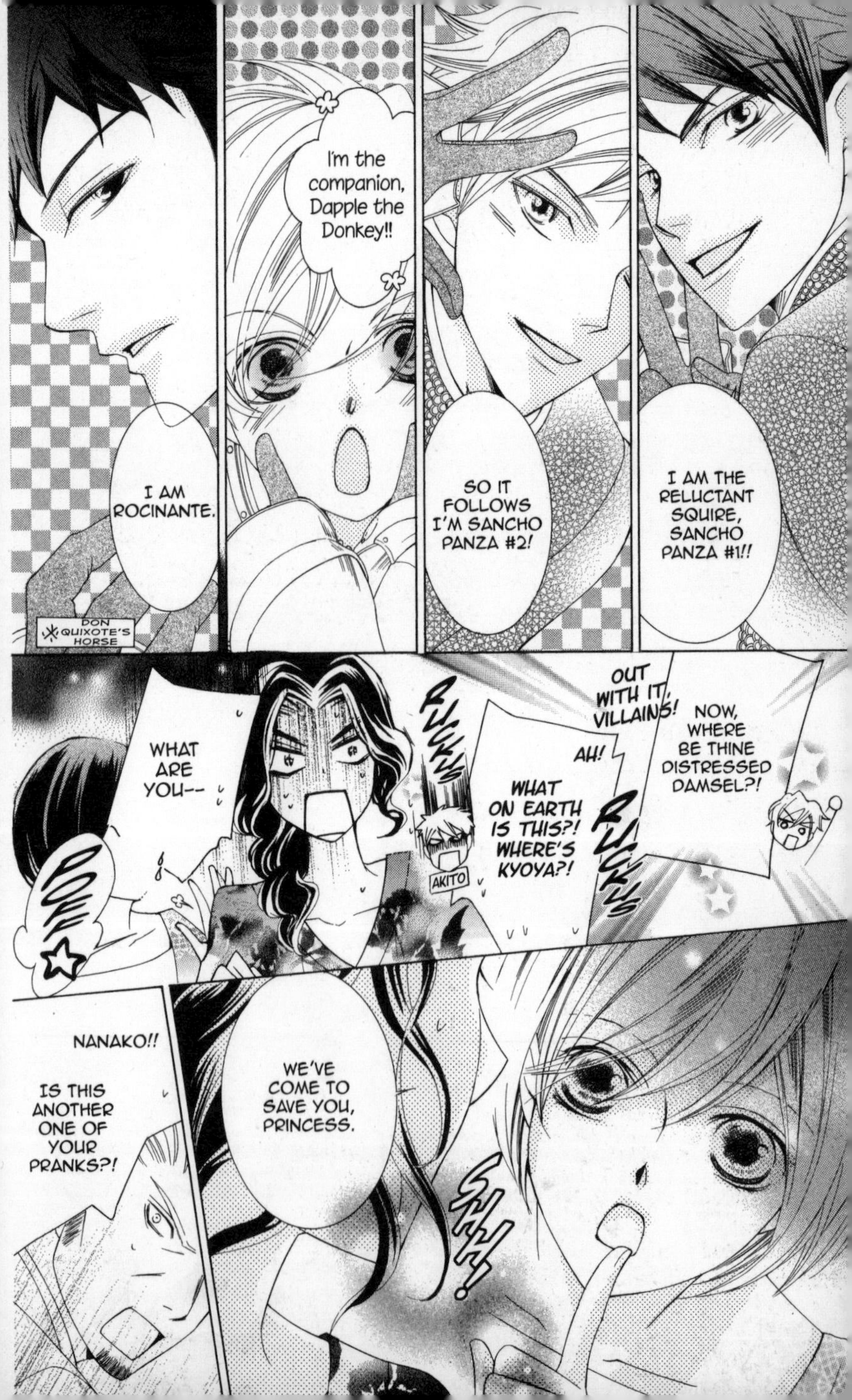
I AM THE RELUCTANT SQUIRE, SANCHO PANZA #1!!
SO IT FOLLOWS I'M SANCHO PANZA #2!
I'm the companion, Dapple the Donkey!!
I AM ROCINANTE.
※DON QUIXOTE'S HORSE
NOW, WHERE BE THINE DISTRESSED DAMSEL?!
OUT WITH IT, VILLAINS!
RUCKUS
AH!
WHAT ON EARTH IS THIS?! WHERE'S KYOYA?!
AKITO
RUCKUS
WHAT ARE YOU--
OOFF
WE'VE COME TO SAVE YOU, PRINCESS.
SHHH!
NANAKO!!
IS THIS ANOTHER ONE OF YOUR PRANKS?!

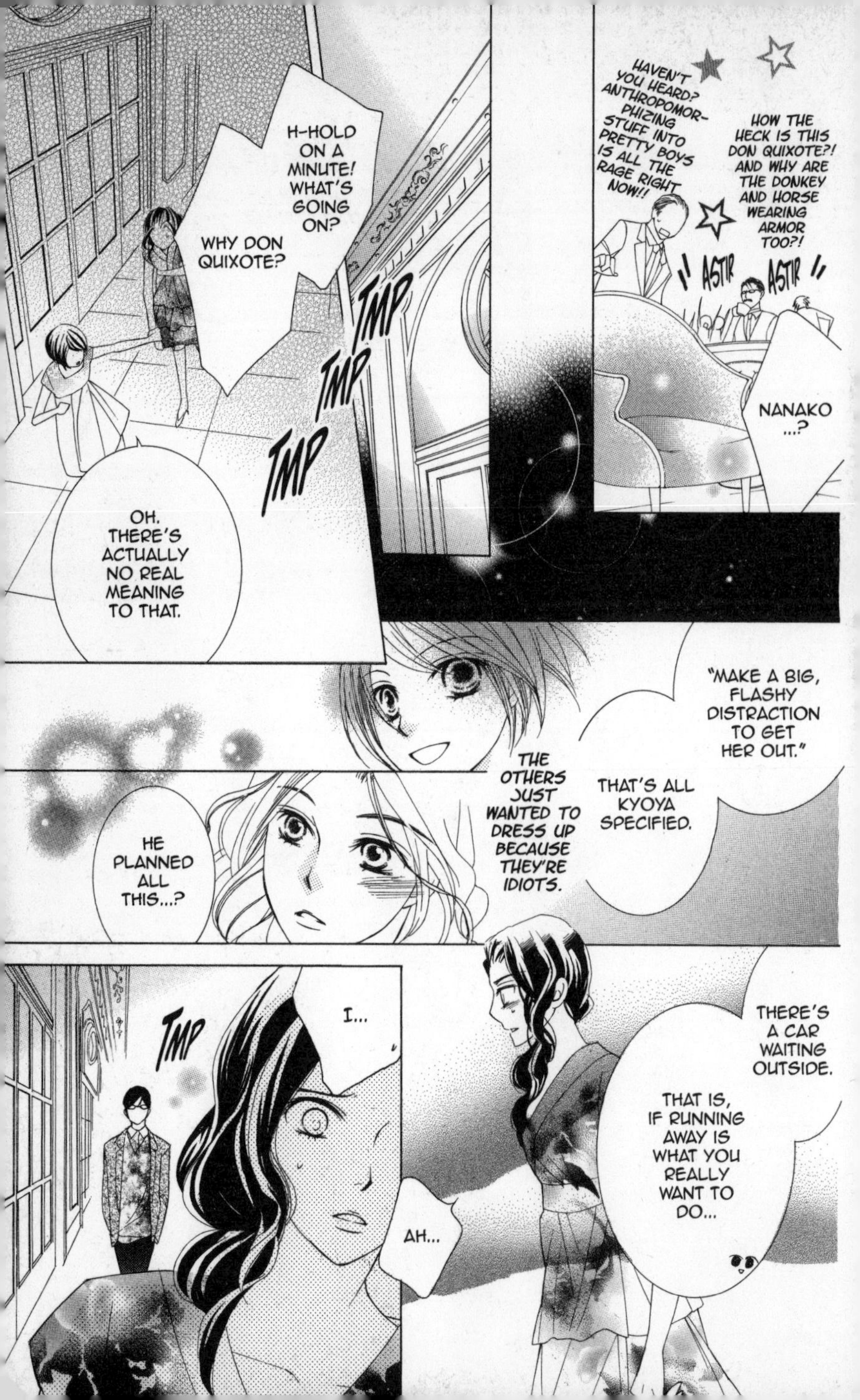
HOW THE HECK IS THIS DON QUIXOTE?! AND WHY ARE THE DONKEY AND HORSE WEARING ARMOR TOO?!
HAVEN'T YOU HEARD? ANTHROPOMOR-PHIZING STUFF INTO PRETTY BOYS IS ALL THE RAGE RIGHT NOW!!
ASTIR ASTIR
NANAKO ...?
TMP TMP TMP
H-HOLD ON A MINUTE! WHAT'S GOING ON?
WHY DON QUIXOTE?
OH. THERE'S ACTUALLY NO REAL MEANING TO THAT.
"MAKE A BIG, FLASHY DISTRACTION TO GET HER OUT."
THAT'S ALL KYOYA SPECIFIED.
THE OTHERS JUST WANTED TO DRESS UP BECAUSE THEY'RE IDIOTS.
HE PLANNED ALL THIS...?
THERE'S A CAR WAITING OUTSIDE.
THAT IS, IF RUNNING AWAY IS WHAT YOU REALLY WANT TO DO...
AH...
I...
TMP

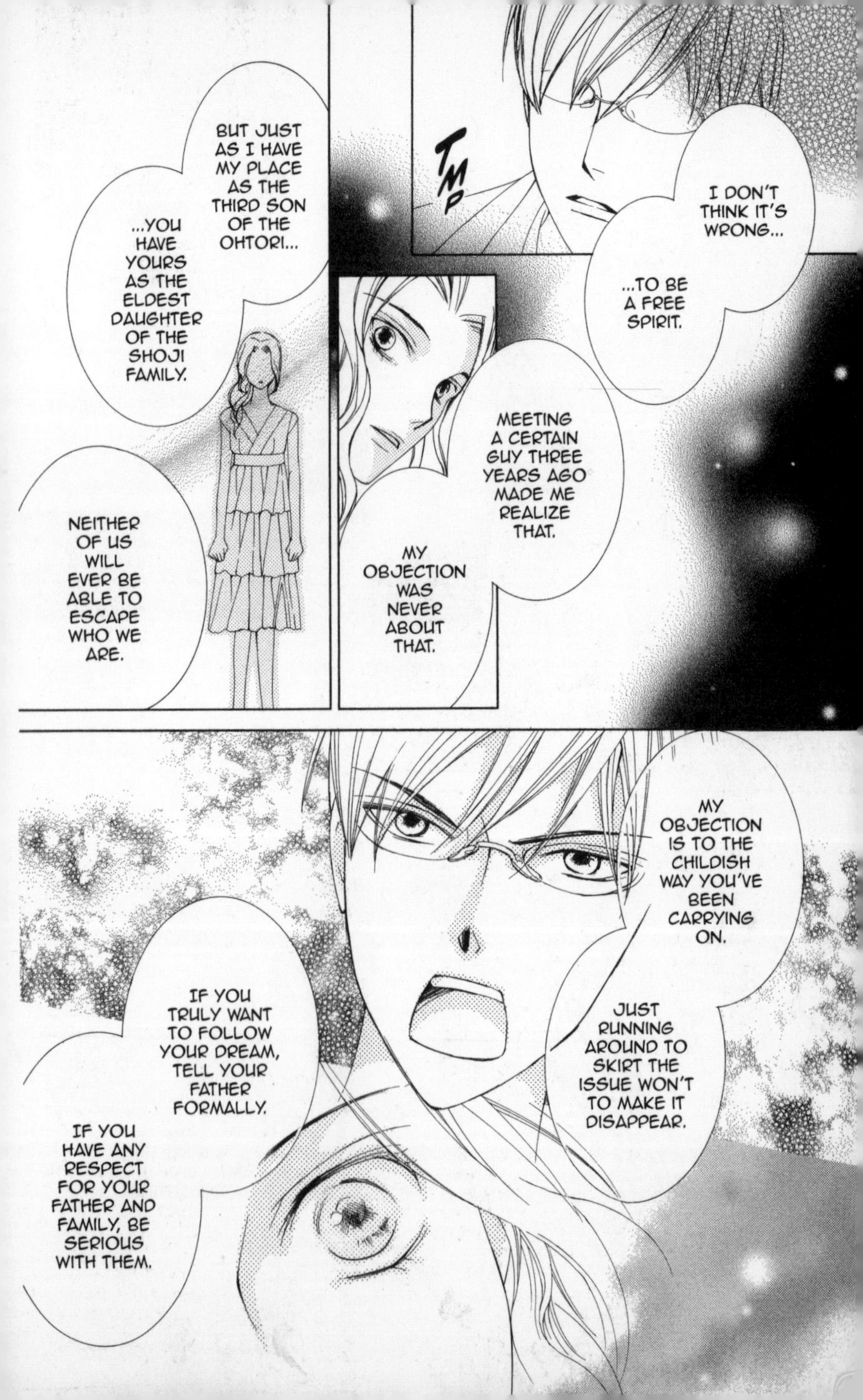
TMP
I DON'T THINK IT'S WRONG...
...TO BE A FREE SPIRIT.
MEETING A CERTAIN GUY THREE YEARS AGO MADE ME REALIZE THAT.
MY OBJECTION WAS NEVER ABOUT THAT.
BUT JUST AS I HAVE MY PLACE AS THE THIRD SON OF THE OHTORI...
...YOU HAVE YOURS AS THE ELDEST DAUGHTER OF THE SHOJI FAMILY.
NEITHER OF US WILL EVER BE ABLE TO ESCAPE WHO WE ARE.
MY OBJECTION IS TO THE CHILDISH WAY YOU'VE BEEN CARRYING ON.
JUST RUNNING AROUND TO SKIRT THE ISSUE WON'T TO MAKE IT DISAPPEAR.
IF YOU TRULY WANT TO FOLLOW YOUR DREAM, TELL YOUR FATHER FORMALLY.
IF YOU HAVE ANY RESPECT FOR YOUR FATHER AND FAMILY, BE SERIOUS WITH THEM.

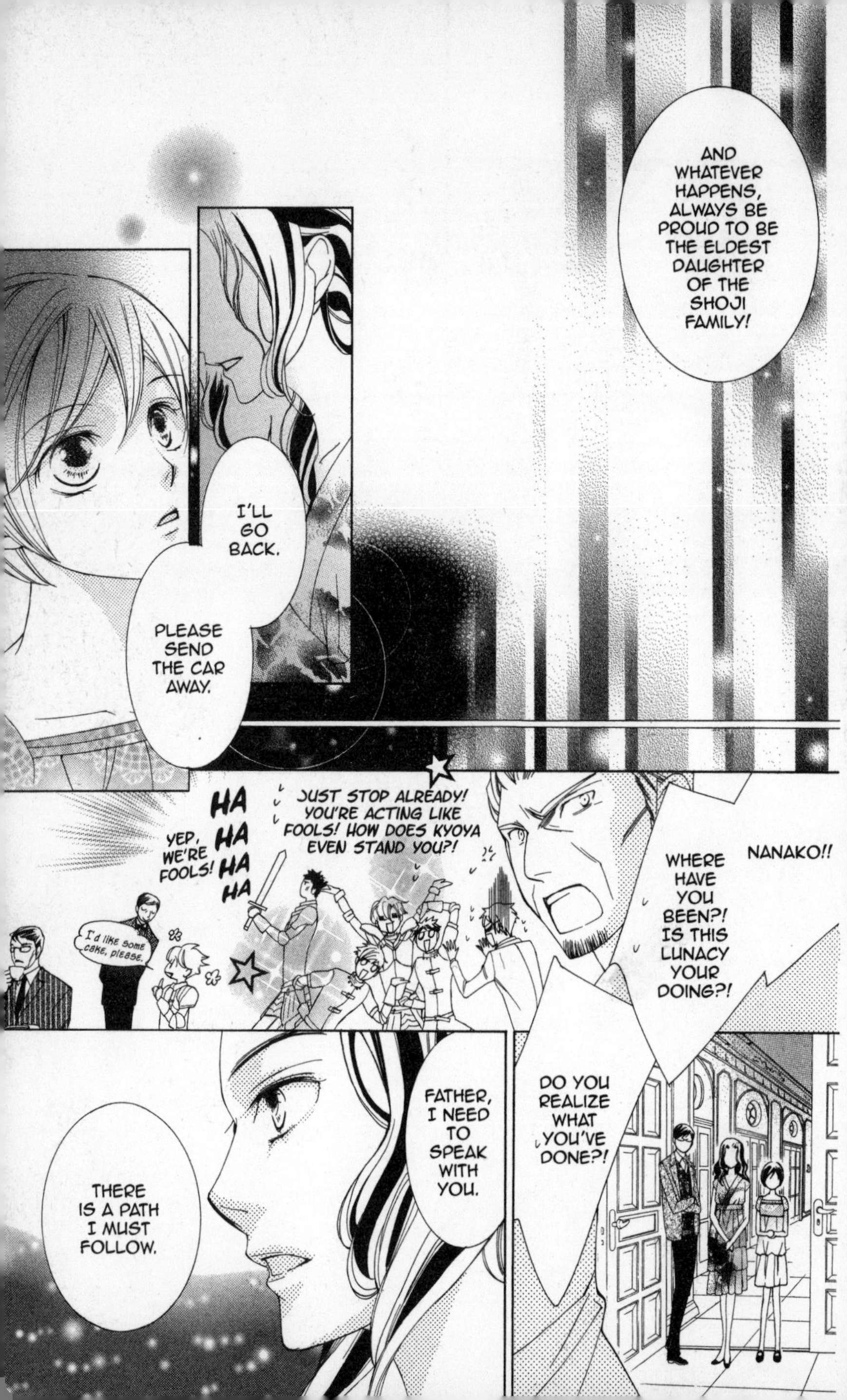
AND WHATEVER HAPPENS, ALWAYS BE PROUD TO BE THE ELDEST DAUGHTER OF THE SHOJI FAMILY!
I'LL GO BACK.
PLEASE SEND THE CAR AWAY.
NANAKO!!
WHERE HAVE YOU BEEN?! IS THIS LUNACY YOUR DOING?!
JUST STOP ALREADY! YOU'RE ACTING LIKE FOOLS! HOW DOES KYOYA EVEN STAND YOU?!
HA HA HA HA
YEP, WE'RE FOOLS!
I'd like some cake, please.
DO YOU REALIZE WHAT YOU'VE DONE?!
FATHER, I NEED TO SPEAK WITH YOU.
THERE IS A PATH I MUST FOLLOW.

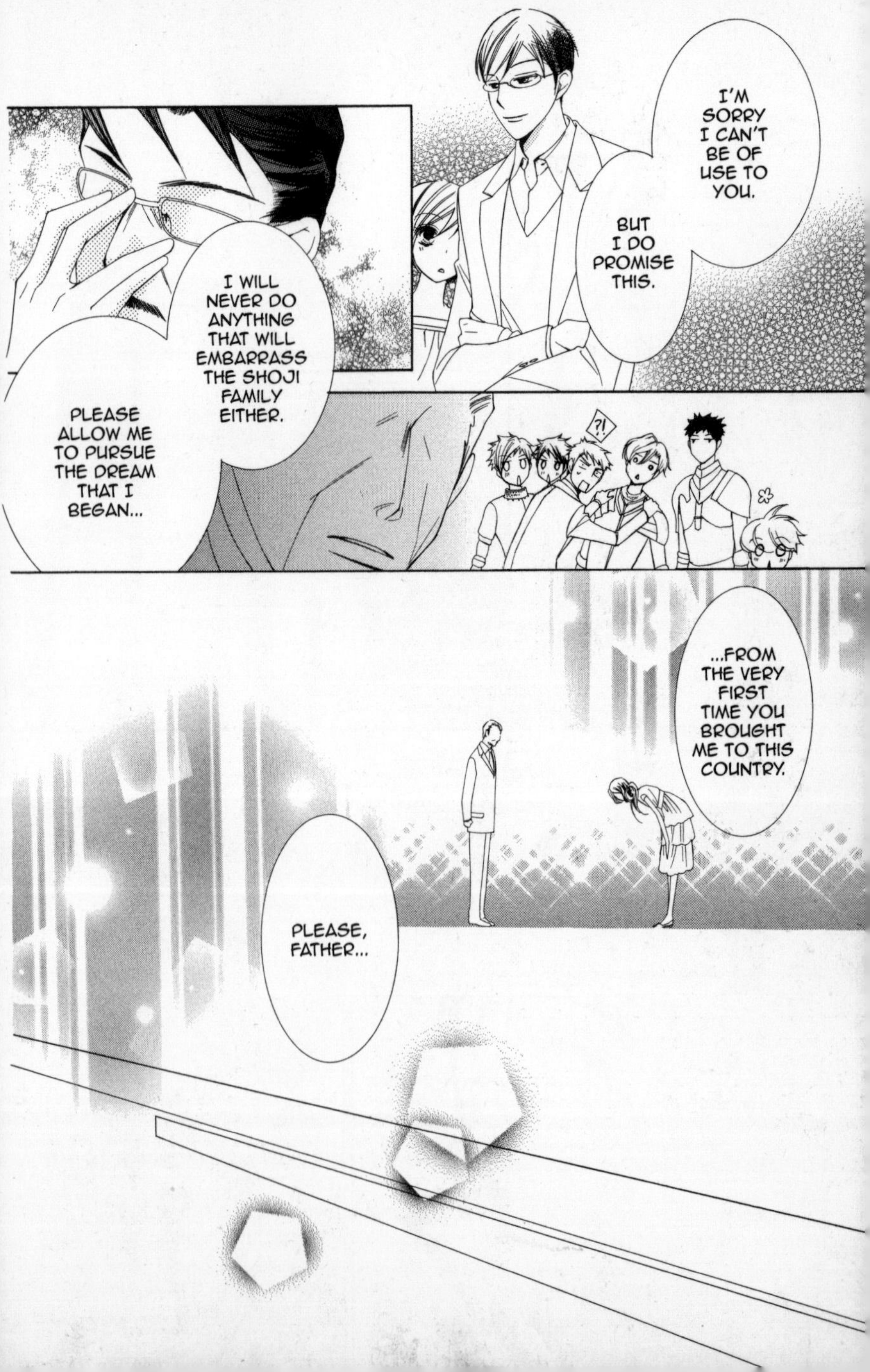
I'M SORRY I CAN'T BE OF USE TO YOU.
BUT I DO PROMISE THIS.
I WILL NEVER DO ANYTHING THAT WILL EMBARRASS THE SHOJI FAMILY EITHER.
?!
PLEASE ALLOW ME TO PURSUE THE DREAM THAT I BEGAN...
...FROM THE VERY FIRST TIME YOU BROUGHT ME TO THIS COUNTRY.
PLEASE, FATHER...

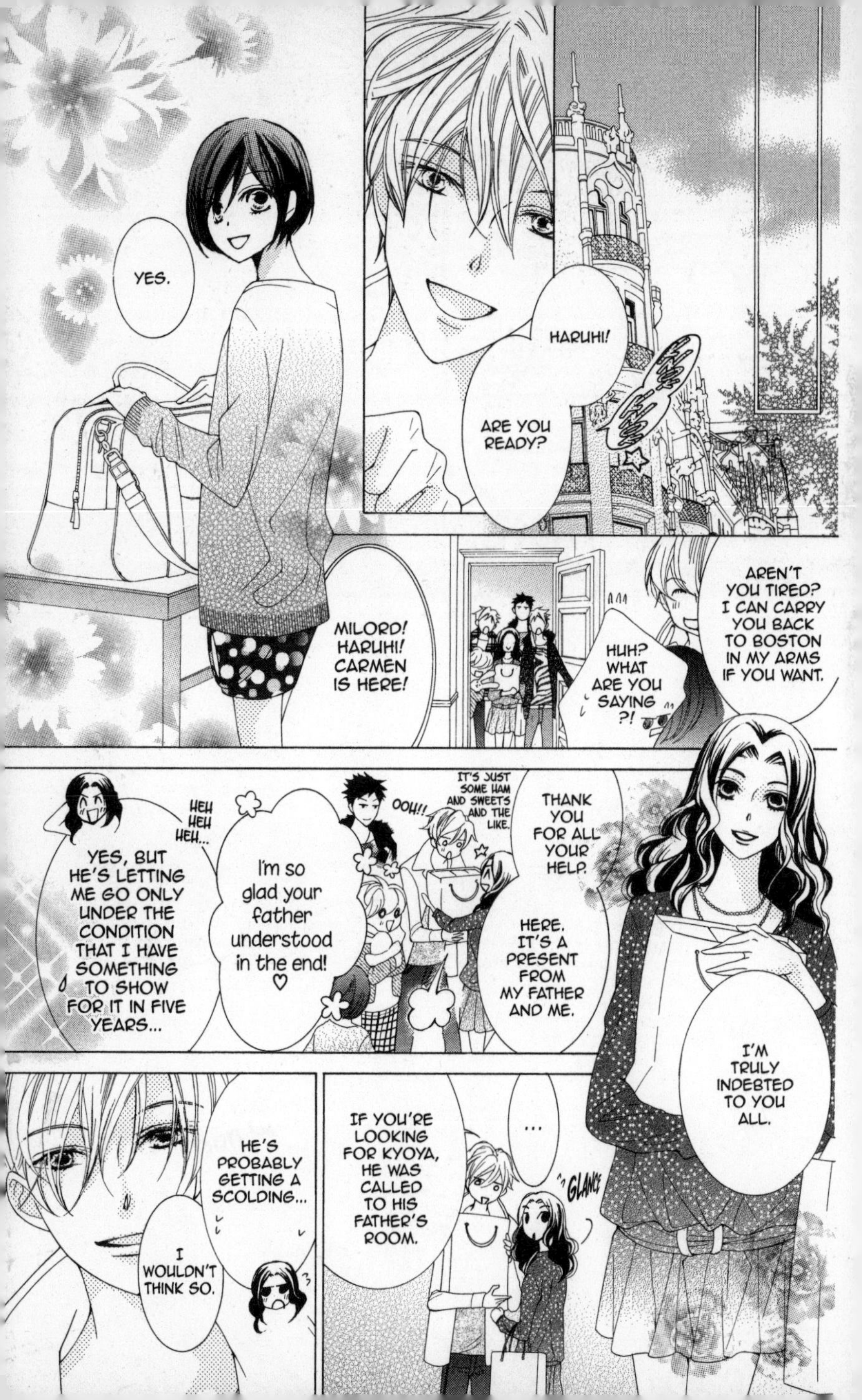
HARUHI!
ARE YOU READY?
AREN'T YOU TIRED? I CAN CARRY YOU BACK TO BOSTON IN MY ARMS IF YOU WANT.
HUH? WHAT ARE YOU SAYING?!
MILORD! HARUHI! CARMEN IS HERE!
YES.
I'M TRULY INDEBTED TO YOU ALL.
THANK YOU FOR ALL YOUR HELP.
HERE. IT'S A PRESENT FROM MY FATHER AND ME.
IT'S JUST SOME HAM AND SWEETS AND THE LIKE.
OOH!!
I'm so glad your father understood in the end! ♡
HEH HEH HEH...
YES, BUT HE'S LETTING ME GO ONLY UNDER THE CONDITION THAT I HAVE SOMETHING TO SHOW FOR IT IN FIVE YEARS...
...
GLANCE
IF YOU'RE LOOKING FOR KYOYA, HE WAS CALLED TO HIS FATHER'S ROOM.
HE'S PROBABLY GETTING A SCOLDING...
I WOULDN'T THINK SO.

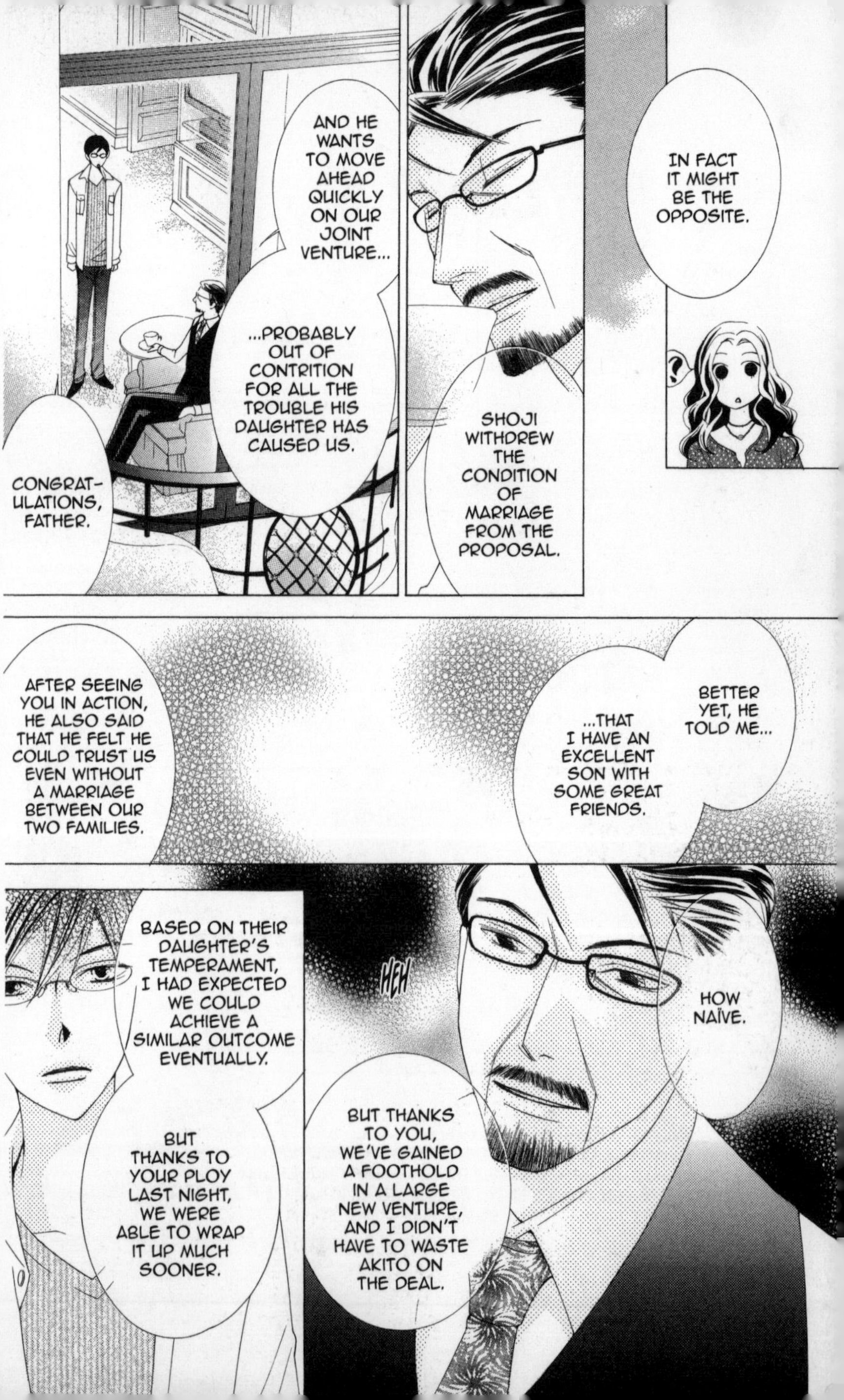

IN FACT IT MIGHT BE THE OPPOSITE.
?
SHOJI WITHDREW THE CONDITION OF MARRIAGE FROM THE PROPOSAL.
AND HE WANTS TO MOVE AHEAD QUICKLY ON OUR JOINT VENTURE...
...PROBABLY OUT OF CONTRITION FOR ALL THE TROUBLE HIS DAUGHTER HAS CAUSED US.
CONGRAT-ULATIONS, FATHER.
BETTER YET, HE TOLD ME...
...THAT I HAVE AN EXCELLENT SON WITH SOME GREAT FRIENDS.
AFTER SEEING YOU IN ACTION, HE ALSO SAID THAT HE FELT HE COULD TRUST US EVEN WITHOUT A MARRIAGE BETWEEN OUR TWO FAMILIES.
HOW NAÏVE.
HEH
BUT THANKS TO YOU, WE'VE GAINED A FOOTHOLD IN A LARGE NEW VENTURE, AND I DIDN'T HAVE TO WASTE AKITO ON THE DEAL.
BASED ON THEIR DAUGHTER'S TEMPERAMENT, I HAD EXPECTED WE COULD ACHIEVE A SIMILAR OUTCOME EVENTUALLY.
BUT THANKS TO YOUR PLOY LAST NIGHT, WE WERE ABLE TO WRAP IT UP MUCH SOONER.

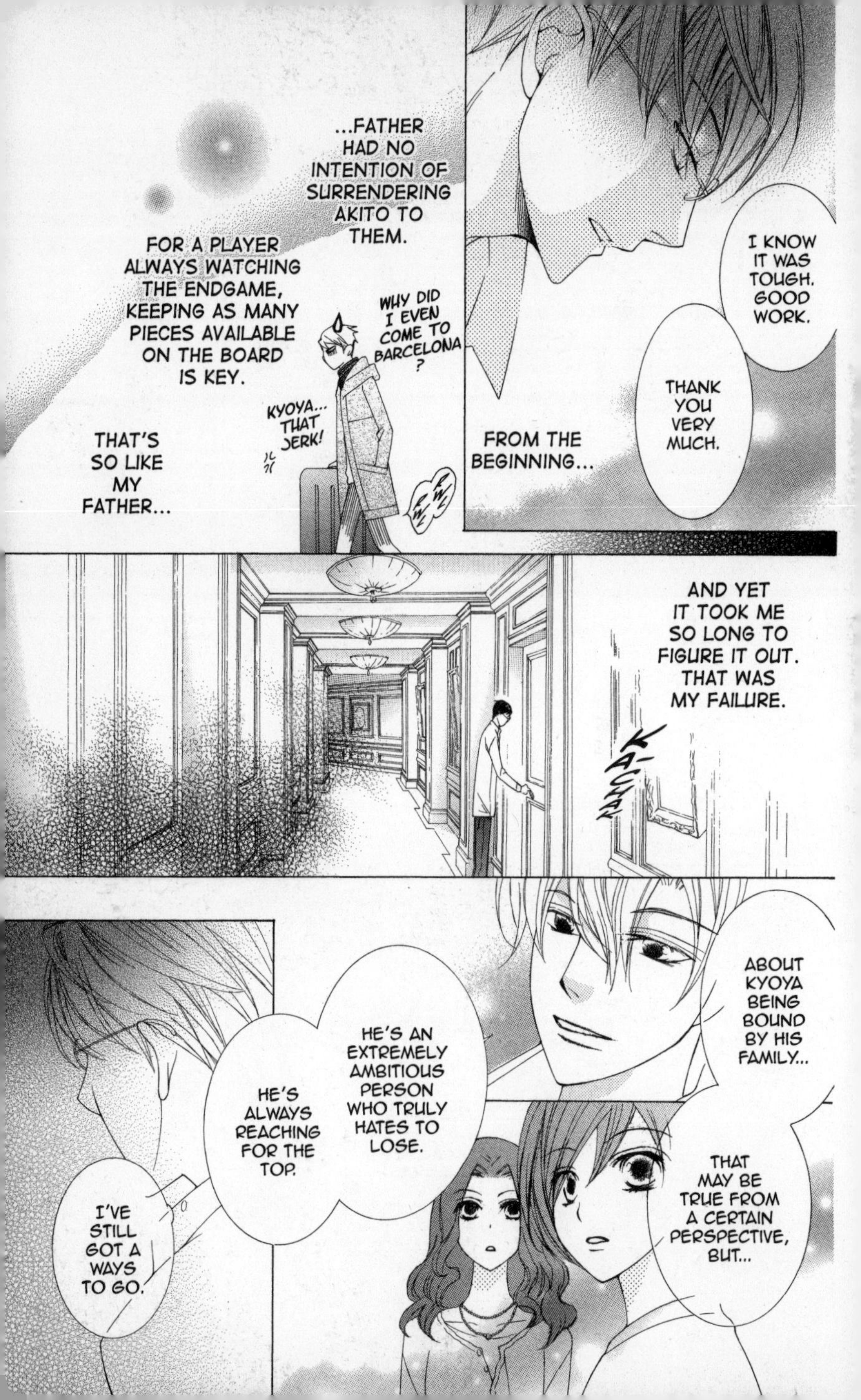
I KNOW IT WAS TOUGH. GOOD WORK.
THANK YOU VERY MUCH.
FROM THE BEGINNING...
...FATHER HAD NO INTENTION OF SURRENDERING AKITO TO THEM.
FOR A PLAYER ALWAYS WATCHING THE ENDGAME, KEEPING AS MANY PIECES AVAILABLE ON THE BOARD IS KEY.
WHY DID I EVEN COME TO BARCELONA?
KYOYA... THAT JERK!
THAT'S SO LIKE MY FATHER...
AND YET IT TOOK ME SO LONG TO FIGURE IT OUT. THAT WAS MY FAILURE.
KACHA
ABOUT KYOYA BEING BOUND BY HIS FAMILY...
THAT MAY BE TRUE FROM A CERTAIN PERSPECTIVE, BUT...
HE'S AN EXTREMELY AMBITIOUS PERSON WHO TRULY HATES TO LOSE.
HE'S ALWAYS REACHING FOR THE TOP.
I'VE STILL GOT A WAYS TO GO.

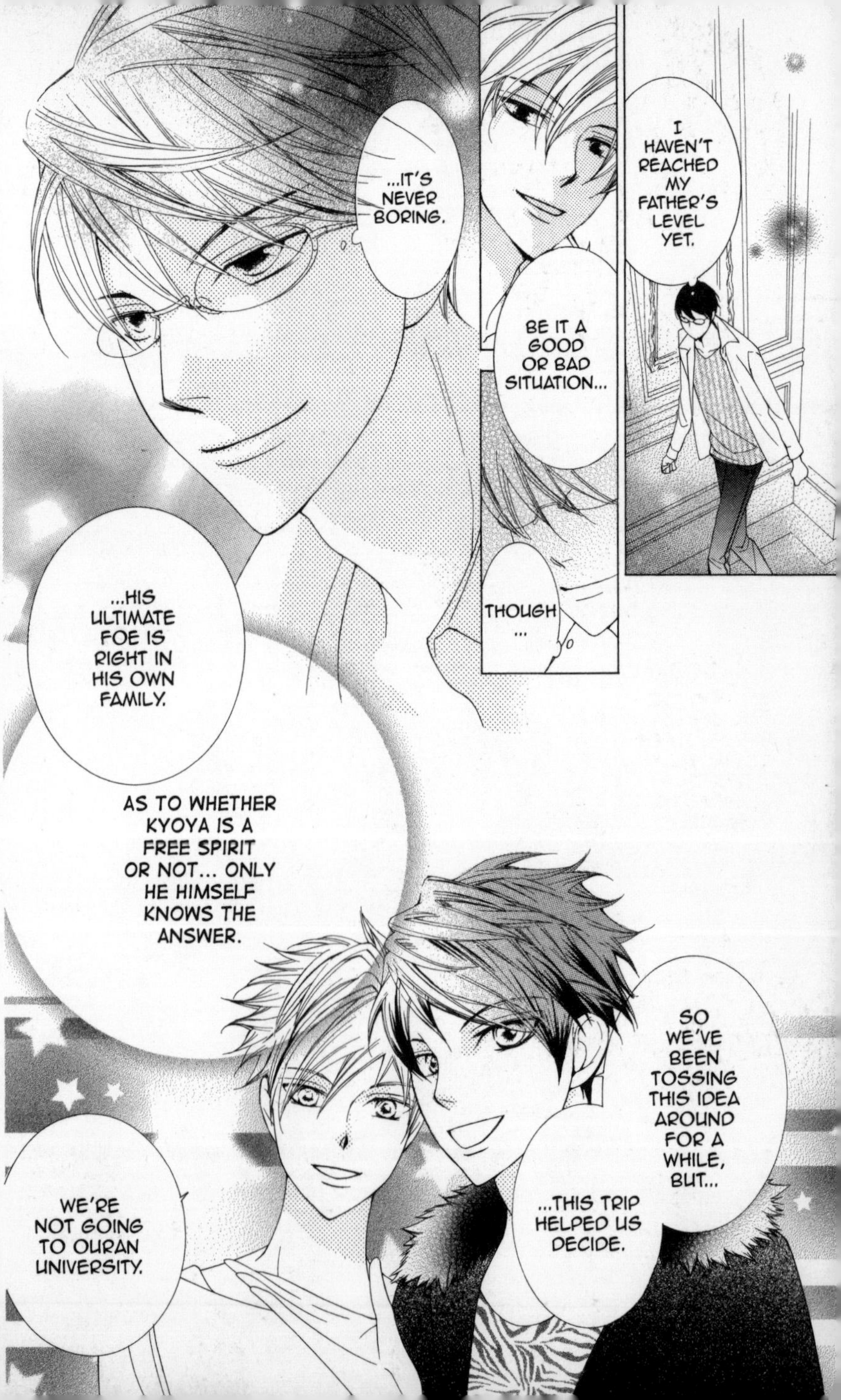
I HAVEN'T REACHED MY FATHER'S LEVEL YET.
BE IT A GOOD OR BAD SITUATION...
...IT'S NEVER BORING.
THOUGH...
...HIS ULTIMATE FOE IS RIGHT IN HIS OWN FAMILY.
AS TO WHETHER KYOYA IS A FREE SPIRIT OR NOT... ONLY HE HIMSELF KNOWS THE ANSWER.
SO WE'VE BEEN TOSSING THIS IDEA AROUND FOR A WHILE, BUT...
...THIS TRIP HELPED US DECIDE.
WE'RE NOT GOING TO OURAN UNIVERSITY.

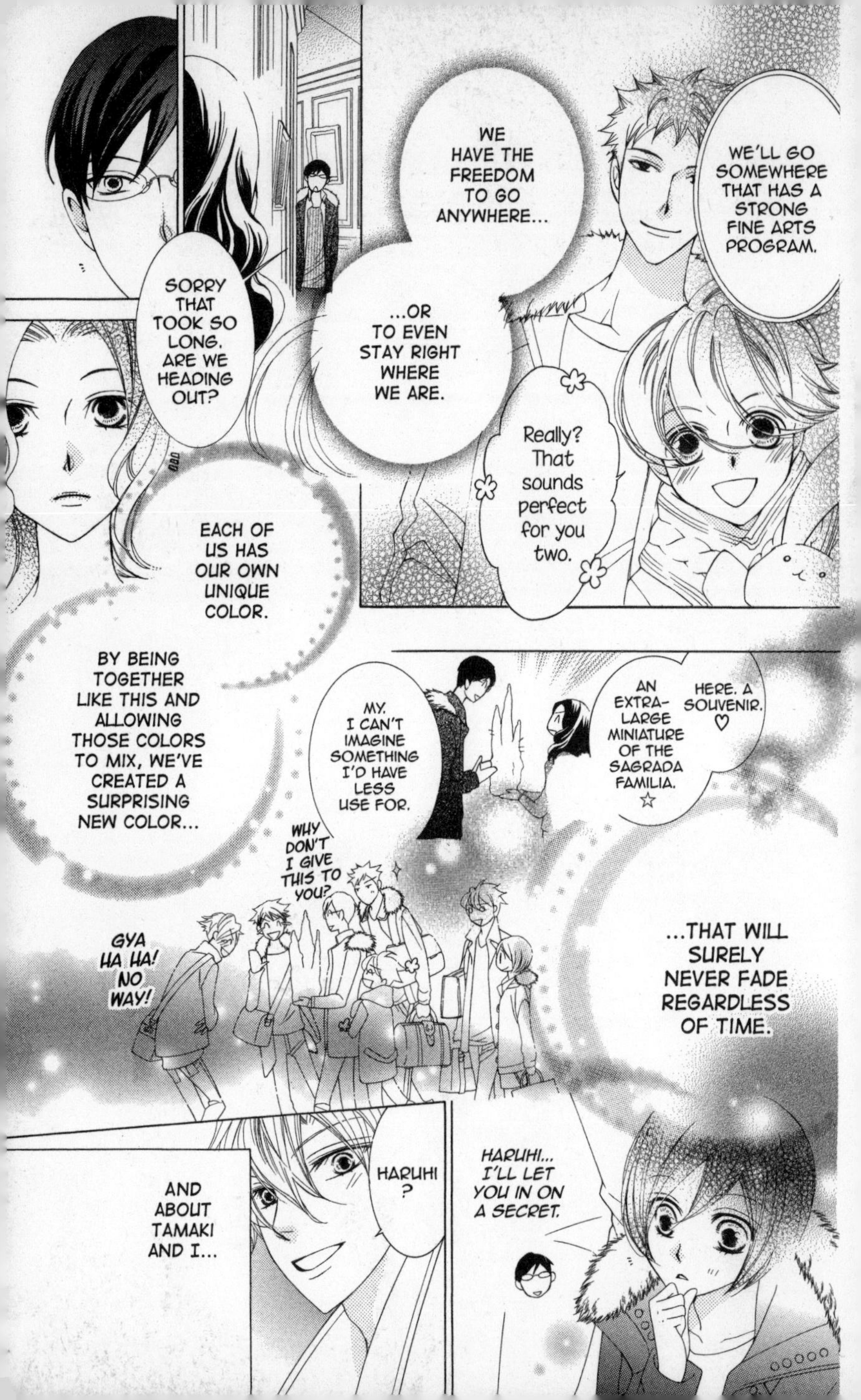
WE'LL GO SOMEWHERE THAT HAS A STRONG FINE ARTS PROGRAM.
WE HAVE THE FREEDOM TO GO ANYWHERE...
...OR TO EVEN STAY RIGHT WHERE WE ARE.
Really? That sounds perfect for you two.
SORRY THAT TOOK SO LONG. ARE WE HEADING OUT?
EACH OF US HAS OUR OWN UNIQUE COLOR.
HERE. A SOUVENIR. ♡
AN EXTRA-LARGE MINIATURE OF THE SAGRADA FAMILIA. ☆
MY. I CAN'T IMAGINE SOMETHING I'D HAVE LESS USE FOR.
BY BEING TOGETHER LIKE THIS AND ALLOWING THOSE COLORS TO MIX, WE'VE CREATED A SURPRISING NEW COLOR...
...THAT WILL SURELY NEVER FADE REGARDLESS OF TIME.
WHY DON'T I GIVE THIS TO YOU?
GYA HA HA! NO WAY!
HARUHI... I'LL LET YOU IN ON A SECRET.
HARUHI?
AND ABOUT TAMAKI AND I...

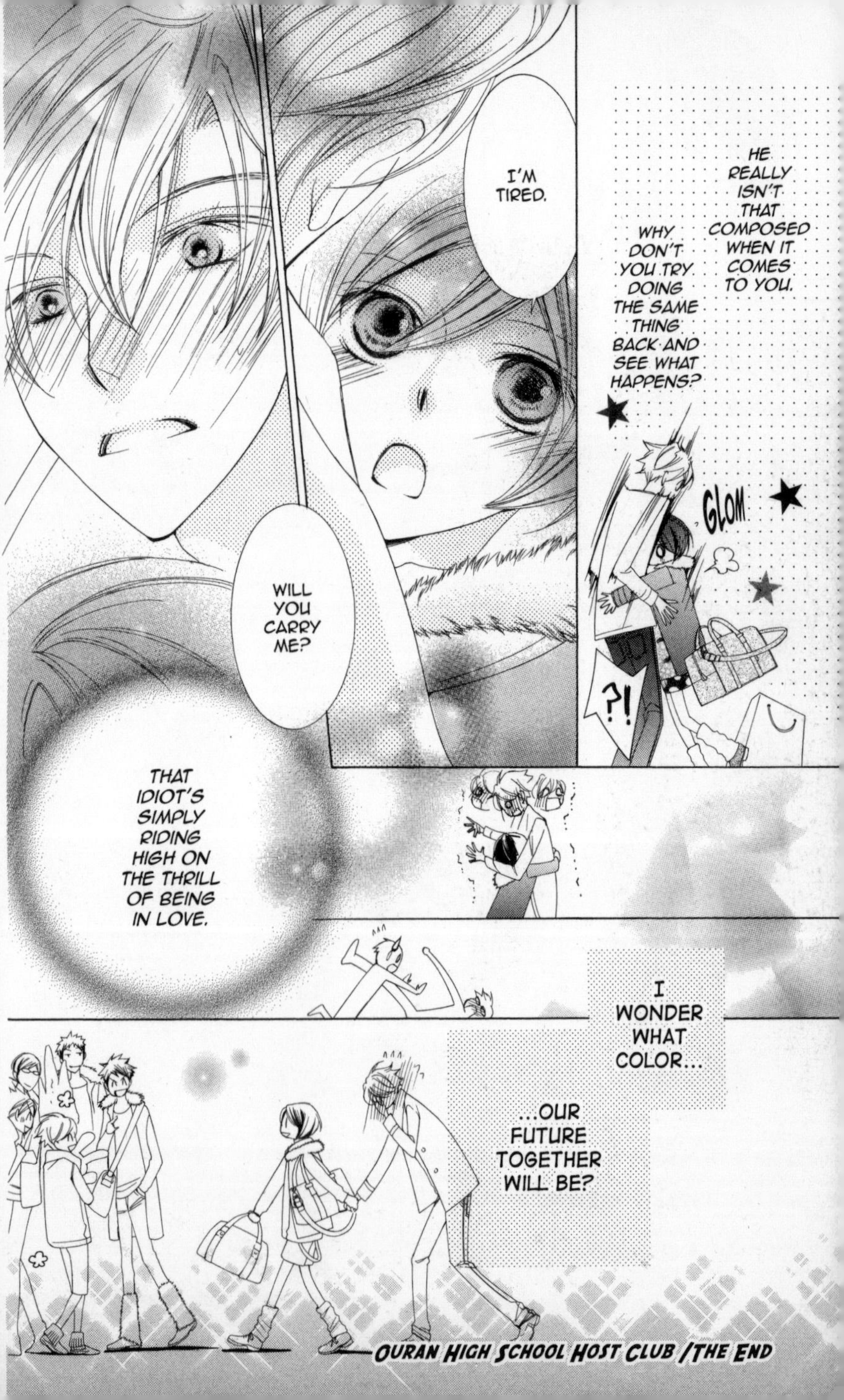
HE REALLY ISN'T THAT COMPOSED WHEN IT COMES TO YOU.
WHY DON'T YOU TRY DOING THE SAME THING BACK AND SEE WHAT HAPPENS?
GLOM
?!
I'M TIRED.
WILL YOU CARRY ME?
THAT IDIOT'S SIMPLY RIDING HIGH ON THE THRILL OF BEING IN LOVE.
I WONDER WHAT COLOR...
...OUR FUTURE TOGETHER WILL BE?
OURAN HIGH SCHOOL HOST CLUB / THE END

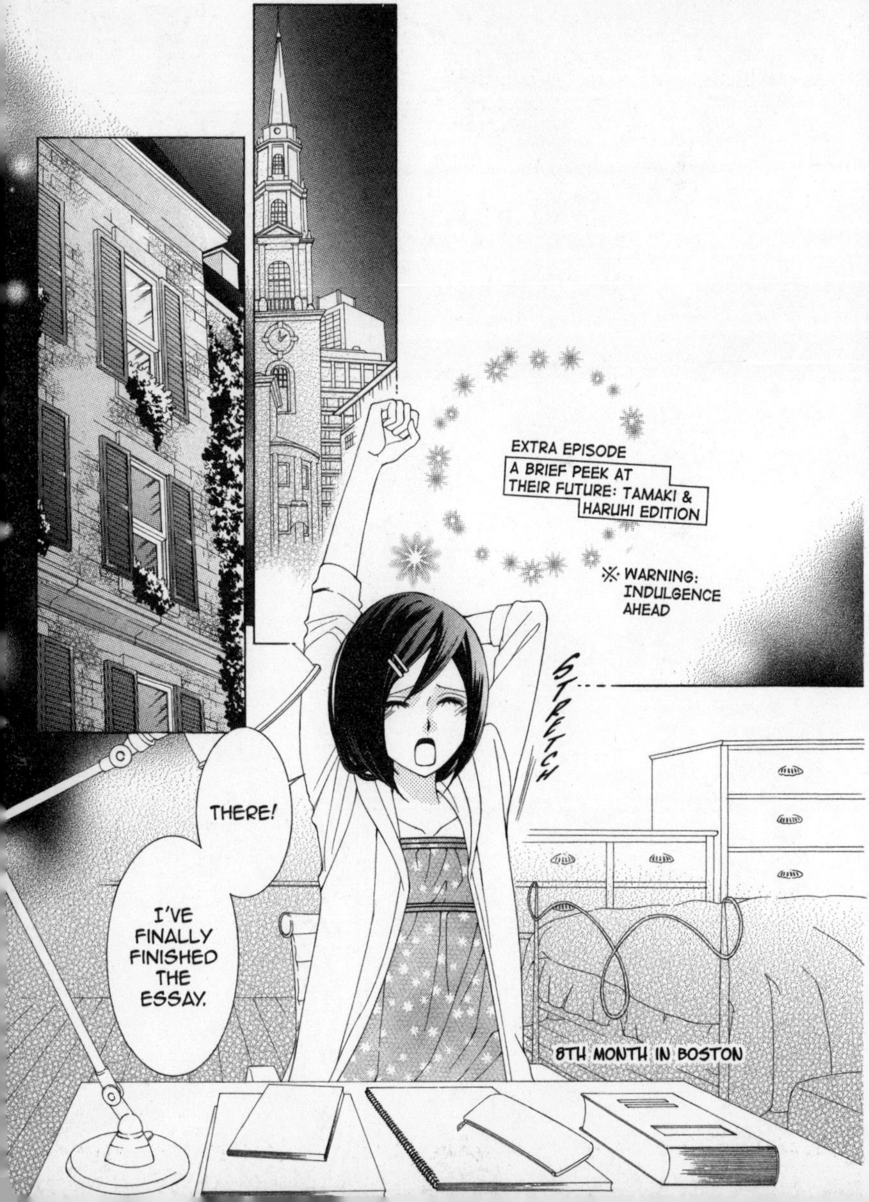
EXTRA EPISODE
A BRIEF PEEK AT THEIR FUTURE: TAMAKI & HARUHI EDITION
※ WARNING: INDULGENCE AHEAD
STRETCH
THERE!
I'VE FINALLY FINISHED THE ESSAY.
8TH MONTH IN BOSTON

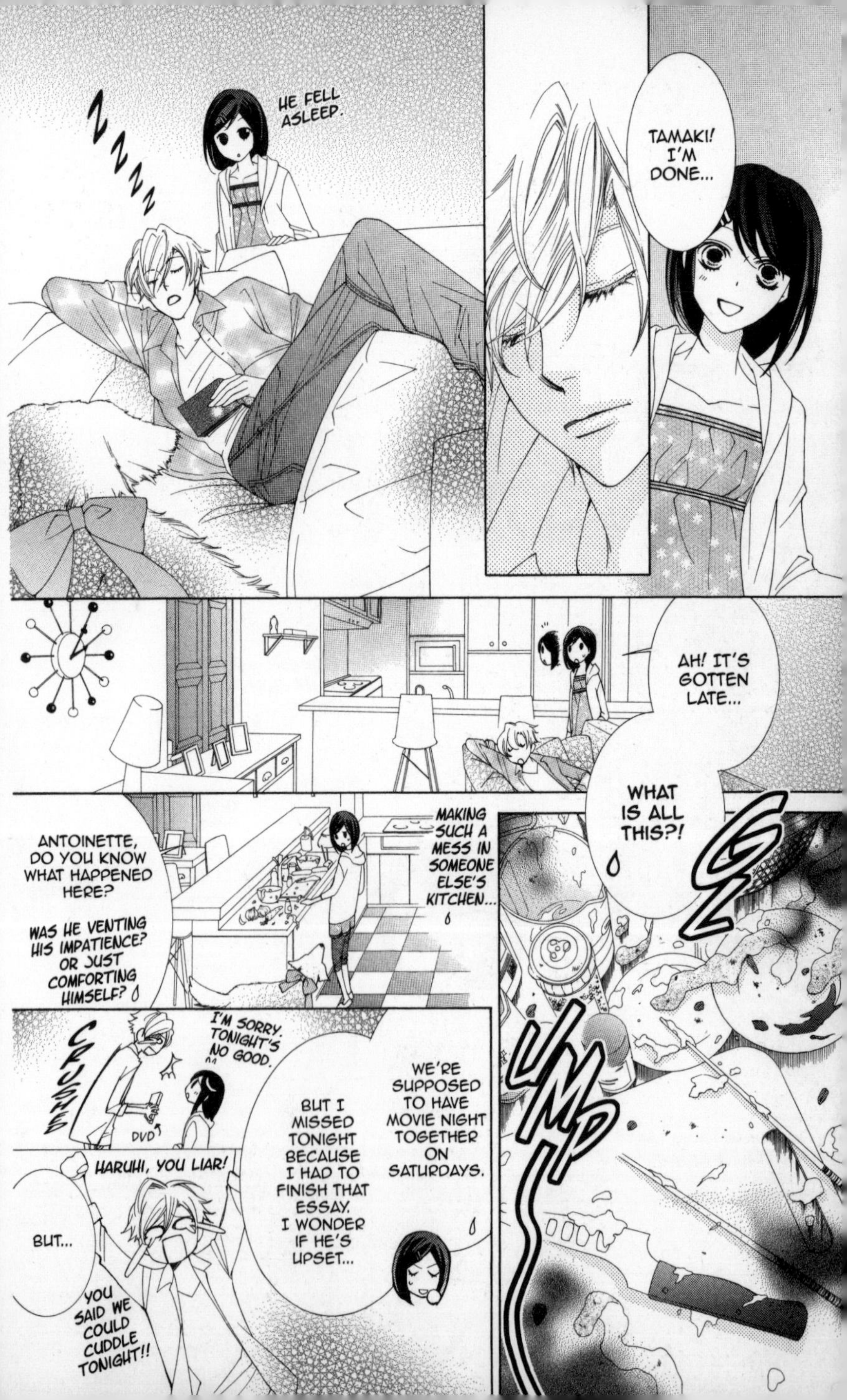
TAMAKI! I'M DONE...
ZZZZ
HE FELL ASLEEP.
AH! IT'S GOTTEN LATE...
WHAT IS ALL THIS?!
MAKING SUCH A MESS IN SOMEONE ELSE'S KITCHEN...
ANTOINETTE, DO YOU KNOW WHAT HAPPENED HERE?
WAS HE VENTING HIS IMPATIENCE? OR JUST COMFORTING HIMSELF?
WE'RE SUPPOSED TO HAVE MOVIE NIGHT TOGETHER ON SATURDAYS.
BUT I MISSED TONIGHT BECAUSE I HAD TO FINISH THAT ESSAY. I WONDER IF HE'S UPSET...
I'M SORRY. TONIGHT'S NO GOOD.
CRUSHED
DVD
HARUHI, YOU LIAR!
BUT...
YOU SAID WE COULD CUDDLE TONIGHT!!

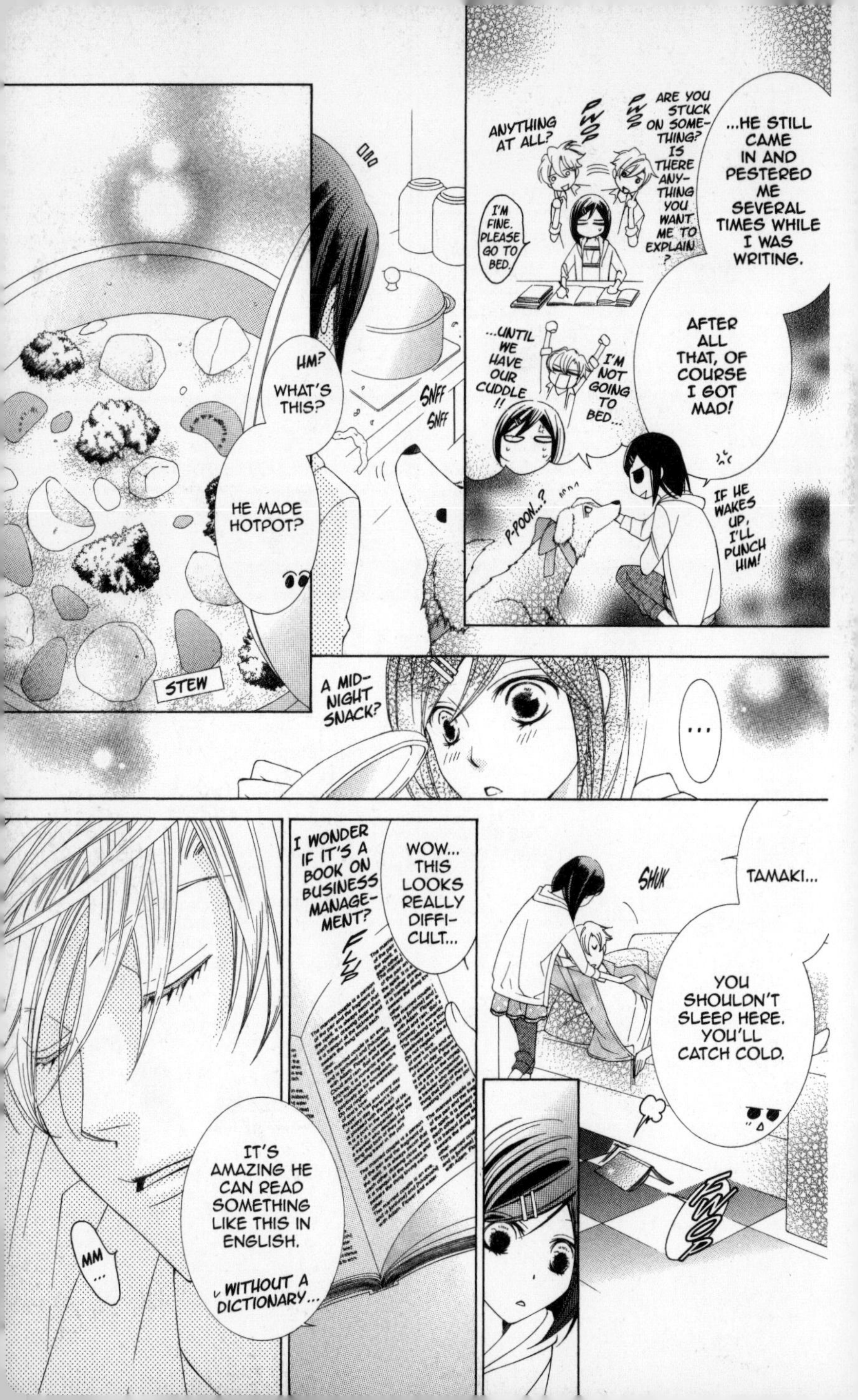
...HE STILL CAME IN AND PESTERED ME SEVERAL TIMES WHILE I WAS WRITING.
ARE YOU STUCK ON SOMETHING? IS THERE ANYTHING YOU WANT ME TO EXPLAIN?
ANYTHING AT ALL?
I'M FINE. PLEASE GO TO BED.
AFTER ALL THAT, OF COURSE I GOT MAD!
I'M NOT GOING TO BED...
...UNTIL WE HAVE OUR CUDDLE!!
IF HE WAKES UP, I'LL PUNCH HIM!
P-POON...?
HM? WHAT'S THIS?
SNFF SNFF
HE MADE HOTPOT?
STEW
...
A MID-NIGHT SNACK?
TAMAKI...
YOU SHOULDN'T SLEEP HERE. YOU'LL CATCH COLD.
SHUK
WOW... THIS LOOKS REALLY DIFFI-CULT...
I WONDER IF IT'S A BOOK ON BUSINESS MANAGE-MENT?
IT'S AMAZING HE CAN READ SOMETHING LIKE THIS IN ENGLISH.
...WITHOUT A DICTIONARY...
MM...

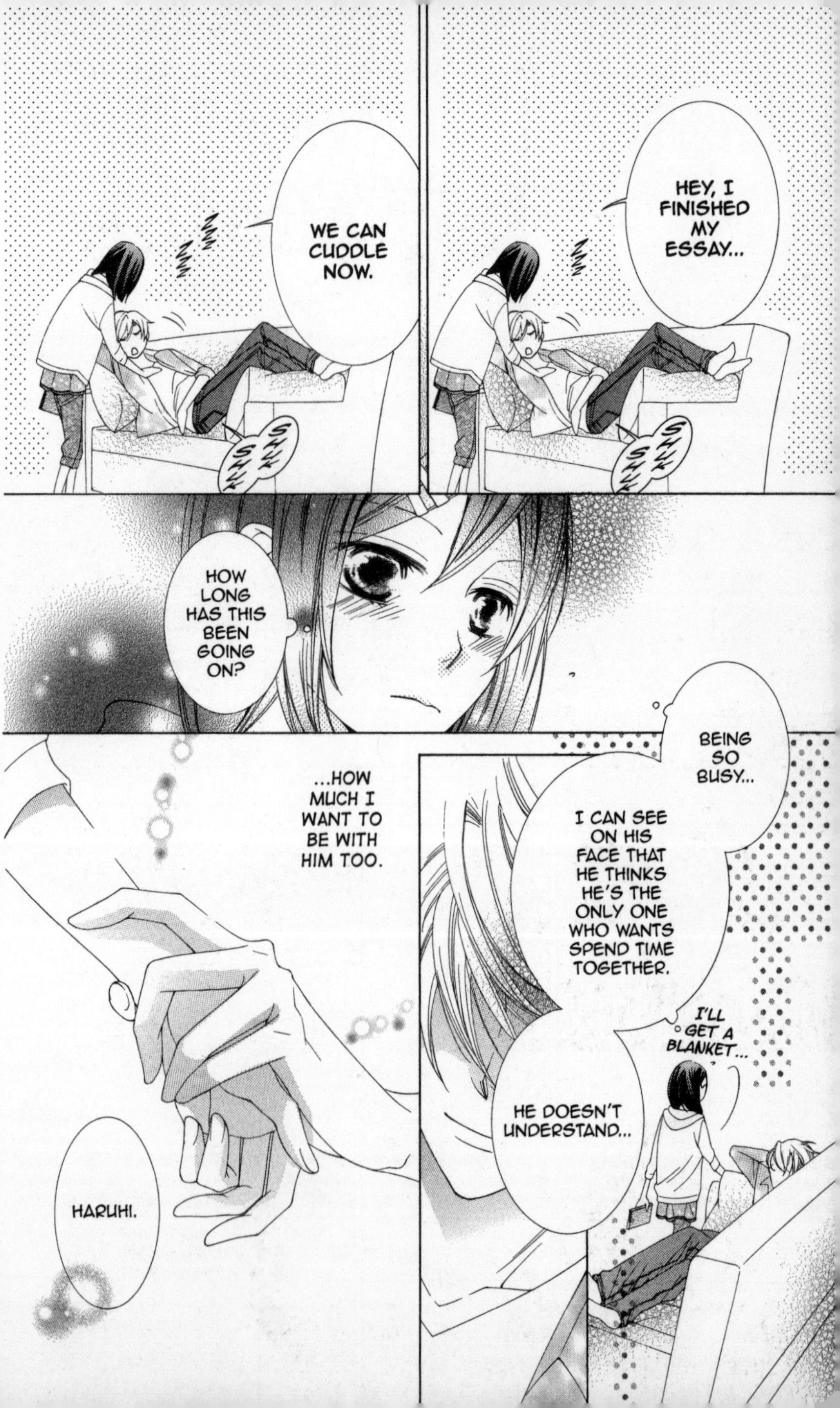
HEY, I FINISHED MY ESSAY...
SHUK SHUK
WE CAN CUDDLE NOW.
SHUK SHUK
HOW LONG HAS THIS BEEN GOING ON?
BEING SO BUSY...
I CAN SEE ON HIS FACE THAT HE THINKS HE'S THE ONLY ONE WHO WANTS SPEND TIME TOGETHER.
I'LL GET A BLANKET...
HE DOESN'T UNDERSTAND...
...HOW MUCH I WANT TO BE WITH HIM TOO.
HARUHI.

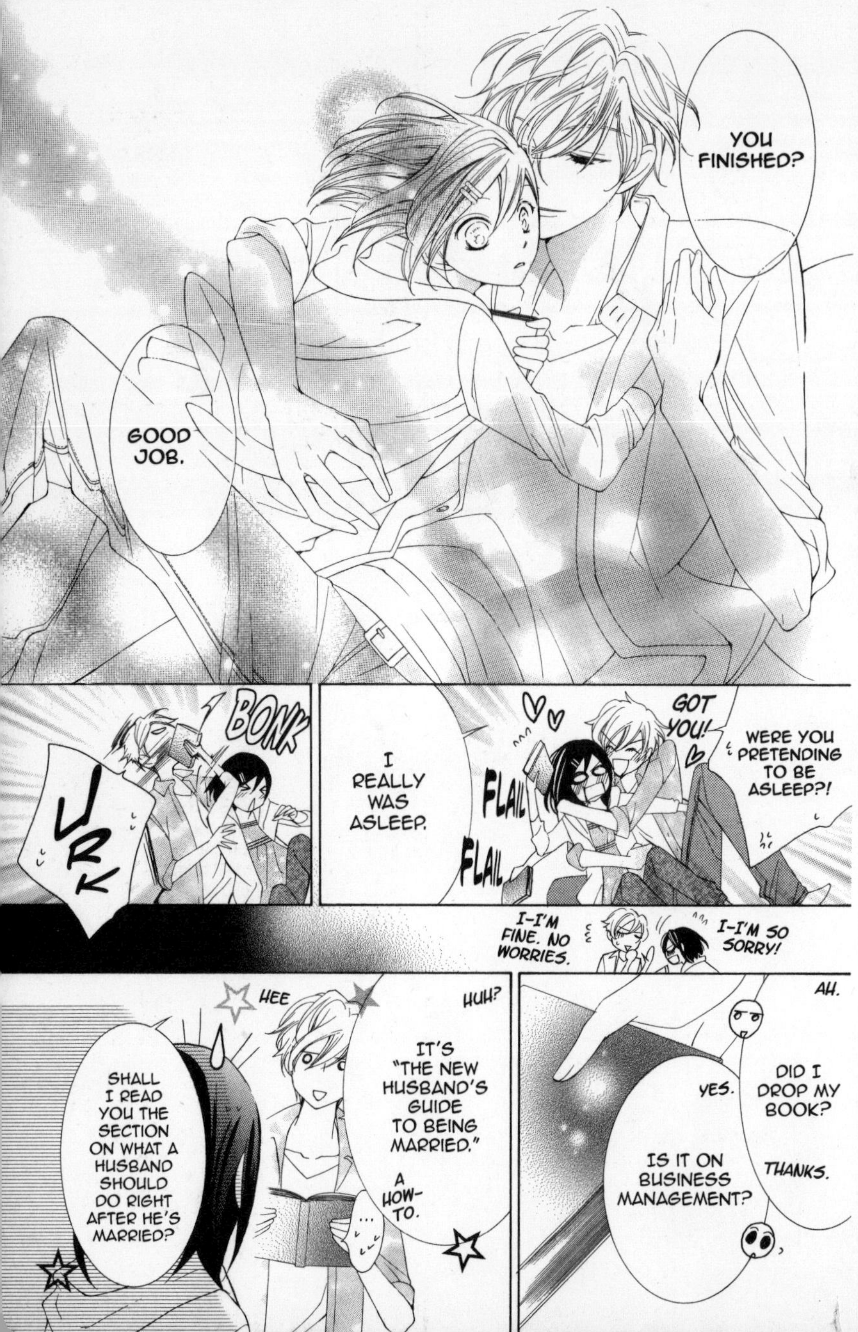
YOU FINISHED?
GOOD JOB.
WERE YOU PRETENDING TO BE ASLEEP?!
GOT YOU!
FLAIL
FLAIL
I REALLY WAS ASLEEP.
BONK
URK
I-I'M SO SORRY!
I-I'M FINE. NO WORRIES.
AH.
DID I DROP MY BOOK?
YES.
THANKS.
IS IT ON BUSINESS MANAGEMENT?
HUH?
HEE
IT'S "THE NEW HUSBAND'S GUIDE TO BEING MARRIED." A HOW-TO.
...
SHALL I READ YOU THE SECTION ON WHAT A HUSBAND SHOULD DO RIGHT AFTER HE'S MARRIED?

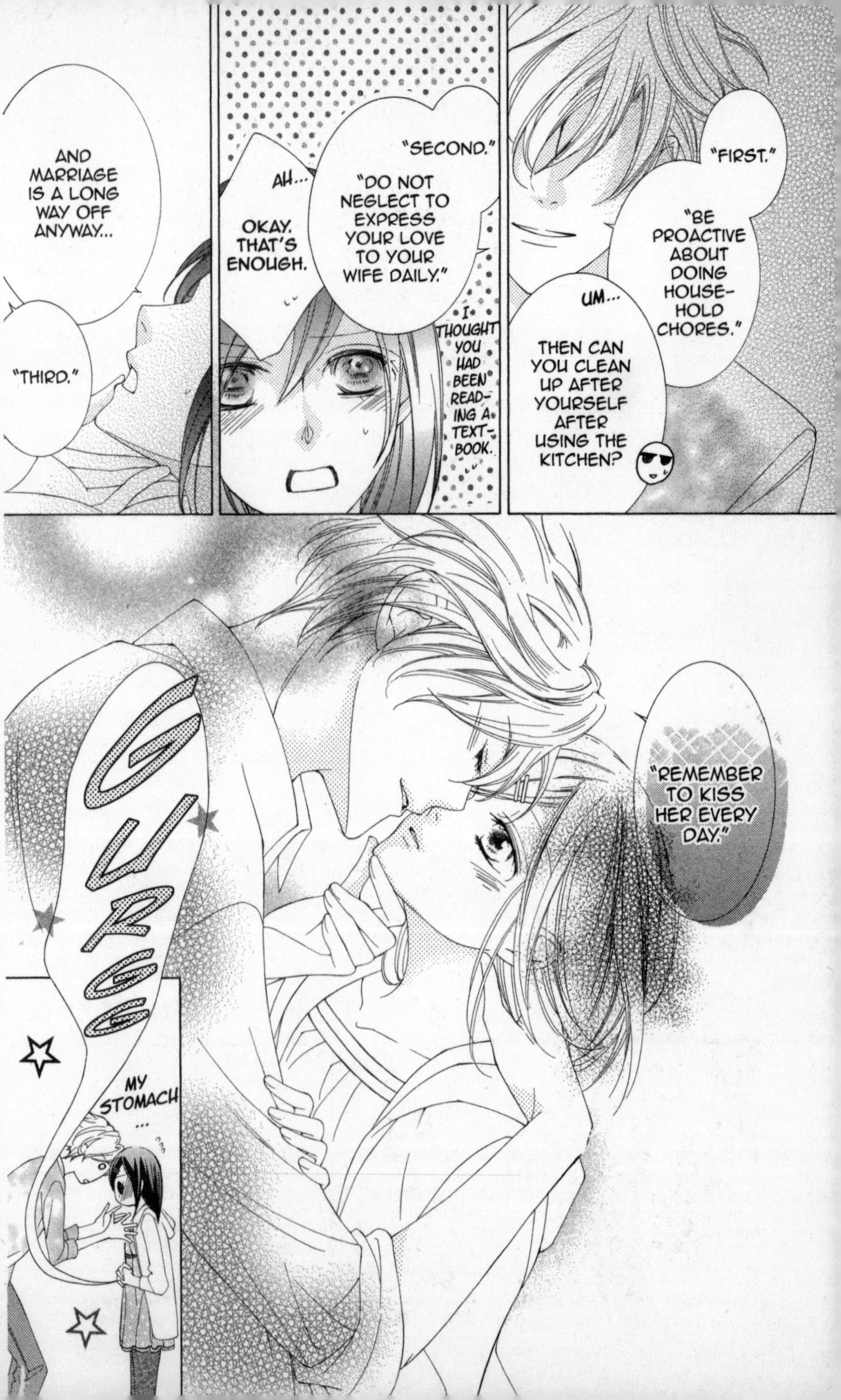
"FIRST."
"BE PROACTIVE ABOUT DOING HOUSE-HOLD CHORES."
UM...
THEN CAN YOU CLEAN UP AFTER YOURSELF AFTER USING THE KITCHEN?
"SECOND."
"DO NOT NEGLECT TO EXPRESS YOUR LOVE TO YOUR WIFE DAILY."
AH...
OKAY. THAT'S ENOUGH.
I THOUGHT YOU HAD BEEN READ-ING A TEXT-BOOK.
AND MARRIAGE IS A LONG WAY OFF ANYWAY...
"THIRD."
"REMEMBER TO KISS HER EVERY DAY."
GURGG
MY STOMACH ...

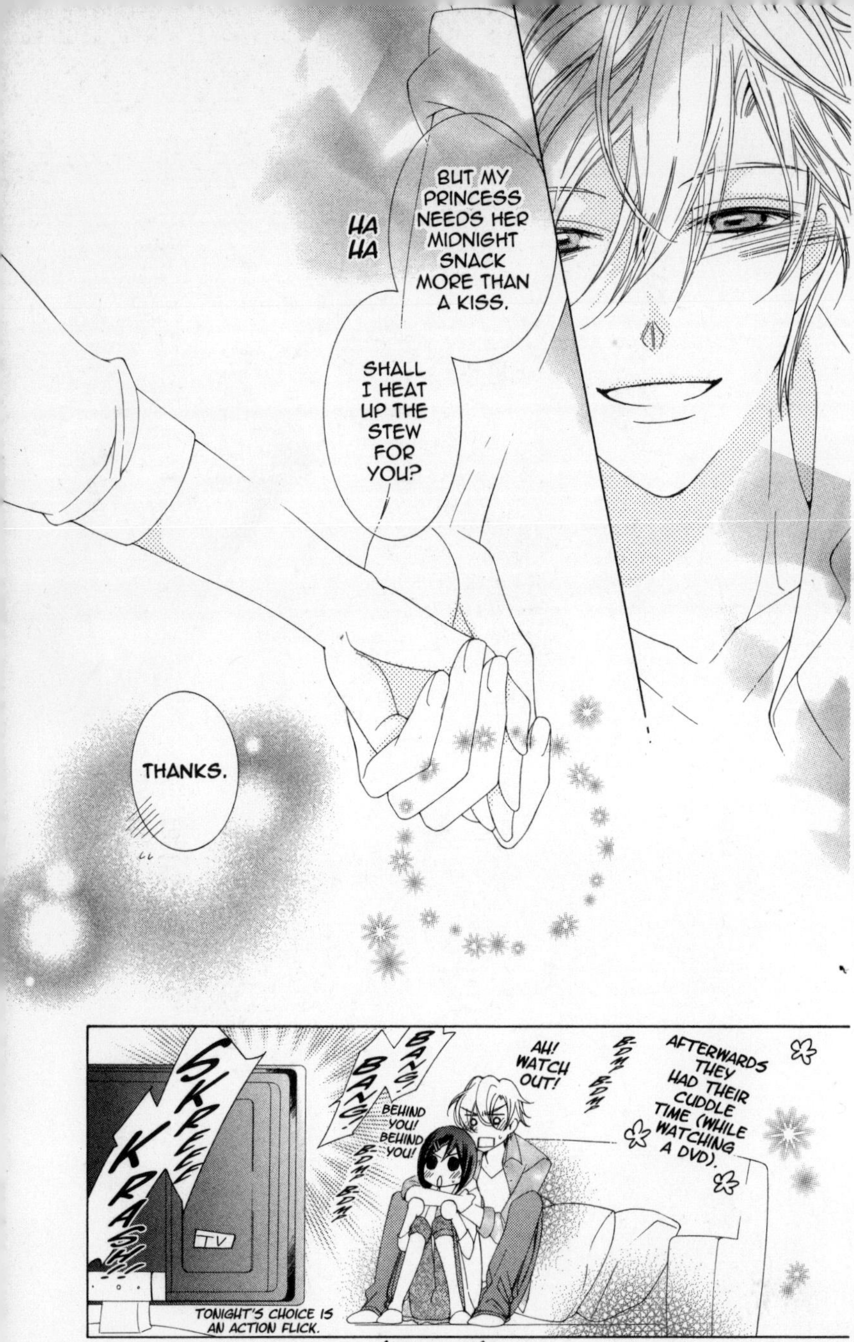
BUT MY PRINCESS NEEDS HER MIDNIGHT SNACK MORE THAN A KISS.
HA HA
SHALL I HEAT UP THE STEW FOR YOU?
THANKS.
AFTERWARDS THEY HAD THEIR CUDDLE TIME (WHILE WATCHING A DVD).
BDM BDM
AH! WATCH OUT!
BEHIND YOU! BEHIND YOU!
BANG! BANG!
BDM BDM
SKREEE
KRASH!!
TV
TONIGHT'S CHOICE IS AN ACTION FLICK.

THE END

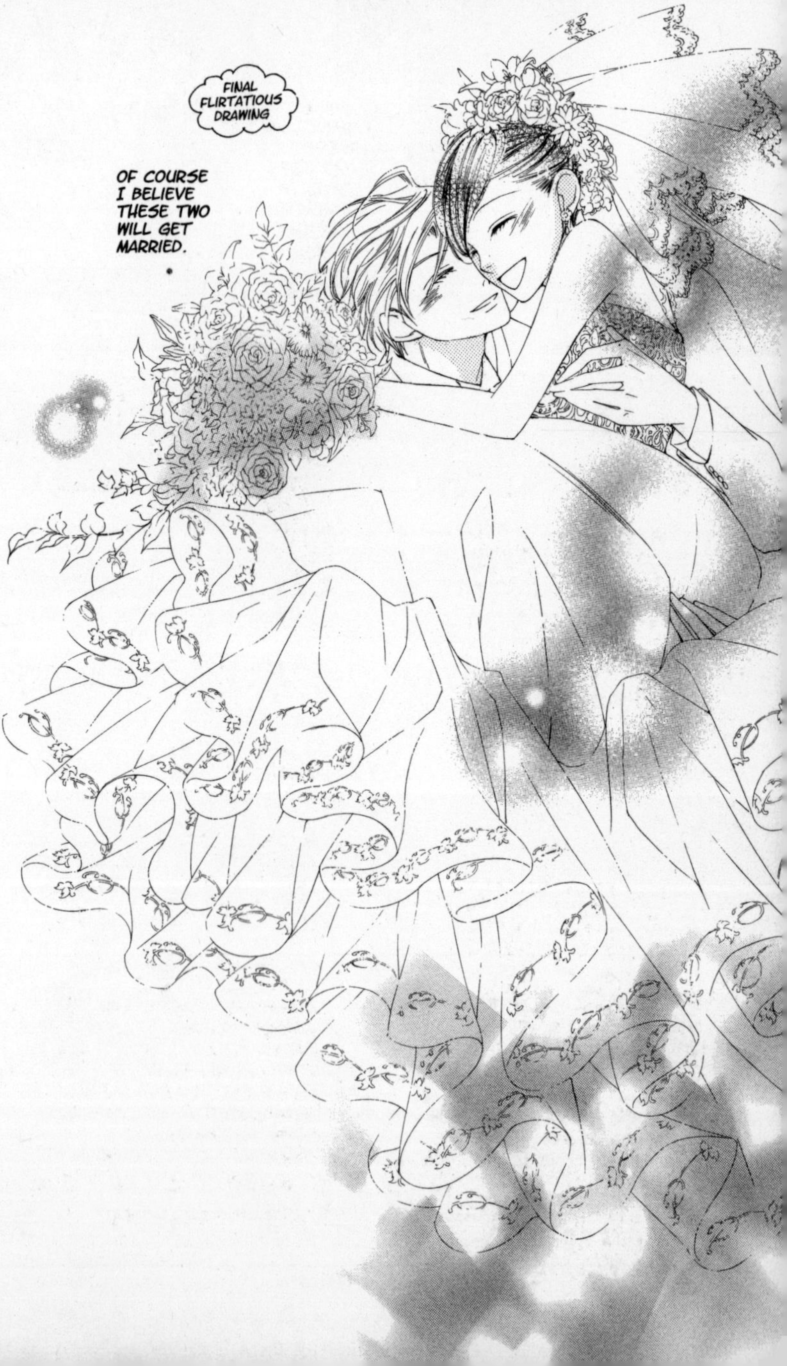
FINAL FLIRTATIOUS DRAWING
OF COURSE I BELIEVE THESE TWO WILL GET MARRIED.

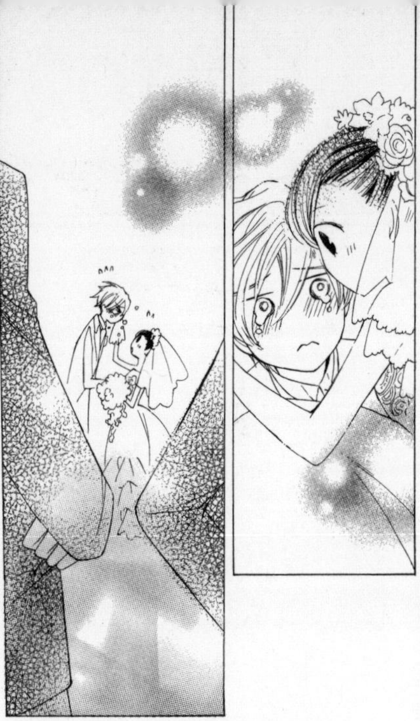

Special Thanks!!

YAMASHITA-SAMA,
MISTRESS T, ICHIKAWA-SAMA,
AND YANAGIZAWA-SAMA

MY ENTIRE STAFF:
YUI NATSUKI, RIKU, AYA AOMURA,
YUTORI HIZAKURA, SHIZURU ONDA,
UMEKO, AND MY MOM
(I LEFT OFF THE HONORIFICS.)

MY AMAZING HELPERS:
AKIRA UCHINO-SAMA, NATSUNA
KAWASE-SAMA, WATARU HIBIKI-SAMA,
AKANE OGURA-SAMA, SHIGEYOSHI
TAKAGI-SAMA, CHIAKI KARAZAWA,
TOKI YAJIMA-SAMA, YOUKO SANO-
SAMA, AKIRA HAGIO-SAMA, KANA-
SAMA, NATSUMI SATOU-SAMA,
KOBATO UCHIDA-SAMA,
AND MIKA MORINAGA-SAMA

ENGLISH CONSULTANT SIMONA

AKIKO YAMADA-SAMA

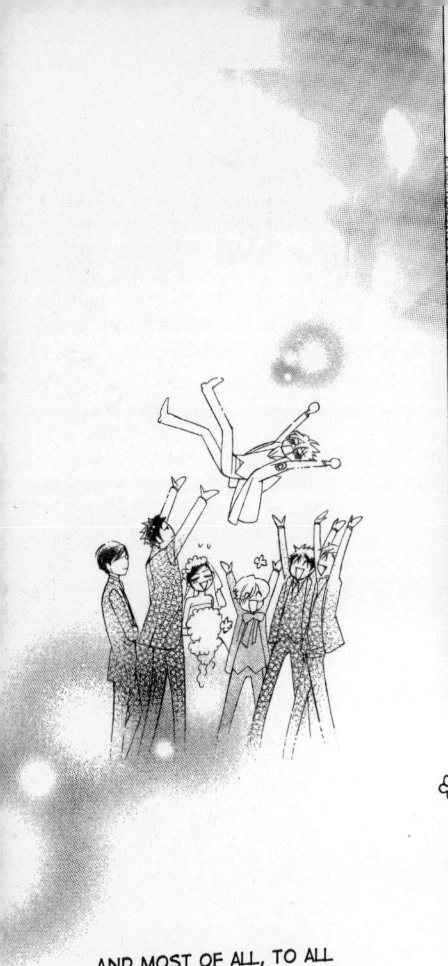

AND MOST OF ALL, TO ALL
OF YOU WHO READ THIS BOOK,
I THANK YOU FROM THE
BOTTOM OF MY HEART.

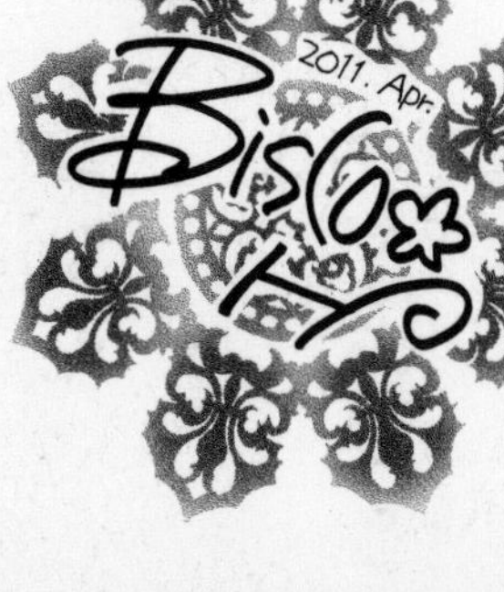
2011. Apr.
Bisco H

EDITOR'S NOTES

EPISODE 81

Page 30: A *sarashi* is a long sash used as an undergarment for the chest.

FINAL EPISODE

Page 153: Usually one traces the kanji for "person" in the palm of their hand to calm down. Tamaki is instead tracing the kanji for "beauty."

FINAL EPISODE

Page 164: An *omiai* is a matchmaking meeting of two people and their families.

Author Bio

Bisco Hatori made her
manga debut with *Isshun
kan no Romance* (A Moment
of Romance) in *LaLa DX*
magazine. The comedy *Ouran
High School Host Club* is her
breakout hit. When she's stuck
thinking up characters' names,
she gets inspired by loud,
upbeat music (her radio is set
to NACK5 FM). She enjoys
reading all kinds of manga, but
she's especially fond of the
sci-fi drama *Please Save My
Earth* and *Slam Dunk*, a
basketball classic.

OURAN HIGH SCHOOL HOST CLUB
Vol. 18
Shojo Beat Edition

STORY AND ART BY BISCO HATORI

Translation/Su Mon Han
Touch-up Art & Lettering/Gia Cam Luc
Graphic Design/Amy Martin
Editor/Nancy Thistlethwaite

Ouran Koko Host Club by Bisco Hatori © Bisco Hatori 2011. All rights reserved.
First published in Japan in 2011 by HAKUSENSHA, Inc., Tokyo. English language
translation rights arranged with HAKUSENSHA, Inc., Tokyo.

The rights of the author(s) of the work(s) in this publication to be so identified have
been asserted in accordance with the Copyright, Designs and Patents Act 1988. A CIP
catalogue record for this book is available from the British Library.

The stories, characters and incidents mentioned in this publication
are entirely fictional.

No portion of this book may be reproduced or transmitted in any form or by any means
without written permission from the copyright holders.

Printed in the U.S.A.

Published by VIZ Media, LLC
P.O. Box 77010
San Francisco, CA 94107

10 9 8 7 6 5 4 3 2 1
First printing, June 2012

www.viz.com   www.shojobeat.com

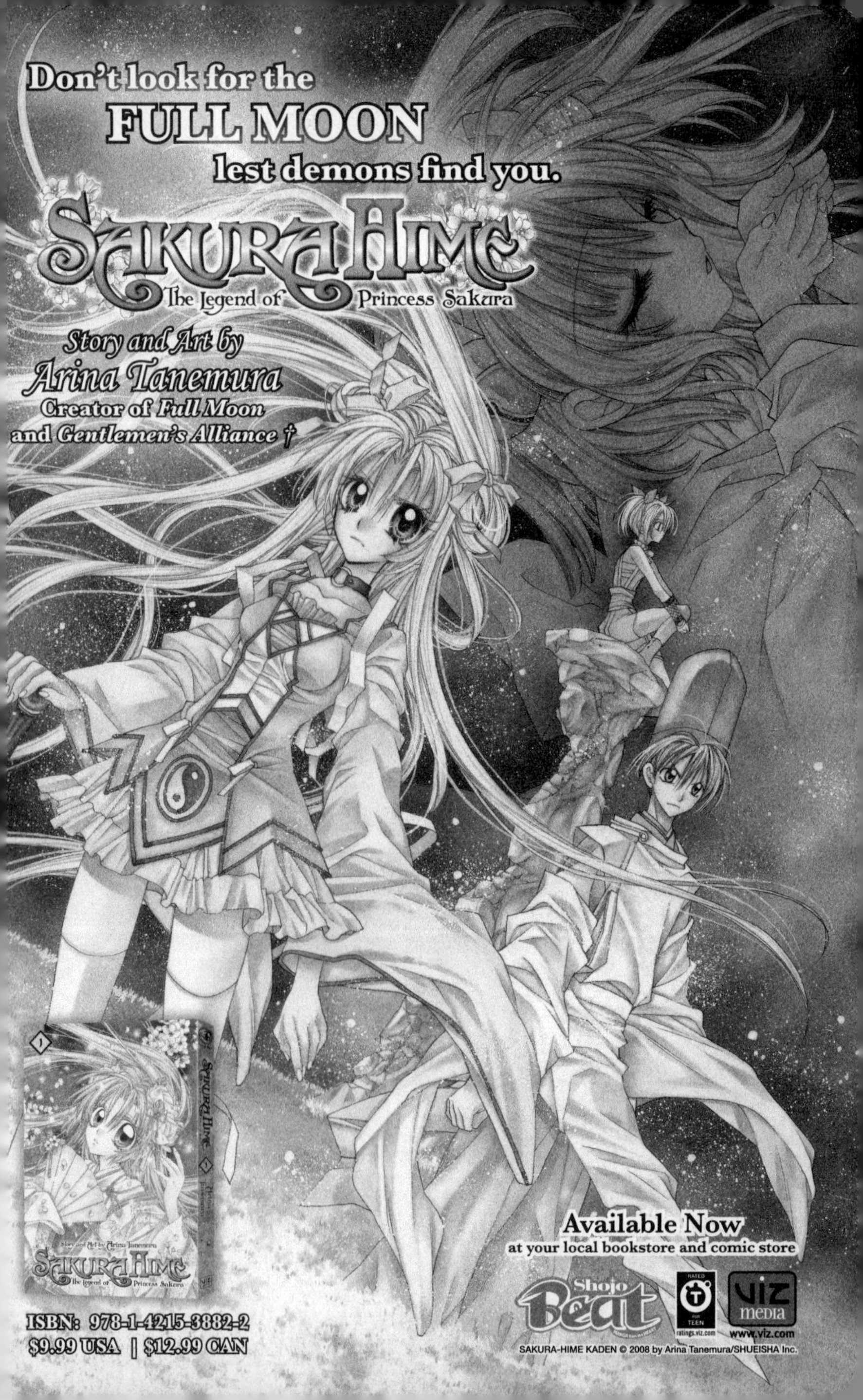

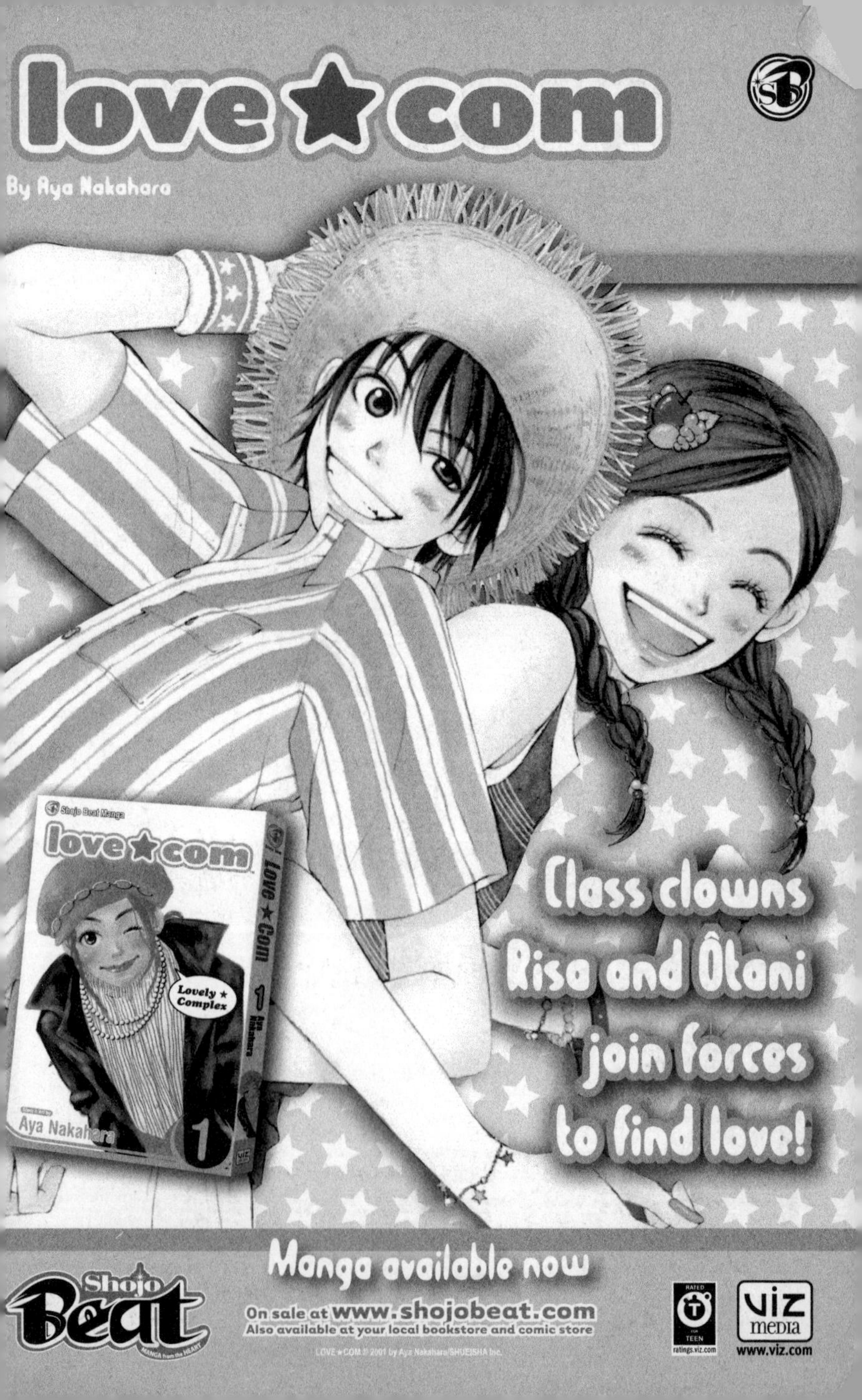
love★com
By Aya Nakahara
Shojo Beat Manga
love★com
Lovely ★ Complex
Love★Com
1
Aya Nakahara
Class clowns Risa and Ôtani join forces to find love!
Manga available now
Shojo Beat
MANGA from the HEART
On sale at www.shojobeat.com
Also available at your local bookstore and comic store
LOVE★COM © 2001 by Aya Nakahara/SHUEISHA Inc.
RATED T TEEN
ratings.viz.com
VIZ MEDIA
www.viz.com